APPLIED NUMERICAL METHODS FOR DIGITAL COMPUTATION

APPLIED NUMERICAL METHODS FOR DIGITAL COMPUTATION

Third Edition

M. L. James
G. M. Smith
J. C. Wolford
University of Nebraska

HARPER & ROW, PUBLISHERS, New York
Cambridge, Philadelphia, San Francisco, Washington,
London, Mexico City, São Paulo, Singapore, Sydney

1817

Sponsoring Editor: Peter Richardson
Project Editor: David Nickol
Cover Design: Betty Sokol
Text Art: Fineline Illustrations, Inc.
Production: Delia Tedoff
Compositor: Waldman Graphics, Inc.
Printer and Binder: The Maple Press

Applied Numerical Methods for Digital Computation with FORTRAN and CSMP, Third Edition

Library of Congress Cataloging in Publication Data
James, M. L. (Merlin L.)
  Applied numerical methods for digital computation.

  Includes index.
  1. Numerical analysis—Data processing.   2. FORTRAN (Computer program language)   3. CSMP (Computer program language)   I. Smith, G. M. (Gerald M.)   II. Wolford, J. C.
III. Title.
QA297.J3   1985   519.4   84-19176
ISBN 0-06-043281-0

88 9 8 7 6

Contents

B Matrix Algebra 701

C Interpolating Polynomials and Application to Numerical Integration and Differentiation 710

Index 743

Preface

In view of the success of the second edition and the favorable comments from its users, no major changes have been made in the arrangement or scope of the material coverage in the third edition. The revisions, for the most part, involve modification or reinforcement of several areas to enhance understanding of the subject matter. Several methods have been replaced by ones considered to be more efficient or more current. Throughout the text, problems have been modified and a number of new problems added, some of which can be solved on today's pocket calculators, to illustrate computational procedures. Present-day personal microcomputers and available FORTRAN sofware may be used to solve essentially all the problems at the ends of the chapters with the exception of Chapter 9, which discusses CSMP (IBM's Continuous System Modeling Program). The authors have encountered no difficulty in solving a considerable number of the problems throughout the book using a microcomputer (64K bytes RAM, CP/M operating system, and 200K disk storage) with Microsoft FORTRAN-80.

In Chapter 2 Graeffe's root-squaring method for determining the roots of polynomials has been deleted, since its use on the digital computer is rather cumbersome. Bairstow's method, which is better suited for the computer in finding real and complex roots of polynomials, has been retained in the new edition.

In Chapter 3, a discussion of the solution of tridiagonal systems of algebraic equations has been added. Several changes have also been made in the discussion of eigenvalue problems. The determination of eigenvalues by the polynomial method has been retained, but the determination of eigenvectors by the polynomial method has been deleted in favor of more suitable methods for determining both eigenvalues and eigenvectors for problems involving matrices of order greater than 2. Iteration by the power method for obtaining the lowest, or highest, eigenvalue and corresponding eigenvector has been retained. The iteration procedure for obtaining intermediate eigenvalues and eigenvectors has been completely revised, with a detailed discussion of a simple and easily understood sweeping method known as Hotelling's deflation method. A brief discussion and program for using Jacobi's method on moderately sized matrices has been added, since this method yields all eigenvalues and eigenvectors with equal accuracy.

The discussion in Chapter 4 on curve fitting has been modified to enhance understanding of why a least-squares fit is a good approach to use with experimental data. To facilitate the formulation of the simultaneous algebraic equations that must be solved for curve fitting to experimental data, a matrix equation with summations has been added. The discussion of curve fitting involving exponential functions has been modified to show the difference between minimizing the summation of the deviations of the data from the assumed function curve and minimizing the summation of the natural logs of the deviations. A discussion of the spline fit has also been added to extend the coverage of curve fitting.

Consideration was given to moving the material on interpolating polynomials, found in Appendix C, into a separate chapter preceding the chapter on numerical integration and differentiation. However, it was decided to leave this material in an appendix because some users do not utilize the general interpolating polynomial approach in the derivation of numerical integration and differentiation formulas. The material is readily available in Appendix C for those who wish to use this more general approach.

As in the second edition, the arrangement and scope of the material permits the text to be used for different course levels. The mathematics required for the first five chapters involves differential and integral calculus and elementary matrix algebra. The basic concepts and operations of matrix algebra are reviewed in Appendix B for those who lack the necessary background in this area. A background in differential equations is essential for study beyond Chapter 5.

This edition continues to reflect the philosophy that the most effective approach to learning numerical methods is to integrate theoretical study with the solving of physical problems on the computer. Such problems have physical characteristics that enable students to recognize whether they are obtaining correct results or results indicating errors in their mathematical models or in their programs. Students also obtain practice in interpreting and analyzing numerical results, and gain a "feel" for the effect of various parameters on the behavior of particular systems. Throughout the text, theoretical discussions of numerical methods are complemented by the formulation of FORTRAN programs for the solution of typical problems from the various engineering disciplines.

Chapter 1 presents the elements of FORTRAN IV and FORTRAN 77. This chapter may serve as a reference, a review, or an introduction for those not already familiar with the FORTRAN language. Chapter 2 presents the most commonly used methods for obtaining the roots of algebraic and transcendental equations. In addition, Bairstow's method for obtaining roots (real or complex) of polynomials, along with synthetic division, are discussed in considerable detail. Chapter 3 presents the most commonly used methods for the solution of simultaneous linear algebraic equations, and also includes discussions of the solution of nonlinear equations and the eigenvalue problem. Chapter 4 presents curve fitting of experimental data by the method of least squares and also by the spline fit. Chapters 5 through 7 present many of the most commonly used methods for numerical integration and differentiation, and for integration of ordinary differential equations involving initial-value problems and boundary-value problems. Chapter 8 gives an introduction to the numerical solution of partial differential equations, and the concluding Chapter 9 presents the Continuous System Modeling Program (CSMP) with numerous examples to illustrate the power and simplicity of using a typical higher-level language.

Appendices A, B, and C contain supplemental material that may be helpful to some users of the text. Conversion factors relating English and SI systems of units are given in Appendix A. As mentioned previously, Appendix B reviews the basic concepts and operations of matrix algebra. Appendix C gives a rather extensive coverage of interpolating polynomials and their applications. This will be of interest to those who prefer the use of interpolating polynomials in certain derivations and uses in numerical methods.

The authors wish to acknowledge the many individuals who have contributed valuable suggestions for this revised edition. We are particularly grateful to Professors J. L. Barlow, S. I. Chou, R. E. Ekstrom, M. K. Householder, K. P. Meade, J. E. Panarelli, W. J. Remillard, V. C. Rideout, C. S. Rudisill, N. S. Salamon, T. E. Shoup, and R. C. Umholtz for their valuable suggestions. We are also grateful to our wives, Jane, Eunice, and Joan, for their patience and understanding during the preparation of this text. The authors also commend the staff of Harper & Row for the excellent and professional job done in the planning and production of this text.

M.L.J.
G.M.S.
J.C.W.

Chapter 1
Digital Computer Principles and FORTRAN IV and FORTRAN 77

1-1 INTRODUCTION

Primitive man did his counting and simple arithmetic with the aid of his fingers, pebbles, and sticks, by relating these objects to other objects such as sheep, goats, cattle, and so on. His pile of sticks or stones constituted the earliest primitive digital computer. The abacus, developed some 3000 years ago, represents the first great advance in digital computation.

In 1642 Blaise Pascal, a French religious philosopher, scientist, and mathematician, developed the first mechanical adding machine, which was similar in principle to present-day machines. This machine is now on display in a French museum. In 1671 the German philosopher and mathematician Gottfried Wilhelm von Leibniz independently conceived a more advanced mechanical calculator, which he completed in 1694.

Automatic mechanical calculators were suggested as early as the eighteenth century, but the technical knowledge required to build them was lacking. Joseph Jacquard, a French loom designer, perfected an automatic pattern loom in 1804 which contributed to the development of computers. The sequence of operations for the loom was controlled by punched cards, and the loom made intricate patterns as easily as other looms made plain cloth.

About 1833 the British mathematician Charles Babbage conceived and designed on paper the first automatic digital computer, which he called an "analytical engine." It had many features of modern computers. It was proposed to use a variation of the control mechanism of the Jacquard loom to control the sequence of arithmetic operations. These operations were to be specified, in advance, by means of punched cards. All calculations were to be done mechanically, and numbers were to be stored by the position of counter wheels. Unfortunately, this automatic computer was never built, owing to technical and financial difficulties, and an embittered Babbage died in 1871 without completing a working model, and with few people having even taken his work seriously.

It was not until 1937 that work was again begun on a computer similar in principle to the one conceived by Babbage. The design of the Automatic Sequence-Controlled Calculator, or Mark I, was begun at that time by Howard Aiken of Harvard University, and was completed with the help of the International Business Machine (IBM) Company in 1944. The Mark I was capable of performing a fixed sequence of operations controlled by punched tape. It consisted mainly of mechanical and electromechanical components and had a memory capable of storing 72 numbers of 24 digits each.

Shortly after Professor Aiken had begun work on the Mark I *electromechanical* computer, Dr. John V. Atanasoff of Iowa State College (now Iowa State University) conceived the principles upon which he hoped to build an *electronic* computer, using vacuum tubes for storage and arithmetic-logic functions. With the help of graduate assistant Clifford Berry and some very modest funding, they completed the Atanasoff-Berry computer, or ABC, in 1939. It was not a general-purpose computer but was wired to solve sets of simultaneous equations. It incorporated the very important principle of using binary arithmetic.

John W. Mauchly, who had met Atanasoff at a scientific meeting in 1940, visited the Iowa State professor in his home in Ames, Iowa, in June of 1941. The following September, Mauchly joined the faculty of the Moore School of Electrical Engineering at the University of Pennsylvania where he teamed with J. P. Eckert in designing an electronic computer. Army Ordnance funding was obtained in 1943, and the Electronic Numerical Integrator and Calculator (ENIAC) was completed in 1946. In later years a controversy arose (actually a court case was involved) over who invented the first electronic computer. Mauchly at that time claimed to have received little if any information of use for his design work on the ENIAC during his visit to Ames. The result of the court case, however, was that the patent on ENIAC was invalidated.

ENIAC did not employ binary arithmetic, and it depended upon an externally wired plugboard for sequence control. While ENIAC was under construction, Dr. John von Neumann of the Institute for Advanced Study at Princeton began consulting with the computer design group at the University of Pennsylvania on the design of a second electronic computer. In 1945 von Neumann wrote a report giving the requirements for the design of a computer using binary arithmetic and the very important principle of the *internally stored program.* Because the report was written by von Neumann, he has often been given all the credit for the idea of the internally stored program although the idea may well have evolved from group discussions that included von Neumann, Eckert, and Mauchly. Their computer, the Electronic Discrete Variable Automatic Computer (EDVAC) was operational by 1952. A computer operating on similar principles, the Electronic Delay Storage Automatic Computer (EDSAC), was completed at Cambridge University in 1949, well before EDVAC was operational.

The speed and reliability of computers were enhanced in the early 1950s by Dr. Jay Forrester's invention of the magnetic core memory, which was the predominantly used primary memory element of computers from about 1960 to the mid-1970s.

Digital computer installations were constructed at only a moderate rate in the early 1950s, since it was felt that all of the computing requirements of this country could be handled at a few large installations. However, the demand for computing facilities grew much faster than had been anticipated, and in the early 1960s computer manufacturers were putting their primary efforts into designing larger and faster computers. Toward the mid-1960s, some manufacturers began to recognize that not all users required these large and fast computers nor would they be able to afford them. It was recognized that even users of large computers might be able to utilize smaller computers to handle various specialized control functions and other specific applications more efficiently. Miniaturization of components, particularly the developments in integrated-circuit technology, had made it possible to build fairly powerful computers of comparatively small size. These were called *minicomputers*, and some are now faster and more powerful than large central computers of a few years ago. Most are capable of operating in a time-sharing mode, and high-level programming languages are available for them. Their cost ranges from several thousand dollars up to about $200,000 for the larger models with peripherals.

Further developments in integrated-circuit technology in the 1970s made it possible to put the entire computer processor and primary memory on a few silicon chips (or even on one chip), which led to the development of *microcomputers* (see Fig. 1-1). These are the smallest systems which have all the functional elements of larger systems. BASIC is the principal microcomputer language, but other high-level programming languages such as FORTRAN, PASCAL, and COBOL can be used with most microcomputers of today. Microcomputers are characterized by their low cost, which may range from less than $100 up to about $10,000. Today they are used by organizations as well as by millions of individuals as home or personal computers.

The so-called *mainframe* computers or large central computers are typified by those in use by large organizations serving many users that require extensive computations. Their cost may range from approximately $80,000 for the pro-

Figure 1-1 Microcomputer. (Courtesy of Apple Computer, Inc., Cupertino, California)

cessor and primary storage up to approximately $5,000,000 for the most powerful mainframe with peripherals.

At some government research laboratories, such as weather forecasting centers, and so forth, a need exists for faster computation than the mainframe computers can provide. These organizations use the largest and fastest computers made, called *supercomputers,* which may cost up to $10,000,000 or more. Even the 100 million calculations per second which is available today is insufficient for some applications, and research continues on still faster and more powerful computer architecture.

Large central computers are not ideally suited for handling large numbers of users needing only small computational capability. Therefore, there has been a trend for organizations to disperse smaller computers throughout their organization. In order to share computing and software resources, *networking* of computers has developed. Some networks include a number of computers having the same computing power while others may include microcomputers, minicomputers, and one or more mainframes. Jobs requiring small computational capability are handled by the microcomputers. Large "number-crunching" jobs are handled by the mainframes, with jobs requiring medium computational power being done by the minicomputers.

Owing to the use of high-level programming languages such as FORTRAN, it is not necessary to be familiar with the details of the internal computing processes of a digital computer. It is helpful, however, to have a general concept of the operational characteristics of the computer in order to understand its capabilities and limitations. Therefore, a brief discussion of computer components and operations is included here, along with a review of the most commonly used features of FORTRAN IV and FORTRAN 77.

1-2 DIGITAL-COMPUTER COMPONENTS

The modern electronic digital computer performs its functions by utilizing sequences of numerical operations performed upon discrete numbers. Five basic components are employed: (1) the *input* unit, which is used to provide data and instructions to the computer; (2) the *memory* or *storage* unit, in which data and instructions are stored; (3) the *arithmetic-logic* unit, which performs the arithmetic operations and provides the "decision-making" ability, or logic, of the computer; (4) the *control* unit, which controls the computer operations; and (5) the *output* unit, from which the computer results are obtained. The control unit and arithmetic-logic unit are often considered as a single unit, called the *central-processing* unit (CPU). Often primary memory is also considered as part of the CPU since the three components are usually physically housed together as a unit (they are on the same silicon chip in some microcomputers). The relationships of these components are shown symbolically in Fig. 1-2, where the lines indicate the flow of instructions and data or control information.

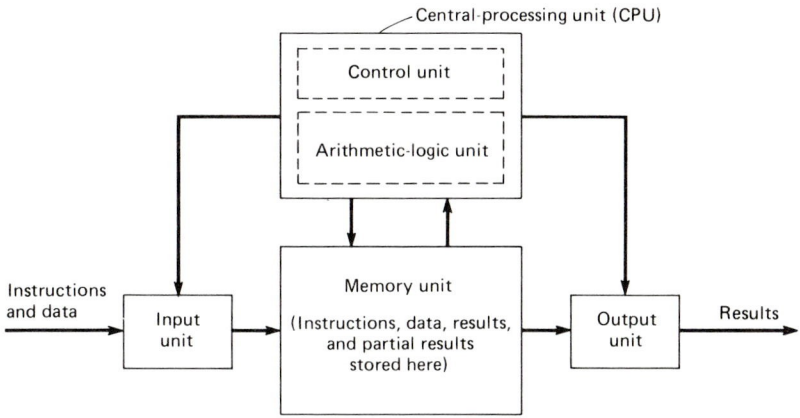

Figure 1-2 Basic components of a digital computer

Input Unit

The most common input device for today's computers is a terminal keyboard which, in some instances, may be very remote from the computer. The input unit may also be one of the following devices: a card reader, a paper-tape reader, a magnetic tape unit, or in some instances specialized input devices such as magnetic-ink character readers or optical-character readers. Magnetic disk drives may also serve as input (and output) units, but they are generally thought of as being auxiliary storage devices. The input device generally sends the program and data to auxiliary storage where it awaits further processing before actual computation begins.

Primary Memory or Storage Unit

The primary memory or storage unit must be capable of storing the program instructions and data when execution is ready to begin. Although many devices have been employed as storage elements, the two types in use today are magnetic cores and semiconductor chips, with the latter being used in the newer models of most manufacturers. The numbers stored are in some form of the binary number system. Numbers can be represented in this system by just two digits (0 and 1), corresponding very conveniently to the two polarity states of a magnetic core or a charged capacitor on a semiconductor chip. Research is currently being done on new types of storage elements, including the *Josephson junction*, which would operate at a temperature a few degrees above absolute zero.

The memory unit receives instructions and data and stores them in separately assigned locations. Each of these storage locations is designated by a numerical address which identifies the location to the computer. Once the data and instructions have been stored, they are subsequently always referred to by their numerical address. In addition to storing data and instructions, the memory unit is also utilized to store intermediate and final results for subsequent use or readout.

Arithmetic-Logic Unit

The arithmetic-logic unit consists of all the electronic circuitry necessary for performing the various arithmetic operations and for supplying computer logic. The latter is usually accomplished by performing tests on certain conditions existing in the computer to decide which of alternate sequences of steps will be followed.

Control Unit

The control unit consists of the circuitry required to take the instructions from memory, interpret them, and cause them to be executed. Normally, the instructions in memory are followed in sequential order, unless the control unit is instructed by the program to interrupt the sequence.

Output Unit

The results obtained as a consequence of the arithmetic operations performed by the computer must be communicated to the user. This is accomplished by some type of output unit. Output units usually consist of one of the following devices: a high-speed printer, a magnetic-tape unit, a card punch, a paper-tape punch, a visual display unit, a special typewriter, or a graphical plotter. Generally the computed results first go to an auxiliary storage device (perhaps to a print queue to await printing) or to a small storage device called a *buffer* that accepts data at high speeds from the CPU and releases it at the slower speed of the particular output device.

1-3 PREPARING A DIGITAL-COMPUTER PROGRAM

The first phase in programming a problem to the digital computer is to decide on the approach or method to be used in obtaining the solution. Since the digital computer is capable of performing only arithmetic operations, problems which cannot be solved by arithmetic procedures, when in their usual form, must be put in a form consistent with such procedures. Obviously, a problem in addition can be solved per se, since its solution is inherently an arithmetic operation. However, the closed-form solution of a differential equation, for example, is not an arithmetic operation. An arithmetic procedure for solving such an equation must be developed. Such procedures are discussed in detail in subsequent chapters.

Once a method of solution has been selected, the problem must be programmed to the computer as a definite step-by-step procedure. This is called an *algorithm*. One method of expressing the algorithm is to write the steps in a numbered sequence. More frequently, however, the algorithm is stated graphically by means of a *flow chart*, in which the steps are displayed in the form of a block diagram. A flow chart may show the required steps in considerable detail, or it may merely outline the general procedure necessary to obtain a computer solution to the problem. In general, excessively detailed procedures should be avoided in the flow chart, since its primary purpose is merely to outline the overall process, which will be implemented by the more specific steps appearing in the finished computer program. The use of a flow chart is illustrated in Ex. 1-1 (Fig. 1-4).

The computer must be instructed very specifically for it to perform its operations. In fact, each step must be initiated by an instruction. The instructions which the computer interprets and executes must be transmitted to it in a *coded* form it can interpret. The program in this form is called a *machine-language* program.

Writing a machine-language program is a tedious task if done manually, but this is seldom done. The computer itself can be programmed to write the machine-language program. The desired program is first written in a less-detailed and much simpler language very similar to ordinary English and algebra. The simpler program is then translated into machine language by the computer. To accomplish this translation, the computer must first have a specially written machine-language program loaded into its memory. Such a special program is called a *translator,* a *processor,* or a *compiler.* The FORTRAN processor, or compiler, is an example of such a special program.

The machine-language program generated by the computer generally goes to a direct-access storage device such as a disk file where it is available for immediate execution or where it is stored for later execution. This completes the programming and translation phases of the process. The execution phase, involving the actual computation, follows.

EXAMPLE 1-1

As an example of flow charting, let us consider the following problem. It is desired to find the first positive nonzero solution of the equation

$$1 + 5.25x - \sec\sqrt{0.68x} = 0$$

An approximate graph of the function $F(x) = 1 + 5.25x - \sec\sqrt{0.68x}$ is shown in Fig. 1-3. We must determine the first point at which the graph of the function crosses the x axis, as shown. For small values of x, the function will be positive. The technique will consist of calculating $F(x)$ for successively larger values of x, starting at $x = \Delta x$, and incrementing x by successive values

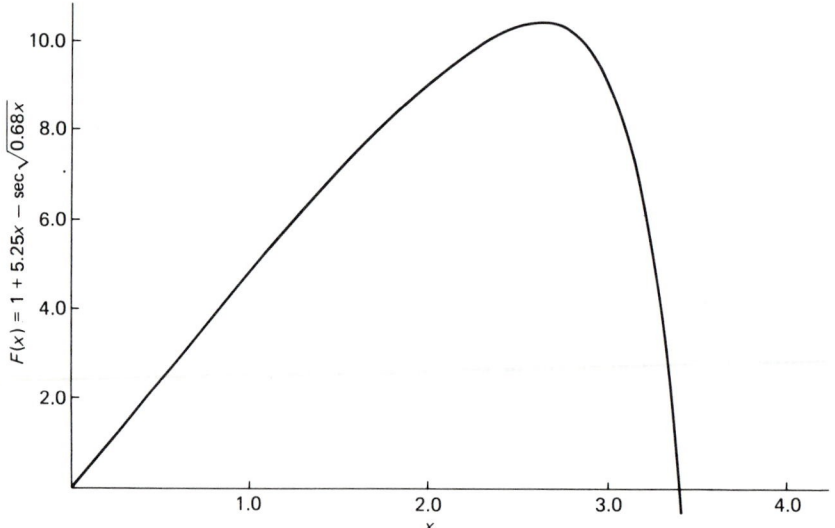

Figure 1-3 Approximate graph of $F(x) = 1 + 5.25x - \sec\sqrt{0.68x}$

of $\Delta x = 0.1$, until the function becomes negative. We will then know that the x value for which the function will be zero has been exceeded. We then revert to the immediately preceding x value and again increase x, this time incrementing by a smaller amount, say, one-tenth of the previously used Δx. Incrementing continues until the function again becomes negative. Again, we revert to the immediately preceding value of x and begin to increase x with still smaller increments. This procedure continues until the value of x which represents the first positive nonzero solution is obtained with the desired accuracy. The result is then printed.

As crude as this method may appear to be, a computer solution can be rapidly obtained by its use, since the computer performs the indicated operations so swiftly. Convergence to a solution can be obtained even more rapidly if we refine the preceding technique by writing a slightly more complicated program, using, for example, the Newton-Raphson method (illustrated in Sec. 2-6).

A flow chart for the foregoing solution is shown in Fig. 1-4. At this point, the reader should study the flow chart and correlate the notes in the blocks with the preceding problem discussion. Note that the flow chart merely outlines the general procedure to be followed. The actual program would be written by following this outline and detailing to the computer the specific instructions necessary to implement the procedures outlined in the blocks. The block symbols used for this flow chart, which will also be used in subsequent discussions in the text, are described in Fig. 1-5.

1-4 LARGE COMPUTER OPERATING SYSTEMS

Many computers operate under the control of an *operating system*. The user communicates with the operating system by means of a special language called, in some systems, the job-control language (JCL). The operating system consists of a number of machine-language programs stored in an auxiliary storage device, from which they can be brought into main memory. Typical system programs include program loaders, a job-control program for reading job-control language, a supervisor program for general supervisory tasks, the compilers for the various languages, and various service programs.

As an abbreviated example of how the operating system works, let us assume a user has written a program in FORTRAN, the high-level language used by most engineers. This FORTRAN program is called the *source program*. The source program along with the data required for the problem may be entered from a terminal, or in some instances, they may be punched on cards and entered via a card reader. Certain control statements are used to control the translation and execution of the FORTRAN program. One such control statement, for example, might specify that the program is to be compiled in FORTRAN. Such a statement would cause the system loader to locate the FORTRAN compiler and load it into the primary memory. Processing of the source statements would then be handled by this compiler.

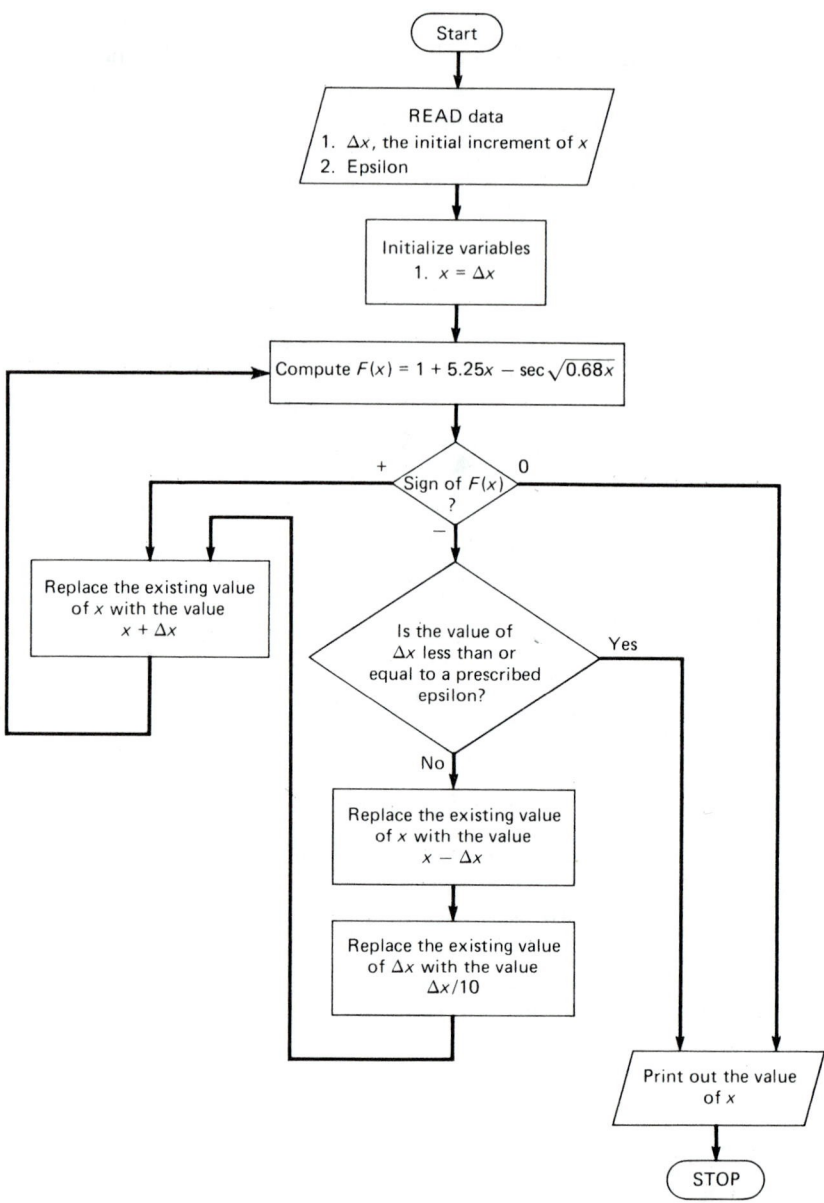

Figure 1-4 Flow chart for Ex. 1-1

The output of the compilation process is called the *object program*. The object program may not be in final form for execution but may require a certain amount of editing first. A service program, called the *linkage-editor* in some systems, does this task. This editing includes assigning final main storage addresses to the program instructions. The resulting machine-language program,

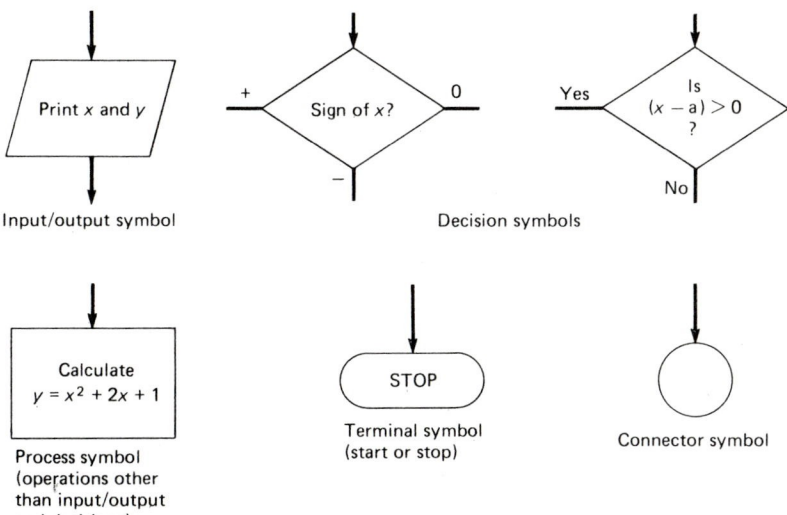

Figure 1-5   Symbols used in flow charts

ready for execution, is called the *load module* in some systems. In other systems it is known simply as the object program.

The final load module then goes to direct-access storage for immediate execution as in a "compile-and-go" operation, or to a file for later execution if desired.

At some computer installations, jobs are not run in the order in which they are received by the system input devices. Instead they go to a queue on an auxiliary storage device from which they are processed according to some selected priority system.

1-5 FORTRAN

As we have seen, the modern method of solving engineering problems on the digital computer involves the use of compilers to simplify the programming procedures. One of the most frequently used compilers is FORTRAN, first developed for the IBM 704 computer in 1956. The name FORTRAN is derived from FORmula TRANslator. It was designed primarily for use by engineers and scientists in handling problems involving considerable amounts of numerical computation. The use of the FORTRAN compiler permits the engineer to write a program in a simple language closely resembling that of ordinary English and algebra and involving a minimum of programming steps. The computer itself thus performs the tedious task of coding the program into the machine language understood by the computer. FORTRAN has evolved considerably since 1956, with earlier versions being supplanted by newer and more sophisticated versions.

Currently the most widely used versions are FORTRAN IV and FORTRAN 77.

FORTRAN 77 is the designation given to the most recent standard for FORTRAN of the American National Standards Institute (ANSI) approved in 1978.[1] Most of standard FORTRAN IV is also valid in FORTRAN 77. FORTRAN IV along with the extensions of FORTRAN 77 are reviewed in the sections which follow.

1-6 THE ELEMENTS OF FORTRAN

The sentences of FORTRAN are called *statements*. Most versions list from five to nine different types of statements (FORTRAN 77 specifies five types). These statements will be discussed later, but first we will review the elements used to form such statements. These include constants, variables, subscripted variables, operation symbols, expressions, and mathematical functions.

1-7 CONSTANTS

A constant is a fixed, unchanging quantity. There are three principal types of constants: (1) numerical, (2) logical, and (3) literal (called *character* constants in FORTRAN 77). Numerical constants may be further subdivided into *integer* constants, *real* constants, and *complex* constants. Both real and complex constants may be *single-precision* or *double-precision*. We will now discuss each of the above in the order mentioned.

Integer Constants

An integer constant is a number written without a decimal point and can thus be only a whole number. The use of a sign is optional except when the number is negative. Embedded commas are not permitted, and there is a maximum magnitude which cannot be exceeded, the magnitude depending upon the computer being used. The following are examples of valid integer constants:

0   216   1   −42963

Real Constants

Real constants are numbers written with a decimal point. As with integer constants, embedded commas are not permitted. There are two basic forms, *ordinary decimal* form such as −983.12, and *exponent* form, which consists of the use of a real constant followed by an E and either a positive or negative power of 10. The following are examples of valid exponent forms:

1.573E+13   −2.746E+11   −1.86E−12   20E+4

The first one, for example, specifies that the real constant 1.573 is multiplied

---

[1] American National Standard Programming Language FORTRAN, ANSI X3.9-1978.

by 10 to the 13th power. The last one illustrates that if the real constant is a whole number, it is permissible to omit the decimal point in using the exponent form. If the power of ten is positive, the positive sign after the E is optional. The maximum number of significant digits varies with the FORTRAN version used but is usually from seven to nine. The minimum and maximum magnitudes of real constants also vary with the FORTRAN version used. Typical limits on the magnitude of real constants, for example, might be approximately 10^{-78} to 10^{75}. The real constants discussed in this paragraph are *single-precision*.

Double-Precision Real Constants

Double-precision real constants, called simply double-precision constants in some FORTRAN versions, use the letter D in the exponent instead of E. The maximum number of significant digits varies from approximately 14 to 29 but is typically about 16 or 17. For example,

987654321.234567D−26

is a valid double-precision real constant. In some versions constants may be double-precision by virtue of the fact that they contain more digits than are valid for real constants, and the D exponent is not required to make it double-precision. However, it is recommended that double-precision constants always be written with a D exponent, since double-precision is sometimes lost when it is not used, even though the system reference manual may imply that it will not be. The minimum and maximum magnitudes of double-precision real constants are the same as for single-precision as mentioned in the preceding paragraph.

Complex Constants

Complex constants are represented by an ordered pair of real constants. The two real constants are separated by a comma and enclosed in parentheses. The first real constant is the *real* part of the complex constant, and the second is the *imaginary* part. For example,

(5.71, −2.95)   represents 5.71 − 2.95i

Double-precision complex constants, for which both parts are double-precision real, are not available in all FORTRAN versions.

Logical Constants

Logical constants specify the logical values "true" and "false." When appearing in a source program, they are written as

.TRUE.   and   .FALSE.

The periods shown are required.

Literal or Character Constants

A literal constant is a string of alphabetic, numeric, or special characters, which are either enclosed in apostrophes or preceded by wH, where w is the number of characters in the string. When the characters are preceded by wH, they are often referred to as a *Hollerith constant*. For example,

38HDYNAMIC CHARACTERISTICS OF A MECHANISM

illustrates the Hollerith form, and

'DISPLACEMENT VELOCITY ACCELERATION'

shows the use of apostrophes.

In FORTRAN 77, the character string enclosed in apostrophes is called a *character constant*.

1-8 VARIABLES

A FORTRAN variable is a symbolic name for a quantity that is stored in computer memory. It consists of from one to six alphabetic and numeric (alphanumeric) characters, the first of which must be alphabetic. FORTRAN IV provides for integer, real, complex, and logical variables. Real and complex variables may be either single-precision or double-precision. FORTRAN 77 provides for character variables in addition to those in FORTRAN IV.

Integer Variables

The first character of an integer variable name is I, J, K, L, M, or N. A different character than those listed may be used if the name appears in an INTEGER explicit type specification statement, or if the variable is specified as integer by an IMPLICIT type specification statement (these statements are discussed later under Specification Statements). If the variable is specified as integer by virtue of its first character being I, J, K, L, M, or N, its type is said to be specified by the *predefined specification*. JOBNO is a valid integer variable name, for example.

Real Variables

If a real variable has its type specified by the predefined specification, its name will begin with any alphabetic character other than I, J, K, L, M, or N. An example would be VELOC.

Double-Precision Real, Complex, Double-Precision Complex, and Logical Variables

These variables must have their type specified by either the explicit or the IMPLICIT type specification, as there is no predefined specification for these variables. As mentioned earlier, these statements are discussed later under Specification Statements.

Character Variables

In FORTRAN 77, character variables must be explicitly typed with a CHARACTER type statement, or typed by means of an IMPLICIT statement. These statements will be discussed later under Specification Statements.

1-9 ARRAYS

A FORTRAN *array* is a set of variables identified by a single name. The different elements of the array are differentiated from one another by using subscripts with the array name. Thus the array elements are *subscripted variables.* The rules for choosing the array name are the same as those that govern nonsubscripted variables. They may also be the same modes (integer, real, and so forth) as nonsubscripted variables. The number of elements in an array must be specified by giving the number of subscripts and the maximum value of each subscript in a DIMENSION, COMMON, or explicit type specification statement. For example, the statement

```
DIMENSION AMATR(50,50)
```

indicates that there are two subscripts, each having a maximum value of 50. Each has a minimum value of one by default. (In FORTRAN 77, a DIMENSION statement may specify a *lower bound* for a subscript, which may be positive, negative, or zero. See the discussion of FORTRAN 77 subscripts in the following section and the discussion of DIMENSION statements in Sec. 1-23 on specification statements.) The array name is AMATR, and AMATR(10,25) would be a particular element of the array. AMATR(I,J) would represent any particular element corresponding to the values of I and J. Arrays are stored in computer memory in ascending storage locations, with the value of the first subscript increasing most rapidly and the value of the last subscript increasing least rapidly. Most FORTRAN IV versions permit up to three subscripts (three-dimensional arrays), but in some versions up to seven-dimensional arrays are possible. Standard FORTRAN 77 permits up to seven-dimensional arrays.

   FORTRAN 77 provides for character type arrays in addition to the types valid in FORTRAN IV.

1-10 SUBSCRIPTS

Subscripts are most often used in one of the following forms:

Symbolic Form	FORTRAN Form
v	JMAX
c	3
$v + c$	I+1
$v - c$	J-1

where v represents an unsigned, nonsubscripted integer variable, and c represents an unsigned integer constant. The numerical value of the subscript must be positive in FORTRAN IV.

Most versions of FORTRAN IV also permit the following forms:

Symbolic Form	FORTRAN Form
$c*v$	3*JOB
$c*v + c'$	6*I+7
$c*v - c'$	4*N-2

In some FORTRAN IV versions considerably more freedom is allowed in the choice of subscript forms. Function names, subscripted variables, and all the arithmetic operators may appear in expressions used as subscripts. It is also permissible in these versions to mix real and integer modes in subscript expressions. The values of all expressions used in subscripts are converted to integer mode after evaluation if they are not already integer, and the resulting subscript values must always be greater than or equal to 1.

FORTRAN 77 permits negative and zero subscripts. In order to use a negative or zero subscript, however, the DIMENSION statement must specify a lower dimension bound which is negative or zero. If no lower bound is specified, it is 1 by default. (See the discussion of DIMENSION statements in Sec. 1-23 on Specification Statements for the method of specifying a lower bound for a subscript.) An array subscript can be an integer constant, variable, or expression, and up to seven-dimensional arrays are permitted.

1-11 ARITHMETIC EXPRESSIONS

The most simple arithmetic expression is a single constant, variable, or function. More complicated expressions are formed by combining constants, variables, and functions with arithmetic operators. These operators are

Operator	Operation	Hierarchy Level
**	Exponentiation	1st
* and /	Multiplication and division	2nd
+ and −	Addition and subtraction	3rd

The hierarchy determines which of two consecutive operations is performed first. A group of operations of the same hierarchy are performed from left to right, except that when exponentiation operators appear consecutively, evaluation is from right to left. Parentheses may also be used to form groupings and thus control the order of operations just as they are used in ordinary algebra. Evaluation starts with the innermost parentheses and works outward with operations performed according to hierarchy within the parentheses.

In some FORTRAN IV versions, modes cannot be mixed except for permitting real quantities to be raised to integer powers. FORTRAN 77 and some FORTRAN IV versions allow mixed mode expressions. A general rule in mixing modes is that real takes precedence over integer and complex takes precedence over both integer and real. That is, an integer quantity times a real quantity will be real, and a real or integer quantity times a complex quantity will be complex.

Care should be exercised in using any pure integer quotient in an expression. For example, the quotient J/2 with J = 7 gives a value of 3 since integer quotients are truncated. Using J/2. (assuming mixed-mode expressions are permitted) would result in a value of 3.5 for the quotient.

If a positive quantity is being raised to a whole number power, an integer type exponent is preferable. Negative quantities *cannot* be raised to a real power even though the power is a whole number.

A positive or negative sign (to be distinguished from a plus or minus indicating addition or subtraction) is treated in the hierarchy the same as the plus or minus in addition and subtraction. Thus C = − A∗B is treated as C = − (A∗B).

No two arithmetic operators may appear sequentially in an expression. Thus A∗ − B must be written as A∗(− B). A typical valid FORTRAN expression is

```
((A+B)*C-D)/F
```

which represents the algebraic expression

$$\frac{(a + b)c - d}{f}$$

Blank spaces may be used as desired in FORTRAN expressions: for example, to increase readability.

1-12 LOGICAL EXPRESSIONS

A logical expression always has the value "true" or "false." One of the more common uses of logical expressions is in the Logical IF statement which is discussed later. The simplest form of a logical expression is a single logical constant, a single logical variable, or a single logical function. More complicated logical expressions state conditions which are either true or false. One such logical expression is called a *relational* expression, which simply makes a declaration regarding the relative magnitudes of two arithmetic expressions. For example, it might state that A + B is greater than C∗D. In FORTRAN IV or 77 this is stated by writing the two arithmetic expressions separated by the relational operator .GT. which gives

A + B   .GT.   C∗D

The relational operators available in FORTRAN IV or 77 are as follows:

Relational Operator	Definition
.GT.	Greater than
.GE.	Greater than or equal to
.EQ.	Equal to
.NE.	Not equal to
.LT.	Less than
.LE.	Less than or equal to

Only single- and double-precision real and integer arithmetic expressions may be combined by relational operators. In some FORTRAN IV versions arithmetic expressions of different modes cannot be combined by relational operators, but in other FORTRAN IV versions and in FORTRAN 77, mixing of real, double-precision real, and integer modes across the relational operator is permissible. Complex and logical quantities cannot be used in relational expressions.

More complicated logical expressions can be formed by combining relational expressions, logical constants, logical functions, and logical variables with the logical operators .AND., .OR., and .NOT.. Suppose X and Y represent any of the logical quantities mentioned above (relational expressions, logical constants, and so forth). Then

.NOT.   X

is true if X is false, or false if X is true. The logical expression

X   .AND.   Y

is true if and only if both X and Y are true. The logical expression

X   .OR.   Y

is true if either X or Y or both are true, and false if *both* X and Y are false.

Still more complicated logical expressions involving several logical operators are possible. Parentheses may be used to control the order in which operations are performed in logical expressions. When parentheses are not used, a hierarchy determines the order of performing operations which is as follows:

Operation	Hierarchy
Evaluation of functions	1st
**	2nd
* and /	3rd
+ and −	4th
Application of relational operators	
.GT., .LT., etc.	5th
Application of .NOT.	6th
Application of .AND.	7th
Application of .OR.	8th

1-13 CHARACTER EXPRESSIONS (FORTRAN 77 ONLY)

FORTRAN 77 permits the use of character expressions of the form

```
character element//character element//character element . . .
```

where a character element is a character constant, variable, function reference, or expression. The operator // is called the concatenation operator and is the only operator available for character expressions. The character expression

```
'FOR'//'TRAN'
```

is equivalent to

```
'FORTRAN'
```

Spaces, if they occur, are considered as characters.

Character expressions may be compared in relational expressions according to a collating sequence (usually the ASCII collating sequence). This feature may be used for alphabetizing lists of character strings, searching for particular words or other character strings, and so forth. To use this feature, and for functional uses of the concatenation operator, refer to your computer FORTRAN reference manual.

1-14 FORTRAN-SUPPLIED MATHEMATICAL FUNCTION SUBPROGRAMS

Certain commonly used mathematical operations have had their procedures for evaluation preprogrammed as function subprograms. These preprogrammed procedures are in a library (such as in a disk file) and are available to the FORTRAN compiler. To use the functions, it is only necessary to write the function name in the expression in which it is required and to supply the argument(s). This is often called *referencing the function*.

Arguments in general are expressions but often are just single variables. In the statement

```
Y = SQRT(X) + B
```

SQRT is the name of a FORTRAN-supplied function used for obtaining the square root of an argument. The variable X is the argument which has been supplied by the programmer. The square root of the argument is obtained and the value of variable B added to it. When there is more than one argument, they are separated by commas as illustrated in the statement

```
M = MOD(I,J) + 1
```

Some commonly used FORTRAN IV mathematical function subprograms are given in the following table. The numbers following the function and argument types refer to 8-bit bytes of memory in a computer in which *single-precision* and *double-precision* real quantities are stored in 4 and 8 bytes of memory, respectively. Complex quantities require twice as much memory space as real quantities so 16 bytes, for example, could be required for a double-precision complex quantity.

Function Name	Number of Arguments	Function Type	Argument Type	Definition (a is argument)
EXP	1	Real(4)	Real(4)	
DEXP	1	Real(8)	Real(8)	e^a
CEXP	1	Complex(8)	Complex(8)	
CDEXP	1	Complex(16)	Complex(16)	
ALOG	1	Real(4)	Real(4)	
DLOG	1	Real(8)	Real(8)	$\log_e (a)$
CLOG	1	Complex(8)	Complex(8)	
CDLOG	1	Complex(16)	Complex(16)	
ALOG10	1	Real(4)	Real(4)	$\log_{10} (a)$
DLOG10	1	Real(8)	Real(8)	
ARSIN	1	Real(4)	Real(4)	arc sin (a)
DARSIN	1	Real(8)	Real(8)	(in radians)
ARCOS	1	Real(4)	Real(4)	arc cos (a)
DARCOS	1	Real(8)	Real(8)	(in radians)
ATAN	1	Real(4)	Real(4)	arc tan (a)
ATAN2	2	Real(4)	Real(4)	arc tan (a_1/a_2)
DATAN	1	Real(8)	Real(8)	arc tan (a)
DATAN2	2	Real(8)	Real(8)	arc tan (a_1/a_2)

Function Name	Number of Arguments	Function Type	Argument Type	Definition (a is argument)
SIN	1	Real(4)	Real(4)	
DSIN	1	Real(8)	Real(8)	sin (a)
CSIN	1	Complex(8)	Complex(8)	(a is in radians)
CDSIN	1	Complex(16)	Complex(16)	
COS	1	Real(4)	Real(4)	
DCOS	1	Real(8)	Real(8)	cos (a)
CCOS	1	Complex(8)	Complex(8)	(a is in radians)
CDCOS	1	Complex(16)	Complex(16)	
TAN	1	Real(4)	Real(4)	tan (a)
DTAN	1	Real(8)	Real(8)	(a is in radians)
COTAN	1	Real(4)	Real(4)	cotan (a)
DCOTAN	1	Real(8)	Real(8)	(a is in radians)
SQRT	1	Real(4)	Real(4)	
DSQRT	1	Real(8)	Real(8)	$\sqrt{a}$
CSQRT	1	Complex(8)	Complex(8)	
CDSQRT	1	Complex(16)	Complex(16)	
TANH	1	Real(4)	Real(4)	tanh (a)
DTANH	1	Real(8)	Real(8)	
SINH	1	Real(4)	Real(4)	sinh (a)
DSINH	1	Real(8)	Real(8)	
COSH	1	Real(4)	Real(4)	cosh (a)
DCOSH	1	Real(8)	Real(8)	
ABS	1	Real(4)	Real(4)	$|a|$
IABS	1	Integer(4)	Integer(4)	
DABS	1	Real(8)	Real(8)	$\sqrt{a^2 + b^2}$
CABS	1	Real(4)	Complex (8)	for argument
CDABS	1	Real(8)	Complex(16)	$a + ib$
INT	1	Integer(4)	Real(4)	Truncates argument to largest integer having an absolute value less than or equal to argument. Sign same as sign of argument
AINT	1	Real(4)	Real(4)	
IDINT	1	Integer(4)	Real(8)	

(Continued)

Function Name	Number of Arguments	Function Type	Argument Type	Definition (a is argument)
AMOD	2	Real(4)	Real(4)	Defined as
MOD	2	Integer(4)	Integer(4)	$a_1 - [a_1/a_2]a_2$
DMOD	2	Real(8)	Real(8)	where $[a_1/a_2]$ is truncated value of the quotient
REAL	1	Real(4)	Complex(8)	Obtains the real part of a complex argument
AIMAG	1	Real(4)	Complex(8)	Obtains the imaginary part of complex argument
CMPLX	2	Complex(8)	Real(4)	Expresses two
DCMPLX	2	Complex(16)	Real(8)	real arguments in complex form
CONJG	1	Complex(8)	Complex(8)	Obtains conju-
DCONJG	1	Complex(16)	Complex(16)	gate of a complex argument

The functions listed in the table above are all standard in FORTRAN 77 except for the cotangent and double-precision complex functions, which are available in some FORTRAN 77 versions as extensions. The spellings of the arc sine and arc cosine functions have been changed from ARSIN, DARSIN, ARCOS, and DARCOS in FORTRAN IV to ASIN, DASIN, ACOS, and DACOS in FORTRAN 77. Also FORTRAN 77 permits the use of *generic names* for most of the functions shown in the table as well as the *specific names* listed in the table. For example, the generic name SQRT can be used instead of one of the specific names SQRT, DSQRT, or CSQRT, with the function type being determined by the argument type. For example, using the generic name SQRT, SQRT(RAD) would be single-precision real if RAD were single-precision real; it would be double-precision real if RAD were double-precision real, and so forth. Standard FORTRAN 77 generic names corresponding to the functions listed in the table are EXP, LOG, LOG10, ASIN, ACOS, ATAN, ATAN2, SIN, COS, TAN, SQRT, TANH, SINH, COSH, ABS, IABS, INT, MOD, CONJ, and CMPLX.

1-15 FORTRAN STATEMENTS

A FORTRAN source program consists of a sequence of statements (instructions) written in FORTRAN language. Statements are grouped into two general classes, executable and nonexecutable, with each class consisting of several types.

Standard FORTRAN IV uses eight types of statements, but these are reduced to five in FORTRAN 77 by combining some of the eight types as shown below. Of the eight types, three are executable. They are

1. arithmetic- and logical-assignment
2. control
3. input/output

The five types of nonexecutable statements are

1. FORMAT
2. DATA initialization   } Grouped as specification statements
3. specification   in FORTRAN 77
4. statement function definition } Grouped as subprogram statements
5. subprogram   in FORTRAN 77

In the next four sections we will discuss *executable* statements.

1-16 ARITHMETIC-ASSIGNMENT STATEMENTS

The arithmetic-assignment statement consists of a single subscripted or non-subscripted variable to the left of an equal sign and an arithmetic expression on the right of the equal sign. In executing the statement, the arithmetic expression is evaluated, and the resulting value is assigned to the variable to the left of the equal sign. The following is a typical arithmetic-assignment statement:

```
X=(−B+SQRT(B*B−4*A*C))/(2.*A)
```

If x has a value prior to the execution of the statement, this value will be *replaced* by the value calculated during the execution. In FORTRAN the equality sign does not have the customary mathematical meaning of "is equal to." Instead it means "is to be replaced by." For example, the FORTRAN statement

```
J=J+2
```

is a perfectly valid arithmetic-assignment statement, with the FORTRAN interpretation of the equality sign given above. This statement instructs the computer to add 2 to the existing value of J, and to then replace the existing value of J by the sum obtained.

It is sometimes necessary or convenient to use different modes on both sides of an equality sign, and such a procedure is valid. That is, the expression on the right side of the equality sign need not be in the same mode as the variable on the left side. For example, if we have the statement

```
A=I+1
```

the value of the expression $I+1$ will be calculated in integer mode, and this value will then be stored in the location referred to by the variable name A in real mode. In the statement

```
J = X**2 - B
```

the expression on the right is evaluated in real mode, and the result is then truncated to the next lowest integer value and stored in integer mode in the location referred to by the variable name J.

1-17 LOGICAL-ASSIGNMENT STATEMENTS

Statements consisting of a logical variable on the left of an equal sign and a logical expression on the right side are called logical-assignment statements. The expression on the right is evaluated as either "true" or "false," and this logical value is then assigned to the variable on the left. The following are examples of valid logical-assignment statements, where the variables on the left have been specified as logical variables:

```
LV1 = .TRUE.
G = X.GT.Y
F = A.GT.B .AND. C.EQ.D
```

When logical quantities are involved, no mixing of modes across the equal sign is permitted.

1-18 CONTROL STATEMENTS

A FORTRAN program consists of a number of statements which are executed sequentially unless the sequence is changed by a control statement. Control statements may alter the sequence by causing a direct transfer from one location in the program to another, by conditional branching, or by looping. They also provide a means of temporarily suspending execution of a program and of terminating execution of the object program. In all transfer of control statements, the statement to which control is transferred must be executable. Various control statements are discussed in the following paragraphs.

Unconditional GO TO Statement

This statement, referred to as an unconditional branch or transfer statement, is used to interrupt the usual sequential execution of statements by an unconditional transfer of control to a specified *numbered* statement. For example, the statement

```
GO TO 16
```

instructs the computer to execute immediately the statement numbered 16, regardless of the position of the statement in the program sequence. Any executable statement immediately following a GO TO statement must be numbered, or it can never be executed.

Computed GO TO Statement

This statement is a conditional branch or transfer type of control statement, since the transfer of control depends on the value of a nonsubscripted integer variable which is a part of the computed GO TO statement. For example, the statement

```
GO TO (3,8,11,24),J
```

will transfer control to statement 3 if the value of J is 1, to statement 8 if J is 2, and so on. Any number of statements to which control can be transferred is permissible. If the integer variable in the computed GO TO statement (J in the example above) has a value greater than the number of statements referred to in the parentheses, the next statement is executed.

Arithmetic IF Statement

The arithmetic IF statement is a conditional branching type of control statement. It provides for control to be transferred to any one of three numbered statements, depending on the value of the expression enclosed in parentheses which is part of the IF statement. For example, the statement

```
IF(X−A)14,13,7
```

transfers control to statement 14 if the quantity $(X - A)$ is *negative*, to statement 13 if $(X - A)$ is equal to *zero*, and to statement 7 if $(X - A)$ is *positive*. The parenthetical portion of the IF statement may contain any legitimate arithmetic expression other than a complex expression, including a single variable name.

Logical IF Statement

The logical IF statement has the general form

```
IF(e)s
```

where e represents a *logical expression* and s represents any executable FORTRAN statement except a DO or another logical IF. For example, if A and B are real variables and LV1, LV2, and LV3 are logical variables, the following are valid logical IF statements:

```
IF(A .GT. B)GO TO 16
IF(LV1)Y=A/B
IF(LV2 .AND. A .LE. B)LV3=.TRUE.
```

If the logical expression in parentheses (symbolized by e in the general expression) is true, the statement following (symbolized by s) is executed. The statement following the logical IF statement is then executed unless statement s is a transfer-of-control statement. In the latter instance, control is transferred as specified by statement s. If the logical expression e is false, control passes to the next statement in the program following the logical IF statement. In the first of the examples of valid logical IF statements shown above, control would be transferred to statement 16 if A were greater than B. If A were not greater than B, control would transfer to the statement in the program following the logical IF statement.

The Block IF Statement (FORTRAN 77 Only)

The block IF and associated statements have the basic form

```
IF(e)THEN
. . . . .
. . . .          } a block of statements
. . . . .
ENDIF
```

where e represents a logical expression. The block statements following IF(e)THEN consist of one or more statements which are executed if the logical expression e is true. If e is false, control jumps to the first statement following ENDIF and the block of statements is skipped.

An alternate form of the block IF and associated statements is

```
IF(e)THEN
. . . . .
. . . .          } first block of statements
. . . . .
ELSE
. . . . .
. . . .          } second block of statements
. . . . .
ENDIF
```

If the logical expression e is true, the first block of statements (called the THEN block) is executed followed by control jumping to the first statement after ENDIF; that is, the second block of statements is skipped. If e is false, the first block of statements is skipped and control jumps to the first statement of the second block (called the ELSE block). The ELSE block is next executed followed by control jumping to the first statement following ENDIF. It is not permissible to transfer into a THEN or ELSE block from outside that particular block other than in the manner just described.

DO Statement

The use of DO loops in FORTRAN IV will be discussed first. This will be followed by a discussion of the differences found and extensions permitted in FORTRAN 77.

The DO statement causes the computer to repeat a specific sequence of statements, within a given program, a prescribed number of times. The statements in the sequence to be repeated are known as the *range* of the DO statement. This type of statement is convenient to use when a known number of repetitions, or loops, is required for a given sequence of statements. It may also be used when a maximum number of repetitions is specified, with a transfer from the DO loop *possibly* occurring before the maximum number of repetitions specified has been completed. The IF statement, discussed previously, may also be used to accomplish the same type of repetitive operation, but it generally is not so convenient as the DO statement.

The general form of the DO statement is

DO n i = m_1, m_2, m_3

in which n represents the number of the last statement in the range of the DO, i represents a nonsubscripted integer variable known as the *index* or DO *variable*, and m_1, m_2, and m_3 represent unsigned integer constants or non-subscripted integer variables called *indexing parameters*. Individually, they are called, respectively, the *initial value*, the *test value*, and the *increment*. All indexing parameters have values greater than zero.

The DO statement causes the statements within the range to be executed repeatedly. For the first execution of the range, the index has the value of m_1, the initial value. After each execution of the statements in the range, the index is incremented by the value of m_3, the increment. The index is then compared with the value of m_2, the test value. If it is less than or equal to the test value, execution of the statements in the range is carried out again. If the index value exceeds the test value, the execution of the DO loop ceases, and control passes to the first statement following the end of the range of the DO. The DO statement is then said to be satisfied, and the exit from the DO loop is known as a *normal exit*.

Let us consider the DO statement

DO 6I = 1,100,2

as an example. The number 6 identifies statement number 6 as the last statement of the group of statements which are to be executed repeatedly. The integer variable 1 is the index in this example. The index may be used in statements within the range for any purpose for which any other integer variable would be permissible. It is most commonly used as a subscript for a subscripted variable. However, it is not necessary that the index be used in any of the statements in the range. If it is not, it merely serves as a counter and is incremented by the value of m_3 after each execution of the range. The index in this example would have a value of 1 during the first execution. Following each execution of the loop, the index would be incremented by the value of 2. When the value of the index reached 99, an additional execution of the loop would be made. The index would then assume a value of 101. This value would then be compared with the test value of 100, and, since it exceeds the test value, execution of the DO loop would cease.

After a normal exit, the integer variable assigned as the index may or may not be defined and available for use in a subsequent portion of the program, depending upon the version of FORTRAN being used. Usually, it is not. If control is transferred from a statement in the DO loop to a statement outside the DO loop before the DO statement is satisfied (a transfer of this type is permitted at any time), the index remains defined and may be used, as so defined, in a subsequent portion of the program.

It is permissible to have one or more other DO statements within the range of a DO loop. In this instance, the set of DO loops is referred to as nested DOs. If the range of a DO statement includes another DO statement, the former is called the *outer* or *major* DO, and the latter is called the *inner* or *minor* DO. All the statements in the range of an inner DO must also be in the range of the outer DO. This rule allows the inner and outer DO loops to end with a statement common to each loop, if this is desired. A set of nested DOs, as a portion of an overall program, might appear as follows:

```
      . . . . .
      READ (5,2)M
    2 FORMAT (I4)
      N = M + 1
      DO 9 I = 2,M
      DO 9 J = 2,N
      L = J - 1
      SUM = 0.
      DO 8 K = 1,L
    8 SUM = SUM + B(I,K)*T(K,J)
    9 B(I,J) = A(I,J) - SUM
      . . . . .
      . . . . .
```

In the normal sequence of operations of a set of nested DOs, control is first passed to the outer DO from the preceding portion of the program. The statements in the outer DO range preceding the inner DO statement are then executed in some type of sequence until that sequence arrives at the inner DO statement, to which control then passes. After the inner DO is satisfied, or after exit from it occurs by a transfer, any remaining statements in the outer DO are executed, completing the first cycle of the outer DO. Unless exit occurs from an inner DO by a transfer, it cycles the specified number of times and is satisfied for each separate execution of the range of the outer DO.

It is not permissible to transfer from outside the range of a DO to a statement inside the range of the DO, except that a transfer may be made into the *innermost* DO loop of a nest of DOs provided there has previously been a transfer *out* of this innermost DO loop, and the index or indexing parameters have not been changed by statements executed between the transfer out and the transfer back in. However, it is permissible to transfer out of any DO loop to a *subprogram*, and to then return from it. That is, a subprogram may be used within any DO loop in a nest of DOs.

If the constant or variable in the DO statement, defining the increment, is omitted (along with the comma which would precede it), the index will be incremented by 1 after each execution.

There are certain restrictions placed on the statements in the range of the DO which must be observed. They are

1. No statement within the range of the DO should redefine the index or any of the indexing parameters.
2. The last statement in the range of a DO loop must be an executable statement, but it cannot be a GO TO statement (unconditional or computed), an arithmetic IF statement, another DO statement, a PAUSE, STOP, or RETURN statement, or a logical IF containing any of these statements.

In FORTRAN 77, the DO variable is not restricted to being an integer variable as it is in FORTRAN IV but may be either integer or real. The indexing parameters are not restricted to being integer constants or variables but may be arithmetic expressions. If expressions are used, they are first evaluated and then converted to the same type as the DO variable (integer or real). Unlike FORTRAN IV, the initial value and test value can be negative or zero, and the increment can be negative, which will cause decrementing. The increment cannot be zero.

In FORTRAN 77, there is not necessarily always at least one pass through the loop as is the case in standard FORTRAN IV. For example, the DO statement

```
DO 6I=2,1,1
```

would not cause execution of any of the statements in the range of the DO since the initial value of I exceeds the test value, and the increment is positive.

CONTINUE Statement

The CONTINUE statement is a dummy statement that may be placed anywhere in the source program without having any effect on the execution of the program. However, it is usually used as the last statement in the range of a DO loop to avoid the error of ending the DO loop with one of the prohibited types of statements outlined in the previous paragraph.

The use of the CONTINUE statement is illustrated in the following partial program for finding the largest element of an array A consisting of 100 elements.

```
. . . . . . . . . . . . . . . .
  N = 1
  BIG = ABS(A(1))
  DO 4I = 2,100
  IF(BIG - ABS(A(I)))3,4,4
3 BIG = ABS(A(I))
  N = I
4 CONTINUE
. . . . . . . . . . . . . . . .
```

If the absolute value of A(I) is not bigger than the value of BIG in the IF statement, statement 3 and the statement following it must be by-passed. To increment the index, control must pass to the last statement in the range of the DO. We might be tempted to use a GO TO statement as this last statement, to transfer control back to the first statement in the range of the DO. However, this is not permissible, so a CONTINUE statement is used as the last statement in the range. When control is transferred to the CONTINUE statement, the index I is incremented by 1, and either the execution of the range is repeated, or a normal exit is made from the DO loop, depending upon whether or not the DO statement has been satisfied.

PAUSE Statement

The PAUSE statement has one of the forms

```
PAUSE or PAUSE n
```

where n represents a string of one through five decimal digits. On some computers, the statement causes a temporary termination of execution, and operator intervention is required to resume execution. On larger systems running in batch mode, execution is not generally suspended. PAUSE or PAUSE n may be written to the system output file, but execution continues. In FORTRAN 77 the form PAUSE 'message' may also be used, where 'message' is a character (literal) constant. If the program is running in interactive mode, the message is usually displayed at the user's terminal when the PAUSE statement is executed. If there is no character constant, just FORTRAN PAUSE would normally be displayed. The terminal user would then have to make some response, such as entering CONTINUE to cause execution to resume or EXIT to cause execution to terminate.

STOP Statement

This statement has the form

```
STOP or STOP n
```

where n is a string of one through five decimal digits. The statement terminates execution of the object program and STOP or STOP n is written to the system output file. In larger systems operating in batch mode, control returns to the operating system, and execution of the next job begins.

In FORTRAN 77 the form STOP 'message' may also be used where 'message' is a character (literal) constant. If the user is operating from a terminal, the message will be displayed at the terminal, and control returned to the operating system.

END Statement

The END statement, although classified as a control statement, is not an executable statement in FORTRAN IV. It produces no machine-language instructions, but is used to indicate the end of a source program or subprogram to the FORTRAN compiler. Physically, it is always the last statement of a source program or subprogram.

In FORTRAN 77, the END statement in a main program may also be used to terminate execution of the program. Use of both STOP and END is not required. In a subprogram, the END statement may also be used to cause a RETURN to be executed. Use of both RETURN and END is not required.

1-19 INPUT AND OUTPUT STATEMENTS

The input/output statements control the transmission of data between the computer and the input or output devices or files used. The following discussion will be concerned with one basic input statement, the READ statement, and one basic output statement, the WRITE statement. In some versions of FORTRAN IV, there are different forms of these two statements available, but we will confine our discussion to forms for *formatted* READ and WRITE (data transmitted under control of a FORMAT statement) which are available in all versions of FORTRAN IV.

The basic form of the formatted READ statement is

READ(r,n)list

where n is the statement number of an accompanying FORMAT statement (to be discussed later) and r represents an unsigned integer constant or variable specifying the device or file from which input data will be read. It is often called a logical unit number (LUN). In the I/O examples which follow we will assume that input is read from some device (such as a terminal) with logical unit number 5, and that output will be to a device or file with the logical unit number 6. The *list* is a list of variables, separated by commas, whose values are to be transmitted from the input unit to the computer. A typical READ statement might appear as

```
READ(5,13)A,DISPL,X
```

This statement would cause three data values to be read from logical unit 5 and assigned to the three variable names in the list. A FORMAT statement having statement number 13 would have to be used in conjunction with this READ statement to specify the form of the data.

The basic form of the formatted WRITE statement is

```
WRITE(r,n)list
```

where r and n have the same meaning as they do in the READ statement. In FORTRAN IV, the list is a list of variables, separated by commas, whose values are to be transmitted from the computer to the output device or file. In FORTRAN 77, the list may contain not only variables, but also arithmetic expressions and character constants. A typical WRITE statement is

```
WRITE(6,14)J,ARRAY(3),YDIST
```

The values of the three variables in the list would be transmitted to the output device or file. For example, if the output device specified is a line printer, the values of the three variables would be printed by the line printer.

FORTRAN 77 permits the use of what is called *list-directed* input. The READ statement has the form

```
READ(r,*)list
```

where r and list have the same meanings as previously given. The input data is not arranged according to the specifications of a FORMAT statement since there is none accompanying a list-directed READ statement. The data is arranged so that there is a blank column or a comma separating each of the data values. The input data for the statement

```
READ(5,*)SK,THCL,DELT,EPSI,J
```

for example, might be

```
.669,3.27,.0001,.00003,36
```

List-directed input is particularly useful to a terminal user since, in entering data, it would not be necessary to count columns on the terminal screen.

List-directed output is also permitted in FORTRAN 77. The statement

```
WRITE(6,*)A/B,C,K
```

would transmit the values of the expression A/B and the two variables to the output device or file. The output would be in one record. (A *record* is a collection of data fields that are logically related and processed as a unit. On a line printer, one record of output data goes on one line.) Each execution of a list-directed READ or WRITE statement transmits one record of data. For a list-directed WRITE statement, real variable or expression values would be put in ordinary decimal form unless they are very large or very small, in which case they would be put in E form. List-directed formatting may vary with different computers.

The input and output of character quantities in FORTRAN 77 will be discussed later in Sec. 1-23 after discussion of CHARACTER type statements.

Input and Output of Entire Arrays

In illustrating the input and output of arrays, FORMAT statements will be used even though they have not been discussed. For the reader using this material for review or reference, this will not present a problem. A reader learning FORTRAN for the first time may wish to review this material on transmission of arrays after studying FORMAT statements.

One possible way of transmitting (reading into memory or printing out from memory) an entire one-dimensional array or a part of it is to use a single DO loop. Similarly, a two-dimensional array can be transmitted by using a double DO loop. For example, the appearance in a program of the statements

```
47 FORMAT (1Hᵇ,F10.2)
   DO 6J=1,N
   DO 6I=J,N
 6 WRITE(6,47) A(I,J)
```

would cause the printout (assuming that logical unit 6 is the line printer) of the elements

a_{11}

a_{21} a_{22}

a_{31} a_{32} a_{33}

$\quad\vdots\qquad\quad\vdots$

$a_{n1}\cdots\cdots\cdots a_{n4}\cdots\cdots a_{nn}$

of an array. These elements would not appear in the form shown above but would be printed out, one element to a line, in one long column, their order being $a_{11}, a_{21}, a_{31}, \ldots, a_{n1}, a_{22}, a_{32}, \ldots, a_{n2}, a_{33}, a_{43}, \ldots, a_{n3}$, and so forth. If the entire array were to be printed out, instead of just the elements shown, the statements referred to could be used by simply changing the initial value (first indexing parameter), in the second DO statement, from a J to a 1.

Another method of printing an entire array is by using a set of statements such as

```
DIMENSION B(10)
. . . . . . . . . .
49 FORMAT(1Hᵇ,F10.2)
   WRITE(6,49)B
```

in which the array name B appears in the list in nonsubscripted form. In printing the one-dimensional array B, all ten elements would be printed consecutively in a column, with one element to a line. By changing statement 49 to FORMAT(1Hᵇ,10F10.2) all ten elements of the array would be printed out consecutively on a single line. The input of an entire array may be handled in a similar manner.

If the array to be handled is two-dimensional or greater, a set of statements, such as those in the preceding paragraph, will read in or print out the elements in an order in which the *first* subscript progresses most rapidly, the second subscript progresses the next most rapidly, and so forth. For example, the elements of a 3-by-3-by-3 three-dimensional array would print out as a_{111}, a_{211}, a_{311}, a_{121}, a_{221}, a_{321}, a_{131}, a_{231}, a_{331}, a_{112}, a_{212}, a_{312}, a_{122}, a_{222}, a_{322}, and so forth.

Indexing Within an Input or Output List (Implied DO)

Arrays in an input or output list may have their subscripts incremented without the use of DO statements. For example, the statements

```
27 FORMAT(10F7.1)
   READ(5,27)(A(I), I=1,10)
```

would cause the reading of ten data values, and these values would be assigned to A(1), A(2), . . . , A(10), respectively. This indexing of subscripted variables within an input or output list is referred to as an *implied* DO. It has the advantage over the explicit use of the DO statement such as

```
27 FORMAT(F7.1)
   DO 7I=1,10
 7 READ(5,27)A(I)
```

in that, in the explicit use of the DO, each input value must be in a separate input record. Changing the FORMAT specification to 10F7.1, for example, would not alter this requirement. Only the first F7.1 specification would be used each time the READ statement was executed. On the other hand, in the implied DO example shown, all ten values would be in the same input record.

Implied DOs may also be nested. For example, the statements

```
49 FORMAT(1Hᵇ,10F7.1)
   WRITE(6,49)((A(I,J),J=1,10),I=1,10)
```

would cause the a_{ij} array to be written in the form

a_{11} a_{12} a_{13} · · · · $a_{1,10}$

a_{21} a_{22} a_{23}

a_{31}

$a_{10,1}$ $a_{10,2}$ · · · · · · · $a_{10,10}$

This form is obtained since the subscript J progresses the fastest because it is in the inner implied DO in the WRITE statement shown. Note that this is not the order in which the elements would be written if the array were transmitted by using the array name in the list in nonsubscripted form, as discussed under input and output of entire arrays.

In the examples thus far, the increment of the index has been assumed to be 1, but it can be given any other value by using a third indexing parameter, just as in the DO statement. The statements

```
29 FORMAT(1Hᵇ,5F9.2)
   WRITE(6,29)(A(I),I=2,10,2)
```

would cause the values of A(2), A(4), A(6), A(8), and A(10) to be written on one line.

Manipulative I/O Statements

Three manipulative statements are used with auxiliary memory devices such as tape units or disks. The statement

```
BACKSPACE 2
```

for example, would cause device number 2 to backspace one record. The statement

```
REWIND 3
```

would direct device number 3 to the start of the file so that a subsequent READ or WRITE statement referring to device number 3 would read data from or write data into the first record of the file. The statement

```
ENDFILE 4
```

would define the end of the file associated with the number 4. If the number 4 refers to a data set being transmitted by a magnetic-tape unit, for example, an end-of-file mark would be written on the tape.

1-20 NONEXECUTABLE FORTRAN STATEMENTS

In the next sections, we will discuss nonexecutable FORTRAN statements. As mentioned previously, there are five types of nonexecutable statements:

1. FORMAT statements
2. DATA initialization statements
3. specification statements
4. statement function definition statements
5. subprogram statements

A transfer of control cannot be made to any of these nonexecutable statements. None of them may appear as the last statement in the range of a DO loop, nor may any of them appear as the last statement which is part of the logical IF statement. They will now be discussed in the order given.

1-21 FORMAT STATEMENTS

FORMAT statements are used with both READ and WRITE statements to supply information to the processor regarding the structure of the data *fields* and *records* which are to be read in or written. Records have been defined previously; fields will be defined subsequently. A complete listing of the order in which the programmer should arrange the various kinds of statements in his source program will be given after all of the kinds of statements have been discussed, but it should be noted here that FORMAT statements may be placed anywhere in the source program after the IMPLICIT statement, if one is used, and before the END statement, except where the use of a nonexecutable statement is prohibited.

The general form of a FORMAT statement is

n FORMAT $(s_1, s_2, s_3, \ldots, s_m)$

where n is the statement number consisting of from one to five decimal digits, and s_1, s_2, s_3, . . . , s_m are *format specifications* (also called *format codes, field specifications,* or *field descriptors*). We will now discuss the eleven different types of format specifications used to describe data fields. They are:

Type	General Form	Example	Remarks
I	aIw	3I6	Describes data fields for transmission of integer quantities
F	aFw.d	2F10.3	Describes data fields for transmission of real quantities
E	aEw.d	2E14.7	Describes data fields for transmission of real quantities
D	aDw.d	4D20.13	Describes data fields for transmission of double-precision real quantities
G	aGw.s	3G14.7	A generalized specification for transmission of integer, real, complex, or logical quantities
X	wX	5X	Indicates a field of w columns is to be skipped on input, or a field of w columns is to be filled with blanks on output
H	wHtext	7HDENSITY	Used for transmission of w characters of literal data indicated by text in general form
literal	'text'	'DENSITY'	Used for transmission of literal data indicated by text in general form (not available in all versions of FORTRAN IV)
A	aAw	5A4	Used for transmission of alphameric characters
L	aLw	5L4	Used for transmission of logical quantities
T	Tr	T35	Used to specify the record position where transmission of data begins (not available in all versions of FORTRAN IV)

In the general form, a is a repeat constant. That is, the specification 3I6 is equivalent to I6,I6,I6. The field width is symbolized by the letter w, and the number of places to the right of the decimal point by the letter d. In the G specification, the s is used only for output and symbolizes the number of significant digits to be written. In the T specification, the r symbolizes an integer constant designating the position in a FORTRAN record at which the transmission of data is to begin. In the following paragraphs, we will discuss the various types of format specifications in more detail.

In the subsequent discussion of output specifications, we will assume that logical unit number 6 refers to the line printer and that the output is printed, although the descriptions also apply to output on a terminal screen.

I-Type Specification (Output)

The statements

```
    WRITE(6,17)NUM
17 FORMAT(1Hᵇ,I5)
```

would cause the value of NUM to be printed by the line printer. Five spaces (printer columns) would be allocated for the printout of the digits and the sign (if negative) because of the field width of 5 specified in the I5 specification. These five spaces constitute a *field* in which the value of NUM is printed. If less than five spaces are required, the spaces to the left of the field are filled with blanks. If more than five are required, there would either be a deletion of the sign and/or of some digits. In some FORTRAN versions asterisks would be printed instead of a value. The latter method, or some printout equivalent to it, in which the printout of an incorrect value is avoided, is characteristic of the newer processors. When the repeat constant is 1, as it is in the above example, it may be omitted.

In the example above, there is an H specification (also called a Hollerith specification) preceding the I specification. This type has not yet been discussed, but its purpose in the FORMAT statement shown is for carriage control. It makes the first character of the output record a blank. This first character is not printed but is used for carriage control. A blank causes the printer to advance one line before printing, giving, in general, normal single spacing. Carriage control will be discussed in more detail after the H and literal specifications are explained.

F-Type Specification (Output)

This specification is used in a FORMAT statement accompanying a WRITE statement when a real value is to be printed out in ordinary decimal form. The statements

```
    WRITE(6,10)XDIST
10 FORMAT(1Hᵇ,F10.3)
```

would cause the value of XDIST to be printed out. There would be three digits after the decimal point, and a total field of ten spaces (printer columns) would be used. The ten spaces must be enough to accommodate the digits of the number and the decimal point, as well as the sign if the output value is negative. If the field width is insufficient, there may be a deletion of the sign and/or some of the digits. With the more modern processors, an incorrect value will not be printed when the error is due to too small a field width. Typically the field would be filled with asterisks.

E-Type Specification (Output)

This specification is used for printing out real quantities in exponent form. Exponent form is usually required if the value is very large or very small, or if the programmer has no way of estimating the order of magnitude. The statements

```
  WRITE(6,7)X2
7 FORMAT(1Hᵇ,E14.7)
```

might cause the value of X2 to be printed out as

-0.1234567Eᵇ03

if the value of X2 were

-123.4567

A sign is usually printed only if the quantity is negative, and a leading zero (a zero to the left of the decimal point) is generally printed only if sufficient field width has been provided for it. It is specified in the example format specification that seven digits will be printed out after the decimal point. The most significant digit is immediately to the right of the decimal point in most FORTRAN versions, providing that a scale factor has not been used (scale factors will be discussed later). In general, four places are required for the exponent, one for the decimal point, one for a sign if required, and one for the zero. Thus a field width $w \geq d + 7$ should be used in most FORTRAN versions, where d is the number of digits to be printed after the decimal point. If the field width provided is insufficient, there will be some characters deleted or, more likely, asterisks will be printed in the field.

I-Type Specification (Input)

The statements

```
  READ(5,2)LP
2 FORMAT(I4)
```

cause an integer value to be read from an input device, and the value is assigned to the variable LP. The value to be read would be entered in the first four columns of a terminal screen (or punched in the first four columns of a card). Since leading, trailing, or embedded blanks are generally interpreted as zeros, the number should be entered so that it is as far as possible to the right in the field on the screen (or card).

F-Type Specification (Input)

If the statements

```
   READ(5,3)XDOT
3 FORMAT(F10.3)
```

appear in a program, the value of XDOT, if entered from a terminal keyboard, must appear in the first ten columns of the terminal screen. (It must be punched in the first ten columns of a data card if input is from a card reader.) It can be entered with three digits after the decimal point as specified by the 3 in the F specification. However, the actual location of the decimal point overrides the specification. Therefore, many programmers would use the specification (F10.0) in this example and enter a decimal point wherever it appeared in the number. If no decimal point is used in the value entered as data, it is located by the d value (3 in this example) in the F specification; that is, the decimal point would precede the last 3 digits. If the number is not as far as possible to the right in the input data field, the trailing blanks are interpreted as zeros, but this causes no change in the value of the number if a decimal point has been used. When a decimal point is used, some programmers, for convenience, will always begin the data value in the extreme left column of the field.

E-Type Specification (Input)

As with the F specification, the data being read in with this specification can be entered on the terminal screen just as it would be written out from a WRITE statement using the E specification. For example, if 0.1257691×10^4 were being read in and assigned to a variable BMAX by the statements

```
   READ(5,4)BMAX
4 FORMAT(E14.7)
```

the value could be entered in the first 14 columns of a terminal screen as follows:

^{b}0.1257691E^{b}04

which is the form in which the number would be written out in most FORTRAN versions. However, it could also be entered in a number of other forms, such as

^{bb}.1257691E^{b}04	^{bb}.1257691E+04
^{bbb}.1257691E+4	^{bbbb}1257691E+4
^{bbbb}.1257691+4	^{bbbbb}1257691E4

The data value must be entered in the field of 14 terminal screen columns, and as far to the right in the field as possible so that one or more zeros are not placed after the desired exponent. Where no decimal point is entered in the above examples, it is located by the value of d in the specification.

D-Type Specification (Output and Input)

The D specification is similar to the E specification except that it is used to transmit double-precision quantities. The variable associated with a D specification should be defined as a double-precision variable in a type statement. The number of significant digits which can be read in or written out for the value of a double-precision variable varies with different computers from about 14 to 29, but 16 or 17 significant digits is typical.

G-Type Specifications (Input and Output-FORTRAN 77)

The G FORMAT specification (FORMAT specifications are called field descriptors in FORTRAN 77) is found in some FORTRAN IV versions as an extension but is standard in FORTRAN 77. It is a generalized specification that may be used for input or output of real data types or for the real and imaginary parts of a complex quantity. However, it is really only useful for output, so we will discuss its use for that purpose.

Sometimes we have little knowledge of the magnitude of variable values that are to be written out. Perhaps we would like to have the quantities expressed in ordinary decimal form if it could be done within reasonable field widths. If not we would accept the E form of output. Use of the G specification makes this possible. The s in the specification Gw.s gives the number of significant digits to be written, and it also has some control over whether the number will be written in ordinary decimal form or exponent form. It does not give the number of places that will appear after the decimal point unless the variable is written in E form. The data value will be written in ordinary decimal form if the magnitude of the number is not too small or too large. Otherwise it will be written in E form. Typically, if the data value is greater than 0.1 but less than 10^s, it will be written in ordinary decimal form. If the magnitude is outside this range, it will apear in E form. If the magnitude of the number should be written in E form, the field width w must be large enough to include room for the exponent (four positions), the decimal point, and the sign if it is negative.

Transmission of Several Variable Values

When the values of several variables are to be transmitted, there must be a format specification for each variable. If different format specifications are used, they are separated by commas. If the same format specification is used for each variable, a repeat constant can be used with a single specification. For example, the FORMAT statement

```
12 FORMAT(1Hᵇ,3F10.3)
```

is equivalent to

```
12 FORMAT(1Hᵇ,F10.3,F10.3,F10.3)
```

Let us consider the FORMAT statement below which is used to describe the output of four variable values.

```
   WRITE(6,13)Y1,Y2,Y3,N
13 FORMAT(1Hᵇ,E15.7,2F10.3,I6)
```

Between the parentheses of the FORMAT statement one *record* of output data is specified. One record of output data corresponds to one line of output. Therefore, the maximum length of an output record will vary with different line printers and terminal screens. For example, for a typical high-speed line printer, a maximum of 132 output characters plus one for carriage control can be specified. Carriage control will be discussed later. The term was originated for output by a printer but is used for terminal output also. In the above example there are 41 characters in the output record plus one blank for carriage control.

If more variables were added to the above example without adding corresponding format specifications, control would return to the first specification, and the added variable values would be in a new output record and would be written on a new line.

In a FORMAT statement used with a READ statement, a maximum of 80 input characters can be specified. This corresponded originally to the 80 columns on a card.

The following is a typical READ statement, with its associated FORMAT statement, containing all three types of field specifications:

```
  READ(5,3)X,Y,XDOT,YDOT,N
3 FORMAT(F3.0,F4.1,E8.3,E10.4,I3)
```

Input for read-in by the above statements might be entered as follows:

```
col. 1
 ↓
 1.2  1356  −63125E1  ᵇ2.1513E+2  ᵇ21
 └─┘  └──┘  └──────┘  └────────┘  └─┘
  X    Y     XDOT       YDOT       N
```

where the fields are indicated by the brackets shown.

The FORMAT statement

```
16 FORMAT(1Hᵇ,E14.7,3(F10.3,F5.2))
```

contains a *group* format specification. The group is within the inner parentheses and is preceded by the repeat constant 3. The specifications F10.3, F5.2 are repeated three times. If there are more variables in the list than there are specifications in such a FORMAT statement, control returns to the last group specification, and a new record is begun.

The X Specification (Blank Field Specification)

When the programmer wishes to leave blank spaces (blank output columns, not blank lines) in the output, or when terminal or card columns are to be ignored on input, the X specification is used in the FORMAT statement. Suppose, for example, that the values of time, displacement, velocity, and acceleration of a rocket are to be written for specified time increments over a specified time interval, and that all four values at each time increment are to be written on a single line. A more readable output would be obtained if a number of blank spaces were used to separate the various columns of figures and their headings.

The X specification has the general form wX, where w is an integer constant specifying the number of blank spaces to be provided in the output record. As an example, the FORMAT statement

```
3 FORMAT(5X,F6.2,6X,F5.1)
```

associated with a WRITE statement listing two variables might cause output as

^{bbbb} −34.61 ^{bbbbbb} ᵇ89.1

where the fields are indicated by the brackets shown. It should be noted that while the first blank field specification has a w value of 5, only four blank spaces appear in the first field. It has been mentioned previously that the first character of the output record is not written but is used for carriage control. In the previous examples, the specification 1Hᵇ has been used to put a blank in as the first character of the output record. The specification 5X puts five blanks in the output record, but the first is used for carriage control, and only four of the blanks appear in the output.

The blank field specification 20X would cause 20 terminal or card columns to be skipped if used in an input. Such a specification could be used where it was not desired to read some of the data, or where the columns skipped contained information other than data.

The H Specification (Hollerith Specification)

The H specification is used for writing out alphameric (alphabetic, numeric, and special characters) text. Titles, names, dates, and so forth, are written out with this specification. It may also be used for input of alphameric characters.

The H format specification has the general form

wHtext

in which w is an integer constant indicating the number of alphameric characters in the text to be written out (the field width). The text, a literal constant, also called Hollerith text or literal data, follows the letter H. Any desired blank spaces in the text are included in the field width count. The statements

```
WRITE(6,2)
2 FORMAT(1Hᵇ,34HSOLUTION OF SIMULTANEOUS EQUATIONS)
```

appearing in a source program would result in an output of the text shown following the letter H.

Hollerith text can also be written along with the numerical values of variables in the output. This is best illustrated by an example such as

```
WRITE(6,3)DISPL,VEL,ACCEL
3 FORMAT(1Hᵇ,F7.1,3HᵇFT,F9.2,7HᵇFT/SEC,F7.2,11HᵇFT/SEC/SEC)
```

where the b's indicate blanks. Hollerith text is written following each variable value so that the output might appear as

ᵇ1326.5 ᵇFT ᵇᵇᵇ165.21 ᵇFT/SEC ᵇᵇ28.61 ᵇFT/SEC/SEC

where the brackets (which do not appear in the output) are added to indicate the conformance of the numerical output to the field specifications shown in the FORMAT statement.

The H specification for input is used to replace Hollerith text in a FORMAT statement with data read from a terminal or a card. This is illustrated by the following example. Let us assume the two statements

```
READ(5,33)
33 FORMAT(16HᵇUSERSᵇNAMEᵇHERE)
```

appear in a source program. These statements would cause 16 characters to be read. They would replace, in storage, the 16 characters of the FORMAT statement following the H. Suppose the 16 characters read were

ᵇWILLIAMᵇBROWNᵇᵇ

A subsequent statement

```
WRITE(6,33)
```

in the source program would cause output of the name WILLIAM BROWN. The first blank in the field read in would not be written but would be used for carriage control.

The Literal Specification

The literal specification may be used in place of the H specification. It has the advantage that the number of characters in the field need not be counted in making the specification. The literal data in this specification are simply enclosed in apostrophes. The statements

```
  WRITE(6,4)
4 FORMAT(1Hᵇ,'DYNAMIC CHARACTERISTICS OF A ROCKET')
```

would result in the output of the literal data.

The literal specification may be used in a FORMAT statement associated with a READ statement in a manner similar to the use of the H specification for input.

Carriage Control

As has been noted previously, the first character of the output record does not actually appear on the terminal screen or is not printed by a printer but is used for carriage control. The following tabulation shows some normally used control characters, the corresponding H and literal specifications (either of which could be used to insert the control character into the output record), and the control function performed by each control character.

Control Character	H Specification	Literal Specification	Printer Carriage Advance Before Printing	Terminal Screen Action
blank	1Hᵇ	' '	One line	Line feed to new line
0 (zero)	1H0	'0'	Two lines	Skip a line
+	1H+	'+'	No advance	Suppress line feed
1	1H1	'1'	To first line of new page	Clear screen

The x specification, IX, may also be used to put a blank into the output record for carriage control.

The T Specification

The T specification is found in some FORTRAN IV versions as an extension and is standard in FORTRAN 77. It may be used in a FORMAT statement for output to indicate the position in a record at which the output of data is to begin. It has the general form

```
Tr
```

where r specifies the record position. If the output is being *printed*, the print position will be $r - 1$, since the first character of the output record is used for carriage control of the printer. For example, used in conjunction with a literal specification, the statements

```
17 FORMAT(T1,'bDISPLACEMENT',T38,'ACCELERATION',T21,
                                            'VELOCITY')
   WRITE(6,17)
```

would cause the following printout:

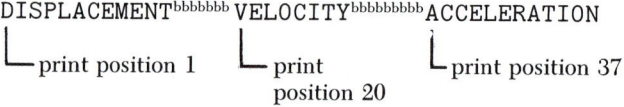

In this example the literal specification causing the printout of VELOCITY follows the literal specification for ACCELERATION in the FORMAT statement. However, printout begins in the position specified, less 1. DISPLACEMENT begins in position 1, because the first character of the literal specification is a blank for carriage control of the printer. When output is to be displayed on a terminal screen, the T specification gives positional tabulation just as described above for printed output.

With input, the T specification can be used to indicate at which external input record position the reading will begin for the following field. Thus the statements

```
   READ(5,29)A,B
29 FORMAT(T15,E17.8,T1,E12.0)
```

would cause the reading of a 17-character field containing the value of A, beginning in record position 15. Beginning in position 1, a 12-character field containing the value of B would be read.

The A Specification

We will first describe the use of the A specification in FORTRAN IV and then discuss the A field descriptor, as it is called, in FORTRAN 77.

The A format specification may be used for the input and output of alphameric characters. It differs from the H and literal specifications in that groups of characters transmitted by the A format are assigned to variable names. One application of the A specification which is discussed later is its use in storing FORMAT information which is read in at the time the program is executed.

The general form of the A specification is

Aw

where w is an integer constant specifying the number of characters to be read into or written from the memory location, or locations, associated with a particular variable name. Corresponding to each variable name, some maximum number of characters m can be stored. The value of m ranges from about 4 to 16 for various computers and variable types to which characters are assigned. The magnitude of m usually depends upon the number of bytes of storage associated with the corresponding variable in the I/O list. Typically m would be 4 for single-precision real variables and integer variables of standard length (those integer variables which have not been specified in a type statement as having their values stored in 2 bytes, as can be done in some FORTRAN IV versions). In the case of double-precision real variables, m would be 8. Normally w will not exceed m for input, but if it does, only the m characters the farthest to the right in the input field of width w will be read in. If w is less than m, the storage location will be filled with blanks *following* the w characters. For output, if w exceeds m, only m characters will be written. These characters will be preceded by w − m blanks. If w is less than m, the first w characters in the storage location (the w characters farthest to the left) will be written.

If the alphameric data to be stored contain more characters than can be assigned to one variable name (more than m characters), several successive A fields can be specified in the usual manner of specifying successive fields having the same format. That is, the specification 10A4 would indicate ten successive A fields, each with a field width of four spaces, and ten variable names would be required to refer to the storage locations in which the alphameric characters were stored. A subscripted-variable name could be conveniently used for this purpose. Thus, the ten groups of characters might be stored in locations referred to by the names C(1), C(2), . . . , C(10). The statements

```
20 FORMAT(10A4)
   READ(5,20)(C(I),I=1,10)
```

could then be used to read the 40 alphameric characters to be stored as the values of the ten variables $c(i)$.

Suppose that one wished to write out the contents of just the storage locations referred to by the variable names $c(5)$ through $c(10)$. This could be accomplished with the use of the statements

```
16 FORMAT(1Hᵇ,6A4)
   WRITE(6,16)(C(I),I=5,10)
```

In FORTRAN 77, the A field descriptor may be used slightly differently than the A field specification of FORTRAN IV. It is used for the transfer (input or output) of character quantities as it is in FORTRAN IV, but the w is not limited to some small value such as 4. In one FORTRAN version, for example, it can have any value up to 32767. With a READ statement, the A field descriptor causes transfer of w characters from the external field to internal storage as the "value" of the corresponding variable in the READ list. The value of w usually agrees with the length (number of characters) associated with this variable as specified in a CHARACTER type statement (to be discussed later). If w does agree with this length specification, then w may optionally be omitted. If a CHARACTER type statement is not used, then the A field descriptor of FORTRAN 77 is used just like the A field specification of FORTRAN IV. If w is greater than the length associated with the corresponding character variable, only the rightmost of the w characters read are assigned as the variable value. If w is less than the length specification, w characters are assigned, left justified, as the variable value. The remaining spaces are filled with blanks.

With a WRITE statement, the A field descriptor causes output of the value of a character variable to an external field w characters long. If w is greater than the variable size, the characters appear right justified in the field, with leading blanks. If w is less than the length of the variable in the WRITE statement list, only the leftmost w characters of the variable will be written.

The L Specification

This specification is used for input and output of logical quantities. The general form is

Lw

where w represents an integer constant which specifies the data field width. On input, the first T or F encountered in the w characters of the input field would cause a value of "true" or "false," respectively, to be assigned to the logical variable in the I/O list which is associated with the L specification. If the input field is entirely filled with blanks, a value of "false" is assigned.

For output, a specification of L4 would allot four spaces (terminal screen or printer columns) for the value of the logical variable. If the value of the logical variable is "true," a T is written in the extreme right position of the field. If the value of the logical variable is "false," an F is written in that position. A specification of L1 would obviously suffice, but larger data fields might be desired for spacing and for the appearance of the data.

Format Specifications for Input and Output of Complex Quantities

As discussed previously, a complex constant is represented by an ordered pair of real constants. The first real constant is the real part of the complex number and the second is the imaginary part. The input and output of complex quantities requires a field specification for each of the real numbers representing the real and imaginary parts of the complex number. For example, if COMP is a complex variable, the statements

```
    WRITE(6,12)COMP
12 FORMAT(1Hᵇ,F8.3,F9.2)
```

might be used for output. The specification F8.3 would be used for the real part of COMP and the specification F9.2 for the imaginary part. As another example, if COMP1, COMP2, and COMP3 are complex variables, and A is a real variable, the statements

```
    WRITE(6,17)COMP1,COMP2,COMP3,A
17 FORMAT(1Hᵇ,E10.4,E12.4,2(E13.5,F9.2),F7.1)
```

might be used for output. The specifications E10.4 and E12.4 would be associated with the real and imaginary parts, respectively, of COMP1. The specifications E13.5 and F9.2 would be associated with the real and imaginary parts, respectively, of COMP2 and COMP3, and the specification F7.1 would be associated with the real variable A.

The Use of Slashes and the Multiple Use of Field Specifications

In a FORMAT statement, a slash (/) can be used to indicate the end of a record of input or output data. A slash is used to separate field specifications in a FORMAT statement when the FORMAT statement is associated with a READ or WRITE statement which is to read in or write out more than one record of data. Thus, if the FORMAT statement

```
3 FORMAT(1Hᵇ,F9.2/1Hᵇ,F10.4)
```

were associated with a WRITE statement having two variables in its list, the values of these variables would be written out on separate lines. If the FORMAT statement

```
4 FORMAT(F9.2/F10.4)
```

were associated with a READ statement listing two variables, the 2 values to be read in would be in separate records (on separate terminal screen lines or on separate cards).

Suppose that the FORMAT statement

```
9 FORMAT(2F6.2,3E14.8/I5)
```

were used with an input statement which was to transmit a large number of variable values. The field specifications would then be used over and over for the input of a number of records. It would specify a format of (2F6.2,3E14.8) for the first and succeeding odd-numbered records and a format of (I5) for the second and succeeding even-numbered records.

Consecutive slashes can be used to create blank output records (leave blank lines) or to skip input records. Using n consecutive slashes at the beginning or end of the format specifications in the FORMAT statement would create n blank lines upon output if the carriage control character specifies that the line feed or carriage advance be one line before writing. On input from cards, n cards would be skipped. If n slashes appear between format specifications, n − 1 blank lines are created or that number of input records are skipped on output and input, respectively. Thus the statements

```
   WRITE(6,2)A,B
2 FORMAT(1Hᵇ,F9.2///1Hᵇ,F10.4)
```

would cause two blank lines to be introduced between the values of A and B.

Scale Factors

In discussing the output of the value of a real variable using the E specification, it was stated that the value had the form of a number between 0.1 and 1.0 multiplied by some power of 10 in most FORTRAN versions. If it is desired that the value have the form of a number between 1.0 and 10 multiplied by a power of 10, a 1P is added in front of the E specification. The 1 preceding the P is called the *scale factor*. If it is desired that the value have the form of a number between 10 and 100 multiplied by a power of 10, a 2P precedes the E specification. For example, the statements

```
   WRITE(6,2)A,B
2 FORMAT(1Hᵇ,1P2E13.6)
```

might cause the following output:

```
-3.123456E-01ᵇ7.543212E 06
```

A positive scale factor multiplies the number by $(10)^{\text{scale factor}}$ and decreases the exponent a corresponding amount. The scale factor applies to all E and F field specifications which follow it within the FORMAT statement. This applies to multiple-record formats as well as single-record formats. To change back to a zero scale factor for a subsequent and following specifications in the FORMAT statement, a 0P (zero followed by P) may be used preceding the specification.

Scale factors have no effect on I-type specifications. With output, a scale factor will cause data values with F-type specifications to be multiplied by $(10)^{\text{scale factor}}$. Such multiplication is generally not desirable, although it is conceivable that it might be desired to convert units such as amperes to milliamperes or meters to centimeters, and so forth, by this method. For example, a value, with the units of amperes, stored in memory could be printed out as the value in milliamperes by using a scale factor of 3.

With input, scale factors may be used only with the F-type specification. The scale factor is then defined as follows:

$$(\text{External quantity})(10)^{-\text{scale factor}} = (\text{internal quantity})$$

For example, if the FORMAT statement

```
2 FORMAT(2PF6.2)
```

were used in conjunction with a READ statement, a data value 312.24 would be read into the computer and stored as 3.1224.

In FORTRAN 77 and as an extension in some FORTRAN IV versions, the scale factor can also be used with the E field descriptor for input, but it has no effect if the input form of the data value is in exponent form. If it is in ordinary decimal form, the internal value is given by the above formula.

Reading in FORMAT Statements at Object Time

Many programs are general in nature and are not written just for a specific set of input data. The magnitude of the variable values read in as data, and the number of significant digits required for these values, may vary considerably from one program application to another. The same may be true of variable values which are to be written out. It may not be practical to write FORMAT statements in a program which are suitable for all possible applications to which the program may be put. FORTRAN IV and 77 handle this problem by making it possible to read FORMAT statements directly into memory at object time (at the time the program is executed) using the A field specification. The word FORMAT and the statement number are omitted in this process. Only the FORMAT specifications and the left and right parentheses enclosing them are read into memory. This alphameric information is stored in locations referred to by a subscripted variable, or in FORTRAN 77 by a single CHARACTER variable. The READ or WRITE statement then uses the array or single variable name in place of a FORMAT-statement number. Thus instead of writing

```
READ(5,64)A,B,C
```

with the FORMAT information given in statement 64, the statements

```
  DIMENSION SPC(5)
2 FORMAT(5A4)
  READ(5,2)(SPC(I),I=1,5)
  READ(5,SPC)A,B,C
```

could be used. The first READ statement reads five fields of four alphameric characters each, and stores them in locations referred to by the names SPC(1), SPC(2), . . . , SPC(5). The assumption is made here that FORTRAN IV is being used and that the computer can store four alphameric characters per storage location. The alphameric characters must be the desired FORMAT specifications for the second READ statement and must include the left and right parentheses. The input record read by the first READ statement might contain, for example, (F10.3, E14.7, F12.4). Then the array name SPC is used in place of a FORMAT statement number in the second READ statement. The array name may be chosen arbitrarily, and it must be dimensioned in a DIMENSION, COMMON, or explicit type specification statement, even if there is only one element in the array.

1-22 THE DATA INITIALIZATION STATEMENT

In many programs, variables are assigned values which do not vary throughout the execution of the program. Thus the value of the acceleration of gravity, 32.17 ft/sec^2, might be assigned to the name G. The variable G, rather than the longer constant 32.17, would then be used in any calculation involving the acceleration of gravity. Other variables in a program may have values which vary during the execution but which always have the same value at the start of execution each time the program is run. These variables, whose values are either invariant throughout the program or at the start of every run of the program, are usually not assigned values which are read in as data; instead, arithmetic-assignment statements of the form

```
G=32.17
TERM=160.
T=0.
X=0.
Y=0.
YD=125.
```

are used.

The DATA statement of FORTRAN IV and 77 provides an alternate method of assigning values to the sort of variables just discussed. If there is not a large number of data values to be assigned, some programmers use a DATA statement for the input even though the values may change for different runs of the program. In this case, the DATA statement must be changed for each different run of the program. DATA statements may also be used to assign alphameric characters to variable names without reading A fields. The DATA statement is a nonexecutable statement having the general form

DATA $v_1, v_2, \ldots, v_n/d_1, d_2, \ldots, d_n/, v_a, v_b, \ldots, v_i/d_a, d_b, \ldots, d_i/, \ldots$

in which the v's represent variable or array names and the d's are their respective values. The d's are constants, but are not necessarily numerical constants. They may also be logical or literal constants. Logical constants may be written as .TRUE. and .FALSE. or just as T or F. There is a one-to-one correspondence between the variables in a list and the constants which follow between a given pair of slashes.

As a simple example, let us enter the data (previously shown as being entered by arithmetic-assignment statements) by the use of a DATA statement. This statement might appear as

```
DATA G,TERM,T,X,Y,YD/32.17,160.0,0.0,0.0,0.0,125.0/
```

The following two statements are alternate DATA statements which could be used to enter the same information:

```
DATA G/32.17/,TERM/160./,T/0./,X/0./,Y/0./,YD/125./
```

or

```
DATA G,TERM/32.17,160./, T,X/0.,0./, Y,YD/0.,125./
```

In using DATA statements, the assigned values are stored in memory upon loading the object program. The variables listed in a DATA statement may subsequently take on other values as the execution proceeds, but control cannot revert to the DATA statement for reassigning the original values, since the DATA statement is not an executable statement.

Any of the variables in the list of a DATA statement may be subscripted with integer constants, or an array name may be used without subscripts where the values of all the elements of the array must be listed. For example, in the statements

```
DIMENSION B(4),C(9)
        .  .   .  .
DATA C(4),B/8.4,3.2,6.7,5.3,9.7/
```

only the value of the particular element C(4) of the C array would be listed (8.4), but all four values of the B array would have to be listed as shown. Some versions of FORTRAN IV permit the use of the implied DO in the list to specify particular elements of an array. Use of the implied DO in the list is standard in FORTRAN 77.

Any of the constants may be preceded by k*, giving it the form

```
k*d
```

in which k is an unsigned integer constant and d is the numerical, logical, or literal constant to be assigned. This form means that k consecutive list variables are to be assigned the particular value d.

For example, the statement

```
DATA X,Y,YD/3*0.0/
```

would cause values of zero to be assigned to the variables X, Y, and YD.

The following example illustrates the use of the implied DO in the list of a DATA statement and the use of Hollerith constants. Literal (character) constants could be used instead of the Hollerith constants shown. Recall that this example would not be valid in standard FORTRAN IV, but it is in some versions as an extension and it is in FORTRAN 77.

```
DATA(CODE(I), I=1,4)/1H*,1H.,1H-,1H+/
```

Using this statement, an asterisk would be stored in a location referred to by the name CODE(1). It would be stored in a memory location such that, on output of the contents of the memory location, the asterisk would be on the left, followed by blanks. A period would be stored in the location referred to by the name CODE(2), and so forth.

Each Hollerith constant in the above example contains a single character. Several characters (the exact number depends upon the CHARACTER type statement if FORTRAN 77 is being used, or upon the computer if FORTRAN IV is being used) may be stored as the "value" of a variable. Suppose that for a particular computer, four alphameric characters may be assigned to a variable name. If a particular literal constant contained 16 characters, four variable names would have to be used to store that constant.

The statements

```
DIMENSION TITLE(6)
DATA TITLE/21HACCELERATION ANALYSIS/
```

would cause the literal constant to be stored in locations referred to by the names TITLE(1), TITLE(2), . . . , TITLE(6). TITLE(6) would be assigned the last alphabetic character, S, and three blanks. The statements

```
DIMENSION TITLE(6)
DATA TITLE/'ACCELERATION ANALYSIS'/
```

could be used for the same purpose.

A DATA initialization statement cannot precede any specification statements (an explicit type specification statement, for example) that refer to any of the variables listed in the DATA statement. It also cannot precede an IMPLICIT statement. Otherwise, for most computers, it can appear anywhere in the program except where a nonexecutable statement is prohibited. A few compilers require that DATA statements precede all executable statements.

A variable which is initialized in a DATA statement should not appear in a blank COMMON statement (discussed later). In FORTRAN 77, DATA statements can be intermixed with statement functions and executable statements but must follow the IMPLICIT statement and all other specification statements except FORMAT statements.

1-23 SPECIFICATION STATEMENTS

Specification statements are nonexecutable statements which provide certain types of information for the compiler. The specification statements of FORTRAN IV include DIMENSION, IMPLICIT type specification, explicit type specification, COMMON, EQUIVALENCE, and EXTERNAL statements. COMMON and EXTERNAL statements will be discussed later with the presentation of subprograms, since they are used with subprograms. Specification statements are often required to be placed before the executable statements and statement function definitions, although there are variations from this requirement.

In FORTRAN 77, DATA and FORMAT statements, which have previously been discussed, are classified as specification statements. One additional FORTRAN 77 specification statement which is not standard in FORTRAN IV, the PARAMETER statement, will be discussed here, and a second, the INTRINSIC statement, will be discussed later with the EXTERNAL statement.

DIMENSION Statements

These statements are used to specify the maximum size of arrays. This information is required by the compiler for the allocation of storage. The array size must be represented by integer constants if the DIMENSION statement is in a main program. *Adjustable dimensions*, in which the array size is represented by integer variables, may be used in subprograms and will be discussed along with the later presentation of subprograms.

As an example of a DIMENSION statement, suppose that a two-dimensional array T(I,J) is to be used in a program in which I and J are to have maximum values of 10 and 20, respectively. The statement

```
DIMENSION T(10,20)
```

in the source program would allocate storage space for 200 array element values.

A single DIMENSION statement may be used for as many array names as desired. When more than one array name appears in the DIMENSION statement, they are separated by commas. For example, the statement

```
DIMENSION A(15,10),B(15,15),T(10,10),X(15)
```

reserves space for four arrays.

In FORTRAN 77, the general form of the DIMENSION statement is

```
DIMENSION a([d₁]:d₂, . . .)
```

where a represents the array name, d_1 represents the lower dimension bound specification, and d_2 represents the upper dimension bound specification. The brackets around the lower bound specification symbolize that this specification is optional. The lower bound is *one* if the specification d_1 is omitted. For example, if we have the DIMENSION statement

```
DIMENSION A(0:5),B(−3:6,10),C(10,10)
```

A is a one-dimensional 6-element array beginning with A(0) and ending with A(5); B is a two-dimensional array containing 100 elements beginning with B(−3,1) and ending with B(6,10); and C is a two-dimensional array containing 100 elements, beginning with C(1,1) and ending with C(10,10).

Type Statements

The type specification of variables by means of the predefined specification has been presented previously. It should be recalled that with this specification the variable is integer if the first character of the name is I, J, K, L, M, or N, and is real if the name begins with any other alphabetic character. This specification applies unless it is overridden by one of the two kinds of type statements: the IMPLICIT statement or the explicit specification statement. IMPLICIT or explicit type specification statements *must* be used to specify double-precision real, single or double-precision complex, or logical variables, since these types are not included in the predefined specification.

In FORTRAN 77, CHARACTER type declarations may be made with either the IMPLICIT statement or an explicit type specification (or declaration) statement.

The IMPLICIT Statement

This statement is not available in standard FORTRAN IV, but it is found in some versions as an extension and is standard in FORTRAN 77. It is used to specify types of variables which begin with certain designated letters. Thus, type specification by use of the IMPLICIT statement is similar to type specification by the predefined specification except that the programmer can select which initial letters are to specify a certain type of variable. The IMPLICIT statement can be used to specify initial letters for all types of variables—integer, real, complex, and logical—whereas the predefined specification applies only to integer and single-precision real variables. In addition, in some FORTRAN IV and 77 versions, the IMPLICIT statement can specify the number of bytes of storage for integer, real, complex, and logical variables. Only specification of the length of CHARACTER variables is standard in FORTRAN 77. In versions where it is permissible, the programmer can specify a standard or optional length (number of bytes) for each type of variable as follows:

Variable Type	Standard Length	Optional Length
Integer	4	2
Real	4	8
Complex	8	16
Logical	4	1 or 2
Character (FORTRAN 77 only)	—	Equal to the number of characters to be assigned to the variables

If 8 bytes are specified for real variables, they are double-precision real, and if 16 bytes are specified for complex variables, they are double-precision complex.

In versions where type lengths may be specified, the general form of the IMPLICIT statement is

IMPLICIT type*$s_1(a_1,a_2 \ldots)$, $\ldots$, type*$s_2(b_1,b_2, \ldots)$

In versions where type lengths cannot be specified, the "*s's" following "type" are omitted and standard lengths are assigned. In these versions, the type specifier DOUBLE PRECISION (standard in all versions) would have to be used instead of REAL*8. The word "type" in the general form symbolizes one of the type specifiers REAL, DOUBLE PRECISION, COMPLEX, LOGICAL, or CHARACTER. The letters $s_1, \ldots , s_2$ represent standard or optional lengths, and the a's and b's represent single alphabetic characters separated by commas, or a range of alphabetic characters. A range of alphabetic characters—for example, B, C, D, E, F—is denoted by B $-$ F. The first and last characters of the range are given, and are separated by a "minus" symbol. For example, the statement

IMPLICIT REAL*8(A−K, O−Z)

specifies that all variables in the program beginning with the letters A through K and O through Z are real, double-precision variables. The statement

IMPLICIT INTEGER*2(I,J,K)

specifies that all variables beginning with the letters I, J, and K are integer variables, occupying only two memory locations each. The last statement above might also have been written as

```
IMPLICIT INTEGER*2(I−K)
```

Several different type specifications can be included in a single IMPLICIT statement, and if a length specification is not included with the type of variable, the standard length is specified. For example, the statement

```
IMPLICIT INTEGER(A,B,D−F),REAL*8(G−K),COMPLEX(C),
                                        LOGICAL(L−N)
```

specifies that all variables beginning with the letters A, B, and D through F are integer variables with a standard number of memory locations for each; that all variables beginning with the letters G through K are real, double-precision variables with eight memory locations reserved for each; that all variables beginning with the letter C are complex with a standard number of eight memory locations for each; and that all variables beginning with the letters L through N are logical variables with a standard number of memory locations reserved. All initial letters not included in the IMPLICIT statement follow the predefined convention.

An IMPLICIT statement, if one is used, must be the first in a main program and the second in a subprogram (in which it follows immediately after the function or subroutine statement, as discussed later). In most FORTRAN IV versions which permit the IMPLICIT statement, only one may be used in a main program or in a subprogram. However, in FORTRAN 77, more than one can be used, but the same letter should not be used more than once in all the IMPLICIT statements in any one program unit.

Explicit Specification Statements

Types of variables may be specified explicitly in standard FORTRAN IV and 77 as shown by the following examples:

```
REAL I,MASS,FORCE
INTEGER X,Y,Z,A(15,15)
DOUBLE PRECISION A,B
COMPLEX AMP,VOLT
LOGICAL LOG1, LOG2
CHARACTER*24 CHAR1, CHAR2    (FORTRAN 77 ONLY)
```

As many variables as necessary may be included in a single type statement. In the first statement above, the variables I, MASS, and FORCE are specified as real. Note that the variable FORCE would not need to be included in the explicit specification statement since it is already real by the predefined specification. However, it is permissible to include it as shown.

The array A is dimensioned in the second type statement shown. Arrays can be dimensioned in any of the kinds of explicit type statements shown, but if a variable is dimensioned in a type statement, it may not be dimensioned elsewhere (such as in a DIMENSION statement). The CHARACTER type statement of FORTRAN 77 will be discussed in a separate subsection which follows. In some versions of FORTRAN IV and 77, a more general explicit specification statement is permissible as an extension having the form

type*s a(k$_1$)/X$_1$/,b(k$_2$)/X$_2$/,c(k$_3$)/X$_3$/, . . .

in which the word "type" symbolizes one of the words INTEGER, REAL, LOG-ICAL, or COMPLEX; the s symbolizes a standard or optional length and its inclusion is optional; a, b, c, . . . symbolize variable, array, or function names; the k's symbolize dimensions and are optional, but may be used if the associated variable name is an array name; and the X's represent initial values of the variables or array elements. Let us use some examples to illustrate this general form of the explicit specification statement.

The type statement

```
REAL*8 DBL1, DBL2, DBL3
```

specifies the listed variables as real, double-precision variables since the *8 following REAL specifies that eight memory locations are to be reserved for each variable, rather than the standard four locations. If the *8 were deleted from the above statement, the absence of this length specification would provide the standard number of memory locations for each variable.

The type statement

```
REAL INV, JOB
```

would specify the listed variables as real variables, overriding the predefined convention, and four memory locations would be provided for each variable.

If it is known that the magnitude of certain integer variables will never exceed $32,767$ ($2^{15} - 1$), in FORTRAN versions which permit length specification in a type statement, memory space may be saved by specifying that these variables are to occupy only two bytes of memory. The statement

```
INTEGER*2 I,V,LL
```

will reserve two bytes for the value of each of the variables listed.

The following statements illustrate the assignment of initial values to variables in type statements, an option permitted in some FORTRAN IV versions and in FORTRAN 77 extensions.

```
COMPLEX*16 D,TAU/(3.92,1.54)/
DOUBLE PRECISION A(10,10)/90*0.0,10*1.0/,C(5)/5*0.0/
```

In the first statement, D and TAU are specified as complex, double-precision variables, with 16 bytes reserved for each. The variable TAU is also assigned the initial value (3.92, 1.54).

In the second statement, the array A is dimensioned and made double precision, and the first 90 elements of the 100-element array are assigned initial values of 0.0, while the last 10 elements are initialized as 1.0. (The order of the array elements in memory are A(1,1), A(2,1), A(3,1), . . . , A(1,2), A(2,2), A(3,2), . . . , A(1,3), A(2,3), A(3,3), . . . , and so forth, up to A(10,10), with the first subscript varying the fastest.) Array C is dimensioned and will be double precision. Space will be reserved for the 5 elements of array C, and all of the initial values will be 0.0.

CHARACTER Type Statements (FORTRAN 77 only)

In FORTRAN 77, strings of alphanumeric characters can be assigned to variable names for convenience in manipulating the character strings. For this to be done, the variable must be declared to be of character type with a statement such as

```
CHARACTER CHAR1*24, CHAR2*15
```

or as

```
CHARACTER*24 CHAR1, CHAR2*15
```

These both declare that the variable name CHAR1 is of character type and will have a string of 24 characters assigned to it as its "value." CHAR2 will also be of character type with a string of 15 characters assigned to it. If both variables were to have strings of 24 characters assigned to them, the statement

```
CHARACTER*24 CHAR1, CHAR2
```

could be used.

Character arrays can be dimensioned in a CHARACTER statement. For example, CHARACTER ARRAY(100)*30 declares that there are up to 100 elements in ARRAY, each having up to 30 characters assigned to it.

Character constants (or character expressions using concatenation) can be assigned to variable names with assignment statements such as

```
CHAR1 = 'THE VELOCITY IS STABLE'
```

Input and Output of Character Quantities (FORTRAN 77)

Formatted input and output of character quantities use the AW field specification as previously discussed under field specifications. The w, however, may be optionally omitted in FORTRAN 77, and it will be considered to be equal to the length specification of the corresponding variable in the CHARACTER type statement. List-directed input and output do not require FORMAT statements and therefore do not use the A field specification. The following statements illustrate reading in some text material and storing it in an array LINE(I).

```
   . . .
   CHARACTER LINE(3)*40
   . . .
   DO 2 I = 1,3
 2 READ(5,*)LINE(I)
   . . .
   END
```

The input for this READ statement might be

```
'PRIMITIVE MAN DID HIS COUNTING'
'AND SIMPLE ARITHMETIC WITH THE'
'AID OF HIS FINGERS, PEBBLES, AND STICKS.'
```

The READ statement is executed 3 times, and each time it reads a new record of up to 40 characters and stores them as the value of one of the elements of LINE(I). If there are less than 40 characters in the input record, the character value is padded with blanks on the right.

The statement

```
WRITE(6,*)LINE(2)
```

in the program would output the character quantity assigned to LINE(2). This would be:

```
AND SIMPLE ARITHMETIC WITH THE
```

Character constants can be written out using list-directed output as follows:

```
WRITE(6,*)'THE FINGERS OF A MAN''S HAND'
```

The double apostrophe must be used if apostrophes appear as part of the character string. This form of output is useful for writing messages to the terminal screen in an *interactive* program. Suppose the following statements appear in an interactive program:

```
. . .
WRITE(6,*)'ENTER THE INITIAL VELOCITYᵇ'
READ(5,*)VINIT
. . .
```

The message to enter the initial velocity would appear on the terminal screen, and the user would respond by typing in the magnitude of VINIT immediately after the output field. Thus we might have on the screen

```
ENTER THE INITIAL VELOCITYᵇ 425.0
```
        output   input

Upon the execution of the READ statement, 425.0 would be assigned as the value of the variable VINIT. Character constants can be written out in the manner described above along with the values of variables, if desired. For example, the statement

```
WRITE(6,*)'THE MINIMUM VELOCITY IS',VMIN,'FPS'
```

might write out

```
THE MINIMUM VELOCITY IS ᵇ154.000ᵇᵇᵇᵇFPS
```

Typically 6 significant digits might be written for the variable value in 12 spaces.

FORTRAN 77 has the capability of doing such character processing as alphabetizing character strings and searching text stored in computer memory for a particular word or combination of words. Methods for doing such character processing will not be discussed in this text, however, since numeric programming is used for implementing the numerical methods discussed later. Use of character quantities will be limited to writing column headings, identifying variable values, and writing messages on a terminal screen.

The PARAMETER Statement (FORTRAN 77)

A PARAMETER statement such as

```
PARAMETER(PI=3.141593, SIG=0.173E-8, TWOPI=PI*2.)
```

assigns symbolic names to constants. In the above example, PI is the symbolic name assigned to 3.141593 and SIG is the symbolic name assigned to $0.173E-8$. The name PI, for example, can be used throughout the program as desired, and then before the program is executed, the constant 3.141593 is substituted everywhere for it by the compiler. Thus, the effect is that of writing 3.141593 throughout the program. This is more efficient than assigning a value to the variable name PI and using that throughout. The symbolic name TWOPI is given to the constant 6.283186. This is done by using an expression containing the constant 2 and the symbolic name PI. This is valid, but use of an ordinary variable in the expression would not be. The value of a symbolic name cannot be changed by statements in the program.

PARAMETER statements must precede statement function definitions and all executable statements. They may precede or follow IMPLICIT statements and other specification statements.

The EQUIVALENCE Statement

In most programs, the values of variables are normally assigned to unique locations in memory. In a large program, where there is often a shortage of memory space, it frequently is desirable, where feasible, to let different variables share locations in memory. With the use of the EQUIVALENCE statement, such an arrangement is possible. Since the storage of large arrays is a common source of memory shortage, subscripted variables are more frequently equivalenced (made to share memory locations) than are nonsubscripted variables.

To take advantage of such a technique, the program must obviously be such that it is never necessary for the values of different variables, which share the same locations, to be stored in memory at the same time. For example, if an array is used only in the early portion of a program, and another array is used only in a later part of the same program, the two arrays could be stored in the same locations in memory but at different times. However, if values from both arrays must be available in memory throughout the program, they obviously cannot share the same memory space, unless they happen to have identical values.

The general form of the EQUIVALENCE statement is

```
EQUIVALENCE (a, b, . . .),(e, f, . . .),(x, y, . . .)
```

In this general form the characters in the parentheses represent a series of variables which are equivalenced; that is, the variable values within a set of parentheses will be stored in the same location in memory but at different times. The order of the variables is not important. Any required number of equivalences (sets of parentheses) may be used. For example, the statement

```
EQUIVALENCE(A,B,C),(X,Y),(I,N)
```

would cause the values of A, B, and C to be stored in a single location in memory at different times, the values of X and Y would share another memory location in the same manner, and the values of I and N would share yet another location.

Equivalence variables may be nonsubscripted, as in the above example, but, as mentioned earlier, subscripted variables are most often necessarily equivalenced. When the latter are equivalenced, they must be single-subscripted variables or else the number of subscripts must equal the number of dimensions of the array in which the variables appear. Some FORTRAN versions *require* that a single subscript be used. In this case the double-subscripted array

```
B(1,1), B(2,1), B(3,1), B(1,2), B(2,2), B(3,2), B(1,3),
                                        B(2,3), B(3,3)
```

which is shown in what is termed its *usual order* (with the first subscript progressing the fastest), would be single-subscripted by taking advantage of the order in which the elements appear in the *usual order*. For example, the element B(3,2), shown above, would be listed in the equivalence statement as B(6), since it is the 6th element in the order shown above. Such a procedure allows the identification of the elements of a higher-subscripted array by the use of single subscripts. Using this technique, the statements

```
DIMENSION A(5,5),B(10)
    . . . .
EQUIVALENCE(A(21),B(1))
```

would cause the values of A(1,5) and B(1) to share the same memory location. (The former is the 21st element of the 5-by-5 array *in its usual order*, and the latter is the 1st element of the one-dimensional array B.) It would also cause the values of A(2,5) and B(2), A(3,5) and B(3), and so forth (through the 25th element of the A array and the 5th element of the B array), to share memory locations. Thus, the two arrays would be stored in memory in the following staggered form

```
A(1,1)
A(2,1)
A(3,1)
   .
   .
   .
A(3,4)
A(4,4)
A(5,4)
A(1,5)    B(1)
A(2,5)    B(2)
A(3,5)    B(3)
A(4,5)    B(4)
A(5,5)    B(5)
          B(6)
           .
           .
           .
          B(10)
```

where only the five matching elements shown would share memory space.

Some versions of FORTRAN IV permit the EQUIVALENCE statement to appear anywhere in the source program, but it is often required that they precede all executable statements and any statement function definitions.

1-24 SUBPROGRAMS

Sometimes a particular routine is used so frequently in a program, or perhaps in many programs, that it becomes convenient to write the routine as a subprogram and simply refer to this subprogram whenever the routine is required.

Some subprograms are supplied as part of the FORTRAN library. These include the mathematical function subprograms discussed in Sec. 1-14. Other library subprograms may be written by programmers at a particular computer installation. In addition, there are two classes of subprograms which the individual programmer may write and use with other programs which refer to them. These are called *function* subprograms and *subroutine* subprograms. Statement functions are similar in their use to function subprograms, so they will be discussed along with subprograms.

Statement Functions

Although not generally classified as subprograms, statement functions are used like function subprograms. They must be capable of being defined by a single statement. This statement function definition is part of a program unit rather than being a separate program unit with its own END statement. It is in this respect that it differs from a true subprogram. A statement function can be referenced (a function is referenced when its name, followed by its arguments in parentheses, appears in a FORTRAN expression) only in the program unit of which it is a part. A subprogram can be referenced from any program unit.

A statement function definition has the general form

name(a, b, . . .) = expression

where "name" represents the function name, the letters a, b, . . . represent the dummy arguments of the function, and "expression" represents a FORTRAN expression which is a function of the arguments.

The same rules apply in choosing a function name as in choosing a variable name. Type declaration of statement function names is also the same as the type declaration of variable names. If the predefined convention is not used, the type statement declaring the type of a statement function name must appear prior to the function definition. Statement function definitions immediately precede the executable statements of the program.

The arguments of the function in the definition are "dummy" arguments which are replaced by the values of the actual arguments which appear in the function reference. For example, the statement function definition

```
DRAG(S,V) =COEFF*RHO*S*V**2/2.
```

might appear in a source program to define a function with the name DRAG. The variables in the expression on the right, which are in addition to the arguments s and v, are known as *parameters* of the function. During compilation, the FORTRAN compiler sets up the necessary machine-language instructions to calculate the value of the function DRAG. These instructions are then used whenever the function is called for later in the program in a FORTRAN expression, using the values of whatever quantities are supplied for the dummy arguments S and V. For example, the arithmetic-assignment statement

```
F=FP-D1-DRAG(AREA,VEL)
```

might appear later in the source program. The value of DRAG would be calculated by using the current values of the arguments AREA and VEL for the dummy arguments S and V, respectively, in the function definition. The variables COEFF and RHO also appear in the definition, and their current values are used in the calculation. This value of DRAG would then be included in the calculation of F. The advantage of using arguments in the statement function definition rather than parameters is that the former are more flexible. For example, the current value of X + DELTX/2. might be the actual argument which replaces a dummy argument X. If X were a parameter rather than a dummy argument, only the current value of X could be used in the calculation of the statement function.

The dummy arguments S and V in the statement function definition could be used in other statement function definitions, if desired, with no relationship existing between these same variables in the different function definitions. They could also be used elsewhere in the program unit of which the statement function definition is a part, as names for other variables if desired. No relationship would exist between the latter and the dummy arguments. That is, the dummy arguments are said to be *local* to the definition statements in which they appear.

The dummy arguments of a statement function cannot be subscripted, since the expression on the right of the equal sign in the function definition cannot contain subscripted variables. However, when the statement function is referenced in a FORTRAN expression, the actual arguments may be expressions in general, and may contain subscripted variables. For example, the arithmetic-assignment statement

```
D2=DRAG(A(2), VEL+100.)
```

would constitute a valid use of the previously defined function DRAG, where A(2) and VEL + 100. are the actual arguments corresponding to the dummy arguments S and V, respectively. *The actual arguments in a function reference must agree in number, order, and type with the dummy arguments.*

It is possible for the actual arguments used in the function reference to be the same as the dummy arguments used in the definition. For examle, the statement function FUNC might be defined as

```
FUNC(X,Y)=0.5*(1+X)*Y**3
```

and might be referenced in the program unit in the statement

```
AK1=DELTX*FUNC(X,Y)
```

using actual arguments X and Y. The values of X and Y in the program replace the dummy arguments X and Y in the definition, and a value of FUNC is obtained which is then used in the calculation of AK1. To again point out the desirability of using X and Y as dummy arguments rather than parameters in the statement function definition (aside from the fact that a statement function must have at least one argument), note that the function FUNC might be referenced again as

```
AK2 = DELTX*FUNC(X + DELTX/2., Y + AK1/2.)
```

If X and Y were parameters rather than dummy arguments, only the current values of X and Y could be sent to the statement function definition for calculations.

Statement functions are defined only in the program unit in which the definition appears. A subprogram, for example, cannot reference a statement function defined in a main program.

Function Subprograms

A function subprogram is similar in many ways to the statement function just discussed, except that it is written as a separate program unit with its own END statement and may be referenced by any other program unit (main program or subprogram). In addition, the function subprogram definition is not limited to one statement. For example, a statement function definition

```
AVG(A,B,C,D) = (A + B + C + D)/4.
```

might appear in a program unit to be referenced whenever it were necessary to find the average of four quantities. Alternatively, a function subprogram could be used which might be written as

```
FUNCTION AVG(A,B,C,D)
SUM = A + B + C + D
AVG = SUM/4.
RETURN
END
```

This subprogram could be referenced from any program unit. For both the statement function and the function subprogram the values of the actual arguments replace the dummy arguments A, B, C, and D when the function is referenced, and a value of AVG is determined. Both are referenced in the same manner, by using the name followed by the arguments in parentheses in the same manner as for the supplied mathematical functions SIN, COS, ATAN2, and so forth. Variables such as SUM in the above example will not have their values available to the referencing program. The same name could be used in the referencing program, for example, or in any other program unit, with a completely different value assigned to it. Variables (and also statement numbers) of a subprogram are *local* to that subprogram. The general form of a function subprogram is

Type FUNCTION name $(a_1, a_2, \ldots, a_m)$

.
.
.

name = expression
RETURN
END

Type in the general statement above would actually be INTEGER, REAL, COMPLEX, or LOGICAL. The function name has a type like a variable name, and its type must be specified in both the referencing program and in the subprogram. If the predefined specification is used, then the type specification may be omitted in the FUNCTION statement. The specification may also be made by an IMPLICIT or explicit specification within the subprogram in most FORTRAN versions, in which case the type in the FUNCTION statement is generally omitted. However, if the function type is specified as shown in the general form above, it overrides a conflicting specification within the subprogram.

The word "name" in the general form of the FUNCTION statement is the name assigned to the function. It must receive a value in the subprogram. The function name could get its value by appearing in a READ statement or as an argument in a CALL statement (discussed later), but it usually gets its value by appearing to the left of an equal sign as shown in the general form of the function subprogram given above. In some FORTRAN versions the name may optionally have a length specification with it. For example, a FUNCTION statement

REAL FUNCTION INT*8(XMIN, XMAX, N, DUMMYF)

would specify the name INT to be double-precision real.

The dummy arguments are represented in the general form by a_1, a_2, $\ldots$, a_m. They must be single nonsubscripted variable or array names, or dummy names of subprograms. The use of subprogram names as arguments of other subprograms will be discussed later.

A function subprogram must have at least one argument. The actual arguments in the function reference must correspond in number, order, and type to the corresponding dummy arguments in the FUNCTION statement, just as when referencing a statement function. If one of the dummy arguments is an array name, a suitable DIMENSION statement must be used in the subprogram. The corresponding actual argument in the function reference must also be an array name, and must be dimensioned in the referencing program. Both the dummy and the actual arrays are generally given the same size in their respective DIMENSION statements, except when adjustable dimensions (discussed later) are used. Some FORTRAN versions require that the dummy and actual arrays have the same dimensions specified, but others require only that the size of the dummy array not exceed the size of the actual array.

When the RETURN statement is reached in the subprogram, control reverts to the referencing program at the point where the function subprogram was referenced, with the function name having the value assigned to it in the subprogram. More than one RETURN statement may appear if branching in the subprogram results in the function values being determined at one of several possible places in the subprogram.

The END statement is always the last statement in the subprogram.

Let us look at an example of the use of a function subprogram called by a main program. Only the pertinent statements of the main program are shown.

Calling Program

```
. . .
. . .
STR=PRESS(THICK,DI)*D/(4.*THICK)
. . .
. . .
P=PRESS(.025,1.25)
. . .
. . .
```

Function Subprogram

```
      FUNCTION PRESS(T,D)
      RATIO=T/D
      IF(RATIO .LE.  .023)GO TO 3
      PRESS=86670.*RATIO-1386.
      RETURN
    3 RAD=1.-1600.*RATIO**2
      PRESS=1000.*(1.-SQRT(RAD))
      RETURN
      END
```

The function PRESS is called two times, in the calling program, by writing the function name and listing the actual arguments to be used in evaluating the function. When the value of the function PRESS is calculated the first time, the value of the variable THICK would be used where T appears in the defining statements, and the value of the variable DI would be used where D appears. For the second calculation of the value of PRESS, .025 would be used for T and 1.25 for D. Note that in the first reference the actual arguments are variables, but in the second they are constants. Any suitable real expressions would be valid arguments in this example. Their mode would have to be real, since T and D are real. Note that the function subprogram PRESS calls on the library function SQRT.

Function subprograms are generally used when only a single value is to be returned to the referencing program, that being the value assigned to the function name. However, it is possible to return several values. This may be done by including one or more undefined variables in the actual argument list. Then the corresponding dummy arguments have values assigned to them in the subprogram, and the actual arguments take on these values in the referencing program and are available for use in the referencing program after the function has been referenced. For example, if we have a function subprogram defined as follows:

```
FUNCTION AVG(A,B,C,D,SUM)
SUM=A+B+C+D
AVG=SUM/4.
RETURN
END
```

and this subprogram is referenced with the statement

```
GRADE=AVG(HW,T1,T2,FIN,TOTAL)
```

the variable TOTAL in the referencing program takes on the value calculated as SUM in the subprogram. Generally, when values are to be returned to a calling program through the arguments as illustrated here, subroutine subprograms are used. Such subprograms are discussed next.

Subroutine Subprograms

These programs are similar to function subprograms in many respects. The rules for naming the subprograms are the same, with the exception that the name of a subroutine subprogram does not have a type. They both may have dummy arguments. They both consist of a set of commonly used statements which are used many times in general, and they both require an END statement as the last statement. They both return control to the calling program by use of a RETURN statement. The dummy arguments of a subroutine subprogram, like those of a function subprogram, may be nonsubscripted variables or array names, or dummy names of subroutine or function subprograms. As with function subprograms, the actual arguments of a subroutine subprogram must agree in number, order, and type with the dummy arguments. If array names are used as arguments, they must be dimensioned in both the calling program and the subprogram, and in some FORTRAN versions with the same dimensions. In other FORTRAN versions, it is only necessary that the dummy array dimensions do not exceed the size of the actual array dimensions. Subroutine subprograms do, however, differ from function subprograms in three important respects which follow.

1. Function subprograms usually return just one value to the referencing program, this being the value of the function name. Subroutine subprograms, on the other hand, may return many values, or no values at all. When the subroutine subprogram is called, usually some of the real arguments have values and some do not. The values replace corresponding dummy argu-

ments in the subroutine subprogram, and thus become inputs to the subprogram. The other dummy arguments become outputs of the subprogram and return values to the calling program. Their values are usually determined in the subprogram by their appearance to the left of an equal sign in an assignment statement. However, their values may also be determined by being in an input list somewhere in the subprogram, or as an argument of a CALL statement or function reference used in the subprogram. The corresponding actual arguments in the calling program, which prior to the subroutine subprogram being called had no value, take on the values, calculated or otherwise specified, in the subprogram. *The name of the subroutine subprogram does not receive a value,* whereas a function subprogram name always does.

2. A subroutine subprogram is called differently than is a function subprogram. A subroutine subprogram cannot be called by simply listing its name in a FORTRAN expression as a function subprogram can, since its name does not take on a value. A special CALL statement (discussed later) is used.

3. Since a subroutine subprogram name has no value associated with it, it cannot be of a particular type, such as real or integer. Thus the first letter of a subroutine subprogram name has no special significance.

The subroutine subprogram begins with a SUBROUTINE statement and ends with an END statement. The general form is

```
SUBROUTINE  n (a₁, a₂, a₃, . . . , aₘ)
   . . .
(FORTRAN  statements)
   . . .
RETURN
END
```

where n represents the subprogram name and the a's represent dummy arguments which correspond to the actual arguments listed in the CALL statement.

The CALL statement, used to call a subroutine subprogram, has the general form

```
CALL  n (x₁, x₂, x₃, . . . , xₘ)
```

where n represents the subprogram name; the x's represent the actual arguments. Those arguments which have values may be expressions, while those arguments which are to receive values from the subprogram are single variables, subscripted variables, or array names.

To illustrate the operation of a subroutine subprogram, let us consider the following simple example. Suppose that the addition of two n-by-m matrices is a very common operation in some particular program, and it is desired to use a subprogram to perform this operation each time it is required. The following might be used:

Calling Program

```
. . . . . . . . .
DIMENSION X(15,15), Y(15,15), Z(15,15)
. . . . . . . . . .
CALL ADD(X,Y,Z,K,L)
   . . . . . . . . .
```

Subroutine Subprogram

```
   SUBROUTINE ADD(A,B,C,N,M)
   DIMENSION A(15,15), B(15,15), C(15,15)
   DO 7I=1,N
   DO 7J=1,M
 7 C(I,J)=A(I,J)+B(I,J)
   RETURN
   END
```

Arrays X and Y are available in the calling program. They have K rows and L columns. The values of the X and Y array elements replace the elements of A and B in the subprogram, and the values of K and L replace N and M, respectively. The values of array C are calculated in the subprogram and are stored in memory, where they are available to the calling program by use of the variable name Z. These values of Z are available after the CALL statement has brought the subprogram into operation. Control returns from the subprogram to the statement following the CALL statement in the calling program.

A subroutine subprogram need not return any values to the calling program, as mentioned previously. If there also were no input to the subprogram, no arguments would be listed in the CALL or SUBROUTINE statements. Such a subprogram might be used, for example, to print out column headings at the top of each page for a program having many pages of output data.

When the program execution reaches the RETURN statement, control is transferred back to the calling program, which is the statement immediately after the CALL statement. This is the normal sequence of operation. Some FORTRAN versions, however, provide for returning to any numbered statement in the calling program by the use of a RETURN statement having the general form

```
RETURN i
```

where i represents an integer constant or variable whose value denotes the position of a statement number in the actual argument list. For example, if the subprogram

```
      SUBROUTINE QDRTIC(A,B,C,R1,R2,*,*)
      IF(B**2-4.*A*C)30,20,10
   10 R1=...
      R2=...
      RETURN
   20 RETURN 1
   30 RETURN 2
      END
```

is called by the CALL statement shown below

```
C     MAIN PROGRAM
          .
          .
          .
      CALL QDRTIC(A1,B1,X+Y,ROOT1,ROOT2,&25,&50)
          .
          .
          .
      END
```

and if B**2-4.*A*C is negative, the return will be to statement number 50 of the calling program, since RETURN 2 is executed following the IF statement. The 2 indicates the second statement number in the actual argument list, which is the number 50. Statement numbers 25 and 50 must be the labels of executable statements in the program issuing the CALL. The statement numbers in the actual argument list are preceded by the ampersand symbol, and the corresponding positions in the dummy argument list contain asterisks.

FORTRAN 77 uses an asterisk instead of the ampersand in the CALL statement. However, some versions also permit the use of the ampersand.

Multiple Entry Points in a Subprogram (FORTRAN 77)

When a function subprogram is referenced or a subroutine subprogram is CALLed, execution of the subprogram begins with the first executable statement after the FUNCTION or SUBROUTINE statement. If, on some executions of the subprogram, the programmer would like to have a block of executable statements at the beginning of the program skipped, he can cause entry into the subprogram at a point other than at the beginning by inserting an ENTRY statement in the subprogram at the point where the secondary entry is desired. An ENTRY statement in a subroutine subprogram, for example, might be

```
ENTRY PROD2(X,PROD)
```

where PROD2 is the entry name and X and PROD are dummy arguments. If PROD1 is the subroutine name, then CALLing PROD1 would start execution of the subprogram at the beginning while CALLing PROD2 would start execution of the program immediately after the ENTRY statement. In entering a function subprogram at a secondary entry point, the entry name is used instead of the function name in the referencing statement. Several ENTRY statements may be used, if desired.

1-25 THE COMMON STATEMENT

The COMMON statement is most often used in linking a main program with its subprograms, without using arguments in the CALL and SUBROUTINE statements. Before discussing the applications of the COMMON statement, let us first consider the statement itself. It has the general form

```
COMMON a, b, c, . . .
```

where a, b, c, . . . are variables, including array names that may be dimensioned. As an example, consider the statement

```
COMMON DISPL,VEL,ACCEL,N
```

appearing in a source program. The values of the variables listed would be stored in memory in the sequence in which they appear in the list in the statement. The block of memory in which these variables would be stored is referred to as a COMMON *block.* COMMON blocks can be labeled with names assigned by the programmer, but, in the example above, no name is assigned, and the block is known as a *blank* COMMON. The blank COMMON block is used more frequently, so it will be discussed first.

It is impossible for two variables listed in a COMMON statement to be equivalenced, since the variables listed could not have their values stored sequentially in separate locations and, at the same time, have two of them share the same location. This would be somewhat like attempting to equivalence two elements of an array, which is also invalid. It is also invalid to equivalence two variables in different COMMON blocks.

The size of a COMMON block, indicated by the number of variables listed in the COMMON statement, can be increased when an EQUIVALENCE statement is used in the following manner:

```
DIMENSION A(4)
. . . . . .
COMMON X,Y,Z,
EQUIVALENCE(Z,A,(1))
```

The variable values would occupy storage locations as shown below, with X in the lowest numbered location and Z and A(1) sharing the same location in memory:

```
X, Y, Z
      A(1), A(2), A(3), A(4)
```

In this case the COMMON block has been extended to higher locations and includes six memory locations instead of three. An extension cannot be made to lower locations. For example, the statements

```
DIMENSION A(4)
COMMON X,Y,Z
EQUIVALENCE (X,A(4))
```

would be invalid.

If a blank COMMON statement appears in both a main program and a subprogram or subprograms, the variables in these COMMON statements share the same COMMON block in memory. For example, if the statement

```
COMMON E,F,G,N
```

appears in a main program, and the statement

```
COMMON P,Q,R,I
```

appears in a subprogram of the main program, the values of E and P, F and Q, and so forth, share locations in memory. (The variable names E and P, F and Q, and so forth, refer to the same memory locations.) If the statement

```
CALL SUB(E,F,G,N)
```

appears in a main program, and the statement

```
SUBROUTINE SUB(P,Q,R,I)
```

appears in a subprogram of the main program, the variables, in some FORTRAN versions, again share locations in memory, as just described. (In other versions, the *values* of the actual arguments rather than their addresses are brought from the calling program to the subprogram.) Thus, in both instances, the effect of equivalencing is obtained, but without the use of the EQUIVALENCE statement. The same effect could not be obtained by equivalencing E and P, F and Q, and so forth, with the use of the EQUIVALENCE statement, since only variables appearing in the *same* program or subprogram can be equivalenced.

Using the statements shown in either of the last two examples, if E is a variable which has been defined in the main program, the appearance of P in the subprogram will cause the value stored as E to be used in the subprogram calculation, since the variable names E and P refer to the same memory location. Similarly, if the value of R is defined in the subprogram, this value will be stored in memory and will be available for use in the main program by using the name G. Since both sets of statements in the last two examples accomplish the same result, the use of two COMMON statements in a main program and a subprogram, respectively, allows the omission of the lists of arguments in the CALL and SUBROUTINE statements. Such a use of the COMMON statements results in a more efficient object program.

Another advantage of using COMMON statements is in dimensioning array names while linking elements between programs. For example, if the statement

```
COMMON A,B,C(50)
```

appears in a main program, and the statement

```
COMMON X,Y,Z(50)
```

appears in a subprogram of the main program, the values of A and X and of B and Y share memory locations, as described before, and the values of C(1) through C(50) share memory locations with Z(1) through Z(50), respectively. When the COMMON statement is used for dimensioning, the arrays dimensioned in it must *not* be listed in a DIMENSION statement or a type statement containing dimension information.

Common statements are often used when a long program is written in segments consisting of a main program and a number of subprograms, so that the individual segments can be checked independently. In this instance a variable defined in one segment may be required for use in one or more other segments. The variable would not be automatically available in different segments, since the variables used in a main program and in individual subprograms are independent of each other, even if the same variable names are used in the different programs. The variables can be made available where required by using a COMMON statement which lists all of the variables of the various program units which are used by other program units. Identical COMMON statements can be used in each segment of the overall program, thus avoiding the chance of errors which might arise in using arguments with the various CALL and SUBROUTINE statements (the arguments of the CALL and SUBROUTINE statements are omitted if COMMON statements are used in this way).

To avoid listing all the variables of a program in the COMMON statement of each subprogram, when any particular subprogram does not require the use of all the variables, a number of COMMON blocks may be set up in memory, each with its own name and each containing certain variables appropriate to the requirements for using the variables in the various subprograms. Such blocks are known as *labeled* COMMON blocks. Before illustrating the preceding discussion, let us consider the statements used to set up labeled COMMON blocks. The statement has the general form

```
COMMON / n / a₁, a₂, . . . , aₘ/ n₁/ b₁, b₂, . . . , bₘ . . .
```

where the n's represent names assigned to the block of variables following them. These block names should consist of one to six alphameric characters, the first of which is alphabetic. The a's and b's are the variables listed for each block, and they appear in the block in the order given in the list.

To illustrate the labeled COMMON block and its use in avoiding the listing of all program variables in each subprogram, let us consider the following:

Main Program
Variables A, C, and E defined; variables B, D, and F required

```
. . .
COMMON/NAMA/A,B/NAMB/C,D/NAMC/E,F

. . .
A = . . .
CALL SUB1

. . .
C = . . .
CALL SUB2

. . .
E = . . .
CALL SUB3

. . .
TILT = B*D/F

. . .
```

First Subprogram
Variable A required; variable B defined

```
SUBROUTINE SUB1
COMMON/NAMA/A,B

. . .
B = A + . . .
RETURN

. . .
B = 2.*A + . . .
RETURN
END
```

Second Subprogram
Variable C required; variable D defined

```
SUBROUTINE SUB2
COMMON/NAMB/C,D

. . .
D = C**2 + . . .
RETURN

. . .
D = C**3 + . . .
RETURN
END
```

Third Subprogram
Variable E required; variable F defined

```
SUBROUTINE SUB3
COMMON/NAMC/E,F

. . .
F = 5.*E + . . .
RETURN

. . .
F = 10.*E + . . .
RETURN
END
```

The COMMON statement in the main program would cause three blocks to be set up in memory, having the names NAMA, NAMB, and NAMC. The labeled COMMON statement in each subprogram contains only the variables whose values are required or calculated in that subprogram. For example, the first subprogram uses the value of the variable A, as defined in the main program, and calculates a value of the variable B which is used, in turn, to calculate the value of TILT in the main program.

The COMMON statement in the first subprogram lists only variables A and B. Thus, by using labeled COMMON blocks, certain variables of a main program might share a certain block of memory with the same variables in one or more subprograms, variables common to several subprograms might share a block, and so forth. As should be evident, there is more chance of introducing an error in using the labeled COMMON in this manner than in using identical blank COMMON statements in each segment. Usually, only professional programmers make extensive use of the labeled COMMON.

Since COMMON statements are specification statements, they must precede any statement function definitions, and the executable statements.

1-26 ADJUSTABLE (OBJECT-TIME) DIMENSIONS

It has been pointed out previously that the arguments of both function subprograms and subroutine subprograms may contain array names. These arrays must be dimensioned in both the calling program and the subprogram. It should be recalled that some FORTRAN versions require that the dimensions be the same in the calling program and subprogram. Since a subprogram may be used with various calling programs, it would be impossible to specify explicitly the size of the arrays in the subprogram for use with various calling programs. To avoid having to specify explicitly the size of an array in a subprogram, FORTRAN IV and 77 provide for *adjustable dimensions* in the subprogram. The use of adjustable dimensions would not be as necessary in those FORTRAN versions in which the DIMENSION statement in the subprogram is not used for allocation of storage, but only to identify names as being array names. Such versions require only that the dimensions of the arrays in the subprogram be less than or equal to the dimensions of the corresponding arrays declared in the calling program.

To give adjustable dimensions to an array appearing in a subprogram, integer variables are used in place of integer constants in the DIMENSION statement of the subprogram. When the subprogram is called, the integer variables which specify the array dimensions of the subprogram array receive values from the calling program. This is accomplished by placing the integer variables in the argument list of the SUBROUTINE statement in the subprogram, and specifying values for these variables in the CALL statement of the calling program (or in the FUNCTION statement of the subprogram and function reference, respectively).

As an example, consider the following:

Calling Program	Subprogram

```
Calling Program                    Subprogram
                                   SUBROUTINE MATI(...,XS,I,J,...)
. . .                              DIMENSION XS(I,J)
DIMENSION X(5,5)
CALL MATI(...,X,5,5,...)           . . .
. . .                              . . .
                                   RETURN
                                   END
```

With the dimensions of the array which is to be used in the subprogram known, these dimensions are specified in the CALL statement of the calling program, as shown above. The array XS of the subprogram corresponds to the array X of the calling program. Each of the variables I and J in the subprogram receives the value of 5 from the calling program, specifying the size of the array which is to be used in the subprogram.

Adjustable dimensions cannot be altered within a subprogram, and arrays listed in a COMMON statement may not have adjustable dimensions. If the adjustable dimension feature is used in a FORTRAN version which does not require that the dimensions of arrays in a subprogram be the same as those for corresponding arrays in the calling program, it is only necessary that the dimensions assigned to the subprogram arrays at object time be less than or equal to the dimensions specified in the DIMENSION statement of the calling program.

1-27 SUBPROGRAM NAMES AS ARGUMENTS OF OTHER SUBPROGRAMS–THE EXTERNAL AND INTRINSIC STATEMENTS

It has been mentioned before that, in FORTRAN IV, a function subprogram or subroutine subprogram name can be used as an argument of another subprogram. To distinguish a subprogram name in an argument list from an ordinary variable name, it must appear in an EXTERNAL statement. This statement has the general form

EXTERNAL a, b, c, . . .

where a, b, c, . . . represent the names of subprograms used as arguments of other subprograms. In the statements below, for example, the function name COS would be listed in an EXTERNAL statement to distinguish it as a subprogram name in the CALL statement shown.

```
EXTERNAL COS
. . .
CALL SUBX(E,COS,G)
. . .
```

To illustrate the use of a function name as an argument, consider the following:

Calling Program
$\Bigg\{$
```
    . . .
    EXTERNAL FUNC
    . . .
    CALL CALC(X,FUNC,Y,Z)
    . . .
```

First Subprogram
$\Bigg\{$
```
    SUBROUTINE CALC(A,F,C,D)
    G=F(C,D)
    . . .
    A = . . .
    . . .
    RETURN
    END
```

Second Subprogram
$\Bigg\{$
```
    FUNCTION FUNC(G,H)
    IF(G-H)1,1,2
  1 FUNC=2.*G*H
    RETURN
  2 FUNC=5.*G/H
    RETURN
    END
```

The function name FUNC replaces the dummy variable F in the first subprogram. The values of the variables Y and Z are used as the arguments of the function FUNC in the calculation of its value in the second subprogram. The function FUNC is shown in this example as a function subprogram with two arguments, written by the programmer. The supplied function subprograms (mathematical functions) EXP, ALOG, ALOG10, SIN, COS, TANH, SQRT, ATAN, CABS, and so forth, may also be used as arguments of other subprograms if they are listed in an EXTERNAL statement.

The EXTERNAL statement is a specification statement, and thus must precede statement function definitions and the executable statements.

In FORTRAN 77, the subprogram names listed in the EXTERNAL statement cannot be any of the FORTRAN-supplied functions such as SIN, COS, and so forth. They can only be the names of user-supplied functions. If a FORTRAN-supplied function name is to be used in the argument list of another subprogram, it must appear in an INTRINSIC statement. For example, if the FORTRAN-supplied function name COS is to be used as an argument, the statement

```
INTRINSIC COS
```

would have to appear in the calling or referencing program instead of

```
EXTERNAL COS
```

1-28 THE FORTRAN SOURCE PROGRAM

Having reviewed the various types of FORTRAN statements, let us next review how these statements are written and how they are entered at a terminal or punched on cards. Preferably, a FORTRAN source program is written on a *coding form* such as the one shown in Fig. 1-6. Coding-form columns 1 through 80 correspond to the 80 columns on a standard punch card or terminal screen. Each line of the coding form corresponds to one card or one line on a terminal screen.

As previously mentioned, some statements must be numbered. The statement numbers are written in columns 1 through 5 of the coding form and, in most FORTRAN versions, consist of from one to five digits written without a decimal point. The numbers assigned to statements need not have any particular sequence as long as a statement number is not repeated. The number 0 is not permitted as a statement number. The statements proper are written, one to a line, in columns 7 through 72. Blanks may be used, as desired, to increase readability, but they are ignored by the compiler. If a statement is too long to write on a single line, it may be continued on successive lines by placing any character (other than a blank or a zero) in column 6 of each continuation line. Columns 73 through 80 are ignored by the compiler and may be used for numbering cards, identifying the program, miscellaneous information, and so forth.

When the source program is entered at a terminal, the statements are entered exactly as they are written on the coding form. Each column of the

Figure 1-6   A FORTRAN source program written on a FORTRAN coding form coding form corresponds to a terminal screen column. If a source deck is punched, the statements are punched in the cards just as they are written on the coding form. Each column of the coding form corresponds to a card column of a standard 80-column card.

Comments may be included in the source program merely to provide information to the reader about the program. Comments are not translated by the compiler but are printed out in the source program listing obtained during compilation. In FORTRAN IV comments are indicated by placing a C in column 1. In FORTRAN 77 either the letter C or an asterisk in column 1 indicates that the line is a comment. In some versions of FORTRAN IV comments may occupy columns 2 through 80, whereas in others the comments cannot extend past column 72. Standard FORTRAN 77 permits the use of columns 2 through 72 for comments.

The Order of Statements in a Program or Subprogram

The following ordering of various types of statements in a source program is applicable to most versions of FORTRAN IV and is generally compatible with FORTRAN 77 ordering.

1. FUNCTION or SUBROUTINE statement if the program unit is a subprogram
2. IMPLICIT statements (or statements in FORTRAN 77), if used
3. other specification statements such as DIMENSION, COMMON, explicit type specification statements, EQUIVALENCE, EXTERNAL statements (and INTRINSIC and PARAMETER statements in FORTRAN 77). The PARAMETER statement may precede the IMPLICIT statement(s) in FORTRAN 77.
4. statement function definitions, if used
5. the executable statements
6. the END statement

FORMAT and DATA statements, in most FORTRAN IV versions and in FORTRAN 77, can appear anywhere in a program between the IMPLICIT and END statements where nonexecutable statements are not specifically prohibited. In some FORTRAN IV versions, DATA statements must follow any specification statement that contains variable or array names which are used in the DATA statement.

Chapter 2
Roots of Algebraic and Transcendental Equations

2-1 INTRODUCTION

A problem commonly encountered in engineering is that of determining the roots of an equation of the form

$$f(x) = 0 \tag{2-1}$$

In this chapter we will consider six methods of finding the *real* roots of such algebraic and transcendental equations: (1) the incremental-search method, (2) the bisection method, (3) the method of false position, (4) the secant method, (5) the Newton-Raphson method, and (6) Newton's second-order method.

If $f(x)$ is a polynomial in x with real coefficients, it may have both real and complex roots. Of the various methods available for finding both real and complex roots, Bairstow's iterative method will be presented.

2-2 THE INCREMENTAL-SEARCH METHOD

In this approach we determine values of $f(x)$ for successive values of x in some interval to be searched until a sign change occurs for $f(x)$. A sign change occurs between x_i and $x_i + \Delta x$ if $f(x_i)f(x_{i+1}) < 0$. The sign change generally indicates

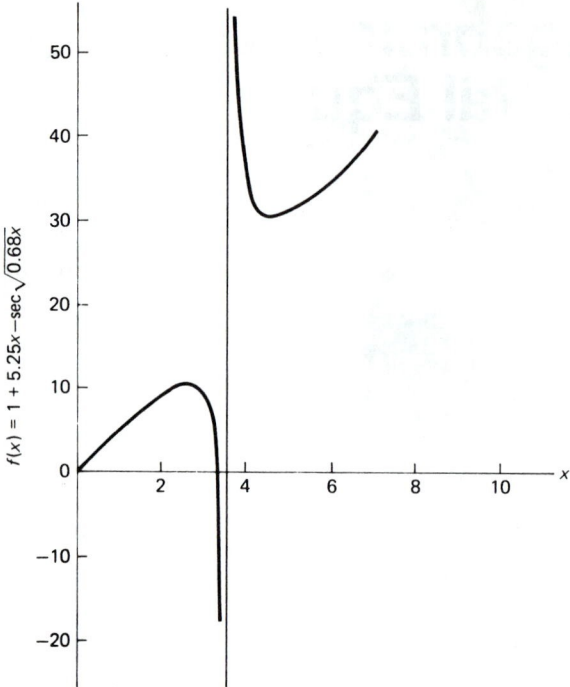

Figure 2-1 Approximate graph of $f(x) = 1 + 5.25x - \sec \sqrt{0.68x}$

that a root has been passed (it could also indicate a discontinuity in the function as shown in Fig. 2-1). A closer approximation to the value of the root may then be obtained by reverting to the last x value preceding the sign change and, beginning with this x value, again determining values of $f(x)$ for successive values of x, using a smaller increment than was used initially, until the sign of $f(x)$ changes again. This procedure is repeated with progressively smaller increments of x until a sufficiently accurate value of the root is obtained. If additional roots are desired, the incrementation of x can be continued until the next root is approximately located by another sign change of $f(x)$, and so on.

Care must be exercised in selecting the initial value by which x is to be incremented, so that roots are not by-passed in an instance when two roots are close together in value. This is usually not a problem, if fairly small increments are used in the initial sequence. The following example will illustrate the use of the incremental-search method just described.

EXAMPLE 2-1

It is desired to determine the first positive nonzero root of the equation

$$1 + 5.25x - \sec \sqrt{0.68x} = 0 \tag{2-2}$$

by the searching method. A plot of the function is shown in Fig. 2-1. The first step is to sketch a flow chart outlining the general procedure (Fig. 2-2). The initial value of Δx, an epsilon value, the initial value of x, and the maximum value of x are read in as data. In locating a root, Δx is decreased until it is less than or equal to epsilon. The initial and maximum values of x specify the range of x to be searched.

Note from Fig. 2-1 that the function approaches negative infinity as x approaches 3.6285 from the left and positive infinity as x approaches 3.6285 from the right. The search interval in this example was taken from $x = 0.1$ to $x = 4.0$ so it would include this discontinuity in the curve. Successive function values, $f(x_i)$ and $f(x_{i+1})$, will have opposite signs if x_i and $x_i + \Delta x$ lie on opposite sides of $x = 3.6285$. A possible root is indicated by the sign change. The x value reverts to the value preceding the sign change and incrementing continues with a smaller increment. When the absolute value of $f(x_{i+1})$ exceeds some predefined large value ($1/\varepsilon$ in this program), a message is printed indicating the function is approaching infinity in the neighborhood of the particular x value. The comparatively large initial step size is again assigned to Δx, and incrementing continues, generally by-passing the discontinuity without the search being stopped due to computer overflow.

In writing the source program, the following variable names were selected for the corresponding quantities:

Variable Name	Quantity	Value
X	x	0.1 initially
FX	$f(x_i)$	
FX1	$f(x_{i+1})$	
DXI	Initial Δx	0.1
EPSI	ε	0.0001
XMAX	Maximum x value	4.0
DELTX	Δx	0.1 initially

A FORTRAN IV source program is shown below followed by the printed computer output.

```
C     REAL ROOTS BY SEARCHING METHOD
      WRITE(6,2)
    2 FORMAT('1',5X,'ROOT DETERMINATION BY SEARCHING METHOD'//)
      READ(5,3) DXI,EPSI,X,XMAX
    3 FORMAT(4F10.0)
      WRITE(6,4) DXI,EPSI
    4 FORMAT(' ',5X,'INITIAL DELTX=',F4.2,9X,'EPSI=',F6.4//)
    5 DELTX=DXI
      FX=1.+5.25*X-1./COS(SQRT(.68*X))
    6 X=X+DELTX
      FX1=1.+5.25*X-1./COS(SQRT(.68*X))
      IF(ABS(FX1).GT.1./EPSI) GO TO 7
      GO TO 9
```

Figure 2-2 Flow chart of Ex. 2-1

```
 7 WRITE(6,8) X
 8 FORMAT(' ','FUNCTION APPROACHING INFINITY FOR X=',F7.4)
   X=X+DXI
   GO TO 5
 9 IF(FX*FX1) 11,13,10
10 IF(X.GT.XMAX) STOP
   FX=FX1
   GO TO 6
11 IF(DELTX-EPSI) 13,13,12
12 X=X-DELTX
   DELTX=DELTX/10.
   GO TO 6
13 WRITE(6,14) X
14 FORMAT(' ','X=',F8.4, ' IS A REAL ROOT')
   X=X+EPSI
   GO TO 5
   END

   ROOT DETERMINATION BY SEARCHING METHOD

   INITIAL DELTX=0.10              EPSI=0.0001

X=   3.3867 IS A REAL ROOT
FUNCTION APPROACHING INFINITY FOR X= 3.6288
```

2-3 THE BISECTION METHOD

After the searching method described in Sec. 2-2 has revealed a change in sign of the function and thus a possible root, there are several ways of converging more rapidly to the root than by continuing the search as described in that section. One of the more reliable of these is the *bisection method*, also known as the half-interval method and the Bolzano method.

We begin with the assumption that an interval between x_i and x_{i+1} has been found such that $f(x_i) \cdot f(x_{i+1}) < 0$. This interval is next cut into two subintervals, the first extending from x_i to $x_{i+1/2}$ and the second from $x_{i+1/2}$ to x_{i+1} where

$$x_{i+1/2} = 0.5(x_i + x_{i+1}) \tag{2-3}$$

These two subintervals are shown in Fig. 2-3. The subinterval containing the root (the left subinterval in Fig. 2-3) must be selected for further bisection. This is easily done by checking the sign of $f(x_i) \cdot f(x_{i+1/2})$. If it is negative, the root lies in the first subinterval. If it is positive, the root lies in the second subinterval. If the product is exactly equal to zero, $x_{i+1/2}$ is an exact root. In general the root will be in one of the subintervals and this subinterval is then

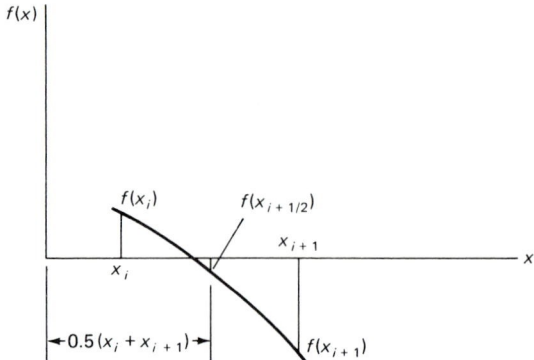

Figure 2-3 Interval bisection

bisected, and the half containing the root is again selected. Bisection continues until the interval becomes small enough that the final x value resulting from bisection of the interval is sufficiently close to a root.

It should be noted that after n bisections, the original interval has been reduced by a factor of 2^n. Thus a large number of bisections are not required to converge to an accurate value of the root. For example, 20 bisections will reduce an interval by a factor of more than one million ($2^{20} = 1{,}048{,}576$). Accuracy greater than that given by 20 bisections would seldom be required.

EXAMPLE 2-2

To illustrate how we might search over a range of x by the incremental-search method of Sec. 2-2 until an interval is found containing a possible root, and then switch to the bisection method for fairly rapid convergence to the root, we again consider the function given by Eq. 2-2 and shown in Fig. 2-1. Our region of search will again be from 0.1 to 4.0, and possible roots will be indicated by sign changes of the function in the neighborhood of 3.38 and 3.63. However, only the first interval (around $x = 3.38$) contains a root as we see from Fig. 2-1. The bisection method applied to an interval containing $x = 3.6285$ will result in overflow if provision is not made to avoid it. We will do this by checking the magnitude of $f[0.5(x_i + x_{i+1})]$ each time it is calculated. If it exceeds some predetermined large value, we assume we are not converging to a root and print a message that the function is approaching infinity for the x value equal to $0.5(x_i + x_{i+1})$.

The flow chart for the combined incremental-search method of Sec. 2-2 and the bisection method of this section is shown in Fig. 2-4. A thorough study of the flow chart will help in understanding how the successive bisections are carried out, with the root always being in the subinterval to be bisected next.

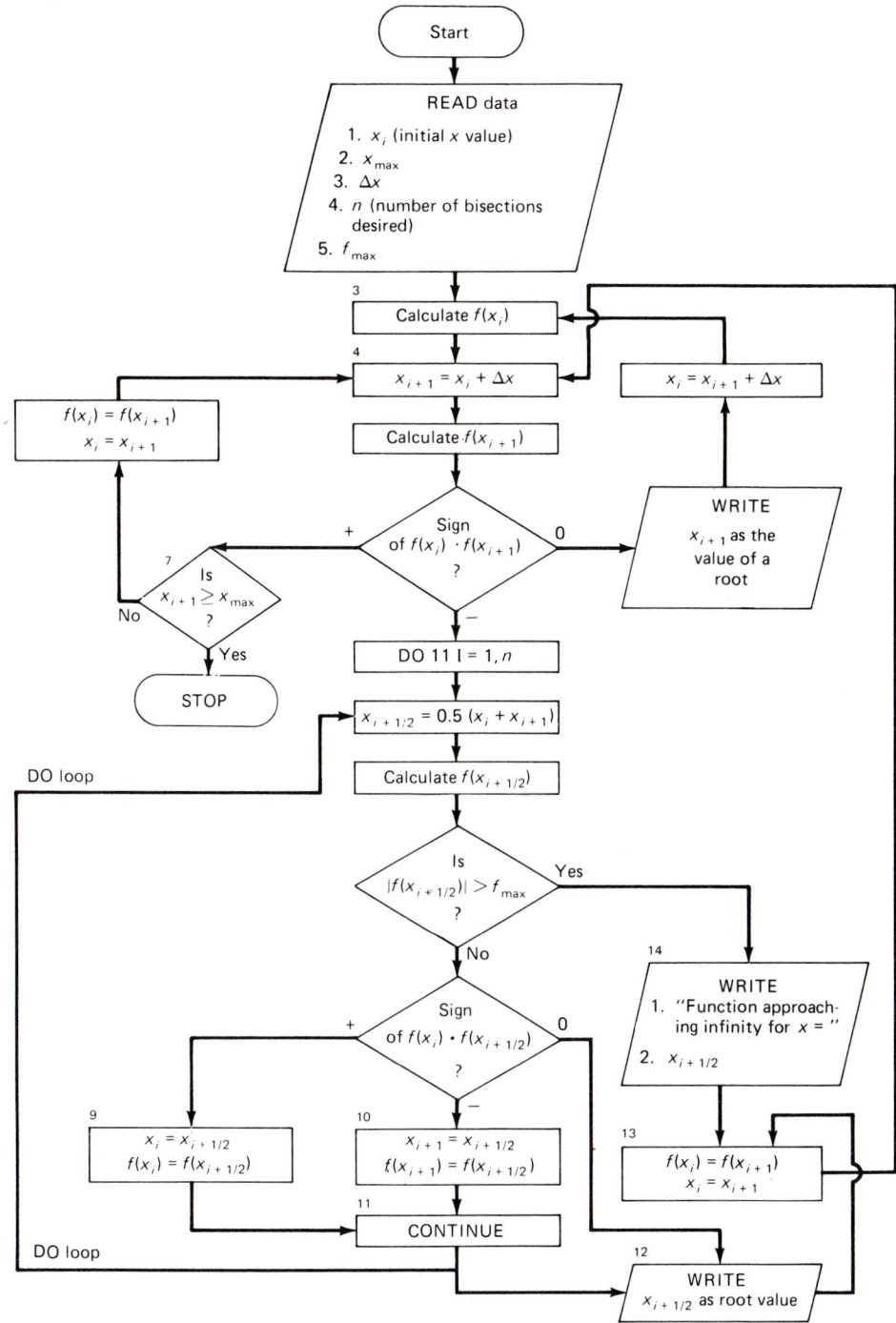

Figure 2-4 Flow chart for Ex. 2-2

The FORTRAN program and output results follow the flow chart. The variable names and the quantities which they represent are as follows:

Variable Name	Quantity	Values Used
X	x_i	Initial value, 0.1
XMAX	x_{max}	4.0
DELTX	Δx	0.1 initially
FMAX	f_{max}	10,000
N	n	20
FX	$f(x_i)$	
X1	x_{i+1}	
FX1	$f(x_{i+1})$	
XAVG	$0.5(x_i + x_{i+1})$	
FAVG	$f(x_{i+1/2})$	

```
    WRITE(6,1)
  1 FORMAT('1',5X,'ROOT DETERMINATION BY BISECTION METHOD'//)
    READ(5,2) X,XMAX,DELTX,FMAX,N
  2 FORMAT(4F10.0,I2)
  3 FX=1.+5.25*X-1./COS(SQRT(.68*X))
  4 X1=X+DELTX
    FX1=1.+5.25*X1-1./COS(SQRT(.68*X1))
    IF(FX*FX1) 8,5,7
  5 WRITE(6,6) X1
  6 FORMAT(' ','X=',F8.4,' IS A REAL ROOT')
    X=X1+DELTX
    GO TO 3
  7 IF(X1.GE.XMAX) STOP
    X=X1
    FX=FX1
    GO TO 4
  8 DO 11 I=1,N
    XAVG=(X+X1)/2.
    FAVG=1.+5.25*XAVG-1./COS(SQRT(.68*XAVG))
    IF(ABS(FAVG).GT.FMAX) GO TO 14
    IF(FX*FAVG) 10,12,9
  9 X=XAVG
    FX=FAVG
    GO TO 11
 10 X1=XAVG
    FX1=FAVG
 11 CONTINUE
 12 WRITE(6,6) XAVG
 13 FX=FX1
    X=X1
    GO TO 4
 14 WRITE(6,15) XAVG
 15 FORMAT(' ','FUNCTION APPROACHING INFINITY FOR X=',F7.4)
    GO TO 13
    END
    ROOT DETERMINATION BY BISECTION METHOD
X=  3.3866 IS A REAL ROOT
FUNCTION APPROACHING INFINITY FOR X= 3.6288
```

2-4 THE METHOD OF FALSE POSITION (LINEAR INTERPOLATION)

After the incremental-search method of Sec. 2-2 has found an interval which contains a real root of the function $f(x) = 0$, the method of false position, or linear interpolation, may be used to converge to the root. Convergence may be more rapid than by the bisection method discussed in Sec. 2-3, but there is no assurance that this will always be the case. The number of iterations required for satisfactory convergence will depend on the shape of the graph of the function in the interval which has been found to contain a root.

Let us assume that x_i and x_{i+1} are two values of x which bound an interval containing a real root of the function, as shown in Fig. 2-5. For convenience in this discussion, these two x values will be referred to as x_1 and x_2, respectively. A straight line is passed through points p_1 and p_2, and the x value (x_3) where this straight line intersects the x axis is a closer approximation to the root than either x_1 or x_2. The value of x_3 may be obtained from the following relationship based on similar triangles:

$$\frac{f(x_2) - f(x_1)}{x_2 - x_1} = \frac{-f(x_1)}{x_3 - x_1}$$

or

$$x_3 = \frac{x_1 f(x_2) - x_2 f(x_1)}{f(x_2) - f(x_1)} \tag{2-4}$$

Now either x_1 and x_3 or x_3 and x_2 will bound an interval containing the root. We see from Fig. 2-5 that the subinterval containing the root is bounded by x_3 and x_2. In a computer program, the interval containing the root may be determined by noting the sign of $f(x_1) \cdot f(x_3)$. If $f(x_1) \cdot f(x_3) < 0$, x_1 and x_3 bound the interval containing the root, whereas if $f(x_1) \cdot f(x_3) > 0$, x_3 and x_2 bound the interval containing the root. In the latter case, which is illustrated in Fig. 2-5, interpolation continues by assigning the value of x_3 to the name

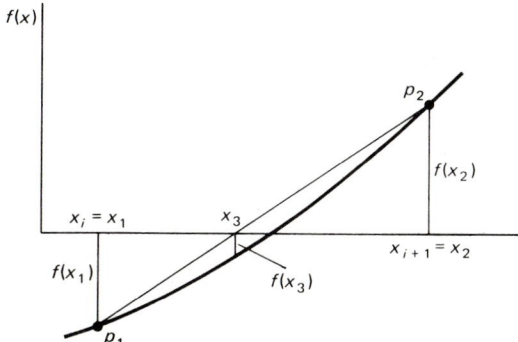

Figure 2-5 Root approximation by linear interpolation

Figure 2-6 Flow chart for the method of false position combined with the incremental-search method

x_1 and the value of $f(x_3)$ to the name $f(x_1)$ and reapplying Eq. 2-4 to obtain a still better approximation to the root. If $f(x_1) \cdot f(x_3) < 0$, the value of x_3 is assigned to the name x_2 and the value of $f(x_3)$ is assigned to the name $f(x_2)$, and Eq. 2-4 is reapplied for an improved approximation to the root. Iteration continues in this manner until $|f(x_3)| < \varepsilon$, where ε is some small number such as perhaps 0.0001.

A flow chart for applying the incremental-search method to find an interval containing a possible root and then applying the method of false position for convergence to the root is shown in Fig. 2-6. Study of the flow chart will reveal that discontinuities in the function such as the one shown in Fig. 2-1 will probably be by-passed without causing overflow, since when $|f(x_3)|$ is larger than some preassigned large number f_{max}, interpolation ceases and the searching method is resumed to search for another interval in which the function changes sign. The range of x searched for roots is from the initial value read in for x_1 to x_{max}.

It is left as an exercise for the reader to write a computer program based on the flow chart of Fig. 2-6 and a particular function (Prob. 2-14c).

2-5 THE SECANT METHOD

The secant method is similar to the method of false position except that the two *most recent* x values and their corresponding function values are used in obtaining a new approximation to the root instead of always using two x values which bound a subinterval containing the root. The method is illustrated in Fig. 2-7 where we assume we have found an interval between x_1 and x_2 which contains a root. A new approximation to the root is then obtained by the use of Eq. 2-4. In the renaming process for iteration, the value of x_2 is always assigned to the name x_1 and the value of x_3 is assigned to the name x_2. Equation 2-4 is then reapplied. Iteration continues until $|f(x)| < \varepsilon$, as in the method of false position.

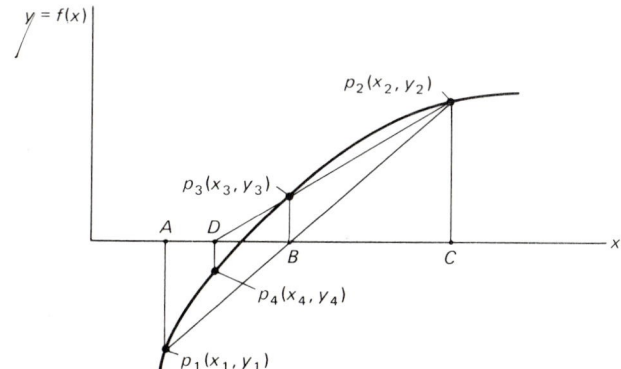

Figure 2-7 Root determination by the secant method

We see from Fig. 2-7 that part of the time we are using linear interpolation and part of the time linear *extrapolation* (when both x values lie on the same side of the root as is the case when we use the straight line, or secant line, joining points p_2 and p_3 to obtain x_4).

It is left as a problem for the reader to revise the flow chart of Fig. 2-6 so that the secant method is used, and to write a computer program based on this flow chart (Prob. 2-17).

2-6 NEWTON-RAPHSON METHOD (NEWTON'S METHOD OF TANGENTS)

This method is very useful for improving a first approximation to a root of an equation of the form $f(x) = 0$, which might have been obtained by the searching method of Sec. 2-2, by an approximate graph of the function, or by some other means.

Consider the graph of $f(x)$ versus x, shown in Fig. 2-8, and assume that x_n is a first approximation of a root. If we draw a tangent line to the curve at $x = x_n$, the tangent line will intersect the x axis at a value x_{n+1}, which is an improved approximation to the root. It can be seen (Fig. 2-8) that the slope of the tangent line is

$$f'(x_n) = \frac{f(x_n)}{x_n - x_{n+1}} \tag{2-5}$$

from which

$$x_{n+1} = x_n - \frac{f(x_n)}{f'(x_n)} \tag{2-6}$$

The value of the function and the value of the derivative of the function are determined at $x = x_n$, and the new approximation to the root, x_{n+1}, is obtained by using Eq. 2-6. The same procedure is repeated, with the new

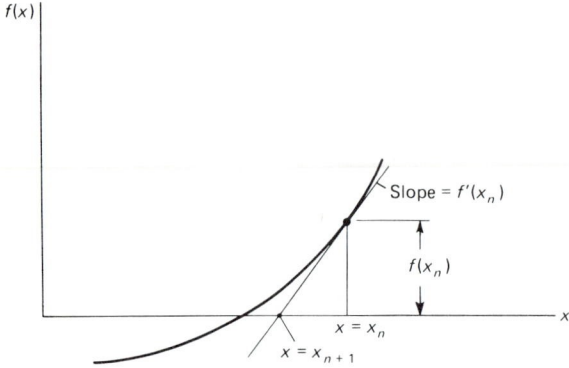

Figure 2-8 Newton-Raphson method

approximation, to get a still better approximation to the root. This continues until successive values of the approximate root differ by less than a prescribed small epsilon which controls the allowable error in the root, or until the value of the function becomes less than some prescribed small value.

The Newton-Raphson method is widely used in practice because of its generally rapid convergence. However, there are cases in which convergence does not occur. One such example is shown in Fig. 2-9(a) where $f''(x)$ changes sign near the root. A second case in which convergence may not occur is illustrated in Fig. 2-9(b). In this example, the initial approximation to the root was not sufficiently close to the true value, and the tangent to the curve for x_n has a very small slope, resulting in x_{n+1} being far to the right where a local maximum in the curve causes the difficulty (oscillation about the local maximum). Other functions could be illustrated in which there is a jump to a root other than the one nearest to the first approximation. These difficulties can be avoided by having the initial approximation sufficiently close to the root value, but sometimes this is not possible.

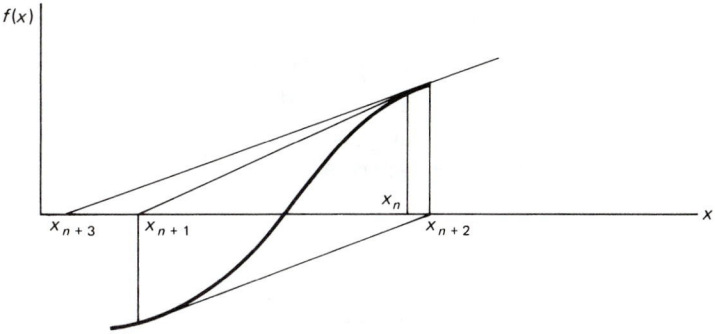

Figure 2-9(a)   A case of no convergence

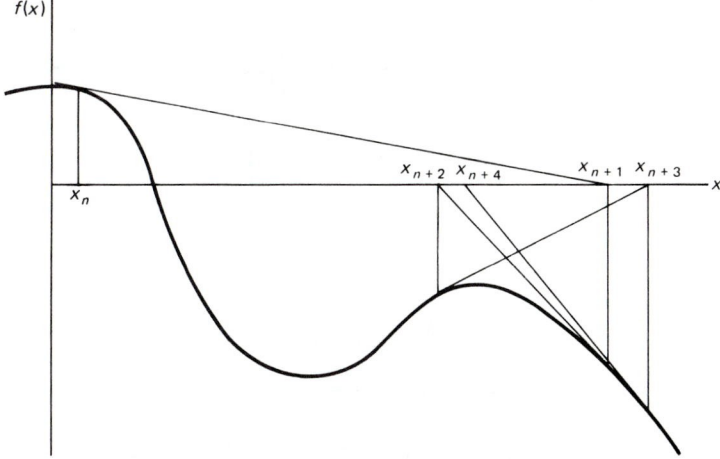

Figure 2-9(b)   A second case of no convergence

As we have seen, the Newton-Raphson method requires the differentiation of the function. If the derivative of the function is very complicated, it may be advantageous to substitute a finite-difference approximation of the derivative for the actual derivative (see Sec. 5-6 for such approximations).

EXAMPLE 2-3

Let us consider the rattrap shown in Fig. 2-10. The trap consists of a movable jaw, trip arm, torsion spring, and trip pan. Upon release of the trip arm owing to a slight disturbance of the trip pan, the torque of the torsion spring closes the movable jaw and kills the rat.

The relationship giving the angular displacement of the jaw as a function of time can be determined as[1]

$$\theta = \frac{T_0}{k} \left(1 - \cos \sqrt{\frac{k}{I_o}}\, t \right) \tag{2-7}$$

where

θ = angular displacement of jaw from "set" position, radians
T_0 = torque exerted by spring on jaw at $\theta = 0$, lb-ft
k = torsional spring constant, lb-ft/radian
I_o = mass moment of inertia of jaw about axis of rotation, lb-ft-sec^2
t = time, sec

[1]See Sec. 6-3.

Figure 2-10 Rattrap shown in open position

With the following trap dimensions (A = 1.125 in., B = 0.5 in., and R = 3.75 in.), we can determine that

θ_k = 2.97 radians or 170.4 deg (angular displacement of jaw upon contact with the rat)

θ_c = 3.27 radians or 187.7 deg (angular displacement of jaw in the closed position)

The torque T_0 is related to the spring constant by the relationship

$$T_0 = T_c + 3.27k \tag{2-8}$$

as indicated in Fig. 2-11 where T_c is the torque when the jaw is in the unset or closed position (θ = 3.27 radians).

The manufacturer of the trap has received complaints that the trap he is marketing closes too slowly (0.0382 sec to strike the rat) and allows too many rats to escape after tripping the trap. Therefore, it is desired to install a new torsion spring which will close the trap on the rat twice as quickly as before, but which will still have the same torque in the closed position (T_c = 0.625 lb-ft), since the existing trap is easily set with this initial torque. It is also desired to maintain the same mass moment of inertia (0.0006 lb-ft-sec²) for the jaw, so that increased energy will also be available in the new trap for killing the rat. The value of the new spring constant is to be determined.

Observing these design requirements and utilizing the fact that θ = 2.97 radians when t = 0.0191 sec, Eq. 2-7 can be put in the following form:

$$\frac{0.625 + 0.30k}{0.625 + 3.27k} - \cos\left(\sqrt{\frac{k}{0.0006}}\,(0.0191)\right) = 0 \tag{2-9}$$

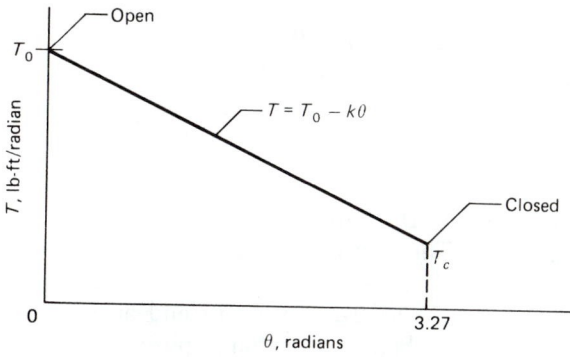

Figure 2-11   Torque-displacement characteristic of torsion spring

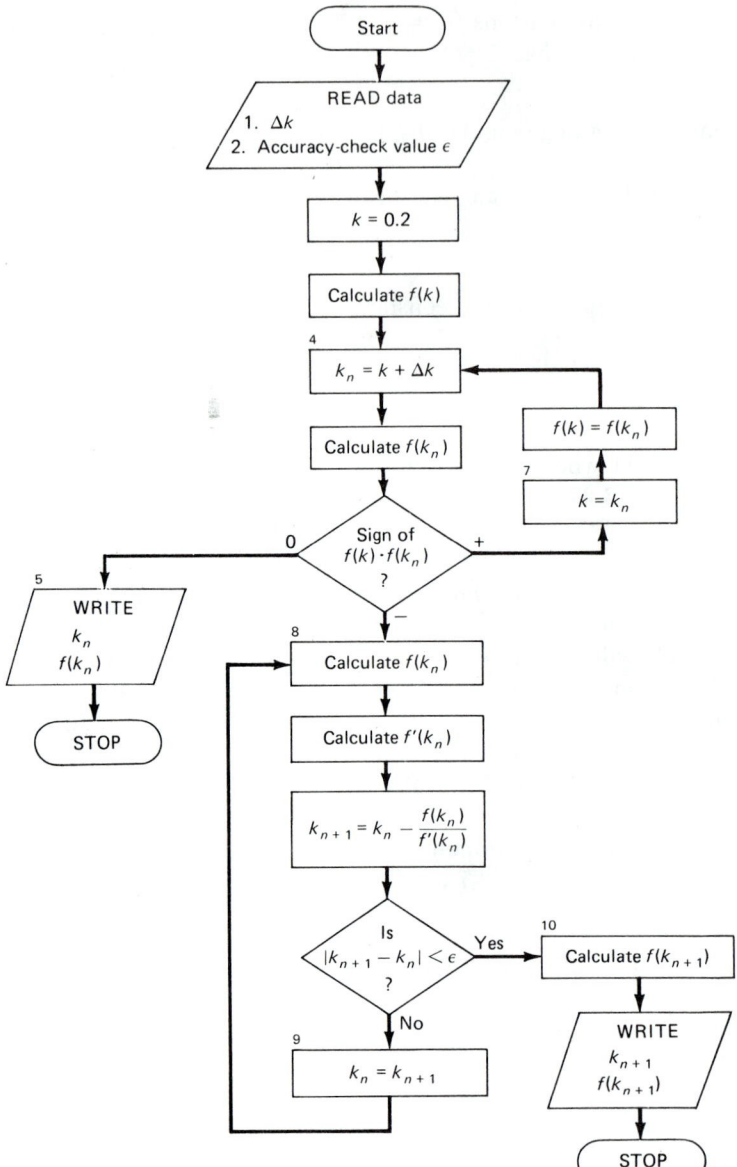

Figure 2-12 Flow chart for Ex. 2-3

A value of $k = 0$ is obviously a root of this equation, but it yields a trivial solution with no physical significance. The solution we desire is that given by the first positive nonzero root.

The incremental-search method of Sec. 2-2 is used to find an approximation to the smallest positive root, and then the Newton-Raphson method is used to converge rapidly to a more accurate approximation. The flow chart for this approach is shown in Fig. 2-12. The FORTRAN variable names represent the quantities shown below.

Variable Name	Quantity	Data Values
K, KN, KN1	Spring constant, k	
DELK	Δk	0.2 lb-ft/radian
EPSI	Accuracy-check value, ε	0.0001 lb-ft/radian
FOFK	$f(k)$	
FOFKN	$f(k_n)$	
FOFKN1	$f(k_{n+1})$	
A	Part of $f'(k_n)$	
B	Part of $f'(k_n)$	
DFOFKN	$f'(k_n)$	

The FORTRAN program is as follows:

```
C REAL ROOT BY SEARCHING WITH CONVERGENCE BY NEWTON-RAPHSON
      REAL K,KN,KN1
      WRITE(6,2)
    2 FORMAT('1','ROOT DETERMINATION BY SEARCHING WITH
                                 CONVERGENCE BY')
      WRITE(6,20)
   20 FORMAT(' ',15X,'NEWTON-RAPHSON METHOD'//)
      READ(5,3) DELK,EPSI
    3 FORMAT(2F10.0)
      K=0.2
      FOFK=(.625+.30*K)/(.625+3.27*K)
                             -COS(SQRT(K/.0006)*.0191)
    4 KN=K+DELK
      FOFKN=(.625+.30*KN)/(.625+3.27*KN)
                             -COS(SQRT(KN/.0006)*.0191)
      IF(FOFK*FOFKN) 8,5,7
    5 WRITE(6,6) KN,FOFKN
    6 FORMAT(' ','NEW SPRING CONSTANT=',F5.3,
                        ' LB-FT/RAD',5X,'FOFKN=',
     *F6.4)
      STOP
    7 K=KN
      FOFK=FOFKN
      GO TO 4
    8 FOFKN=(.625+.30*KN)/(.625+3.27*KN)
                             -COS(SQRT(KN/.0006)*.0191)
      A=((.625+3.27*KN)*.30-(.625+.30*KN)*3.27)/
                             (.625+3.27*KN)**2
      B=.0191/(2.*.0006)*SQRT(.0006/KN)
                             *SIN(SQRT(KN/.0006)*.0191)
      DFOFKN=A+B
      KN1=KN-FOFKN/DFOFKN
      IF(ABS(KN1-KN)-EPSI) 10,10,9
    9 KN=KN1
      GO TO 8
```

```
10 FOFKN1=(.625+.30*KN1)/(.625+3.27*KN1)
                            -COS(SQRT(KN1/.0006)*.0191)
   WRITE(6,11) KN1,FOFKN1
11 FORMAT(' ','NEW SPRING CONSTANT=',F5.3,
                            ' LB-FT/RAD',5X,'FOFKN1=',
   *F6.4)
   STOP
   END
ROOT DETERMINATION BY SEARCHING WITH CONVERGENCE BY
                            NEWTON-RAPHSON METHOD

NEW SPRING CONSTANT=3.362 LB-FT/RAD      FOFKN1=-.0000
```

EXAMPLE 2-4

As another example of the Newton-Raphson method, let us consider the problem of relating the input and output crank angles of a four-bar mechanism. These angles, θ and ϕ, respectively, are measured from the line of the fixed pivots, as shown in Fig. 2-13. The moving links are a, b, and c, and the fixed link is d. Considering the links as vectors, as indicated by the arrows shown in the figure, it follows that their vector sum must always be equal to zero, since they constitute a closed polygon. Setting the sum of the x components and the y components equal to zero, respectively, yields the following equations:

$$b \cos \beta - c \cos \phi + d + a \cos \theta = 0 \tag{2-10}$$

$$b \sin \beta - c \sin \phi + a \sin \theta = 0 \tag{2-11}$$

Solving Eqs. 2-10 and 2-11 for $b \cos \beta$ and $b \sin \beta$, respectively, and squaring both sides of the resulting equations yields

$$b^2 \cos^2 \beta = (c \cos \phi - d - a \cos \theta)^2 \tag{2-12}$$

$$b^2 \sin^2 \beta = (c \sin \phi - a \sin \theta)^2 \tag{2-13}$$

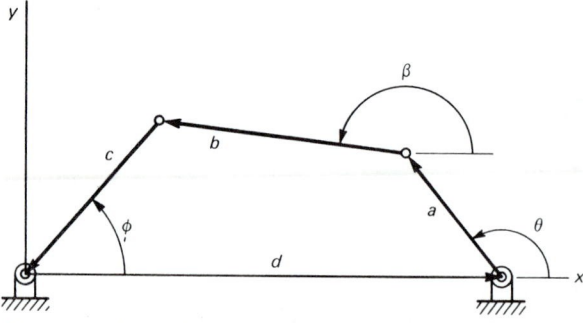

Figure 2-13 Reference diagram for development of the relation between input and output crank angles of a four-bar mechanism

Adding Eqs. 2-12 and 2-13 gives

$$b^2 = c^2 + d^2 + a^2 - 2dc \cos \phi - 2ca \cos \phi \cos \theta \qquad (2\text{-}14)$$
$$- 2ca \sin \phi \sin \theta + 2da \cos \theta$$

Dividing both sides of Eq. 2-14 by $2ca$ and letting

$$R_1 = d/c$$

$$R_2 = d/a$$

$$R_3 = (d^2 + a^2 - b^2 + c^2)/2ca$$

we can write Eq. 2-14 in simpler form as

$$R_1 \cos \theta - R_2 \cos \phi + R_3 - \cos (\theta - \phi) = 0 \qquad (2\text{-}15)$$

This, known as *Freudenstein's equation*, is probably the most useful form of the relation between input and output crank angles of a four-bar mechanism. It should be noted that this equation cannot be readily solved directly for ϕ as a single-valued function of θ.

   Let us select a particular four-bar mechanism so that R_1, R_2, and R_3 are defined, and program a computer solution of Eq. 2-15 which will yield the output angle ϕ for each corresponding input angle θ over the full range of motion of the mechanism, using successive values of θ varying by increments of 5 deg. If we select the following linkage dimensions,

a = length of input crank = 1 in.

b = length of coupler link = 2 in.

c = length of output crank = 2 in.

d = length of fixed link = 2 in.

the proportions of these dimensions define a *crank-and-lever* mechanism in which the input crank has 360 deg of motion while the output lever oscillates.

   Our approach to the problem will consist of substituting successive values of θ into Eq. 2-15 and determining the root (the value of ϕ which satisfies the equation) of each resulting equation by the Newton-Raphson method. The initial approximation of ϕ required in this method may be obtained graphically, for the first value assigned to θ, by sketching the mechanism. The value of ϕ, for this first value of θ, is then calculated to the desired degree of accuracy by the steps outlined in the discussion of the Newton-Raphson method. This calculated value of ϕ_1 is then used as the initial approximation of ϕ_2 in the calculations involved in determining the value of ϕ for the second assigned value of θ. This procedure continues until θ has passed through a 360-deg

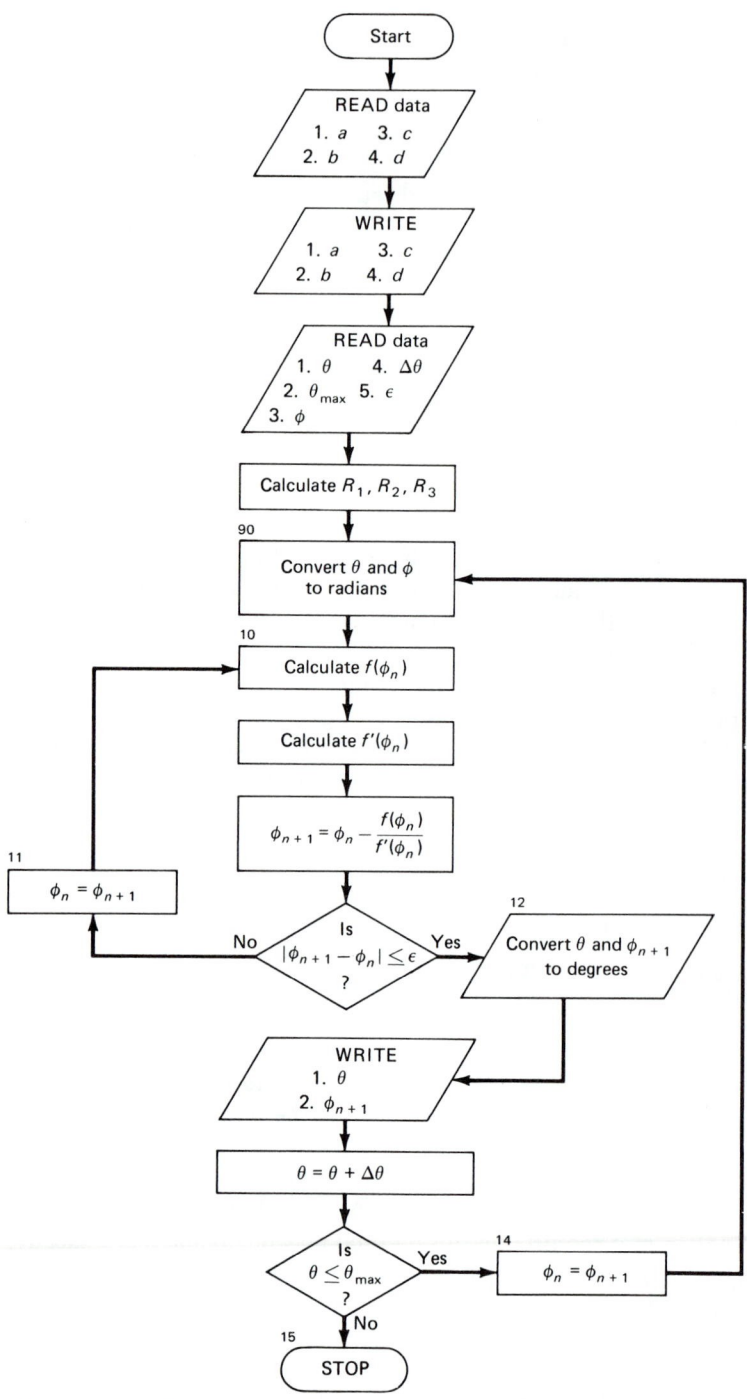

Figure 2-14 Flow chart for Ex. 2-4

range of values. For each position of the mechanism (each value of θ), the iterative process involved in converging on the root value continues until two successive values of ϕ differ by less than the value of some prescribed small epsilon. The flow chart outlining the procedure is shown in Fig. 2-14.

The FORTRAN names assigned to the various quantities are shown below:

FORTRAN Name	Quantity	Given Value
A	Length of input crank a, in.	1
B	Length of coupler link b, in.	2
C	Length of output lever c, in.	2
D	Length of fixed link d, in.	2
DELTH	Increment of input angle $\Delta\theta$, deg	5
TH	Value of input angle θ, deg	Initial value = 0
THMX	Maximum value of input angle θ, deg	360
R1,R2,R3	Constants calculated from link lengths	
PHI	Value of output angle ϕ, deg and radians	Initial guess 41 deg
PHI1	Improved value of output angle ϕ, deg and radians	
FOFPH	$f(\phi) = R_1 \cos\theta - R_2 \cos\phi + R_3 - \cos(\theta - \phi)$	
DFOFPH	$f'(\phi) = R_2 \sin\phi - \sin(\theta - \phi)$	
EPSI	Accuracy-check value, radians	0.00001

The program for this example is as follows:

```
C FOUR BAR LINKAGE ANALYSIS PROGRAM
      WRITE(6,2)
    2 FORMAT('1',12X,'4-BAR LINKAGE INPUT-OUTPUT'/)
      WRITE(6,3)
    3 FORMAT(' ',9X,'NEWTON-RAPHSON METHOD APPLIED TO')
      WRITE(6,4)
    4 FORMAT(' ',14X,'FREUDENSTEIN EQUATION'//)
      READ(5,5) A,B,C,D
    5 FORMAT(4F10.0)
      WRITE(6,6)
    6 FORMAT(' ',18X,'LINK LENGTHS')
      WRITE(6,7) A,B,C,D
    7 FORMAT(' ','A=',F7.3,7X,'B =',F7.3,7X,'C =',
                          F7.3,7X,'D =',F7.3//)

      WRITE(6,8)
    8 FORMAT(' ',20X,'THETA',11X,'PHI'/)
      READ(5,9) TH,THMAX,PHI,DELTH,EPSI
```

```
  9 FORMAT(5F10.0)
    R1=D/C
    R2=D/A
    R3=(D*D+A*A-B*B+C*C)/(2.*C*A)
 90 TH=TH*.01745329
    PHI=PHI*.01745329
 10 FOFPH=R1*COS(TH)-R2*COS(PHI)+R3-COS(TH-PHI)
    DFOFPH=R2*SIN(PHI)-SIN(TH-PHI)
    PHI1=PHI-FOFPH/DFOFPH
    IF(ABS(PHI1-PHI)-EPSI) 12,12,11
 11 PHI=PHI1
    GO TO 10
 12 TH=TH/.01745329
    PHI1=PHI1/.01745329
    WRITE(6,13) TH,PHI1
 13 FORMAT(' ',21X,F4.0,10X,F5.1)
    TH=TH+DELTH
    IF(TH-THMAX) 14,14,15
 14 PHI=PHI1
    GO TO 90
 15 STOP
    END
```

The output results are as follows (for simplicity of printing, the format of the output shown does not completely conform to the FORMAT statements of the program):

```
4-BAR LINKAGE INPUT-OUTPUT

NEWTON-RAPHSON METHOD APPLIED TO
FREUDENSTEIN EQUATION


LINK LENGTHS
A= 1.000        B= 2.000        C= 2.000        D= 2.000
```

THETA	PHI	THETA	PHI
0.	41.4	185.	70.4
5.	43.1	190.	65.4
10.	45.0	195.	60.5
15.	46.9	200.	56.0
20.	48.9	205.	51.8
25.	51.0	210.	48.2
30.	53.2	215.	44.9
35.	55.5	220.	42.1
40.	57.9	225.	39.7
45.	60.3	230.	37.6
50.	62.7	235.	35.9
55.	65.2	240.	34.3
60.	67.7	245.	33.1
65.	70.2	250.	32.0

70.	72.7	255.	31.1
75.	75.3	260.	30.4
80.	77.7	265.	29.9
85.	80.2	270.	29.4
90.	82.6	275.	29.2
95.	84.9	280.	29.0
100.	87.1	285.	29.0
105.	89.2	290.	29.0
110.	91.1	295.	29.2
115.	92.8	300.	29.5
120.	94.3	305.	29.9
125.	95.6	310.	30.4
130.	96.5	315.	31.0
135.	97.1	320.	31.7
140.	97.2	325.	32.5
145.	96.7	330.	33.4
150.	95.7	335.	34.5
155.	94.1	340.	35.6
160.	91.7	345.	36.9
165.	88.6	350.	38.3
170.	84.8	355.	39.8
175.	80.4	360.	41.4
180.	75.5		

2-7 NEWTON'S SECOND-ORDER METHOD

When it is necessary to determine very accurately the value of a root of an equation, Newton's second-order method has the advantage of converging rapidly to a solution, and an extremely close approximation of the value of the root may be obtained with a minimum of calculations. However, this method is limited, in a practical sense, to use on equations which have fairly simple higher-order derivatives (second order, at least), since the time consumed in obtaining and programming involved derivatives outweighs the advantage of rapid convergence. This will be understood more clearly after the following discussion.

Consider, once again, an equation of the form

$$f(x) = 0$$

A graph of the function plotted against x is shown in Fig. 2-15. Suppose that an approximate value of the root, $x = x_n$, has been determined by some method such as a graphical approximation. Expanding $f(x)$ in a Taylor series about $x = x_n$ gives

$$f(x_{n+1}) = f(x_n) + f'(x_n)(\Delta x) + \frac{f''(x_n)(\Delta x)^2}{2!} + \frac{f'''(x_n)(\Delta x)^3}{3!} + \cdots \qquad \text{(2-16)}$$

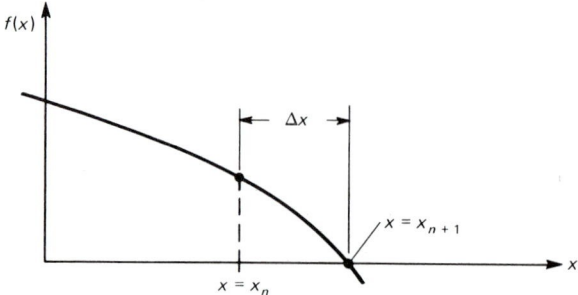

Figure 2-15   Newton's second-order method

If Δx were the particular increment of x which, added to x_n, would result in a zero value for the series, then the quantity $(x_n + \Delta x)$ would be the exact root. Since we are interested in a practical means of determining a value of Δx which will make the series sum to zero, let us set the right side of Eq. 2-16 equal to zero, using just three terms of the series. We obtain the approximate equality

$$f(x_n) + \Delta x \left[f'(x_n) + \frac{f''(x_n)(\Delta x)}{2} \right] = 0 \qquad (2\text{-}17)$$

A value of Δx determined from Eq. 2-17, when added to x_n, will not yield the exact value of the root, since only three terms of an infinite series were utilized in evaluating Δx. However, a much closer approximation to the value of the root will be obtained. Inspection reveals that Eq. 2-17 is a quadratic in Δx and can be solved as such. However, such a solution involves the problem of determining which root is the correct one. This can be avoided, at the cost of slightly slower convergence, by substituting the following expression (from Eq. 2-5) for the Δx within the brackets of Eq. 2-17,

$$\Delta x = -\frac{f(x_n)}{f'(x_n)} \qquad\qquad (\Delta x = x_{n+1} - x_n)$$

and writing Eq. 2-17 in the new form

$$f(x_n) + \Delta x \left[f'(x_n) - \frac{f''(x_n)f(x_n)}{2f'(x_n)} \right] = 0 \qquad (2\text{-}18)$$

Solving Eq. 2-18 for Δx, we obtain

$$\Delta x = -\left[\frac{f(x_n)}{f'(x_n) - \left(\dfrac{f''(x_n)f(x_n)}{2f'(x_n)} \right)} \right] \qquad (2\text{-}19)$$

Since $\Delta x = x_{n+1} - x_n$, we may rewrite Eq. 2-19 as

$$x_{n+1} = x_n - \left[\frac{f(x_n)}{f'(x_n) - \left(\dfrac{f''(x_n)f(x_n)}{2f'(x_n)}\right)}\right] \tag{2-20}$$

which may be used to obtain successively closer approximations to a root by successive applications.

EXAMPLE 2-5

Let us determine the positive real root of the equation

$$2 \cos x - e^x = 0 \tag{2-21}$$

Inspection of Eq. 2-21 reveals that it has an infinite number of negative real roots but only one positive real root. This can best be seen by sketching separately the graphs of $y_1 = 2 \cos x$ and $y_2 = e^x$, as shown in Fig. 2-16, and noting the intersection of the curves. The positive real root lies between $x = 0.5$ and $x = 0.6$. To demonstrate the rapidity of convergence of this method, even when the initial approximation is not too close, we will take $x = 0.4$ as a first approximation and apply Eq. 2-20 successively until we obtain a solution

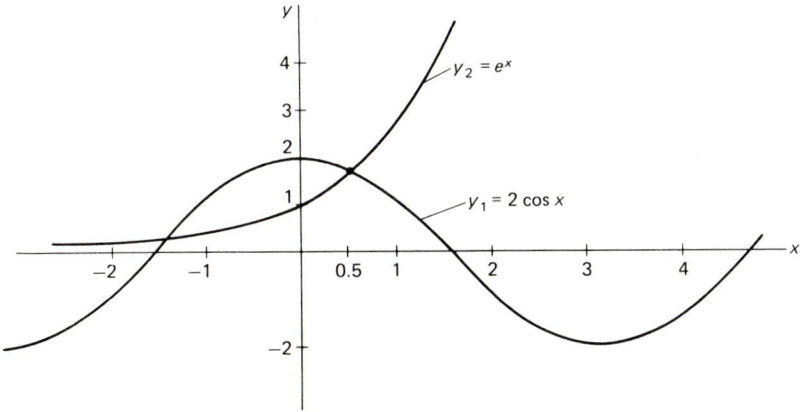

Figure 2-16 Approximate location of the positive real root of the transcendental equation $2 \cos x - e^x = 0$

of the desired accuracy. The results, calculated to three decimal places, are shown herewith.

x	$f(x) =$ $2 \cos x - e^x$	$f'(x) =$ $-2 \sin x - e^x$	$f''(x) =$ $-2 \cos x - e^x$	FR^*
$x_n = 0.4$	0.350	−2.270	−3.334	−0.139
$x_{n+1} = 0.539$	0.003	−2.741	−3.433	−0.001
$x_{n+2} = 0.540$	0.000			

*FR is the bracketed expression in Eq. 2-20.

2-8 ROOTS OF POLYNOMIALS

The analysis of certain types of physical systems involves the solution of polynomial equations of the form

$$x^n + a_1 x^{n-1} + a_2 x^{n-2} + a_3 x^{n-3} + \cdots + a_n = 0 \tag{2-22}$$

where $a_1, a_2, \ldots, a_n$ are real coefficients. For example, the frequency equation of a lumped-mass system with n degrees of freedom is an nth-degree polynomial. The roots of second-degree polynomials are readily determined by the use of the quadratic formula. Various formulas exist for determining the roots of third- and fourth-degree polynomials, but, in general, they are difficult to apply.

There are a number of methods available for finding the roots of polynomials. Unfortunately, each method has certain limitations or disadvantages. For example, the Newton-Raphson method, previously discussed in Sec. 2-6, may be used to find real and distinct roots but requires the use of complex arithmetic for finding complex roots. The quotient-difference method may be used to find complex roots, but it is slow to converge and as a result the method is not very efficient.

In Sec. 2-9 we shall discuss Bairstow's iterative method, which is one of the more commonly used methods which is capable of finding both the real and complex roots of polynomials.

To establish a background for the discussion which follows in Sec. 2-9, let us review the general characteristics of an nth-degree polynomial

$$x^n + a_1 x^{n-1} + a_2 x^{n-2} + a_3 x^{n-3} + \cdots + a_n = 0$$

where the coefficients $a_1, a_2, \ldots, a_n$ are real numbers. For such polynomials, the following facts apply:

1. There will be n roots.
2. There will always be at least one real root if n is an odd integer.
3. Descartes' rule states that the number of positive roots is equal to the number of sign changes of the coefficients *or* is less than this number by

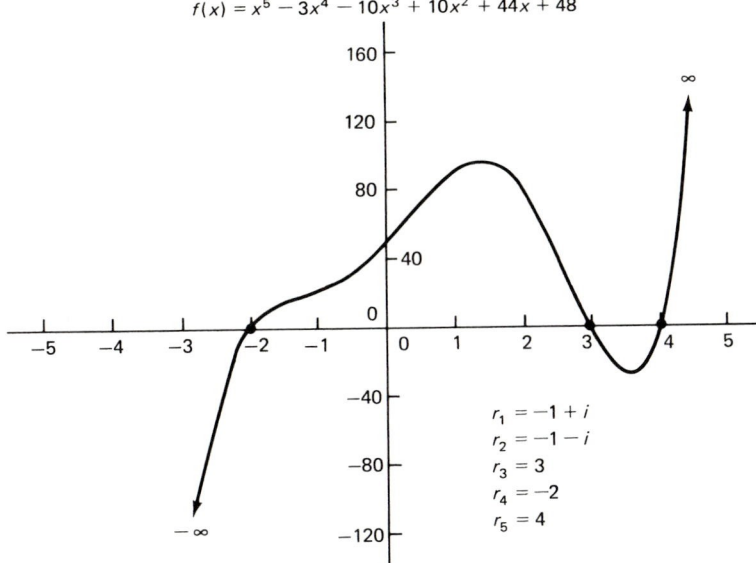

$$f(x) = x^5 - 3x^4 - 10x^3 + 10x^2 + 44x + 48$$

$r_1 = -1 + i$
$r_2 = -1 - i$
$r_3 = 3$
$r_4 = -2$
$r_5 = 4$

Figure 2-17 Plot of 5th degree polynomial

an *even* integer. By transforming the polynomial to $f(-x) = 0$, the number of negative roots is equal to the number of sign changes *or* is less than this number by an *even* integer.
4. It is possible that equal roots exist.
5. When complex roots exist, they occur in conjugate pairs.

Figure 2-17 shows the graph of a 5th degree polynomial which has 2 real positive roots, 1 real negative root, and a complex pair of roots. Note that the polynomial goes to infinity in both directions.

Synthetic Division

It is recalled from algebra that the division of a polynomial, $f(x)$, by $(x - r)$ can be carried out rapidly by *synthetic division*. If r is not a root, then the remainder resulting from the synthetic division is the value of the polynomial for $x = r$. If r is a root of the polynomial, then the remainder is, of course, zero since $f(r) = 0$.

The value of the derivative, $f'(x)$, of a polynomial for $x = r$ is equal to the remainder obtained by a second synthetic division of the result obtained in the first synthetic division. Therefore, the use of synthetic division facilitates the evaluation of $f(x_n)$ and $f'(x_n)$ when using the Newton-Raphson method (Sec. 2-6) to find the roots of a polynomial.

Since synthetic division is discussed in most college algebra books, we will merely review the process by way of the following example.

EXAMPLE 2-6

Divide the polynomial below by the expression $(x + 4)$ and determine the values of $f(x)$ and $f'(x)$ for $x = -4$ using synthetic division.

$$f(x) = x^5 - 3x^4 - 10x^3 + 10x^2 + 44x + 48$$

In dividing the polynomial by $(x + 4)$, the remainder is the value of the function at $x = -4$. The synthetic division process for dividing the polynomial by $(x + 4)$ is carried out as indicated in the following table.

$$
\begin{array}{r|rrrrrr}
-4 & 1 & -3 & -10 & 10 & 44 & 48 \\
 & & -4 & 28 & -72 & 248 & -1168 \\
\hline
 & 1 & -7 & 18 & -62 & 292 & (-1120)
\end{array}
$$

The first row consists of the coefficients of the polynomial. The second row is generated from left to right by multiplying -4 times the elements generated in the third row, the latter being simply the sum of the first- and second-row elements. The value of the polynomial for $x = -4$ is the remainder (-1120). Thus

$$f(-4) = -1120$$

It is easy to verify by long division that the numbers in the third row are actually the coefficients of the fourth-degree polynomial, with a remainder -1120, resulting from division of the fifth-degree polynomial by $(x + 4)$. That is,

Quotient: $x^4 - 7x^3 + 18x^2 - 62x + 292$; with remainder of -1120

To obtain the value of the derivative, $f'(-4)$, of the fifth-degree polynomial for $x = -4$, a second synthetic division is applied to the third row (quotient) obtained in the first synthetic division process to evaluate $f(-4)$. Hence,

$$
\begin{array}{r|rrrrr}
-4 & 1 & -7 & 18 & -62 & 292 \\
 & & -4 & 44 & -248 & 1240 \\
\hline
 & 1 & -11 & 62 & -310 & (1532)
\end{array}
$$

The remainder of 1532 is the value of $f'(-4)$ in which

$$f'(x) = 5x^4 - 12x^3 - 30x^2 + 20x + 44$$

2-9 BAIRSTOW'S METHOD

Bairstow's method is an iterative method which involves finding quadratic factors, $f(x) = x^2 + ux + v$, of the polynomial.[2] From appropriate starting values for u and v, the iteration process converges to the correct values of u and v so that two roots (r_1, r_2) may be determined from the quadratic factor. That is,

$$r_{1,2} = \frac{-u \pm \sqrt{u^2 - 4v}}{2} \tag{2-23}$$

The first quadratic factor obtained from the iteration process gives two roots of the polynomial. Two more roots are then obtained by repeating the iteration process to obtain a quadratic factor of the $n - 2$ degree polynomial resulting from the extraction of the quadratic factor for the first two roots. Thus, the formulation of a quadratic factor of the polynomial resulting from the extraction of a prior quadratic factor will yield additional roots. This procedure may be continued to find all the roots of the original polynomial.

If the quantity under the radical of Eq. 2-23 is negative, the roots, of course, form a pair of complex conjugates.

In a computer program it must be determined whether the value of $u^2 - 4v$ is positive, zero, or negative. In the case of a negative quantity, the sign is changed and the square root of the positive quantity divided by 2 is assigned the value of the complex part of the pair of complex conjugates. If $u^2 - 4v = 0$, then the roots are real and equal. Two real and distinct roots occur when $u^2 - 4v > 0$.

Unfortunately, the iteration process may not converge for some starting (initial) values selected for u and v. It is common practice to select starting values of zero for both u and v, and if convergence does not occur after a number of iterations, new starting values are selected for the iteration procedure. Frequently, suitable starting values of u and v may be determined from $u = a_{n-1}/a_{n-2}$ and $v = a_n/a_{n-2}$, where the a's are the coefficients of the nth-degree polynomial.

We will now develop the equations for the iteration procedure. The extraction of a quadratic factor $x^2 + ux + v$ from an nth-degree polynomial may be written in the form

$$(x^2 + ux + v)(x^{n-2} + b_1 x^{n-3} + b_2 x^{n-4} + \cdots + b_{n-3} x + b_{n-2})$$
$$+ \text{ remainder} \tag{2-24}$$

Dividing an nth-degree polynomial by the quadratic factor gives the following expressions for the b's and *remainder:*

---

[2]The polynomial is of the form given by Eq. 2-22. If the coefficient of x^n is not 1, the equation should be divided through by the coefficient of x^n to make it so.

$$b_0 = 1$$
$$b_1 = a_1 - u$$
$$b_2 = a_2 - b_1 u - v$$
$$b_3 = a_3 - b_2 u - b_1 v$$
$$b_4 = a_4 - b_3 u - b_2 v$$
$$\vdots$$

$$b_k = a_k - b_{k-1} u - b_{k-2} v \qquad\qquad\qquad\text{(2-25)}$$

$$\vdots$$

$$b_{n-1} = a_{n-1} - b_{n-2} u - b_{n-3} v$$
$$b_n = a_n - b_{n-1} u - b_{n-2} v$$

and

$$\text{remainder} = (x + u)b_{n-1} + b_n$$

If u and v have values such that the quadratic factor $x^2 + ux + v$ contains two roots to the nth-degree polynomial, then the remainder is zero. Therefore, b_n and b_{n-1} must both be zero for the remainder to be zero.

Before proceeding with the development of Bairstow's method, let us show that the b's given by Eq. 2-25 can also be obtained by a synthetic division procedure. For illustration purposes, we will use a fifth-degree polynomial ($n = 5$), Eq. 2-26, with $u = v = 1$.

$$x^5 - 3x^4 - 10x^3 + 10x^2 + 44x + 48 = 0 \qquad\qquad\text{(2-26)}$$

$$(n = 5)$$

	a_0	a_1	a_2	a_3	a_4	a_5
$-u = -1$	1	-3	-10	10	44	48
		-1	4	7	-21	-30
$-v = -1$		—	-1	4	7	-21
	1	-4	-7	21	30	-3

$$b_{n-5}\;b_1 = b_{n-4}\;b_2 = b_{n-3}\;b_3 = b_{n-2}\;b_4 = b_{n-1}\;b_5 = b_n$$

It is noted that $b_0 = 1$ and that $b_1 = a_1 - u$. The procedure for the synthetic division is evident if we compare the columns of the table above with the expressions for the b's in Eq. 2-25. From the results of the table we can write the fifth-degree polynomial as

$$(x^2 + x + 1)(x^3 - 4x^2 - 7x + 21) + (x + 1)30 - 3$$

where the remainder is $(x + 1)30 - 3$ or $30x + 27$. As we shall see later, the iteration process will be carried out until b_{n-1} and b_n become essentially zero.

The basic concept of Bairstow's method is to reduce the remainder terms to as near zero as required for a satisfactory approximation of the roots. This means that b_{n-1} and b_n must be reduced to near zero. However, we see from Eq. 2.25 that the b's are functions of both u and v. If we consider Δu and Δv as increments to be added to u and v, respectively, to make the remainder zero, we can express b_n and b_{n-1} in the form of a Taylor-series expansion for a function of two variables. Assuming that Δu and Δv are small so that the higher order terms are negligible, the Taylor-series expansions give

$$b_n(u + \Delta u, v + \Delta v) = 0 \cong b_n + \frac{\partial b_n}{\partial u} \Delta u + \frac{\partial b_n}{\partial v} \Delta v$$

$$b_{n-1}(u + \Delta u, v + \Delta v) = 0 \cong b_{n-1} + \frac{\partial b_{n-1}}{\partial u} \Delta u + \frac{\partial b_{n-1}}{\partial v} \Delta v \tag{2-27}$$

where the terms on the right are evaluated for values of u and v and not for values of $u + \Delta u$ and $v + \Delta v$.

The required partial derivatives in Eq. 2-27 may be obtained from differentiating the expressions of Eq. 2-25. Furthermore, the partial derivatives can be expressed in terms of a set of c's which can be determined from the b's by the synthetic division procedure previously demonstrated for obtaining the b's from the a's, or from a set of equations similar to Eq. 2-25 which can be used for obtaining the b's from the a's. Taking partial derivatives of the expressions of Eq. 2-25 with respect to u and defining these in terms of c's, we obtain the following:

$$\frac{\partial b_1}{\partial u} = -1 = -c_0$$

$$\frac{\partial b_2}{\partial u} = u - b_1 = -c_1$$

$$\frac{\partial b_3}{\partial u} = -b_2 + c_1 u + v = -c_2$$

$$\frac{\partial b_4}{\partial u} = -b_3 + c_2 u + c_1 v = -c_3 \tag{2-28}$$

$$\vdots \qquad\qquad \vdots \qquad\qquad \vdots$$

$$\frac{\partial b_{n-1}}{\partial u} = -b_{n-2} + c_{n-3} u + c_{n-4} v = -c_{n-2}$$

$$\frac{\partial b_n}{\partial u} = -b_{n-1} + c_{n-2} u + c_{n-3} v = -c_{n-1}$$

In a similar manner, taking the partial derviatives with respect to v results in the following:

$$\frac{\partial b_1}{\partial v} = 0$$

$$\frac{\partial b_2}{\partial v} = -1 = -c_0$$

$$\frac{\partial b_3}{\partial v} = u - b_1 = -c_1$$

$$\frac{\partial b_4}{\partial v} = -b_2 + c_1 u + v = -c_2 \tag{2-29}$$

$$\vdots \qquad \vdots \qquad \vdots$$

$$\frac{\partial b_{n-1}}{\partial v} = -b_{n-3} + c_{n-4} u + c_{n-5} v = -c_{n-3}$$

$$\frac{\partial b_n}{\partial v} = -b_{n-2} + c_{n-3} u + c_{n-4} v = -c_{n-2}$$

From either Eq. 2-28 or 2-29, we see that

$$c_k = b_k - c_{k-1} u - c_{k-2} v \qquad (k = 2, 3, \ldots, n-1) \tag{2-30}$$

where $c_0 = 1$ and $c_1 = b_1 - u$. Equation 2-30 is analogous to the expression for b_k in terms of a_k, u, and v of Eq. 2-25. Thus, the partial derivatives, or c's, can be obtained from the b's by the synthetic division procedure previously shown as well as from Eq. 2-30.

From Eqs. 2-28 and 2-29, it is apparent that Eq. 2-27 may be written in the form

$$\left. \begin{aligned} b_n &= c_{n-1} \, \Delta u + c_{n-2} \, \Delta v \\ b_{n-1} &= c_{n-2} \, \Delta u + c_{n-3} \, \Delta v \end{aligned} \right\} \tag{2-31}$$

Solving these two simultaneous equations gives

$$\Delta u = \frac{\begin{vmatrix} b_n & c_{n-2} \\ b_{n-1} & c_{n-3} \end{vmatrix}}{\begin{vmatrix} c_{n-1} & c_{n-2} \\ c_{n-2} & c_{n-3} \end{vmatrix}} \tag{2-32}$$

and

$$\Delta v = \frac{\begin{vmatrix} c_{n-1} & b_n \\ c_{n-2} & b_{n-1} \end{vmatrix}}{\begin{vmatrix} c_{n-1} & c_{n-2} \\ c_{n-2} & c_{n-3} \end{vmatrix}} \tag{2-33}$$

In Eqs. 2-32 and 2-33, n denotes the degree of the polynomial from which the quadratic factor is being extracted.

Bairstow's method may now be summarized by the following step-by-step procedure:

1. Select initial values for u and v. Most frequently these are taken as $u_1 = v_1 = 0$.
2. Calculate $b_1, b_2, \ldots, b_n$ from

$$b_k = a_k - b_{k-1}u - b_{k-2}v \quad (k = 2, 3, \ldots, n) \tag{2-34}$$

   where $b_0 = 1$ and $b_1 = a_1 - u$ as shown in Eq. 2-25 and the synthetic division procedure.
3. Calculate $c_1, c_2, c_3, \ldots, c_{n-1}$ from

$$c_k = b_k - c_{k-1}u - c_{k-2}v \quad (k = 2, 3, \ldots, n - 1) \tag{2-35}$$

   where $c_0 = 1$ and $c_1 = b_1 - u$ as shown in Eq. 2-29.
4. Calculate Δu and Δv from Eqs. 2-32 and 2-33.
5. Increment u and v by Δu and Δv:

$$\left. \begin{array}{l} u_{i+1} = u_i + \Delta u_i \\ v_{i+1} = v_i + \Delta v_i \end{array} \right\} \tag{2-36}$$

   where i denotes the iteration number.
6. Return to step 2 and repeat the procedure until Δu and Δv approach zero to within some preassigned value ε such that

$$|\Delta u_{i+1}| + |\Delta v_{i+1}| < \varepsilon \tag{2-37}$$

For machine computation, an upper limit of iterations should be specified to protect against nonconvergence. If convergence to the desired result does not occur after the specified number of iterations, then new starting values should be selected. Frequently, suitable starting values of u and v may be determined from $u_1 = a_{n-1}/a_{n-2}$ and $v_1 = a_n/a_{n-2}$.

7. Calculate the two roots from the quadratic formula, Eq. 2-23.
8. Obtain additional roots by starting with step 1 and the reduced polynomial which is formulated from the final values of the b's obtained at the end of step 6.

EXAMPLE 2-7

To illustrate Bairstow's method, the roots will be determined for the polynomial

$$x^5 - 3x^4 - 10x^3 + 10x^2 + 44x + 48 = 0$$

To facilitate the required computations in using an electronic pocket calculator, the synthetic division scheme previously explained in Example 2-6 will be used to determine the b's and c's.

In starting with the initial values of $u_1 = v_1 = 0$, the computations with an electronic pocket calculator did not appear to be converging (convergence did occur with these starting values in a subsequent computer program after 14 iterations). Therefore, we select starting values of $u_1 = v_1 = 1.5$ which result in convergence after 5 iterations on the pocket calculator. With these starting values, the synthetic division scheme results in the following for the first iteration:

$$(n = 5)$$

	a_0	a_1	a_2	a_3	a_4	a_5
$-u_1 = -1.5$	1	-3	-10	10	44	48
		-1.5	6.75	7.13	-35.82	-22.97
$-v_1 = -1.5$		—	-1.5	6.75	7.13	-35.82
	1	-4.5	-4.75	23.88	15.31	-10.79
		-1.5	9.00	-4.13	-43.13	
		—	-1.50	9.00	-4.13	
	1	-6.0	2.75	28.75	-31.95	

Substituting the appropriate values into Eqs. 2-32 and 2-33 gives

$$\Delta u_1 = \frac{\begin{vmatrix} -10.79 & 28.75 \\ 15.31 & 2.75 \end{vmatrix}}{\begin{vmatrix} -31.95 & 28.75 \\ 28.75 & 2.75 \end{vmatrix}} = \frac{-469.84}{-914.4} = 0.51$$

$$\Delta v_1 = \frac{\begin{vmatrix} -31.95 & -10.79 \\ 28.75 & 15.31 \end{vmatrix}}{-914.4} = \frac{-178.94}{-914.4} = 0.20$$

$u_2 = 1.5 + 0.51 = 2.01$

$v_2 = 1.5 + 0.20 = 1.70$

For the second iteration, we obtain

	a_0	a_1	a_2	a_3	a_4	a_5
$-2.01 \rfloor$	1	-3	-10	10	44	48
		-2.01	10.07	3.28	-43.80	-5.97
$-1.70 \rfloor$		—	-1.70	8.51	2.77	-37.04
	1	-5.01	-1.63	21.79	2.97	4.99
		-2.01	14.11	-21.67	-24.22	
		—	-1.70	11.93	-18.33	
	1	-7.02	10.78	12.05	-39.58	

$$\Delta u_2 = \frac{\begin{vmatrix} 4.99 & 12.05 \\ 2.97 & 10.78 \end{vmatrix}}{\begin{vmatrix} -39.58 & 12.05 \\ 12.05 & 10.78 \end{vmatrix}} = \frac{18.00}{-571.87} = -0.03$$

$$\Delta v_2 = \frac{\begin{vmatrix} -39.57 & 4.99 \\ 12.05 & 2.97 \end{vmatrix}}{-571.87} = \frac{-177.65}{-571.87} = 0.31$$

$u_3 = 2.01 - 0.03 = 1.98$

$v_3 = 1.70 + 0.31 = 2.01$

The third and fourth iterations yield the following:

$$u_4 = 1.98 + 0.01 = 1.99$$

$$v_4 = 2.01 + 0.00 = 2.01$$

$$u_5 = 1.99 + 0.01 = 2.00$$

$$v_5 = 2.01 - 0.01 = 2.00$$

Since the final b values are required to continue the process to find additional roots, the fifth and last iteration is shown.

	a_0	a_1	a_2	a_3	a_4	a_5
-2.0	1	-3	-10	10	44	48
		-2	10	4	-48	0
-2.0		—	-2	10	4	-48
	1	-5	-2	24	0	0
		-2	14	-20	-36	
		—	-2	14	-20	
	1	-7	10	18	-56	

$\Delta u_6 = 0$ and $\Delta v_6 = 0$

Hence the values of u and v are

$u = 2$ and $v = 2$

Substituting these values into Eq. 2-23 gives

$r_1 = -1 + i$ and $r_2 = -1 - i$

It is noted that the remainder converged to zero since $b_4 = b_5 = 0$. Thus the original polynomial may be written as

$$(x^2 + 2x + 2)(x^3 - 5x^2 - 2x + 24) = 0$$

To obtain the next two roots, we determine the quadratic factor for the third-degree polynomial, $x^3 - 5x^2 - 2x + 24 = 0$. Selecting starting values of $u_1 = v_1 = 0$ and noting that $n = 3$, the first iteration results in the following:

$$(n = 3)$$

	a_0	a_1	a_2	a_3
$u_1 = 0$	1	-5	-2	24
		0	0	0
$v_1 = 0$		—	0	0
	1	-5	-2	24
		0	0	
		—	0	
	1	-5	-2	

$$-b_n = b_3$$

$$c_{n-1} = c_2$$

$$\Delta u_1 = \frac{\begin{vmatrix} 24 & -5 \\ -2 & 1 \end{vmatrix}}{\begin{vmatrix} -2 & -5 \\ -5 & 1 \end{vmatrix}} = \frac{14}{-27} = -0.52$$

$$\Delta v_1 = \frac{\begin{vmatrix} -2 & 24 \\ -5 & -2 \end{vmatrix}}{-27} = \frac{124}{-27} = -4.59$$

$$u_2 = 0.0 - 0.52 = -0.52$$

$$v_2 = 0.0 - 4.59 = -4.59$$

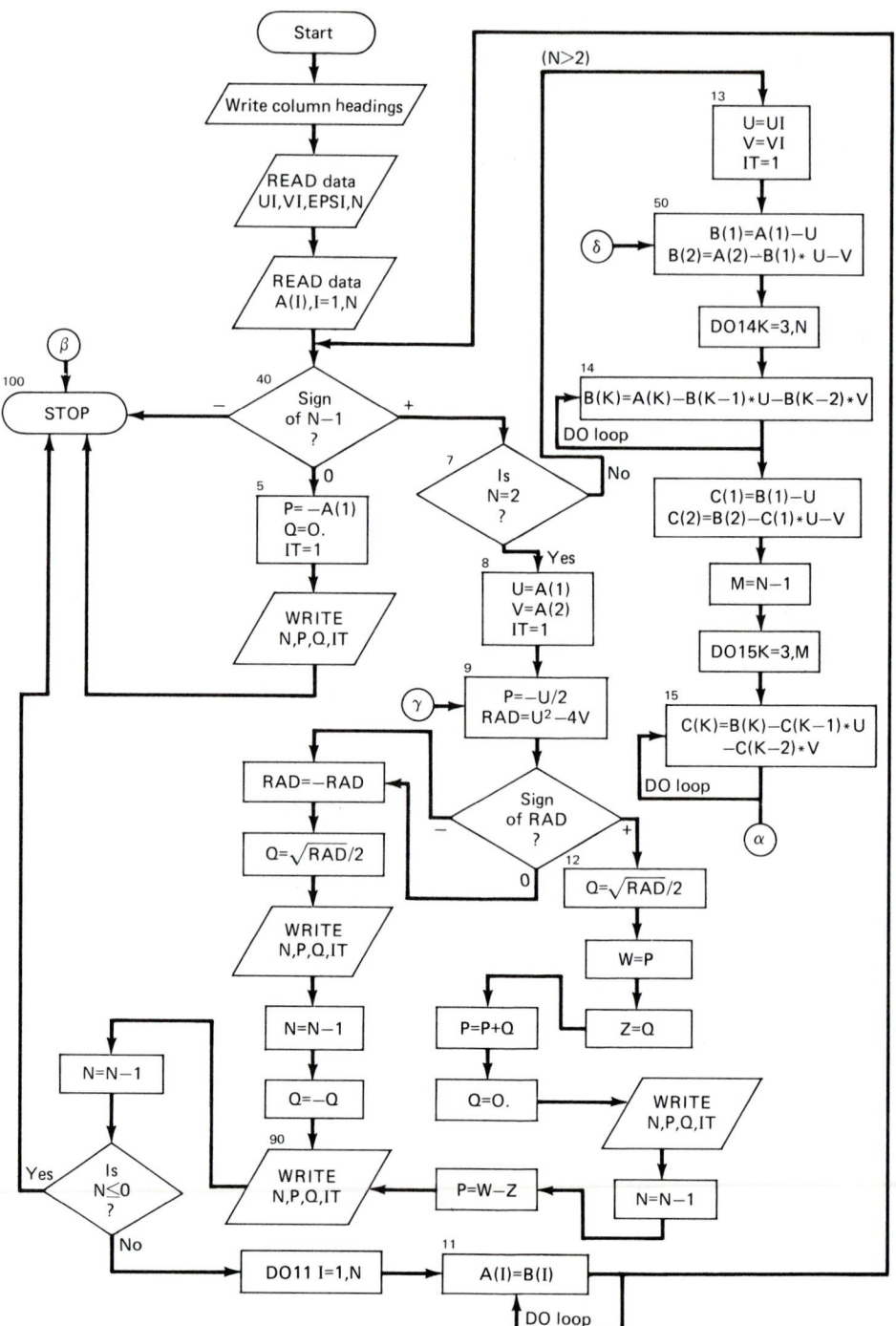

Figure 2-18(a) Flow chart for Bairstow's method

Figure 2-18(b) Flow chart for Bairstow's method (*cont.*)

After two more iterations, the fourth and last iteration results in the following:

$$(n = 3)$$

	a_0	a_1	a_2	a_3
$-u_4 = 1.0$	1	-5	-2	24
		1.0	-4	0.03
$-v_4 = 6.03$		—	6.03	-24.12
	1	-4	0.03	-0.09
		1.0	-3.00	
		—	6.03	
	1	-3.0	3.06	

$$u = u_5 = -1.0 + 0.0 = -1.0$$
$$v = v_5 = -6.03 + 0.03 = -6.0$$

Substituting these values of u and v into Eq. 2-23 gives

$$r_3 = 3$$
$$r_4 = -2$$

Noting that $b_1 = -4$ from the last iteration, the factored form of the fifth-degree polynomial is

$$(x^2 + 2x + 2)(x^2 - x - 6)(x - 4) = 0$$

Thus $r_5 = 4$, and the roots to the fifth-degree polynomial are found to be

$$r_1 = -1 + i$$
$$r_2 = -1 - i$$
$$r_3 = 3$$
$$r_4 = -2$$
$$r_5 = 4$$

The polynomial just solved is shown graphically in Fig. 2-17 in Sec. 2-8.

A flow chart for finding all of the roots of a polynomial by Bairstow's method using the digital computer is shown in Fig. 2-18. The FORTRAN program implementing the flow chart and the results obtained for the roots of the polynomial of Example 2-7 follow. In the FORTRAN program $u_1 = 0$ and $v_1 = 0$. Many of the variable names which appear in the FORTRAN program are also used in the flow chart. Reference to the following variable names and the quantities which they represent will facilitate study of the flow chart.

Variable Name	Quantity Represented
A(I),B(I),C(I)	The a's, b's, and c's of Eqs. 2-22, 2-25, and 2-30, respectively
EPSI	ε of Eq. 2-37
N	The degree of the polynomial
UI and VI	Initial values of u and v
P and Q	The real and imaginary parts of a root, $p + iq$
U and V	The u and v of Eq. 2-24
DELU and DELV	Increments of u and v, Δu and Δv, as given by Eqs. 2-32 and 2-33
RAD	$u^2 - 4v$ of Eq. 2-23
W	$-u/2$ when $u^2 - 4v$ is positive
Z	$\sqrt{u^2 - 4v}/2$ when $u^2 - 4v$ is positive
IT	The number of iterations
DENOM	The denominator of Eqs. 2-32 and 2-33
SUM	$|\Delta u| + |\Delta v|$
STORE	The first value of $|\Delta u| + |\Delta v|$ calculated

It should be noted in studying the flow chart that the first value of $|\Delta u| + |\Delta v|$ calculated is stored and later compared with the fiftieth value, if that many iterations are used. If the fiftieth value exceeds the first value, a message is printed that divergence is occurring and execution stops after printing current values of u, v, Δu, and Δv. If divergence is not occurring but the condition $|\Delta u| + |\Delta v| < \varepsilon$ has not been satisfied after 100 iterations, a message is printed that convergence is slow, current values of u, v, Δu, and Δv are printed, and iterating continues. If the condition $|\Delta u| + |\Delta v| < \varepsilon$ has not been satisfied after 200 iterations, a message is printed that iterating is being stopped after 200 iterations, and current values of u, v, and Δu, and Δv are printed.

```
C ROOTS OF POLYNOMIAL BY BAIRSTOWS METHOD
      DIMENSION A(30),B(30),C(30)
      WRITE(6,2)
```

```
      2 FORMAT('1',9X,'REAL PART',3X,'IMAGINARY PART',3X,
                                          'ITERATIONS'//)
        READ(5,3) UI,VI,EPSI,N
      3 FORMAT(3F10.0,I2)
        READ(5,4) (A(I),I=1,N)
      4 FORMAT(10F8.0)
C SEE IF N=0,N=1,OR N IS GREATER THAN 1
     40 IF(N-1) 100,5,7
      5 P=-A(1)
        Q=0.
        IT=1
        WRITE(6,6) N,P,Q,IT
      6 FORMAT(' ','X(',I2,') =',2X,F8.4,6X,F8.4,10X,I3)
        GO TO 100
C SEE IF N=2 OR IF N IS GREATER THAN 2
      7 IF(N.EQ.2) GO TO 8
        GO TO 13
      8 U=A(1)
        V=A(2)
        IT=1
      9 P=-U/2.
        RAD=U**2-4.*V
C CHECK THE SIGN OF U**2-4.*V
        IF(RAD.GT.0.) GO TO 12
        RAD=-RAD
        Q=SQRT(RAD)/2.
        WRITE(6,6) N,P,Q,IT
        N=N-1
        Q=-Q
     90 WRITE(6,6) N,P,Q,IT
     10 N=N-1
C CHECK TO SEE IF N IS GREATER THAN ZERO
        IF(N.LE.0) GO TO 100
        DO 11 I=1,N
     11 A(I)=B(I)
        GO TO 40
     12 Q=SQRT(RAD)/2.
        W=P
        Z=Q
        P=P+Q
        Q=0.
        WRITE(6,6) N,P,Q,IT
        N=N-1
        P=W-Z
        GO TO 90
     13 U=UI
        V=VI
        IT=1
C CALCULATE THE B VALUES
     50 B(1)=A(1)-U
        B(2)=A(2)-B(1)*U-V
        DO 14 K=3,N
     14 B(K)=A(K)-B(K-1)*U-B(K-2)*V
```

```
C CALCULATE THE C VALUES
      C(1)=B(1)-U
      C(2)=B(2)-C(1)*U-V
      M=N-1
      DO 15 K=3,M
   15 C(K)=B(K)-C(K-1)*U-C(K-2)*V
C CALCULATE DELU AND DELV
      IF(N.GT.3) GO TO 17
      DENOM=C(N-1)-C(N-2)**2
      IF(DENOM.EQ.0.) GO TO 30
      DELU=(B(N)-B(N-1)*C(N-2))/DENOM
   16 DELV=(C(N-1)*B(N-1)-C(N-2)*B(N))/DENOM
      GO TO 18
   17 DENOM=C(N-1)*C(N-3)-C(N-2)**2
      IF(DENOM.EQ.0.) GO TO 30
      DELU=(B(N)*C(N-3)-B(N-1)*C(N-2))/DENOM
      GO TO 16
C CALCULATE NEW U AND V VALUES
   18 U=U+DELU
      V=V+DELV
      SUM=ABS(DELU)+ABS(DELV)
C STORE THE FIRST SUM CALCULATED
      IF(IT.EQ.1) GO TO 19
      GO TO 20
   19 STORE=SUM
      GO TO 21
   20 IF(IT.EQ.50) GO TO 28
      IF(IT.GE.200) GO TO 26
   21 IF(SUM.LE.EPSI) GO TO 9
      IF(IT.EQ.100) GO TO 23
   22 IT=IT+1
      GO TO 50
   23 WRITE(6,24)
   24 FORMAT(' ',10X,'CONVERGENCE IS SLOW')
      WRITE(6,25) U,V,DELU,DELV
   25 FORMAT(' ','U=',E14.7,3X,'V=',E14.7,3X,'DELU=',
                                    E14.7,3X,'DELV=',
     *E14.7)
      GO TO 22
   26 WRITE(6,27)
   27 FORMAT(' ',10X,'ITERATING STOPPED AFTER 200 ITERATIONS')
      WRITE(6,25) U,V,DELU,DELV
      GO TO 100
C SEE IF SUM AFTER 50 ITERATIONS EXCEEDS FIRST SUM STORED
   28 IF(SUM.LT.STORE) GO TO 21
      WRITE(6,29)
   29 FORMAT(' ',10X,'DIVERGENCE OCCURRING')
      WRITE(6,25) U,V,DELU,DELV
      GO TO 100
   30 WRITE(6,31)
   31 FORMAT(' ',10X,'DENOM IS ZERO')
      GO TO 100
  100 STOP
      END
```

The roots of the polynomial determined by the computer program are

	REAL PART	IMAGINARY PART	ITERATIONS
X(5) =	3.0000	0.0	14
X(4) =	-2.0000	0.0	14
X(3) =	-1.0000	1.0000	3
X(2) =	-1.0000	-1.0000	3
X(1) =	4.0000	0.0	1

The polynomial which has the roots determined above is shown graphically in Fig. 2-17 in Sec. 2-8.

Scaling of Polynomials

Bairstow's method may converge very slowly, or not at all, to the roots of polynomials involving very large coefficients and corresponding large roots. In such cases, convergence problems can usually be avoided by scaling the polynomials.

In general, the scale factor α for an nth degree polynomial is simply

$$\alpha = |a_n|^{1/n}$$

and the scaled coefficients, $\bar{a}_i$, are related to the actual coefficients, a_i, by

$$\bar{a}_i = a_i/\alpha^i \qquad (i = 1, 2, \ldots, n)$$

The actual roots, r_i, are related to the scaled roots, $\bar{r}_i$, by

$$r_i = \alpha \bar{r}_i$$

As an example, the polynomial

$$x^3 - 14(10)^5 x^2 + 56(10)^{10}x - 64(10)^{15} = 0$$

would have a scale factor of

$$\alpha = |64(10)^{15}|^{1/3} = 4(10)^5$$

The scaled polynomial is then

$$x^3 - 3.5x^2 + 3.5x - 1 = 0$$

Solving this scaled polynomial give the scaled roots as

$$\bar{x}_1 = 0.5, \quad \bar{x}_2 = 1.0, \quad \bar{x}_3 = 2.0$$

from which the actual roots to the unscaled polynomial would be

$$x_1 = 2(10)^5, \quad x_2 = 4(10)^5, \quad x_3 = 8(10)^5$$

PROBLEMS

2-1. Make an approximate plot of the 2 functions $x^2 - 1$ and $\sin x$ versus x on the same graph. From the intersections of the curves make a rough estimate of the real roots of the function

$$f(x) = x^2 - \sin x - 1$$

Using a pocket calculator, determine the roots of the function to 3 significant decimal digits by applying the following methods:
a. incremental-search method
b. Newton-Raphson method
c. Newton's second-order method
(answer: $x_1 = 1.410$, $x_2 = -0.637$)

2-2. Flexible cables appear in numerous engineering applications such as transmission lines, suspension bridges, and so on. Cables which carry a load uniformly distributed horizontally, such as some in suspension bridges, assume a parabolic form. Cables used as transmission lines must carry their own uniformly distributed weight and assume the form of a catenary curve as shown approximately in the accompanying figure.

Using an origin for the $x-y$ coordinate system a distance c below the lowest point of the cable, the equation for the catenary is

$$y = c \cosh \frac{x}{c}$$

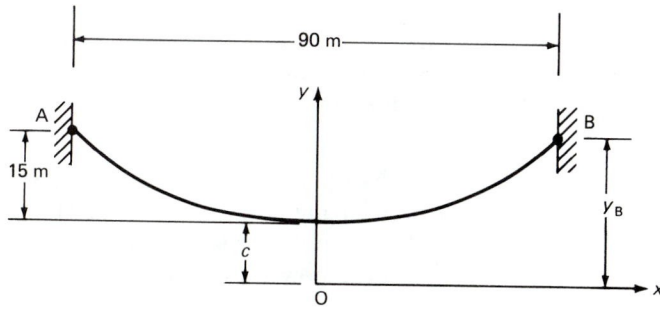

Problem 2-2

The minimum tension in the cable occurs at $y = c$, and the maximum tension occurs at $y = A$ and $y = B$. These tensions may be calculated from the equations

$$T_{min} = wc$$
$$T_{max} = wy_B$$

in which w is the weight of the cable per unit length.

Determine the maximum and minimum tensions in a catenary cable having a span of 90 meters and a maximum deflection of 15 meters as shown in the figure. The weight of the cable is 45 N/m. Use a pocket calculator and a method of your choice, and determine the root of the transcendental equation which is necessary for obtaining the desired solutions.

(answer: $T_{min} = 3143.7$ N, $T_{max} = 3818.7$ N)

2-3. Determine the first three positive nonzero roots of the equation

$$\cos x \cosh x = 1$$

using any of the following:
a. the incremental-search method
b. the incremental-search method combined with the bisection method
c. the incremental-search method combined with the false position method
d. the incremental-search method combined with the secant method
e. each of the above

2-4. Determine the first four positive roots of the equation

$$\cos x \cosh x = -1$$

using the incremental-search method to locate approximate values of the roots, and the Newton-Raphson method for convergence to the root values. (partial answer: $x_4 = 10.9955$)

2-5. Refer to Ex. 2-3 and convert the problem parameter values to the SI system of units and obtain Eq. 2-9 with k having units of N·m/rad.

2-6. Refer to Ex. 2-3 and convert the problem parameter values to the SI system of units and obtain Eq. 2-9 with k having units of N·m/rad. Then make the necessary modifications in the computer program given in the example to work in SI units, and obtain the new spring constant value. (answer: $k = 4.558$ N·m/rad)

2-7. Make a rough plot of the function $2x^2 + 1$ versus x. On the same graph make a rough plot of the function e^x versus x. From the intersection of the two curves, make a rough guess of the value of the nonzero root of the function

$$2x^2 + 1 - e^x = 0$$

Using a pocket calculator and applying Newton's second-order method, find an accurate value of the root.

2-8. Make a rough plot of the function $x^2 + 1$ versus x, and the function $2e^{-x}$ versus x, on the same graph. From the intersection of the two curves make a rough estimate of the positive root of the function

$$x^2 + 1 - 2e^{-x} = 0$$

Using a pocket calculator and applying Newton's second-order method, determine an accurate value of the root.
(answer: $x = 0.48326$)

2-9. Determine the first nonzero positive root of the transcendental equation

$$\tan kl = kl$$

using a pocket calculator and the method of your choice. Begin by roughly plotting each of the functions $\tan kl$ and kl versus kl to obtain an approximate value of the root.

2-10. The accompanying figure shows a mass m attached to an elastic spring of stiffness k and to a tightly stretched cable of length l. A solution of

Problem 2-10

the one-dimensional wave equation with the appropriate boundary conditions results in the frequency equation (transcendental)

$$\tan \frac{2\pi fl}{a} = \frac{T_0\left(\frac{2\pi fl}{a}\right)}{kl\left[\frac{m}{kl^2} a^2 \left(\frac{2\pi fl}{a}\right)^2 - 1\right]}$$

in which

f = frequency, Hz

l = cable length = 500 in.

T_0 = cable tensile load = 7500 lb

γ = cable mass per unit length = 0.0005 lb-sec^2/in.^{2}

$a = \sqrt{T_0/\gamma}$

k = spring constant = 100 lb/in.

m = mass of rigid body = 0.025 lb-sec^2/in.

Letting $u = 2\pi fl/a$, the transcendental equation becomes

$$\tan u = \frac{T_0 u}{kl\left[\frac{ma^2}{kl^2}(u)^2 - 1\right]}$$

Make an approximate sketch of each side of the above equation on the same graph and determine how many roots the equation has.

Then using the incremental-search method, determine the first 3 positive roots and corresponding natural frequencies f_1, f_2, and f_3. (partial answer: $f_2 = 6.5759$ Hz)

2-11. The axial load P which will cause failure of an eccentrically loaded column is frequently determined from the well-known secant formula

$$\frac{P}{A} = \frac{\sigma_{max}}{1 + \frac{ec}{r^2} \sec\left(\frac{L}{2r}\sqrt{\frac{P}{EA}}\right)} \qquad (e > 0)$$

which can be found in most mechanics of materials texts. In this equation

(a)

Problem 2-11(a)

P = load to produce failure, lb

A = cross-sectional area of column, in.^{2}

L = effective column length, in.

e = eccentricity, in.

c = distance from neutral axis of column to outermost fiber, in.

I = least centroidal area moment of inertia of column, in.^{4}

r = least radius of gyration of column, $\sqrt{I/A}$, in.

ec/r^2 = eccentricity ratio, dimensionless

L/r = slenderness ratio, dimensionless

E = modulus of elasticity, psi

σ_{max} = maximum stress in column (usually taken as proportional limit) psi

By considering the ratio ec/r^2 as a parameter, average unit loads P/A can be determined as roots of the secant formula for specified slenderness ratios L/r to obtain a family of curves for design purposes. A typical plot of 1 curve of such a family of curves for 6061-T6 aluminum is shown in the accompanying figure for $ec/r^2 = 0.35$. Euler's equation

$$\frac{P_{cr}}{A} = \frac{\pi^2 E}{\left(\dfrac{L}{r}\right)^2}$$

for slender columns is also shown.

Problem 2-11(b)

a. Using the incremental-search method of Sec. 2-2 and a pocket calculator, determine the root values of P/A for an aluminum column ($\sigma_{max} = 40,000$ psi and $E = 10(10)^6$ psi) for an eccentricity ratio of $ec/r^2 = 0.1$.

b. Write a computer program to determine a family of curves for an aluminum column for eccentricity ratios of $ec/r^2 = 0.1, 0.2, 0.3,$ and 0.4. Use the incremental-search method of Sec. 2-2 to establish fairly close bounds on the values of the roots (P/A), and then converge to the root values using the bisection method. (Hint: If a step size of 500 psi is used in the incremental search, 10 bisections will locate the values of P/A within less than 0.5 psi.)

  If graphics capabilities are available, it is suggested that the family of curves be generated by computer-aided graphics.

2-12. One method which can be used to determine the modulus of elasticity of a material consists of gluing piezoelectric crystals of equal mass to the ends of a slender specimen of the material as shown in the accompanying figure. A sinusoidal voltage of variable frequency is applied to 1 crystal which subjects the system to a sinusoidal exciting force. The other crystal acts as a transducer for monitoring the response of the system at varying excitation frequencies. These responses are used to determine the system's resonant frequencies which depend upon the density and modulus of elasticity of the material. The system can be modeled by the 1-dimensional wave equation

$$\sigma = \text{stress} = E\frac{\partial u}{\partial x}$$

$$\epsilon = \text{strain} = \frac{\partial u}{\partial x}$$

E = modulus of elasticity
γ = mass density of specimen material
A = cross-sectional area of specimen
$m = \gamma A \ell$ = mass of specimen

Problem 2-12

$$\frac{E}{\gamma}\frac{\partial^2 u}{\partial x^2} = \frac{\partial^2 u}{\partial t^2}$$

in which

u = displacement of an element of specimen in the x direction

t = time

E = modulus of elasticity of specimen

γ = mass density of specimen

x = distance along x axis of specimen

Using the method of separation of variables, it can be shown that the solution of the 1-dimensional wave equation is

$$u(x, t) = \left(C \cos \frac{px}{a} + D \sin \frac{px}{a} \right) \sin pt$$

in which

C and D = constants

p = natural circular frequency, radians/sec

$a = \sqrt{E/\gamma}$ = velocity of sound in specimen material

a. Utilizing the free body diagrams shown for the crystals, Newton's 2nd law, and the fact that $\sigma = E \partial u / \partial x$, the 2 necessary boundary conditions are found to be

$$EA \frac{\partial u}{\partial x} (0,t) = M \frac{\partial^2 u}{\partial t^2} (0,t) \qquad\qquad (x = 0)$$

$$- EA \frac{\partial u}{\partial x} (l, t) = M \frac{\partial^2 u}{\partial t^2} (l,t) \qquad\qquad (x = l)$$

Apply these boundary conditions to the solution of the wave equation, and show that the frequency equation is the transcendental equation

$$\tan \beta = \frac{-2\lambda\beta}{1 - \lambda^2\beta^2}$$

in which

$$\beta = \frac{pl}{a} = \frac{2\pi f l}{\sqrt{E/\gamma}}$$

$$\lambda = \frac{M}{\gamma A l} = \frac{\text{mass of crystal}}{\text{mass of specimen}}$$

A = cross-sectional area of specimen

f = natural frequency, Hz

(*Hint:* The determinant of the coefficients of C and D must equal zero.)

b. Make an approximate plot of each side of the transcendental frequency equation of part a versus β for positive values of β with $\lambda = 0.2$, and determine the first 3 positive roots of the equation.

2-13. To study the effect of the mass ratio parameter $\lambda = M/m$ on the frequency of the system shown in the figure for Prob. 2-12, it is desired to determine the first 3 positive nonzero roots of the equation

$$\tan \beta + \frac{2\lambda\beta}{1 - \lambda^2\beta^2} = 0$$

for a range of λ values from 0.05 to 0.5 in increments of 0.05. To do this begin with $\lambda = 0.05$, determine the first 3 positive roots, then increment λ and again determine the first 3 positive roots, and so forth. Use the incremental-search method to determine close bounds on the root values, and then converge to the root values by the bisection method. Plot the root values versus the mass ratio parameter λ obtaining three curves: one for the first positive nonzero root values, another for the second root values, and a third curve for the third root values.

   Suggested procedure: Do the incremental search in the main program using 0.1 as the increment of β beginning with $\beta = 0.111$ (this value is selected so that $1 - \lambda^2\beta^2$ will never equal zero as the incrementing progresses). Increment λ in the main program and also keep a tally there of the number of roots found. Convert the bisection portion of the program of Example 2-2 to a subroutine subprogram BISECT which is called whenever the incremental search produces a sign change in the function

$$\tan \beta + \frac{2\lambda\beta}{1 - \lambda^2\beta^2}$$

Define this function using a function subprogram. Use a "dummy" function name for this function as an argument of BISECT and for referencing the function within the subprogram BISECT. The real name of the function is supplied by using it as an argument of the CALL statement that calls BISECT. Remember to include the real function name in an EXTERNAL statement in the main program. In the bisection subprogram, assume that the function value is approaching infinity when its value exceeds 1000. (It may be possible to use a considerably larger maximum function value than 1000 with some compilers, but the value must be small enough that the value of β in the bisection procedure never gets in the range where the compiler assumes an error has been made due to $\tan \beta$ approaching infinity, and therefore possibly stops execution.)

   (Hint: To avoid missing a root that may be very close to a value of β that gives a very large value for $\tan \beta$, make $\Delta\beta$ small. Try $\Delta\beta \leq 0.05$.)

2-14. The equation

$$x^2(1 - \cos x \cosh x) - \gamma \sin x \sinh x = 0$$

is associated with the flexural vibrations of a missile subjected to a thrust T. The thrust is directly related to the parameter γ appearing in the equation, and the positive roots of the equation determine the configurations and natural frequencies of oscillation of a missile in flight. This information is pertinent to the design of guidance and control systems for such missiles.

   Determine the first three positive (nonzero) roots of the equation for a range of γ from 0.1 to 3.0 $(0.1 \leq \gamma \leq 3.0)$. Use increments of 0.1 for γ until $\gamma = 1.0$, after which increments of 0.5 should be used until the final value of $\gamma = 3.0$ is reached.

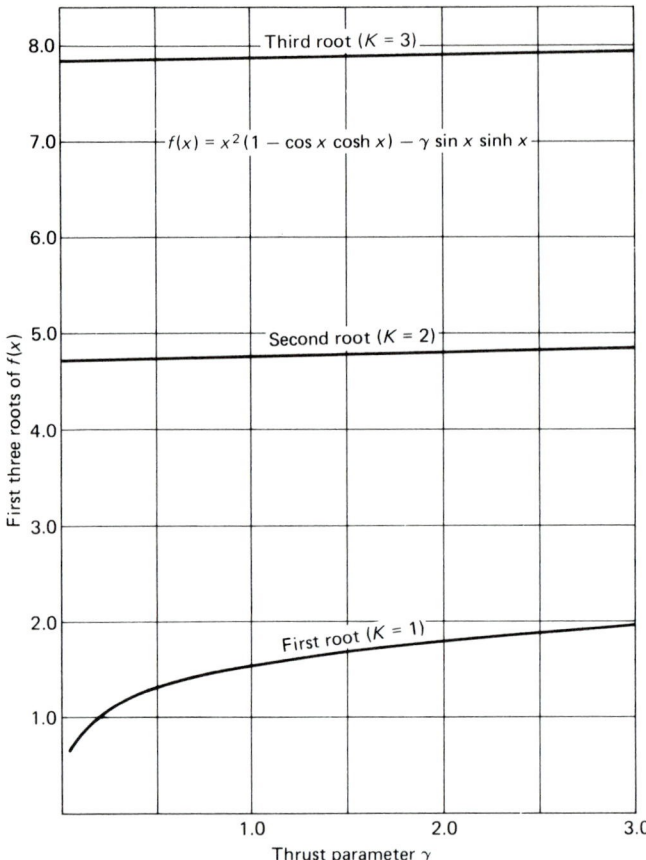

Problem 2-14 Roots of $f(x)$ for Prob. 2-14

Beginning with $\gamma = 0.1$, determine the first three positive roots of the equation. Then increment γ, and again determine the first three positive roots of the equation, and so forth. It is obvious from inspection of the equation that $x = 0$ is a root, so an initial value of $x = 0.1$ may be used to start the search for the roots required. Use the incremental-search method of Sec. 2-2 to locate approximate values of the roots, and then converge to the root values using any of the following:

a. a continuation of the incremental-search method
b. the bisection method
c. the false-position method
d. the secant method
e. each of the above methods

Compare your results with the curves given in the figure accompanying this problem.

2-15. The frequency equation of the vibrating beam shown in the accompanying figure is

Problem 2-15

$$\cos kl \cosh kl = -1$$

where

$$k^2 = \frac{p}{a}$$

$$a^2 = \frac{EIg}{A\gamma}$$

p = natural circular frequency of beam, radians/sec

l = 120 in. (length of beam)

I = 170.6 in.^{4} (area moment of inertia of beam)

E = $3(10)^6$ lb/in.^{2} (elastic modulus of beam material)

γ = 0.066 lb/in.^{3} (density of beam material)

A = 32 in.^{2} (cross-sectional area of beam)

g = 386 in./sec^2 (acceleration of gravity)

Write a program for determining the natural circular frequency of the beam for the first three modes of vibration, by:

a. the incremental-search method
b. the incremental-search method combined with the Newton-Raphson method

2-16. Refer to Prob. 2-15 and use the following data:

$$l = 4 \text{ m}$$
$$I = 8 \times 10^{-5} \text{ m}^4$$
$$E = 200 \text{ GPa}$$
$$\gamma = 76 \times 10^3 \text{ N/m}^3$$
$$A = 0.02 \text{ m}^2$$
$$g = 9.81 \text{ m/s}^2$$

Write a program for determining the natural circular frequency of the beam of the first 3 modes of vibration by:
a. the incremental-search method
b. the incremental-search method combined with the Newton-Raphson method

2-17. Revise the flow chart of Fig. 2-6 so that the secant method is used, and write a computer program based on this flow chart for solving Ex. 2-1.

2-18. Example 2-4 illustrated the application of the Newton-Raphson method of solving Freudenstein's equation. This method was used in the example to determine the angle ϕ which the output crank of a four-bar mechanism made with the line of fixed pivots for each corresponding angle θ which the input crank made with the same line.

Write a computer program, patterned after the one shown in Ex. 2-4 but using Newton's second-order method for solving Freudenstein's equation.

2-19. The frequency equations for elastic beams with various boundary conditions may be found in most texts in the field of vibrations. The frequency equation for a beam of length l, fixed at $x = 0$ and pinned at $x = l$, is

$$\tan kl = \tanh kl$$

By determining the real positive roots of this equation, the natural circular frequencies p of the various beam modes of a particular beam could be determined from the relation

$$p = k^2 \sqrt{\frac{EI}{\gamma}}$$

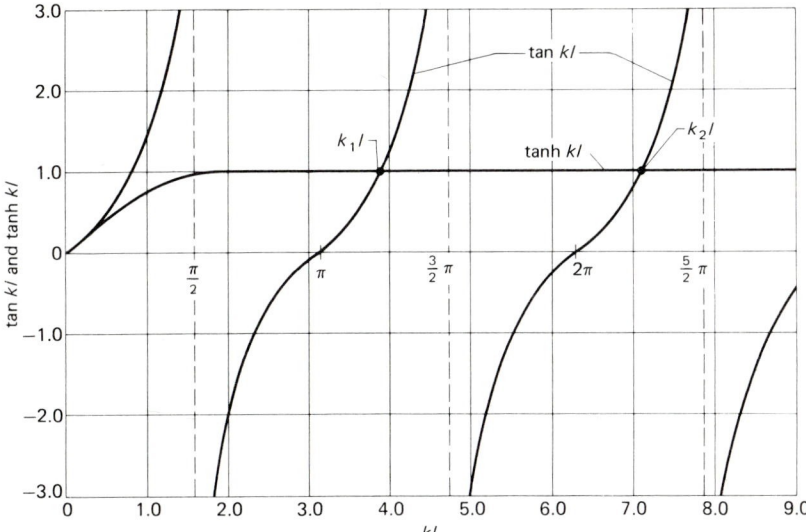

Problem 2-19

where

E = modulus of elasticity of beam

I = moment of inertia of cross section of beam

γ = mass of beam per unit length

Write a FORTRAN program for determining the first three real positive roots of the given frequency equation. Approximate values of the first two real positive roots are shown in the accompanying figure. Combine the incremental-search method with a method of your choice (or a method assigned) for converging to the roots. Incorporate in your program a feature which will prevent overflow for kl values near $\pi/2$, $3\pi/2$, and so forth.

2-20. An automatic washer transmission uses the linkage shown in the accompanying figure to convert rotary motion from the drive motor to a large oscillating output of the agitator shaft G. It consists of two 4-bar linkages in series.

Determine the angle β for values of θ from 0 to 360 deg, using 5-deg increments. Begin with $\theta = 0$ deg, and from a rough sketch of the linkage in this position, guess at the angles ϕ and β. Then using Freudenstein's equation and the Newton-Raphson method (see Ex. 2-4) converge to the correct value of ϕ. Add a constant to ϕ to determine α,

79-tooth helical gear

12-tooth helical pinion

Link lengths
DA = 1.94 in.
AB = 6.86 in.   Automatic washer drive
CB = 2.36 in.
EF = 1.87 in.
GF = 1.26 in.
DC = 7.00 in.
CG = 1.25 in.
CE = 2.39 in.

Problem 2-20

and again using Freudenstein's equation and the Newton-Raphson method, converge to the correct value of β. For the $\theta = 5$-deg position of the linkage, the first approximations to the values of ϕ and β will be the final values obtained for the 0-deg position of the mechanism. This procedure is used for the full cycle of the mechanism.
(partial answer: $\theta = 360°$, $\phi = 24.4°$, $\beta = 65.0°$)

2-21. An interesting problem in space dynamics involves the interception and rendezvous of two vehicles orbiting the earth. One of the simplest cases is concerned with the rendezvousing of two vehicles which are initially orbiting in the same circular orbit.

Referring to the figure accompanying this problem, it can be seen that vehicles 1 and 2 are moving in a circular orbit of radius r_o, each with a velocity v_o. Vehicle 2 is leading vehicle 1 by the angle ϕ_{12}, as shown. If vehicle 1 is to intercept vehicle 2 at some position 3, vehicle 1 must be transferred into a new orbit (usually hyperbolic), as indicated by the dashed line in the figure. Vehicle 1 is placed in the transfer orbit by an impulsive thrust which causes the velocity increment Δv. The velocity v_1 of vehicle 1 on the transfer orbit is the vector sum of v_o and Δv, as shown. At position 3, vehicle 1 is given another impulsive thrust, causing a resulting Δv such that vehicle 1 again assumes a velocity v_o in the same direction as the velocity of vehicle 2, and the two vehicles move off together.

To determine Δv at either position 1 or position 3, for given values of r_o, ϕ_{12}, and ϕ_{23}, the eccentricity e of the transfer orbit must be known.

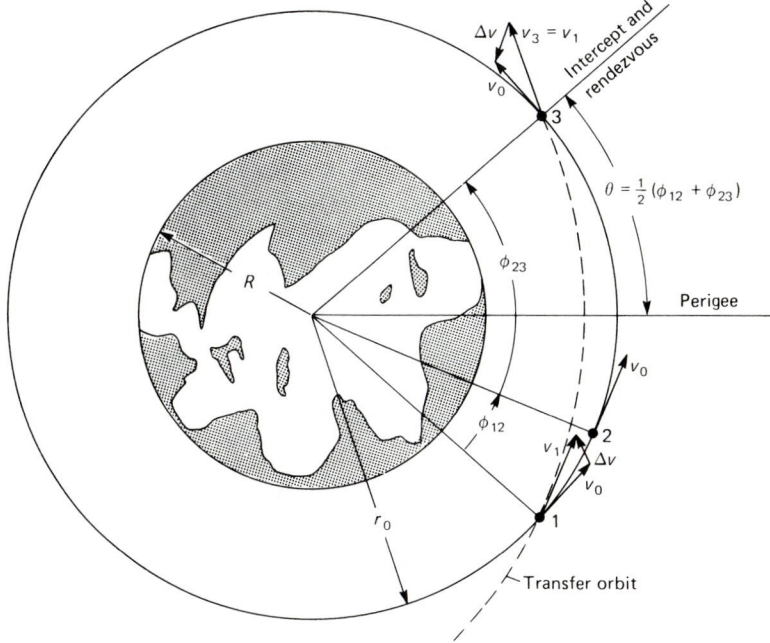

Problem 2-21

This eccentricity is determined from the fact that the time t_{23} for vehicle 2 to move to position 3 must equal the time t_{13} for vehicle 1 to move to position 3. Using the equations of motion of a body in a central force field, and the geometry of conic sections, the transcendental equation resulting from making $t_{13} = t_{23}$ is

$$\frac{\pi \phi_{23}}{360} = \sqrt{\left(\frac{1 + e \cos \theta}{e^2 - 1}\right)^3}$$

$$\times \left[\frac{e\sqrt{e^2 - 1}}{1 + e \cos \theta} \sin \theta - \ln \left(\frac{\sqrt{e + 1} + \sqrt{e - 1} \tan \theta/2}{\sqrt{e + 1} - \sqrt{e - 1} \tan \theta/2}\right)\right]$$

$$(e > 1)$$

where $\theta = (\phi_{12} + \phi_{23})/2$, and a hyperbolic transfer orbit has been used.

Select a suitable method for solving the transcendental equation for e, and write a general FORTRAN program for obtaining values of e for the following data:

$\phi_{12} = 30$ deg
$\phi_{23} = 20, 30, 40, 50$ deg

The eccentricity e will be greater than 1 for hyperbolic orbits.

2-22. (The background material for this problem is given in Prob. 2-21.) When $20 \deg \leq \phi_{23} \leq 50 \deg$ and $\phi_{12} = 30 \deg$, as in Prob. 2-21, the transfer orbits are hyperbolic, and the transcendental equation for such transfer orbits is satisfied by values of e greater than 1.

However, if ϕ_{12} is kept at 30 deg and ϕ_{23} is increased to above 50 deg, the transfer orbits will change from hyperbolic to elliptic, some-where in the range of $55 \deg < \phi_{23} < 75 \deg$. At this point it will be impossible to satisfy the transcendental equation, given in Prob. 2-21, by any value of e. An equation for elliptic orbits must then be used to obtain the required eccentricity of the elliptic transfer orbits. This equa-tion is

$$\frac{\pi \phi_{23}}{360} = \left(\frac{1 + e \cos \theta}{1 - e^2}\right)^{3/2}$$
$$\times \left[2 \tan^{-1} \left(\sqrt{\frac{1 - e}{1 + e}} \tan \frac{\theta}{2}\right) - \frac{e \sqrt{1 - e^2} \sin \theta}{1 + e \cos \theta} \right] \quad (e < 1)$$

and, as indicated, is satisfied only for values of $e \leq 1$.

Thus to write a general FORTRAN program for determining the ec-centricity of the transfer orbits for the data

$$\phi_{12} = 30 \deg$$
$$20 \deg \leq \phi_{23} \leq 120 \deg \quad \text{(use 10-deg increments)}$$

it will be necessary to utilize both the equation given in Prob. 2-21 and the equation given above.

Write a general FORTRAN program for determining the eccentricity of the transfer orbits for the range of data given. (*Hint:* Since $e < 1$ for elliptic orbits and is thus bounded by 0 and 1, while e may approach infinity for hyperbolic orbits, begin with $\phi_{23} = 120 \deg$ and then de-crease by 10-deg increments.)

2-23. Make an approximate plot of the polynomial

$$f(x) = x^5 - 9x^4 + 25x^3 - 5x^2 - 26x + 24$$

and determine the values of all the real roots by the incremental-search method.

2-24. In the following polynomials both positive and negative real roots may be present, and all root values are less than 10 in absolute magnitude.
  a. $x^4 - 10x^3 + 35x^2 - 50x + 24 = 0$
  b. $x^5 - 15x^4 + 85x^3 - 225x^2 + 274x - 120 = 0$
  c. $x^5 - 3x^4 - 23x^3 + 55x^2 + 74x - 120 = 0$

  a. Determine the roots of the polynomials by the incremental-search method combined with either the bisection method, the false-position method, the secant method, or the Newton-Raphson method. Program your root-finder routine as a subroutine subprogram capable of finding the roots of any function defined by a function subprogram. The function name in the root finder will be a dummy name. It will appear as an argument in the root-finder argument list, and will be replaced by the real function name. Store the roots as they are determined in a one-dimensional array for return to the calling program. The calling program will print out the roots of the polynomials given above.

  b. Could a program such as the one discussed above be used to find repeated or complex roots?

2-25. Determine the roots of the polynomial

$$x^4 - 5x^3 + 13x^2 - 19x + 10 = 0$$

using Bairstow's method and a pocket calculator.
(answer: $r_1 = 1.0$, $r_2 = 2.0$, $r_3 = 1 + 2i$, $r_4 = 1 - 2i$)

  In problems 2-26 through 2-33, utilize the program written for Bairstow's method in Sec. 2-10 to determine the roots of the given polynomials.

2-26. $x^4 - 5x^3 + 13x^2 - 19x + 10 = 0$

2-27. $x^5 - 2x^4 - 2x^3 + 20x^2 - 47x + 30 = 0$

2-28. $x^6 + x^5 - 8x^4 + 14x^3 + 13x^2 - 111x + 90 = 0$

2-29. $x^4 - 6x^3 + 29x^2 - 52x + 80 = 0$

2-30. $x^4 - 2x^3 + 3x^2 + 4x + 4 = 0$

2-31. $x^8 + x^7 - 9x^6 + 13x^5 + 21x^4 - 125x^3 + 77x^2 + 111x - 90 = 0$

2-32. $x^6 - 8x^5 + 25x^4 - 32x^3 - x^2 + 40x - 25 = 0$

2-33. $x^8 - 7x^7 + 11x^6 + 41x^5 - 183x^4 + 231x^3 + 21x^2 - 265x + 150 = 0$

2-34. In the Bairstow derivation of this chapter, an nth-degree polynomial is divided by a quadratic factor $x^2 + ux + v$ to give an $n - 2$ degree polynomial plus a remainder. The remainder has the form

$$(x + u)b_{n-1} + b_n$$

as given in Eq. 2-25. If u and v have values such that the quadratic factor contains two roots of the nth-degree polynomial, the remainder must equal zero. Values of u and v are found which make b_n and b_{n-1} go to zero. An alternate approach is to express the remainder as

$$xb_{n-1} + (ub_{n-1} + b_n) = rx + s$$

and find values of u and v which make r and s go to zero. This may be done by expanding $r(u + \Delta u, v + \Delta v)$ and $s(u + \Delta u, v + \Delta v)$ in a Taylor series similar to the expansions of Eq. 2-27. Values of Δu and Δv are then determined which make r and s approximately zero. That is,

$$r(u + \Delta u, v + \Delta v) = b_{n-1}(u + \Delta u, v + \Delta v)$$

$$= 0 \cong b_{n-1} + \frac{\partial b_{n-1}}{\partial u} \Delta u + \frac{\partial b_{n-1}}{\partial v} \Delta v \qquad (a)$$

$$s(u + \Delta u, v + \Delta v) = ub_{n-1}(u + \Delta u, v + \Delta v) + b_n(u + \Delta u, v + \Delta v)$$

$$= 0 \cong ub_{n-1} + b_n + \frac{\partial [ub_{n-1} + b_n]}{\partial u} \Delta u$$

$$+ \frac{\partial [ub_{n-1} + b_n]}{\partial v} \Delta v \qquad (b)$$

From Eqs. 2-28 and 2-29, Eq. a becomes

$$b_{n-1} = c_{n-2} \Delta u + c_{n-3} \Delta v \qquad (c)$$

Equation b may be written as

$$0 = ub_{n-1} + b_n + \left[u \frac{\partial b_{n-1}}{\partial u} + b_{n-1} + \frac{\partial b_n}{\partial u} \right] \Delta u$$

$$+ \left[u \frac{\partial b_{n-1}}{\partial v} + \frac{\partial b_n}{\partial v} \right] \Delta v \qquad (d)$$

Replacing the partial derivatives with their corresponding c values from Eqs. 2-28 and 2-29, and replacing ub_{n-1} with

$$u[c_{n-2} \Delta u + c_{n-3} \Delta v]$$

using Eq. c, we obtain

$$b_n = [c_{n-1} - b_{n-1}] \Delta u + c_{n-2} \Delta v \qquad (e)$$

Solving for Δu and Δv from Eqs. c and e, we have

$$\Delta u = \frac{\begin{vmatrix} b_{n-1} & c_{n-3} \\ b_n & c_{n-2} \end{vmatrix}}{\begin{vmatrix} c_{n-2} & c_{n-3} \\ (c_{n-1} - b_{n-1}) & c_{n-2} \end{vmatrix}} \tag{f}$$

and

$$\Delta v = \frac{\begin{vmatrix} c_{n-2} & b_{n-1} \\ (c_{n-1} - b_{n-1}) & b_n \end{vmatrix}}{\begin{vmatrix} c_{n-2} & c_{n-3} \\ (c_{n-1} - b_{n-1}) & c_{n-2} \end{vmatrix}} \tag{g}$$

Rewrite the Bairstow computer program given in Chap. 2 to incorporate Eqs. f and g for finding u and v instead of the expressions given by Eqs. 2-32 and 2-33. Find the roots of polynomials chosen from those given in Probs. 2-26 through 2-33 with the program you have written.

2-35. Revise the program on page 123 for finding roots of polynomials by Bairstow's method to include scaling (as explained on page 126) and double-precision arithmetic. The revised program should
   a. read in the coefficients of the unscaled polynomial
   b. scale the polynomial as described on page 126
   c. determine the roots of the scaled polynomial
   d. convert the scaled roots obtained to the roots of the unscaled polynomial

Use this revised program to determine the roots of the polynomial

$$x^8 - x^7 - 39x^6 + 37x^5 + 446x^4 - 108x^3 - 1928x^2 - 256x + 1920$$

Use 1.0 for the initial value of both U and V, and use an epsi value of 0.0000001. (Note the root multiplicities in the answer; a condition said to cause most classical methods to fail.)
(answer: $-2.0, -2.0, -2.0, 4.0, 4.0, 1.0, 3.0, -5.0$)

Chapter 3
Solution of Simultaneous Algebraic Equations

3-1 INTRODUCTION

Engineers frequently encounter problems involving the solution of sets of simultaneous algebraic equations. Very frequently the equations are *linear*, so our discussion in this chapter will be primarily concerned with methods applicable for solving sets of linear equations. However, the last section of this chapter (Sec. 3-14) will be devoted to a discussion of the more difficult problem of solving *nonlinear* simultaneous equations.

Problems involving simultaneous linear equations arise in the areas of elasticity, electric-circuit analysis, heat transfer, vibrations, and so forth. We will see later that the numerical integration of some types of ordinary and partial differential equations may be reduced to the solution of such a set of equations.

From a study of algebra, we are familiar with two common methods of solving simultaneous equations: the elimination of unknowns by combining equations, and the use of determinants (Cramer's rule). When three simultaneous equations are to be solved, Cramer's rule appears to have an advantage over the elimination method. However, the method of determinants with expansion by minors is completely impractical when large numbers of equations must be solved simultaneously. Forsythe[1] points out that the solution of n simultaneous equations by Cramer's rule, evaluating determinants in the usual manner of expansion by minors, requires $(n - 1)(n + 1)!$ multiplications. Thus, the solution of ten simultaneous equations by determinants would require 359,251,200 multiplications. With the multiplications performed on the computer at the rate of 2600/sec, approximately 38 hr would be required to obtain a solution. For $n = 26$, $3(10)^{18}$ *years* would be required to obtain a solution. Yet in some engineering problems it may be necessary to solve hundreds, or even thousands, of simultaneous equations. Obviously a solution involving the use of determinants with expansion by minors is not practical. Even if the determinants are evaluated in a more efficient manner such as by the use of an elimination method (see Sec. 3-2), the use of Cramer's rule is very inefficient.

In this chapter we will consider the solution of both *homogeneous* and *nonhomogeneous* sets of linear algebraic equations, since both types appear in engineering problems. The sets of equations with which we will be concerned will involve n equations in n unknowns having the general form

$$
\begin{aligned}
a_{11}x_1 + a_{12}x_2 + \cdots + a_{1n}x_n &= C_1 \quad &\text{(a)} \\
a_{21}x_1 + a_{22}x_2 + \cdots + a_{2n}x_n &= C_2 \quad &\text{(b)} \\
a_{31}x_1 + a_{32}x_2 + \cdots + a_{3n}x_n &= C_3 \quad &\text{(c)} \\
&\ \ \vdots \\
a_{n1}x_1 + a_{n2}x_2 + \cdots + a_{nn}x_n &= C_n
\end{aligned}
\tag{3-1}
$$

If the C's are not all zero, the set of equations is *nonhomogeneous*, and we will find that all the equations must be independent to obtain *unique* solutions. If the C's are all zero, the set of equations is *homogeneous*, and we will find that *nontrivial* solutions exist only if all the equations are *not* independent.

The *coefficient matrix* of the set of equations in Eq. 3-1 is

$$
\mathbf{A} =
\begin{bmatrix}
a_{11} & a_{12} & \cdots & a_{1n} \\
a_{21} & & \cdots & a_{2n} \\
\vdots & & & \vdots \\
a_{n1} & & \cdots & a_{nn}
\end{bmatrix}
\tag{3-2}
$$

[1] Edwin F. Beckenbach, ed., *Modern Mathematics for the Engineer*, University of California Engineering Extension Series (New York: McGraw-Hill Book Company, 1956), p. 436.

A comparison of Eqs. 3-1 and 3-2 shows that a coefficient matrix is a matrix whose elements are the coefficients of the unknowns in the set of equations. If the constants of Eq. 3-1 are added to the coefficient matrix as a column of elements in the position shown in Eq. 3-3, the *augmented matrix* of Eq. 3-1 is formed as

$$
\mathbf{A} =
\begin{bmatrix}
a_{11} & a_{12} & \cdots & a_{1n} & C_1 \\
a_{21} & a_{22} & \cdots & a_{2n} & C_2 \\
\vdots & & & & \vdots \\
a_{n1} & & \cdots & a_{nn} & C_n
\end{bmatrix}
\tag{3-3}
$$

In many instances in computer programming, it may be found convenient to express the column of C's (the constants) as simply an additional column of a_{ij}'s. In such an instance the matrix of Eq. 3-3 might be expressed as

$$
\mathbf{A} =
\begin{bmatrix}
a_{11} & a_{12} & \cdots & a_{1n} & a_{1,n+1} \\
a_{21} & a_{22} & \cdots & a_{2n} & a_{2,n+1} \\
\vdots & & & & \vdots \\
a_{n1} & & \cdots & a_{nn} & a_{n,n+1}
\end{bmatrix}
\tag{3-4}
$$

This form will be used in the discussions in the sections to follow.

We first consider the solution of nonhomogeneous equations, and five methods commonly used on the computer will be discussed. There are two general types of methods available. Methods of the first type are called elimination methods, reduction methods, or direct methods. Of these we will consider Gauss's elimination method, the Gauss-Jordan elimination method, Cholesky's (Crout's) method, and the use of matrix inversion.

Methods of the second type are called indirect or iterative methods. Of these only the widely used Gauss-Seidel method will be presented in this chapter.

Since a nonhomogeneous set of equations, such as Eq. 3-1, describing a physical system, generally consists of linearly independent equations, it will be assumed that such is the case for the sets of equations considered, so that unique solutions exist. A unique solution exists for such a set of simultaneous equations if the coefficient matrix of the set (see Eq. 3-2) is *nonsingular*; that is, if it has linearly independent rows (and columns) or, stated in another way, if the *determinant* of the coefficient matrix is *nonzero*. We will now consider the first of the five methods.

3-2 GAUSS'S ELIMINATION METHOD

The first method usually presented in algebra for the solution of simultaneous linear algebraic equations is one in which the unknowns are eliminated by combining equations. Such a method is known as an *elimination* method. It is called *Gaussian elimination* if a particular systematic scheme, attributed to Gauss, is used in the elimination process.

Using Gauss's method, a set of n equations in n unknowns is reduced to an *equivalent* triangular set (an equivalent set is a set having identical solution values), which is then easily solved by "back substitution," a simple procedure which will be illustrated in the following explanation.

Gauss's scheme begins by reducing a set of simultaneous equations, such as those given by Eq. 3-1, to an equivalent triangular set such as

$$a_{11}x_1 + a_{12}x_2 + a_{13}x_3 + a_{14}x_4 + \cdots \cdots + a_{1n}x_n = C_1$$

$$a'_{22}x_2 + a'_{23}x_3 + a'_{24}x_4 + \cdots + a'_{2n}x_n = C'_2$$

$$a''_{33}x_3 + a''_{34}x_4 + \cdots + a''_{3n}x_n = C''_3$$

$$\cdots \cdots \cdots \cdots \cdots \cdots \cdots \cdots \cdots \cdots \cdots \cdots \tag{3-5}$$

$$a^{n-2}_{n-1,n-1}x_{n-1} + a^{n-2}_{n-1,n}x_n = C^{n-2}_{n-1}$$

$$a^{n-1}_{nn}x_n = C^{n-1}_n$$

where the prime superscripts indicate the new coefficients which are formed in the reduction process. The actual reduction is accomplished in the following manner:

1. Equation 3-1a is divided by the coefficient of x_1 in that equation to obtain

$$x_1 + \frac{a_{12}}{a_{11}}x_2 + \frac{a_{13}}{a_{11}}x_3 + \cdots + \frac{a_{1n}}{a_{11}}x_n = \frac{C_1}{a_{11}} \tag{3-6}$$

Equation 3-6 is next multiplied by the coefficient of x_1 in Eq. 3-1b, and the resulting equation is subtracted from Eq. 3-1b, thus eliminating x_1 from Eq. 3-1b. Equation 3-6 is then multiplied by the coefficient of x_1 in Eq. 3-1c, and the resulting equation is subtracted from Eq. 3-1c to eliminate

x_1 from Eq. 3-1c. In a similar manner, x_1 is eliminated from all equations of the set except the first, so that the set assumes the form

$$
\begin{aligned}
a_{11}x_1 + a_{12}x_2 + a_{13}x_3 + \cdots + a_{1n}x_n &= C_1 \quad \text{(a)} \\
a'_{22}x_2 + a'_{23}x_3 + \cdots + a'_{2n}x_n &= C'_2 \quad \text{(b)} \\
a'_{32}x_2 + a'_{33}x_3 + \cdots + a'_{3n}x_n &= C'_3 \quad \text{(c)} \\
\vdots \qquad \vdots \qquad\qquad \vdots \qquad \vdots \quad\ \vdots& \\
a'_{n2}x_2 + a'_{n3}x_3 + \cdots + a'_{nn}x_n &= C'_n
\end{aligned}
$$

$$\text{(3-7)}$$

The equation used to eliminate the unknowns in the equations which follow it is called the *pivot equation* (Eq. 3-1a in the preceding steps). In the pivot equation the coefficient of the unknown which is to be eliminated from subsequent equations is known as the *pivot coefficient* (a_{11} in the preceding steps).

2. Following the above steps, Eq. 3-7b becomes the pivot equation, and the steps of part 1 are repeated to eliminate x_2 from all the equations following this pivot equation. This reduction yields

$$
\begin{aligned}
a_{11}x_1 + a_{12}x_2 + a_{13}x_3 + \cdots + a_{1n}x_n &= C_1 \quad \text{(a)} \\
a'_{22}x_2 + a'_{23}x_3 + \cdots + a'_{2n}x_n &= C'_2 \quad \text{(b)} \\
a''_{3n}x_3 + \cdots + a''_{3n}x_n &= C''_3 \quad \text{(c)} \\
a''_{43}x_3 + \cdots + a''_{4n}x_n &= C''_4 \quad \text{(d)} \\
\vdots \qquad\qquad \vdots \qquad \vdots \qquad \vdots& \\
a''_{n3}x_3 + \cdots + a''_{nn}x_n &= C''_n
\end{aligned}
$$

$$\text{(3-8)}$$

3. Equation 3-8c is next used as the pivot equation, and the procedure described is used to eliminate x_3 from all equations following Eq. 3-8c. This procedure, using successive pivot equations, is continued until the original set of equations has been reduced to a triangular set, such as that given by Eq. 3-5.

4. After the triangular set of equations has been obtained, the last equation in this equivalent set yields the value of x_n directly (see Eq. 3-5). This value is then substituted into the next-to-the-last equation of the triangular set to obtain a value of x_{n-1}, which is, in turn, used along with the value of x_n in the second-to-the-last equation to obtain a value of x_{n-2}, and so on. This is the *back-substitution* procedure referred to earlier.

To illustrate the method with a numerical example, let us apply these procedures to solving the following set of equations:

$$2x_1 + 8x_2 + 2x_3 = 14$$
$$x_1 + 6x_2 - x_3 = 13 \tag{3-9}$$
$$2x_1 - x_2 + 2x_3 = 5$$

Using the first equation as the pivot equation (the pivot coefficient is 2), we obtain

$$2x_1 + 8x_2 + 2x_3 = 14$$
$$2x_2 - 2x_3 = 6 \tag{3-10}$$
$$-9x_2 + (0)x_3 = -9$$

Next, using the second equation of Eq. 3-10 as the pivot equation, and repeating the procedure, the following triangular set of equations is obtained:

$$2x_1 + 8x_2 + 2x_3 = 14$$
$$2x_2 - 2x_3 = 6 \tag{3-11}$$
$$-9x_3 = 18$$

Finally, through back substitution, beginning with the last of Eqs. 3-11, the following values are obtained:

$$x_3 = -2$$
$$x_2 = 1$$
$$x_1 = 5$$

In the above example the solution yielded values which were exact, since only whole numbers were encountered in the elimination process. In most instances, however, fractions will be encountered in the reduction process. The computer handles fractions in decimal form to a certain limited number of decimal places, and in handling fractions which transform to nonterminating decimals, an error is introduced in the computer solution. This is called *roundoff error*.

When only a small number of equations is to be solved, the roundoff error is small and usually does not substantially affect the accuracy of the results, but if many equations are to be solved simultaneously, the *cumulative* effect of roundoff error can introduce relatively large solution errors. For this reason, the number of simultaneous equations which can be satisfactorily solved by Gauss's elimination method, using seven to ten significant digits in the arithmetic operations, is generally limited to 15 to 20 when most or all of the unknowns are present in all of the equations (the coefficient matrix is dense). On the other hand, if only a few unknowns are present in each equation (the coefficient matrix is sparse), many more equations may be satisfactorily handled.

The number of equations which can be accurately solved also depends to a great extent on the *condition* of the system of equations. If a small relative change in one or more of the coefficients of a system of equations results in a small relative change in the solution, the system of equations is called a *well-conditioned* system. If, however, a small relative change in one or more of the coefficient values results in a large relative change in solution values, the system of equations is said to be *ill conditioned*. Ill-conditioned equations generally result from physical systems in which small changes in one or more system parameters result in large changes in system performance. Since small changes in the coefficients of an equation may result from roundoff error, the use of double-precision arithmetic and *partial pivoting* (described later in this section) or *complete pivoting* becomes very important in obtaining meaningful solutions of such sets of equations. If coefficient errors result from experimental error, then no amount of accuracy in the solution method can be expected to yield meaningful results.

As an example of an extremely ill-conditioned set, consider the following equations:

$$1.000000x + 1.000000y = 0$$
$$1.000000x + 0.999999y = 1$$

with solution

$$y = -10^6$$
$$x = +10^6$$

Now, if we make a change of 0.000002 (only 0.0002 percent) in the coefficient of y in the second equation, making the set

$$1.000000x + 1.000000y = 0$$
$$1.000000x + 1.000001y = 1$$

the solution becomes

$$y = +10^6$$

$$x = -10^6$$

One method that has been used to measure the condition of a set of equations is to divide each equation by the square root of the sum of the squares of its coefficients, and then evaluate the determinant of the coefficient matrix. The smaller the magnitude in comparison with ± 1, the more ill conditioned the set is. An extensive discussion of the solution of ill-conditioned linear equations is given by Wilkinson.[2]

Let us now turn our attention to the implementation of Gauss's elimination method on the computer. Since the computer can handle only numerical data, the use of matrices is required in programming. Referring again to the set of equations given in Eq. 3-9, we can write the augmented matrix of this set as

$$\mathbf{A} = \begin{bmatrix} 2 & 8 & 2 & 14 \\ 1 & 6 & -1 & 13 \\ 2 & -1 & 2 & 5 \end{bmatrix} \tag{3-12}$$

The computer solution is involved with the reduction of this augmented matrix to the augmented matrix of the equivalent triangular set of equations in Eq. 3-11. The necessary successive matrix reductions are accomplished by the same procedures given in steps 1 through 3 above, although in working with matrices we are now concerned with the *pivot row* and *pivot element* rather than with the pivot equation and pivot coefficient, as before.

The first matrix reduction should result in the augmented matrix of Eq. 3-10, which is

$$\mathbf{A}' = \begin{bmatrix} 2 & 8 & 2 & 14 \\ 0 & 2 & -2 & 6 \\ 0 & -9 & 0 & -9 \end{bmatrix} \tag{3-13}$$

Reviewing the procedure outlined in step 1, it can be seen that the elements of the reduced matrix $\mathbf{A}'$ can be written directly from the original matrix $\mathbf{A}$, using the following formula:

$$a'_{ij} = a_{ij} - \frac{a_{ik}}{a_{kk}}(a_{kj}) \quad \begin{Bmatrix} k \leq j \leq m \\ k + 1 \leq i \leq n \end{Bmatrix} \quad k = 1, 2, \ldots, n \geq 1 \tag{3-14}$$

[2]*Mathematical Methods for Digital Computers*, Vol. 2, ed. Anthony Ralston and Herbert S. Wilf (New York: John Wiley & Sons, 1967), pp. 65–93.

where

a = an element of original matrix $\mathbf{A}$

a' = an element of reduced matrix $\mathbf{A'}$

i = row number of matrices

j = column number of matrices

k = number identifying pivot row

n = number of rows in matrices

m = number of columns in matrices

At this point the reader should utilize Eq. 3-14 with $k = 1$ to confirm several of the elements of the matrix $\mathbf{A'}$ given by Eq. 3-13. Then confirm several of the elements of the next reduced matrix

$$\mathbf{A''} = \begin{bmatrix} 2 & 8 & 2 & 14 \\ 0 & 2 & -2 & 6 \\ 0 & 0 & -9 & 18 \end{bmatrix} \tag{3-15}$$

which is determined from the matrix $\mathbf{A'}$ utilizing Eq. 3-14 with $k = 2$. Note that the matrix of Eq. 3-15 is the augmented matrix of Eq. 3-11.

After obtaining the augmented matrix of the equivalent triangular set of equations, the x_i values are obtained by back substitution. (The procedure will be generalized in a following paragraph.)

Having studied the general procedure for reducing matrices, let us now concern ourselves with an efficient way of programming Gauss's elimination method for the computer. We can rewrite Eq. 3-14 as

$$a_{ij}^k = a_{ij}^{k-1} - \frac{a_{kj}^{k-1}}{a_{kk}^{k-1}} (a_{ik}^{k-1}) \begin{Bmatrix} k+1 \le j \le m \\ k+1 \le i \le n \end{Bmatrix} \quad k = 1, 2, \ldots, n-1 \tag{3-16}$$

where the i's, j's, k's, and so on, are as previously defined. The superscripts shown merely correspond to the primes used in identifying successive reduced matrices in preceding discussions, and are not needed in a computer program. Note that in Eq. 3-16 the lower limit of j is $k + 1$ instead of k, as in Eq. 3-14. This limit is used because there is no need to calculate the initial zero values which occur in each row owing to the reduction process, since we know the sequence of these zero values. Furthermore, these zero values are not pertinent to the back-substitution process, so they need not appear as values in the computer.

The back-substitution procedure may be generalized in the form of the following set of equations:

$$x_n = \frac{a_{nm}}{a_{nn}}$$

$$x_i = \frac{a_{im} - \sum_{j=i+1}^{n} a_{ij}x_j}{a_{ii}} \qquad i = n - 1, n - 2, \ldots, 1$$

$$(3\text{-}17)$$

The reader should pause here to use Eq. 3-17, with the augmented matrix given by Eq. 3-15, to confirm the values of x_1, x_2, and x_3 given following Eq. 3-11.

There are two important points we have not yet considered. First, it has been tacitly assumed thus far that every pivot element encountered in the reduction process has been a nonzero element. If this is not the case, the procedure, as discussed, must be modified. If the pivot row has a zero pivot element, the row may be interchanged with any row *following* it which, upon becoming the pivot row, will not have a zero pivot element. For example, suppose that the pivot element of the matrix of Eq. 3-13, a_{22}, were zero instead of 2, as shown. This row could be interchanged with the last row, which would provide a new pivot row with a pivot element having a value of -9, and the procedure could then be continued.

If a pivot element should theoretically have a value of zero, but actually retains a very small nonzero value due to roundoff error, we will find that it will still be desirable to utilize row interchanges. This leads us to the second important point, namely, the effect of the magnitude of the pivot elements on the accuracy of the solution. It can be demonstrated that if the magnitude of the pivot element is appreciably smaller than the magnitude, in general, of the other elements in the matrix, the use of the small pivot element will cause a decrease in solution accuracy.[3] Therefore, for overall accuracy, each reduction should be made by using as a pivot row the row having the largest pivot element. For example, suppose that we were ready to reduce the augmented matrix of the set of equations in Eq. 3-7. The value of a'_{22} would be checked against the values of $a'_{32} \cdots a'_{n2}$, and a row interchange would be made if one or more of these latter values were larger than a'_{22}, so that the row containing the largest of these elements would become the pivot row for that reduction. This procedure is known as *partial pivoting*. Such a provision should always be incorporated in a computer program that is to solve fairly large numbers of simultaneous equations. *Complete pivoting* consists of interchanging columns as well as rows.

---

[3]The magnitudes referred to in this paragraph are the absolute values of the elements.

The results shown below indicate the improvement in solution accuracy obtained in a particular case by using partial pivoting. The exact solutions are the whole numbers 1 through 10.

	Without Largest Pivot Element	With Largest Pivot Element
$x_1 =$	1.0000000	0.9999996
$x_2 =$	1.9999955	1.9999992
$x_3 =$	2.9999983	3.0000001
$x_4 =$	4.0000302	4.0000109
$x_5 =$	5.0000021	4.9999999
$x_6 =$	5.9999964	6.0000039
$x_7 =$	6.9999956	7.0000094
$x_8 =$	8.0000311	8.0000036
$x_9 =$	8.9999557	8.9999822
$x_{10} =$	9.9999531	9.9999913

SOLUTION OF TRIDIAGONAL SYSTEMS OF EQUATIONS

In many engineering problems involving the solution of simultaneous algebraic equations, not all of the unknowns are present in each equation. Frequently the nonzero elements of the coefficient matrix form a band along the main diagonal of the matrix (from upper left to lower right). Such matrices are referred to as *banded* matrices, and one of the most frequently encountered banded matrices is the *tridiagonal* matrix. Such a matrix might have the form

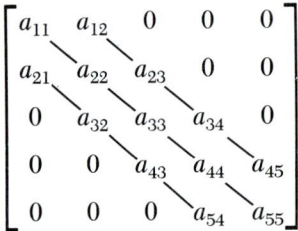

$$
\begin{bmatrix}
a_{11} & a_{12} & 0 & 0 & 0 \\
a_{21} & a_{22} & a_{23} & 0 & 0 \\
0 & a_{32} & a_{33} & a_{34} & 0 \\
0 & 0 & a_{43} & a_{44} & a_{45} \\
0 & 0 & 0 & a_{54} & a_{55}
\end{bmatrix}
$$

for example.

In solving a set of simultaneous equations involving a tridiagonal coefficient matrix, Eq. 3-16 can be applied in the manner previously discussed. However, because of the zero elements in the coefficient matrix, many of the elements would not change. None of the elements outside the tridiagonal band would change from zero, for example.

Let us consider a 5 by 6 augmented matrix. In applying Eq. 3-16 with $k = 1$, the reader can pause here to verify that only 2 elements would be altered. The element a_{22} would become $a_{22} - a_{21}a_{12}/a_{11}$ and the element a_{26} would become $a_{26} - a_{21}a_{16}/a_{11}$. Had Eq. 3-14 been used instead of Eq. 3-16, element a_{21} would have been calculated as being zero. However, there is no need to calculate this zero value because, as previously explained following Eq. 3-16, it is not used in the subsequent back-substitution process. With $k = 2$, the reader should also verify that again only 2 elements would be changed. Element a_{33} would become $a_{33} - a_{32}a_{23}/a'_{22}$, and element a_{36} would become $a_{36} - a_{32}a'_{26}/a'_{22}$, in which a'_{22} and a'_{26} represent the new values of a_{22} and a_{26} previously determined with $k = 1$. Similarly, it can be verified that only 2 elements will be altered for each k value through k equal to $n - 1$. In verifying the above, the reader should have noted that the application of Eq. 3-16 would result in a number of unnecessary calculations involving zeros. Obviously, computer time can be saved by performing only the necessary calculations.

As part of the discussion of the procedure, let us make a change of notation so that a 5 by 6 augmented matrix is represented as

$$\begin{bmatrix} b_1 & c_1 & 0 & 0 & 0 & S_1 \\ a_2 & b_2 & c_2 & 0 & 0 & S_2 \\ 0 & a_3 & b_3 & c_3 & 0 & S_3 \\ 0 & 0 & a_4 & b_4 & c_4 & S_4 \\ 0 & 0 & 0 & a_5 & b_5 & S_5 \end{bmatrix}$$

where the S's forming the augmented column are the constants of the set of simultaneous equations being solved. With this notation, all the elements of the augmented matrix can be stored as 4 one-dimensional arrays (vectors), saving storage space by not storing the zeros.

New values of the elements which are altered by the Gaussian-elimination procedure can be calculated by the application of the equations

$$b_{i+1} = b_{i+1} - \frac{a_{i+1}c_i}{b_i}$$

and $\qquad\qquad i = 1, 2, \ldots, n - 1$ $\qquad\qquad$ (3-18)

$$S_{i+1} = S_{i+1} - \frac{a_{i+1}S_i}{b_i}$$

It should be noted that in these equations i is used to indicate the pivot row instead of k as in Eq. 3-16.

After the application of Eqs. 3-18, the original 5 by 6 augmented matrix shown previously would have the form

$$
\begin{bmatrix}
b_1 & c_1 & 0 & 0 & 0 & S_1 \\
0 & b_2' & c_2 & 0 & 0 & S_2' \\
0 & 0 & b_3'' & c_3 & 0 & S_3'' \\
0 & 0 & 0 & b_4''' & c_4 & S_4''' \\
0 & 0 & 0 & 0 & b_5'''' & S_5''''
\end{bmatrix}
$$

where a single prime indicates a new element value calculated with $i = 1$, a double prime indicates an element calculated with $i = 2$, and so forth. The a elements are shown as having been altered to zero values (as they would have been in the Gaussian-elimination procedure). However, these values are not actually calculated using Eqs. 3-18.

The unknowns of the set of simultaneous equations are obtained by back-substitution utilizing the following:

$$
X_5 = \frac{S_5''''}{b_5''''}
$$

$$
X_4 = \frac{S_4''' - c_4 X_5}{b_4'''}
$$

$$
X_3 = \frac{S_3'' - c_3 X_4}{b_3''}
$$

$$
\vdots \qquad \vdots
$$

and so forth. From above, the general back-substitution equations are seen to be

$$
X_n = \frac{S_n}{b_n}
$$

$$
X_i = \frac{S_i - c_i X_{i+1}}{b_i}
$$

(3-19)

in which $i = n - l$ for $l = 1, 2, \ldots, n - 1$.

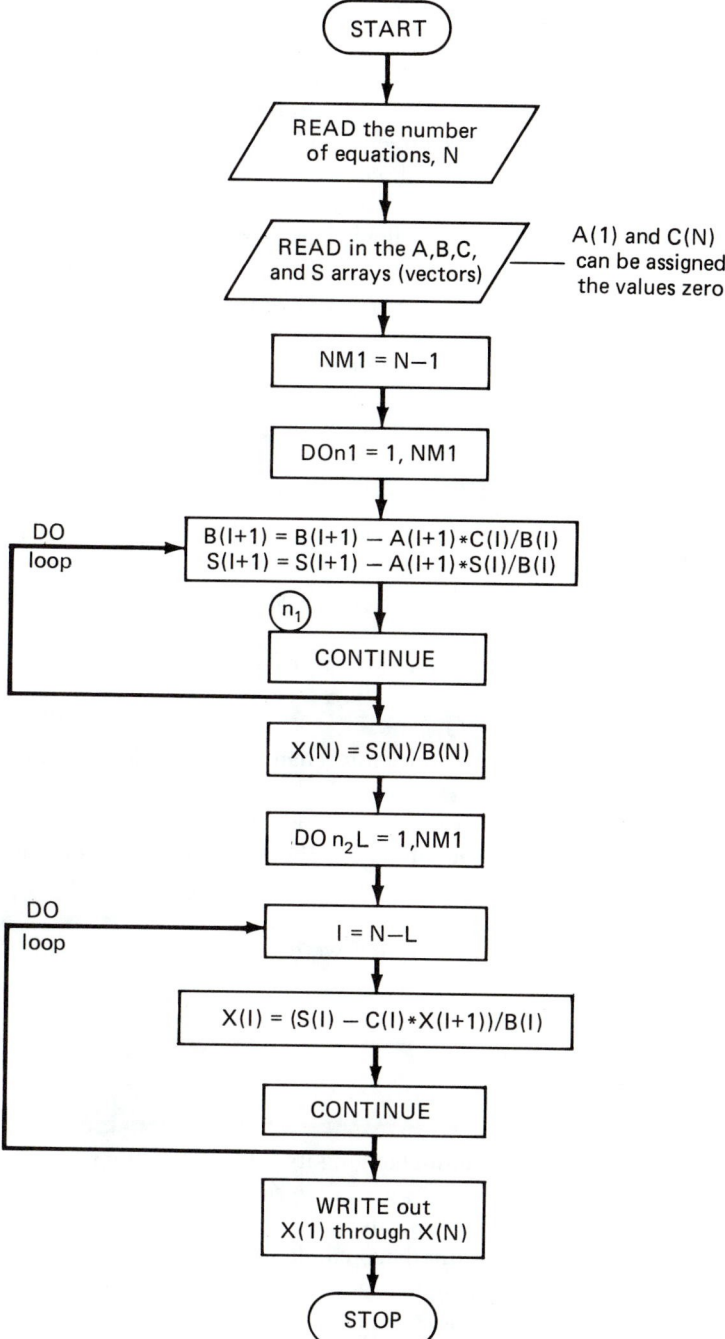

Figure 3-1 Solution of a tridiagonal set of equations using a Gaussian elimination procedure

The application of Eqs. 3-18 and 3-19 are equivalent to a solution by Gaussian elimination using Eqs. 3-16 and 3-17, but with only the necessary calculations being performed. For large sets of equations far fewer calculations are performed, so that large tridiagonal sets (hundreds or even thousands of equations) can be solved without the accuracy problems due to the round-off error inherent in solving large sets with full coefficient matrices.

The flow chart for the solution of a tridiagonal set of equations is shown in Fig. 3-1. No pivoting is indicated in the flow chart since this would destroy the tridiagonal form of the coefficient matrix. From an accuracy standpoint, pivoting would generally not be necessary anyway. Pivoting will be illustrated in the Gaussian-elimination program in Ex. 3-1 later on.

It will be left as a problem for the reader to write a FORTRAN program implementing the flow chart given (see Prob. 3-15).

Gaussian Elimination Used in Determinant Evaluation

Although the use of Cramer's rule is not recommended for the solution of linear simultaneous equations, it may at times be necessary to evaluate a determinant. For larger determinants, the use of Gaussian elimination is much more efficient than expansion by minors.

From the definition of a determinant and the rules of expansion by minors, it may be shown that

1. A determinant is changed only in sign by interchanging any two of its rows (or columns).
2. A determinant is not changed in value if we add (or subtract) a constant multiple of the elements of a row (or column) to the corresponding elements of another row (or column).

From the second statement above, we see that we can apply Eq. 3-16 with

$$k + 1 \leq j \leq n$$
$$k + 1 \leq i \leq n$$

to the elements of a determinant without changing its value. Thus, by repeated application of Eq. 3-16 with $k = 1, 2, \ldots, n - 1$ we can reduce a determinant to upper triangular form without changing its value. The value of the determinant is then simply the product of the diagonal elements (this may easily be verified by expanding an upper triangular determinant by minors). Partial pivoting may be used to avoid having a zero pivot element and to increase the accuracy, but the sign changes resulting from the row interchanges as indicated by the first statement must be kept track of to keep the signs of the determinants correct.

The Gaussian reduction procedure is illustrated by evaluating the determinant of the coefficient matrix of Eq. 3-9. The determinant is

$$\begin{vmatrix} 2 & 8 & 2 \\ 1 & 6 & -1 \\ 2 & -1 & 2 \end{vmatrix} \tag{3-20}$$

Applying Eq. 3-16 with $k = 1$ and simply replacing the second and third elements of column 1 with zeros, we obtain

$$\begin{vmatrix} 2 & 8 & 2 \\ 1 & 6 & -1 \\ 2 & -1 & 2 \end{vmatrix} = \begin{vmatrix} 2 & 8 & 2 \\ 0 & 2 & -2 \\ 0 & -9 & 0 \end{vmatrix} \tag{3-21}$$

Now, applying Eq. 3-16 with $k = 2$ and replacing the third element of the second column with zero, we obtain

$$\begin{vmatrix} 2 & 8 & 2 \\ 0 & 2 & -2 \\ 0 & -9 & 0 \end{vmatrix} = \begin{vmatrix} 2 & 8 & 2 \\ 0 & 2 & -2 \\ 0 & 0 & -9 \end{vmatrix} \tag{3-22}$$

The value of the determinant given by the product of the main diagonal elements is -36.

EXAMPLE 3-1

Let us write a general FORTRAN program for solving up to 15 simultaneous linear algebraic equations (limited to 15 only by the DIMENSION statement).

The FORTRAN names used in the program, and the quantities they represent, are as follows:

FORTRAN Name	Quantity
N	Number of simultaneous equations (number of rows in the augmented matrix)
M	Number of columns in the augmented matrix
L	$N - 1$
A(I,J)	Elements of the augmented matrices
I	Matrix row number
J	Matrix column number
JJ	Takes on values of the row numbers which are possible pivot rows, eventually taking on the value identifying the row having the largest pivot element

FORTRAN Name	Quantity
BIG	Takes on values of the elements in the column containing possible pivot elements, eventually taking on the value of the pivot element used
TEMP	Temporary name used for the elements of the row selected to become the pivot row, before the interchange is made
K	Index of a DO loop taking on values from 1 to $n - 1$; it identifies the column containing possible pivot elements and the pivot row
KP1	$K + 1$
AB	Absolute value of a_{ik}
QUOT	Quotient a_{ik}/a_{kk}
X(I)	Unknowns of the set of equations being solved
SUM	$\sum_{j=i+1}^{n} a_{ij}x_j$
NN	Index of a DO loop taking on values from 1 to $n - 1$
IP1	$I + 1$

The flow chart for the program is shown in Fig. 3-2. The FORTRAN IV program is as follows:

```
C SOLUTION OF SIMULTANEOUS EQUATIONS BY GAUSSIAN ELIMINATION
      DIMENSION A(15,16),X(15)
      READ(5,3) N
    3 FORMAT(I3)
      M=N+1
      L=N-1
      READ(5,4) ((A(I,J),J=1,M),I=1,N)
    4 FORMAT(8F10.0)
      DO 12 K=1,L
      JJ=K
      BIG=ABS(A(K,K))
      KP1=K+1
C
C SEARCH FOR LARGEST POSSIBLE PIVOT ELEMENT
      DO 7 I=KP1,N
      AB=ABS(A(I,K))
      IF(BIG-AB) 6,7,7
    6 BIG=AB
      JJ=I
    7 CONTINUE
C
C DECISION ON NECESSITY OF ROW INTERCHANGE
      IF(JJ-K) 8,10,8
C
C ROW INTERCHANGE
    8 DO 9 J=K,M
      TEMP=A(JJ,J)
      A(JJ,J)=A(K,J)
```

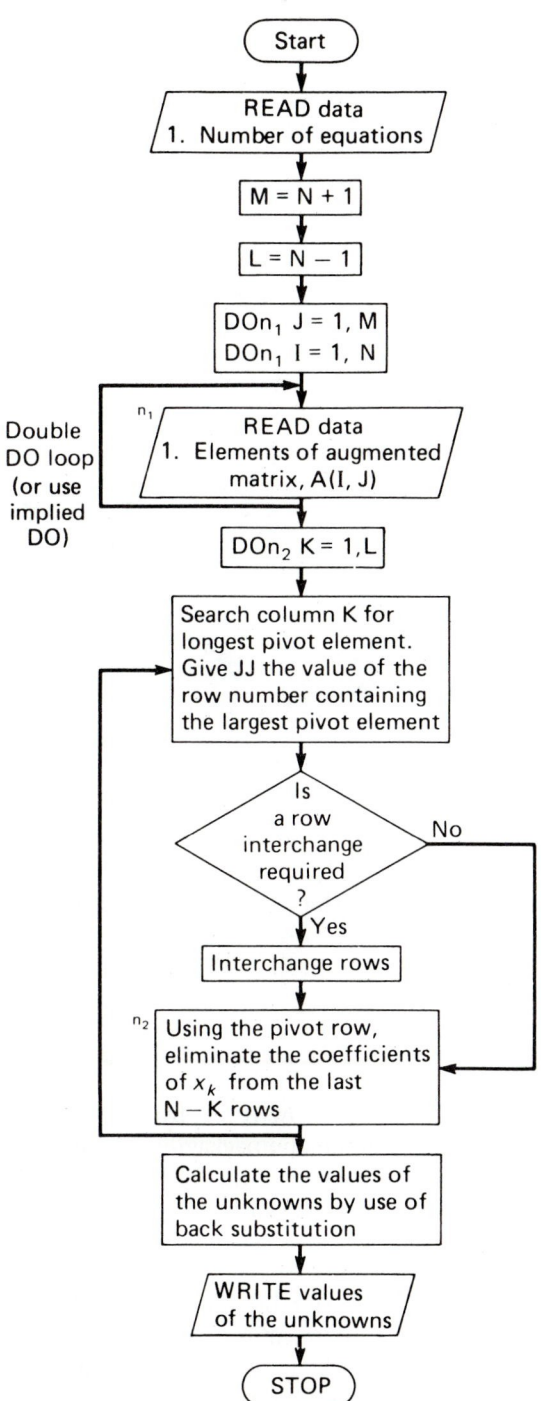

Figure 3-2   Flow chart of Ex. 3-1

```
9 A(K,J)=TEMP
C
C CALCULATION OF ELEMENTS OF NEW MATRIX
   10 DO 11 I=KP1,N
      QUOT=A(I,K)/A(K,K)
      DO 11 J=KP1,M
   11 A(I,J)=A(I,J)-QUOT*A(K,J)
      DO 12 I=KP1,N
   12 A(I,K)=0.
C
C FIRST STEP IN BACK SUBSTITUTION
      X(N)=A(N,M)/A(N,N)
C
C REMAINDER OF BACK-SUBSTITUTION PROCESS
      DO 14 NN=1,L
      SUM=0.
      I=N-NN
      IP1=I+1
      DO 13 J=IP1,N
   13 SUM=SUM+A(I,J)*X(J)
   14 X(I)=(A(I,M)-SUM)/A(I,I)
      WRITE(6,1)
    1 FORMAT('1','X(1) THROUGH X(N)'/)
      DO 15 I=1,N
   15 WRITE(6,2) X(I)
    2 FORMAT(' ',E14.8)
      STOP
      END
```

In the above program, various groups of statements have been identified with respect to their functions by means of comments. Note the correlation of this breakdown with the flow chart of Fig. 3-2. The reader may find it helpful to make such correlations in analyzing the various programs which follow. An application of this general program will be made in the following example.

EXAMPLE 3-2

The five equations in five unknowns appearing below result from the design of a mechanism which is a component of an automatic packaging machine. In this device it is required that a point on the mechanism link be constrained to move over a path having the approximate shape shown in Fig. 3-3. The five points E_1 through E_5 are selected on this curve, with the requirement that the driven point E must pass through each of these five points. A crank length OA is selected, the crank circle is drawn, and for a suitable length EA (arbitrary within limits), the five positions of line EA are determined. A point C is then arbitrarily selected on the link containing line EA. The five positions of point C will in general lie on a conic section since five points determine a conic

Figure 3-3 Design of a linkage to guide a point E through five specified positions

section. To complete the design of the mechanism, the equation of the conic section passing through the five positions of point C must be determined.[4]

From analytical geometry we recall that the general equation of a conic section is

$$Ax^2 + Bxy + Cy^2 + Dx + Ey + F = 0$$

The coefficient A may be considered to have a magnitude of unity, since the entire equation may be divided by the coefficient of x^2 to establish this value. Appropriate values of the remaining coefficients B, C, D, E, and F will establish the equation of a conic curve passing through points C_1 through C_5. These coefficient values are determined by solving the five equations formed by substituting the coordinates of each point into the general equation above.

[4]For complete synthesis of the mechanism, see M. L. James, G. M. Smith, and J. C. Wolford, *Applied Numerical Methods for Digital Computation*, 1st ed. (New York: International Textbook Company, 1967), pp. 195–198.

Performing these substitutions, we obtain the following five equations in five unknowns:

$$8.77B + 2.40C + 5.66D + 1.55E + 1.0F = -32.04$$
$$4.93B + 1.21C + 4.48D + 1.10E + 1.0F = -20.07$$
$$3.53B + 1.46C + 2.92D + 1.21E + 1.0F = -8.53 \qquad (3\text{-}23)$$
$$5.05B + 4.04C + 2.51D + 2.01E + 1.0F = -6.30$$
$$3.54B + 1.04C + 3.47D + 1.02E + 1.0F = -12.04$$

Using the computer program developed in Ex. 3-1 with the coefficient values and the constants of Eq. 3-23 as input data, the values of the unknowns B through F are given, respectively, by the following computer printout:

```
X(1) THROUGH X(N)
-.14649792E 01
0.14580536E 01
-.60047874E 01
-.22087317E 01
0.14719152E 02
```

3-3 GAUSS-JORDAN ELIMINATION METHOD

This method, which is a variation of the Gaussian elimination method, is suitable for solving as many as 15 to 20 simultaneous equations, with 7 to 10 significant digits used in the arithmetic operations of the computer. This procedure varies from the Gaussian method in that when an unknown is eliminated, it is eliminated from *all* the other equations, that is, from those preceding the pivot equation as well as those following it. For example, in the preceding section describing Gauss's method, Eq. 3-7b was used as the pivot equation in eliminating x_2 from all the equations below it in obtaining Eq. 3-8. In the Gauss-Jordan method, the pivot equation would be used to eliminate x_2 from Eq. 3-7a as well. In the subsequent step, in which Eq. 3-8c was used as the pivot equation, x_3 would be eliminated from Eqs. 3-8a and 3-8b as well as from the equations below the pivot equation. This eliminates the necessity of using the back-substitution process employed in Gauss's method.

To illustrate the Gauss-Jordan elimination method, let us solve the following set of equations:

$$2x_1 - 2x_2 + 5x_3 = 13 \qquad (a)$$
$$2x_1 + 3x_2 + 4x_3 = 20 \qquad (b) \qquad (3\text{-}24)$$
$$3x_1 - x_2 + 3x_3 = 10 \qquad (c)$$

We begin by dividing the first equation of the set, Eq. 3-24a, by the coefficient of the *first* unknown in that equation, which gives us Eq. 3-25a below. We then multiply Eq. 3-25a, respectively, by the coefficient of the *first* unknown in each of the remaining equations (Eqs. 3-24b and c) to get

$$x_1 - x_2 + \tfrac{5}{2}x_3 = \tfrac{13}{2} \quad \text{(a)}$$

$$2x_1 - 2x_2 + 5x_3 = 13 \quad \text{(b)} \qquad \qquad (3\text{-}25)$$

$$3x_1 - 3x_2 + \tfrac{15}{2}x_3 = \tfrac{39}{2} \quad \text{(c)}$$

Now we subtract Eq. 3-25b from Eq. 3-24b and Eq. 3-25c from Eq. 3-24c, and we let Eq. 3-25a become Eq. 3-26c, obtaining

$$5x_2 - x_3 = 7 \quad \text{(a)}$$

$$2x_2 - \tfrac{9}{2}x_3 = -\tfrac{19}{2} \quad \text{(b)} \qquad \qquad (3\text{-}26)$$

$$x_1 - x_2 + \tfrac{5}{2}x_3 = \tfrac{13}{2} \quad \text{(c)}$$

Next, we divide Eq. 3-26a by the coefficient of the *first* unknown in that equation (the coefficient of x_2) to obtain Eq. 3-27a. We then multiply Eq. 3-27a, respectively, by the coefficient of the x_2 term in each of Eqs. 3-26b and c. This yields

$$x_2 - \tfrac{1}{5}x_3 = \tfrac{7}{5} \quad \text{(a)}$$

$$2x_2 - \tfrac{2}{5}x_3 = \tfrac{14}{5} \quad \text{(b)} \qquad \qquad (3\text{-}27)$$

$$-x_2 + \tfrac{1}{5}x_3 = -\tfrac{7}{5} \quad \text{(c)}$$

We next subtract Eq. 3-27b from Eq. 3-26b and Eq. 3-27c from Eq. 3-26c, and we let Eq. 3-27a become Eq. 3-28c, obtaining

$$-\tfrac{41}{10}x_3 = -\tfrac{123}{10} \quad \text{(a)}$$

$$x_1 + \tfrac{23}{10}x_3 = \tfrac{79}{10} \quad \text{(b)} \qquad \qquad (3\text{-}28)$$

$$x_2 - \tfrac{1}{5}x_3 = \tfrac{7}{5} \quad \text{(c)}$$

Repeating the procedure yields

$$x_3 = 3 \quad \text{(a)}$$

$$\tfrac{23}{10}x_3 = \tfrac{69}{10} \quad \text{(b)} \qquad \qquad (3\text{-}29)$$

$$-\tfrac{1}{5}x_3 = -\tfrac{3}{5} \quad \text{(c)}$$

and finally

$$x_1 = 1 \quad \text{(a)}$$

$$x_2 = 2 \quad \text{(b)} \tag{3-30}$$

$$x_3 = 3 \quad \text{(c)}$$

which constitutes the desired solution of the simultaneous equations.

Having solved Eq. 3-24 by the procedure shown, let us see how we can obtain the same result by working with just the coefficients and constants of these equations. Associated with Eq. 3-24 is a matrix $\mathbf{A}$, which is the *augmented* matrix of the set of equations. This matrix is

$$\mathbf{A} = \begin{bmatrix} 2 & -2 & 5 & 13 \\ 2 & 3 & 4 & 20 \\ 3 & -1 & 3 & 10 \end{bmatrix}$$

We next associate an augmented matrix $\mathbf{B}$ with Eq. 3-26, in which the first column of coefficients (0, 0, and 1) is omitted, and we write

$$\mathbf{B} = \begin{bmatrix} 5 & -1 & 7 \\ 2 & -\frac{9}{2} & -\frac{19}{2} \\ -1 & \frac{5}{2} & \frac{13}{2} \end{bmatrix}$$

Having established matrix $\mathbf{B}$ from Eq. 3-26, we note, from the way in which Eq. 3-26 was obtained from Eq. 3-24 in the first procedure, that we can write the elements of $\mathbf{B}$ directly from the elements of $\mathbf{A}$ by using the following formulas:

$$b_{i-1,j-1} = a_{ij} - \frac{a_{1j} a_{i1}}{a_{11}} \quad \begin{cases} 1 < i \le n \\ 1 < j \le m \\ a_{11} \ne 0 \end{cases} \tag{3-31}$$

$$b_{n,j-1} = \frac{a_{1j}}{a_{11}} \quad \begin{cases} 1 < j \le m \\ a_{11} \ne 0 \end{cases} \tag{3-32}$$

Equation 3-31 is used to find all elements of the new matrix $\mathbf{B}$ except those making up the last row of that matrix. For determining the elements of the last row of the new matrix, Eq. 3-32 is used. In these equations,

i = row number of old matrix **A**

j = column number of old matrix **A**

n = maximum row number

m = maximum column number

a = an element of old matrix **A**

b = an element of new matrix **B**

Now, if we write the augmented matrix of Eq. 3-28, this time omitting the first two columns (elements 0, 1, 0 and 0, 0, 1), we get

$$\mathbf{C} = \begin{bmatrix} -\frac{41}{10} & -\frac{123}{10} \\ \frac{23}{10} & \frac{79}{10} \\ -\frac{1}{5} & \frac{7}{5} \end{bmatrix}$$

Again, we note that the elements of **C** can be obtained directly from the elements of **B** by utilizing Eqs. 3-31 and 3-32, where **C** is now the *new* matrix and **B** is the *old* matrix.

The augmented matrix of Eq. 3-30, with the first three columns (1, 0, 0; 0, 1, 0; and 0, 0, 1) omitted, is simply the matrix whose elements are the solution of the set of simultaneous equations with which we started,

$$\mathbf{D} = \begin{Bmatrix} 1 \\ 2 \\ 3 \end{Bmatrix}$$

Just as with the previous matrices, matrix **D** can be obtained from matrix **C** by application of Eqs. 3-31 and 3-32. The elements shown in **D** are associated, respectively, with x_1, x_2, and x_3 by the above procedure.

Thus, it can be seen that the roots of a set of n simultaneous equations can be obtained by successive applications of Eqs. 3-31 and 3-32 to get n new matrices, the last of which will be a *column* matrix whose elements are the roots of the set of simultaneous equations.

In a computer program employing the method just described, only the FORTRAN names A and B would be used for pairs of successive matrices, rather than calling them A, B, C, D, and so forth, as was done in describing the method. After obtaining the **B** matrix from the **A** matrix, the elements of **B** would be assigned to the name A, and a new matrix with the name B obtained. This will be illustrated in the program shown in Ex. 3-3 which follows later in this section.

It is possible that the pivot element a_{11} of one or more of the matrices obtained during the elimination process could have a zero value, in which case divisions by a_{11} in Eqs. 3-31 and 3-32 would be invalid. If this occurs, the first row can be interchanged with one of the first $m - 1$ rows of the matrix which has a first element not equal to zero, where m is the number of columns in the current matrix. The use of a row beyond row $m - 1$ as a pivot row in the elimination process would reintroduce one of the previously eliminated unknowns into the equations. The elimination process then continues as before, until a solution is reached.

In instances in which a_{11} is not zero but is very small in comparison with the general magnitude of the other elements of the matrix, its use could cause a decrease in solution accuracy, as discussed in Gauss's elimination method. For improved accuracy the applicable row having the largest potential pivot element (the row among the first $m - 1$ rows having the largest pivot element) should be placed in the first or pivot position if it is not already there. This would be accomplished by checking the absolute value of a_{11} against the absolute values of a_{21}, a_{31}, . . . , $a_{m-1,1}$ and making the appropriate row interchange if one of these latter values were larger than $|a_{11}|$. This procedure, called *partial pivoting*, should always be incorporated in a computer program for solving fairly large numbers of simultaneous equations.

It should be noted that, if it were desired to solve a second set of simultaneous equations which differed from a first set only in the constant terms which appeared, both sets could be solved at the same time by representing each set of constants as a separate column in augmenting the coefficient matrix. Actually, two or more sets of simultaneous equations, differing only in their constant terms, can be solved in a single elimination procedure by placing the constants of each set in a separate column to the right of the coefficient columns in the augmented matrix, and applying Eqs. 3-31 and 3-32 until a reduced matrix is obtained which has the same number of columns as the number of *sets* of simultaneous equations being solved. Such a solution will be illustrated in Sec. 3-6.

An Improved Gauss-Jordan Algorithm

In the computer program of Ex. 3-3 at the end of this section, storage space is reserved for both the **A** and **B** arrays. To provide memory space for both matrices would generally not be a problem. However, if a fairly large number of equations were being solved on a smaller computer, or if the program were to be frequently used on a computer where charges were based in part on the amount of memory used, it would be desirable to store the new matrix generated by Eqs. 3-31 and 3-32 in the same location as the original matrix. To see how these equations must be modified to accomplish this space-saving feature, let us consider the system of equations given earlier by Eqs. 3-9 and 3-12, which are repeated here for convenience.

$$2x_1 + 8x_2 + 2x_3 = 14$$

$$x_1 + 6x_2 - x_3 = 13 \tag{3-33}$$

$$2x_1 - x_2 + 2x_3 = 5$$

and augmented matrix

$$\mathbf{A} = \begin{bmatrix} 2 & 8 & 2 & 14 \\ 1 & 6 & -1 & 13 \\ 2 & -1 & 2 & 5 \end{bmatrix} \tag{3-34}$$

The first step in the Gauss-Jordan elimination method is to divide the pivot equation (the first of Eq. 3-33) through by the coefficient of x_1 in that equation. The pivot row in matrix $\mathbf{A}$ is identified by k, and $k = 1$ in the first reduction. The pivot equation is then multiplied by the coefficients of x_1 in the second and third equations, and the resulting pivot equations are subtracted, respectively, from the second and third equations to yield an equivalent set in which x_1 has been eliminated from the second and third equations. In the Gauss-Jordan procedure previously given, the pivot equation (or row) divided by the pivot element was brought to the bottom position so that the new pivot equation (or row) was always in the top position. However, if we wish to store the new reduced matrix in the same location as the old matrix, it is not convenient to do this. The new matrix of the first reduction, with the pivot equation of this reduction divided through by the pivot element a_{kk}, is

$$\mathbf{A'} = \begin{bmatrix} 1 & 4 & 1 & 7 \\ 0 & 2 & -2 & 6 \\ 0 & -9 & 0 & -9 \end{bmatrix} \tag{3-35}$$

We observe from the manner in which the new equivalent set is determined that the elements of $\mathbf{A'}$ may be obtained from the elements of $\mathbf{A}$ by use of the equations

$$a'_{kj} = \frac{a_{kj}}{a_{kk}} \tag{a}$$

$$a'_{ij} = a_{ij} - a_{ik}a'_{kj} \tag{b}$$

$$\left. \begin{array}{c} \end{array} \right\} \quad (3\text{-}36)$$

where Eq. 3-36a is applied first, and

$$1 \le i \le 3 \quad (\text{except that } i \ne k)$$

$$1 \le j \le 4$$

$$\left. \begin{array}{c} \end{array} \right\} \quad k = 1$$

If the elements of $\mathbf{A}'$ were to be stored in locations different from the elements of $\mathbf{A}$, the use of Eq. 3-36 would present no problem. However, with the elements of $\mathbf{A}'$ actually replacing the elements of $\mathbf{A}$ in memory, the following difficulties are noted:

1. When Eq. 3-36a is applied with $j = k$ (1 in this case), the pivot element a_{kk} is replaced with a new value (unity). This new pivot value would be used in subsequent calculations of a'_{kj} (with $j = 2$, 3, and 4 in this case), whereas the old one should be used.
2. In applying Eq. 3-36b, the element a_{ik} ($k = 1$, $i = 2$) is used in the calculation of all of the elements a'_{ij} of row 2, and a_{ik} ($k = 1$, $i = 3$) is used in calculating all a'_{ij} of row 3. These elements a_{ik} would be replaced by their new values (zero) whenever $j = k$ (1 in this case). The use of the zero values instead of the old values of 1 and 2 (a_{21} and a_{31}, respectively) would give incorrect values for subsequent a'_{ij} values calculated in this step.

These difficulties may be overcome by observing that the elements of column 1 of the $\mathbf{A}'$ matrix, Eq. 3-35, are never used in any later steps of the reduction process. Therefore, they can be left just as they were in the $\mathbf{A}$ matrix (which they need to be for the present step), without affecting calculations in subsequent steps. This may be accomplished by letting the range of j be given by

$$2 \le j \le 4$$

in Eq. 3-36, so that the $\mathbf{A}'$ matrix as actually stored is

$$\mathbf{A}' = \begin{bmatrix} (2) & 4 & 1 & 7 \\ (1) & 2 & -2 & 6 \\ (2) & -9 & 0 & -9 \end{bmatrix} \tag{3-37}$$

The elements of the first column are shown in parentheses since they would normally be 1, 0, 0 at the end of the first reduction step. It should be recalled that in the previous Gauss-Jordan procedure, this column was not carried in the $\mathbf{B}$ matrix.

The $\mathbf{A}'$ matrix of Eq. 3-37 will now be considered an $\mathbf{A}$ matrix, and a new $\mathbf{A}'$ matrix determined by using the second row as the pivot row ($k = 2$). Thus,

$$\mathbf{A} = \begin{bmatrix} (2) & 4 & \overset{\text{pivot element}}{1} & 7 \\ (1) & 2 & -2 & 6 \\ (2) & -9 & 0 & -9 \end{bmatrix} \tag{3-38}$$

The pivot equation is now used to eliminate x_2 from the first and third equations. The pivot equation is first divided through by the pivot element 2. It is then multiplied by the coefficients of x_2 in the first and third equations, and the resulting equations subtracted, respectively, from the first and third equations of the set to give a new equivalent set in which x_2 has been eliminated from the first and third equations. With the pivot equation of the second reduction divided through by the pivot element 2, this equivalent set is

$$1x_1 + 0x_2 + 5x_3 = -5$$

$$0x_1 + 1x_2 - 1x_3 = 3 \tag{3-39}$$

$$0x_1 + 0x_2 - 9x_3 = 18$$

with augmented matrix

$$\mathbf{A'} = \begin{bmatrix} (2) & 0 & 5 & -5 \\ (1) & 1 & -1 & 3 \\ (2) & 0 & -9 & 18 \end{bmatrix} \tag{3-40}$$

Again we note that the $\mathbf{A'}$ matrix of Eq. 3-40 could be obtained from the $\mathbf{A}$ matrix of Eq. 3-38 by the use of Eq. 3-36 with

$$k = 2$$

$$1 \le i \le 3 \qquad \text{(except that } i \ne k)$$

$$2 \le j \le 4$$

The same difficulties previously described again occur when the elements of the second column of $\mathbf{A}$, Eq. 3-38, are replaced by the new elements shown in column 2 of the matrix $\mathbf{A'}$, Eq. 3-40, before the new elements of columns 3 and 4 are calculated. As before, we simply change the range of j so that it becomes

$$3 \le j \le 4$$

and the elements of column 2 are left unchanged. The $\mathbf{A'}$ matrix as it is actually stored, now called the $\mathbf{A}$ matrix in preparation for the final step, is

pivot element

$$\mathbf{A} = \begin{bmatrix} (2) & (4) & 5 & -5 \\ (1) & (2) & -1 & 3 \\ (2) & (-9) & -9 & 18 \end{bmatrix} \tag{3-41}$$

The final equivalent set is determined using the third equation as the pivot equation. It is divided through by the pivot element -9 in Eq. 3-41, and then multiplied by the coefficients of x_3 in the first and second equations. The resulting pivot equations are subtracted, respectively, from the first and second equations, and the pivot equation divided by the pivot element to give the final equivalent set

$$1x_1 + 0x_2 + 0x_3 = 5$$
$$0x_1 + 1x_2 + 0x_3 = 1 \tag{3-42}$$
$$0x_1 + 0x_2 + 1x_3 = -2$$

with augmented matrix

$$\mathbf{A'} = \begin{bmatrix} (2) & (4) & 0 & 5 \\ (1) & (2) & 0 & 1 \\ (2) & (-9) & 1 & -2 \end{bmatrix} \tag{3-43}$$

This matrix $\mathbf{A'}$ can be obtained from the $\mathbf{A}$ matrix of Eq. 3-41 by the application of Eq. 3-36 with

$$k = 3$$
$$1 \le i \le 3 \quad \text{(except that } i = k)$$
$$3 \le j \le 4$$

As before, however, we change the range of j to

$$4 \le j \le 4 \quad \text{(or } j = 4)$$

and do not actually calculate the new elements for the third column of $\mathbf{A'}$, Eq. 3-43. The final $\mathbf{A'}$ matrix as actually stored is

$$\mathbf{A'} = \begin{bmatrix} (2) & (4) & (5) & 5 \\ (1) & (2) & (-1) & 1 \\ (2) & (-9) & (-9) & -2 \end{bmatrix} \tag{3-44}$$

The values of the unknowns, x_1, x_2, and x_3 are 5, 1, and -2, respectively (the elements of the fourth column of the final $\mathbf{A'}$ matrix).

Equation 3-36 can be made general for all steps of the reduction process as follows:

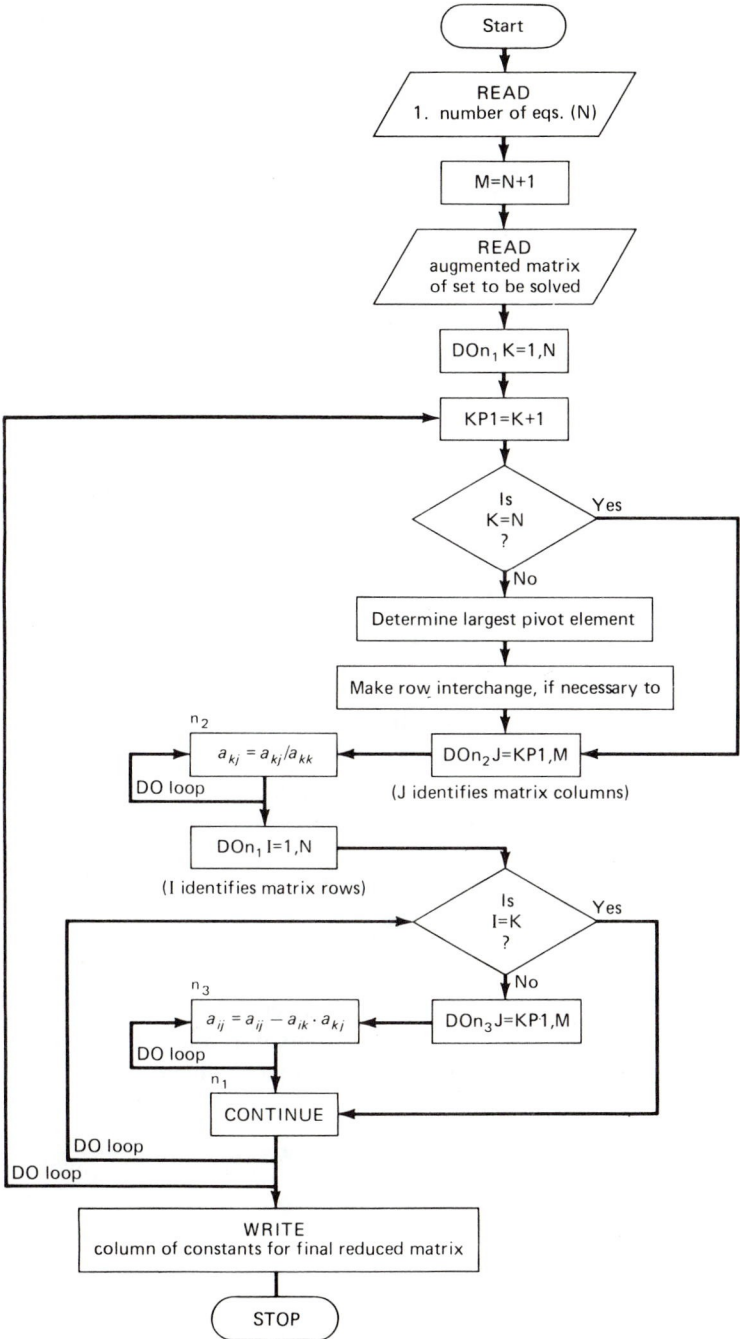

Figure 3-4 Flow chart for improved Gauss-Jordan algorithm

$$
\left. \begin{array}{l}
a'_{kj} = \dfrac{a_{kj}}{a_{kk}} \qquad\qquad\qquad\qquad\qquad\qquad\quad \text{(a)} \\[3ex]
a'_{ij} = a_{ij} - a_{ik}a'_{kj} \qquad\qquad\qquad\qquad\quad \text{(b)} \\[3ex]
\qquad\qquad\qquad\qquad k = 1, 2, 3, \ldots, n \\[2ex]
\quad 1 \le i \le n \qquad\qquad (\text{except that } i \ne k) \\[2ex]
k + 1 \le j \le n + 1
\end{array} \right\} \quad \text{(3-45)}
$$

where Eq. 3-45a is applied first with $k = 1$, say, and j cycling from $k + 1$ to $n + 1$. Then Eq. 3-45b is applied with k still equal to the same value and with i and j both cycling. This procedure is repeated for each k value. Since the a' elements actually replace the a elements in memory, the name A(I, J) in a computer program would be used for both a_{ij} and a'_{ij}, and the name A(K, J) would be used for both a_{kj} and a'_{kj}.

The Gauss-Jordan algorithm just described is flow-charted in Fig. 3-4. It includes partial pivoting for improved accuracy and to insure that a pivot element will not have a value of zero. It is left as a problem for the student to write a computer program utilizing this space-saving Gauss-Jordan algorithm (see Prob. 3-18 at the end of this chapter).

EXAMPLE 3-3

Let us write a FORTRAN program for solving Eq. 3-23 by the Gauss-Jordan elimination method using the procedure which employs Eqs. 3-31 and 3-32. Although the set we are solving contains only 5 simultaneous equations, we will write a program capable of handling up to 15 simultaneous equations. Partial pivoting will be used in the program.

The variable names used in the FORTRAN program represent the following quantities:

FORTRAN Name	Quantity
A(I,J)	Elements of augmented and reduced matrices
B(I,J)	Temporary name for elements of reduced matrices
N	Number of equations in set being solved
M	Number of columns in augmented and reduced matrices
K	Number of rows in matrix which are possible pivot rows (equal to $M - 1$)
JJ	A variable which takes on the value of the row having the largest pivot element
BIG	Takes on values of the elements in column 1 which are possible pivot elements, eventually taking on the value of the pivot element used
TEMP	Temporary name used for the elements of the row selected to become the pivot row before interchange is made

The FORTRAN program is as follows:

```
C SOLUTION OF SIMULTANEOUS EQUATIONS BY GAUSS-JORDAN METHOD
C THIS PROGRAM USES PARTIAL PIVOTING
      DIMENSION A(15,16),B(15,15)
      WRITE(6,1)
    1 FORMAT('1','SOLUTION OF SIMULTANEOUS EQUATIONS')
      WRITE(6,2)
    2 FORMAT(' ','BY GAUSS-JORDAN ELIMINATION METHOD'/)
      WRITE(6,3)
    3 FORMAT(' ',7X,'X(1) THROUGH X(N)'/)
C READ NUMBER OF EQUATIONS TO BE SOLVED
      READ(5,4) N
    4 FORMAT(I2)
      M=N+1
C READ AUGMENTED MATRIX OF SET TO BE SOLVED
      READ(5,5) ((A(I,J),J=1,M),I=1,N)
    5 FORMAT(8F10.0)
C SEARCH FOR LARGEST PIVOT ELEMENT
    6 K=M-1
      IF(K.EQ.1) GO TO 11
      JJ=1
      BIG=ABS(A(1,1))
      DO 8 I=2,K
      AB=ABS(A(I,1))
      IF(BIG-AB) 7,8,8
    7 BIG=AB
      JJ=I
    8 CONTINUE
C MAKE DECISION ON ROW INTERCHANGE
      IF(JJ-1) 9,11,9
C MAKE ROW INTERCHANGE
    9 DO 10 J=1,M
      TEMP=A(JJ,J)
      A(JJ,J)=A(1,J)
   10 A(1,J)=TEMP
C CALCULATE THE ELEMENTS OF THE B MATRIX
   11 DO 12 J=2,M
      DO 12 I=2,N
   12 B(I-1,J-1)=A(I,J)-A(1,J)*A(I,1)/A(1,1)
      DO 13 J=2,M
   13 B(N,J-1)=A(1,J)/A(1,1)
C REDUCE COLUMN COUNTER BY ONE
      M=M-1
C ASSIGN THE B MATRIX TO THE NAME A
      DO 14 J=1,M
      DO 14 I=1,N
   14 A(I,J)=B(I,J)
C CHECK TO SEE IF THE A MATRIX CONSISTS OF JUST ONE COLUMN
      IF(M-1) 6,15,6
C PRINT THE SINGLE COLUMN OF THE A MATRIX
   15 WRITE(6,16) (A(I,1),I=1,N)
   16 FORMAT(' ',10X,E14.7)
      STOP
      END
```

The output results of the program are shown below:

```
SOLUTION OF SIMULTANEOUS EQUATIONS
BY GAUSS-JORDAN ELIMINATION METHOD
        X(1) THROUGH X(N)
          -0.1464931E 01
           0.1458158E 01
          -0.6004849E 01
          -0.2209171E 01
           0.1471957E 02
```

3-4 CHOLESKY'S METHOD

Cholesky's method, also known as Crout's method, the method of matrix decomposition, and the method of matrix factorization, is more economical of computer time than other elimination methods. As a result it has been used extensively in some of the larger structural analysis programs.[5]

For illustrative purposes, let us discuss the solution of three simultaneous equations in three unknowns. The set is represented by the matrix equation[6]

$$
\begin{bmatrix} a_{11} & a_{12} & a_{13} \\ a_{21} & a_{22} & a_{23} \\ a_{31} & a_{32} & a_{33} \end{bmatrix} \begin{Bmatrix} x_1 \\ x_2 \\ x_3 \end{Bmatrix}^* = \begin{Bmatrix} c_1 \\ c_2 \\ c_3 \end{Bmatrix}^* \tag{3-46}
$$

(*The braces shown will be used henceforth in the text to signify a column matrix.)

If we let **A** represent the coefficient matrix, $\{X\}$ the column matrix of the unknowns, and $\{C\}$ the column matrix of the constants, we can replace Eq. 3-46 by

$$
\mathbf{A}\{X\} - \{C\} = 0 \tag{3-47}
$$

If we could reduce the system of equations to an equivalent system of the form

$$
\begin{bmatrix} 1 & u_{12} & u_{13} \\ 0 & 1 & u_{23} \\ 0 & 0 & 1 \end{bmatrix} \begin{Bmatrix} x_1 \\ x_2 \\ x_3 \end{Bmatrix} = \begin{Bmatrix} d_1 \\ d_2 \\ d_3 \end{Bmatrix} \tag{3-48}
$$

---

[5]William Weaver, Jr., *Computer Programs for Structural Analysis* (Princeton, N.J.: D. Van Nostrand Co., Inc., 1967), pp. 56–64.

[6]For a review of matrix multiplication, see App. B.

they could readily be solved by back substitution as discussed under Gaussian elimination. The upper unit triangular matrix in Eq. 3-48 will be represented by **U**. Then Eq. 3-48 can be written as

$$\mathbf{U}\{X\} - \{D\} = 0 \tag{3-49}$$

Suppose there exists a lower triangular matrix

$$\begin{bmatrix} l_{11} & 0 & 0 \\ l_{21} & l_{22} & 0 \\ l_{31} & l_{32} & l_{33} \end{bmatrix}$$

which we represent by **L** and which has the following property: When we premultiply the left side of Eq. 3-49 by **L**, it will give us the left side of Eq. 3-47. The existence of such a matrix **L** has not been proved at this point, but we will assume for the moment that it does exist. In accordance with the above property of **L**, we have

$$\mathbf{L}(\mathbf{U}\{X\} - \{D\}) = \mathbf{A}\{X\} - \{C\} \tag{3-50}$$

Therefore,

$$\mathbf{LU} = \mathbf{A} \tag{3-51}$$

and

$$\mathbf{L}\{D\} = \{C\} \tag{3-52}$$

Equations 3-51 and 3-52 may be combined into the single matrix equation

$$\begin{bmatrix} l_{11} & 0 & 0 \\ l_{21} & l_{22} & 0 \\ l_{31} & l_{32} & l_{33} \end{bmatrix} \begin{bmatrix} 1 & u_{12} & u_{13} & d_1 \\ 0 & 1 & u_{23} & d_2 \\ 0 & 0 & 1 & d_3 \end{bmatrix} = \begin{bmatrix} a_{11} & a_{12} & a_{13} & c_1 \\ a_{21} & a_{22} & a_{23} & c_2 \\ a_{31} & a_{32} & a_{33} & c_3 \end{bmatrix} \tag{3-53}$$

For the sake of convenience, let the c's be represented by a_{i4} and the d's by u_{i4} to obtain Eq. 3-53 as

$$\begin{bmatrix} l_{11} & 0 & 0 \\ l_{21} & l_{22} & 0 \\ l_{31} & l_{32} & l_{33} \end{bmatrix} \begin{bmatrix} 1 & u_{12} & u_{13} & u_{14} \\ 0 & 1 & u_{23} & u_{24} \\ 0 & 0 & 1 & u_{34} \end{bmatrix} = \begin{bmatrix} a_{11} & a_{12} & a_{13} & a_{14} \\ a_{21} & a_{22} & a_{23} & a_{24} \\ a_{31} & a_{32} & a_{33} & a_{34} \end{bmatrix} \tag{3-54}$$

The l_{ij} and u_{ij} elements may be determined from Eq. 3-54. The augmented $\mathbf{U}$ matrix of Eq. 3-54 is the augmented matrix of the equivalent triangular set given by Eq. 3-48. Therefore, with the u_{ij} determined, the unknown x_i values may be determined by back substitution.

From the rules of matrix multiplication, we note that the first column of matrix $\mathbf{L}$ is identical with the first column of the augmented $\mathbf{A}$ matrix. That is,

$$l_{i1} = a_{i1} \tag{3-55}$$

We also note that

$$l_{11}u_{12} = a_{12}$$
$$l_{11}u_{13} = a_{13}$$
$$l_{11}u_{14} = a_{14}$$

Therefore, we can obtain the first row of the $\mathbf{U}$ matrix as the first row of $\mathbf{A}$ divided by l_{11} (or a_{11}). That is,

$$u_{1j} = \frac{a_{1j}}{l_{11}} \tag{3-56}$$

We have determined the first column of $\mathbf{L}$ and the first row of $\mathbf{U}$. We can now proceed to determine the second column of $\mathbf{L}$, followed by the second row of $\mathbf{U}$.

From matrix multiplication, we have

$$l_{21}u_{12} + l_{22} \cdot 1 = a_{22}$$
$$l_{31}u_{12} + l_{32} \cdot 1 = a_{32}$$

from which we obtain

$$l_{22} = a_{22} - l_{21}u_{12} \tag{3-57}$$
$$l_{32} = a_{32} - l_{31}u_{12}$$

Having the second column of $\mathbf{L}$, we get the second row of $\mathbf{U}$ from

$$l_{21}u_{13} + l_{22}u_{23} = a_{23}$$
$$l_{21}u_{14} + l_{22}u_{24} = a_{24}$$

or

$$u_{23} = \frac{a_{23} - l_{21}u_{13}}{l_{22}}$$

$$u_{24} = \frac{a_{24} - l_{21}u_{14}}{l_{22}} \tag{3-58}$$

Next we get the third column of **L** followed by the third row of **U**. The third column of **L** is obtained from

$$l_{31}u_{13} + l_{32}u_{23} + l_{33} = a_{33}$$

or

$$l_{33} = a_{33} - [l_{31}u_{13} + l_{32}u_{23}] \tag{3-59}$$

The element u_{34}, the only element in the third row of **U** except the 1, is obtained from

$$l_{31}u_{14} + l_{32}u_{24} + l_{33}u_{34} = a_{34}$$

or

$$u_{34} = \frac{a_{34} - [l_{31}u_{14} + l_{32}u_{24}]}{l_{33}} \tag{3-60}$$

The general equations for the elements of the **L** and augmented **U** matrices, for n equations in n unknowns, are

$$l_{i1} = a_{i1} \qquad \text{for} \begin{cases} i = 1, 2, \ldots, n \\ j = 1 \end{cases}$$

$$u_{1j} = \frac{a_{1j}}{a_{11}} \qquad \text{for} \begin{cases} j = 2, 3, \ldots, n+1 \\ i = 1 \end{cases}$$

$$l_{ij} = a_{ij} - \sum_{k=1}^{j-1} l_{ik}u_{kj} \qquad \text{for} \begin{cases} j = 2, 3, \ldots, n \\ i = j, j+1, \ldots, n \end{cases} \tag{3-61}$$
$$\text{(for each value of } j)$$

$$u_{ij} = \frac{a_{ij} - \sum_{k=1}^{i-1} l_{ik}u_{kj}}{l_{ii}} \qquad \text{for} \begin{cases} i = 2, 3, \ldots, n \\ j = i+1, i+2, \ldots, n+1 \end{cases}$$
$$\text{(for each value of } i)$$

After the first and second equations of the above set are applied over their ranges of i and j, respectively, the third equation is applied with $j = 2$ and i ranging from j to n. Then the fourth equation is applied with $i = 2$ and j ranging from $i + 1$ to $n + 1$. Then the third equation is applied with $j = 3$ and i ranging from j to n, the fourth with $i = 3$ and j ranging from $i + 1$ to $n + 1$, and so on.

The back-substitution formulas are

$$x_n = u_{n,n+1} \qquad\qquad\qquad\qquad\qquad\qquad (3\text{-}62)$$

$$x_i = u_{i,n+1} - \sum_{j=i+1}^{n} u_{ij}x_j \qquad \text{for } i = n - 1, n - 2, \dots, 1$$

If the matrix decomposition

$$\mathbf{LU} = \mathbf{A} \qquad\qquad\qquad\qquad\qquad\qquad (3\text{-}63)$$

exists, then the divisions in Eq. 3-61 will always be defined since the l_{ii} elements will be nonzero. This can be seen by noting that since the above decomposition equation holds, the determinant of $\mathbf{L}$ times the determinant of $\mathbf{U}$ equals the determinant of $\mathbf{A}$. That is,[7]

$$|\mathbf{L}|\,|\mathbf{U}| = |\mathbf{A}|$$

We are assuming independent equations, so the determinant of $\mathbf{A}$ is nonzero. Therefore, the determinant of $\mathbf{L}$ must be nonzero. Since the determinant of a triangular matrix is equal to the product of the main diagonal elements, it follows that the l_{ii} elements must all be nonzero. Unfortunately, however, the decomposition

$$\mathbf{LU} = \mathbf{A}$$

may not always be possible, and in applying the Cholesky method to the solution of a set of simultaneous equations, 1 or more of the l_{ii} elements can turn out to be equal to zero. To avoid any possibility of a division by zero, and at the same time improve the accuracy of the solution, we shall incorporate a row interchange procedure which will be described later in the Cholesky computer program.

For $n > 2$, Cholesky's method requires fewer arithmetic operations than either the Gaussian or Gauss-Jordan methods, making it the fastest of the basic elimination methods. It may also be made economical of storage in the computer by overlaying the $\mathbf{U}$ and $\mathbf{L}$ matrices on the $\mathbf{A}$ matrix (in the same storage locations). This may be done since there is no need to store the zeros and ones

[7]Frank Ayres, Jr., *Matrices* (New York: Schaum Publishing Co., 1962), p. 33.

of the **U** and **L** matrices. The original a_{ij} values of the augmented **A** matrix are first stored in the computer. Then, calling both the u_{ij} and l_{ij} elements simply a_{ij}, the old a_{ij} values are replaced with new a_{ij} values. Then the first of Eq. 3-61 is automatically satisfied with no computer execution. The other equations become

$$a_{1j} = \frac{a_{1j}}{a_{11}} \qquad \text{for } j = 2, 3, \ldots, n + 1$$

$$a_{ij} = a_{ij} - \sum_{k=1}^{j-1} a_{ik}a_{kj} \qquad \text{for } \begin{cases} j = 2, 3, \ldots, n \\ i = j, j + 1, \ldots, n \end{cases}$$

$$\text{(for each } j \text{ value)}$$

$$a_{ij} = \frac{a_{ij} - \sum_{k=1}^{i-1} a_{ik}a_{kj}}{a_{ii}} \qquad \text{for } \begin{cases} i = 2, 3, \ldots, n \\ j = i + 1, i + 2, \ldots, n + 1 \end{cases}$$

$$\text{(for each } i \text{ value)}$$

$$(3\text{-}64)$$

Following the application of the first equation of Eq. 3-64, the second and third equations are applied in the manner previously described for the *third* and *fourth* equations of Eq. 3-61. Carnahan, Luther, and Wilkes[8] have incorporated a row interchange procedure in performing matrix decomposition that they attribute to J. H. Wilkenson. We shall apply this procedure to avoid any possibility of division by zero and at the same time to improve the accuracy of the solution. The procedure is as follows.

The first column of the original matrix **A** will be searched for the largest element (in absolute value), and the row containing this largest element (if it is other than the first) will be interchanged with the first row. Then, after the second equation of Eq. 3-64 has been applied with $j = 2$, the *new* a_{ij}'s just determined for column 2 are searched for the largest element. The entire row in which the largest element is found is then interchanged with the second row.

The third equation of Eq. 3-64 is next applied with $i = 2$, with no chance of the a_{ii} term in the denominator being zero.

The second equation of Eq. 3-64 is then again applied with $j = 3$. The *new* a_{ij}'s calculated for the third column are searched for the largest element, and if an a_{ij} larger than a_{33} is found, the entire row in which that a_{ij} was found is interchanged with the third row. The third equation of Eq. 3-64 is then applied with no chance of division by zero. This procedure continues with alternate applications of the second and third equations of Eq. 3-64 until $j = n$ in the second equation and $i = n$ in the third.

[8]Bruce Carnahan, H. A. Luther, James O. Wilkes, *Applied Numerical Methods*, Vol. I, Preliminary Ed., (New York: John Wiley and Sons, 1964), p. 372.

With row interchange, the decomposition of the original **A** matrix is not accomplished. Instead, the decomposition of a matrix with rows interchanged results. This is equivalent to rearranging the simultaneous equations, which does not affect their solution.

If the decomposition of a specific matrix is desired, the row interchange procedure must be omitted. If division by zero of such a matrix results, then the decomposition of that matrix is not possible.

If the **A** matrix is symmetrical, as it often is in structural-analysis problems, the number of calculations of Cholesky's method may be further reduced.[9] The Cholesky subroutine subprogram is as follows:

```
      SUBROUTINE CHLSKY(A,N,M,X)
      DIMENSION A(N,M),X(N)
C INTERCHANGE ROWS OF THE A MATRIX SO THAT ELEMENT A(1,1) IS
C THE DOMINANT ELEMENT IN THE FIRST COLUMN.
C
C SEARCH THE FIRST COLUMN OF THE A MATRIX FOR THE LARGEST
                                              ELEMENT.
      IROW=1
      BIG=ABS(A(1,1))
      DO 1 I=2,N
      AB=ABS(A(I,1))
      IF(BIG .GE. AB)GO TO 1
      BIG=AB
      IROW=I
    1 CONTINUE
C CHECK TO SEE IF A ROW INTERCHANGE IS TO BE PERFORMED.
      IF(IROW .EQ. 1)GO TO 200
C INTERCHANGE ROWS IROW AND 1 OF THE A MATRIX.
      DO 100 J=1,M
      TEMP=A(IROW,J)
      A(IROW,J)=A(1,J)
  100 A(1,J)=TEMP
  200 CONTINUE
C CALCULATE THE FIRST ROW OF THE NEW MATRIX.
      DO 2 J=2,M
    2 A(1,J)=A(1,J)/A(1,1)
C CALCULATE THE NEW ELEMENTS OF THE ITH COLUMN FROM A(I,I)
                                              TO A(N,I).
      DO 10 I=2,N
      J=I
      DO 4 II=J,N
      SUM=0.
      JM1=J-1
      DO 3 K=1,JM1
    3 SUM=SUM+A(II,K)*A(K,J)
```

[9]See William Weaver, Jr., *Computer Programs for Structural Analysis* (Princeton, N.J.: D. Van Nostrand Co., 1967), pp. 56–58; or see M. G. Salvadori and M. L. Baron, *Numerical Methods in Engineering*, 2d ed. (Englewood Cliffs, N.J.: Prentice-Hall, 1961), p. 29.

```
      4 A(II,J)=A(II,J)-SUM
        IF(I .EQ. N)GO TO 7
C SEARCH FOR THE LARGEST A(II,J) VALUE FROM A(I,I) TO A(N,I).
        IROW=I
        BIG=ABS(A(I,I))
        IP1=I+1
        DO 5 II=IP1,N
        AB=ABS(A(II,I))
        IF(BIG .GE. AB)GO TO 5
        BIG=AB
        IROW=II
      5 CONTINUE
C CHECK TO SEE IF A ROW INTERCHANGE IS TO BE PERFORMED.
        IF(IROW .EQ. I)GO TO 7
C INTERCHANGE ROWS I AND IROW.
        DO 6 J=1,M
        TEMP=A(IROW,J)
        A(IROW,J)=A(I,J)
      6 A(I,J)=TEMP
      7 CONTINUE
C CALCULATE THE NEW ELEMENTS OF THE ITH ROW FROM A(I,I+1)
                                       TO A(I,N+1).
        IP1=I+1
        DO 9 J=IP1,M
        SUM=0.
        IM1=I-1
        DO 8 K=1,IM1
      8 SUM=SUM+A(I,K)*A(K,J)
      9 A(I,J)=(A(I,J)-SUM)/A(I,I)
     10  CONTINUE
C SOLVE FOR X(I) BY BACK SUBSTITUTION.
        X(N)=A(N,N+1)
        L=N-1
        DO 12 NN=1,L
        SUM=0.
        I=N-NN
        IP1=I+1
        DO 11 J=IP1,N
     11 SUM=SUM+A(I,J)*X(J)
     12 X(I)=A(I,M)-SUM
        RETURN
        END
```

3-5 THE USE OF ERROR EQUATIONS

Error equations are used to increase the accuracy with which the roots of simultaneous equations may be determined. For example, when the elimination method, just discussed, is used to find the roots of simultaneous equations, there may be a considerable loss of accuracy in the results, owing to *roundoff error* which accumulates during the large number of arithmetic operations performed in obtaining a solution. (Roundoff error is defined as the error which results from replacing a number having more than n digits by a number having n digits.)

Suppose that the computer were used to solve, for example, 15 to 20 simultaneous equations by the elimination method, and that seven significant digits were retained in the result of each calculation. The final results might have only two- or three-digit accuracy, owing to the cumulative errors introduced by rounding off numbers in the hundreds of arithmetic operations performed.

Error equations can be used to reduce the error introduced by rounding off. Their use is explained in the following discussion.

Consider a set of equations of the form

$$
\begin{aligned}
a_{11}x_1 + a_{12}x_2 + a_{13}x_3 + \cdots + a_{1n}x_n &= C_1 \\
a_{21}x_1 + a_{22}x_2 + a_{23}x_3 + \cdots + a_{2n}x_n &= C_2 \\
&\ \ \vdots \\
a_{n1}x_1 + a_{n2}x_2 + a_{n3}x_3 + \cdots + a_{nn}x_n &= C_n
\end{aligned}
\tag{3-65}
$$

Suppose that we have obtained the approximate roots x_1', x_2', ..., x_n' by the elimination method. Upon substituting these values into Eq. 3-65, we find that the constant values C_1', C_2', ..., C_n' obtained vary from the respective original values C_1, C_2, ..., C_n, since the roots substituted were not exact. Such a substitution may be expressed in equation form as

$$
\begin{aligned}
a_{11}x_1' + a_{12}x_2' + \cdots + a_{1n}x_n' &= C_1' \\
a_{21}x_1' + a_{22}x_2' + \cdots + a_{2n}x_n' &= C_2' \\
&\ \ \vdots \\
a_{n1}x_1' + a_{n2}x_2' + \cdots + a_{nn}x_n' &= C_n'
\end{aligned}
\tag{3-66}
$$

If Δx_1, Δx_2, ..., Δx_n are the corrections which must be added to the approximate root values to obtain the *exact* root values $\bar{x}_1$, $\bar{x}_2$, ..., $\bar{x}_n$, it follows that

$$
\begin{aligned}
\bar{x}_1 &= x_1' + \Delta x_1 \\
\bar{x}_2 &= x_2' + \Delta x_2 \\
&\ \ \vdots \\
\bar{x}_n &= x_n' + \Delta x_n
\end{aligned}
\tag{3-67}
$$

If we substitute these expressions for the exact roots into Eq. 3-65, we obtain

$$a_{11}(x_1' + \Delta x_1) + a_{12}(x_2' + \Delta x_2) + \cdots + a_{1n}(x_n' + \Delta x_n) = C_1$$
$$a_{21}(x_1' + \Delta x_1) + a_{22}(x_2' + \Delta x_2) + \cdots + a_{2n}(x_n' + \Delta x_n) = C_2$$
$$\vdots \qquad\qquad \vdots \qquad\qquad\qquad \vdots \qquad\qquad \vdots$$
$$a_{n1}(x_1' + \Delta x_1) + a_{n2}(x_2' + \Delta x_2) + \cdots + a_{nn}(x_n' + \Delta x_n) = C_n$$

$$(3\text{-}68)$$

If Eq. 3-66 is then subtracted from Eq. 3-68, we obtain the following set of simultaneous equations, involving the root corrections:

$$a_{11}\Delta x_1 + a_{12}\Delta x_2 + \cdots + a_{1n}\Delta x_n = (C_1 - C_1') = e_1$$
$$a_{21}\Delta x_1 + a_{22}\Delta x_2 + \cdots + a_{2n}\Delta x_n = (C_2 - C_2') = e_2$$
$$\vdots \qquad \vdots \qquad\qquad \vdots \qquad\qquad \vdots \qquad \vdots$$
$$a_{n1}\Delta x_1 + a_{n2}\Delta x_2 + \cdots + a_{nn}\Delta x_n = (C_n - C_n') = e_n$$

$$(3\text{-}69)$$

Inspection of Eq. 3-69 reveals that the required root corrections are, themselves, the roots of a set of equations which differs from the original set (Eq. 3-65) only in the respective constant values. The constants e_i of Eq. 3-69 express the error resulting from inaccurate root values, and the equations are called *error equations*.

In a computer solution of a set of simultaneous equations by an elimination method, in which error equations are to be employed, the augmented matrix of the original set of equations should be left stored in memory during its use in obtaining the approximate roots. The corrections to the roots may then be obtained by simply replacing the values in the right-hand column of this matrix by the e_i values calculated, and repeating the reduction of the matrix by the elimination method used. The corrections obtained are then added, respectively, to the approximate root values found in the original elimination process, to obtain more accurate root values.

If still greater accuracy is desired, corrections may be made in the values obtained as the root corrections from solving Eq. 3-69. If we designate the corrections to the corrections by $\Delta^2 x_i$, then the more exact roots $\bar{x}_i$ are given by

$$\bar{x}_i = x_i' + \Delta x_i + \Delta^2 x_i \tag{3-70}$$

This process of using error equations to correct the roots of other error equations can be carried as far as necessary to obtain roots of the desired accuracy. The use of error equations is illustrated in Ex. 3-4.

EXAMPLE 3-4

The following set of simultaneous equations defines the motion of a dwell-return-dwell polynomial cam in which the C's are unknown polynomial coefficients.

$$
\begin{aligned}
C_4 + C_5 + C_6 + C_7 &= -1 \\
4C_4 + 5C_5 + 6C_6 + 7C_7 &= 0 \\
6C_4 + 10C_5 + 15C_6 + 21C_7 &= 0 \\
12C_4 + 30C_5 + 60C_6 + 105C_7 &= 0
\end{aligned}
\tag{3-71}
$$

The roots of this set of equations have been determined by the Gauss-Jordan elimination method and have the following values:

$$
\begin{aligned}
C_4 &= -35 \\
C_5 &= 84 \\
C_6 &= -70 \\
C_7 &= 20
\end{aligned}
$$

Since all the coefficients of Eq. 3-71 are whole numbers, and since the arithmetic operations used in solving the roots did not involve any numbers with sufficient significant digits to exceed the computer capacity, no roundoff error occurred in obtaining the roots, which are whole numbers themselves and are thus the exact roots of Eq. 3-71.

However, for the purpose of illustrating the use of error equations, let us suppose that roundoff has occurred and that the roots have been found to be

$$
\begin{aligned}
C_4' &= -35.1 \\
C_5' &= 83.9 \\
C_6' &= -70.3 \\
C_7' &= 20.2
\end{aligned}
$$

If we substitute these roots into Eq. 3-71 to determine how accurate they are, we find that

$$
\begin{aligned}
C_4 + C_5 + C_6 + C_7 &= -1.3 \\
4C_4 + 5C_5 + 6C_6 + 7C_7 &= -1.3 \\
6C_4 + 10C_5 + 15C_6 + 21C_7 &= -1.9 \\
12C_4 + 30C_5 + 60C_6 + 105C_7 &= -1.2
\end{aligned}
\tag{3-72}
$$

A comparison of the constant values of Eq. 3-72 with the respective constant values of Eq. 3-71 reveals that considerable error exists in the roots. Therefore, we introduce the use of error equations to determine more accurate values. Referring to Eqs. 3-69 and 3-72, we obtain the following set of error equations:

$$\Delta C_4 + \Delta C_5 + \Delta C_6 + \Delta C_7 = -1.0 - (-1.3) = 0.3$$

$$4\Delta C_4 + 5\Delta C_4 + 6\Delta C_6 + 7\Delta C_7 = 0.0 - (-1.3) = 1.3$$

$$6\Delta C_4 + 10\Delta C_5 + 15\Delta C_6 + 21\Delta C_7 = 0.0 - (-1.9) = 1.9$$

$$12\Delta C_4 + 30\Delta C_5 + 60\Delta C_6 + 105\Delta C_7 = 0.0 - (-1.2) = 1.2$$

(3-73)

Using the matrix-reduction method (the matrix form of the Gauss-Jordan elimination method), we find that the augmented and reduced matrices are

$$\mathbf{A} = \begin{bmatrix} 1 & 1 & 1 & 1 & 0.3 \\ 4 & 5 & 6 & 7 & 1.3 \\ 6 & 10 & 15 & 21 & 1.9 \\ 12 & 30 & 60 & 105 & 1.2 \end{bmatrix}$$

$$\mathbf{B} = \begin{bmatrix} 1 & 2 & 3 & 0.10 \\ 4 & 9 & 15 & 0.10 \\ 18 & 48 & 93 & -2.40 \\ 1 & 1 & 1 & 0.30 \end{bmatrix}$$

$$\mathbf{C} = \begin{bmatrix} 1 & 3 & -0.30 \\ 12 & 39 & -4.20 \\ -1 & -2 & 0.20 \\ 2 & 3 & 0.10 \end{bmatrix}$$

$$\mathbf{D} = \begin{bmatrix} 3 & -0.6 \\ 1 & -0.1 \\ -3 & 0.7 \\ 3 & -0.3 \end{bmatrix}$$

$$\mathbf{E} = \begin{Bmatrix} 0.1 \\ 0.1 \\ 0.3 \\ -0.2 \end{Bmatrix}$$

Using the corrections shown in the column matrix, the corrected values of the roots are

$$
\begin{aligned}
C_4 &= C_4' + \Delta C_4 = -35.1 + \quad 0.1 \;\; = -35.0 \\
C_5 &= C_5' + \Delta C_5 = \quad 83.9 + \quad 0.1 \;\; = \quad 84.0 \\
C_6 &= C_6' + \Delta C_6 = -70.3 + \quad 0.3 \;\; = -70.0 \\
C_7 &= C_7' + \Delta C_7 = \quad 20.2 + (-0.2) = \quad 20.0
\end{aligned}
\tag{3-74}
$$

Since no roundoff error was introduced in solving the error equations, the corrections are exact corrections and, when added to the approximate values of the roots assumed, yield the exact roots determined in the actual solution.

As was evident at the beginning of this discussion, this example does not involve equations whose solution requires the use of error equations. Such an example was used, for the sake of simplicity, to illustrate the actual matrix reductions which resulted in the root corrections. It should be obvious to the reader, at this point, why error equations would be necessary in solving a set of, say, 30 simultaneous equations, involving coefficients as follows, on a computer having the capacity of handling perhaps only seven significant digits:

$$
\begin{aligned}
0.86746C_1 + 0.97121C_2 + 1.67543C_3 + \cdots + 0.23456C_{30} &= 1.76408 \\
0.34657C_1 + 0.78645C_2 + \cdots \qquad\qquad\qquad\qquad\;\; &= 2.67823 \\
\vdots \qquad\qquad \vdots \qquad\qquad\qquad\qquad\qquad\quad\; &\;\;\;\;\vdots \\
0.54236C_1 + \cdots \qquad\qquad\qquad\qquad\qquad\qquad\;\; &= 1.53266
\end{aligned}
\tag{3-75}
$$

The procedure discussed in this example would be used to obtain roots of the desired accuracy for Eq. 3-75, except that the whole procedure would be programmed to let the computer perform all the tedious reduction operations, which are complicated by the numerical values of the coefficients.

3-6 MATRIX-INVERSION METHOD

When it is necessary to solve a large number of different *sets* of simultaneous equations which differ only by the constant values appearing in the respective equations, the matrix-inversion method may be used to advantage in reducing the number of operations required.

Before proceeding with this method, the reader may wish to review the rules governing the multiplication of matrices given in App. B.

Let us consider again the set of simultaneous equations given by Eq. 3-65. From the rules of matrix multiplication, it can be seen that Eq. 3-65 may be expressed by the single matrix equation

$$\begin{bmatrix} a_{11} & a_{12} & \cdots & a_{1n} \\ a_{21} & a_{22} & \cdots & a_{2n} \\ \vdots & \vdots & & \vdots \\ & & & a_{nn} \end{bmatrix} \begin{Bmatrix} x_1 \\ x_2 \\ \vdots \\ x_n \end{Bmatrix} = \begin{Bmatrix} c_1 \\ c_2 \\ \vdots \\ c_n \end{Bmatrix} \tag{3-76}$$

If we let A represent the coefficient matrix, $\{X\}$ the column matrix of the unknowns, and $\{C\}$ the column matrix of the constants, we can express Eq. 3-76 as

$$A\{X\} = \{C\} \quad \text{or} \quad AX = C \tag{3-77}$$

If the given set of equations (Eq. 3-65) has a unique solution, the coefficient matrix A is nonsingular, and, as such, there exists for A an inverse matrix A^{-1} such that

$$A^{-1}A = I$$

where I is the *identity* or *unit* matrix. The identity matrix, which is an n-by-n matrix with its main diagonal consisting of *ones* and zeros everywhere else (see Eq. 3-80), is to matrix algebra what the identity number (1) is to ordinary algebra; that is, $IA = A$ or $AI = A$.

Premultiplying both sides of Eq. 3-77 by A^{-1} gives

$$(A^{-1}A)\{X\} = A^{-1}\{C\}$$
$$I\{X\} = A^{-1}\{C\} \tag{3-78}$$
$$\{X\} = A^{-1}\{C\}$$

Inspection of Eq. 3-78 reveals that if A^{-1} is known, the elements of $\{X\}$ can easily be determined for any number of different $\{C\}$ matrices by merely premultiplying the particular constant matrix by the inverse matrix.

The inverse of A can be determined from the equation

$$AA^{-1} = I \tag{3-79}$$

If we let a_{ij} be the general element of A and b_{ij} be the general element of A^{-1}, Eq. 3-79 may be expressed as

$$\begin{bmatrix} a_{11} & a_{12} & \cdots & a_{1n} \\ a_{21} & a_{22} & \cdots & a_{2n} \\ \vdots & \vdots & & \vdots \\ a_{n1} & a_{n2} & \cdots & a_{nn} \end{bmatrix} \begin{bmatrix} b_{11} & b_{12} & \cdots & b_{1n} \\ b_{21} & b_{22} & \cdots & b_{2n} \\ \vdots & \vdots & & \vdots \\ b_{n1} & b_{n2} & \cdots & b_{nn} \end{bmatrix} = \begin{bmatrix} 1 & 0 & \cdots & 0 \\ 0 & 1 & & 0 \\ \vdots & & & \vdots \\ 0 & 0 & \cdots & 1 \end{bmatrix} \tag{3-80}$$

where the identity matrix on the right side of the equation has the same n-by-n order as the $\mathbf{A}$ and $\mathbf{A}^{-1}$ matrices.

From the rules of matrix multiplication, Eq. 3-80 is equivalent to the following n *sets* of simultaneous equations:

$$
\left.
\begin{aligned}
a_{11}b_{11} + a_{12}b_{21} + \cdots + a_{1n}b_{n1} &= 1 \\
a_{21}b_{11} + a_{22}b_{21} + \cdots + a_{2n}b_{n1} &= 0 \\
\vdots \qquad\quad \vdots \qquad\qquad \vdots \qquad\quad \vdots \\
a_{n1}b_{11} + a_{n2}b_{21} + \cdots + a_{nn}b_{n1} &= 0
\end{aligned}
\right\} \quad (1)
$$

$$
\left.
\begin{aligned}
a_{11}b_{12} + a_{12}b_{22} + \cdots + a_{1n}b_{n2} &= 0 \\
a_{21}b_{12} + a_{22}b_{22} + \cdots + a_{2n}b_{n2} &= 1 \\
\vdots \qquad\quad \vdots \qquad\qquad \vdots \qquad\quad \vdots \\
a_{n1}b_{12} + a_{n2}b_{22} + \cdots + a_{nn}b_{n2} &= 0
\end{aligned}
\right\} \quad (2)
$$

$$
\vdots \qquad\qquad\qquad\qquad \vdots
$$

$$
\left.
\begin{aligned}
a_{11}b_{1n} + a_{12}b_{2n} + \cdots + a_{1n}b_{nn} &= 0 \\
a_{21}b_{1n} + a_{22}b_{2n} + \cdots + a_{2n}b_{nn} &= 0 \\
\vdots \qquad\quad \vdots \qquad\qquad \vdots \qquad\quad \vdots \\
a_{n1}b_{1n} + a_{n2}b_{2n} + \cdots + a_{nn}b_{nn} &= 1
\end{aligned}
\right\} \quad (n)
$$

$$(3\text{-}81)$$

Inspection of Eq. 3-81 reveals that all the n sets of equations have identical known coefficients a_{ij}, and that each set contains one column of elements of the inverse matrix $\mathbf{A}^{-1}$ as unknowns and the corresponding column of the identity matrix $\mathbf{I}$ (see Eq. 3-80) as constants. Thus, we have n sets of simultaneous equations which differ only by the constants associated with each set.

It was stated in Sec. 3-3 that the Gauss-Jordan elimination method could be utilized to solve simultaneously n sets of simultaneous equations, differing only in their constants, by including the column of constants associated with each set of equations on the right side of the coefficient matrix in the augmented matrix. Utilizing the Gauss-Jordan elimination method, we first form the augmented matrix

$$
\begin{bmatrix}
a_{11} & a_{12} & \cdots & a_{1n} & 1 & 0 & \cdots & 0 \\
a_{21} & a_{22} & \cdots & a_{2n} & 0 & 1 & \cdots & 0 \\
\vdots & \vdots & & \vdots & \vdots & \vdots & & \vdots \\
a_{n1} & a_{n2} & \cdots & a_{nn} & 0 & 0 & \cdots & 1
\end{bmatrix}
$$

The elements of the inverse matrix (the b_{ij}'s) may then be obtained by successive applications of Eqs. 3-31 and 3-32, continuing the reduction process until n columns remain, or by application of Eq. 3-45, modified for $2n$ columns instead of $n + 1$ columns. The following example utilizes the first reduction method for matrix inversion.

EXAMPLE 3-5

Let us solve Eq. 3-71 of Ex. 3-4 using the matrix-inversion method. The coefficient matrix is

$$
\mathbf{A} = \begin{bmatrix} 1 & 1 & 1 & 1 \\ 4 & 5 & 6 & 7 \\ 6 & 10 & 15 & 21 \\ 12 & 30 & 60 & 105 \end{bmatrix}
$$

We begin the matrix reduction with the augmented matrix

$$
\begin{bmatrix} 1 & 1 & 1 & 1 & 1 & 0 & 0 & 0 \\ 4 & 5 & 6 & 7 & 0 & 1 & 0 & 0 \\ 6 & 10 & 15 & 21 & 0 & 0 & 1 & 0 \\ 12 & 30 & 60 & 105 & 0 & 0 & 0 & 1 \end{bmatrix}
$$

Successive reductions, applying Eqs. 3-31 and 3-32, yield the inverted matrix

$$
\mathbf{A}^{-1} = \begin{bmatrix} 35 & -15 & 5 & -\frac{1}{3} \\ -84 & 39 & -14 & 1 \\ 70 & -34 & 13 & -1 \\ -20 & 10 & -4 & \frac{1}{3} \end{bmatrix}
$$

The correctness of the inverse matrix can easily be checked by multiplying it by the matrix $\mathbf{A}$. If it is correct, the resulting product will be the identity matrix.

If $\{K\}$ represents the column matrix of the constants of Eq. 3-71, and $\{C\}$ represents the column matrix of the unknowns C_4, C_5, C_6, and C_7, then, from Eq. 3-78,

$$\{C\} = \mathbf{A}^{-1}\{K\}$$

or

$$\{C\} = \begin{bmatrix} 35 & -15 & 5 & -\frac{1}{3} \\ -84 & 39 & -14 & 1 \\ 70 & -34 & 13 & -1 \\ -20 & 10 & -4 & \frac{1}{3} \end{bmatrix} \begin{Bmatrix} -1 \\ 0 \\ 0 \\ 0 \end{Bmatrix} = \begin{Bmatrix} -35 \\ 84 \\ -70 \\ 20 \end{Bmatrix}$$

These are the same values which were obtained much more simply by the elimination method illustrated in Ex. 3-4. Comparing the two methods, it is evident that the matrix-inversion method is not practical for solving a single set (or even two or three sets) of simultaneous equations, because of the amount of calculation involved in determining the inverse matrix. If, however, 20 sets of ten simultaneous equations, differing only in their constants, were to be solved, an augmented matrix containing 20 columns of constants would be used in the elimination method, and the matrix-inversion method could be used to advantage.

Matrix Inversion in Place

In accomplishing the matrix reductions on the computer by either of the Gauss-Jordan algorithms given in Sec. 3-3, it would not be necessary to read in the elements of the appended identity matrix as data values. If they are to be stored in memory at all (and they need not be, at the cost of a slightly more complicated inversion program), they can be readily generated by statements in the program. Such statements might be as follows:

```
   . . .
   DO 8J=NP1,M
   DO 8I=1,N
   IF(J-N-I)7,6,7
 6 A(I,J)=1.
   GO TO 8
 7 A(I,J)=0.
 8 CONTINUE
   . . .
```

where NP1 = N + 1 and M is the number of columns in the augmented matrix.

If fairly large matrices are being inverted, and it is important to save as much primary memory as possible, it is preferable to use the second Gauss-Jordan algorithm given in Sec. 3-3, which lays the reduced matrix over the original augmented matrix in memory. A further saving of memory space can be accomplished by not storing the identity matrix. The matrix to be inverted is stored in memory and is replaced by its inverse. This is called "inversion in place."

A problem arises in the use of partial pivoting with inversion in place. When rows of a matrix are interchanged, the rows containing zeros and ones in the appended matrix must also be interchanged. If the identity matrix is not present in core, this required interchange must be taken into account. A discussion of this problem will be postponed until we have first studied *inversion in place* without row interchange.

Let us consider inversion of the matrix

$$\begin{bmatrix} 3 & -2 & -1 \\ -4 & 1 & -1 \\ 2 & 0 & 1 \end{bmatrix}$$

With the appended identity matrix, it becomes

$$\begin{bmatrix} 3 & -2 & -1 & 1 & 0 & 0 \\ -4 & 1 & -1 & 0 & 1 & 0 \\ 2 & 0 & 1 & 0 & 0 & 1 \end{bmatrix}$$

Applying Eq. 3-45 with $2n$ columns instead of $n + 1$ columns, the first step in the reduction process results in

$$\begin{bmatrix} 3 & -2 & -1 & 1 & 0 & 0 \\ -4 & 1 & -1 & 0 & 1 & 0 \\ 2 & 0 & 1 & 0 & 0 & 1 \end{bmatrix} \rightarrow \begin{bmatrix} 1 & -\frac{2}{3} & -\frac{1}{3} & \frac{1}{3} & 0 & 0 \\ 0 & -\frac{5}{3} & -\frac{7}{3} & \frac{4}{3} & 1 & 0 \\ 0 & \frac{4}{3} & \frac{5}{3} & -\frac{2}{3} & 0 & 1 \end{bmatrix}$$

The first column of the reduced matrix consists of zeros and a one, and they are not used in further steps of the reduction process. Therefore, the fourth column could be stored in its place. Only three columns are required to store the vital elements resulting from this reduction step. With matrix inversion in place, the matrix in memory at this stage would be

$$\begin{bmatrix} \frac{1}{3} & -\frac{2}{3} & -\frac{1}{3} \\ \frac{4}{3} & -\frac{5}{3} & -\frac{7}{3} \\ -\frac{2}{3} & \frac{4}{3} & \frac{5}{3} \end{bmatrix}$$

The second step in the reduction process results in

$$\begin{bmatrix} 1 & -\frac{2}{3} & -\frac{1}{3} & \frac{1}{3} & 0 & 0 \\ 0 & -\frac{5}{3} & -\frac{7}{3} & \frac{4}{3} & 1 & 0 \\ 0 & \frac{4}{3} & \frac{5}{3} & -\frac{2}{3} & 0 & 1 \end{bmatrix} \rightarrow \begin{bmatrix} 1 & 0 & \frac{3}{5} & -\frac{1}{5} & -\frac{2}{5} & 0 \\ 0 & 1 & \frac{7}{5} & -\frac{4}{5} & -\frac{3}{5} & 0 \\ 0 & 0 & -\frac{1}{5} & \frac{2}{5} & \frac{4}{5} & 1 \end{bmatrix}$$

Again, the fourth column could be stored where the first column is, and the fifth column could replace the second column. With matrix inversion in place, we would have in memory

$$\begin{bmatrix} -\frac{1}{5} & -\frac{2}{5} & \frac{3}{5} \\ -\frac{4}{5} & -\frac{3}{5} & \frac{7}{5} \\ \frac{2}{5} & \frac{4}{5} & -\frac{1}{5} \end{bmatrix}$$

After one more reduction step, the final matrix would be

$$\begin{bmatrix} 1 & 0 & 0 & 1 & 2 & 3 \\ 0 & 1 & 0 & 2 & 5 & 7 \\ 0 & 0 & 1 & -2 & -4 & -5 \end{bmatrix}$$

or for inversion in place, simply

$$\begin{bmatrix} 1 & 2 & 3 \\ 2 & 5 & 7 \\ -2 & -4 & -5 \end{bmatrix}$$

We note that the matrix reduction in place can be accomplished with the following equations applied in the order listed; first with $k = 1$ for all equations and j and i cycling as indicated for each equation; then applied again in the same manner with $k = 2$, and so forth, up to $k = n$, where n is the order of the matrix.

1. $a'_{kj} = \dfrac{a_{kj}}{a_{kk}}$ for $j = 1, 2, \ldots, n$ (except $j \neq k$)

2. $a'_{kk} = \dfrac{1}{a_{kk}}$

3. $a'_{ij} = a_{ij} - a'_{kj} a_{ik}$ for $\begin{cases} i = 1, 2, \ldots, n \ (\text{except } i \neq k) \\ j = 1, 2, \ldots, n \ \text{for each } i \end{cases}$ (3-82)

         (except $j \neq k$)

4. $a'_{ik} = 0 - a_{ik} a'_{kk}$ for $i = 1, 2, \ldots, n$ (except $i \neq k$)

     To aid in the study of matrix inversion in place, a computer program applying Eq. 3-82 is presented next. The student should correlate this program with the preceding discussion. Partial pivoting is not used, so the computer would stop execution because of overflow upon attempted division by zero in the event that a pivot element were very small or exactly zero. Partial pivoting, which is used to avoid this problem, is discussed in the next subsection.

```
C MATRIX INVERSION USING GAUSS-JORDAN REDUCTION
C INVERTED MATRIX OVERLAYS ORIGINAL MATRIX IN MEMORY
C PARTIAL PIVOTING IS NOT USED
C STATEMENT 8 SHOULD BE CHANGED AS REQUIRED BY ORDER OF
                                                      MATRIX
      DIMENSION A(15,15)
C READ IN ORDER OF MATRIX
      READ(5,2) N
    2 FORMAT(I2)
C READ IN MATRIX TO BE INVERTED
      READ(5,3) ((A(I,J),J=1,N),I=1,N)
    3 FORMAT(8F10.0)
C CALCULATE ELEMENTS OF REDUCED MATRIX
      DO 6 K=1,N
C CALCULATE NEW ELEMENTS OF PIVOT ROW
      DO 4 J=1,N
      IF(J.EQ.K) GO TO 4
      A(K,J)=A(K,J)/A(K,K)
    4 CONTINUE
C CALCULATE ELEMENT REPLACING PIVOT ELEMENT
      A(K,K)=1./A(K,K)
C CALCULATE NEW ELEMENTS NOT IN PIVOT ROW OR PIVOT COLUMN
      DO 5 I=1,N
      IF(I.EQ.K) GO TO 5
      DO 5 J=1,N
      IF(J.EQ.K) GO TO 5
      A(I,J)=A(I,J)-A(K,J)*A(I,K)
    5 CONTINUE
C CALCULATE REPLACEMENT ELEMENTS FOR PIVOT COLUMN-EXCEPT
                                             PIVOT ELEMENT
      DO 6 I=1,N
      IF(I.EQ.K) GO TO 6
      A(I,K)=-A(I,K)*A(K,K)
    6 CONTINUE
C WRITE OUT INVERTED MATRIX
      WRITE(6,7)
    7 FORMAT('1','INVERTED MATRIX'/)
      WRITE(6,8) ((A(I,J),J=1,N),I=1,N)
    8 FORMAT(' ',3F16.4)
      STOP
      END
```

Matrix Inversion In Place with Partial Pivoting

Let us again suppose that the matrix

$$\begin{bmatrix} -3 & -2 & -1 \\ -4 & 1 & -1 \\ 2 & 0 & 1 \end{bmatrix}$$

is to be inverted, but that we wish to interchange the first and second rows to utilize the largest value in the pivot column as the pivot element. The appended identity matrix must also have its first and second rows interchanged, giving

$$\begin{bmatrix} 0 & 1 & 0 \\ 1 & 0 & 0 \\ 0 & 0 & 1 \end{bmatrix}$$

We observe that we could obtain the same appended matrix by interchanging the first and second *columns* of the original appended identity matrix. Next we consider the effect of failing to make the column interchange in the appended matrix (since it is not present in memory). By referring to Eqs. 3-80 and 3-81, we see that changing the first and second rows of matrix **A,** without changing the first and second columns of the identity matrix, has the same effect as changing the first and second columns of the identity matrix without the row interchange in the **A** matrix. Therefore, the question arises as to the effect of changing only the first and second column of the identity matrix. In Eq. 3-81(1), we would actually be solving for b_{12}, b_{22}, b_{32}, . . . instead of b_{11}, b_{21}, b_{31}, ... In Eq. 3-81(2) we would be solving for b_{11}, b_{21}, b_{31}, . . . instead of for b_{12}, b_{22}, b_{32}, ... Thus, the inverted matrix would have its first and second columns interchanged. This is also the effect of changing the first and second rows of the matrix to be inverted, with no change in the rows containing the zeros and one in the appended matrix. Therefore, if partial pivoting is used in the program, we must keep track of all row interchanges and reorder the columns of the final matrix obtained in the reduction process. If the last row interchange involved the fourth and sixth rows, then the fourth and sixth columns of the final matrix would have to be interchanged first. If the next-to-the-last row interchange involved the third and fourth rows, the third and fourth columns of the final matrix would have to be interchanged *following the interchange of columns* 4 and 6. The complete procedure of matrix inversion in place with partial pivoting is outlined in the flow chart given in Fig. 3-5. It is left as a problem for the student to write a computer program implementing this flow chart (see Prob. 3-19 at the end of the chapter).

3-7 GAUSS-SEIDEL METHOD

The elimination methods of solving simultaneous equations usually yield sufficiently accurate solutions for approximately 15 to 20 simultaneous equations, where most of the unknowns are present in all of the equations. The exact number depends on the number of significant digits retained in the results of the arithmetic operations, and the actual equations being solved. When the coefficient matrix is sparse, a considerably larger number of equations can be handled by the elimination methods. Error equations can be used to increase

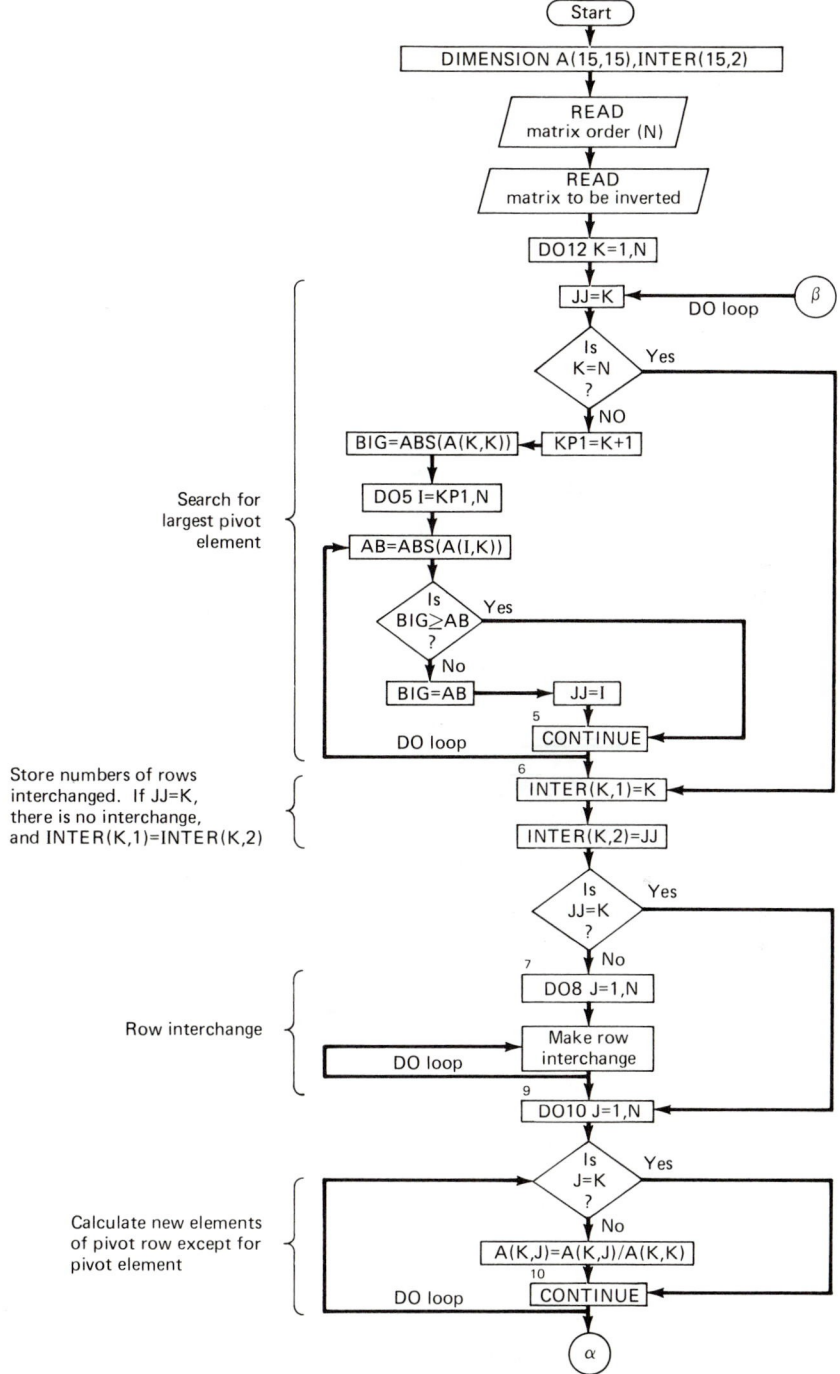

Figure 3-5(a)   Flow chart for matrix inversion in place with partial pivoting

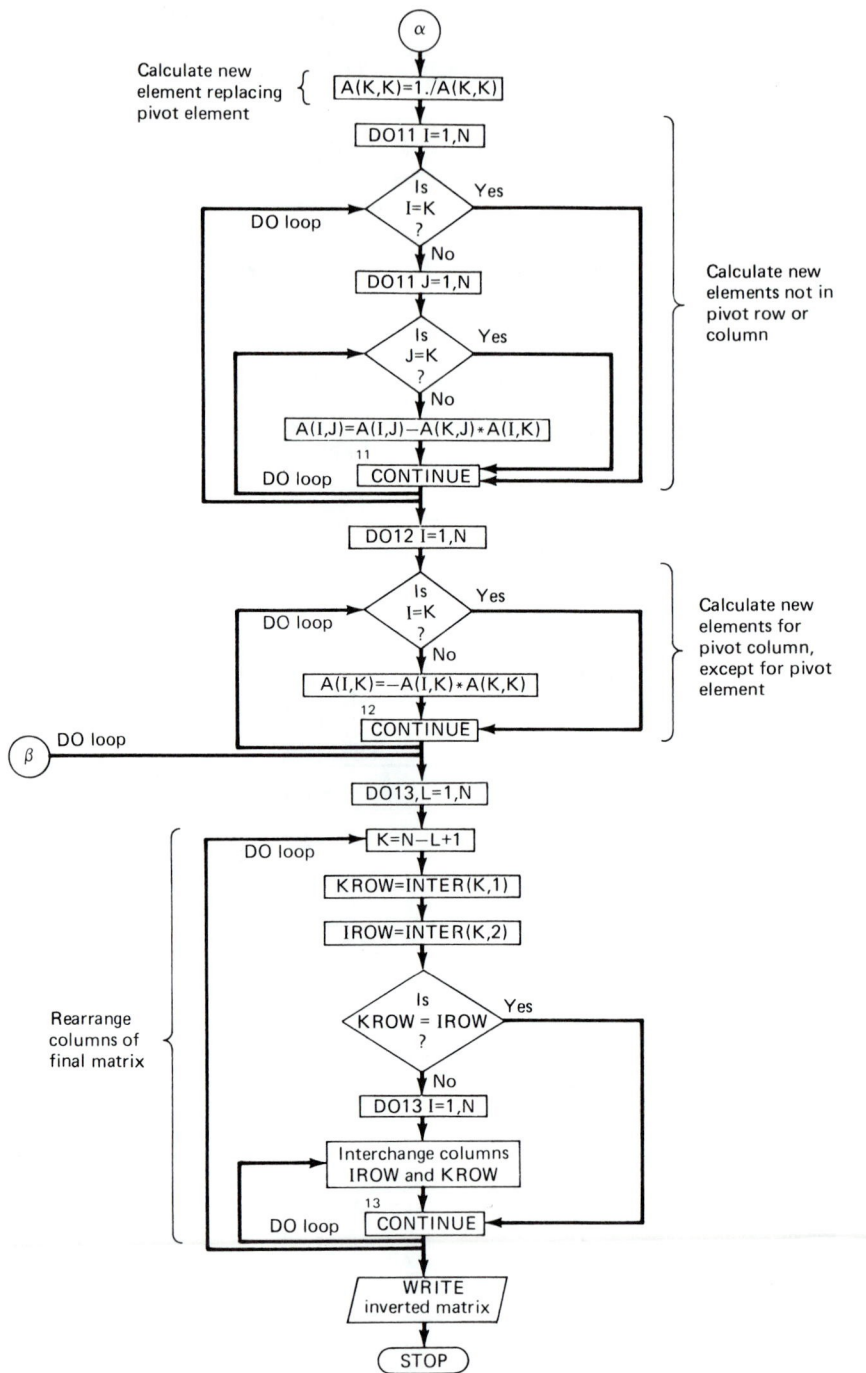

Figure 3-5(b) Flow chart for matrix inversion in place with partial pivoting (*cont.*)

the number which can be accurately solved, but elimination methods are generally impractical when many hundreds or thousands of equations must be solved simultaneously.

There are, however, several techniques which can be used to solve large numbers of simultaneous equations. One of the most useful is the Gauss-Seidel method. None of the several approaches is completely satisfactory, and the Gauss-Seidel method has the disadvantages of not always converging to a solution and of sometimes converging very slowly when it does converge. However, this method will always converge to a solution when the magnitude of a coefficient of a different unknown, in each equation of the set, is sufficiently dominant with respect to the magnitudes of the other coefficients in that equation. It is difficult to define the exact minimum margin by which such a coefficient must dominate the other coefficients to ensure convergence, and it is even more difficult to predict the rate of convergence for some combination of coefficient values when convergence exists. However, when the absolute value of the dominant coefficient for a different unknown in each equation is larger than the sum of the absolute values of the other coefficients in that equation, convergence is assured. Such a set of linear simultaneous equations is known as a *diagonal* system. A diagonal system is *sufficient* to ensure convergence but is not *necessary*. Fortunately, the linear simultaneous equations which derive from many engineering problems are of the type in which dominant coefficients are present.

As a simple example of a set of simultaneous equations which are solvable by the Gauss-Seidel method, let us consider

$$10x_1 + x_2 + 2x_3 = 44$$
$$2x_1 + 10x_2 + x_3 = 51 \qquad\qquad (3\text{-}83)$$
$$x_1 + 2x_2 + 10x_3 = 61$$

It can be seen that the coefficient of x_1 is dominant in the first equation of the set, and that the coefficients of x_2 and x_3 are dominant in the second and third equations, respectively. Since the dominant coefficient in each equation is larger than the sum of the other coefficients in that equation, Eq. 3-83 represents a diagonal system, and convergence is assured.

The sequence of steps constituting the Gauss-Seidel method is as follows:

1. Assign an initial value for each unknown appearing in the set. If it is possible to make a reasonable assumption of these values, do so. If not, any arbitrarily selected values may be assigned. The initial values used will not affect the convergence, as such, but will affect the number of iterations required for convergence.
2. Starting with the first equation, solve that equation for a new value of the unknown which has the largest coefficient in that equation, using the assumed values for the other unknowns.

3. Go to the second equation and solve it for the unknown having the largest coefficient in that equation, using the value calculated for the unknown in step 2 and the assumed values for the remaining unknowns.
4. Proceed with the remaining equations, always solving for the unknown having the largest coefficient in the particular equation, and always using the *last calculated* values for the other unknowns in the equation. (During the first iteration, assumed values must be used for the unknowns until a calculated value has been obtained.) When the final equation has been solved, yielding a value for the last unknown, one iteration is said to have been completed.
5. Continue iterating until the value of each unknown determined in a particular iteration differs from its respective value obtained in the preceding iteration by an amount less than some arbitrarily selected epsilon. The procedure is then complete.

Referring to step 5, the smaller the magnitude of the epsilon selected, the greater will be the accuracy of the solution. However, the magnitude of epsilon does not specify the error which may exist in the values obtained for the unknowns, as this is a function of the rate of convergence. The faster the rate of convergence, the greater will be the accuracy obtained in the values of the unknowns for a given epsilon.

As a simple illustration of the steps just discussed, let us solve Eq. 3-83, using a value of $\varepsilon = 0.02$. Assuming initial values of zero for all three unknowns, the steps appear as follows:

$$\left[\begin{array}{l} 10x_1 + 0 + 0 = 44 \\ \qquad\qquad x_1 = 4.40 \end{array}\right] \quad (1)$$

$$\left[\begin{array}{l} 2(4.40) + 10x_2 + 0 = 51 \\ \qquad\qquad x_2 = 4.22 \end{array}\right] \quad (2)$$

$$\left[\begin{array}{l} 4.40 + 2(4.22) + 10x_3 = 61 \\ \qquad\qquad x_3 = 4.81 \end{array}\right] \quad (3)$$

The first iteration has now been completed. A second iteration yields

$$\left[\begin{array}{l} 10x_1 + 4.22 + 2(4.81) = 44 \\ \qquad\qquad x_1 = 3.01 \end{array}\right] \quad (1)$$

$$\left[\begin{array}{l} 2(3.01) + 10x_2 + 4.81 = 51 \\ \qquad\qquad x_2 = 4.01 \end{array}\right] \quad (2)$$

$$\left[\begin{array}{l} 3.01 + 2(4.01) + 10x_3 = 61 \\ \qquad\qquad x_3 = 4.99 \end{array}\right] \quad (3)$$

Comparing the last values with the respective values obtained in the previous iteration, it can be seen that Δx_1, Δx_2, and Δx_3 are all greater than the ε chosen. Therefore, a third iteration is indicated. This iteration yields

$$x_1 = 3.00$$

$$x_2 = 4.00$$

$$x_3 = 5.00$$

Comparing these values with the respective values obtained in the previous iteration, it can be seen that Δx_1, Δx_2, and Δx_3 are all less than ε, indicating that only three iterations are required. In this example, a fourth iteration would be found to give no change in the values of the unknowns, indicating that an exact solution has been reached.

In obtaining the above solution, only three digits were retained in the result of each calculation. This was done by arbitrarily lopping off all the excess digits which appeared. In a computer solution the computer might retain approximately seven to twelve digits in the result of each calculation, depending on the computer being used. Although this example is a simple one, it serves very well to illustrate the Gauss-Seidel method, since the solution of a much larger set of simultaneous equations would proceed in exactly the same manner, differing only in that many more calculations would be required.

The Gauss-Siedel method is used frequently in the solution of Laplace's and Poisson's partial differential equations, and an example of an engineering problem in which this method is employed will be discussed in Sec. 8-2.

3-8 HOMOGENEOUS ALGEBRAIC EQUATIONS— EIGENVALUE PROBLEMS

In the preceding sections several methods were presented for solving n nonhomogeneous simultaneous linear algebraic equations in n unknowns. It was assumed that the equations were such that their solutions yielded unique values for the unknowns, since that is generally the case for nonhomogeneous equations describing the characteristics of physical systems. It was noted that the determinants of the coefficient matrices of the sets of equations had to be nonzero (all the equations of the set had to be linearly independent) before unique solutions could be obtained.

Let us now consider the solution of *homogeneous* simultaneous linear algebraic equations which have the general form

$$a_{11}x_1 + a_{12}x_2 + a_{13}x_3 + \cdots + a_{1n}x_n = 0$$

$$a_{21}x_1 + a_{22}x_2 + \cdots\cdots\cdots + a_{2n}x_n = 0$$

$$\vdots \qquad\qquad \vdots \quad \vdots$$

$$a_{n1}x_1 + \cdots\cdots\cdots\cdots\cdots + a_{nn}x_n = 0$$

(3-84)

or, in matrix notation,

$$
\begin{bmatrix}
a_{11} & a_{12} & \cdots & a_{1n} \\
a_{21} & a_{22} & \cdots & a_{2n} \\
\vdots & & \vdots & \\
a_{n1} & a_{n2} & \cdots & a_{nn}
\end{bmatrix}
\begin{Bmatrix}
x_1 \\
x_2 \\
\vdots \\
x_n
\end{Bmatrix} = 0 \tag{3-85}
$$

In linear algebra it is proved that any system of m linear algebraic equations in n unknowns has a solution if, and only if, the coefficient matrix and the augmented matrix of the set have the same *rank*.[10] Therefore, a set of homogeneous equations such as Eq. 3-85 always has a solution (that is, they are consistent), since the augmented matrix and the coefficient matrix of the set are always necessarily of the same rank.

Any system of homogeneous linear algebraic equations always has a trivial solution $(x_1 = x_2 = \cdots = x_n = 0)$. If the rank r of the coefficient matrix of the set of equations is equal to the order n, only a trivial solution will exist. *Nontrivial solutions* exist for a set of homogeneous equations if, and only if, the rank r of the coefficient matrix of the set is *less* than the order n. For such a set of equations, the determinant of the coefficient matrix is *zero*, and the set will consist of r linearly independent equations and $n - r$ dependent equations which are linear combinations of the independent equations. In obtaining nontrivial solutions of a set of homogeneous equations, unique values are not obtained for the unknowns. Rather, *relationships* are established between the unknowns (the x's of Eq. 3-84). Any combination of x_i values which satisfies these relationships constitutes a solution. Such solutions will be discussed further later in this section.

To understand the application of homogeneous equations in the analysis of engineering problems, let us consider the solution of *eigenvalue problems* (*characteristic-value* problems) which occur in the areas of vibration analysis, electric-circuit analysis, theory of elasticity, and so on. In developing the mathematical models of systems in these areas, the equations generally have the form

$$
\begin{aligned}
(a_{11} - \lambda)x_1 + \quad & a_{12}x_2 + \quad a_{13}x_3 + \cdots + a_{1n}x_n = 0 \\
a_{21}x_1 + \quad & (a_{22} - \lambda)x_2 + \quad a_{23}x_3 + \cdots + a_{2n}x_n = 0 \\
a_{31}x_1 + \quad & a_{32}x_2 + (a_{33} - \lambda)x_3 + \cdots + a_{3n}x_n = 0 \\
& \vdots \qquad\qquad\qquad\qquad \vdots \quad \vdots \\
a_{n1}x_1 + \quad & \cdots\cdots\cdots\cdots\cdots\cdots + (a_{nn} - \lambda)x_n = 0
\end{aligned} \tag{3-86}
$$

[10] The rank of a matrix is the order of the largest nonzero determinant which can be obtained considering all minors of the matrix. Or, stated in another way, it is the number of linearly independent rows (or columns) of the matrix.

where the coefficients a_{ij} are real, the x's are system variables, and λ is a particular parameter of the system having unknown values. For example, in a vibrating system having several degrees of freedom, such as the one shown in Fig. 3-6, the coefficient values would derive from the m_i and k_i values (masses and spring constants, respectively), and x_i would be the displacements of the respective masses, and the values of λ would be the squares of the natural circular frequencies of the system.

In matrix notation Eq. 3-86 is expressed as

$$
\begin{bmatrix}
(a_{11} - \lambda) & a_{12} & a_{13} \cdots\cdots a_{1n} \\
a_{21} & (a_{22} - \lambda) & a_{23} \cdots\cdots a_{2n} \\
a_{31} & a_{32} & (a_{33} - \lambda) \cdots a_{3n} \\
\vdots & \vdots & \vdots \qquad\quad \vdots \\
a_{n1} & \cdots\cdots & \cdots\cdots (a_{nn} - \lambda)
\end{bmatrix}
\begin{Bmatrix}
x_1 \\
x_2 \\
x_3 \\
\vdots \\
x_n
\end{Bmatrix} = \mathbf{0}
\tag{3-87}
$$

or more compactly as

$$(\mathbf{A} - \lambda\mathbf{I})\mathbf{X} = \mathbf{0} \tag{3-88}$$

where the use of the *identity* matrix $\mathbf{I}$ allows us to use $(\mathbf{A} - \lambda\mathbf{I})$ as a coefficient matrix. The column matrix $\mathbf{X}$ is frequently referred to as an *eigenvector*, with

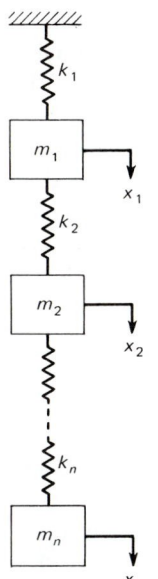

Figure 3-6 Vibrating system with multiple degrees of freedom

$x_1, x_2, x_3, \ldots, x_n$ considered as the *components* of the eigenvector. The values obtained for λ are known as *eigenvalues* or *characteristic values* of the matrix **A.**

Thinking of Eq. 3-86 or Eq. 3-87 as being the mathematical model of a physical system, it is obvious that the trivial solution has no physical significance and that we are interested in nontrivial solutions. As stated earlier, nontrivial solutions exist if the determinant of the coefficient matrix is equal to zero. With λ appearing as an unknown in the coefficient matrix, we may arbitrarily set the determinant of the coefficient matrix equal to zero,

$$|D| = \begin{vmatrix} (a_{11} - \lambda) & a_{12} & a_{13} & a_{1n} \\ a_{21} & (a_{22} - \lambda) & a_{23} & a_{2n} \\ a_{31} & a_{32} & (a_{33} - \lambda) & a_{3n} \\ \vdots & \vdots & \vdots & \vdots \\ a_{n1} & \cdots & \cdots & \cdots (a_{nn} - \lambda) \end{vmatrix} = 0$$

and find values of λ which will make the determinant equal to zero.

The expansion of such a determinant results in an nth-degree polynomial

$$\lambda^n + b_1\lambda^{n-1} + b_2\lambda^{n-2} + \cdots + b_n = 0 \tag{3-89}$$

which is solved to obtain the λ_i values that will make $|D| = 0$. (There will be n values of λ appearing as the n roots of the polynomial.) This polynomial is referred to as the *characteristic equation* of the matrix **A,** and the roots of the polynomial are known as *eigenvalues* or *characteristic values*.

After determining the eigenvalues, these values may be substituted, one value at a time, back into the given set of equations to obtain a corresponding *set of relationships* between the unknowns x_i for each substitution. The relationships obtained will depend upon the rank r of the coefficient matrix $(\mathbf{A} - \lambda\mathbf{I})$. If $r = n - 1$, the relationships will be such that the assumption of a value for one unknown will yield a corresponding value for each of the remaining unknowns; if $r = n - 2$, the relationships will be such that values will have to be assumed for two unknowns in order to obtain a corresponding value for each of the remaining unknowns; and so forth.

In many engineering applications the rank of the coefficient matrix is one less than the order (this corresponds to only one linearly *dependent* equation in the set), and the relationships between the unknowns may be obtained as the ratios $x_1/x_2 = \alpha_1$, $x_1/x_3 = \alpha_2$, $\ldots$, $x_1/x_n = \alpha_{n-1}$. The unknowns x_i are known as *eigenvector components*.

When n is small ($n = 2$ or 3), the expansion of the determinant by minors to obtain the polynomial in λ is not difficult, nor is the subsequent determination of the roots of the polynomial. However, when n becomes larger, the determination of the coefficients of the polynomial becomes more difficult, and a procedure more practical than an expansion by minors must be employed. (Such a procedure will be discussed in Sec. 3-10.) These higher degree polynomials may be solved by one of the methods discussed in Chap. 2 (preferably Bairstow's method).

EXAMPLE 3-6

To make the preceding discussion a little more specific, let us consider a simple set of just two equations,

$$(a_{11} - \lambda)x_1 + a_{12}x_2 = 0 \tag{3-90}$$
$$a_{21}x_1 + (a_{22} - \lambda)x_2 = 0$$

which may be written in matrix notation as

$$\begin{bmatrix} (a_{11} - \lambda) & a_{12} \\ a_{21} & (a_{22} - \lambda) \end{bmatrix} \begin{Bmatrix} x_1 \\ x_2 \end{Bmatrix} = 0 \tag{3-91}$$

Using Cramer's rule to solve for x_1 and x_2, we obtain

$$x_1 = \cfrac{0}{\begin{vmatrix} (a_{11} - \lambda) & a_{12} \\ a_{21} & (a_{22} - \lambda) \end{vmatrix}} \quad \text{and} \quad x_2 = \cfrac{0}{\begin{vmatrix} (a_{11} - \lambda) & a_{12} \\ a_{21} & (a_{22} - \lambda) \end{vmatrix}} \tag{3-92}$$

Looking at Eq. 3-92 it is obvious that if the determinant of the coefficient matrix appearing in the denominator of each equation is nonzero, only a trivial solution will be obtained. However, if $|D| = 0$,

$$x_1 = \frac{0}{0} \quad \text{and} \quad x_2 = \frac{0}{0} \tag{3-93}$$

which shows that nontrivial solutions *may* exist. We know from the previous discussion that when $|D| = 0$, nontrivial solutions *do* exist.

Expanding the determinant yields the characteristic equation

$$\lambda^2 - (a_{11} + a_{22})\lambda + (a_{11}a_{22} - a_{21}a_{12}) = 0 \tag{3-94}$$

which is a second-degree polynomial in this simple example. The roots λ_1 and λ_2 (the eigenvalues) of Eq. 3-94 are the two values of λ which will make the determinant of the coefficient matrix of Eq. 3-91 equal to zero, thus yielding a nontrivial solution.

After obtaining λ_1 and λ_2, their substitution into either Eq. 3-90 or Eq. 3-91 yields two relationships between the unknowns x_1 and x_2. For example, using λ_1 in Eq. 3-90, we obtain

$$x_1 = \frac{-a_{12}x_2}{(a_{11} - \lambda_1)} = \frac{-(a_{22} - \lambda_1)x_2}{a_{21}} \tag{3-95}$$

Similarly, using λ_2 in Eq. 3-90 yields another relationship

$$x_1 = \frac{-a_{12}x_2}{(a_{11} - \lambda_2)} = \frac{-(a_{22} - \lambda_2)x_2}{a_{21}} \tag{3-96}$$

It is apparent, from an inspection of Eqs. 3-95 and 3-96, that unique values of x_1 and x_2 cannot be determined. However, any *combination* of values of x_1 and x_2 constitutes a solution of Eq. 3-90, as long as the combination satisfies Eq. 3-95 when λ_1 is used, or Eq. 3-96 when λ_2 is used.

EXAMPLE 3-7

To illustrate the solution of a physically significant characteristic-value problem, let us determine the principal stresses at a point in a body in a state of plane stress.

Figure 3-7(a) shows an infinitesimal element of material subjected to the normal stresses σ_x and σ_y and the shear stress τ_{xy}. Since all stresses in the z direction are zero, the element is in a state of plane stress. In deriving the

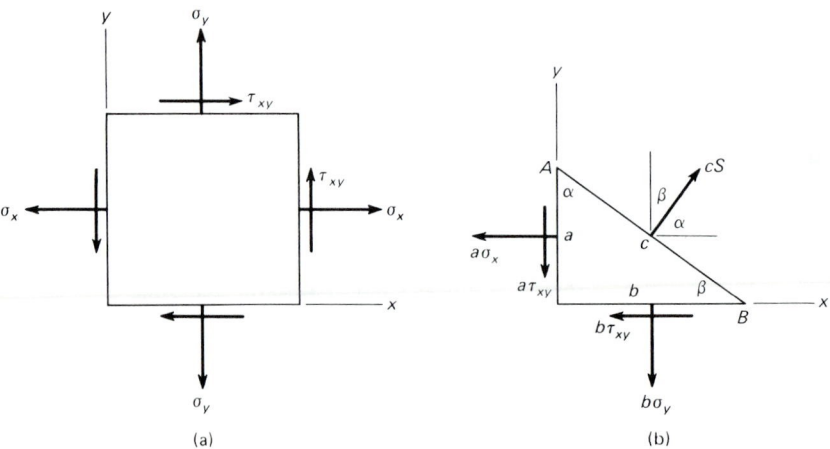

Figure 3-7 Element of material in a state of plane stress

equilibrium equations, we consider a wedge-shaped portion of the element formed by cutting the element with an inclined plane at some angle α to the yz plane. This plane AB is arbitrarily designated as a principal plane upon which one of the principal normal stresses acts. We know, from mechanics-of-materials theory, that the shear stress is zero on a principal plane. Therefore, the only stress shown acting on plane AB is the principal normal stress, which will be designated by S. Considering the element to have a depth of unity, with sides of lengths a, b, and c, as shown, the corresponding areas of the sides upon which the stresses act are of magnitudes a, b, and c. The forces shown in Fig. 3-7(b) which maintain the wedge-shaped element in equilibrium are obtained by multiplying the stresses acting on these areas by the respective areas of the element.

Since the element is in equilibrium,

$$\sum F_x = 0 = cS \cos \alpha - a\sigma_x - b\tau_{xy}$$

from which

$$\frac{a}{c} \sigma_x - S \cos \alpha + \frac{b}{c} \tau_{xy} = 0 \tag{3-97}$$

Also,

$$\sum F_y = 0 = cS \cos \beta - a\tau_{xy} - b\sigma_y$$

from which

$$\frac{a}{c} \tau_{xy} - S \cos \beta + \frac{b}{c} \sigma_y = 0 \tag{3-98}$$

Denoting the direction cosines l and m of the normal to the principal plane as

$$l = \cos \alpha = \frac{a}{c}$$

$$m = \cos \beta = \frac{b}{c}$$

Eqs. 3-97 and 3-98 may be written as

$$(\sigma_x - S)l + \tau_{xy}m = 0$$
$$\tau_{xy}l + (\sigma_y - S)m = 0 \tag{3-99}$$

or, in matrix notation, as

$$\begin{bmatrix} (\sigma_x - S) & \tau_{xy} \\ \tau_{xy} & (\sigma_y - S) \end{bmatrix} \begin{Bmatrix} l \\ m \end{Bmatrix} = 0 \tag{3-100}$$

Comparing Eq. 3-100 with Eq. 3-87, we see that the normal and shear stresses correspond to the coefficients a_{ij}, the direction cosines correspond to the unknowns x_i, and the principal stresses S are λ's, or the eigenvalues, necessary to satisfy the equilibrium equations of Eq. 3-99.

Remembering that the determinant of the coefficient matrix of Eq. 3-100 must equal zero to obtain a nontrivial solution,

$$|D| = \begin{vmatrix} (\sigma_x - S) & \tau_{xy} \\ \tau_{xy} & (\sigma_y - S) \end{vmatrix} = 0 \tag{3-101}$$

Expanding the determinant yields

$$S^2 - (\sigma_x + \sigma_y)S + \sigma_x\sigma_y - \tau_{xy}^2 = 0 \tag{3-102}$$

Using the quadratic formula, the roots or eigenvalues of Eq. 3-102 are found to be

$$S_{1,2} = \frac{\sigma_x + \sigma_y}{2} \pm \sqrt{\left(\frac{\sigma_x - \sigma_y}{2}\right)^2 + \tau_{xy}^2} \tag{3-103}$$

Equation 3-103 is the familiar equation, found in mechanics of materials, relating the principal stresses to the stresses acting on any two orthogonal planes.

Suppose that the orthogonal stresses at the point are given by

$$\sigma_x = 1000 \text{ psi}$$

$$\sigma_y = 500 \text{ psi}$$

$$\tau_{xy} = 500 \text{ psi}$$

From Eq. 3-103 we can compute the principal stresses as

$$S_1 = 1310 \text{ psi}$$
$$S_2 = 190 \text{ psi}$$

Then the relationships between the direction cosines l and m may be determined by substituting the principal-stress values into Eq. 3-100. Using the value of S_2

$$\begin{bmatrix} (1000 - 190) & 500 \\ 500 & (500 - 190) \end{bmatrix} \begin{Bmatrix} l \\ m \end{Bmatrix} = 0 \tag{3-104}$$

which yields the relationship

$$\frac{m}{l} = \frac{\cos \beta}{\cos \alpha} = -\frac{810}{500} \tag{3-105}$$

The direction-cosine relationships for the principal stress S_1 are determined similarly, where

$$\begin{bmatrix} (1000 - 1310) & 500 \\ 500 & (500 - 1310) \end{bmatrix} \begin{Bmatrix} l \\ m \end{Bmatrix} = 0 \tag{3-106}$$

which yields

$$\frac{m}{l} = \frac{\cos \beta}{\cos \alpha} = \frac{310}{500} \tag{3-107}$$

In this particular example unique values may be determined for l and m, since an additional relationship exists in that the angles α and β are complementary angles. Thus, since $\sin \alpha = \cos \beta$,

$$\tan \alpha = -\frac{810}{500} \quad \text{(for } S_2\text{)}$$

$$\alpha = -58.3 \text{ deg}$$

$$\tan \alpha = \frac{310}{500} \quad \text{(for } S_1\text{)}$$

$$\alpha = 31.7 \text{ deg}$$

These angles locate the principal planes (the planes upon which the respective principal stresses act) with α measured positive counterclockwise from the y axis and negative clockwise (see Fig. 3-7(b)).

It should be emphasized that the unique values which could be obtained for l and m resulted from the availability of the *additional* relationship between the angles α and β. In general, in characteristic-value problems, such additional relationships will not be available, and only ratios of the components of the eigenvector will be obtainable, as discussed before.

EXAMPLE 3-8

As another example of a characteristic-value problem, let us analyze the free undamped vibrational characteristics of the three-degrees-of-freedom system shown schematically in Fig. 3-8. The system consists of the three masses m_1, m_2, and m_3, connected by the three springs shown, with spring constants k_1, k_2, and k_3. The displacements of the masses are defined by the generalized coordinates x_1, x_2, and x_3, respectively, each displacement being measured from the static-equilibrium position of the respective mass.

Utilizing either Lagrange's equation (see Prob. 3-46) or Newton's second law, the differential equations of motion of the system are found to be

$$m_1\ddot{x}_1 + (k_1 + k_2)x_1 - k_2x_2 = 0$$
$$m_2\ddot{x}_2 - k_2x_1 + (k_2 + k_3)x_2 - k_3x_3 = 0 \tag{3-108}$$
$$m_3\ddot{x}_3 - k_3x_2 + k_3x_3 = 0$$

It is well known, from vibration theory, that the solution of Eq. 3-108 may be taken in the form

$$x_1 = X_1 \sin pt$$
$$x_2 = X_2 \sin pt \tag{3-109}$$
$$x_3 = X_3 \sin pt$$

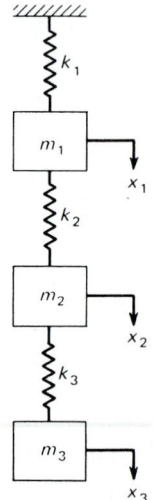

$m_1 = m_2 = m_3 = 14.59$ kg (kilograms)
$k_1 = k_2 = k_3 = 145.9$ N/m (newtons/meter)

Figure 3-8   Three-degrees-of-freedom system

where X_1, X_2, and X_3 are the *amplitudes* of motion of the respective masses, and p denotes the natural circular frequencies corresponding to the principal modes of vibration of the system.

Substituting Eq. 3-109 and appropriate derivatives of these expressions into Eq. 3-108, and using the spring-constant and mass values shown in Fig. 3-8, we obtain the following set of homogeneous algebraic equations:

$$\begin{aligned}
(20 - p^2)X_1 \quad - 10X_2 \quad\quad\quad &= 0 \\
- 10X_1 + (20 - p^2)X_2 \quad - 10X_3 &= 0 \\
- 10X_2 + (10 - p^2)X_3 &= 0
\end{aligned} \tag{3-110}$$

To obtain a nontrivial solution of Eq. 3-110, we know that the determinant of the coefficients of X_i must be equal to zero, so that

$$|D| = \begin{vmatrix} (20 - p^2) & -10 & 0 \\ -10 & (20 - p^2) & -10 \\ 0 & -10 & (10 - p^2) \end{vmatrix} = 0 \tag{3-111}$$

Expansion of this determinant results in the characteristic polynomial

$$p^6 - 50p^4 + 600p^2 - 1000 = 0 \tag{3-112}$$

which may be written as a cubic equation in p^2 as

$$(p^2)^3 - 50(p^2)^2 + 600(p^2) - 1000 = 0 \tag{3-113}$$

The roots of Eq. 3-113 are found to be

$$p_1^2 = 1.98 \text{ s}^{-2}$$
$$p_2^2 = 15.5 \text{ s}^{-2}$$
$$p_3^2 = 32.5 \text{ s}^{-2}$$

These eigenvalues are the squares of the natural circular frequencies of the first, second, and third modes of vibration of the system, respectively.

Since Eq. 3-110 constitutes a homogeneous set of simultaneous equations, a unique set of values cannot be obtained for X_1, X_2, and X_3. However, various ratios of the amplitudes may be determined which will yield the configuration of the system for the various modes when the amplitude of any one of the masses is defined. For example, substituting $p_1^2 = 1.98$ into Eq. 3-110 yields the following configuration for the *first* mode:

$$\left.\begin{array}{l} X_2 = 1.80X_1 \\ X_3 = 2.24X_1 \end{array}\right\} \quad \text{first mode} \qquad (3\text{-}114)$$

Similarly, the second- and third-mode configurations, using $p_2^2 = 15.5$ and $p_3^2 = 32.5$, respectively, are

$$\left.\begin{array}{l} X_2 = 0.45X_1 \\ X_3 = -0.82X_1 \end{array}\right\} \quad \text{second mode} \qquad (3\text{-}115)$$

$$\left.\begin{array}{l} X_2 = -1.25X_1 \\ X_3 = 0.555X_1 \end{array}\right\} \quad \text{third mode} \qquad (3\text{-}116)$$

From the last three equations it can be seen that if the amplitude of any one of the three masses is known or assumed for a particular mode of vibration, the configuration of the system may be determined for that mode. Since Eqs. 3-114 through 3-116 consist of ratios of amplitudes X_i, the substitution of Eq. 3-109 into these equations reveals that the ratios shown are also the ratios of the *displacements*. For example, when m_1 has a displacement of 0.01 m and the system is vibrating in the second mode, the corresponding displacements of m_2 and m_3 will be 0.0045 m and -0.0082 m, respectively, and the motion of m_3 will be 180 deg out of phase with that of m_1. It might be added here that the configuration of a system, as given by the above ratios, also defines the *initial* displacements which would have to be given to the masses to have the system vibrate in the mode associated with that configuration, with no other harmonics present, when the system is released from rest.

3-9 METHODS FOR SOLUTION OF EIGENVALUE PROBLEMS—GENERAL

Through the years, various methods and techniques for the solution of eigenvalue problems have evolved because of their importance in engineering, science, and mathematics. The characteristic polynomial method was used in the previous section to develop an "insight" into the nature of the eigenvalue problem. We shall discuss some of the more widely used methods, which include the polynomial method (Sec. 3-10), the iteration (or power) method (Sec. 3-11), Hotelling's deflation method in conjunction with the iteration method (Sec. 3-12), and Jacobi's method (Sec. 3-13).

In general, the most suitable method to use for the solution of eigenvalue problems depends to some extent upon the size of the matrix, whether only the eigenvalues are to be determined, or whether both eigenvalues and corresponding eigenvectors are to be determined.

The polynomial method discussed briefly in Sec. 3-8 will be discussed in the next section in more detail relative to computer computation. The use of the computer to obtain the characteristic polynomial and corresponding roots (eigenvalues) of moderately sized matrices ($n \leq 10$) is fairly straightforward. However, its use to determine *both* eigenvalues and corresponding eigenvectors of matrices by the polynomial method is somewhat cumbersome. Therefore, the discussion of the polynomial method will be limited to the use of the *Faddeev-Leverrier method* for generating the coefficients of the characteristic equation.

We shall present Sec. 3-11 in some detail. It presents an iteration, or power, method which is frequently used when only the *smallest* and/or *largest* eigenvalue(s) of a matrix are desired. An advantage of the iteration method over most other methods is that the eigenvalue(s) and corresponding eigenvector(s) are obtained simultaneously in the iteration process. Furthermore, the iteration method may be easily carried out using today's pocket calculator in the solution of eigenvalue problems involving small matrices of order $n \leq 5$. In Sec. 3-12, we shall present Hotelling's deflation method for "sweeping" out previously determined eigenvalues and corresponding eigenvectors so that intermediate eigenvalues and eigenvectors can be determined by the iteration method. The iteration method used in conjunction with Hotelling's deflation method may be used for finding *all* the eigenvalues and eigenvectors for matrices up to approximately order 10, but it is particularly well suited for problems involving matrices much larger than order 10 in which only a relatively small number of eigenvalues and eigenvectors are required. In the solution of problems which involve matrices of order greater than approximately 10 by this method, a loss of accuracy in the higher eigenvalues begins to show up due to roundoff errors. For example, for a matrix of order 20, perhaps the first 14 eigenvalues and eigenvectors would be sufficiently accurate to be usable, but the higher ones would not be.

Jacobi's method, Sec. 3-13, is perhaps one of the most reliable methods, but it is not very efficient in comparison to some of the other methods for matrices of order larger than approximately 20. One advantage of the Jacobi method is that it obtains all eigenvalues and eigenvectors simultaneously and with excellent and uniform accuracy.

Today it is generally recognized that one of the most efficient and accurate methods for obtaining all of the eigenvalues and eigenvectors of large matrices (20 to several hundred) is Householder's method in conjunction with an algorithm called QL. Householder's method is based upon an orthogonal transformation which produces a large number of zeros in a given row to yield a *tridiagonalized* matrix. Various techniques, including the QL algorithm, are then used to determine the eigenvalues from the tridiagonalized matrix. A detailed discussion of Householder's method is beyond the scope of this text, and the reader is referred to a discussion of the Householder method by Ortega.[11]

3-10 POLYNOMIAL METHOD—EIGENVALUE PROBLEMS

In the examples presented in Sec. 3-8, the determination of the eigenvalues involved two major steps: (1) obtaining the characteristic polynomial by expanding the determinant of the coefficient matrix $(\mathbf{A} - \lambda\mathbf{I})$ and (2) solving for the roots of the polynomial. Both steps employed familiar elementary methods, since we were concerned with matrices of low order. When the order of the matrices becomes larger, computer methods should be used to accomplish each of these steps efficiently.

As we shall see, it is relatively easy to obtain the polynomial (the characteristic equation) and corresponding roots of moderately sized matrices on the computer. However, the determination of the corresponding eigenvectors is rather cumbersome. Therefore, if both the eigenvalues and the corresponding eigenvectors are required in problems involving matrices of order greater than 2, it is recommended that an iterative method (Secs. 3-11 and 3-12) or Jacobi's method (Sec. 3-13) be used instead of the polynomial method.

Because of the difficulty in determining the eigenvectors by the polynomial method, our discussion of it will be limited to the generation of the characteristic equation (the polynomial). The roots (the eigenvalues) could then be determined using Bairstow's method, for example.

Computer Determination of Characteristic Polynomials

As mentioned in the preceding paragraph, our discussion here will be concerned only with a computer method for determining the characteristic equation.[12]

Many methods have been proposed for generating the coefficients p_k of the characteristic equation

$$\lambda^n + p_1\lambda^{n-1} + p_2\lambda^{n-2} + p_3\lambda^{n-3} + \cdots + p_n = 0 \qquad (k = 1, 2, \ldots, n)$$

$$(3\text{-}117)$$

---

[11]James Ortega, *Mathematical Methods for Digital Computers*, Vol. II, ed. A. Ralston and H. S. Wilf (New York: John Wiley & Sons, 1967), pp. 94–115.

[12]In Ex. 7-3 (Chap. 7) a characteristic-value problem arising from the finite-difference form of a differential equation is solved, in which Bairstow's method is used to find the roots of the characteristic polynomial.

when the order n of the set of algebraic equations is large. Of these methods, we will discuss the *Faddeev-Leverrier method*, an efficient technique which is equally suitable for generating the polynomial coefficients whether the coefficient matrix of the equations is symmetrical or unsymmetrical. This method has an additional feature in that the *inverse* of the matrix for which the eigenvalues are desired is, essentially, obtained in the process of generating the coefficients of the characteristic polynomial. This is advantageous in instances where one may wish to check the accuracy of the eigenvalues obtained by the polynomial method, by using an iterative method, since an inversion of the matrix may be desired in an iterative procedure (see Sec. 3-11). Proof of the validity of the Faddeev-Leverrier method is beyond the intended scope of this text, but it may be found elsewhere.[13] (This reference also includes numerous other methods and their derivations.)

Before outlining the method we have chosen, let us define the *trace* of a matrix, since it is an integral part of the method. Given the matrix

$$\begin{bmatrix} a_{11} & a_{12} & a_{13} & \cdots & a_{1n} \\ a_{21} & a_{22} & a_{23} & \cdots & a_{2n} \\ a_{31} & a_{32} & a_{33} & \cdots & a_{3n} \\ \vdots & \vdots & & & \vdots \\ a_{n1} & a_{n2} & \cdots & \cdots & a_{nn} \end{bmatrix} \qquad (3\text{-}118)$$

the trace of the matrix, written as "tr $\mathbf{A}$," is

$$\text{tr } \mathbf{A} = a_{11} + a_{22} + a_{33} + \cdots + a_{nn} \qquad (3\text{-}119)$$

The Faddeev-Leverrier method generates the polynomial coefficients $p_k(k = 1, 2, 3, \ldots, n)$ from the matrix $\mathbf{A}$ of the given set of equations written as

$$(\mathbf{A} - \lambda \mathbf{I})\mathbf{X} = 0 \qquad (3\text{-}120)$$

[13]See D. K. Faddeev and U. N. Faddeeva, *Computational Methods of Linear Algebra*, trans. Robert C. Williams (San Francisco: W. H. Freeman & Co., 1963). For other methods see Leon Lapidus, *Digital Computation for Chemical Engineers* (New York: McGraw-Hill Book Company, 1962).

by forming a *sequence* of matrices $\mathbf{B}_1$, $\mathbf{B}_2$, ..., $\mathbf{B}_n$ from which the p_k values are determined. These p_k values are then substituted in the following basic form of the characteristic polynomial:

$$(-1)^n(\lambda^n - p_1\lambda^{n-1} - p_2\lambda^{n-2} - p_3\lambda^{n-3} - \cdots - p_n) = 0 \tag{3-121}$$

where the $(-1)^n$ is used merely to give the terms of the polynomial the same signs that they would have if the polynomial were generated by expanding a determinant. The p_k values are determined as follows:

$$\mathbf{B}_1 = \mathbf{A} \qquad \text{and} \qquad p_1 = \text{tr } \mathbf{B}_1$$

$$\mathbf{B}_2 = \mathbf{A}(\mathbf{B}_1 - p_1\mathbf{I}) \qquad \text{and} \qquad p_2 = \frac{1}{2}\text{tr } \mathbf{B}_2$$

$$\mathbf{B}_3 = \mathbf{A}(\mathbf{B}_2 - p_2\mathbf{I}) \qquad \text{and} \qquad p_3 = \frac{1}{3}\text{tr } \mathbf{B}_3$$

$$\vdots \qquad\qquad\qquad \vdots \tag{3-122}$$

$$\mathbf{B}_k = \mathbf{A}(\mathbf{B}_{k-1} - p_{k-1}\mathbf{I}) \qquad \text{and} \qquad p_k = \frac{1}{k}\text{tr } \mathbf{B}_k$$

$$\vdots \qquad\qquad\qquad \vdots$$

$$\mathbf{B}_n = \mathbf{A}(\mathbf{B}_{n-1} - p_{n-1}\mathbf{I}) \qquad \text{and} \qquad p_n = \frac{1}{n}\text{tr } \mathbf{B}_n$$

Referring to the generation of the inverse of the matrix for which the eigenvalues are desired, mentioned earlier, Faddeev has shown that the inverse of $\mathbf{A}$ can be determined from

$$\mathbf{A}^{-1} = \frac{1}{p_n}(\mathbf{B}_{n-1} - p_{n-1}\mathbf{I}) \tag{3-123}$$

EXAMPLE 3-9

Let us suppose that the homogeneous set of algebraic equations

$$
\begin{aligned}
(3 - \lambda)x_1 + \qquad 2x_2 + \qquad 4x_3 &= 0 \\
2x_1 + (0 - \lambda)x_2 + \qquad 2x_3 &= 0 \\
4x_1 + \qquad 2x_2 + (3 - \lambda)x_3 &= 0
\end{aligned}
\tag{3-124}
$$

has been obtained as the mathematical model of some physical system which we are analyzing. In matrix notation, Eq. 3-124 appears as

$$\begin{bmatrix} (3-\lambda) & 2 & 4 \\ 2 & (0-\lambda) & 2 \\ 4 & 2 & (3-\lambda) \end{bmatrix} \begin{Bmatrix} x_1 \\ x_2 \\ x_3 \end{Bmatrix} = 0 \tag{3-125}$$

Our problem will be to find the characteristic polynomial, using the Faddeev-Leverrier method, and then to solve the resulting polynomial for its roots which are the eigenvalues of the matrix

$$\mathbf{A} = \begin{bmatrix} 3 & 2 & 4 \\ 2 & 0 & 2 \\ 4 & 2 & 3 \end{bmatrix}$$

of the equation

$$(\mathbf{A} - \lambda\mathbf{I})\mathbf{X} = 0 \tag{3-126}$$

Using the procedure indicated in Eq. 3-122,

$$\mathbf{B}_1 = \mathbf{A} = \begin{bmatrix} 3 & 2 & 4 \\ 2 & 0 & 2 \\ 4 & 2 & 3 \end{bmatrix}$$

and

$$p_1 = \text{tr } \mathbf{B}_1 = 3 + 0 + 3 = 6$$

$$\mathbf{B}_2 = \mathbf{A}(\mathbf{B}_1 - p_1\mathbf{I}) = \begin{bmatrix} 3 & 2 & 4 \\ 2 & 0 & 2 \\ 4 & 2 & 3 \end{bmatrix} \left(\begin{bmatrix} 3 & 2 & 4 \\ 2 & 0 & 2 \\ 4 & 2 & 3 \end{bmatrix} - \begin{bmatrix} 6 & 0 & 0 \\ 0 & 6 & 0 \\ 0 & 0 & 6 \end{bmatrix} \right)$$

$$= \begin{bmatrix} 3 & 2 & 4 \\ 2 & 0 & 2 \\ 4 & 2 & 3 \end{bmatrix} \begin{bmatrix} -3 & 2 & 4 \\ 2 & -6 & 2 \\ 4 & 2 & -3 \end{bmatrix}$$

$$= \begin{bmatrix} 11 & 2 & 4 \\ 2 & 8 & 2 \\ 4 & 2 & 11 \end{bmatrix}$$

and

$$p_2 = \tfrac{1}{2} \operatorname{tr} \mathbf{B}_2 = \tfrac{1}{2}(11 + 8 + 11) = 15$$

$$\mathbf{B}_3 = \mathbf{A}(\mathbf{B}_2 - p_2\mathbf{I}) = \begin{bmatrix} 3 & 2 & 4 \\ 2 & 0 & 2 \\ 4 & 2 & 3 \end{bmatrix} \left(\begin{bmatrix} 11 & 2 & 4 \\ 2 & 8 & 2 \\ 4 & 2 & 11 \end{bmatrix} - \begin{bmatrix} 15 & 0 & 0 \\ 0 & 15 & 0 \\ 0 & 0 & 15 \end{bmatrix} \right)$$

$$\begin{bmatrix} 3 & 2 & 4 \\ 2 & 0 & 2 \\ 4 & 2 & 3 \end{bmatrix} \begin{bmatrix} -4 & 2 & 4 \\ 2 & -7 & 2 \\ 4 & 2 & -4 \end{bmatrix} = \begin{bmatrix} 8 & 0 & 0 \\ 0 & 8 & 0 \\ 0 & 0 & 8 \end{bmatrix}$$

and

$$p_3 = \tfrac{1}{3} \operatorname{tr} \mathbf{B}_3 = \tfrac{1}{3}(8 + 8 + 8) = 8$$

Substituting the values of p_1, p_2, and p_3 into Eq. 3-121, we obtain

$$(-1)^3(\lambda^3 - 6\lambda^2 - 15\lambda - 8) = 0 \tag{3-127}$$

The roots of Eq. 3-127 are simply obtained, since the polynomial may be factored as

$$(\lambda - 8)(\lambda + 1)(\lambda + 1) = 0 \tag{3-128}$$

from which the eigenvalues are

$$\begin{aligned} \lambda_1 &= 8 \\ \lambda_2 &= -1 \\ \lambda_3 &= -1 \end{aligned} \tag{3-129}$$

Reviewing the determination of the coefficient p_3 in the procedure just finished, we observe that

$$\mathbf{B}_3 = p_3\mathbf{I} \tag{3-130}$$

Faddeev has proved that for an nth-order matrix

$$\mathbf{B}_n = p_n\mathbf{I} \tag{3-131}$$

from which we see that we can always obtain p_n simply as

$$p_n = b_{11} = b_{22} = b_{33} = \cdots = b_{nn} \tag{3-132}$$

where the b_{ii} are *identical* elements composing the trace of $\mathbf{B}_n$.

At this point the interested reader might expand the determinant of the coefficient matrix of Eq. 3-125,

$$|D| = \begin{vmatrix} (3-\lambda) & 2 & 4 \\ 2 & (0-\lambda) & 2 \\ 4 & 2 & (3-\lambda) \end{vmatrix} = 0$$

by minors and check the polynomial obtained in Eq. 3-127.

The generation of the coefficients of the characteristic polynomial, by the Faddeev-Leverrier method, on the computer is outlined in the flow chart of Fig. 3-9. The variable names and the quantities they represent in the FORTRAN source program are as follows:

FORTRAN Name	Quantity
N	Order of the **A** matrix for which the characteristic polynomial is to be determined
A(I,J)	Elements of the **A** matrix
B(I,J)	Elements of the $\mathbf{B}_k$ matrices formed by the Faddeev-Leverrier method; also used for elements of $(\mathbf{B}_k - p_k\mathbf{I})$
I	Row numbers of **A** and $\mathbf{B}_k$ matrices
J	Column numbers of **A** and $\mathbf{B}_k$ matrices
M	$N - 1$
TRACE	Traces of $\mathbf{B}_k$ matrices
P(K)	Coefficients of characteristic polynomial
K	Subscript of P(K) used as index of a DO loop
AK	Real name for the integer subscript K of P(K)
COLB(I)	Elements of the columns of the $(\mathbf{B}_{k-1} - p_{k-1}\mathbf{I})$ matrices

The source program, written to implement the flow chart of Fig. 3-9, is as follows:

```
      DIMENSION A(15,15),B(15,15),P(15),COLB(15)
      READ(5,1) N
    1 FORMAT(I3)
      READ(5,2) ((A(I,J),J=1,N),I=1,N)
    2 FORMAT(8F10.0)
      DO 3 I=1,N
      DO 3 J=1,N
    3 B(I,J)=A(I,J)
      M=N-1
      DO 10 K=1,M
      TRACE=0.
      DO 7 I=1,N
```

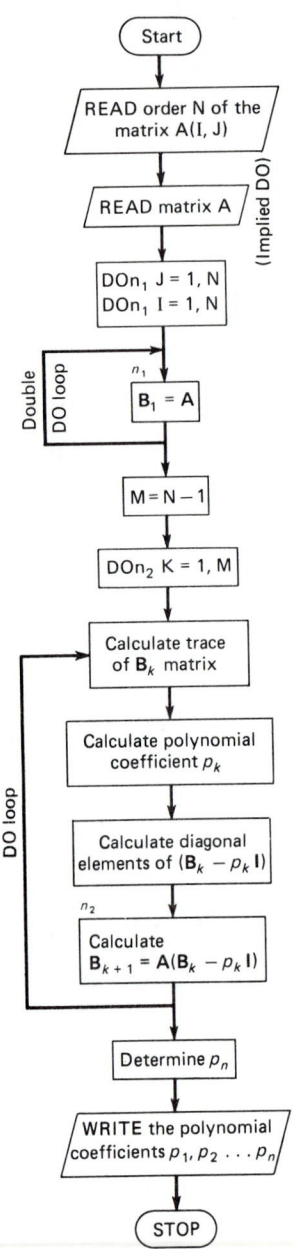

Figure 3-9 Flow chart for generating coefficients of a characteristic polynomial

```
  7 TRACE=TRACE+B(I,I)
    AK=K
    P(K)=TRACE/AK
    DO 8 I=1,N
  8 B(I,I)=B(I,I)-P(K)
    DO 10 J=1,N
    DO 9 I=1,N
  9 COLB(I)=B(I,J)
    DO 10 I=1,N
    B(I,J)=0.
    DO 10 L=1,N
 10 B(I,J)=B(I,J)+A(I,L)*COLB(L)
    P(N)=B(1,1)
    WRITE(6,4)
  4 FORMAT('1','THE CHARACTERISTIC POLYNOMIAL COEFFICIENTS')
    WRITE(6,5)
  5 FORMAT(' ',10X,'P(1) THROUGH P(N)'/)
    WRITE(6,6) (P(K),K=1,N)
  6 FORMAT(' ',14X,E14.7)
    STOP
    END
```

3-11 ITERATION METHOD—EIGENVALUE PROBLEMS

In addition to the polynomial method discussed in the preceding section, there are various iterative methods to determine eigenvalues. Of these, the one most commonly used in engineering problems is the *power method.*

An iterative method is used most frequently when only the *smallest* and/or *largest* eigenvalue(s) of a matrix are desired, but may also be used when intermediate eigenvalues and eigenvectors are to be found. For finding the intermediate eigenvalues and eigenvectors, a sweeping technique discussed in Sec. 3-12 may be used. An advantage of the iterative method is that the eigenvectors are obtained simultaneously with the associated eigenvalues rather than requiring separate operations, as in the polynomial method.

To illustrate the power method, let us first use it to determine the largest eigenvalue of a matrix. We will assume that both the elements of the matrix and its eigenvalues are real, although the use of iterative methods is not thus restricted.

Suppose that, in the analysis of a physical system, we have obtained from a mathematical model of the system the following set of simultaneous homogeneous linear algebraic equations:

$$
\begin{aligned}
(a_{11} - \lambda)x_1 + &\quad a_{12}x_2 + a_{13}x_3 + \cdots + &a_{1n}x_n = 0 \\
a_{21}x_1 + &(a_{22} - \lambda)x_2 + a_{23}x_3 + \cdots + &a_{2n}x_n = 0 \\
\vdots \qquad &\qquad \vdots \qquad\qquad &\vdots \\
a_{n1}x_1 + &\quad a_{n2}x_2 + a_{n3}x_3 + \cdots + &(a_{nn} - \lambda)x_n = 0
\end{aligned}
\tag{3-133}
$$

which may be expressed more compactly, in matrix notation, as

$$(A - \lambda I)X = 0 \qquad (3\text{-}134)$$

To find the largest eigenvalue λ_1, we rewrite Eq. 3-134 in the form

$$AX = \lambda X \qquad (3\text{-}135)$$

and carry out the following steps:

1. Arbitrarily assume values for the components of the eigenvector $X = (x_1, x_2, \ldots, x_n)$. This assumed vector will subsequently be referred to as X_0. Choosing all components of X_0 equal to unity is generally satisfactory. Upon substituting the components of X_0 into the left side of Eq. 3-135 as the elements of the matrix X and carrying out the matrix multiplication, a first approximation to the right side of Eq. 3-135 is obtained, where

$$\lambda X = \begin{Bmatrix} \lambda x_1 \\ \lambda x_2 \\ \lambda x_3 \\ \vdots \\ \lambda x_n \end{Bmatrix} \qquad (3\text{-}136)$$

2. Normalize the vector λX obtained in step 1. This is done by dividing the vector by the magnitude of its first component, by its largest component, or by normalizing the vector X to a unit length. In this case, let us normalize by dividing the vector by the magnitude of the first component, reducing that component to unity.
3. Use the components of the normalized vector as improved values of x_i to be substituted into the left side of Eq. 3-135. Carrying out the matrix multiplication, another approximation of the right-hand side of Eq. 3-135 is obtained.
4. Repeat steps 2 and 3 until Eq. 3-135 is essentially satisfied; that is, until the eigenvector components in step 2 vary from the previously obtained values by less than some small preassigned ε value, in two successive iterations. The normalizing factor will be the *largest eigenvalue* λ_1, and the elements of X will be the components of the eigenvector associated with it.[14]

---

[14]See Appendix B-6 for proof of convergence to the largest eigenvalue and associated eigenvector.

In carrying out the iteration procedure we are, in effect, forming a sequence of vectors AX_0, A^2X_0, A^3X_0, . . . , A^kX_0, where X_0 is the arbitrary vector initially assumed. (The name "power method" comes from the fact that the sequence is made up of powers of the matrix A.)

To illustrate the steps just outlined, let us consider the equations

$$(2 - \lambda)x_1 + 4x_2 = 0$$
$$3x_1 + (13 - \lambda)x_2 = 0$$

(3-137)

and determine the value of λ_1, the *largest eigenvalue*. Putting Eq. 3-137 in the form of Eq. 3-135, we have

$$\begin{bmatrix} 2 & 4 \\ 3 & 13 \end{bmatrix} \begin{Bmatrix} x_1 \\ x_2 \end{Bmatrix} = \lambda \begin{Bmatrix} x_1 \\ x_2 \end{Bmatrix}$$

Carrying out steps 1 and 2, we obtain

$$\begin{bmatrix} 2 & 4 \\ 3 & 13 \end{bmatrix} \begin{Bmatrix} 1 \\ 1 \end{Bmatrix} = \begin{Bmatrix} 6 \\ 16 \end{Bmatrix} = 6 \begin{Bmatrix} 1 \\ \frac{16}{6} \end{Bmatrix}$$

Applying step 3 gives

$$\begin{bmatrix} 2 & 4 \\ 3 & 13 \end{bmatrix} \begin{Bmatrix} 1 \\ \frac{16}{6} \end{Bmatrix} = \begin{Bmatrix} \frac{38}{3} \\ \frac{113}{3} \end{Bmatrix} = \frac{38}{3} \begin{Bmatrix} 1 \\ \frac{113}{38} \end{Bmatrix}$$

The next iteration yields

$$\begin{bmatrix} 2 & 4 \\ 3 & 13 \end{bmatrix} \begin{Bmatrix} 1 \\ \frac{113}{38} \end{Bmatrix} = \begin{Bmatrix} \frac{264}{19} \\ \frac{1538}{38} \end{Bmatrix} = 13.9 \begin{Bmatrix} 1 \\ 2.998 \end{Bmatrix}$$

Comparing the normalizing factors of the *second* and *third* iterations ($\frac{38}{3}$ and 13.9), it is apparent that the third iteration results in only a minor change of the normalizing factor obtained in the second iteration. Thus, a good approximation to λ_1 is $\lambda_1 = 13.9$. The eigenvector associated with λ_1 is $X = (1, 2.998)$. A fourth iteration would, of course, yield a still better approximation to λ_1 and the corresponding components of the eigenvector. Application of the polynomial method readily reveals that the exact values are $\lambda_1 = 14$ and $X = (1, 3)$.

In many physical problems the *smallest* eigenvalue turns out to be the one of primary importance. To arrange the matrix equation in a form in which the iteration converges to the smallest eigenvalue, we first premultiply Eq. 3-135 by the inverse matrix $\mathbf{A}^{-1}$, obtaining

$$\mathbf{A}^{-1}\mathbf{A}\mathbf{X} = \mathbf{A}^{-1}\lambda\mathbf{X} = \lambda\mathbf{A}^{-1}\mathbf{X}$$

or

$$\mathbf{X} = \lambda\mathbf{A}^{-1}\mathbf{X} \tag{3-138}$$

Dividing Eq. 3-138 by λ gives

$$\mathbf{A}^{-1}\mathbf{X} = \frac{1}{\lambda}\mathbf{X} \tag{3-139}$$

Equation 3-139 is in a form which will result in convergence to the largest value of $1/\lambda$, which corresponds to the smallest eigenvalue λ of the $\mathbf{A}$ matrix. It should be noted that if we denote $1/\lambda = \lambda'$, then λ' is actually the eigenvalue of $\mathbf{A}^{-1}$ since $\mathbf{A}^{-1}\mathbf{X} = \lambda'\mathbf{X}$. However, in the discussion in this section and in Sec. 3-12, values for the λ's will be determined as the eigenvalues of the $\mathbf{A}$ matrix.

Let us now find the smallest eigenvalue of the same matrix

$$\mathbf{A} = \begin{bmatrix} 2 & 4 \\ 3 & 13 \end{bmatrix}$$

for which we previously found the largest eigenvalue. Using the procedure discussed in Sec. 3-6, the inverse matrix $\mathbf{A}^{-1}$ is readily found to be

$$\mathbf{A}^{-1} = \begin{bmatrix} \frac{13}{14} & -\frac{2}{7} \\ -\frac{3}{14} & \frac{1}{7} \end{bmatrix}$$

Proceeding as outlined in steps 1 through 4, we obtain

$$\begin{bmatrix} \frac{13}{14} & -\frac{2}{7} \\ -\frac{3}{14} & \frac{1}{7} \end{bmatrix} \begin{Bmatrix} 1 \\ 1 \end{Bmatrix} = \begin{Bmatrix} \frac{9}{14} \\ -\frac{1}{14} \end{Bmatrix} = \frac{9}{14} \begin{Bmatrix} 1 \\ -\frac{1}{9} \end{Bmatrix}$$

$$\begin{bmatrix} \frac{13}{14} & -\frac{2}{7} \\ -\frac{3}{14} & \frac{1}{7} \end{bmatrix} \begin{Bmatrix} 1 \\ -\frac{1}{9} \end{Bmatrix} = \begin{Bmatrix} \frac{121}{126} \\ -\frac{29}{126} \end{Bmatrix} = \frac{121}{126} \begin{Bmatrix} 1 \\ -\frac{29}{121} \end{Bmatrix}$$

$$\begin{bmatrix} \frac{13}{14} & -\frac{2}{7} \\ -\frac{3}{14} & \frac{1}{7} \end{bmatrix} \begin{Bmatrix} 1 \\ -\frac{29}{121} \end{Bmatrix} = \begin{Bmatrix} \frac{1689}{1694} \\ -\frac{421}{1694} \end{Bmatrix} = \frac{1689}{1694} \begin{Bmatrix} 1 \\ -\frac{421}{1689} \end{Bmatrix}$$

Therefore, we find that for the matrix $\mathbf{A}$ the *smallest* eigenvalue is $\lambda_2 \cong 1.003$, and that the associated vector $\mathbf{X} = (1, -0.2493)$. The polynomial solution shows that the exact solution is $\lambda_2 = 1$ and $\mathbf{X} = (1, -0.25)$.

It should be apparent, from the discussion thus far, that the iteration method is ideally suited for computer calculation. In the solution of engineering problems there is rarely any difficulty in its use. If the largest and next-to-the-largest or the smallest and next-to-the-smallest eigenvalues have nearly the same value, convergence to the largest or smallest value, respectively, may be slow. If the largest eigenvalue has a multiplicity of 2 ($\lambda_1 = \lambda_2$), convergence is to the largest eigenvalue, but the components of the eigenvector converge to any of the eigenvectors (which usually form a two-dimensional space) associated with λ_1. The eigenvector obtained depends on the vector assumed initially.

In the event that the vector initially assumed is *orthogonal* to the eigenvector associated with the largest eigenvalue of the *transposed* matrix (their dot product is equal to zero), convergence will be to the *second-largest* eigenvalue instead of to the *largest*. To illustrate this point, consider the matrix

$$\mathbf{A} = \begin{bmatrix} 1 & 0 & -1 \\ 1 & 2 & 1 \\ 2 & 2 & 3 \end{bmatrix}$$

in which the second-largest and the largest eigenvalues are $\lambda_2 = 2$ and $\lambda_1 = 3$, respectively. The transpose of matrix $\mathbf{A}$, formed by interchanging rows and columns, is

$$\mathbf{A}^{\mathrm{T}} = \begin{bmatrix} 1 & 1 & 2 \\ 0 & 2 & 2 \\ -1 & 1 & 3 \end{bmatrix}$$

The largest eigenvalue of the transposed matrix is $\lambda = 3$ with the associated eigenvector $(1, 1, \frac{1}{2})$. An arbitrary vector orthogonal to this eigenvector is $(4, -3, -2)$. That is, the dot product of the two orthogonal vectors is

$$1(4) + 1(-3) + \tfrac{1}{2}(-2) = 0$$

If we use the vector $(4, -3, -2)$ as the initially assumed vector in determining the largest eigenvalue of the matrix $\mathbf{A}$, we write, for the first iteration

$$\begin{bmatrix} 1 & 0 & -1 \\ 1 & 2 & 1 \\ 2 & 2 & 3 \end{bmatrix} \begin{Bmatrix} 4 \\ -3 \\ -2 \end{Bmatrix} = 6 \begin{Bmatrix} 1 \\ -\tfrac{2}{3} \\ -\tfrac{2}{3} \end{Bmatrix}$$

After three more iterations we finally obtain

$$
\begin{bmatrix}
1 & 0 & -1 \\
1 & 2 & 1 \\
2 & 2 & 3
\end{bmatrix}
\begin{Bmatrix}
1 \\
-\frac{5}{9} \\
-\frac{8}{9}
\end{Bmatrix}
=
\frac{17}{9}
\begin{Bmatrix}
1 \\
-\frac{9}{17} \\
-\frac{16}{17}
\end{Bmatrix}
$$

which is converging to $\lambda_2 = 2$ with the associated eigenvector $(1, -\frac{1}{2}, -1)$ rather than to $\lambda_1 = 3$ with the associated eigenvector $(1, -1, -2)$.

Other special cases, which would be encountered only rarely in engineering analysis, are discussed by Faddeev and Faddeeva.[15]

3-12 ITERATION FOR INTERMEDIATE EIGENVALUES AND EIGENVECTORS—HOTELLING'S DEFLATION METHOD

The iteration procedure discussed in Sec. 3-11 can be extended to determine intermediate eigenvalues and associated eigenvectors which occur between the smallest and largest eigenvalues. The procedure discussed herein is known as Hotelling's deflation method. As previously mentioned in Sec. 3-9, Hotelling's deflation method may be used along with the iteration method to obtain the eigenvalues and eigenvectors for matrices up to approximately 10, and it is particularly well suited for matrices much larger than 10 when only a relatively small number of eigenvalues and eigenvectors is required for problems such as occur in structural dynamics.

It can be seen in Sec. 3-11 that the iteration process applied to Eq. 3-135,

$$\mathbf{AX} = \lambda \mathbf{X}$$

converges to the largest eigenvalue λ and corresponding eigenvector $\mathbf{X}$. The same process applied to Eq. 3-139,

$$\mathbf{A}^{-1}\mathbf{X} = \frac{1}{\lambda} \mathbf{X}$$

converges to the largest value of $1/\lambda$ which corresponds to the smallest eigenvalue λ and corresponding eigenvector of matrix $\mathbf{A}$. The extension to obtain intermediate eigenvalues and associated eigenvectors requires that $\mathbf{A}$ be a symmetric matrix since the orthogonality principle of symmetric matrices discussed in Appendix B is used.

The method discussed in this section for obtaining eigenvalues in descending order involves the formation of a new matrix $\mathbf{A}_{i+1}$ from $\mathbf{A}_i$ which will have eigenvectors identical to those of $\mathbf{A}_i$ and will have all of its eigenvalues *but one*

---

[15]Faddeev and Faddeeva, *op. cit.*

identical to those of $\mathbf{A}_i$. This singular one eigenvalue of $\mathbf{A}_{i+1}$ will have the value zero, and its associated eigenvector is identical to the eigenvector of $\mathbf{A}_i$ associated with the largest eigenvalue of $\mathbf{A}_i$. Thus, the largest eigenvalue of $\mathbf{A}_i$ is not one of the eigenvalues of $\mathbf{A}_{i+1}$ and is said to have been "swept out" (actually it has been replaced by a zero-valued eigenvalue). The largest eigenvalue of the new matrix $\mathbf{A}_{i+1}$ is identical to the second largest of $\mathbf{A}_i$. The iteration procedure of Sec. 3-11 applied to Eq. 3-135 with $\mathbf{A}_{i+1}$ in place of the $\mathbf{A}$ matrix of that equation will converge to the largest eigenvalue of $\mathbf{A}_{i+1}$ which is the second largest of $\mathbf{A}_i$. A similar procedure is used for obtaining eigenvalues in ascending order. Having discussed the general procedure, we shall next consider the details of the method.

Sweeping for Eigenvalues in Descending Order

Let us first consider the sweeping technique using Eq. 3-135 in which the original matrix $\mathbf{A}$ will be denoted as $\mathbf{A}_1$ and used in the iteration process to obtain the largest eigenvalue λ_1 and associated eigenvector $\mathbf{X}_1$ (let us denote the eigenvalues of $\mathbf{A}_1$ such that $\lambda_1 > \lambda_2 > \ldots > \lambda_n$). Having determined λ_1 and $\mathbf{X}_1$, a new matrix $\mathbf{A}_2$ is formed from

$$\mathbf{A}_2 = \mathbf{A}_1 - \lambda_1 \mathbf{X}_1 \mathbf{X}_1^T \tag{3-140}$$

Using this new matrix in Eq. 3-135, the iteration process will result in convergence to λ_2 and corresponding eigenvector $\mathbf{X}_2$. To show this, Eq. 3-140 is postmultiplied on both sides by $\mathbf{X}_1$ to obtain

$$\mathbf{A}_2 \mathbf{X}_1 = \mathbf{A}_1 \mathbf{X}_1 - \lambda_1 \mathbf{X}_1 \mathbf{X}_1^T \mathbf{X}_1 \tag{3-141}$$

The orthogonality principle for symmetric matrices (see App. B) states that eigenvectors $\mathbf{X}_i$ and $\mathbf{X}_j$ are orthogonal. That is

$$\mathbf{X}_i^T \mathbf{X}_j = \begin{Bmatrix} 0 & i \neq j \\ 1 & i = j \end{Bmatrix}$$

when the components of $\mathbf{X}_i$ are normalized so that $\mathbf{X}_i^T \mathbf{X}_i = 1$ (the sum of the squares of the components of $\mathbf{X}_i$ is equal to 1). With $\mathbf{X}_1^T \mathbf{X}_1 = 1$, and noting from Eq. 3-135 that after the iteration is completed $\mathbf{A}_1 \mathbf{X}_1 = \lambda_1 \mathbf{X}_1$, Eq. 3-141 reduces to

$$\mathbf{A}_2 \mathbf{X}_1 = \mathbf{A}_1 \mathbf{X}_1 - \lambda_1 \mathbf{X}_1 = 0 \tag{3-142}$$

This shows that $\mathbf{A}_2 \mathbf{X}_1 = 0$ from which $\lambda = 0$, $\mathbf{X} = \mathbf{X}_1$ is a solution to the equation

$$\mathbf{A}_2 \mathbf{X} = \lambda \mathbf{X} \tag{3-143}$$

Thus, eigenvalue λ_1 of $\mathbf{A}_1$ is not an eigenvalue associated with eigenvector $\mathbf{X}_1$ of $\mathbf{A}_2$ but has been replaced by a zero value.

We have yet to show that $\lambda_2, \lambda_3, \ldots, \lambda_n$ and the associated eigenvectors $\mathbf{X}_2, \mathbf{X}_3, \ldots, \mathbf{X}_n$ are eigenvalues and eigenvectors of $\mathbf{A}_2$. To show this, Eq. 3-140 is postmultiplied by $\mathbf{X}_2$ to obtain

$$\mathbf{A}_2\mathbf{X}_2 = \mathbf{A}_1\mathbf{X}_2 - \lambda_1\mathbf{X}_1\mathbf{X}_1^\mathrm{T}\mathbf{X}_2 \tag{3-144}$$

Referring again to the orthogonality principle above, we note that $\mathbf{X}_1^\mathrm{T}\mathbf{X}_2 = 0$ so that Eq. 3-144 reduces to

$$\mathbf{A}_2\mathbf{X}_2 = \mathbf{A}_1\mathbf{X}_2$$

and since $\mathbf{A}_1\mathbf{X}_2 = \lambda_2\mathbf{X}_2$ (recall that $\lambda = \lambda_1, \mathbf{X} = \mathbf{X}_1; \lambda = \lambda_2, \mathbf{X} = \mathbf{X}_2; \ldots; \lambda = \lambda_n, \mathbf{X} = \mathbf{X}_n$ are solutions of $\mathbf{A}_1\mathbf{X} = \lambda\mathbf{X}$),

$$\mathbf{A}_2\mathbf{X}_2 = \lambda_2\mathbf{X}_2 \tag{3-145}$$

Postmultiplying Eq. 3-140 successively by $\mathbf{X}_3, \ldots, \mathbf{X}_n$ we can similarly show that

$$\mathbf{A}_2\mathbf{X}_3 = \lambda_3\mathbf{X}_3$$
$$\mathbf{A}_2\mathbf{X}_4 = \lambda_4\mathbf{X}_4$$

$$\cdot \quad \cdot \quad \cdot$$

$$\mathbf{A}_2\mathbf{X}_n = \lambda_n\mathbf{X}_n$$

Thus, the new matrix $\mathbf{A}_2$ has eigenvalues $\lambda_2, \ldots, \lambda_n$ with associated eigenvectors $\mathbf{X}_2, \ldots, \mathbf{X}_n$ and a zero eigenvalue associated with the eigenvector $\mathbf{X}_1$. The largest eigenvalue of $\mathbf{A}_2$ is λ_2 and the iteration of Eq. 3-143 will result in convergence to λ_2 and an associated eigenvector $\mathbf{X}_2$. Similarly, it can be shown that a new matrix

$$\mathbf{A}_3 = \mathbf{A}_2 - \lambda_2\mathbf{X}_2\mathbf{X}_2^\mathrm{T} \tag{3-146}$$

sweeps out λ_2 as an eigenvalue of $\mathbf{A}_3$ leaving λ_3 as its largest eigenvalue, so that the iteration of Eq. 3-135, with $\mathbf{A}_3$ replacing the original matrix $\mathbf{A}_1$, converges to λ_3 and the corresponding eigenvector $\mathbf{X}_3$. To show this, we postmultiply Eq. 3-146 by $\mathbf{X}_2$ to obtain

$$\mathbf{A}_3\mathbf{X}_2 = \mathbf{A}_2\mathbf{X}_2 - \lambda_2\mathbf{X}_2\mathbf{X}_2^\mathrm{T}\mathbf{X}_2 \tag{3-147}$$

Since $\mathbf{X}_2^\mathrm{T}\mathbf{X}_2 = 1$ and $\mathbf{A}_2\mathbf{X}_2 = \lambda_2\mathbf{X}_2$ (Eq. 3-145), the right side of Eq. 3-147 is equal to zero. Therefore, $A_3X_2 = 0$, which shows that $\lambda = 0$, $X = X_2$ is a solution to the equation $A_3X = \lambda X$. Therefore, λ_2 is not the eigenvalue of A_3 associated with eigenvector X_2 but has been replaced by $\lambda = 0$. To show that λ_3 is now the largest of the eigenvalues of A_3, Eq. 3-146 is postmultiplied by X_3 to obtain

$$A_3X_3 = A_2X_3 - \lambda_2X_2X_2^TX_3 \tag{3-148}$$

Substituting the expression for A_2 shown in Eq. 3-140 into Eq. 3-148 yields

$$A_3X_3 = A_1X_3 - \lambda_1X_1X_1^TX_3 - \lambda_2X_2X_2^TX_3 \tag{3-149}$$

Noting that $X_1^TX_3 = X_2^TX_3 = 0$ and that $A_1X_3 = \lambda_3X_3$ we can rewrite Eq. 3-149 as

$$A_3X_3 = \lambda_3X_3 \tag{3-150}$$

Therefore, $\lambda = \lambda_3$, $X = X_3$ is a solution to the equation $A_3X = \lambda X$. We next show that the other nonzero eigenvalues of A_3 are $\lambda_4, \ldots, \lambda_n$ with associated eigenvectors $X_4, \ldots, X_n$. Successively postmultiplying Eq. 3-146 by $X_4, \ldots, X_n$, it becomes apparent that

$$A_3X_4 = \lambda_4X_4$$
$$A_3X_5 = \lambda_5X_5$$

$$\cdot \quad \cdot \quad \cdot$$

$$A_3X_n = \lambda_nX_n$$

Thus the new matrix A_3 has the eigenvectors $\lambda_3, \ldots, \lambda_n$ with associated eigenvectors $X_3, \ldots, X_n$ and, as shown previously, a $\lambda = 0$ associated with $X = X_2$. We will next show that the eigenvalue of A_3 associated with the other eigenvector X_1 is also equal to zero. We postmultiply both sides of Eq. 3-146 with X_1 so that

$$A_3X_1 = A_2X_1 - \lambda_2X_2X_2^TX_1$$

From Eq. 3-142, $A_2X_1 = 0$ and from the orthogonality principle $X_2^TX_1 = 0$ so that $A_3X_1 = 0$. Therefore, $\lambda = 0$, $X = X_1$ is a solution of $A_3X = \lambda X$, and thus are an eigenvalue and eigenvector, respectively, of A_3. With λ_3, therefore, being the largest eigenvalue of A_3, the iteration method of Sec. 3-11 applied to Eq. 3-135 with $A = A_3$ will converge to λ_3 and the associated X_3.

Continuing in this manner, it could be shown that new matrices could be similarly formed, each of which would have one of the intermediate eigenvalues of A_1 as its maximum eigenvalue which could then be determined by the iteration method of Sec. 3-11 (the power method).

Summarizing the preceding discussion, we can write a set of equations for iteration and sweeping s times to obtain $s + 1$ eigenvalues and associated eigenvectors in *descending order* $(\lambda_1 > \lambda_2 > \ldots > \lambda_{s+1})$ as

$$\mathbf{A}_1\mathbf{X} = \lambda\mathbf{X} \qquad \text{(iteration to } \lambda_1 \text{ and } \mathbf{X}_1) \qquad \text{(a)}$$

$$\mathbf{X}_i^\mathrm{T}\mathbf{X}_i = 1 \qquad \text{(normalization)} \qquad \text{(b)}$$

$$\mathbf{A}_{i+1} = \mathbf{A}_i - \lambda_i\mathbf{X}_i\mathbf{X}_i^\mathrm{T} \qquad \text{(formation of new matrix)} \qquad \text{(c)}$$

$$\mathbf{A}_{i+1}\mathbf{X} = \lambda\mathbf{X} \qquad \text{(iteration to } \lambda_{i+1} \text{ and } \mathbf{X}_{i+1}) \qquad \text{(d)}$$

$$i = 1, 2, 3, \ldots, s$$

(3-151)

in which the original matrix becomes $\mathbf{A}_1$ in the first iteration to obtain the largest eigenvalue λ_1 and associated eigenvector $\mathbf{X}_1 (i = 1)$. Steps (b), (c), and (d) are then used to obtain eigenvalue λ_2 and associated eigenvector $\mathbf{X}_2$. Then $\mathbf{X}_2$ is used in step (b)$(i = 2)$, steps (c) and (d) are performed, and λ_3 and $\mathbf{X}_3$ are obtained. The process then again reverts to step (b), and so forth.

Sweeping for Eigenvalues in Ascending Order

The iteration of Eq. 3-139 with sweeping s times will yield $s + 1$ eigenvalues and associated eigenvectors in ascending order $(\lambda_1 < \lambda_2 < \ldots < \lambda_{s+1})$ where λ_1 now denotes the smallest eigenvalue. To simplify the notation, let us write Eq. 3-139 as

$$\mathbf{B}_1\mathbf{X} = \frac{1}{\lambda}\mathbf{X} \qquad (3\text{-}152)$$

in which $\mathbf{B}_1 = \mathbf{A}_1^{-1}$ is the original matrix used in the initial iteration process to obtain the smallest eigenvalue λ_1 and associated eigenvector $\mathbf{X}_1$ of matrix $\mathbf{A}$. Sometimes it is possible to form $\mathbf{A}^{-1}$ directly from the physical nature of the problem, which eliminates the need to invert the $\mathbf{A}$ matrix.

In a manner similar to that used to verify the sweeping effect of the new matrix formed by Eq. 3-140, it can be shown that the new matrix

$$\mathbf{B}_2 = \mathbf{B}_1 - \frac{1}{\lambda_1}\mathbf{X}_1\mathbf{X}_1^\mathrm{T} \qquad (3\text{-}153)$$

will result in convergence to the largest value of $1/\lambda$ which corresponds to eigenvalue λ_2 and associated eigenvector $\mathbf{X}_2$ when used for iteration in Eq. 3-152 in place of $\mathbf{B}_1$. Similarly, iteration with the new matrix

$$\mathbf{B}_3 = \mathbf{B}_2 - \frac{1}{\lambda_2}\mathbf{X}_2\mathbf{X}_2^\mathrm{T} \qquad (3\text{-}154)$$

will converge to the largest value of $1/\lambda$ which corresponds to λ_3 and $\mathbf{X}_3$.

Thus, the system of equations for iteration and sweeping s times to obtain $s + 1$ eigenvalues and associated eigenvectors in ascending order ($\lambda_1 < \lambda_2$, ..., $< \lambda_{s+1}$) is

$$\mathbf{B}_1\mathbf{X} = \frac{1}{\lambda}\mathbf{X} \qquad \text{(iteration to } \lambda_1 \text{ and } \mathbf{X}_1) \qquad \text{(a)}$$

$$\mathbf{X}_i^T\mathbf{X}_i = 1 \qquad \text{(normalization)} \qquad \text{(b)}$$

$$\mathbf{B}_{i+1} = \mathbf{B}_i - \frac{1}{\lambda_i}\mathbf{X}_i\mathbf{X}_i^T \qquad \text{(formation of new matrix)} \qquad \text{(c)}$$

$$\mathbf{B}_{i+1}\mathbf{X} = \frac{1}{\lambda}\mathbf{X} \qquad \begin{array}{l} \text{(iteration to } \lambda_{i+1} \text{ and } \mathbf{X}_{i+1}) \qquad \text{(d)} \\ i = 1, 2, 3, \ldots s \end{array}$$

(3-155)

in which the original matrix $\mathbf{A}^{-1}$ is used as $\mathbf{B}_1$ in the first iteration process in step (a) above to obtain the smallest eigenvalue λ_1 and associated eigenvector $\mathbf{X}_1$ of matrix $\mathbf{A}$. The steps in Eq. 3-155 are then used as described immediately after Eq. 3-151 to obtain eigenvalue λ_2 and associated eigenvector $\mathbf{X}_2$, and so forth.

It should be pointed out at this time that the iteration method with sweeping is subject to the accumulation of roundoff errors and errors due to less than perfect convergence in the iteration procedures. Due to this accumulation it may not always be possible to obtain accurate values for *all* of the eigenvalues and eigenvectors of large matrices. However, in many engineering problems this is not a serious drawback, either because the matrices are not large or because of the information desired as a solution. For example, in structural dynamics (see Ex. 3-11) the first few lowest eigenvalues (squares of natural circular frequencies) and associated eigenvectors (mode shapes) are the most important in a dynamic response analysis, and they may be obtained quite accurately by sweeping in ascending order. If the largest eigenvalues were of primary importance in some other type of problem, they could be obtained by sweeping in descending order.

EXAMPLE 3-10

Before writing a general computer program for determining eigenvalues and eigenvectors by the sweeping method just discussed, let us determine the two smallest eigenvalues and associated eigenvectors of matrix $\mathbf{A}$ using just a hand calculator where the inverse of $\mathbf{A}$ is

$$\mathbf{B}_1 = \mathbf{A}^{-1} = \begin{bmatrix} 0.1 & 0.1 & 0.1 \\ 0.1 & 0.2 & 0.2 \\ 0.1 & 0.2 & 0.3 \end{bmatrix}$$

Using the iteration procedure of Sec. 3-11, the smallest eigenvalue λ_1 and corresponding eigenvector $\mathbf{X}_1$ are found to be

$$\lambda_1 = 1.981$$

$$\mathbf{X}_1 = \begin{Bmatrix} 1.000 \\ 1.802 \\ 2.247 \end{Bmatrix}$$

The next step is to normalize $\mathbf{X}_1$ so that $\mathbf{X}_1^T\mathbf{X}_1 = 1$ (see Eq. 3-155b). The normalizing factor is

$$\sqrt{(1.000)^2 + (1.802)^2 + (2.247)^2} = 3.049$$

Dividing each component of $\mathbf{X}_1$ shown above by 3.049 yields the unit vector

$$\mathbf{X}_1 = \begin{Bmatrix} 0.328 \\ 0.591 \\ 0.737 \end{Bmatrix}$$

so that

$$\mathbf{X}_1^T\mathbf{X}_1 = (0.328)^2 + (0.591)^2 + (0.737)^2 = 1.000$$

Next a new matrix $\mathbf{B}_2$ is formed by using Eq. 3-155c with $i = 1$. This yields

$$\mathbf{B}_2 = \begin{bmatrix} 0.1 & 0.1 & 0.1 \\ 0.1 & 0.2 & 0.2 \\ 0.1 & 0.2 & 0.3 \end{bmatrix} - \frac{1}{1.981} \begin{Bmatrix} 0.328 \\ 0.591 \\ 0.737 \end{Bmatrix} \begin{bmatrix} 0.328 & 0.591 & 0.737 \end{bmatrix}$$

which reduces to

$$\mathbf{B}_2 = \begin{bmatrix} (0.1-0.054) & (0.1-0.098) & (0.1-0.122) \\ (0.1-0.098) & (0.2-0.176) & (0.2-0.220) \\ (0.1-0.122) & (0.2-0.220) & (0.3-0.274) \end{bmatrix}$$

and in turn to

$$\mathbf{B}_2 = \begin{bmatrix} 0.046 & 0.002 & -0.022 \\ 0.002 & 0.024 & -0.020 \\ -0.022 & -0.020 & 0.026 \end{bmatrix}$$

This matrix is now used in Eq. 3-155d for iteration to obtain λ_2 and $\mathbf{X}_2$. Carrying out steps 1 and 2 of the iteration procedure given in Sec. 3-11 yields

$$\begin{bmatrix} 0.046 & 0.002 & -0.022 \\ 0.002 & 0.024 & -0.020 \\ -0.022 & -0.020 & 0.026 \end{bmatrix} \begin{Bmatrix} 1 \\ 1 \\ 1 \end{Bmatrix} = \begin{Bmatrix} 0.026 \\ 0.006 \\ -0.016 \end{Bmatrix} = 0.026 \begin{Bmatrix} 1.000 \\ 0.210 \\ -0.615 \end{Bmatrix}$$

from which

$$\lambda_2 \cong \frac{1}{0.026} = 38.46$$

Applying step 3 (Sec. 3-11) of the iteration procedure yields

$$\begin{bmatrix} 0.046 & 0.002 & -0.022 \\ 0.002 & 0.024 & -0.020 \\ -0.022 & -0.020 & 0.026 \end{bmatrix} \begin{Bmatrix} 1.000 \\ 0.210 \\ -0.615 \end{Bmatrix} = 0.060 \begin{Bmatrix} 1.000 \\ 0.323 \\ -0.704 \end{Bmatrix}$$

from which

$$\lambda_2 \cong \frac{1}{0.060} = 16.67$$

After 6 more iterations, we finally obtain the following values for λ_2 and $\mathbf{X}_2$,

$$\lambda_2 = 15.63 \qquad \mathbf{X}_2 = \begin{Bmatrix} 1.000 \\ 0.443 \\ -0.801 \end{Bmatrix}$$

which have the desired accuracy.

To obtain eigenvalue λ_3 and corresponding $\mathbf{X}_3$, which in this particular case is the last one, a new matrix $\mathbf{B}_3(i = 2)$ would be formed from $\mathbf{B}_2$, λ_2, and $\mathbf{X}_2$ following the procedure given in Eq. 3-155c. That is,

$$\mathbf{B}_3 = \mathbf{B}_2 - \frac{1}{\lambda_2} \mathbf{X}_2 \mathbf{X}_2^{\mathsf{T}}$$

in which $\mathbf{X}_2$ would be normalized so that $\mathbf{X}_2^{\mathsf{T}} \mathbf{X}_2 = 1$. The iteration process would then be carried out using $\mathbf{B}_3$ until the desired accuracy was obtained for the values of λ_3 and $\mathbf{X}_3$.

The computer program which follows is for obtaining the smallest eigenvalues and eigenvectors in ascending order, utilizing the procedure of Eq. 3-155. The order of the matrix and the number of eigenvalues to be found are entered by means of a DATA statement. The DIMENSION statement in the main program and in the subprogram POWER should be replaced for each new problem involving a different order matrix and/or different number of eigenvalues to be found.

Variable Name	Quantity
B(I,J)	The inverse of matrix **A**. **A** is the matrix for which the smallest eigenvalue and intermediate eigenvalues in ascending order are to be found. **B** changes as successive eigenvalues are swept from it.
LAMBDA(I)	The eigenvalues of matrix **A**
LPRIME	An eigenvalue of matrix **B** and equal to 1/LAMBDA
X(I)	An eigenvector of **A** or **B**
XX(I,J)	A two-dimensional array in which the eigenvectors are stored as columns
XIXIT(I,J)	The matrix $\mathbf{X}_i\mathbf{X}_i^T$
ITER(I) and IT	A counter for the number of iterations used in converging to an eigenvalue and corresponding eigenvector
SP1	$s + 1$, where s is the number of eigenvalues to be swept out. The value of $s + 1$ equals the total number of eigenvalues to be found.
N	The order of matrix **B**
EPSI	A small quantity (1×10^{-12} in this problem) used to control convergence of the iterative procedure for finding eigenvalues
II	A FORTRAN DO variable which corresponds to i of equations 3-155
XMAG	Normalizing factor for making an eigenvector a unit vector
I,J,K	DO variables
PROD	The product of the first and $(s + 1)$th eigenvectors
A	Dummy name for the matrix in subroutine POWER for which largest eigenvalue is found
D(I)	Name for vector **AX** in subroutine POWER (also equal to $\lambda\mathbf{X}$)
Z(I)	Name for normalized D(I) (with D(I) normalized so that $D(1) = 1.0$)
DIFF	The difference between two successive eigenvector component values in the iterative procedure of subroutine POWER

The computer printout after the program that follows gives the values of all 3 eigenvalues and corresponding eigenvectors of the matrix of Ex. 3-10. In that example the first two were solved by means of a hand calculator.

```
C THIS PROGRAM FINDS S+1 EIGENVALUES OF A MATRIX 'A'
C IN ASCENDING ORDER AND ALSO THE ASSOCIATED EIGENVECTORS
C USING THE SWEEPING METHOD FOR INTERMEDIATE EIGENVALUES.
C 'S' IS THE NUMBER OF EIGENVALUES SWEPT OUT, BUT THIS
                                                    VARIABLE
C DOES NOT APPEAR AS A FORTRAN VARIABLE IN THE PROGRAM.
C S+1 (FORTRAN NAME SP1) IS USED INSTEAD AS A PROGRAM
                                                    VARIABLE.
C THE INVERSE OF THE 'A' MATRIX CALLED THE 'B' MATRIX
C IS READ IN AS DATA FOR THIS PROGRAM.
      IMPLICIT REAL*8(A-H,O-Z)
      REAL*8 LAMBDA,LPRIME
      INTEGER SP1
C REPLACE THE FOLLOWING DIMENSION STATEMENT FOR EACH NEW
C PROBLEM SO THAT THE DIMENSIONS AGREE WITH THE ACTUAL
C SIZES OF THE ARRAYS USED.  THIS WILL AVOID PROBLEMS
C WHICH MIGHT ARISE WITH CERTAIN FORTRAN COMPILERS IN
C USING SUBROUTINE 'POWER' WITH THE PROGRAM.
C ALSO REPLACE THE DIMENSION STATEMENT IN SUBROUTINE POWER
C SO THAT DIMENSIONS AGREE WITH CORRESPONDING QUANTITIES
C IN THE MAIN PROGRAM.
      DIMENSION B(3,3),LAMBDA(3),X(3),XX(3,3),XIXIT(3,3),
                                                    ITER(3)
C ASSIGN THE NUMBER OF EIGENVALUES TO BE FOUND, THE ORDER
C OF THE MATRIX 'B', AND A SMALL QUANTITY TO BE SENT TO
C SUBROUTINE 'POWER' TO CONTROL CONVERGENCE.
      DATA SP1,N,EPSI/3,3,.000000000001/
C READ IN THE UPPER TRIANGULAR ELEMENTS OF
C SYMMETRIC MATRIX 'B' BY ROWS.
      READ(5,2)((B(I,J),J=I,N),I=1,N)
    2 FORMAT(8F10.0)
C ASSIGN VALUES TO SYMMETRIC ELEMENTS BELOW MAIN DIAGONAL.
      DO 3I=2,N
      IMIN1=I-1
      DO 3J=1,IMIN1
    3 B(I,J)=B(J,I)
C WRITE OUT THE SYMMETRIC B MATRIX
      WRITE(6,4)
    4 FORMAT('1','THE SYMMETRIC B MATRIX IS AS FOLLOWS:',//)
      WRITE(6,40) ((B(I,J),J=1,N),I=1,N)
C THE FOLLOWING FORMAT STATEMENT SHOULD BE CHANGED FOR EACH
C DIFFERENT SIZE MATRIX.
   40 FORMAT(' ',3F15.4)
      DO 100 II=1,SP1
      CALL POWER(B,LPRIME,X,N,EPSI,IT)
      ITER(II)=IT
      LAMBDA(II)=1./LPRIME
C ASSIGN THE EIGENVECTOR COMPONENTS RETURNED FROM SUBROUTINE
C 'POWER' AS A COLUMN OF THE TWO-DIMENSIONAL ARRAY XX.
      DO 5I=1,N
```

```
    5 XX(I,II)=X(I)
C CALCULATE NORMALIZING FACTOR XMAG FOR MAKING
C EIGENVECTOR RETURNED BY SUBROUTINE 'POWER' A UNIT VECTOR.
      SUM=0.0
      DO 6I=1,N
    6 SUM=SUM+X(I)**2
      XMAG=DSQRT(SUM)
C DIVIDE EACH COMPONENT OF X BY XMAG.
      DO 7I=1,N
    7 X(I)=X(I)/XMAG
C GET PRODUCT OF X(I) AND X(I)TRANSPOSE.
      DO 8I=1,N
      DO 8J=1,N
    8 XIXIT(I,J)=X(I)*X(J)
C GET NEW MATRIX B.
      DO 9I=1,N
      DO 9J=1,N
    9 B(I,J)=B(I,J)-XIXIT(I,J)/LAMBDA(II)
  100 CONTINUE
C WRITE OUT THE EIGENVALUES AND EIGENVECTORS.
      DO 13I=1,SP1
      WRITE(6,10) I,LAMBDA(I),ITER(I)
   10 FORMAT(///,' ','LAMBDA(',I2,')=',E14.7,' USING',I4,
     $' ITERATIONS')
      WRITE(6,11)
   11 FORMAT(/,' ','THE ASSOCIATED EIGENVECTOR COMPONENTS
                                            ARE:'/)
      WRITE(6,12)(XX(K,I),K=1,N)
   12 FORMAT(' ',13X,E14.7)
   13 CONTINUE
C CHECK ON THE ORTHOGONALITY OF THE FIRST AND (S+1)TH
C EIGENVECTORS AS AN INDICATION OF THE ACCURACY ATTAINED.
      PROD=0.0
      DO 14I=1,N
      PROD=PROD+XX(I,1)*XX(I,SP1)
   14 CONTINUE
      WRITE(6,15)PROD
   15 FORMAT(///,' ','THE PRODUCT OF THE FIRST AND (S+1)TH',
     $' EIGENVECTORS IS ',F20.17)
      STOP
      END

      SUBROUTINE POWER(A,LAMBDA,X,N,EPSI,IT)
C SUBROUTINE POWER FINDS THE LARGEST EIGENVALUE OF A MATRIX
C AND THE ASSOCIATED EIGENVECTOR COMPONENTS BY THE ITERATIVE
C PROCEDURE CALLED THE POWER METHOD.
C 'A' IS THE MATRIX FOR WHICH LARGEST EIGENVALUE IS FOUND.
C 'LAMBDA' IS THE LARGEST EIGENVALUE.
C 'X(I)' IS THE EIGENVECTOR ASSOCIATED WITH LAMBDA.
C 'N' IS THE ORDER OF THE A MATRIX.
C 'EPSI' IS A SMALL VALUE USED IN DETERMINING CONVERGENCE.
C 'IT' IS THE NUMBER OF ITERATIONS USED.
      IMPLICIT REAL*8(A-H,O-Z)
      REAL*8 LAMBDA
      DIMENSION A(3,3),X(3),D(3),Z(3)
```

```
C ASSIGN VALUES OF UNITY TO COMPONENTS OF VECTOR X.
      DO 2I=1,N
    2 X(I)=1.
C CALCULATE COMPONENTS OF THE VECTOR AX=LAMBDA*X.
C THIS VECTOR IS CALLED D(I)
      IT=0
    3 DO 4I=1,N
      D(I)=0.
      DO4J=1,N
      D(I)=D(I)+A(I,J)*X(J)
    4 CONTINUE
      IT=IT+1
C NORMALIZE THE VECTOR D(I) AND CALL IT Z(I)
      DO 5I=1,N
    5 Z(I)=D(I)/D(1)
C CHECK TO SEE IF REQUIRED ACCURACY HAS BEEN ATTAINED.
      DO 6I=1,N
      DIFF=X(I)-Z(I)
      IF(DABS(DIFF)-EPSI*DABS(Z(I)))6,6,7
    6 CONTINUE
      GO TO 9
C REQUIRED ACCURACY HAS NOT BEEN ATTAINED.  ASSIGN COM-
C PONENTS OF THE Z VECTOR TO X AND ITERATE AGAIN.
    7 DO 8I=1,N
    8 X(I)=Z(I)
      IF(IT .GE. 100)GO TO 10
      GO TO 3
C REQUIRED ACCURACY HAS BEEN ATTAINED
    9 DO 20I=1,N
   20 X(I)=Z(I)
C OR MAXIMUM NUMBER OF ITERATIONS HAS BEEN REACHED.
   10 LAMBDA=D(1)
      RETURN
      END
```

THE SYMMETRIC B MATRIX IS AS FOLLOWS:

0.1000	0.1000	0.1000
0.1000	0.2000	0.2000
0.1000	0.2000	0.3000

LAMBDA(1)= 0.1980623D 01 USING 15 ITERATIONS
THE ASSOCIATED EIGENVECTOR COMPONENTS ARE:

```
0.1000000D 01
0.1801938D 01
0.2246980D 01
```

LAMBDA(2)= 0.1554958D 02 USING 38 ITERATIONS
THE ASSOCIATED EIGENVECTOR COMPONENTS ARE:

```
 0.1000000D 01
 0.4450419D 00
-0.8019377D 00
```

```
LAMBDA( 3)= 0.3246980D 02 USING  3 ITERATIONS
THE ASSOCIATED EIGENVECTOR COMPONENTS ARE:

              0.1000000D 01
             -0.1246980D 01
              0.5549581D 00

THE PRODUCT OF THE FIRST AND (S+1)TH EIGENVECTORS IS
                                  0.00000000000000289
```

EXAMPLE 3-11

Frequently the matrix equations for real physical problems do not occur in the standard form of Eqs. 3-135 or 3-139. So, let us consider a problem in structural dynamics in which the matrix equations are not of the standard form, and write a general FORTRAN program for obtaining the smallest eigenvalues (squares of natural circular frequencies) and eigenvectors (mode configurations) in ascending order. It will be left as an exercise for the reader to modify the program to determine the largest eigenvalues and eigenvectors in descending order (see Prob. 3-43 at the end of this chapter).

To illustrate the use of the program, the data for the four-story building shown in Fig. 3-10 will be used as input data. The eigenvalues λ_i and associated eigenvectors X_i will correspond to the squares of the natural circular frequencies ω_i^2 and the mode configurations, respectively.

The four-story building is shown schematically in Fig. 3-10(a). It is assumed that the mass distribution of the building may be represented in the form of concentrated masses at each floor level, as shown. It is further assumed that the girders of the structure are infinitely rigid, in comparison with the supporting columns, so that a general configuration between floors will be obtained, as shown in Fig. 3-10(b). The spring constants in the figure are equivalent constants representing the aggregate stiffness of the number of columns supporting a given floor, and they were obtained by considering the columns as springs in parallel.

In structural dynamics the matrix equations may be formulated in terms of a *stiffness* matrix K (symmetric) or in terms of a *flexibility* matrix B (symmetric) which is the inverse of K. While the stiffness matrix is sometimes obtained by deriving the differential equations of motion of a system, both it and the flexibility matrix can often be derived in an easier and more direct manner as will be explained in succeeding paragraphs.

Considering the use of the stiffness matrix first, the matrix equation in terms of K is

$$KX = \lambda MX$$

If we then premultiply this equation by M^{-1}, it has the form

$$M^{-1}KX = \lambda X \tag{3-156}$$

Figure 3-10 Model of a four-story building

which is a more convenient form for purposes of iteration. In these equations λ is the square of the natural circular frequency ω, $\mathbf{M}$ is the mass matrix containing only elements on the diagonal, and $\mathbf{M}^{-1}$ is its inverse; that is,

$$
\mathbf{M} = \begin{bmatrix}
m_1 & 0 & 0 & \cdots & 0 \\
0 & m_2 & 0 & \cdots & 0 \\
0 & 0 & m_3 & \cdots & 0 \\
\multicolumn{5}{c}{\cdots\cdots\cdots\cdots\cdots\cdots} \\
0 & 0 & 0 & \cdots & m_n
\end{bmatrix}
$$

$$
\mathbf{M}^{-1} = \begin{bmatrix}
1/m_1 & 0 & 0 & \cdots & 0 \\
0 & 1/m_2 & 0 & \cdots & 0 \\
0 & 0 & 1/m_3 & \cdots & 0 \\
\multicolumn{5}{c}{\cdots\cdots\cdots\cdots\cdots\cdots} \\
0 & 0 & 0 & \cdots & 1/m_n
\end{bmatrix}
$$

The diagonal elements of the stiffness matrix can be determined by defining k_{ii} as the force required at station i, with all of the other stations held fixed. The nondiagonal elements of the stiffness matrix can be determined by defining element k_{ij} as the force which would have to be applied to the mass at station i to keep it fixed if the mass at station j were given a positive *unit* displacement, with all of the other stations fixed. The direction chosen as positive is arbitrary, but it should be the same for both the displacements and the forces. Both positive and negative elements will appear in stiffness matrices (see Prob. 3-45), and they could be moments instead of forces (see Prob. 3-42).

It can be shown that the iteration procedure applied to Eq. 3-156 along with Hotelling's deflation method will converge to the eigenvalues and associated eigenvectors in descending order (see Prob. 3-43).

Next the use of the flexibility matrix is considered. The matrix equation in terms of **B** is

$$\mathbf{BMX} = \frac{1}{\lambda} \mathbf{X} \tag{3-157}$$

The flexibility matrix may be obtained by defining the element b_{ij} as the displacement of the mass at station i due to a *unit* force applied to the mass at station j, with the mass at each station free to displace. In many types of problems the elements of the flexibility matrix (frequently referred to as *influence coefficients*) will all have the same sign. However, there are physical systems in which both positive and negative elements will appear (see Prob. 3-50).

It will be shown that the iteration procedure applied to Eq. 3-157 along with Hotelling's deflation method will converge to the largest values of $1/\lambda$ in descending order (the smallest values of λ in *ascending* order).

With the preceding discussion in mind, it can be seen that we can write our program for the building using either Eq. 3-156 or Eq. 3-157. However, since the lowest frequencies and mode shapes are generally of the most importance, let us use Eq. 3-157. This means that we need to determine the flexibility matrix for input to the FORTRAN program.

From the definition of b_{ij} above, and the spring constant values in Fig. 3-10,

$$b_{11} = b_{12} = b_{13} = b_{14} = \frac{1}{k_1} = 8.333333333333332(10)^{-8}$$

$$b_{21} = b_{12}$$

$$b_{22} = b_{23} = b_{24} = \frac{1}{k_1} + \frac{1}{k_2} = 18.33333333333333(10)^{-8}$$

$$b_{31} = b_{13}$$

$$b_{32} = b_{23}$$

$$b_{33} = b_{34} = \frac{1}{k_1} + \frac{1}{k_2} + \frac{1}{k_3} = 30.83333333333333(10)^{-8}$$

$$b_{41} = b_{14}$$

$$b_{42} = b_{24}$$

$$b_{43} = b_{34}$$

$$b_{44} = \frac{1}{k_1} + \frac{1}{k_2} + \frac{1}{k_3} + \frac{1}{k_4} = 47.5(10)^{-8}$$

From Fig. 3-10, we see that the mass matrix $\mathbf{M}$ is

$$\mathbf{M} = (10)^3 \begin{bmatrix} 6 & 0 & 0 & 0 \\ 0 & 5 & 0 & 0 \\ 0 & 0 & 4 & 0 \\ 0 & 0 & 0 & 3 \end{bmatrix}$$

The expressions which make up Eq. 3-155 must be modified slightly for use in the iteration and sweeping technique to obtain values of λ and associated eigenvectors. The modified expressions for finding them in ascending order are

$$\mathbf{B}_1\mathbf{M}\mathbf{X} = \frac{1}{\lambda}\mathbf{X} \qquad \text{(iteration for } \lambda_1 \text{ and } \mathbf{X}_1) \qquad \text{(a)}$$

$$\mathbf{X}_i^\mathsf{T}\mathbf{M}\mathbf{X}_i = 1 \qquad \text{(normalization)} \qquad \text{(b)}$$

$$\text{(3-158)}$$

$$\mathbf{B}_{i+1}\mathbf{M} = \mathbf{B}_i\mathbf{M} - \frac{1}{\lambda_i}\mathbf{X}_i\mathbf{X}_i^\mathsf{T}\mathbf{M} \qquad \text{(formation of new matrix)} \qquad \text{(c)}$$

$$\mathbf{B}_{i+1}\mathbf{M}\mathbf{X} = \frac{1}{\lambda}\mathbf{X} \qquad \text{(iteration for } \lambda_{i+1} \text{ and } \mathbf{X}_{i+1}) \qquad \text{(d)}$$

$$i = 1, 2, 3, \ldots, s$$

in which the original flexibility matrix $\mathbf{B}$ is used as $\mathbf{B}_1(i = 1)$ for the first iteration process in Eq. 3-158a. Equation 3-158b follows from the orthogonality principle (see App. B-5) which is

$$\mathbf{X}_i^\mathsf{T}\mathbf{M}\mathbf{X}_j = \begin{Bmatrix} 0 & i \neq j \\ 1 & i = j \end{Bmatrix} \qquad \text{(3-159)}$$

where the components of $\mathbf{X}_i$ are normalized to make $\mathbf{X}_i^\mathsf{T}\mathbf{M}\mathbf{X}_i = 1$.

After obtaining λ_i and $\mathbf{X}_i$ from the iteration process, Eq. 3-158c is used to form a new matrix $\mathbf{B}_{i+1}\mathbf{M}$ in which $1/\lambda_i$ has been swept out. This matrix is then used in Eq. 3-158d so that the iteration process will converge to the next smallest value λ_{i+1} ($\lambda_i < \lambda_{i+1}$) and eigenvector $\mathbf{X}_{i+1}$.

For example, with $i = 1$, and having iterated to obtain λ_1 and $\mathbf{X}_1$, the new matrix $\mathbf{B}_2\mathbf{M}$ which is needed for iteration to obtain λ_2 and $\mathbf{X}_2$ is

$$\mathbf{B}_2\mathbf{M} = \mathbf{B}_1\mathbf{M} - \frac{1}{\lambda_1}\mathbf{X}_1\mathbf{X}_1^T\mathbf{M} \tag{3-160}$$

Postmultiplying Eq. 3-160 by $\mathbf{X}_1$ yields

$$\mathbf{B}_2\mathbf{M}\mathbf{X}_1 = \mathbf{B}_1\mathbf{M}\mathbf{X}_1 - \frac{1}{\lambda_1}\mathbf{X}_1\mathbf{X}_1^T\mathbf{M}\mathbf{X}_1 \tag{3-161}$$

Normalizing $\mathbf{X}_1$ so that

$$\mathbf{X}_1^T\mathbf{M}\mathbf{X}_1 = 1 \tag{3-162}$$

and realizing from Eq. 3-158d that with the initial iteration completed

$$\mathbf{B}_1\mathbf{M}\mathbf{X}_1 = \frac{1}{\lambda_1}\mathbf{X}_1$$

the substitution of the last two expressions into Eq. 3-161 shows that

$$\mathbf{B}_2\mathbf{M}\mathbf{X}_1 = 0$$

This shows that $1/\lambda_1$ ($i = 1$) has been swept out of the equation

$$\mathbf{B}_2\mathbf{M}\mathbf{X} = \frac{1}{\lambda}\mathbf{X} \tag{3-163}$$

which upon iteration converges to $1/\lambda_2$, which gives the next smallest value, λ_2, and corresponding $\mathbf{X}_2$.

To show that the next smallest value λ_2 ($\lambda_1 < \lambda_2$) and eigenvector $\mathbf{X}_2$ are present in Eq. 3-163, Eq. 3-160 is postmultiplied by $\mathbf{X}_2$ to obtain

$$\mathbf{B}_2\mathbf{M}\mathbf{X}_2 = \mathbf{B}_1\mathbf{M}\mathbf{X}_2 - \frac{1}{\lambda_1}\mathbf{X}_1\mathbf{X}_1^T\mathbf{M}\mathbf{X}_2 \tag{3-164}$$

Referring to Eq. 3-159 we can see that

$$\mathbf{X}_1^T\mathbf{M}\mathbf{X}_2 = 0$$

so that Eq. 3-164 reduces to

$$\mathbf{B}_2\mathbf{M}\mathbf{X}_2 = \mathbf{B}_1\mathbf{M}\mathbf{X}_2 \tag{3-165}$$

Since

$$\mathbf{B}_1\mathbf{M}\mathbf{X}_2 = \frac{1}{\lambda_2}\,\mathbf{X}_2 \tag{3-166}$$

we see from Eqs. 3-165 and 3-166 that

$$\mathbf{B}_2\mathbf{M}\mathbf{X}_2 = \frac{1}{\lambda_2}\,\mathbf{X}_2 \tag{3-167}$$

Thus, iteration of Eq. 3-158d with the new matrix $\mathbf{B}_2$ will result in convergence to the next smallest value λ_2 and associated eigenvector $\mathbf{X}_2$.

In a similar manner it can be shown that iteration with the new matrix

$$\mathbf{B}_3\mathbf{M} = \mathbf{B}_2\mathbf{M} - \frac{1}{\lambda_2}\,\mathbf{X}_2\mathbf{X}_2^\mathsf{T}\mathbf{M}$$

will result in convergence to the next smallest value λ_3 ($\lambda_1 < \lambda_2 < \lambda_3$) and associated eigenvector $\mathbf{X}_3$.

In this particular problem the values of the elements b_{ij} of the $\mathbf{B}$ matrix and the elements of the diagonal mass matrix $\mathbf{M}$ will be used as input data to the FORTRAN program, with the original $\mathbf{B}$ matrix used as $\mathbf{B}_1$ in the initial iteration process.

In using Eq. 3-158, the initial iteration process proceeds as described in Sec. 3-11. However, when we move into the sweeping process it should be noted that the normalization procedure for Eq. 3-158b varies from the process described for Eq. 3-151b and Eq. 3-155b. In the latter, the normalization of $\mathbf{X}_i^\mathsf{T}\mathbf{X}_i$ was accomplished by making $\mathbf{X}_i$ a unit vector as described in the example following Eq. 3-155. However, this is not sufficient in Eq. 3-158b because of the presence of the mass matrix $\mathbf{M}$. We must determine a *normalizing factor* to use with $\mathbf{X}_i$ such that $\mathbf{X}_i^\mathsf{T}\mathbf{M}\mathbf{X}_i = 1$, so that in effect we are not normalizing $\mathbf{X}_i$ as before but finding a value of $\mathbf{X}_i$ that will make $\mathbf{X}_i^\mathsf{T}\mathbf{M}\mathbf{X}_i = 1$.

This normalizing factor can be obtained by noting that

$$\mathbf{X}_i^\mathsf{T}\mathbf{M}\mathbf{X}_i = [x_1\ x_2\ \ldots\ x_n]_i \begin{Bmatrix} m_1 x_1 \\ m_2 x_2 \\ \vdots \\ m_n x_n \end{Bmatrix}_i$$

or that

$$\mathbf{X}_i^\mathsf{T}\mathbf{M}\mathbf{X}_i = [m_1 x_1^2 + m_2 x_2^2 + \ldots + m_n x_n^2]_i \tag{3-168}$$

where the component values of $\mathbf{X}_i$ obtained from the iteration process have been normalized with respect to $x_1 = 1$. The normalizing factor is then obtained as

$$N.F. = \sqrt{[m_1(1)^2 + m_2 x_2^2 + m_3 x_3^2 + \ldots m_n x_n^2]} \tag{3-169}$$

The x_i values for use in Eq. 3-158c are then

$$x_1 = \frac{1}{N.F.}, \; x_2 = \frac{x_2}{N.F.}, \; \ldots, \; x_n = \frac{x_n}{N.F.}$$

The variable names used in the program and the quantities they represent are as follows:

Variable Name	Quantity
B(I,J)	The matrix **B** of the equation $$\mathbf{BMX} = \frac{1}{\lambda}\mathbf{X}$$
LAMBDA(I)	λ of the equation $\mathbf{BMX} = \frac{1}{\lambda}\mathbf{X}$ (Nonsubscripted LAMBDA is the dummy name for the eigenvalue in subroutine subprogram 'POWER')
LPRIME	An eigenvalue of the matrix **BM** and equal to $\frac{1}{\lambda}$
M(I)	The diagonal mass matrix (a two-dimensional matrix but for simplicity the diagonal elements are stored in a one-dimensional array)
NF	Normalizing factor equal to $[m_1(1)^2 + m_2 x_2^2 + \ldots + m_n x_n^2]^{1/2}$
SP1	$s + 1$ where s is the number of eigenvalues to be swept out. $s + 1$ equals the total number of eigenvalues found
BM(I,J)	The product **BM**
X(I)	An eigenvector of the equation $$\mathbf{BMX} = \frac{1}{\lambda}\mathbf{X}$$

Variable Name	Quantity
XX(I,J)	A two-dimensional array in which the eigenvectors are stored as columns
XIXITM(I,J)	The matrix $\mathbf{X}_i\mathbf{X}_i^T\mathbf{M}$
ITER(I) and IT	A counter for the number of iterations to converge to a value of $\dfrac{1}{\lambda_i}$ and corresponding eigenvector
N	The order of matrices $\mathbf{B}$ and $\mathbf{M}$
EPSI	A small quantity (1×10^{-12} in this problem) used to control convergence of the iterative procedure in subroutine subprogram 'POWER'
II	A FORTRAN DO variable which corresponds to i of Eq. 3-158
I,J,K	DO variables
PROD	The product $\mathbf{X}_1^T\mathbf{M}\mathbf{X}_{(s+1)}$
A(I,J)	Dummy name for the matrix in subroutine subprogram 'POWER' for which largest eigenvalue is found
D(I)	Name for the vector $\mathbf{AX}$ in subroutine 'POWER' (also equal to $\lambda\mathbf{X}$)
Z(I)	Name for the normalized D(I) [D(I) normalized so that D(1) = 1.0]
DIFF	The difference between two successive eigenvector component values in the iterative procedure of subroutine 'POWER'

The program is as follows:

```
C THIS PROGRAM FINDS S+1 VALUES OF LAMBDA OF THE
                                          NON-STANDARD
C EIGENVALUE PROBLEM DEFINED BY THE EQUATION
                                  BMX=(1./LAMBDA)X.
C VALUES OF LAMBDA ARE FOUND IN ASCENDING ORDER (AND THE
C ASSOCIATED EIGENVECTORS ARE ALSO FOUND) USING THE SWEEPING
C METHOD.  'S' IS THE NUMBER OF VALUES OF LAMBDA SWEPT
                                                OUT, BUT
C THIS VARIABLE DOES NOT APPEAR AS A PROGRAM VARIABLE.  S+1
C (FORTRAN NAME SP1) IS USED INSTEAD AS A PROGRAM VARIABLE.
      IMPLICIT REAL*8(A-H,O-Z)
      REAL*8 M,LAMBDA,LPRIME,NF
      INTEGER SP1
C REPLACE THE FOLLOWING DIMENSION STATEMENT FOR EACH NEW
C PROBLEM SO THAT THE DIMENSIONS AGREE WITH THE ACTUAL
C SIZES OF THE ARRAYS USED.  THIS WILL AVOID PROBLEMS
```

```
C WHICH MIGHT ARISE WITH CERTAIN FORTRAN COMPILERS IN
C USING SUBROUTINE 'POWER' WITH THE PROGRAM.
C ALSO REPLACE THE DIMENSION STATEMENT IN SUBROUTINE POWER
C SO THAT DIMENSIONS AGREE WITH CORRESPONDING QUANTITIES
C IN THE MAIN PROGRAM.
      DIMENSION B(4,4),BM(4,4),LAMBDA(4),X(4),XX(4,4),
                                              XIXITM(4,4),
     $ITER(4,),M(4)
C ASSIGN THE NUMBER OF VALUES OF LAMBDA TO BE FOUND,
                                          THE ORDER OF
C THE MATRIX 'B', AND A SMALL QUANTITY TO BE SENT TO
C SUBROUTINE 'POWER' TO CONTROL CONVERGENCE.
      DATA SP1,N,EPSI/4,4,.000000000001/
C READ IN THE UPPER TRIANGULAR ELEMENTS OF
C SYMMETRIC MATRIX 'B' BY ROWS.
      READ(5,2)((B(I,J),J=I,N),I=1,N)
    2 FORMAT(4F20.0)
C ASSIGN VALUES TO SYMMETRIC ELEMENTS BELOW MAIN DIAGONAL.
      DO 3I=2,N
      IMIN1=I-1
      DO 3J=1,IMIN1
    3 B(I,J)=B(J,I)
C WRITE OUT THE B MATRIX.
      WRITE(6,4)
    4 FORMAT('1','THE SYMMETRIC B MATRIX IS AS FOLLOWS:',//)
      WRITE(6,5)((B(I,J),J=1,N),I=1,N)
C THE FOLLOWING FORMAT STATEMENT SHOULD BE CHANGED FOR
C EACH DIFFERENT SIZE MATRIX.
    5 FORMAT(' ',4E30.16)
C READ THE DIAGONAL ELEMENTS OF THE M MATRIX INTO A
C ONE-DIMENSIONAL ARRAY.
      READ(5,6)(M(I),I=1,N)
    6 FORMAT(8F10.0)
C WRITE OUT THE DIAGONAL ELEMENTS OF THE M MATRIX.
      WRITE(6,7)
    7 FORMAT(///,' ','THE DIAGONAL ELEMENTS OF THE M MATRIX
                                          ARE:',//)
      WRITE(6,8)(M(I),I=1,N)
C THE FOLLOWING FORMAT STATEMENT SHOULD BE CHANGED FOR EACH
C DIFFERENT SIZE MATRIX.
    8 FORMAT(' ',4F15.2,//)
C DETERMINE THE PRODUCT OF THE B AND M MATRICES.
      DO 9I=1,N
      DO 9J=1,N
    9 BM(I,J)=B(I,J)*M(J)
C BEGIN A MAJOR DO LOOP IN WHICH THE STEPS GIVEN BY
C EQUATIONS 3-158 ARE CARRIED OUT.  DO VARIABLE 'II'
C CORRESPONDS TO LOWER CASE LETTER I OF EQUATIONS 3-158.
      DO 100 II=1,SP1
      CALL POWER(BM,LPRIME,X,N,EPSI,IT)
      ITER(II)=IT
      LAMBDA(II)=1./LPRIME
C ASSIGN THE EIGENVECTOR COMPONENTS RETURNED FROM SUBROUTINE
C 'POWER' AS A COLUMN OF THE TWO-DIMENSIONAL ARRAY XX.
      DO 10I=1,N
```

```
   10 XX(I,II)=X(I)
      IF(II.EQ.SP1)GO TO 100
C CALCULATE NORMALIZING FACTOR NF FOR NORMALIZING
C THE EIGENVECTORS SO THAT (XTRANSPOSE)(M)(X)=1.0 .
      SUM=0.0
      DO11I=1,N
   11 SUM=SUM+M(I)*X(I)**2
      NF=DSQRT(SUM)
C DIVIDE EACH COMPONENT OF X BY NF.
      DO 12I=1,N
   12 X(I)=X(I)/NF
C CALCULATE ELEMENTS OF THE N BY N MATRIX (X)(XTRANSPOSE)(M).
      DO 13I=1,N
      DO 13J=1,N
   13 XIXITM(I,J)=X(I)*X(J)*M(J)
C GET THE NEW (B)(M) MATRIX.
      DO 14I=1,N
      DO 14J=1,N
   14 BM(I,J)=BM(I,J)-XIXITM(I,J)/LAMBDA(II)
  100 CONTINUE
C WRITE OUT THE LAMBDAS AND CORRESPONDING EIGENVECTORS.
      DO 18I=1,SP1
      WRITE(6,15)I,LAMBDA(I),ITER(I)
   15 FORMAT(///,' ','LAMBDA(',I2,')=',F20.10,' USING',I4,
     $' ITERATIONS')
      WRITE(6,16)
   16 FORMAT(/,' ','THE ASSOCIATED EIGENVECTOR COMPONENTS
                                                   ARE:'/)
      WRITE(6,17)(XX(K,I),K=1,N)
   17 FORMAT(' ',13X,D17.10)
   18 CONTINUE
C CHECK ON THE ORTHOGONALITY OF (XTRANSPOSE)(M)(X) USING
C THE FIRST EIGENVECTOR FOR (XTRANSPOSE) AND THE (S+1)TH
C EIGENVECTOR FOR X , AS AN INDICATION OF THE ACCURACY
                                              ATTAINED.
      PROD=0.0
      DO 19I=1,N
      PROD=PROD+XX(I,1)*M(I)*XX(I,SP1)
   19 CONTINUE
      WRITE(6,20)PROD
   20 FORMAT(///,' ','THE PRODUCT (XTRANSPOSE)(M)(X)
                                              USING THE',
     $' FIRST AND (S+1)TH EIGENVECTORS IS ',F20.17)
      STOP
      END


      SUBROUTINE POWER(A,LAMBDA,X,N,EPSI,IT)
C SUBROUTINE POWER FINDS THE LARGEST EIGENVALUE OF A MATRIX
C AND THE ASSOCIATED EIGENVECTOR COMPONENTS BY THE ITERATIVE
C PROCEDURE CALLED THE POWER METHOD.
C 'A' IS THE MATRIX FOR WHICH LARGEST EIGENVALUE IS FOUND.
C 'LAMBDA' IS THE LARGEST EIGENVALUE.
C 'X(I)' IS THE EIGENVECTOR ASSOCIATED WITH LAMBDA.
C 'N' IS THE ORDER OF THE A MATRIX.
```

```
C 'EPSI' IS A SMALL VALUE USED IN DETERMINING CONVERGENCE.
C 'IT' IS THE NUMBER OF ITERATIONS USED.
      IMPLICIT REAL*8(A-H,O-Z)
      REAL*8 LAMBDA
      DIMENSION A(4,4),X(4),D(4),Z(4)
C ASSIGN VALUES OF UNITY TO COMPONENTS OF VECTOR X.
      DO 2I=1,N
    2 X(I)=1.
C CALCULATE COMPONENTS OF THE VECTOR AX=LAMBDA*X.
C THIS VECTOR IS CALLED D(I)
      IT=0
    3 DO 4I=1,N
      D(I)=0.
      DO4J=1,N
      D(I)=D(I)+A(I,J)*X(J)
    4 CONTINUE
      IT=IT+1
C NORMALIZE THE VECTOR D(I) AND CALL IT Z(I)
      DO 5I=1,N
    5 Z(I)=D(I)/D(1)
C CHECK TO SEE IF REQUIRED ACCURACY HAS BEEN ATTAINED.
      DO 6I=1,N
      DIFF=X(I)-Z(I)
      IF(DABS(DIFF)-EPSI*DABS(Z(I)))6,6,7
    6 CONTINUE
      GO TO 9
C REQUIRED ACCURACY HAS NOT BEEN ATTAINED.  ASSIGN COM-
C PONENTS OF THE Z VECTOR TO X AND ITERATE AGAIN.
    7 DO 8I=1,N
    8 X(I)=Z(I)
      IF(IT .GE. 100)GO TO 10
      GO TO 3
C REQUIRED ACCURACY HAS BEEN ATTAINED
    9 DO 20I=1,N
   20 X(I)=Z(I)
C OR MAXIMUM NUMBER OF ITERATIONS HAS BEEN REACHED.
   10 LAMBDA=D(1)
      RETURN
      END
```

The computer printout is as follows:

THE SYMMETRIC B MATRIX IS AS FOLLOWS:

0.8333333333333332D-07	0.8333333333333332D-07
0.8333333333333332D-07	0.1833333333333333D-06
0.8333333333333332D-07	0.1833333333333333D-06
0.8333333333333332D-07	0.1833333333333333D-06
0.8333333333333332D-07	0.8333333333333332D-07
0.1833333333333333D-06	0.1833333333333333D-06
0.3083333333333333D-06	0.3083333333333333D-06
0.3083333333333333D-06	0.4749999999999999D-06

```
THE DIAGONAL ELEMENTS OF THE M MATRIX ARE:

      6000.00           5000.00           4000.00           3000.00

LAMBDA( 1)=       317.6280363493 USING   17 ITERATIONS
THE ASSOCIATED EIGENVECTOR COMPONENTS ARE:

               0.1000000000D 01
               0.2009423178D 01
               0.2872296440D 01
               0.3414579536D 01

LAMBDA( 2)=      1877.3083380413 USING   37 ITERATIONS
THE ASSOCIATED EIGENVECTOR COMPONENTS ARE:

               0.1000000000D 01
               0.1073614997D 01
              -0.9405774763D-01
              -0.1533237811D 01

LAMBDA( 3)=      4233.4402653897 USING   68 ITERATIONS
THE ASSOCIATED EIGENVECTOR COMPONENTS ARE:

               0.1000000000D 01
              -0.3400641592D 00
              -0.1115368543D 01
               0.9987896791D 00

LAMBDA( 4)=      6338.2900268875 USING    3 ITERATIONS
THE ASSOCIATED EIGENVECTOR COMPONENTS ARE:

               0.1000000000D 01
              -0.1602974016D 01
               0.1493379851D 01
              -0.6884647370D 00

THE PRODUCT (XTRANSPOSE)(M)(X) USING THE FIRST AND (S+1)TH
                    EIGENVECTORS IS  -0.00000000002728484
```

The computer printout shows that

$$\lambda_1 = \omega_1^2 = 317.6280$$

Thus the natural circular frequency of the first (the fundamental) mode of vibration is

$$\omega_1 = \sqrt{317.628} = 17.82 \text{ rad/s}$$

$$\lambda_1 = \omega_1^2 = 317.6280$$

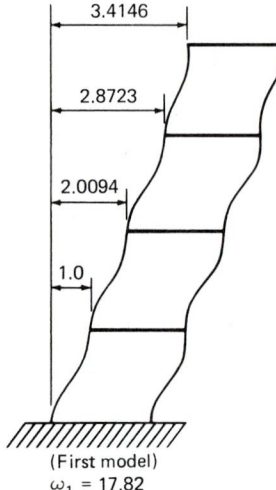

(First model)
$\omega_1 = 17.82$

Figure 3-11   First-mode configuration of the four-story building

The frequency in cycles per second is then

$$f_1 = \frac{\omega_1}{2\pi} = \frac{17.82}{2\pi} = 2.84$$

From the components of the eigenvector corresponding to λ_1, we obtain the configuration for the first mode of vibration shown in Fig. 3-11.

The Power Method with Shifting

In determining the largest eigenvalue λ_1 and associated eigenvector of a matrix **A** by the power method, slow convergence is sometimes encountered. One of the methods that has been used to speed up convergence consists of forming a new matrix

$$\mathbf{B} = \mathbf{A} - \beta\mathbf{I}$$

and finding the largest eigenvalue λ_1' of this matrix. With a proper choice of β, convergence may be improved considerably, and λ_1 is then determined from its relationship to λ_1'. We will show that the eigenvalues of **B** are related to the eigenvalues of **A** by

$$\lambda_i' = \lambda_i - \beta$$

To show that the eigenvalues of **B** are *shifted* from the eigenvalues of **A** by an amount β, we observe that

$$[\mathbf{A} - \beta\mathbf{I}]\mathbf{X} = \mathbf{A}\mathbf{X} - \beta\mathbf{X}$$

Since $\mathbf{A}\mathbf{X} = \lambda\mathbf{X}$, we can write that

$$[\mathbf{A} - \beta\mathbf{I}]\mathbf{X} = \lambda\mathbf{X} - \beta\mathbf{X} = (\lambda - \beta)\mathbf{X}$$

or

$$[\mathbf{A} - \beta\mathbf{I}]\mathbf{X} = \lambda'\mathbf{X}$$

with

$$\lambda' = \lambda - \beta$$

Thus, the eigenvalues of **B** will all be shifted from those of **A** by an amount β. Note that **B** is formed by subtracting β from the diagonal elements of the **A** matrix.

When we iterate to obtain the largest eigenvalue λ_1 of matrix **A,** the rate of convergence depends largely upon the ratio $|\lambda_2|\,/|\lambda_1|$, while in finding the largest eigenvalue of matrix **B,** the rate of convergence will depend largely upon the ratio $|\lambda_2 - \beta|/|\lambda_1 - \beta|$ (see App. B-6). The latter ratio can be made smaller than the former by a suitable choice of the value of β, thus improving the rate of convergence. The value of β which will result in the fastest convergence is given by

$$\beta = \frac{(\lambda_2 + \lambda_n)}{2}$$

This value will make $(\lambda_2 - \beta)$ and $(\lambda_n - \beta)$ equal in magnitude but of opposite sign. For example, if the eigenvalues of **A** are 10, 6, and 4, convergence would depend largely upon the ratio 6/10. The optimum value of β would be (6 + 4)/2 = 5. Remembering that $\lambda' = \lambda - \beta$, the eigenvalues of **B** would be 5, 1, and -1. The rate of convergence to λ_1' would depend largely upon the ratio 1/5, which is a considerable improvement over the ratio 6/10 obtained above. Of course in actually solving for the eigenvalues, λ_2 and λ_n would in general not be known, so the optimum β value could not be calculated. The only practical use of knowing how to determine the optimum value of β would be in cases in which rough estimates of the eigenvalues could be made, perhaps from knowledge of the physical characteristics of a system being modeled.

Convergence to the Smallest (Least Dominant) Eigenvalue by Shifting

With a proper choice of β, the *absolute values* of $\mathbf{B}$ may be reversed in order of magnitude from those of $\mathbf{A}$. For example, if the eigenvalues of $\mathbf{A}$ are 10, 6, and 4, and β is selected as 9, the eigenvalues of $\mathbf{B}$ will be 1, -3, and -5, with the dominant eigenvalue being -5. Convergence by the power method would be to -5, and λ_3, the smallest eigenvalue of $\mathbf{A}$, would be obtained as $-5 + \beta = 4$. To obtain the smallest eigenvalue of $\mathbf{A}$ with the most rapid convergence of $\mathbf{B}$, β should be given the value obtained from

$$\beta = \frac{(\lambda_{n-1} + \lambda_1)}{2}$$

Unfortunately, the value of λ_{n-1} would not be known, so a β value for optimum convergence could not be calculated in an actual problem in which we were solving for the eigenvalues. If λ_1, the largest eigenvalue of $\mathbf{A}$, is found first, and β is made equal to that value, λ_1' of matrix $\mathbf{B}$ will become equal to (be shifted to) zero, and the smallest eigenvalue of matrix $\mathbf{A}$ will be shifted so that its shifted value λ_n' is the most dominant eigenvalue (largest in absolute value) of matrix $\mathbf{B}$, and convergence will always be to it. Thus, the smallest eigenvalue λ_n of matrix $\mathbf{A}$ is obtained from

$$\lambda_n = \lambda_n' + \beta$$

in which $\beta = \lambda_1$.

3-13 JACOBI'S METHOD

Jacobi's method finds all eigenvalues and eigenvectors simultaneously and with uniform (and excellent) accuracy. It is not as efficient a method for large matrices as the Householder tridiagonalization method with the QL algorithm mentioned in Sec. 3-9, but the authors have found it to be quite acceptable for matrices up to approximately order 20. For matrices larger than this, Householder's method should be considered, particularly if many problems of this magnitude are to be solved.

Jacobi's method is limited to symmetric matrices (as is Householder's), but this limitation is less restrictive than one might suppose since many practical problems result in symmetric matrices or matrices that can be transformed into symmetric matrices. Our discussion of Jacobi's method will be limited to its application to real symmetric matrices, in which case the eigenvalues will also be real. We will first consider the basic eigenvalue equation

$$(\mathbf{A} - \lambda\mathbf{I})\mathbf{X} = 0$$

(3-134)
(repeated)

and later consider other forms of eigenvalue equations which result from common physical problems.

Coordinate Transformations

Before beginning our study of the Jacobi method, we may find it helpful to review coordinate transformations from analytic geometry. Figure 3-12 shows a point P in 3-dimensional space in an $x_1x_2x_3$ coordinate system. It is shown in the x_1x_2 plane to simplify showing its x_1 and x_2 coordinates, but it is not restricted to being in this plane. The coordinates of P are x_1, x_2, and x_3. Now suppose there is a rotation of the coordinate system in the counterclockwise sense about the x_3 axis (also called a rotation in the x_1x_2 plane) through the angle θ as shown in the figure so that the x_1 and x_2 axes are located at x_1' and x_2', respectively. The new coordinates of point P are x_1', x_2', and x_3'. Referring to Fig. 3-12, we see that

$$x_1' = x_1 \cos \theta + x_2 \sin \theta + (0)x_3$$
$$x_2' = -x_1 \sin \theta + x_2 \cos \theta + (0)x_3 \tag{3-170}$$
$$x_3' = (0)x_1 + (0)x_2 + (1)x_3$$

Equation 3-170 may be written in matrix form as

$$\begin{Bmatrix} x_1' \\ x_2' \\ x_3' \end{Bmatrix} = \begin{bmatrix} \cos \theta & \sin \theta & 0 \\ -\sin \theta & \cos \theta & 0 \\ 0 & 0 & 1 \end{bmatrix} \begin{Bmatrix} x_1 \\ x_2 \\ x_3 \end{Bmatrix} \tag{3-171}$$

or more simply as

$$\mathbf{X'} = \mathbf{RX} \tag{3-172}$$

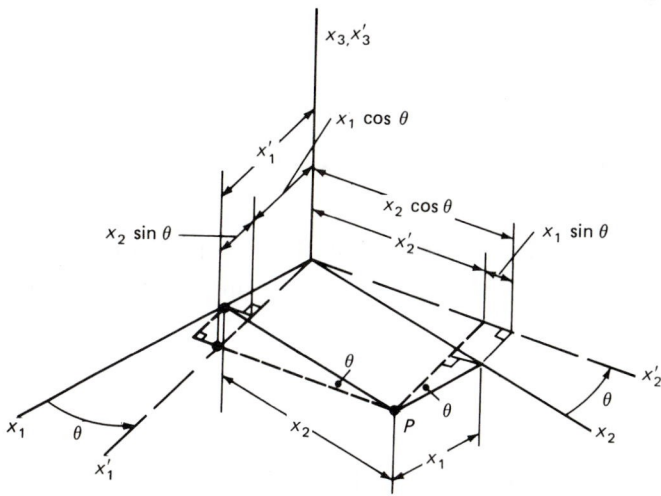

Figure 3-12 Transformation of coordinates due to a rotation of the coordinate system

where $\mathbf{R}$ is known as a rotation matrix. Let us note that with a proper selection of the angle θ we could make either x_1' or x_2' equal to zero.

For non-Euclidean 5-dimensional space, for example, a rotation matrix for rotation in the $x_i x_j$ plane with $i = 2, j = 4$, say, would be

$$
\mathbf{R} = \begin{bmatrix}
1 & 0 & 0 & 0 & 0 \\
0 & \cos\theta & 0 & \sin\theta & 0 \\
0 & 0 & 1 & 0 & 0 \\
0 & -\sin\theta & 0 & \cos\theta & 0 \\
0 & 0 & 0 & 0 & 1
\end{bmatrix}
\tag{3-173}
$$

A rotation matrix of any order n (n-dimensional space) for rotation in the $x_i x_j$ plane is an identity matrix of order n except for the elements r_{ii}, r_{ij}, r_{ji}, and r_{jj} which are

$$
\begin{aligned}
r_{ii} &= \cos\theta & r_{ij} &= \sin\theta \\
r_{ji} &= -\sin\theta & r_{jj} &= \cos\theta
\end{aligned}
\tag{3-174}
$$

A rotation in the $x_i x_j$ plane alters the coordinates x_i and x_j of a point in the n-dimensional space, and a proper selection of the rotation angle θ can make either of the coordinates x_i' or x_j' zero.

At this point we make a special note of the fact that if we form the transpose of a rotation matrix and take the matrix product $\mathbf{R}^T\mathbf{R}$, we obtain

$$
\mathbf{R}^T\mathbf{R} = \mathbf{I}
\tag{3-175}
$$

Any matrix $\mathbf{A}$ which satisfies the condition that $\mathbf{A}^T\mathbf{A}$ is equal to the *identity* matrix is known as an *orthogonal* matrix, so we should keep in mind that rotation matrices are orthogonal matrices.

Let us next consider an extension of the technique of altering the x_i and x_j coordinates of a point (or components of a vector) in n-dimensional space by a rotation in the $x_i x_j$ plane. We will consider the elements of each column of an $n \times n$ matrix $\mathbf{A}$ to be the components of an n-dimensional vector. If we premultiply matrix $\mathbf{A}$ by an $n \times n$ rotation matrix $\mathbf{R}$ for rotation in the $x_i x_j$ plane (we will henceforth designate such a rotation matrix as $\mathbf{R}(i,j)$), we will alter the i-th and j-th elements of *each* column vector of the matrix; that is, all of the elements of the i-th and j-th *rows* of matrix $\mathbf{A}$ will be altered. For example, if we premultiply a 3 by 3 matrix $\mathbf{A}$ by $\mathbf{R}(1, 2)$, we obtain

$$\mathbf{A'} = \begin{bmatrix} \cos\theta & \sin\theta & 0 \\ -\sin\theta & \cos\theta & 0 \\ 0 & 0 & 1 \end{bmatrix} \begin{bmatrix} a_{11} & a_{12} & a_{13} \\ a_{21} & a_{22} & a_{23} \\ a_{31} & a_{32} & a_{33} \end{bmatrix} =$$

$$\begin{bmatrix} (a_{11}\cos\theta + a_{21}\sin\theta) & (a_{12}\cos\theta + a_{22}\sin\theta) & (a_{13}\cos\theta + a_{23}\sin\theta) \\ (-a_{11}\sin\theta + a_{21}\cos\theta) & (-a_{12}\sin\theta + a_{22}\cos\theta) & (-a_{13}\sin\theta + a_{23}\cos\theta) \\ a_{31} & a_{32} & a_{33} \end{bmatrix}$$

$$(3\text{-}176)$$

When we look at the right side of Eq. 3-176, it is apparent that we could determine a value of θ for each altered element that would make that element equal to zero. For example, setting a'_{21} equal to zero gives

$$\tan\theta = \frac{a_{21}}{a_{11}} \qquad\qquad (3\text{-}177)$$

from which we could obtain the values of $\sin\theta$ and $\cos\theta$ in the rotation matrix which makes a'_{21} zero in the altered matrix.

Similarity Transformations

Having considered matrix transformations by premultiplying a matrix by a rotation matrix, let us next consider matrix transformations of a matrix $\mathbf{A}$ of the form $\mathbf{H}^{-1}\mathbf{AH}$. Such a transformation is called a *similarity* transformation and matrix $\mathbf{H}^{-1}\mathbf{AH}$ is said to be *similar* to matrix $\mathbf{A}$. Transformations of this form are of special importance since *the eigenvalues under a similarity transformation are invariant;* that is, the eigenvalues of matrix $\mathbf{H}^{-1}\mathbf{AH}$ are iden' al with the eigenvalues of $\mathbf{A}$. This may be shown as follows. Consider the basic eigenvalue matrix equation

$$(\mathbf{A} - \lambda\mathbf{I})\mathbf{X} = 0$$

or

$$\mathbf{A}\{\mathbf{X}\} = \lambda\{\mathbf{X}\} \qquad\qquad (3\text{-}178)$$

in which the λ values which satisfy Eq. 3-178 are the eigenvalues of matrix $\mathbf{A}$

and the $\{X\}$'s are the corresponding eigenvectors. Noting that a matrix HH^{-1} is simply an identity matrix, we can rewrite Eq. 3-178 as

$$AHH^{-1}\{X\} = \lambda\{X\} \tag{3-179}$$

We now premultiply both sides of Eq. 3-179 by H^{-1} giving

$$H^{-1}AHH^{-1}\{X\} = H^{-1}\lambda\{X\}$$

or

$$[H^{-1}AH]\{H^{-1}X\} = \lambda\{H^{-1}X\} \tag{3-180}$$

Comparing Eq. 3-180 with Eq. 3-178, we see that Eq. 3-180 is a basic eigen-value matrix equation for the matrix $H^{-1}AH$. The lambda values which satisfy Eq. 3-178 and are the eigenvalues of matrix A are the same lambda values which satisfy Eq. 3-180 and are the eigenvalues of matrix $H^{-1}AH$. Although it is not important in our development, we note that the eigenvectors of matrix $H^{-1}AH$ are the eigenvectors of A premultiplied by H^{-1}.

Now let us consider the transformation $R(i, j)AR^T(i, j)$, where $R(i, j)$ is a rotation matrix for rotation in the $x_i x_j$ plane. We have previously noted that R and R^T are the inverses of one another, so this transformation is a *similarity transformation* with eigenvalues invariant under such a transformation. It is also called an *orthogonal transformation* since R and R^T are orthogonal matrices. It should also be noted that if the original matrix is symmetric, the transformed matrix will also be symmetric.

As illustrated by Eq. 3-176, the premultiplication of matrix A by $R(i, j)$ will alter all the elements of the i-th and j-th rows of A. It may be similarly verified that postmultiplication of the matrix RA by $R^T(i, j)$ will alter all the elements of the i-th and j-th *columns* of matrix RA. Therefore, the transformation RAR^T is equivalent to a planar rotation altering the i-th and j-th rows of A, followed by a planar rotation altering the i-th and j-th columns of RA. Thus, all the elements of the i-th and j-th rows and columns of the matrix A (and only those elements) will be altered in each RAR^T transformation. As we will see later, when the RAR^T transformation is used in the Jacobi method, one of the off-diagonal elements of matrix A will be made to transform to zero with each transformation. The $R(i, j)$ and $R^T(i, j)$ matrices will depend upon the plane of rotation selected, and which altered off-diagonal element is made to go to zero in the transformed matrix depends upon the rotation angle θ selected.

A Special Similarity Transformation

Let the solutions of Eq. 3-135 be eigenvalues $\lambda_1, \lambda_2, \ldots, \lambda_n$ with corresponding eigenvectors $\{X_1\}, \{X_2\}, \ldots \{X_n\}$ so that

$$A\{X_i\} = \lambda_i\{X_i\}$$

with $i = 1, 2, \ldots, n$. The n matrix equations of Eq. 3-181 can be written as a single matrix equation

$$A[X] = [X][D] \tag{3-181}$$

where $[D]$ is a diagonal matrix with $\lambda_1, \lambda_2, \ldots, \lambda_n$ on the diagonal and $[X]$ is an n by n matrix with $\{X_i\}$, $i = 1, 2, \ldots, n$, as its columns. Premultiplying both sides of Eq. 3-181 by $[X]^{-1}$ gives

$$[X]^{-1}A[X] = [D] \tag{3-182}$$

Thus, we see that there exists a similarity transformation of matrix A which produces a diagonal matrix with the eigenvalues of A as the diagonal elements. Furthermore, the matrix X used in the transformation contains the eigenvectors of A as its columns.

Jacobi's Method

Jacobi's method consists of performing a sequence of similarity transformations on a sequence of matrices beginning with the matrix A (to be called A_1 in the equations below) whose eigenvalues and eigenvectors are sought. These transformations are of the form

$$
\begin{aligned}
A_2 &= R_1(i, j)A_1R_1^T(i, j) \\
A_3 &= R_2(i, j)A_2R_2^T(i, j) \\
&\vdots \\
A_{r+1} &= R_r(i, j)A_rR_r^T(i, j) \\
&\vdots
\end{aligned}
\tag{3-183}
$$

where the $R(i, j)$'s are plane rotation matrices with the rotation angle θ in the x_ix_j plane. The θ value and the plane x_ix_j for each transformation is selected to make a particular off-diagonal element (a_{ij}) in that transformed matrix equal to zero. We shall call each such transformation a rotation, and the rotations proceed with the transformed matrices A_2, A_3, $\ldots$, A_{r+1} $\ldots$ until the final desired transformed matrix is obtained.

Jacobi selected the plane and the angle to make the largest off-diagonal element in each transformed matrix go to zero. However, in a computer program the off-diagonal elements are usually made to go to zero in some systematic, cyclic manner to save the time involved in a search for the largest off-diagonal element prior to each transformation. We shall make the off-diagonal elements go to zero by *rows* in our subsequent computer program. When all the off-diagonal elements have in turn been initially made to go to zero, it is said that a *sweep* has been completed. The sweeps continue until the transformed matrices approach a diagonal form. A number of sweeps are required because when an off-diagonal element of A_{r+1} is made zero in that similarity transformation, the off-diagonal element of A_r which was made zero in the previous transformation will in general become nonzero. Fortunately, however, the off-diagonal elements all tend toward zero, and with a sufficient number of sweeps the sequence of transformed matrices approaches a final diagonal form. The sweeps cease when all the off-diagonal elements become negligible in magnitude.

As an example of the foregoing discussion, consider a 4 by 4 matrix

$$
A_1 = \begin{bmatrix} a_{11} & a_{12} & a_{13} & a_{14} \\ a_{21} & a_{22} & a_{23} & a_{24} \\ a_{31} & a_{32} & a_{33} & a_{34} \\ a_{41} & a_{42} & a_{43} & a_{44} \end{bmatrix}
$$

With $i = 1$, and $j = 2$, the altered elements of the transformed matrix A_2 are indicated below by the horizontal and vertical lines (the i-th and j-th rows and columns) given by the rotation plane $x_1 x_2$.

$$
A_2 = \begin{bmatrix} a_{11} & a_{12} & a_{13} & a_{14} \\ a_{21} & a_{22} & a_{23} & a_{24} \\ a_{31} & a_{32} & a_{33} & a_{34} \\ a_{41} & a_{42} & a_{43} & a_{44} \end{bmatrix}
$$

The angle θ would be selected to make a_{12} go to zero. The element a_{21} would also go to zero since if the original matrix is symmetric, the transformed matrices will be symmetric. After the above rotation, the next rotation would be in plane $x_1 x_3$ and the altered elements are again shown below by the horizontal and vertical lines.

$$
A_3 = \begin{bmatrix} a_{11} & a_{12} & a_{13} & a_{14} \\ a_{21} & a_{22} & a_{23} & a_{24} \\ a_{31} & a_{32} & a_{33} & a_{34} \\ a_{41} & a_{42} & a_{43} & a_{44} \end{bmatrix}
$$

A θ value is determined to make elements a_{13} and a_{31} equal to zero. Next would come a rotation in plane $x_1 x_4$ in which a θ value would be determined to make elements a_{14} and a_{41} of the transformed matrix A_4 equal to zero. The sequence then steps forward to a rotation in the plane $x_2 x_3$ in which a θ value would be determined to make the off-diagonal elements a_{23} and a_{32} of $\mathbf{A}_5$ equal to zero. The final transformation of the sequence would be with the rotation plane $x_3 x_4$ in which the off-diagonal elements a_{34} and a_{43} of $\mathbf{A}_7$ would be made to equal zero. As stated before, when all the off-diagonal elements have been initially transformed to zero in the row by row procedure just outlined, a sweep has been completed. The operations within a sweep can be specified by

$$i = 1, j = i + 1, i + 2, \ldots, n$$

$$i = 2, j = i + 1, i + 2, \ldots, n$$

$$\vdots$$

$$i = n - 1, j = n$$

The next sweep would begin with the rotation plane $x_1 x_2$ in which the off-diagonal elements a_{12} and a_{21} of $\mathbf{A}_8$ would be transformed to zero by determining a proper θ value. The steps within this second sweep continue through the rotation planes as discussed above until the rotation plane $x_3 x_4$ is reached again and yet another sweep begins. The sweeps then continue until all the off-diagonal elements are of negligible magnitude.

The eigenvalues will have remained invariant under all the similarity transformations mentioned, so the eigenvalues of the final diagonal matrix are the same as those of the original matrix $\mathbf{A}_1$, or $\mathbf{A}$. It can be shown that the diagonal elements of the final matrix are these eigenvalues. The final form of a 4 by 4 matrix would be

$$\mathbf{A}_{\text{final}} = \begin{bmatrix} a_{11} & 0 & 0 & 0 \\ 0 & a_{22} & 0 & 0 \\ 0 & 0 & a_{33} & 0 \\ 0 & 0 & 0 & a_{44} \end{bmatrix}$$

From Sec. 3-8 we know that the eigenvalues of the matrix may be found by setting the determinant

$$\begin{vmatrix} a_{11} - \lambda & 0 & 0 & 0 \\ 0 & a_{22} - \lambda & 0 & 0 \\ 0 & 0 & a_{33} - \lambda & 0 \\ 0 & 0 & 0 & a_{44} - \lambda \end{vmatrix}$$

equal to zero. Thus,

$$(a_{11} - \lambda)(a_{22} - \lambda)(a_{33} - \lambda)(a_{44} - \lambda) = 0$$

from which $a_{11} = \lambda_1$, $a_{22} = \lambda_2$, $a_{33} = \lambda_3$, and $a_{44} = \lambda_4$.

If in Eq. 3-183 we substitute the first equation into the second, the second into the third, and so on for all the rotations, we find that the final equation will be of the form

$$\mathbf{A}_{\text{final}} = \underset{\text{final}}{\mathbf{R}(i, j)} \ldots \mathbf{R}_2(i, j)\mathbf{R}_1(i, j)\mathbf{A}_1\mathbf{R}_1^{\mathrm{T}}(i, j)\mathbf{R}_2^{\mathrm{T}}(i, j) \ldots \underset{\text{final}}{\mathbf{R}^{\mathrm{T}}(i, j)} \qquad \text{(3-184)}$$

Comparing Eq. 3-184 with Eq. 3-182, we see that

$$\mathbf{R}_1^{\mathrm{T}}(i, j)\mathbf{R}_2^{\mathrm{T}}(i, j) \ldots \underset{\text{final}}{\mathbf{R}^{\mathrm{T}}(i, j)} = [\mathbf{X}] \qquad \text{(3-185)}$$

with the columns of $[\mathbf{X}]$ being the eigenvectors $\{\mathbf{X}_i\}$ of $\mathbf{A}_1$, with $\{\mathbf{X}_1\}$ being the eigenvector corresponding to λ_1, with $\{\mathbf{X}_2\}$ being the eigenvector corresponding to λ_2, and so forth.

In the subsequent computer program, the matrix $[\mathbf{X}]$ is formed by beginning with an n by n identity matrix. After the first rotation, this identity matrix is postmultiplied by $\mathbf{R}_1^{\mathrm{T}}$ and the resulting matrix is stored as elements of the FORTRAN array RT. After the second rotation, this stored matrix, which we call here RT, is postmultiplied by $\mathbf{R}_2^{\mathrm{T}}$, and a new matrix RT is formed. This postmultiplication continues after each rotation until finally RT is postmultiplied by $\mathbf{R}_{\text{final}}^{\mathrm{T}}$. The resulting matrix is the matrix $[\mathbf{X}]$ which is stored in the computer as the elements of the final FORTRAN array RT.

Selection of the Rotation Planes and Angles θ

As has been previously noted, a transformation of a matrix $\mathbf{A}$ using the plane rotation matrix $\mathbf{R}(i, j)$ and its transpose $\mathbf{R}^{\mathrm{T}}(i, j)$ will affect only elements of the i-th and j-th rows and columns of $\mathbf{A}$. It may be verified that the new elements resulting from such a transformation are as shown in Eqs. 3-186. The new elements are identified with the superscript $(r + 1)$ and the old elements with the superscript (r).

$$
\left.
\begin{aligned}
a_{li}^{(r+1)} &= a_{li}^{(r)} \cos \theta + a_{lj}^{(r)} \sin \theta \qquad\qquad = a_{il}^{(r+1)} \\
a_{lj}^{(r+1)} &= -a_{li}^{(r)} \sin \theta + a_{lj}^{(r)} \cos \theta \qquad\qquad = a_{jl}^{(r+1)}
\end{aligned}
\right\} \quad l \neq i, j
$$

$$a_{ii}^{(r+1)} = a_{ii}^{(r)} \cos^2 \theta + 2a_{ij}^{(r)} \cos \theta \sin \theta + a_{jj}^r \sin^2 \theta \qquad \text{(3-186)}$$

$$a_{jj}^{(r+1)} = a_{ii}^{(r)} \sin^2 \theta - 2a_{ij}^{(r)} \cos \theta \sin \theta + a_{jj}^{(r)} \cos^2 \theta$$

$$a_{ij}^{(r+1)} = (a_{jj}^{(r)} - a_{ii}^{(r)}) \cos \theta \sin \theta + a_{ij}^{(r)}(\cos^2 \theta - \sin^2 \theta) = a_{ji}^{(r+1)}$$

The angle θ for the transformation $\mathbf{R}_r(i, j)\mathbf{A}_r\mathbf{R}_r^{\mathrm{T}}(i, j)$ will be selected to make $a_{ij}^{(r+1)}$ equal to zero; that is, in each rotation we make a particular off-diagonal element equal to zero. If $a_{ij}^{(r+1)}$ is to be zero, we use the rotation matrix $\mathbf{R}(i, j)$ and its transpose and the angle θ determined from setting the last of Eqs. 3-186 equal to zero. Setting this equation equal to zero, and using the identities $2 \sin \theta \cos \theta = \sin 2\theta$ and $\cos^2 \theta - \sin^2 \theta = \cos 2\theta$, we obtain

$$\tan 2\theta = \frac{2 \, a_{ij}^{(r)}}{(a_{ii}^{(r)} - a_{jj}^{(r)})} \tag{3-187}$$

where the angle 2θ is chosen to satisfy the condition that

$$-\frac{\pi}{2} \le 2\theta \le \frac{\pi}{2}$$

We could solve Eq. 3-187 for θ and then obtain numerical values for $\sin \theta$ and $\cos \theta$ for the rotation, but values of $\sin \theta$ and $\cos \theta$ with a higher degree of accuracy may be obtained by using equations which solve for $\sin \theta$ and $\cos \theta$ directly. Various expressions for $\sin \theta$ and $\cos \theta$ can be derived from the last of Eqs. 3-186 for obtaining values for these quantities in the rotation matrices. However, expressions that give particularly accurate values are

$$\cos \theta = \left[\frac{\sqrt{(a_{ii} - a_{jj})^2 + 4 \, a_{ij}^2} + (a_{ii} - a_{jj})}{2 \, \sqrt{(a_{ii} - a_{jj})^2 + 4 \, a_{ij}^2}} \right]^{1/2} \tag{3-188}$$

and

$$\sin \theta = \frac{a_{ij}}{\sqrt{(a_{ii} - a_{jj})^2 + 4 \, a_{ij}^2} \, \cos \theta} \tag{3-189}$$

Equations 3-188 and 3-189 give highly accurate results since they do not involve taking the difference of two quantities which are of nearly the same magnitude, such as $1 - \cos 2\theta$ for small values of θ.

Ordering the Eigenvalues

When the diagonal matrix $[\mathbf{D}]$ is obtained by the Jacobi procedure outlined above, the eigenvalues on the diagonal are not ordered as to algebraic magnitude as would be desirable. When we perform matrix rotations in our computer program which transform various off-diagonal elements in turn to zero, we will vary i and j values in a given sweep such that i is always less than j; that is, we will sweep through the elements above the main diagonal by rows (because of the symmetry of the successive matrices obtained, symmetric elements below the main diagonal will also be transformed to zero). If a_{ii} is less than a_{jj}, then the elements down the main diagonal are not all decreasing in magnitude as we would like to have them, so that the eigenvalues down the main diagonal of our final matrix will be in descending order (algebraically

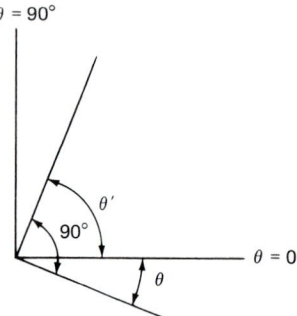

Figure 3-13 Angles θ and θ' for negative θ

largest to smallest). It would be possible to order the eigenvalues without a separate algorithm if, whenever $(a_{ii}^{(r)} - a_{jj}^{(r)})$ is negative, we could use a rotation angle θ' instead of θ that would make $a_{ij}^{(r+1)}$ zero, and at the same time would interchange $a_{ii}^{(r+1)}$ and $a_{jj}^{(r+1)}$ from what they would be if the angle θ were used. Fortunately, this is possible by using an angle θ' which is 90 degrees larger than θ if θ is negative, or 90 deg smaller than θ if θ is positive, as illustrated in Figs. 3-13 and 3-14.

The expression for $\sin \theta'$ will be

$$
\sin \theta' = \pm \left[\frac{\sqrt{(a_{ii} - a_{jj})^2 + 4 a_{ij}^2} - (a_{ii} - a_{jj})}{2 \sqrt{(a_{ii} - a_{jj})^2 + 4 a_{ij}^2}} \right]^{1/2}
\tag{3-190}
$$

which is just like the expression for $\cos \theta$ in Eq. 3-188 except that $(a_{ii} - a_{jj})$ in the numerator is subtracted instead of added because $(a_{ii} - a_{jj})$ is negative. If $a_{ij}^{(r)}$ is a negative quantity, indicating a positive θ (refer to the quotient in Eq. 3-187), then the negative sign is used in Eq. 3-190, since θ' is negative.

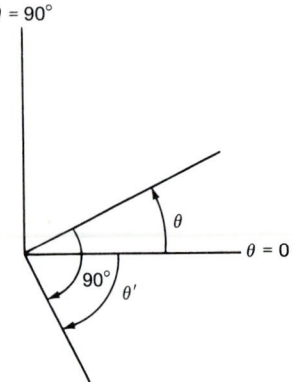

Figure 3-14 Angles θ and θ' for positive θ

The expression for $\cos \theta'$ will be

$$\cos \theta' = \frac{a_{ij}}{\sqrt{(a_{ii} - a_{jj})^2 + 4\,a_{ij}^2}\, \sin \theta'} \tag{3-191}$$

This is just like the expression for $\sin \theta$ in Eq. 3-189 except that $\cos \theta$ has been replaced by $\sin \theta'$ in the denominator. We note that $\cos \theta'$ will always be positive.

The variable names used in the flow chart and in the FORTRAN program which follows it and the quantities these names represent are as follows:

Variable Name	Quantity
A(I,J)	The array name of the original symmetric matrix for which eigenvalues and eigenvectors are to be found and also the name of all the transformed matrices
RT(I,J)	Originally an N by N identity matrix which eventually becomes the product matrix of all the transposed rotation matrices, and therefore the matrix containing the eigenvectors
N	The order of the matrix **A**
IMIN1	$I - 1$
NSWEEP	A counter which counts the number of sweeps
NRSKIP	A counter which counts the number of rotations skipped in a given sweep
NMIN1	$N - 1$
IP1	$I + 1$
AV	$(a_{ij} + a_{ji})/2$
DIFF	$(a_{ii} - a_{jj})$
RAD	$\sqrt{(a_{ii} - a_{jj})^2 + 4(\text{AV})^2}$
SINE	$\sin \theta$
COSINE	$\cos \theta$
Q	A temporary name for A(I,K), A(K,I), and RT(K,I) for use during calculation of new values of these quantities
PROD	The product of the first and last eigenvectors, which is determined as an accuracy check

A flow chart based upon our discussion of Jacobi's method is shown in Fig. 3-15. It essentially follows the algorithm of Nash.[16]

[16] J. C. Nash, *Compact Numerical Methods for Computers* (New York: John Wiley & Sons, 1979, pp. 106–107).

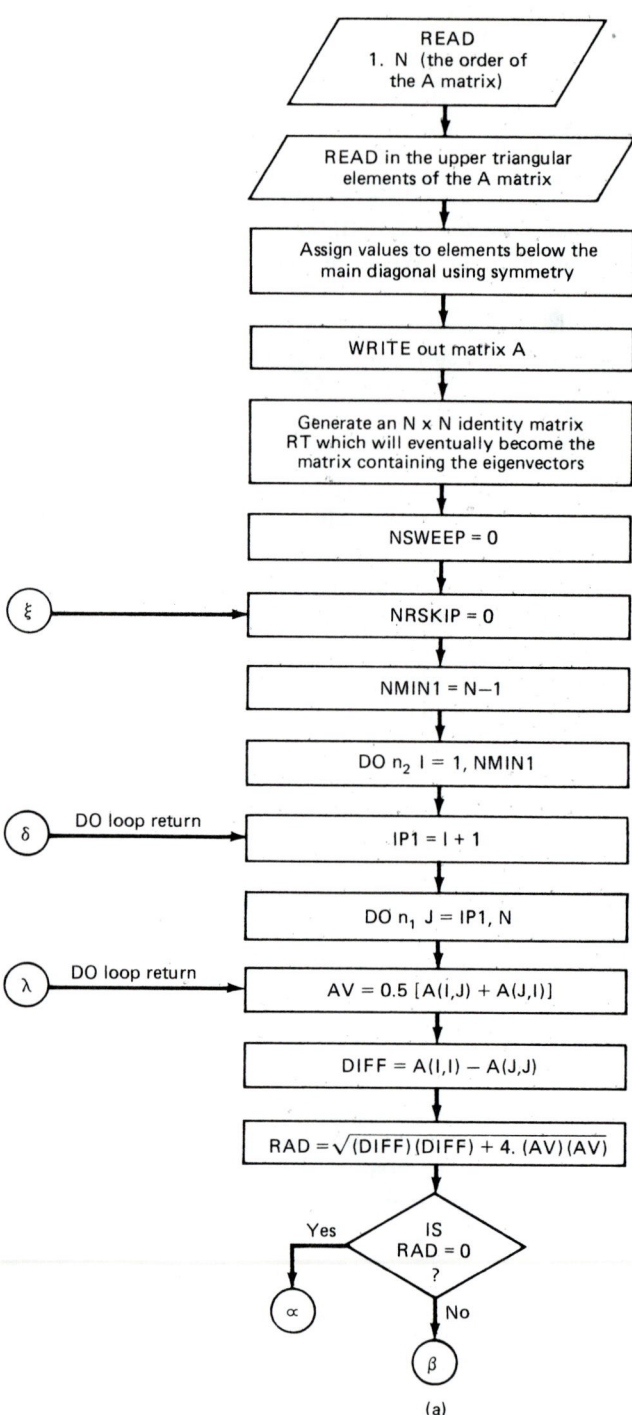

Figure 3-15(a) Flow chart for Jacobi's method

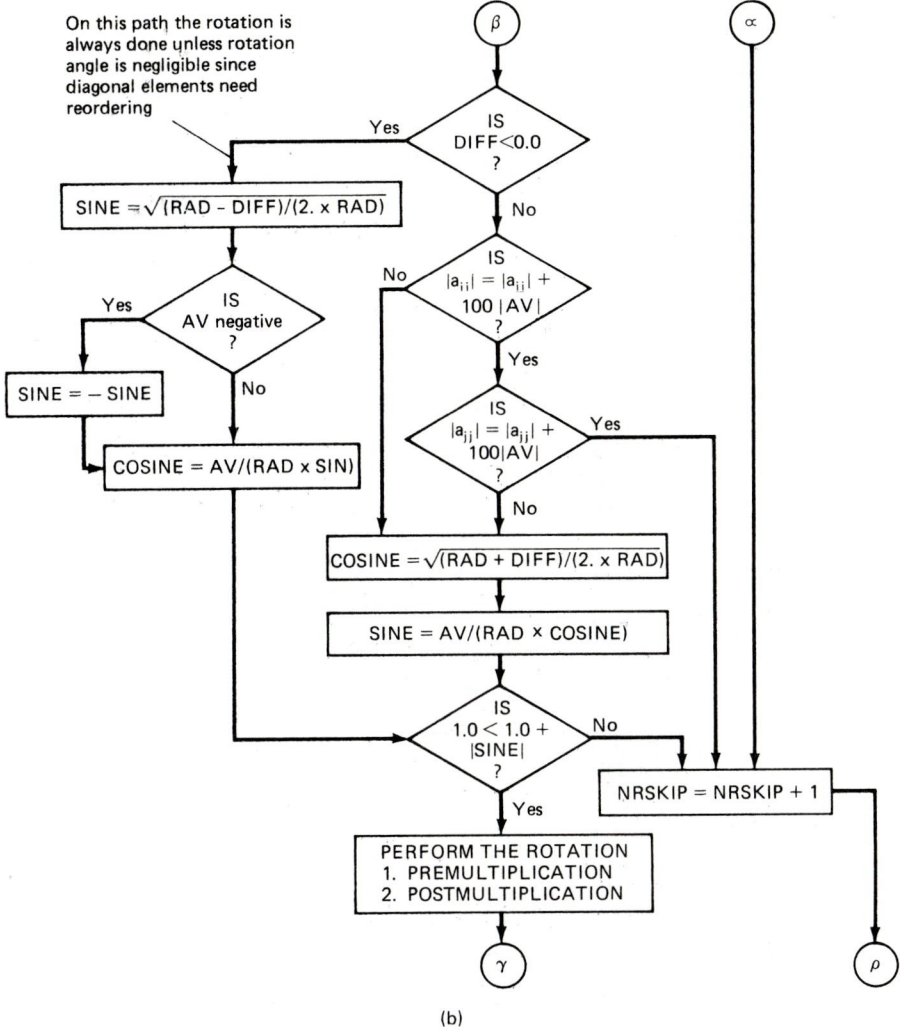

(b)

Figure 3-15(b) Flow chart for Jacobi's method

The FORTRAN program implementing the flow chart of Fig. 3-15 follows. The eigenvalues and eigenvectors of the matrix

$$\begin{bmatrix} 5.0 & 3.0 & 1.0 \\ 3.0 & 9.0 & 3.0 \\ 1.0 & 3.0 & 5.0 \end{bmatrix}$$

are determined by this program and the output results are shown.

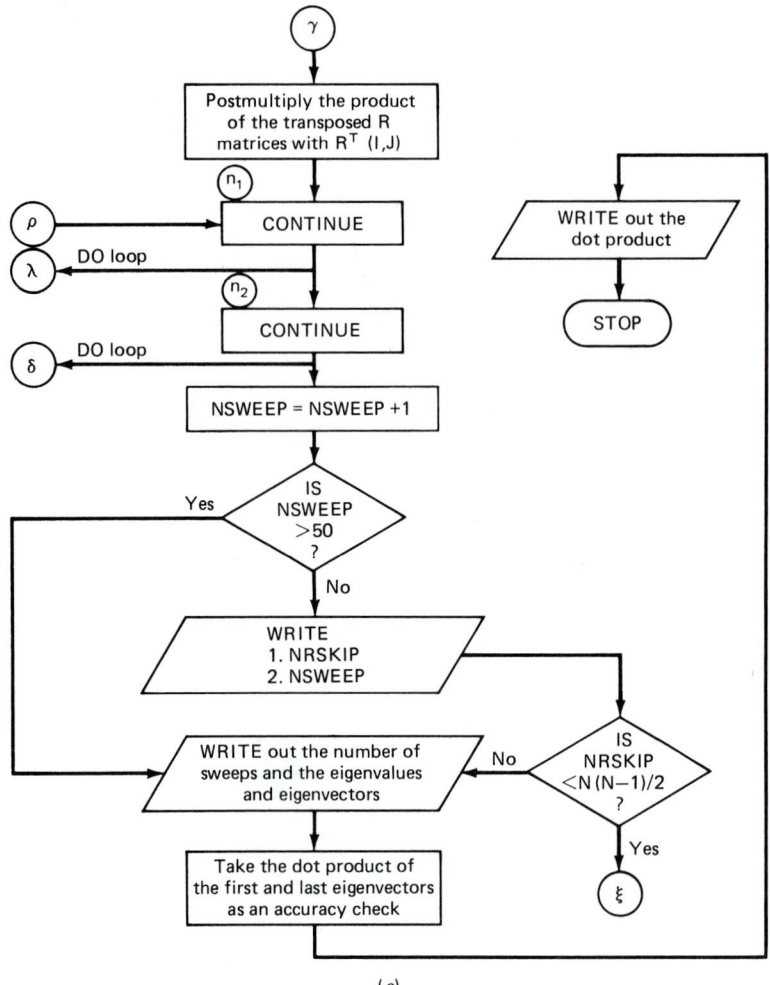

Figure 3-15(c)   Flow chart for Jacobi's method

```
C THIS DOUBLE PRECISION PROGRAM DETERMINES THE EIGENVALUES
C AND EIGENVECTORS OF SYMMETRIC MATRICES BY THE JACOBI
                                        METHOD.   THE
C EIGENVALUES ARE ORDERED FROM ALGEBRAICALLY LARGEST TO
                                        SMALLEST.
C THE EIGENVECTORS ARE NORMALIZED SO THAT THEIR MAGNITUDES
C EQUAL UNITY BUT ADDITIONAL STATEMENTS TO NORMALIZE IN ANY
C WAY DESIRED MAY BE ADDED.
      IMPLICIT REAL*8 (A-H,O-Z)
      DIMENSION A(10,10),RT(10,10)
C READ IN THE ORDER OF THE MATRIX   A   FOR WHICH THE
C EIGENVALUES AND EIGENVECTORS ARE TO BE DETERMINED.
      READ(5,2)N
```

```
    2 FORMAT(I2)
C READ IN THE ELEMENTS OF THE MATRIX  A   ALONG AND ABOVE
C THE MAIN DIAGONAL.
      READ(5,3)((A(I,J),J=I,N),I=1,N)
    3 FORMAT(8F10.0)
C ASSIGN VALUES TO ELEMENTS BELOW THE MAIN DIAGONAL
C USING SYMMETRY.
      DO 4 I=2,N
      IMIN1=I-1
      DO 4 J=1,IMIN1
    4 A(I,J)=A(J,I)
C WRITE OUT SYMMETRIC MATRIX  A.
      WRITE(6,5)
    5 FORMAT('1','SYMMETRIC MATRIX  A  IS AS FOLLOWS:',//)
      WRITE(6,6) ((A(I,J),J=1,N),I=1,N)
C THE FOLLOWING FORMAT STATEMENT MUST AGREE WITH THE ORDER
                                              OF MATRIX  A.
    6 FORMAT(' ',3F15.4)
C GENERATE AN N × N IDENTITY MATRIX RT WHICH WILL
C EVENTUALLY BECOME THE MATRIX CONTAINING THE EIGENVECTORS.
      DO 8 I=1,N
      DO 7 J=1,N
      RT(I,J)=0.0
    7 CONTINUE
      RT(I,I)=1.0
    8 CONTINUE
      NSWEEP=0
    9 NRSKIP=0
C BEGIN A SWEEP WHICH WILL TRANSFORM EACH OFF-DIAGONAL
C ELEMENT IN TURN TO ZERO.
      NMIN1=N-1
      DO 19 I=1,NMIN1
      IP1=I+1
      DO 18 J=IP1,N
      AV=0.5*(A(I,J)+A(J,I))
      DIFF=A(I,I)-A(J,J)
      RAD=DSQRT(DIFF*DIFF+4.*AV*AV)
C CHECK TO SEE IF RAD IS ZERO.  IF IT IS, NO ROTATION
C WILL BE PERFORMED SINCE CALCULATION OF SINE AND
C COSINE WOULD CAUSE OVERFLOW.
      IF(RAD .EQ. 0.0)GO TO 14
C CHECK TO SEE IF DIFF IS NEGATIVE.  IF IT IS, THE ELEMENTS
C A(I,I) AND A(J,J) ON THE DIAGONAL NEED TO BE
C INTERCHANGED AND THEREFORE A ROTATION WILL BE PERFORMED.
      IF(DIFF .LT. 0.0)GO TO 12
      IF(DABS(A(I,I)) .EQ. DABS(A(I,I))+100.*DABS(AV))GO
                                              TO 10
      GO TO 11
   10 IF(DABS(A(J,J)) .EQ. DABS(A(J,J))+100.*DABS(AV))GO
                                              TO 14
   11 COSINE=DSQRT((RAD+DIFF)/(2.*RAD))
      SINE=AV/(RAD*COSINE)
      GO TO 13
C ON THIS PATH, ROTATIONS WILL ALWAYS BE PERFORMED SINCE
C ELEMENTS ON THE DIAGONAL NEED REORDERING.
```

```
   12 SINE=DSQRT((RAD-DIFF)/(2.*RAD))
      IF(AV .LT. 0.0)SINE=-SINE
      COSINE=AV/(RAD*SINE)
C CHECK TO SEE IF SIN(THETA) IS NEGLIGIBLE.  IF IT IS,
C SKIP THE ROTATION.
   13 IF(1. .LT. 1. + DABS(SINE))GO TO 15
   14 NRSKIP=NRSKIP + 1
      GO TO 18
C PERFORM THE ROTATION.
C PREMULTIPLY BY THE ROTATION MATRIX.
   15 DO 16 K=1,N
      Q=A(I,K)
      A(I,K)=COSINE*Q+SINE*A(J,K)
      A(J,K)=-SINE*Q+COSINE*A(J,K)
   16 CONTINUE
C POSTMULTIPLY BY THE TRANSFORM OF THE ROTATION MATRIX.
      DO 17 K=1,N
      Q=A(K,I)
      A(K,I)=COSINE*Q+SINE*A(K,J)
      A(K,J)=-SINE*Q+COSINE*A(K,J)
C POSTMULTIPLY THE CURRENT PRODUCT OF ALL THE RT MATRICES
C UP TO THIS POINT BY THE CURRENT RT MATRIX.  THIS PRODUCT
C OF RT MATRICES WHICH HAS THE FORTRAN VARIABLE NAME  RT
C WILL EVENTUALLY BECOME THE MATRIX CONTAINING THE
                                            EIGENVECTORS.
      Q=RT(K,I)
      RT(K,I)=COSINE*Q+SINE*RT(K,J)
      RT(K,J)=-SINE*Q+COSINE*RT(K,J)
   17 CONTINUE
   18 CONTINUE
   19 CONTINUE
C KEEP A TALLY OF THE NUMBER OF SWEEPS.
      NSWEEP=NSWEEP+1
      IF(NSWEEP .GT. 50)GO TO 21
      WRITE(6,20)NRSKIP,NSWEEP
   20 FORMAT(' ','THERE WERE ',I2,
     $' ROTATIONS SKIPPED ON SWEEP NUMBER ',I2)
C SEE IF THE NUMBER OF ROTATIONS SKIPPED IS LESS THAN OR
                                                    EQUAL
C TO THE NUMBER OF ELEMENTS ABOVE THE MAIN DIAGONAL.  IF
C EQUAL TO, THEN CONVERGENCE HAS OCCURRED.
      IF(NRSKIP .LT. N*(N-1)/2)GO TO 9
   21 WRITE(6,22)NSWEEP
   22 FORMAT(' ',//,' THERE WERE ',I2,' SWEEPS PERFORMED.',
     $/' THE EIGENVALUES AND EIGENVECTORS FOLLOW:')
      DO 27 J=1,N
      WRITE(6,23)J,A(J,J)
   23 FORMAT(/,' ','LAMBDA (',I2,') = ',F20.10)
      WRITE(6,24)
   24 FORMAT(/,' ','THE ASSOCIATED EIGENVECTOR IS:')
      DO 25 I=1,N
   25 WRITE(6,26)RT(I,J)
   26 FORMAT(' ',5X,D17.10)
```

```
   27 CONTINUE
C AS AN ACCURACY CHECK, SEE IF THE DOT PRODUCT OF THE FIRST
                                                        AND LAST
C EIGENVECTORS IS NEAR ZERO.
      PROD=0.0
      DO 28 J=1,N
      PROD=PROD+RT(J,1)*RT(J,N)
   28 CONTINUE
      WRITE(6,29)PROD
   29 FORMAT(///,' ','THE PRODUCT OF THE FIRST AND LAST',
     $' EIGENVECTORS IS ',F18.16)
      STOP
      END
```

```
SYMMETRIC MATRIX  A  IS AS FOLLOWS:

           5.0000          3.0000          1.0000
           3.0000          9.0000          3.0000
           1.0000          3.0000          5.0000
THERE WERE  0 ROTATIONS SKIPPED ON SWEEP NUMBER  1
THERE WERE  0 ROTATIONS SKIPPED ON SWEEP NUMBER  2
THERE WERE  0 ROTATIONS SKIPPED ON SWEEP NUMBER  3
THERE WERE  3 ROTATIONS SKIPPED ON SWEEP NUMBER  4


THERE WERE  4 SWEEPS PERFORMED.
THE EIGENVALUES AND EIGENVECTORS FOLLOW:

LAMBDA ( 1) =         12.0000000000

THE ASSOCIATED EIGENVECTOR IS:
        0.4082482905D+00
        0.8164965809D+00
        0.4082482905D+00

LAMBDA ( 2) =          4.0000000000

THE ASSOCIATED EIGENVECTOR IS:
      - 0.7071067812D+00
      - 0.1548221893D-15
        0.7071067812D+00

LAMBDA ( 3) =          3.0000000000

THE ASSOCIATED EIGENVECTOR IS:
        0.5773502692D+00
      - 0.5773502692D+00
        0.5773502692D+00


THE PRODUCT OF THE FIRST AND LAST EIGENVECTOR IS
                                    - .0000000000000000
```

The Eigenvalue Problem $KX = \lambda MX$

As we noted in Ex. 3-11, matrix eigenvalue equations for physical problems do not always occur in the standard form of Eq. 3-135 or Eq. 3-139. In structural dynamics, for example, the matrix equation

$$KX = \lambda MX$$

(3-156)
(repeated)

occurs frequently, where $\mathbf{K}$ is the stiffness matrix (symmetric) and $\mathbf{M}$ is the mass matrix containing elements only on the diagonal. This eigenvalue problem may be solved by reducing it to a standard symmetric eigenvalue problem and solving by Jacobi's method.

Let $\mathbf{M}$ be a 3 by 3 mass matrix for purposes of illustrating that the mass matrix can be decomposed as follows:

$$\begin{bmatrix} m_1 & 0 & 0 \\ 0 & m_2 & 0 \\ 0 & 0 & m_3 \end{bmatrix} = \begin{bmatrix} \sqrt{m_1} & 0 & 0 \\ 0 & \sqrt{m_2} & 0 \\ 0 & 0 & \sqrt{m_3} \end{bmatrix} \begin{bmatrix} \sqrt{m_1} & 0 & 0 \\ 0 & \sqrt{m_2} & 0 \\ 0 & 0 & \sqrt{m_3} \end{bmatrix}$$

or

$$\mathbf{M} = \left[\sqrt{m}\right]\left[\sqrt{m}\right]$$

(3-192)

where $\left[\sqrt{m}\right]$ represents a diagonal matrix as illustrated above. We can therefore rewrite Eq. 3-156 as

$$KX = \lambda\left[\sqrt{m}\right]\left[\sqrt{m}\right] X$$

(3-193)

Let $\left[1/\sqrt{m}\right]$ represent a diagonal matrix with $1/\sqrt{m_1}$, $1/\sqrt{m_2}$, and so on, on the diagonal. It is easy to show that

$$\left[\frac{1}{\sqrt{m}}\right]\left[\sqrt{m}\right] = \mathbf{I}$$

(3-194)

Then Eq. 3-193 can be written as

$$K\left[\frac{1}{\sqrt{m}}\right]\left[\sqrt{m}\right] X = \lambda\left[\sqrt{m}\right]\left[\sqrt{m}\right] X$$

(3-195)

Premultiplying both sides by $\left[1/\sqrt{m}\right]$ gives

$$\left[\frac{1}{\sqrt{m}}\right] \mathbf{K} \left[\frac{1}{\sqrt{m}}\right]\left[\sqrt{m}\right] \mathbf{X} = \lambda\left[\frac{1}{\sqrt{m}}\right]\left[\sqrt{m}\right]\left[\sqrt{m}\right] \mathbf{X}$$

or

$$\left[\left[\frac{1}{\sqrt{m}}\right] \mathbf{K} \left[\frac{1}{\sqrt{m}}\right]\right] \left[\left[\sqrt{m}\right] \mathbf{X}\right] = \lambda\left[\left[\sqrt{m}\right] \mathbf{X}\right] \qquad (3\text{-}196)$$

The matrix $\left[\dfrac{1}{\sqrt{m}}\right] \mathbf{K} \left[\dfrac{1}{\sqrt{m}}\right]$ is symmetric and has elements $\dfrac{k_{ij}}{\sqrt{m_i}\ \sqrt{m_j}}$ so
Eq. 3-196 is in standard form. The eigenvalues determined from this standard
form are identical to those of Eq. 3-156, but the eigenvector components
obtained from the solution of Eq. 3-196 must be divided by $\sqrt{m_i}$ to get the
eigenvectors of Eq. 3-156 (see Prob. 3-51).

The Eigenvalue Problem $\mathbf{BMX} = \dfrac{1}{\lambda}\mathbf{X}$

In Ex. 3-11 we noted that in structural dynamics the eigenvalue matrix equation

$$\mathbf{BMX} = \frac{1}{\lambda}\mathbf{X} = \lambda'\mathbf{X} \qquad \begin{array}{l}(3\text{-}157)\\ (\text{repeated})\end{array}$$

is written when the flexibility matrix (symmetric) is used rather than the stiffness matrix $\mathbf{K}$. The flexibility matrix is the inverse of the stiffness matrix. Matrix
$\mathbf{B}$ is symmetric, but unfortunately when the product of $\mathbf{B}$ and $\mathbf{M}$ is formed it
is not in general symmetric. Therefore, a reduction of Eq. 3-157 to standard
form must be carried out for a solution by Jacobi's method.

Using Eq. 3-192, we can write Eq. 3-157 as

$$\mathbf{B}\left[\sqrt{m}\right]\left[\sqrt{m}\right] \mathbf{X} = \lambda'\mathbf{X} \qquad (3\text{-}197)$$

Premultiplying both sides by $\left[\sqrt{m}\right]$ gives

$$\left[\left[\sqrt{m}\right] \mathbf{B} \left[\sqrt{m}\right]\right]\left[\left[\sqrt{m}\right] \mathbf{X}\right] = \lambda'\ \sqrt{m}\ \mathbf{X} \qquad (3\text{-}198)$$

The matrix $\mathbf{C} = \left[\sqrt{m}\right] \mathbf{B} \left[\sqrt{m}\right]$ is a symmetric matrix having elements
$b_{ij}\ \sqrt{m_i}\ \sqrt{m_j}$ and its eigenvalues are λ'. From $\lambda' = 1/\lambda$, lambdas corresponding to those of Eq. 3-156 may be found.

The eigenvectors of matrix $[\mathbf{BM}]$ may be found by dividing the eigenvector
components of the eigenvectors of matrix $\mathbf{C}$ by $\sqrt{m_i}$. (See Prob. 3-52.)

Other Nonstandard Eigenvalue Problems

Other nonstandard eigenvalue problems include those of the form

$$\mathbf{AX} = \lambda\mathbf{BX} \tag{3-199}$$

where $\mathbf{A}$ is symmetric and $\mathbf{B}$ is symmetric and positive definite (Eq. 3-156 is a special case of Eq. 3-199), and

$$\mathbf{ABX} = \lambda\mathbf{X} \tag{3-200}$$

where $\mathbf{A}$ and $\mathbf{B}$ are symmetric and one or both are positive definite (Eq. 3-157 is a special case of Eq. 3-200). Readers interested in these more general problems are referred to Gourlay and Watson.[17]

3-14 NONLINEAR SIMULTANEOUS EQUATIONS

There are no direct methods available for solving nonlinear simultaneous equations such as are available for linear sets. In general, iterative approaches must be used, which require initial guesses or approximations of the solution values to get started. The iterative approach which we will consider makes use of Taylor's series for functions of several variables[18] to find real roots of nonlinear sets.

Let us consider the two nonlinear equations

$$
\begin{aligned}
f(x, y) &= 0 \\
g(x, y) &= 0
\end{aligned} \tag{3-201}
$$

with $x = x_r$ and $y = y_r$ an exact solution to the set. If $x = x_i$, $y = y_i$ are approximations to the solution, a Taylor series expansion about x_i, y_i yields

$$
\begin{aligned}
f(x_r, y_r) &= f(x_i, y_i) + h\left(\frac{\partial f}{\partial x}\right)_i + j\left(\frac{\partial f}{\partial y}\right)_i + \cdots = 0 \\
g(x_r, y_r) &= g(x_i, y_i) + h\left(\frac{\partial g}{\partial x}\right)_i + j\left(\frac{\partial g}{\partial y}\right)_i + \cdots = 0
\end{aligned} \tag{3-202}
$$

where

$$x_r = x_i + h \qquad y_r = y_i + j$$

---

[17]A. R. Gourlay and G. A. Watson, *Computational Methods for Matrix Eigenproblems* (New York: John Wiley & Sons, 1973).
[18]For a discussion of Taylor's series for functions of several variables, see any advanced calculus book. Also see Sec. 6-5.

and

$$\left.\frac{\partial f}{\partial x}\right)_i = \frac{\partial f}{\partial x}\bigg]_{\substack{x=x_i\\y=y_i}}, \quad \left.\frac{\partial g}{\partial x}\right)_i = \frac{\partial g}{\partial x}\bigg]_{\substack{x=x_i\\y=y_i}}, \quad \text{and so forth.}$$

If we truncate the Taylor series of Eq. 3-202 to only linear terms, we then have two linear equations in the two unknowns h and j. However, since the Taylor series has been truncated, h and j are only approximations to $x_r - x_i$ and $y_r - y_i$, respectively. Therefore, solving the two linear equations for h and j, we can only obtain improved values for x and y (assuming that x_i and y_i are close enough to x_r and y_r for convergence) rather than exact solution values. That is,

$$x_{i+1} = x_i + h \tag{3-203}$$
$$y_{i+1} = y_i + j$$

where x_{i+1} and y_{i+1} are improved approximations to x_r and y_r. They are used as x_i and y_i, respectively, in obtaining still better solution values. Iteration continues until the values of x and y stabilize.

For three equations in three unknowns (say, x, y, and z), the three functions $f(x, y, z)$, $g(x, y, z)$, and $F(x, y, z)$ would be expanded in a Taylor series for functions of three variables. Proceeding as for two equations, three linear equations in the unknowns h, j, and k would be obtained. The remaining procedure would parallel the case discussed above for two equations. Extension may be made to more than three equations.

EXAMPLE 3-12

Let us find the roots of the set

$$f(x, y) = x^2 + 2y^2 - 22.0 = 0 \tag{3-204}$$
$$g(x, y) = -2x^2 + xy - 3y + 11.0 = 0$$

The partial derivatives needed in Eq. 3-202 are

$$\frac{\partial f}{\partial x} = 2x \qquad \frac{\partial g}{\partial x} = -4x + y$$

$$\frac{\partial f}{\partial y} = 4y \qquad \frac{\partial g}{\partial y} = x - 3$$

Suppose that our first approximation of a solution (perhaps arrived at by trial and error) is $x = 1.5$, $y = 2.0$. Evaluating $f(x, y)$, $g(x, y)$, and the above partial derivatives at $x_i = 1.5$, $y_i = 2.0$, we obtain

$$f(x_i, y_i) = (1.5)^2 + 2(2.0)^2 - 22.0 = -11.75$$

$$g(x_i, y_i) = -2(1.5)^2 + (1.5)(2.0) - 3(2.0) + 11.0 = 3.5$$

$$\left.\frac{\partial f}{\partial x}\right)_i = 2(1.5) = 3.0 \qquad\qquad \left.\frac{\partial f}{\partial y}\right)_i = 4(2.0) = 8.0$$

$$\left.\frac{\partial g}{\partial x}\right)_i = -4(1.5) + 2.0 = -4.0 \qquad\qquad \left.\frac{\partial g}{\partial y}\right)_i = 1.5 - 3 = -1.5$$

Then from Eq. 3-202

$$3h + 8j = 11.75$$
$$-4h - 1.5j = -3.5$$

from which

$$h = 0.377$$
$$j = 1.327$$

and

$$x_{i+1} = 1.5 + 0.377 = 1.877$$
$$y_{i+1} = 2.0 + 1.327 = 3.327$$

Using these values for x_i and y_i, one more iteration yields

$$h = 0.136$$
$$j = -0.313$$

and

$$x_{i+1} = 1.877 + 0.136 = 2.013$$
$$y_{i+1} = 3.327 - 0.313 = 3.014$$

The exact solution values are $x = 2.000$, $y = 3.000$.

PROBLEMS

Problems 3-1 through 3-5 involve some elementary operations of matrix algebra used in Chap. 3. The reader is referred to App. B in working these problems.

3-1. Determine the products **AB**, **AC**, **DA**, and **CD** for the matrices below.

$$
\mathbf{A} = \begin{bmatrix} 2 & 4 & 1 \\ 6 & 3 & 5 \\ 1 & 3 & 9 \end{bmatrix} \quad
\mathbf{B} = \begin{bmatrix} 3 & 2 & 5 \\ 2 & 4 & -8 \\ 1 & 2 & 7 \end{bmatrix}
$$

$$
\mathbf{C} = \begin{Bmatrix} 7 \\ -2 \\ 4 \end{Bmatrix} \quad \mathbf{D} = \begin{bmatrix} 7 & 2 & 4 \end{bmatrix}
$$

3-2. Refer to the matrices shown in Prob. 3-1 and list any products which would not be valid in matrix multiplication.

3-3. For the matrices **A** and **B** shown in Prob. 3-1, determine $\mathbf{A}^{\mathrm{T}}$, $\mathbf{B}^{\mathrm{T}}$, and $[\mathbf{AB}]^{\mathrm{T}}$.

3-4. Referring to the matrices in Prob. 3-1, postmultiply the product **AB** by **C**.

3-5. Prove that $\mathbf{B} = \mathbf{A}^{-1}$ using the matrices given below.

$$
\mathbf{A} = \begin{bmatrix} 1 & 2 & 1 \\ 2 & 1 & 2 \\ 1 & 1 & 3 \end{bmatrix} \quad
\mathbf{B} = \begin{bmatrix} -\frac{1}{6} & \frac{5}{6} & -\frac{1}{2} \\ \frac{2}{3} & -\frac{1}{3} & 0 \\ -\frac{1}{6} & -\frac{1}{6} & \frac{1}{2} \end{bmatrix}
$$

3-6. Using a pocket calculator, determine $\{x_i\}$ for the simultaneous equations indicated below by the Gauss-Jordan method.

$$
\begin{bmatrix} 1 & 1 & 1 & -1 \\ 1 & -1 & -1 & 1 \\ 2 & 1 & -1 & 2 \\ 3 & 1 & 2 & -1 \end{bmatrix}
\begin{Bmatrix} x_1 \\ x_2 \\ x_3 \\ x_4 \end{Bmatrix} =
\begin{Bmatrix} -2.00 \\ 4.00 \\ 5.50 \\ 3.50 \end{Bmatrix}
$$

(answer: $x_1 = 1$, $x_2 = -2$, $x_3 = 3.5$, $x_4 = 4.5$)

3-7. A parabola having an equation of the form $y = Ax^2 + Bx + C$ goes through the points (1, 8), (2,13), and (3, 20). Using a pocket calculator and the Gauss-Jordan method, determine the equation of this parabola.

3-8. Determine the equation of the third-degree polynomial of the form $y = Ax^3 + Bx^2 + Cx + D$ which passes through the points $(1, 10)$, $(2, 26)$, $(-1, 2)$, and $(0, 4)$. Use a pocket calculator and the Gauss-Jordan method.

3-9. Determine the coefficients of the polynomial $y = Ax^3 + Bx^2 + Cx + D$ which passes through the points $(1, 10)$, $(2, 26)$, $(-1, 2)$ and has a slope of 10 at the point $(1, 10)$. Use a pocket calculator and a method of your choice unless otherwise specified.

$$(\text{answer: } y = x^3 + 2x^2 + 3x + 4)$$

3-10. Determine the coefficients of the polynomial $y = Ax^4 + Bx^3 + Cx^2 + Dx + E$ which passes through the points $(1, 8)$, $(2, 44)$, $(-1, 2)$, $(-3, 44)$, and $(-2, 8)$. Use a pocket calculator and a method of your choice if not otherwise specified.

3-11. Determine the coefficients of the polynomial shown below using the computer program of Ex. 3-1 which utilizes the Gaussian elimination method.

$$y = Ax^5 + Bx^4 + Cx^3 + Dx^2 + Ex + F$$

It passes through points $(1, -7)$, $(2, 2)$, $(-1, -7)$, $(-2, -34)$, $(3, 121)$, and $(0, -8)$.

3-12. Determine the coefficients of the polynomial shown below using the computer program of Ex. 3-1 which utilizes the Gaussian elimination method.

$$y = Ax^5 + Bx^4 + Cx^3 + Dx^2 + Ex + F$$

It passes through the points $(-2, -34)$, $(1, -7)$, $(2, 2)$, $(-1, -7)$, and has a slope of 0 at the points $(1, -7)$ and $(-1, -7)$.

3-13. The general equation of a conic section can be written as

$$x^2 + Bxy + Cy^2 + Dx + Ey + F = 0$$

a. Determine the equation of the conic section passing through the points $(0, \frac{1}{2})$, $(\frac{1}{2}, \frac{4}{9})$, $(-2, \frac{57}{2})$, $(1, \frac{3}{22})$, and $(-\frac{1}{2}, 0)$ using the computer program of Ex. 3-1.

b. Do part a, but convert the given program to double precision and compare the results of the 2 solutions.

3-14. Determine x_i for the set of simultaneous equations indicated below using a pocket calculator and the matrix-inversion method.

$$\begin{bmatrix} 1 & 1 & 1 & -1 \\ 1 & -1 & -1 & 1 \\ 2 & 1 & -1 & 2 \\ 3 & 1 & 2 & -1 \end{bmatrix} \begin{Bmatrix} x_1 \\ x_2 \\ x_3 \\ x_4 \end{Bmatrix} = \begin{Bmatrix} -2.00 \\ 4.00 \\ 5.50 \\ 3.50 \end{Bmatrix}$$

Compare your answer to that given for Prob. 3-6.

3-15. Write a FORTRAN program implementing the flow chart given in Fig. 3-1 to solve a tridiagonal set of simultaneous equations. Use the program to solve the following tridiagonal set:

$$
\begin{aligned}
4x_1 + x_2 &= 4.0 \\
x_1 + 4x_2 + x_3 &= 11.0 \\
x_2 + 4x_3 + x_4 &= 15.0 \\
x_3 + 4x_4 + x_5 &= 18.0 \\
x_4 + 4x_5 + x_6 &= 21.0 \\
x_5 + 4x_6 + x_7 &= 24.0 \\
x_6 + 4x_7 + x_8 &= 27.0 \\
x_7 + 4x_8 + x_9 &= 30.0 \\
x_8 + 4x_9 + x_{10} &= 37.0 \\
x_9 + 4x_{10} &= 45.5
\end{aligned}
$$

(partial answer: $x_1 = 0.500$ $x_2 = 2.000$ $x_7 = 4.5$)

3-16. A rotating plate cam is to drive a reciprocating radial roller follower such as shown in part (a) of the accompanying figure. During the first 90 deg of cam rotation, the follower is to rise 1 in. and then be followed by a dwell as indicated by the displacement diagram in part (b) of the accompanying figure. When cams have moderate speeds, various standard motions, such as constant acceleration and deceleration or simple harmonic motion, are usually used for such displacements. For high-speed cams, certain restrictions may have to be placed on the acceleration or second-acceleration (jerk or pulse). Polynomial equations are often used to describe the displacement in such cases. The restrictions imposed in this problem are that the follower must have zero velocity, zero acceleration,

Problem 3-16(a)   **Problem 3-16(b)**

and zero second-acceleration at $\theta = 0$ and at $\theta = \pi/2$. Furthermore, when $\theta = \pi/4$, it is desired that the acceleration be zero. Since the angular velocity of the cam $d\theta/dt$ is to be constant, zero velocity, zero acceleration, and zero jerk of the follower imply that $dy/d\theta = 0$, $d^2y/d\theta^2 = 0$, and $d^3y/d\theta^3 = 0$. One further restriction to be imposed is that the value of $dy/d\theta$ should be $4/\pi$ in./radian at $\theta = \pi/4$. The restrictions are summarized as follows: when

a. $\theta = 0 : y = 0$, $y' = 0$, $y'' = 0$, $y''' = 0$
b. $\theta = \pi/2 : y = 1$ in., $y' = 0$, $y'' = 0$, $y''' = 0$
c. $\theta = \pi/4 : y' = 4/\pi$ in./radian, $y'' = 0$

   With ten conditions prescribed, it will be necessary to use ten constants in the polynomial describing the follower motion. That is,

$$y = C_0 + C_1\theta + C_2\theta^2 + C_3\theta^3 + C_4\theta^4 + C_5\theta^5 + C_6\theta^6$$
$$+ C_7\theta^7 + C_8\theta^8 + C_9\theta^9$$

   Differentiate the polynomial three times to obtain expressions for y', y'', and y'''. Applying conditions a, it will be obvious that $C_0 = C_1 = C_2 = C_3 = 0$. Substituting conditions b and c into the equations with the above zero constants, six equations in the remaining six C's will result. Solve the simultaneous equations by the method assigned, and plot curves of y, y', y'', and y''' versus θ.

3-17. Referring to the FORTRAN program written for Ex. 3-3, modify the program to bring the largest *applicable* element in the *matrix* into the pivot position by the use of row and/or column interchange.

3-18. Write a computer program for solving simultaneous linear algebraic equations by the Gauss-Jordan method flow charted in Fig. 3-4.

3-19. Write a computer program for inverting a matrix in place using partial pivoting, following the flow chart given in Fig. 3-5.

3-20. Modify the program written in Prob. 3-19 so that a set of simultaneous equations is solved, and at the same time the coefficient matrix is inverted. Provision will have to be made for a column of constants to be appended to the coefficient matrix.

3-21. Using the Faddeev-Leverrier method, verify the polynomial

$$(p^2)^3 - 50(p^2)^2 + 600(p^2) - 1000 = 0$$

obtained in Ex. 3-8 (see Eq. 3-113). Use a pocket calculator.

3-22 a. Use Faddeev-Leverrier's method and a pocket calculator to determine the polynomial coefficients of the matrix $\mathbf{A}$ of the homogeneous set of algebraic equations given by

$$\begin{bmatrix} (1 - \lambda) & 1 & 0 \\ 1 & (0 - \lambda) & 1 \\ 1 & 2 & (2 - \lambda) \end{bmatrix} \begin{Bmatrix} x_1 \\ x_2 \\ x_3 \end{Bmatrix} = 0$$

Check the polynomial obtained by expanding the appropriate determinant.

b. Determine the matrix $\mathbf{A}^{-1}$.

c. Use the incremental-search method (see Chap. 2) to obtain the eigenvalues of the polynomial obtained.

In Probs. 3-23 through 3-28, determine the coefficients of the characteristic polynomial of the matrix $\mathbf{A}$ by the Faddeev-Leverrier method using a pocket calculator.

3-23.
$$\begin{bmatrix} (3 - \lambda) & -3 & 1 \\ 4 & (3 - \lambda) & -2 \\ 4 & 4 & (-2 - \lambda) \end{bmatrix} \begin{Bmatrix} x_1 \\ x_2 \\ x_3 \end{Bmatrix} = \{0\}$$

3-24.
$$\begin{bmatrix} (1 - \lambda) & 2 & 3 \\ -10 & (0 - \lambda) & 2 \\ -2 & 4 & (8 - \lambda) \end{bmatrix} \begin{Bmatrix} x_1 \\ x_2 \\ x_3 \end{Bmatrix} = \{0\}$$

(answer: $\lambda^3 - 9\lambda^2 + 26\lambda - 24 = 0$)

3-25.
$$\begin{bmatrix} (0-\lambda) & 2 & 3 \\ -10 & (-1-\lambda) & 2 \\ -2 & 4 & (7-\lambda) \end{bmatrix} \begin{Bmatrix} x_1 \\ x_2 \\ x_3 \end{Bmatrix} = \{0\}$$

3-26.
$$\begin{bmatrix} (5-\lambda) & 2 & -1 \\ 2 & (5-\lambda) & 1 \\ 1 & 4 & (5-\lambda) \end{bmatrix} \begin{Bmatrix} x_1 \\ x_2 \\ x_3 \end{Bmatrix} = \{0\}$$

3-27.
$$2x_1 + 2x_2 + 3x_3 = \lambda x_1$$
$$-10x_1 + x_2 + 2x_3 = \lambda x_2$$
$$-2x_1 + 4x_2 + 9x_3 = \lambda x_3$$

3-28.
$$3x_1 - x_2 - x_3 = \lambda x_1$$
$$4x_1 - x_2 - 2x_3 = \lambda x_2$$
$$3x_1 - 2x_2 = \lambda x_3$$

In Probs. 3-29 through 3-31 the eigenvalues are given below the equations. Referring to Ex. 3-8 and taking $x_1 = 1$, determine the eigenvector associated with each eigenvalue given. Use a pocket calculator.

3-29.
$$\begin{bmatrix} (1-\lambda) & 2 & 3 \\ -10 & (0-\lambda) & 2 \\ -2 & 4 & (8-\lambda) \end{bmatrix} \begin{Bmatrix} x_1 \\ x_2 \\ x_3 \end{Bmatrix} = \{0\}$$

$(\lambda_1 = 2, \lambda_2 = 3, \lambda_3 = 4)$

3-30.
$$\begin{bmatrix} (0-\lambda) & 2 & 3 \\ -10 & (-1-\lambda) & 2 \\ -2 & 4 & (7-\lambda) \end{bmatrix} \begin{Bmatrix} x_1 \\ x_2 \\ x_3 \end{Bmatrix} = \{0\}$$

$(\lambda_1 = 1, \lambda_2 = 2, \lambda_3 = 3)$

3-31.
$$\begin{bmatrix} (2-\lambda) & 2 & 3 \\ -10 & (1-\lambda) & 2 \\ -2 & 4 & (9-\lambda) \end{bmatrix} \begin{Bmatrix} x_1 \\ x_2 \\ x_3 \end{Bmatrix} = \{0\}$$

$(\lambda_1 = 3, \lambda_2 = 4, \lambda_3 = 5)$

3-32. Using the iteration method, determine the largest eigenvalue and corresponding eigenvector for the matrix

$$\mathbf{A} = \begin{bmatrix} 10 & 4 & -1 \\ 4 & 2 & 3 \\ -1 & 3 & 1 \end{bmatrix}$$

by means of a pocket calculator. Retain 3 decimal digits in the eigenvalue and the eigenvector at each step.

$$\left(\text{answer: } \lambda = 11.663 \quad \mathbf{X} = \begin{Bmatrix} 1.000 \\ 0.422 \\ 0.025 \end{Bmatrix} \right)$$

3-33. If the voltage drop across an induction coil is $L\ di/dt$ and the voltage drop across a capacitor is $1/C \int i\,dt$, derive the differential equations, for the circuit shown, in terms of the charges q_1, q_2, and q_3 flowing in the respective loops. The currents and charges are related by $i_1 = dq_1/dt$, $i_2 = dq_2/dt$, and $i_3 = dq_3/dt$. (a) Using solutions of the form $q_i = Q_i \sin pt$, and letting $E = 0$, transform the set of simultaneous differential equations, obtained above, into a set of homogeneous linear algebraic equations. (b) Write the set of equations, obtained in part a, in matrix form, and determine, by the iteration method, the largest eigenvalue (p^2) and associated eigenvector, with $L_1 = L_2 = L_3 = 0.001$ henry and $C_1 = C_2 = C_3 = 0.001$ farad. It is suggested that the iterations be made by using a pocket calculator, in order to familiarize the reader with the process.

L - inductance, henries
C - capacitance, farads
i - current, amperes

Problem 3-33

3-34. Referring to Prob. 3-33 and using the data given there, determine, by the iteration method, the smallest eigenvalue (p^2) and associated eigenvector.

3-35. Referring to Prob. 3-33 and using the data given there, determine, by the polynomial method, the eigenvalues and corresponding eigenvectors for the electric circuit.

3-36. A cylinder, shown in the accompanying figure rolls without slipping and has a mass m_1 and a moment of inertia $\bar{I}$. Determine (a) the differential equations of motion in terms of the coordinates θ and x, and (b) the characteristic equation, by assuming a solution of the form $\theta = \Theta \sin pt$ and $x = X \sin pt$.

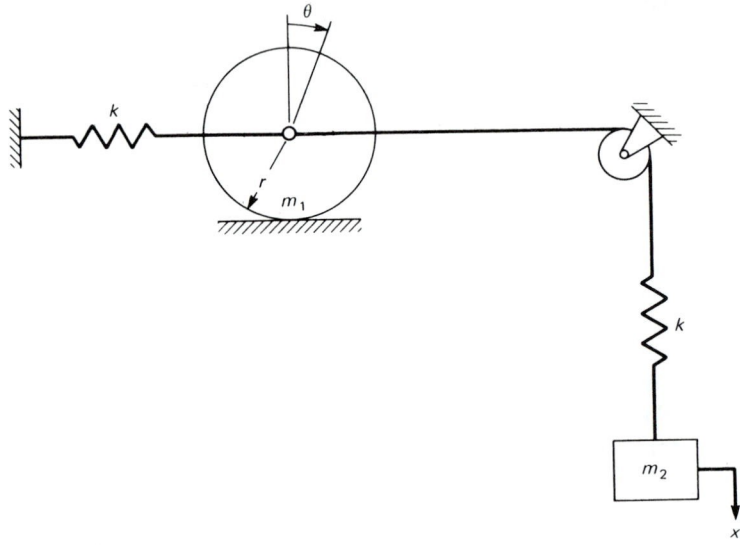

Problem 3-36

3-37. Referring to Prob. 3-36, let $m_1 = m_2 = 2$ lb-sec²/ft, $\bar{I} = 1.0$ lb-ft-sec², $r = 1.0$ ft, and $k = 200$ lb/ft, and determine, by the polynomial method, the eigenvalues and associated eigenvectors.

3-38. Refer to Prob. 3-36 and determine the eigenvalues and eigenvectors by the polynomial method by taking the system data as follows:

$$m_1 = m_2 = 50 \text{ kg}$$

$$\bar{I} = 2 \text{ kg·m}^2$$

$$r = 0.3 \text{ m}$$

$$k = 3500 \text{ N/m}$$

3-39. Referring to Prob. 3-36 and using the data of Prob. 3-37, determine, by the iteration method, the smallest eigenvalue and associated eigenvector.

3-40. Two disks are attached to the ends of a shaft having a torsional spring constant of k lb-in./radian as shown in the accompanying figure. The differential equations of motion of the system are found to be

$$\bar{I}_1 \ddot{\theta}_1 + k\theta_1 - k\theta_2 = 0$$

$$\bar{I}_2 \ddot{\theta}_2 + k\theta_2 - k\theta_1 = 0$$

Assuming a solution of the form $\theta_i = \Theta_i \sin pt$ and noting that $\bar{I}_2 = 2\bar{I}_1$, we obtain the set of homogeneous equations

$$\left(\frac{k}{\bar{I}_1} - \lambda\right) \Theta_1 - \frac{k}{\bar{I}_1} \Theta_2 = 0$$

$$-\frac{k}{2\bar{I}_1} \Theta_1 + \left(\frac{k}{2\bar{I}_1} - \lambda\right) \Theta_2 = 0$$

where $\lambda_i = p_i^2$. Using the polynomial method, the roots of the characteristic equation are found to be

$$\lambda_1 = p_1^2 = \frac{3}{2} \frac{k}{\bar{I}_1}$$

$$\lambda_2 = p_2^2 = 0$$

The value of $\lambda_2 = 0$ describes the system rotating as a rigid body ($\theta_1 = \theta_2$).

Using the iteration method, and assuming values of $\Theta_1 = \Theta_2 = 1$ for the eigenvector components, show that convergence will be to the smallest eigenvalue instead of to the largest eigenvalue. Discuss the significance of this result, with respect to the assumed eigenvector components.

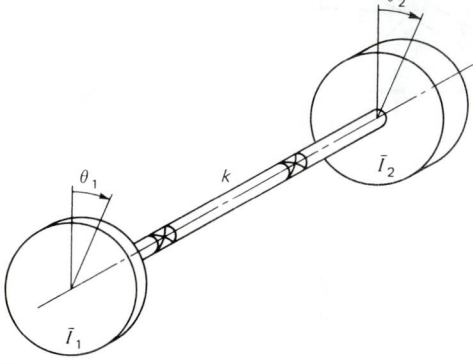

Problem 3-40

3-41. Referring to Prob. 3-40, assume initial values of $\Theta_1 = -1$ and $\Theta_2 = 1$ for the eigenvector components in the iteration procedure, and determine the largest eigenvalue (p^2 when the disks are oscillating 180 deg out of phase with each other).

3-42. The accompanying figure shows 3 disks attached to a shaft which is supported by the 4 bearings indicated. Referring to Eq. 3-156 in Ex. 3-11, the set of homogeneous algebraic equations for free, undamped torsional vibrations can be written as

$$\mathbf{K\Theta} = \lambda \mathbf{M\Theta}$$

or as

$$\mathbf{M}^{-1}\mathbf{K\Theta} = \lambda \mathbf{\Theta}$$

in which $\mathbf{M}$ becomes the mass-moment-of-inertia matrix instead of a mass matrix, and the displacement matrix $\mathbf{X}$ is replaced by the angular-displacement matrix $\mathbf{\Theta}$.

The mass-moment-of-inertia matrix and its inverse are given by

$$\mathbf{M} = \begin{bmatrix} 2 & 0 & 0 \\ 0 & 2 & 0 \\ 0 & 0 & 2 \end{bmatrix} \qquad \mathbf{M}^{-1} = \begin{bmatrix} \frac{1}{2} & 0 & 0 \\ 0 & \frac{1}{2} & 0 \\ 0 & 0 & \frac{1}{2} \end{bmatrix}$$

$$k_1 = k_2 = 4(10)^4 \text{ N·m/rad.}$$
$$k_3 = k_4 = 3(10)^4 \text{ N·m/rad.}$$

$$I_1 = I_2 = I_3 = I_4 = 2 \text{ kg·m}^2 \text{ (mass moment of inertia)}$$

Problem 3-42

The nondiagonal elements of the stiffness matrix are determined by defining element k_{ij} as the moment which would be required at station i to keep it fixed if station j were given a positive angular displacement, with all the other stations fixed. The diagonal elements are determined by considering the moment required at each station to give that station a positive unit angular displacement with all the other stations fixed. Using the torsional stiffness values shown, the stiffness matrix $\mathbf{K}$ is found to be

$$\mathbf{K} = (10)^4 \begin{bmatrix} 8 & -4 & 0 \\ -4 & 7 & -3 \\ 0 & -3 & 6 \end{bmatrix}$$

Noting that $f = \sqrt{\lambda}/2\pi$, determine the largest undamped natural frequency f, and the corresponding mode shape (eigenvector) by the iteration method. Make a sketch to show the physical significance of the mode shape (see Ex. 3-11).

Explain how you would obtain the lowest undamped natural frequency and corresponding mode shape by the iteration method.

$$\left(\text{partial answer: } f_3 = 39.36 \text{ Hz} \quad \Theta_3 = \left\{ \begin{array}{c} 1.00 \\ -1.058 \\ 0.511 \end{array} \right\} \right)$$

3-43. In Ex. 3-11 a FORTRAN program was written for obtaining the smallest eigenvalues and associated eigenvectors in ascending order using the iteration method.

a. Equation 3-156 shows that

$$\mathbf{M}^{-1}\mathbf{K}\mathbf{X} = \lambda\mathbf{X}$$

Considering this relationship, show that the *largest* eigenvalues and associated eigenvectors can be obtained in *descending* order ($\lambda_i > \lambda_{i+1}$) by successive iterations with the new matrix

$$[\mathbf{M}^{-1}\mathbf{K}]_{i+1} = [\mathbf{M}^{-1}\mathbf{K}]_i - \lambda_i\mathbf{X}_i\mathbf{X}_i^T\mathbf{M}$$

b. Modify the program written for Eq. 3-158 in Ex. 3-11 so that it may be used to obtain the largest eigenvalues and associated eigenvectors in descending order.

c. Use the modified program you developed to determine the eigenvalues (natural circular frequencies squared) and associated eigenvectors (mode shapes) of the 4-story building discussed in Ex. 3-11.

3-44. A 10 ft. long aluminum rod is fixed at the right end and free at the left end as shown in the accompanying figure. By solving the one-dimensional wave equation with the appropriate boundary conditions, it can be shown that the natural circular frequencies, ω_i, of the longitudinal vibrations of the rod are given by

$$\omega_i = (i)\frac{\pi}{2l}\sqrt{\frac{E}{\gamma}}$$

in which

$i = 1, 3, 5, \ldots$ (mode number)

$E = 10(10)^6$ psi (modulus of elasticity, aluminum)

$\gamma = 0.1/386$ (mass/in.^{3}, aluminum)

$l =$ length, inches

For the lowest natural frequency (mode) $i = 1$, and

$$\omega_1 = \frac{\pi}{2(120)}\sqrt{\frac{10(10)^6(386)}{0.1}} = 2572 \text{ rad/sec}$$

and

$$f_1 = \frac{\omega_1}{2\pi} = 409 \text{ Hz}$$

Model the rod as 4 lumped masses and stiffness elements k as shown in

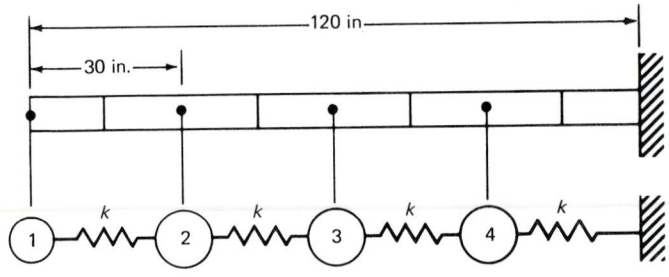

$A = 1$ in.^{2} (cross-sectional area of rod)
$\gamma = 0.1/g$ (mass/in.^{3} of aluminum)
$E = 10 \times 10^6$ psi (modulus of elasicity of Aluminum)
$k = AE/30$ lb/in. (spring constant)

Problem 3-44

the figure. Determine the lowest natural circular frequency ω_1 by iteration of the equation

$$\mathbf{BMX} = \frac{1}{\lambda}\mathbf{X} \qquad (\lambda = \omega_1^2)$$

in which $\mathbf{B}$ (symmetric) and $\mathbf{M}$ (diagonal) are the flexibility matrix and mass matrix, respectively.

The elements of the flexibility matrix $\mathbf{B}$ may be obtained by defining the element b_{ij} as the displacement of the mass at station i due to a unit force applied to the mass at station j with the mass at each station free to displace. For example,

$$b_{11} = \frac{1}{k} + \frac{1}{k} + \frac{1}{k} + \frac{1}{k}$$

$$b_{22} = \frac{1}{k} + \frac{1}{k} + \frac{1}{k}$$

$$b_{31} = \frac{1}{k} + \frac{1}{k}$$

$$b_{41} = \frac{1}{k} = b_{14} = b_{44}$$

and so on. Using the values in the accompanying figure, the matrices involved are

$$\mathbf{B} = \frac{1}{10^7} \begin{bmatrix} 120 & 90 & 60 & 30 \\ 90 & 90 & 60 & 30 \\ 60 & 60 & 60 & 30 \\ 30 & 30 & 30 & 30 \end{bmatrix}$$

$$\mathbf{M} = \frac{1}{10^3} \begin{bmatrix} 3.886 & 0 & 0 & 0 \\ 0 & 7.772 & 0 & 0 \\ 0 & 0 & 7.772 & 0 \\ 0 & 0 & 0 & 7.772 \end{bmatrix}$$

The 4 lumped masses shown correspond to the distributed mass portions directly above them. For example, the lumped mass m_1 is the mass of the left 1.25 ft of the rod, m_2 is the mass of the next 2.5 ft, and so on.

Compare the result obtained from the lumped-mass model with the exact value of $\omega_1 = 2572$ rad/sec.

3-45. The accompanying figure shows a slender rod of length l, cross-sectional area A, modulus of elasticity E, and mass-per-unit-volume γ. It is modeled by 4 lumped masses to obtain a set of equations involving the free, undamped longitudinal vibrations of the rod.

The set of equations in terms of the stiffness matrix $\mathbf{K}$ and the mass matrix $\mathbf{M}$ is of the form (see Eq. 3-156 and attendant discussion)

$$\mathbf{KX} = \lambda\mathbf{MX}$$

or

$$\mathbf{M}^{-1}\mathbf{KX} = \lambda\mathbf{X}$$

in which the mass matrix and its inverse are

$$\mathbf{M} = \begin{bmatrix} m_1 & 0 & 0 & 0 \\ 0 & m_2 & 0 & 0 \\ 0 & 0 & m_3 & 0 \\ 0 & 0 & 0 & m_4 \end{bmatrix} \qquad \mathbf{M}^{-1} = \begin{bmatrix} 1/m_1 & 0 & 0 & 0 \\ 0 & 1/m_2 & 0 & 0 \\ 0 & 0 & 1/m_3 & 0 \\ 0 & 0 & 0 & 1/m_4 \end{bmatrix}$$

The total mass of the rod is $m_r = A\gamma l$ so that

$$m_1 = m_4 = \frac{A\gamma l}{6}$$

$$m_2 = m_3 = \frac{A\gamma l}{3}$$

The elements of the stiffness matrix are determined as discussed just below Eq. 3-156 in Sec. 3-12. With $k = 3AE/l$, the stiffness matrix is

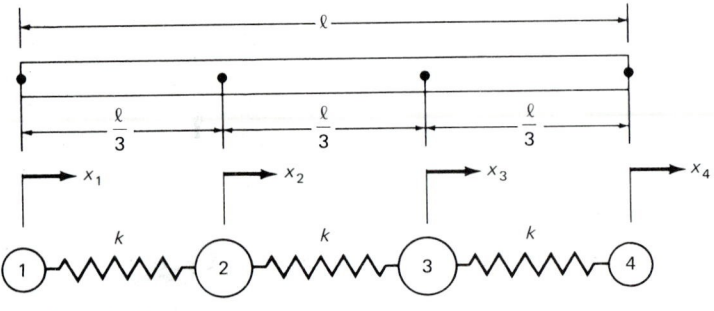

Problem 3-45

$$
\mathbf{K} = \begin{bmatrix} k & -k & 0 & 0 \\ -k & 2k & -k & 0 \\ 0 & -k & 2k & -k \\ 0 & 0 & -k & k \end{bmatrix}
$$

Use the iteration method to determine the largest natural circular frequency of longitudinal vibration $\omega_4 = \sqrt{\lambda_1}$.

After finding $\lambda_1 (\lambda_1 > \lambda_2 > \lambda_3 > \lambda_4)$ obtain the lowest natural circular frequency $\omega_2 = \sqrt{\lambda_3}$ using the shift procedure explained in Sec. 3-12. Compare the latter with the exact solution

$$
\omega_2 = \frac{\pi}{l} \sqrt{\frac{E}{\gamma}}
$$

which is obtained from the solution of the wave equation.

Hint: The lowest frequency $\omega_1 = 0$ with $\lambda_4 = 0$ corresponds to the rigid body motion such that

$$
\mathbf{X}_4 = \begin{Bmatrix} 1 \\ 1 \\ 1 \\ 1 \end{Bmatrix}
$$

3-46. The accompanying figure shows 4 disks supported by 4 bearings and fixed at the right end (this system is analogous to the 4-story building in Ex. 3-11). If 1 or more of the disks is given an initial displacement and released, the disks and shaft will have an angular vibration about the longitudinal axis of the shaft. The mass moment of inertia of each disk and the angular spring constant of each shaft section is given in the figure. The mass-moment-of-inertia of the shaft is small compared to that of the disks and may be neglected.

a. Use Lagrange's equation

$$
\frac{d}{dt}\left(\frac{\partial T}{\partial \dot{\theta}_i} \right) - \frac{\partial T}{\partial \theta_i} + \frac{\partial V}{\partial \theta_i} = 0
$$

to derive the differential equations of motion of the system, where the kinetic energy $T = \frac{1}{2}I(\dot{\theta}_1^2 + \dot{\theta}_2^2 + \dot{\theta}_3^2 + \dot{\theta}_4^2)$ and the strain energy

$$
V = \tfrac{1}{2}k_1(\theta_1 - \theta_2)^2 + \tfrac{1}{2}k_2(\theta_2 - \theta_3)^2 + \tfrac{1}{2}k_3(\theta_3 - \theta_4)^2 + \tfrac{1}{2}k_4(\theta_4)^2
$$

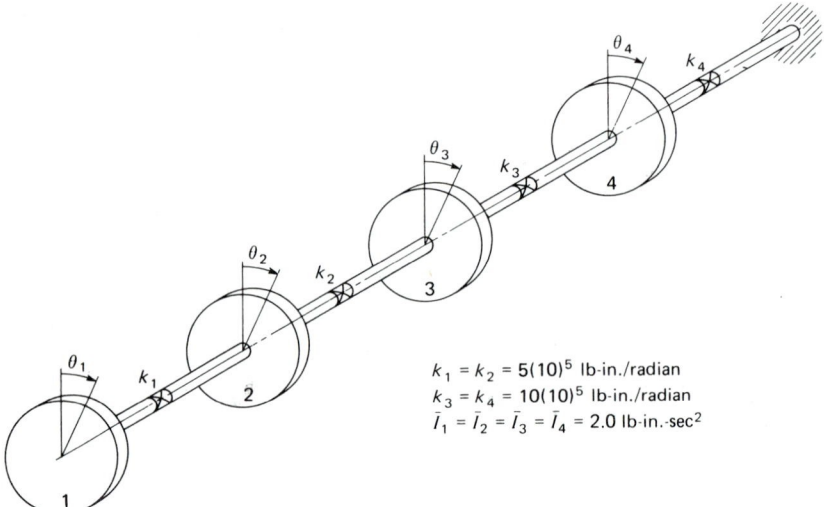

$k_1 = k_2 = 5(10)^5$ lb·in./radian
$k_3 = k_4 = 10(10)^5$ lb·in./radian
$\bar{I}_1 = \bar{I}_2 = \bar{I}_3 = \bar{I}_4 = 2.0$ lb·in.·sec^2

Problem 3-46

b. Assume solutions of the form $\theta_i = \Theta_i \sin \omega t$ for the differential equations and show that the substitution of these solutions gives a set of homogeneous algebraic equations of the form

$$\mathbf{M}^{-1}\mathbf{K}\boldsymbol{\Theta} = \omega^2\boldsymbol{\Theta}$$

which is the form of Eq. 3-156 in which $\lambda = \omega^2$.

c. Considering the matrix equation obtained in part b, show that the largest eigenvalues and associated eigenvectors can be found in descending order ($\lambda_i > \lambda_{i+1}$) by successive iterations with the new matrix

$$[\mathbf{M}^{-1}\mathbf{K}]_{i+1} = [\mathbf{M}^{-1}\mathbf{K}]_i - \lambda_i\mathbf{X}_i\mathbf{X}_i^\mathsf{T}\mathbf{M}$$

d. Modify the program written for Eq. 3-158 in Ex. 3-11 so that it may be used to obtain the largest eigenvalues and associated eigenvectors in descending order, and in turn the natural circular frequencies and mode shapes (relative disk displacements) of the shaft-and-disk system, and determine these values.

3-47. Refer to the figure and data accompanying Prob. 3-46, and convert the data to the SI system of units.

a. Using Lagrange's equation, determine the differential equations of motion of the system.

b. Determine the eigenvalues (squares of the natural circular frequencies) for the 4 principal modes of vibration by the polynomial method (see Ex. 3-8).

3-48. The system shown in Prob. Fig. 3-46 is analogous to the 4-story building in Ex. 3-11, so the computer program in that example can be used to determine the natural circular frequencies and mode shapes (relative disk displacements) of the disk-and-shaft system for its 4 principal modes of vibration.

  a. Change the data given for Prob. 3-46 to the SI system of units. Then, referring to the discussion following Eq. 3-157, formulate the flexibility matrix **B** directly. In this problem, moments and angular displacements replace forces and linear displacements in the example. The diagonal matrix **M** consists of the mass moments of inertias of the disks I_1, I_2, I_3, and I_4 on the diagonal, and the inverse follows from the inverse shown in the example.

  b. Use the program of Ex. 3-11 to determine the natural circular frequencies and mode shapes in ascending order by determining the $(1/\lambda)$'s in descending order.

3-49. Distributed-mass systems, of which beams are an example, are often modeled as lumped-mass systems for purposes of dynamic analysis. The accompanying figure shows a cantilever beam which is to be modeled by 3 lumped masses. Our problem is to determine which of the systems shown, model A or B, is the better model for the cantilever beam.

  The better model will be the one which has a fundamental natural

Model A

$m_1 = m_2 = m_b/3$

$m_3 = m_b/6$

$L = 3\ell$ = length of beam
m_b = total mass of beam
E = modulus of elasticity
I = moment of inertia of beam cross section about neutral axis

Model B

$m_1 = m_2 = m_3 = m_b/3$

Problem 3-49

circular frequency ω_1 (corresponding to the smallest eigenvalue λ) closest to the exact value which is given by

$$\omega_1 = 3.516 \sqrt{\frac{EI}{L^3 m_b}}$$

Since we are interested in the lowest natural circular frequency, the best approach is to use Eq. 3-157, as the iteration procedure with this equation will converge to the largest value of $1/\lambda$ (the smallest value of λ).

The mass matrices for the 2 models are

$$M = \frac{m_b}{3} \begin{bmatrix} 1 & 0 & 0 \\ 0 & 1 & 0 \\ 0 & 0 & \frac{1}{2} \end{bmatrix} \qquad M = \frac{m_b}{3} \begin{bmatrix} 1 & 0 & 0 \\ 0 & 1 & 0 \\ 0 & 0 & 1 \end{bmatrix}$$

$$\text{(model A)} \qquad\qquad\qquad \text{(model B)}$$

Calculating the influence coefficients b_{ij} of the flexibility matrix, we obtain

$$B = \frac{l^3}{3EI} \begin{bmatrix} 1 & 2.5 & 4 \\ 2.5 & 8 & 14 \\ 4 & 14 & 27 \end{bmatrix}$$

Determine the fundamental natural circular frequency ω_1 for each model by using a pocket calculator, and determine which is the better model.

(answer: Model A has 5% error in ω_1, Model B has 34% error in ω_1)

3-50. The accompanying figure shows a steel crossarm made from steel tubing that is pin-connected to a tower structure which carries power transmission lines. The crossarm has the following properties:

$r = 6$ in.   (mean radius of tube)

$t = 0.25$ in.   (wall thickness of tube)

$I = 169.1646$ in.^{4} (area moment of inertia about neutral axis)

$E = 30(10)^6$ psi   (modulus of elasticity)

$\gamma = 0.0069$ lb-sec^2/in.^{2} (crossarm mass per unit length)

$l = 36$ ft   (crossarm length)

Air flowing over the crossarm induces vortex shedding which can subject the crossarm to a sinusoidal exciting force F per unit length of

$$F = \frac{Cv^2 A\rho}{2} \sin 2\pi f\, t$$

in which

C = aerodynamic constant ($C = 1$ for a cylinder)

v = wind velocity over crossarm

A = projected area of crossarm perpendicular to wind

ρ = mass density of air $(2.37(10)^{-3}\text{lb-sec}^2/\text{ft}^4)$

f = vortex shedding frequency, Hz

The vortex shedding frequency is given by

$$f = Sv/d$$

in which

S = Strouhal number (0.2)

d = tube diameter (ft)

v = wind velocity (ft/sec)

For a Reynolds number of $R < 200,000$ the value of the Strouhal number is usually taken as 0.2. If the vortex shedding f is equal to one of the natural circular frequencies of the crossarm, a condition of resonance results and large bending stresses may be caused.

a. Model the crossarm as 8 lumped masses at 4 ft intervals as shown in the accompanying figure, and determine the first 4 lowest natural frequencies of the crossarm by iteration and using Hotelling's deflation method. From Ex. 3-11 the equation for iteration in terms of the flexibility matrix B is

$$\mathbf{BMX} = \frac{1}{\lambda}\mathbf{X} \quad (\lambda_i = \omega_i^2) \quad (\omega_i = 2\pi f)$$

The 8 lumped masses shown in the accompanying figure correspond to the distributed mass portions directly above them. For example, the lumped mass m_1 is the mass of the left 2 ft of the crossarm, m_2 is the mass of the next 4 ft of the crossarm, and so on. From ele-

Problem 3-50

mentary beam theory and the definition of influence coefficients, the flexibility matrix B is found to be:

$$
\mathbf{B} = (10)^{-5}
\begin{bmatrix}
20.28 & 9.05 & -5.22 & -6.95 & -6.08 & -3.48 & 3.62 & 7.24 \\
9.05 & 4.35 & -2.61 & -3.48 & -3.04 & -1.74 & 1.81 & 3.62 \\
-5.22 & -2.61 & 2.32 & 3.26 & 2.90 & 1.67 & -1.74 & -3.48 \\
-6.95 & -3.48 & 3.26 & 5.22 & 4.93 & 2.90 & -3.04 & -6.08 \\
-6.08 & -3.04 & 2.90 & 4.93 & 5.22 & 3.26 & -3.48 & -6.95 \\
-3.48 & -1.74 & 1.67 & 2.90 & 3.26 & 2.32 & -2.61 & -5.22 \\
3.62 & 1.81 & -1.74 & -3.04 & -3.48 & -2.61 & 4.35 & 9.05 \\
7.24 & 3.62 & -3.48 & -6.08 & -6.95 & -5.22 & 9.05 & 20.28
\end{bmatrix}
$$

b. Do any of the natural frequencies of the crossarm equal the vortex-shedding frequency f if the wind velocities encountered have a range of 10 mph (14.67 ft/sec) to 80 mph (117.3 ft/sec)?

(answer: $f_1 = 15.79$ Hz, $v = 53.83$ mph)

3-51. In Sec. 3-13 a computer program was written for use with Jacobi's method to solve the eigenvalue matrix equation

$$AX = \lambda X$$

in which **A** must be a symmetric matrix.

a. Refer to the discussion in Sec. 3-13 on the transformation of nonsymmetric matrices to symmetric forms, and modify the computer program so that it may be used to obtain a solution of the matrix equation

$$KX = \lambda MX$$

by Jacobi's method. The matrices **K** and **M** are stiffness and mass matrices, respectively, and are discussed in Ex. 3-11.

b. Determine the stiffness elements k_{ij} of **K** for the 4-story building shown in Fig. 3-10 using the given equivalent spring constant values.

c. Obtain the eigenvalues and eigenvectors for the structure using the modified program, and compare the results to that obtained in Ex. 3-11.

$$\text{partial answer: } K = 10^6 \begin{bmatrix} 22 & -10 & 0 & 0 \\ -10 & 18 & -8 & 0 \\ 0 & -8 & 14 & -6 \\ 0 & 0 & -6 & 6 \end{bmatrix}$$

3-52. In Sec. 3-13 a computer program was written for Jacobi's method of solving the eigenvalue matrix equation

$$AX = \lambda X$$

in which **A** must be a symmetric matrix for Jacobi's method.

a. Refer to the discussion in Sec. 3-13 on the transformation of nonsymmetric matrices to symmetric form and modify the computer program in Sec. 3-13 to solve the matrix equation

$$BMX = \frac{1}{\lambda} X = \lambda' X$$

by Jacobi's method. This equation was used in Ex. 3-11.

b. Use the modified program to determine the eigenvalues and eigenvectors for the 4-story building of Ex. 3-11, using the data given in that example. Compare the results obtained with that obtained in the example.

3-53. Consider the nonlinear simultaneous equations

$$f(x, y) = x^2 + y^2 - 4 = 0$$

$$g(x, y) = x^3 - y = 0$$

Make a rough sketch of each equation in an xy coordinate system to obtain suitable starting values for x and y, and determine the roots of the equations following the procedures discussed in Sec. 3-14.

$$\left(\begin{array}{l} \text{answer: } x = 1.1742, \; y = 1.6182 \\ \phantom{\text{answer: }} x = -1.1742, \; y = -1.6182 \end{array}\right)$$

3-54. There are 4 pairs of roots to the following nonlinear simultaneous equations:

$$f(x, y) = x^2 + y^2 - 4 = 0$$

$$g(x, y) = x^2 + 9y^2 - 9 = 0$$

a. Make a rough sketch of each equation in an xy coordinate system to obtain suitable starting values of x and y.

b. Select 1 set of suitable starting values, and determine the corresponding roots (x_r and y_r) by the method described in Sec. 3-14.

c. Compare your results with that which can be obtained by using simple algebra to solve this particular set of nonlinear simultaneous equations.

3-55. There are 2 pairs of roots to the following nonlinear simultaneous equations:

$$f(x, y) = x^2 + y^2 - 4 = 0$$

$$g(x, y) = e^{-x} + xy - 1 = 0$$

a. Make a rough sketch of each equation in an xy coordinate system to obtain suitable starting values of x and y.

b. Select 1 set of suitable starting values and determine the corresponding roots (x_r and y_r) by the method discussed in Sec. 3-14. Obtain an answer to 4 significant digits.

Chapter 4
Curve Fitting

4-1 INTRODUCTION

In fitting a curve to given data points, there are two possible approaches. One is to have the graph of the approximating function pass exactly through the given data points. The method of polynomial approximation presented in Appendix C utilizes this approach, as does the spline fit discussed in Sec. 4-8. However, if the data values are experimental, having the scatter frequently found in such data, this method may yield unsatisfactory results. The second approach, which is usually a more satisfactory one for experimental data, uses an approximating function which graphs as a smooth curve having the *general shape* suggested by the data values, but not usually passing exactly through all of the data points. Both approaches are presented in this chapter.

In engineering, curve fitting plays an important role in the analysis and interpretation of experimental data and in its correlation with mathematical models formulated from fundamental engineering principles. In the most general sense, curve fitting involves the determination of a continuous function

$$y = f(x) \tag{4-1}$$

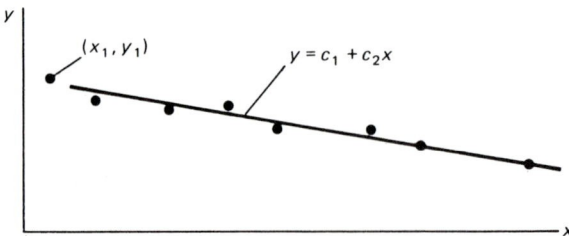

Figure 4-1 Data suggesting straight line

which results in the most "reasonable" or "best" fit of experimentally measured values of (x_1, y_1), (x_2, y_2), and so forth. The particular form of $f(x)$ will in many cases be known in advance from a consideration of the physical laws, or theory, associated with the x and y variables being measured. In other instances, the general appearance of the plotted data may suggest the particular form of $f(x)$. For example, a plot of x and y values as shown in Fig. 4-1 would suggest that the measured data can best be represented by a straight line. That is,

$$y = f(x) = c_1 + c_2 x \tag{4-2}$$

One can, of course, intuitively construct a straight line through the points as shown which will appear as a reasonable average of the plotted points. However, as we will see, the constants c_1 and c_2 can be determined from a "least-squares" criterion (discussed in Sec. 4-2) which will result in a "best-fit" straight-line representation of the experimental data. Other criteria besides least squares could be employed, such as minimizing the maximum error, but the least-squares criterion is the most widely used.

As another example, a plot of experimentally determined x and y values as shown in Fig. 4-2 might suggest a curve fitted by the pure quadratic equation

$$y = c_1 + c_2 x^2 \tag{4-3}$$

where c_1 and c_2 would be determined from the least-squares criterion for a best fit of the function to the measured data.

4-2 METHOD OF LEAST-SQUARES

In general, with a well-chosen approximating function, a least-squares fit will furnish a good representation of experimental data. However, if the approximating function chosen is a poor one, the least-squares fit will probably be a poor one, and only the "best fit" for the type of function chosen could be expected.

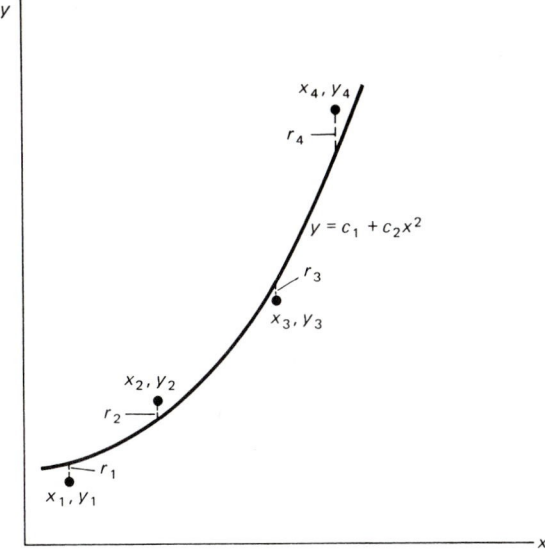

Figure 4-2 Data suggesting quadratic equation

Let us consider an example which will provide some insight into why a least-squares fit is generally a good approach to use with experimental data. Suppose that a surveying crew measures a given distance between 2 points on the ground n times. They will very likely come up with n different results, $d_1, d_2, \ldots, d_n$. We will let D represent some close approximation to the *true* distance. We next form the sum S of the squares of the deviations of the measurements from this unknown value D as

$$S = (d_1 - D)^2 + (d_2 - D)^2 + \cdots + (d_n - D)^2 \tag{4-4}$$

This sum will be either a maximum or a minimum if $dS/dD = 0$. Considering D as a variable and taking the derivative of S with respect to D gives

$$dS/dD = -2(d_1 - D) - 2(d_2 - D) - \cdots - 2(d_n - D)$$
$$= -2 \left(\sum_{i=1}^{n} d_i - nD \right) \tag{4-5}$$

The second derivative is

$$d^2S/dD^2 = 2 + 2 + \cdots + 2 = 2n \tag{4-6}$$

Since $2n$ is always positive, setting $dS/dD = 0$ gives a value of D for which the sum S is a *minimum*.

For $dS/dD = 0$,

$$\sum_{i=1}^{n} d_i - nD = 0$$

or

$$D = \left(\sum_{i=1}^{n} d_i\right) \bigg/ n \qquad (4\text{-}7)$$

The value we obtain for D in Eq. 4-7 by making the sum of the squares of the deviations of the measured values from D a minimum is simply the *arithmetic mean* of the n measurements. If the n measurements are all made with equal care, it would generally be agreed that the best value which could be assigned to the measured distance would be this arithmetic mean of all the measurements.

The above example illustrates the principle of least-squares applied to the experimental determination of a single unknown. We next simply extend this principle to the case where there are two related variables, say x and y. In this case for particular values of x we experimentally determine corresponding y values. Then instead of determining a single value such as D in the above example, we determine a *function*, $y = f(x)$, having some known or assumed form (such as $y = c_1 + c_2x^2$, for example) such that the sum of the squares of the deviations of the measured y values from the function values is a minimum.

As an example, suppose that corresponding to the measured values x_1, x_2, x_3, . . . , x_n of a variable x, we experimentally determine n values of y and designate them as y_1, y_2, y_3, . . . , y_n. Note that the x values are referred to as *measured values* and would therefore be subject to errors of measurement. However, let us simplify the treatment of the problem here and assume that all the error for each pair of values is in the measurement of y_i, and that all the x_i values are exact. Let us assume further that a plot of the data suggests that the points form approximately a straight line. The function we would then choose to fit the data would be of the form

$$y = c_1 + c_2x.$$

The equations for the various data sets are thus

$$y_1 = c_1 + c_2x_1$$
$$y_2 = c_1 + c_2x_2$$
$$y_3 = c_1 + c_2x_3 \qquad (4\text{-}8)$$
$$\vdots$$
$$y_n = c_1 + c_2x_n$$

and are sometimes referred to as the *observation equations*. There are n observation equations corresponding to n data sets and 2 unknown constants, c_1 and c_2. If n is greater than 2, as would usually be the case, it is impossible in most cases to determine two c values which will satisfy *all* n observation equations. This is because in most cases a single straight line cannot be drawn through all the data points. Applying the principle of least squares in such a situation requires that we determine as the best approximation to the unknown c's those values which minimize the sum S of the squares of the deviations of the measured y values from the function values calculated with those c's; that is, we minimize

$$S = [y_1 - (c_1 + c_2 x_1)]^2 + [y_2 - (c_1 + c_2 x_2)]^2 + \cdots \\ + [y_n - (c_1 + c_2 x_n)]^2 \tag{4-9}$$

The bracketed quantities are called the *residuals* and would all be zero for a perfect fit of all the points. Since S is a function of the two unknowns c_1 and c_2, to minimize S we must determine $\partial S/\partial c_1$ and $\partial S/\partial c_2$ and equate them to zero.

$$\partial S/\partial c_1 = -2[y_1 - (c_1 + c_2 x_1)] - 2[y_2 - (c_1 + c_2 x_2)] - \cdots \tag{4-10} \\ - 2[y_n - (c_1 + c_2 x_n)] = 0$$

$$\partial S/\partial c_2 = -2x_1[y_1 - (c_1 + c_2 x_1)] - 2x_2[y_2 - (c_1 + c_2 x_2)] - \cdots \tag{4-11} \\ - 2x_n[y_n - (c_1 + c_2 x_n)] = 0$$

These equations may be rewritten as

$$nc_1 + \left(\sum_{i=1}^{n} x_i\right)c_2 = \sum_{i=1}^{n} y_i$$

$$\left(\sum_{i=1}^{n} x_i\right)c_1 + \left(\sum_{i=1}^{n} x_i^2\right)c_2 = \sum_{i=1}^{n} x_i y_i \tag{4-12}$$

Using Cramer's rule to solve these two equations for the two unknown c values, we obtain

$$c_1 = \frac{\begin{vmatrix} \sum y_i & \sum x_i \\ \sum x_i y_i & \sum x_i^2 \end{vmatrix}}{\begin{vmatrix} n & \sum x_i \\ \sum x_i & \sum x_i^2 \end{vmatrix}} \qquad c_2 = \frac{\begin{vmatrix} n & \sum y_i \\ \sum x_i & \sum x_i y_i \end{vmatrix}}{\begin{vmatrix} n & \sum x_i \\ \sum x_i & \sum x_i^2 \end{vmatrix}} \tag{4-13}$$

where the summation index i goes from $i = 1$ to $i = n$ for all summations.

EXAMPLE 4-1

The percent reduction in area of normalized medium-carbon cast steel speci-
mens in a series of tension tests was found to vary as follows with the carbon
content of the steel:

Carbon Content of Steel, Percent	Reduction of Area Percent
0.20	54.0
0.25	48.8
0.30	45.3
0.35	40.1
0.40	35.2
0.45	32.3
0.50	27.5

Determine a linear relationship between these variables of the form $y = c_1 + c_2 x$ which best fits the given data, where y is the percent reduction in area
and x is the carbon content.

x_i	y_i	x_i^2	$x_i y_i$
0.20	54.0	0.0400	10.800
0.25	48.8	0.0625	12.200
0.30	45.3	0.0900	13.590
0.35	40.1	0.1225	14.035
0.40	35.2	0.1600	14.080
0.45	32.3	0.2025	14.535
0.50	27.5	0.2500	13.750
$\Sigma x_i = 2.45$	$\Sigma y_i = 283.2$	$\Sigma x_i^2 = 0.9275$	$\Sigma x_i y_i = 92.990$

Using the above summations and Cramer's rule, we find that

$$c_1 = \frac{\begin{vmatrix} 283.2 & 2.45 \\ 92.99 & 0.9275 \end{vmatrix}}{\begin{vmatrix} 7 & 2.45 \\ 2.45 & 0.9275 \end{vmatrix}} = \frac{34.8425}{0.49} = 71.1$$

and that

$$c_2 = \frac{\begin{vmatrix} 7 & 283.2 \\ 2.45 & 92.99 \end{vmatrix}}{\begin{vmatrix} 7 & 2.45 \\ 2.45 & 0.9275 \end{vmatrix}} = \frac{-42.91}{0.49} = -87.6$$

which yields the linear relationship

$$y = 71.1 - 87.6x$$

Let us next consider some data such as that plotted in Fig. 4-2 which suggests a fit using a quadratic equation of the form $y = c_1 + c_2 x^2$. The curve-fitting procedure using this function is similar to that for the linear fit previously illustrated. The steps in the procedure will be repeated here, but some of the equations will be written in a more compact form by using the symbol r_i to represent the residuals (the differences between the measured y values, y_i, and the function values $c_1 + c_2 x_i^2$). The observation equations corresponding to the n data points are

$$y_1 = c_1 + c_2 x_1^2$$
$$y_2 = c_1 + c_2 x_2^2$$
$$y_3 = c_1 + c_2 x_3^2 \qquad\qquad (4\text{-}14)$$
$$\vdots \quad \cdots \cdots \cdots$$
$$y_n = c_1 + c_2 x_n^2$$

As noted for the observation equations of the linear fit previously illustrated, there are generally no values of c_1 and c_2 which will satisfy *all* the equations. The residuals are thus

$$c_1 + c_2 x_1^2 - y_1 = r_1$$
$$c_1 + c_2 x_2^2 - y_2 = r_2$$
$$c_1 + c_2 x_3^2 - y_3 = r_3 \qquad\qquad (4\text{-}15)$$
$$\vdots \quad \cdots \cdots \cdots \cdots$$
$$c_1 + c_2 x_n^2 - y_n = r_n$$

In Eq. 4-15 the function values minus the measured y values are shown as the residuals, while in the illustration of the linear fit we used the y values minus the function values. Since the principle of least squares requires a determination of c_1 and c_2 such that the sum of the *squares* of the residuals is minimized, the residuals can obviously be defined in either manner.

From the principle of least squares

$$\sum_{i=1}^{n} (r_i)^2 = \text{a minimum} \qquad\qquad (4\text{-}16)$$

Since the residuals are functions of c_1 and c_2, Eq. 4-16 requires that

$$\frac{\partial \sum_{i=1}^{n} (r_i)^2}{\partial c_k} = 0 \qquad k = 1, 2 \tag{4-17}$$

Since the derivative of a sum is equal to the sum of the derivatives of the individual terms, Eq. 4-17 can be written as

$$\sum_{i=1}^{n} r_i \frac{\partial r_i}{\partial c_k} = 0 \qquad k = 1, 2 \tag{4-18}$$

In this illustration

$$\partial r_1/\partial c_1 = \partial r_2/\partial c_1 = \cdots = \partial r_n/\partial c_1 = 1$$

and

$$\partial r_1/\partial c_2 = x_1^2, \; \partial r_2/\partial c_2 = x_2^2, \; \partial r_3/\partial c_2 = x_3^2, \; \ldots, \; \partial r_n/\partial c_2 = x_n^2$$

Substituting these partial derivatives and the expressions for r_i of Eq. 4-15 into Eq. 4-18, we obtain

$$nc_1 + \left[\sum_{i=1}^{n} (x_i)^2 \right] c_2 = \sum_{i=1}^{n} y_i$$

$$\left[\sum_{i=1}^{n} (x_i)^2 \right] c_1 + \left[\sum_{i=1}^{n} (x_i)^4 \right] c_2 = \sum_{i=1}^{n} x_i^2 y_i \tag{4-19}$$

These 2 equations can be solved simultaneously to obtain the constants c_1 and c_2 of the quadratic equation $y = c_1 + c_2 x^2$ which best fits the n data points.

EXAMPLE 4-2

The experimental data points (1.0, 3.8), (2.5, 15.0), (3.5, 26.0), and (4.0, 33.0) shown in Fig. 4-3 indicate a curve having the form

$$y = c_1 + c_2 x^2$$

Determine the least-squares fit of this function to the data. To begin the solution we substitute the data values into Eq. 4-19 and obtain

$$4c_1 + 35.5c_2 = 77.8$$

$$35.5c_1 + 446c_2 = 944$$

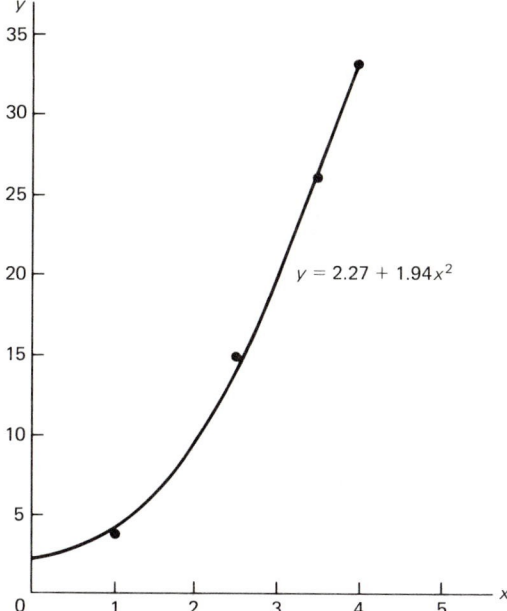

Figure 4-3 Least-squares fit for Ex. 4-2

from which

$$c_1 = 2.27$$

$$c_2 = 1.94$$

Thus, $y = 2.27 + 1.94x^2$ for a least-squares fit to the given data points. The given data points and the resulting function are shown in Fig. 4-3.

It should be emphasized that while the application of the least-squares fit of a specific function, $f(x)$, gives the best fit of that function to the data points, it may be necessary to apply the least-squares criterion to several different functions to determine which function best represents the data. For example, a least-squares fit of a straight-line function, $y = c_1 + c_2x$, could be obtained for the data points shown in Fig. 4-3. However, it should be apparent that the straight-line function would not fit the data nearly as well as the quadratic equation determined in Ex. 4-2.

Curve Fitting with Polynomials

The equations $y = c_1 + c_2x$ and $y = c_1 + c_2x^2$ which we have used thus far for curve fitting are particular examples of *polynomial* equations used in curve fitting. Other polynomials are also frequently used, where in general an $n - 1$ degree polynomial has the form

$$y = c_1 + c_2x + c_3x^2 + \cdots + c_nx^{n-1} \tag{4-20}$$

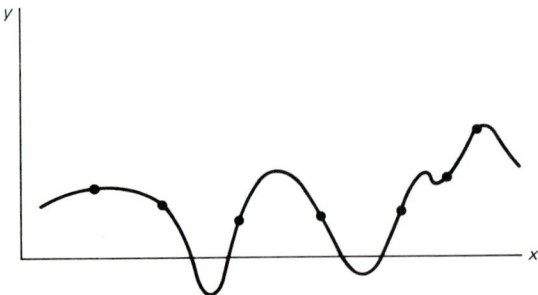

Figure 4-4 Typical fluctuations of a polynomial between data points

The least-squares fit of an $n - 1$ degree polynomial to n data points will of course pass through all the given data points since all the residuals go to zero. However, the polynomial may fluctuate considerably between the data points as shown in Fig. 4-4. To minimize such fluctuations, the degree of the polynomial used should be less than the number of data points used. Although no general rule exists for selecting the most suitable degree, a "rule of thumb" sometimes used is to select the degree of the polynomial somewhere in the neighborhood of $\frac{1}{2}$ to $\frac{3}{4}$ of the number of data points used. The smoothing effect between data points due to using a lower degree polynomial is of course generally accompanied by a curve having a poorer fit to the data points. The rule of thumb given above should not be applied indiscriminately in all cases. In Ex. 4-1 a plot of the data strongly suggests a straight-line fit, and the use of a third- or fourth-degree polynomial as given by the rule of thumb would be inappropriate.

4-3 MATRIX FORMULATION OF LEAST-SQUARES PROCEDURE FOR LINEAR FORMS

Let us consider curve fitting of data with a curve having the form

$$y = f(x, c_1, c_2, \ldots, c_m) = c_1 f_1(x) + c_2 f_2(x) + \cdots + c_m f_m(x) \qquad (4\text{-}21)$$

in which the dependent variable y is linear with respect to the constants $c_1, c_2, \ldots, c_m$; that is, the constants appear only as coefficients and never as part of the arguments. We shall call such equations *linear forms with undetermined constants*. The equations

$$y = c_1 + c_2 x \qquad \text{and} \qquad y = c_1 x + c_2 x^2$$

would be such examples. In the first of these $f_1(x) = 1$ and $f_2(x) = x$, while in the second $f_1(x) = x$ and $f_2(x) = x^2$. An example of a nonlinear form might be $y = c_1 e^{c_2 x}$ in which c_2 appears in the exponent.

When there are more than 2 or 3 constants involved ($m > 2$ or 3 in Eq. 4-21), it is often advantageous to generate the resulting m linear simultaneous algebraic equations in the form of a matrix equation. We shall develop such an equation in the discussion which follows.

The n observation equations for a fit with a function of the form shown in Eq. 4-21 are

$$
\left.
\begin{aligned}
y_1 &= c_1 f_1(x_1) + c_2 f_2(x_1) + \cdots + c_m f_m(x_1) \\
y_2 &= c_1 f_1(x_2) + c_2 f_2(x_2) + \cdots + c_m f_m(x_2) \\
&\ \vdots \quad \ \cdots\cdots\cdots\cdots\cdots\cdots\cdots\cdots\cdots \\
y_n &= c_1 f_1(x_n) + c_2 f_2(x_n) + \cdots + c_m f_m(x_n)
\end{aligned}
\right\}
\qquad (4\text{-}22)
$$

or

$$
y_i = \sum_{k=1}^{m} c_k f_k(x_i) \qquad i = 1, 2, \ldots, n \qquad (4\text{-}23)
$$

Considering the residuals $r_1, r_2 \ldots r_n$ for a least-squares fit, it follows from Eq. 4-23 that

$$
\left.
\begin{aligned}
\sum_{k=1}^{m} c_k f_k(x_1) - y_1 &= r_1 \\
\sum_{k=1}^{m} c_k f_k(x_2) - y_2 &= r_2 \\
\cdots\cdots\cdots\cdots\cdots\cdots \\
\sum_{k=1}^{m} c_k f_k(x_n) - y_n &= r_n
\end{aligned}
\right\}
\qquad (4\text{-}24)
$$

For the sum of the squares of the residuals to be a minimum, it is necessary that

$$
\sum_{i=1}^{n} r_i \frac{\partial r_i}{\partial c_k} = 0 \qquad k = 1, 2, \ldots, m
$$

which may be written in the matrix form

$$[r_1 \ r_2 \cdots r_n] \begin{bmatrix} \dfrac{\partial r_1}{\partial c_1} & \dfrac{\partial r_1}{\partial c_2} & \cdots & \dfrac{\partial r_1}{\partial c_m} \\[2ex] \dfrac{\partial r_2}{\partial c_1} & \dfrac{\partial r_2}{\partial c_2} & \cdots & \dfrac{\partial r_2}{\partial c_m} \\[2ex] \cdots\cdots\cdots\cdots\cdots \\[1ex] \dfrac{\partial r_n}{\partial c_1} & \dfrac{\partial r_n}{\partial c_2} & \cdots & \dfrac{\partial r_n}{\partial c_m} \end{bmatrix} = [0 \ \ 0 \cdots 0] \tag{4-25}$$

where $[r_1 \ r_2 \cdots r_n]$ and $[0 \ \ 0 \cdots 0]$ are row matrices.

It can be seen from Eq. 4-24 that

$$\frac{\partial r_i}{\partial c_k} = f_k(x_i) \tag{4-26}$$

Thus, Eq. 4-25 may be written in the form

$$[r_1 \ r_2 \cdots r_n]\mathbf{F} = [0 \ \ 0 \cdots 0] \tag{4-27}$$

where

$$\mathbf{F} = \begin{bmatrix} f_1(x_1) & f_2(x_1) & \cdots & f_m(x_1) \\ f_1(x_2) & f_2(x_2) & \cdots & f_m(x_2) \\ \cdots\cdots\cdots\cdots\cdots\cdots \\ f_1(x_n) & f_2(x_n) & \cdots & f_m(x_n) \end{bmatrix} \tag{4-28}$$

We now let $[r_1 \ r_2 \cdots r_n] = \mathbf{R}$ and take the *transpose* (see App. B) of Eq. 4-27 to obtain

$$[\mathbf{RF}]^\mathrm{T} = [0 \ \ 0 \cdots 0]^\mathrm{T} \tag{4-29}$$

Since $[\mathbf{RF}]^\mathrm{T} = \mathbf{F}^\mathrm{T}\mathbf{R}^\mathrm{T}$ and $[0 \ \ 0 \cdots 0]^\mathrm{T}$ is a column matrix, Eq. 4-29 takes the form

$$\mathbf{F}^\mathrm{T} \begin{Bmatrix} r_1 \\ r_2 \\ \vdots \\ r_n \end{Bmatrix} = \begin{Bmatrix} 0 \\ 0 \\ \vdots \\ 0 \end{Bmatrix} \tag{4-30}$$

where

$$\mathbf{F}^{\mathrm{T}} = \begin{bmatrix} f_1(x_1) & f_1(x_2) & \cdots & f_1(x_n) \\ f_2(x_1) & f_2(x_2) & \cdots & f_2(x_n) \\ \cdots\cdots\cdots\cdots\cdots\cdots\cdots\cdots \\ f_m(x_1) & f_m(x_2) & \cdots & f_m(x_n) \end{bmatrix} \tag{4-31}$$

and (from Eq. 4-24)

$$\begin{Bmatrix} r_1 \\ r_2 \\ \vdots \\ r_n \end{Bmatrix} = \begin{Bmatrix} \sum_{k=1}^{m} c_k f_k(x_1) \\ \sum_{k=1}^{m} c_k f_k(x_2) \\ \vdots \\ \sum_{k=1}^{m} c_k f_k(x_n) \end{Bmatrix} - \begin{Bmatrix} y_1 \\ y_2 \\ \vdots \\ y_n \end{Bmatrix} \tag{4-32}$$

Substituting Eq. 4-32 into Eq. 4-30, we obtain

$$\mathbf{F}^{\mathrm{T}} \begin{Bmatrix} \sum_{k=1}^{m} c_k f_k(x_1) \\ \sum_{k=1}^{m} c_k f_k(x_2) \\ \vdots \\ \sum_{k=1}^{m} c_k f_k(x_n) \end{Bmatrix} = \mathbf{F}^{\mathrm{T}} \begin{Bmatrix} y_1 \\ y_2 \\ \vdots \\ y_n \end{Bmatrix} \tag{4-33}$$

Finally, we note that

$$\begin{Bmatrix} \sum_{k=1}^{m} c_k f_k(x_1) \\ \sum_{k=1}^{m} c_k f_k(x_2) \\ \vdots \\ \sum_{k=1}^{m} c_k f_k(x_n) \end{Bmatrix} = \mathbf{F} \begin{Bmatrix} c_1 \\ c_2 \\ \vdots \\ c_m \end{Bmatrix} \tag{4-34}$$

Thus, Eq. 4-33 may be written in the form

$$
\mathbf{F}^{\mathrm{T}}\mathbf{F}
\begin{Bmatrix} c_1 \\ c_2 \\ \vdots \\ c_m \end{Bmatrix}
= \mathbf{F}^{\mathrm{T}}
\begin{Bmatrix} y_1 \\ y_2 \\ \vdots \\ y_n \end{Bmatrix}
$$

or more simply as

$$
\mathbf{F}^{\mathrm{T}}\mathbf{F}\{c\} = \mathbf{F}^{\mathrm{T}}\{y\} \tag{4-35}
$$

The use of Eq. 4-35 facilitates the formulation of a system of m linear algebraic equations for the least-squares curve-fitting criterion when m is greater than 2 or 3. The $\mathbf{F}$ matrix is readily generated from the known functions $f_1(x)$, $f_2(x)$, $\ldots$, $f_m(x)$ of Eq. 4-21 and the known data values for x.

To avoid having to perform the matrix multiplication $\mathbf{F}^{\mathrm{T}}\mathbf{F}$ each time a problem is solved, Eqs. 4-28 and 4-31 can be multiplied and the result put in Eq. 4-35 to change it to the following form:

$$
\begin{bmatrix}
\sum [f_1(x_i)]^2 & \sum f_1(x_i)f_2(x_i) & \cdots & \sum f_1(x_i)f_m(x_i) \\
\sum f_2(x_i)f_1(x_i) & \sum [f_2(x_i)]^2 & \cdots & \sum f_2(x_i)f_m(x_i) \\
\vdots & \vdots & \vdots & \vdots \\
\sum f_m(x_i)f_1(x_i) & \sum f_m(x_i)f_2(x_i) & \cdots & \sum [f_m(x_i)]^2
\end{bmatrix}
\begin{Bmatrix} c_1 \\ c_2 \\ \vdots \\ c_m \end{Bmatrix}
=
\begin{bmatrix}
\sum f_1(x_i)y_i \\
\sum f_2(x_i)y_i \\
\vdots \\
\sum f_m(x_i)y_i
\end{bmatrix}
\tag{4-35a}
$$

Inspection of the above reveals that $\mathbf{F}^{\mathrm{T}}\mathbf{F}$ is a symmetric matrix. The summation index goes from $i = 1$ to $i =$ number of data points for all the summations, while m is equal to the number of constants in the approximating function being used. Two previously derived equations, Eqs. 4-12 and 4-19, could also be obtained from the above equation with $m = 2$. However, it is generally more convenient to use those equations directly for the particular approximating functions they were derived for.

EXAMPLE 4-3

Let us use Eq. 4-35a to formulate the algebraic equations determined for the solution of Ex. 4-2. From Eq. 4-35a with $m = 2$, we obtain

$$
\begin{bmatrix}
\sum [f_1(x_i)]^2 & \sum f_1(x_i)f_2(x_i) \\
\sum f_2(x_i)f_1(x_i) & \sum [f_2(x_i)]^2
\end{bmatrix}
\begin{Bmatrix} c_1 \\ c_2 \end{Bmatrix}
=
\begin{Bmatrix}
\sum f_1(x_i)y_i \\
\sum f_2(x_i)y_i
\end{Bmatrix}
$$

in which the index goes from $i = 1$ to $i = 4$.

To facilitate evaluating the summations, the following table is formed:

x_i	y_i	$f_1(x_i) = 1$	$f_2(x_i) = x_i^2$
1	3.8	1	1
2.5	15.0	1	6.25
3.5	26.0	1	12.25
4.0	33.0	1	16.00

From the preceding equation and the table above we obtain

$$\begin{bmatrix} 4 & 35.5 \\ 35.5 & 446 \end{bmatrix} \begin{Bmatrix} c_1 \\ c_2 \end{Bmatrix} = \begin{Bmatrix} 77.8 \\ 944 \end{Bmatrix}$$

or

$$4c_1 + 35.5c_2 = 77.8$$
$$35.5c_1 + 446c_2 = 944$$

which agree with the simultaneous equations determined in Ex. 4-2.

4-4 WEIGHTING FOR LEAST-SQUARES METHOD

Sometimes certain data values obtained in an experiment may be more accurate than other data values because of the range of variables being measured relative to the full-scale accuracy of the equipment used. In such cases it may be desirable to give more "weight" to those data values which are considered to be the most accurately measured quantities. The weighting of certain data points may also be desirable to bring a selected function closer to certain data points. For example, the function

$$y = c_1 + c_2 x^2$$

can be brought into closer agreement with the data point (1.0, 3.8) than is shown in Fig. 4-3 by weighting that data point. The weighting value selected generally depends upon the experience and judgment of the user.

One of the simplest approaches to the weighting of a given data point is to merely make multiple use of the data point as if it were obtained from several different data runs. For example, a weighting factor of 2 can be given to the data point (1.0, 3.8) of Ex. 4-3 by considering the data points shown in the summation table below, which would be used to perform the weighting with the use of Eq. 4-35a.

x_i	y_i	$f_1(x_i)$	$f_2(x_i)$
1	3.8	1	1
1	3.8	1	1
2.5	15.0	1	6.25
3.5	26.0	1	12.25
4.0	33.0	1	16.00

The procedure would be the same as that in Ex. 4-3, with the only difference being in the use of 5 data points instead of 4.

The multiple use of data points for weighting purposes corresponds to minimizing the quantity

$$w_1 r_1^2 + w_2 r_2^2 + \cdots + w_n r_n^2$$

in which the w's are weighting factors which are positive, real numbers. Taking the partials of the above with respect to the constants, the minimization leads to

$$\frac{\partial}{\partial c_k} \sum_{i=1}^{n} w_i r_i^2 = 2 \sum_{i=1}^{n} w_i r_i \frac{\partial r_i}{\partial c_k} = 0 \qquad k = 1, 2, \ldots, m \tag{4-36}$$

and

$$[w_1 r_1 \quad w_2 r_2 \cdots w_n r_n]\mathbf{F} = [0 \quad 0 \cdots 0] \tag{4-37}$$

Taking the transpose of Eq. 4-37 gives

$$\mathbf{F}^\mathrm{T} \begin{Bmatrix} w_1 r_1 \\ w_2 r_2 \\ \vdots \\ w_n r_n \end{Bmatrix} = \begin{Bmatrix} 0 \\ 0 \\ \vdots \\ 0 \end{Bmatrix}$$

or

$$\mathbf{F}^\mathrm{T} \begin{bmatrix} \ddots \\ & w_i \\ & & \ddots \end{bmatrix} \begin{Bmatrix} r_1 \\ r_2 \\ \vdots \\ r_n \end{Bmatrix} = \begin{Bmatrix} 0 \\ 0 \\ \vdots \\ 0 \end{Bmatrix} \tag{4-38}$$

in which

is a diagonal weighting matrix in which the weighting factors, w_i, appear on the diagonal with zeros elsewhere. Following the same steps previously used in going from Eq. 4-30 to Eq. 4-35, we can go from Eq. 4-38 to

$$\mathbf{F}^{\mathrm{T}}\begin{bmatrix}\ddots & & \\ & w_i & \\ & & \ddots\end{bmatrix}\mathbf{F}\{c\} = \mathbf{F}^{\mathrm{T}}\begin{bmatrix}\ddots & & \\ & w_i & \\ & & \ddots\end{bmatrix}\{y\} \tag{4-39}$$

To illustrate the use of Eq. 4-39, let us turn again to Ex. 4-3 and give a weighting factor of 2 to the data point (1.0, 3.8) just as was done previously in illustrating the same weighting using Eq. 4-35a. Equation 4-39 becomes

$$\begin{bmatrix} 1 & 1 & 1 & 1 \\ 1 & 6.25 & 12.25 & 16.00 \end{bmatrix}\begin{bmatrix} 2 & 0 & 0 & 0 \\ 0 & 1 & 0 & 0 \\ 0 & 0 & 1 & 0 \\ 0 & 0 & 0 & 1 \end{bmatrix}\begin{bmatrix} 1 & 1 \\ 1 & 6.25 \\ 1 & 12.25 \\ 1 & 16.00 \end{bmatrix}\begin{Bmatrix} c_1 \\ c_2 \end{Bmatrix}$$

$$= \begin{bmatrix} 1 & 1 & 1 & 1 \\ 1 & 6.25 & 12.25 & 16.00 \end{bmatrix}\begin{bmatrix} 2 & 0 & 0 & 0 \\ 0 & 1 & 0 & 0 \\ 0 & 0 & 1 & 0 \\ 0 & 0 & 0 & 1 \end{bmatrix}\begin{Bmatrix} 3.8 \\ 15 \\ 26 \\ 33 \end{Bmatrix}$$

with all the pertinent values substituted. The reader might pause at this point to compare the procedures using the above equation to obtain the constants c_1 and c_2 to the procedure used with a summation table and Eq. 4-35a as discussed earlier. Before leaving this discussion, it might be pointed out that the weighting factors in a weighting matrix need not always be whole numbers as they are in this case in which they correspond to the number of times a particular data point is to be repeated. We shall see in a subsequent discussion of the use of exponential functions that they may assume other values.

4-5 CURVE FITTING USING EXPONENTIAL FUNCTIONS

Exponential functions appear quite frequently in the mathematical analysis of physical systems, so they are also used for fitting curves to experimental data. However, an undetermined constant will generally appear in the exponent of the function, and as a result the function $f(x)$ will not be a linear form such as discussed in Sec. 4-3. The nonlinear form of $f(x)$, however, can be transformed to a linear form by the use of logarithms so that the least-squares method previously described may be used.

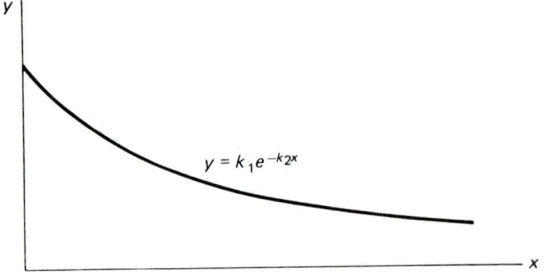

Figure 4-5 General form of the function $y = k_1 e^{-k_2 x}$

Let us first consider the exponential function shown in Fig. 4-5

$$y = k_1 e^{-k_2 x} \tag{4-40}$$

in which k_1 and k_2 are *positive real numbers*. Taking the logarithm of each side of Eq. 4-40 we obtain

$$\ln y = \ln k_1 - k_2 x \tag{4-41}$$

Letting $z = \ln y$, $c_1 = \ln k_1$, and $c_2 = -k_2$, Eq. 4-41 becomes

$$z = c_1 + c_2 x \tag{4-42}$$

which is the equation of a straight line. It tells us that Eq. 4-40 will plot as a straight line on semilog paper when the values of y are plotted as ordinates on the log scale. The constants in Eq. 4-42 may be determined using Eq. 4-12 (with y_i replaced by $\ln y_i$). However, in thus using Eq. 4-12 it should be realized that a least-squares fit is obtained in which $\sum R_i^2$ is minimized rather than $\sum r_i^2$ since

$$R_i = c_1 + c_2 x_i - \ln y_i$$

and

$$r_i = k_1 e^{-k_2 x_i} - y_i$$

It can be seen that the R_i values are errors in $\ln y_i$, whereas the r_i values are errors in y_i.

Let us compare a least-squares fit with $\sum R_i^2$ minimized to one in which $\sum r_i^2$ is minimized, and develop an equation for determining a least-squares fit using an approximating function such as is given by Eq. 4-40 in which $\sum r_i^2$ is minimized. Figure 4-6 shows experimental data points plotted in the x, y coordinate system and the general shape of an approximating curve of the form

$$y = k_1 e^{-k_2 x}$$

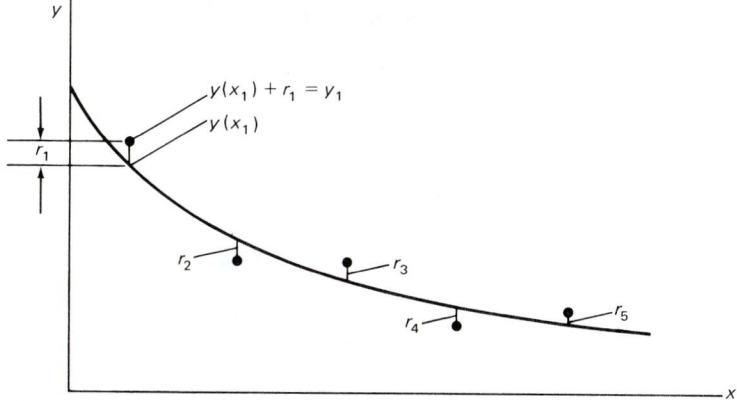

Figure 4-6 Approximating curve of the form $k_1 e^{-k_2 x}$

The exact location of the curve depends on the particular values of k_1 and k_2 found in the curve-fitting procedure.

Let us now think of the approximating curve in Fig. 4-6 as having been transformed to a straight line of the form

$$z = c_1 + c_2 x$$

by the transformation previously discussed. It is shown in this form in Fig. 4-7, along with the transformed experimental data points, in an x, z coordinate system where $z = \ln y$.

Now, if we have the errors r_i between the y_i values of the data points and the y values of the approximating curve shown in Fig. 4-6, the corresponding errors R_i in $\ln y$ are

$$R_i = \ln[y(x_i) + r_i] - \ln[y(x_i)] = \ln\left[\frac{y(x_i) + r_i}{y(x_i)}\right] = \ln\left[1 + \frac{r_i}{y(x_i)}\right] \qquad (4\text{-}43)$$

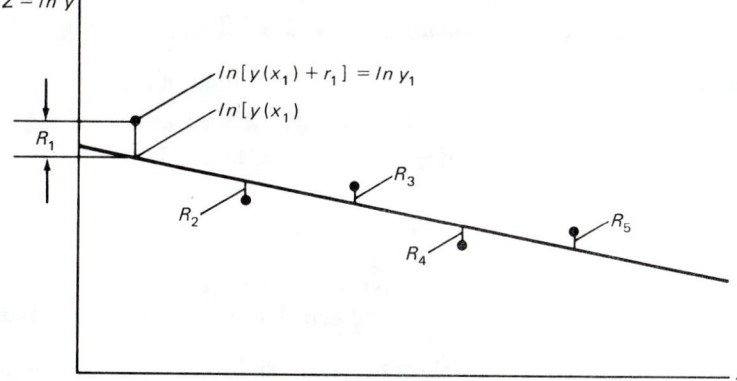

Figure 4-7 Curve of Fig. 4-6 transformed

From Eq. 4-43 and the definition of the natural logarithm,

$$e^{R_i} = 1 + \frac{r_i}{y(x_i)} \tag{4-44}$$

The series expansion for e^{R_i} is

$$e^{R_i} = 1 + R_i + \frac{R_i^2}{2!} + \frac{R_i^3}{3!} + \cdots \tag{4-45}$$

and if R_i is small,

$$e^{R_i} \cong 1 + R_i \tag{4-46}$$

Thus, from Eqs. 4-44 and 4-46

$$1 + \frac{r_i}{y(x_i)} = 1 + R_i$$

so that

$$R_i = \frac{r_i}{y(x_i)} \tag{4-47}$$

or

$$R_i = \frac{r_i}{y_i} \tag{4-48}$$

if we assume that $y(x_i)$ on the curve differs by only a small amount from the measured value y_i. Therefore, if the 2 constants necessary to determine the least-squares location of the approximating curve are solved by minimizing $\sum_{i=1}^{n} R_i^2$, we are approximately minimizing $\sum_{i=1}^{n} (r_i/y_i)^2$ instead of $\sum_{i=1}^{n} r_i^2$; that is in minimizing $\sum_{i=1}^{n} R_i^2$ we have introduced a weighting factor $1/y_i^2$ with each term of the summation $\sum_{i=1}^{n} r_i^2$. This is equivalent to saying that instead of giving equal weight to the errors in y, we are giving equal weight to the *relative errors*, r_i/y_i. Thus, to give equal weight to the errors in y, we must minimize $\sum_{i=1}^{n} y_i^2 R_i^2$ which is approximately equivalent to minimizing $\sum_{i=1}^{n} r_i^2$. Such weighting could be accomplished using a weighting matrix $\left[\overline{y_i^2}\right]$ with the matrix method developed in Sec. 4-4. However, since the matrix method does not provide any advantage when there are only 2 simultaneous equations to solve as in a straight-line fit, let us develop equations similar to Eq. 4-12 which are suitable for either a pocket calculator or a computer.

Minimizing $\sum_{i=1}^{n} y_i^2 R_i^2$ requires that

$$\sum_{i=1}^{n} y_i^2 R_i \frac{\partial R_i}{\partial c_1} = 0 \tag{4-49}$$

and that

$$\sum_{i=1}^{n} y_i^2 R_i \frac{\partial R_i}{\partial c_2} = 0 \tag{4-50}$$

To satisfy Eqs. 4-49 and 4-50, with $R_i = c_1 + c_2 x_i - \ln y_i$, it is necessary that

$$\sum_{i=1}^{n} y_i^2[(c_1 + c_2 x_i) - \ln y_i] = 0 \tag{4-51}$$

and

$$\sum_{i=1}^{n} y_i^2 x_i[(c_1 + c_2 x_i) - \ln y_i] = 0 \tag{4-52}$$

These may be rewritten as

$$\left[\sum_{i=1}^{n} y_i^2\right] c_1 + \left[\sum_{i=1}^{n} y_i^2 x_i\right] c_2 = \sum_{i=1}^{n} y_i^2 \ln y_i$$

$$\left[\sum_{i=1}^{n} y_i^2 x_i\right] c_1 + \left[\sum_{i=1}^{n} y_i^2 x_i^2\right] c_2 = \sum_{i=1}^{n} y_i^2 x_i \ln y_i \tag{4-53}$$

This provides a set of equations which may be used to determine the constants of the approximating function $y = k_1 e^{-k_2 x}$ where equal weight is given to the errors in y. To understand the applications of Eqs. 4-12 and 4-53, we shall next look at 2 examples in which they are employed.

EXAMPLE 4-4

Let us make a least-squares fit of the points (0, 10), (1, 3), and (2, 1) using an approximating function of the form

$$y = k_1 e^{-k_2 x}$$

first by giving equal weight to the errors in y and then by giving equal weight to the errors in $\ln y$, and compare the results.

To give equal weight to the errors in y, we apply Eq. 4-53. The following summations

x_i	y_i	y_i^2	$y_i^2 x_i$	x_i^2	$y_i^2 x_i^2$	$y_i^2 \ln y_i$	$y_i^2 x_i \ln y_i$
0	10	100	0	0	0	230.26	0.00
1	3	9	9	1	9	9.89	9.89
2	1	1	2	4	4	0.00	0.00
		$\Sigma = 110$	$\Sigma = 11$		$\Sigma = 13$	$\Sigma = 240.15$	$\Sigma = 9.89$

are substituted into Eq. 4-53 to obtain

$$110c_1 + 11c_2 = 240.15$$
$$11c_1 + 13c_2 = 9.89$$

The solution of these equations yields $c_1 = 2.302$ and $c_2 = -1.187$, from which $k_1 = e^{c_1} = 9.994$ and $k_2 = -c_2 = 1.187$. The approximating function is

$$y = 9.994e^{-1.187x}$$

which passes through the points (0, 9.99), (1, 3.05), and (2, 0.93).

To give equal weight to the errors in $\ln y$, we use Eq. 4-12 with $\ln y_i$ replacing y_i. The required summations are

x_i	x_i^2	y_i	$\ln y_i$	$x_i \ln y_i$
0	0	10	2.303	0.000
1	1	3	1.099	1.099
2	4	1	0.000	0.000
$\Sigma = 3$	$\Sigma = 5$		$\Sigma = 3.402$	$\Sigma = 1.099$

and the resulting simultaneous equations are

$$3c_1 + 3c_2 = 3.402$$
$$3c_1 + 5c_2 = 1.099$$

Solving these equations simultaneously, we obtain

$$c_1 = 2.286 \qquad k_1 = e^{2.286} = 9.836$$

$$c_2 = -1.152 \qquad k_2 = -c_2 = 1.152$$

The approximating function is then

$$y = 9.836e^{-1.152x}$$

and it passes through the points (0, 9.836), (1, 3.108), and (2, 0.982). Note that the absolute error between the data value and the corresponding value from the approximating curve is much larger at $x = 0$ than at $x = 2$ because of the lesser weight given to the larger data values.

One means of comparing the 2 approximation curves we have just determined is to compare the $(y - y_i)$ values at each data point, where y is computed from the approximating curve and y_i is the data ordinate, and then compute the $\sum(y - y_i)^2$ for all the data points for each curve. Doing this we find that in giving equal weight to the errors in y,

$$(y - y_i)^2 = (9.99 - 10)^2 + (3.05 - 3)^2 + (0.93 - 1)^2 = 0.0075$$

while in giving equal weight to the errors in $\ln y$,

$$(y - y_i)^2 = (9.836 - 10)^2 + (3.108 - 3)^2 + (0.982 - 1)^2 = 0.0389$$

Thus, the first curve obtained is the better approximating function.

In a majority of engineering applications either of the fits just obtained would suffice since the data used would generally be subject to more error than the differences between the values obtained from the 2 equations, making the distinction between minimizing $\sum R_i^2$ instead of $\sum r_i^2$ unimportant in a practical sense.

EXAMPLE 4-5

As a practical example of the use of Eq. 4-40, consider the photograph shown in Fig. 4-8 of an actual oscillograph record of the free-damped vibrations of a small structure. From vibration theory it is known that for viscous damping (damping proportional to velocity) the *envelope* of such a vibration (the curve through the peaks as shown in Fig. 4-9) is an exponential function of the form

$$y = k_1 e^{-2\pi\xi x} \tag{4-54}$$

where x is the cycle number, y is the corresponding amplitude, and ξ is a damping factor which has a magnitude of 1 for critical damping.

The free-damped vibrations of structural systems quite often appear to be

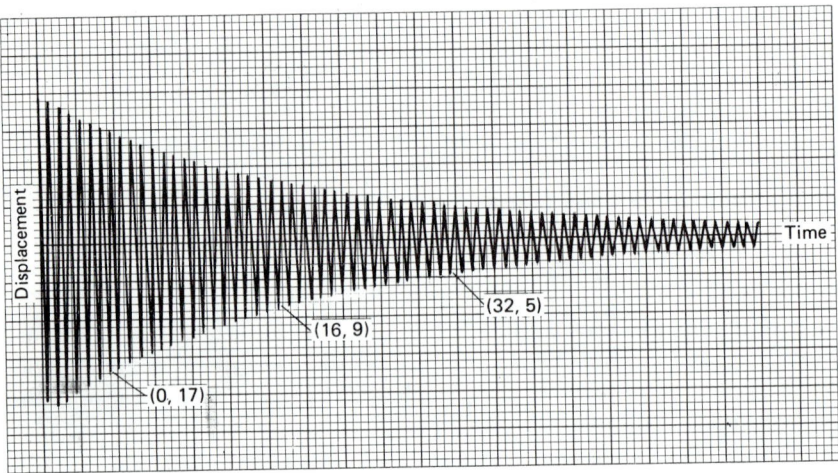

Figure 4-8 Oscillograph record of free-damped vibrations

those of a viscously damped system when actually the damping factor ξ may vary with the amplitude. For viscous damping, the damping factor is independent of amplitude, and a plot of the data (x_i, y_i) is essentially a straight line on semilog paper. For purposes of illustration, we shall consider only those data points (cycle number x and corresponding amplitude y given by the number of small divisions of chart lines) shown in parentheses in Fig. 4-8 to determine the following:

1. whether the free-damped vibrations correspond to a viscous damping model
2. a best fit by the least-squares criterion for the evaluation of the damping factor ξ for a viscous damping model. The data points are (0, 17), (16, 9), and (32, 5). The accuracy of these data points depends upon how closely the values can be interpolated from the oscillograph record.

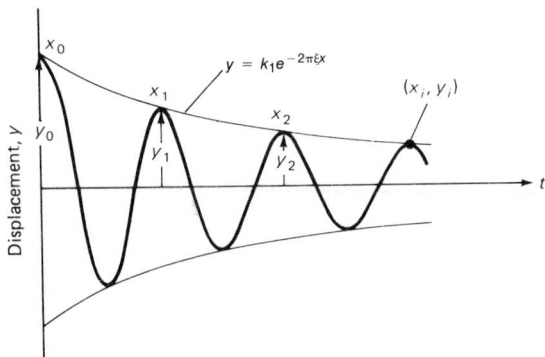

Figure 4-9 Envelope of free-damped vibrations

SOLUTION

To answer the first question above, the 3 data values are plotted on semilog paper as shown in Fig. 4-10. Since the data points appear to be fairly close to a straight-line plot, the damping factor ξ is for all practical purposes independent of amplitude, which means that the system damping can be described by means of a viscous damping model. In this example we know the type of equation to use to fit the data since we know Eq. 4-54. Our purpose then is to determine values of k_1 and ξ to best fit the equation to the data.

For a least-squares fit, we first take the logarithm of Eq. 4-54 so that

$$\ln y = \ln k_1 - 2\pi\xi x \qquad (4\text{-}55)$$

Letting $z = \ln y$, $c_1 = \ln k_1$, and $c_2 = -2\pi\xi$, Eq. 4-55 becomes

$$z = c_1 + c_2 x \qquad (4\text{-}56)$$

In this example we will fit a curve for which equal weight is given to the errors in $\ln y$. It will be left as an exercise for the reader to fit a curve for which equal weight is given to the errors in y (see Prob. 4-18).

In fitting a curve for which equal weight is given to the errors in $\ln y$, the

Figure 4-10   Semilog plot for Ex. 4-5

following table is formed for the summations in Eq. 4-12 in which y_i is replaced with $\ln y_i$.

x_i	y_i	$\ln y_i$	x_i^2	$x_i \ln y_i$
0	17	2.833	0	0
16	9	2.197	256	35.152
32	5	1.609	1024	51.488
48		6.639	1280	86.640

Using these summations, the simultaneous equations are

$$3c_1 + 48c_2 = 6.639$$
$$48c_1 + 1280c_2 = 86.640$$

(4-57)

The simultaneous solution of Eq. 4-57 yields

$$c_1 = \ln k_1 = 2.825$$

$$k_1 = e^{2.825} = 16.86$$

$$c_2 = -2\pi\xi = -0.03825$$

$$\xi = 0.00609$$

and the least-squares fit with equal weight to errors in $\ln y$ gives

$$y = 16.86e^{-2\pi(0.00609)x}$$

(4-58)

or

$$\ln y = 2.825 - 0.03825x$$

(4-59)

The straight line from the least-squares fit is shown in Fig. 4-10 in which the initial value of y is 16.86.

Another exponential function which is frequently encountered in engineering is shown in Fig. 4-11. It is

$$y = k_1 x e^{-k_2 x}$$

(4-60)

in which k_1 and k_2 are positive real numbers. Taking the logarithm of both sides of Eq. 4-60 gives

$$\ln y = \ln(k_1 x) - k_2 x$$

(4-61)

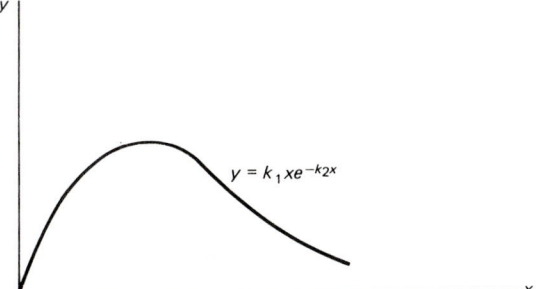

Figure 4-11   General form of the function $y = k_1 x e^{-k_2 x}$

which is a nonlinear form. To obtain a linear form, Eq. 4-61 may be written as

$$\ln \frac{y}{x} = \ln k_1 - k_2 x \tag{4-62}$$

Letting $z = \ln(y/x)$, $c_1 = \ln k_1$, and $c_2 = -k_2$, Eq. 4-62 becomes

$$z = c_1 + c_2 x \tag{4-63}$$

In this form we see that Eq. 4-60 will plot as a straight line on semilog paper when the values of (y/x) are plotted as ordinates on the log scale. We can determine the constants in Eq. 4-63 by utilizing Eq. 4-12 with $\ln(y_i/x_i)$ replacing y_i. Then with $k_i = e^{c_1}$ and $k_2 = -c_2$, we can obtain an approximating equation of the form of Eq. 4-60.

However, in the least-squares fit just discussed, we are minimizing $\sum R_i^2$ and not $\sum r_i^2$. If we want to minimize $\sum r_i^2$, we will have to use weighting with the minimization of $\sum R_i^2$ just as was done with the first exponential function discussed in this section leading to Eq. 4-53. Fig. 4-12 shows exper-

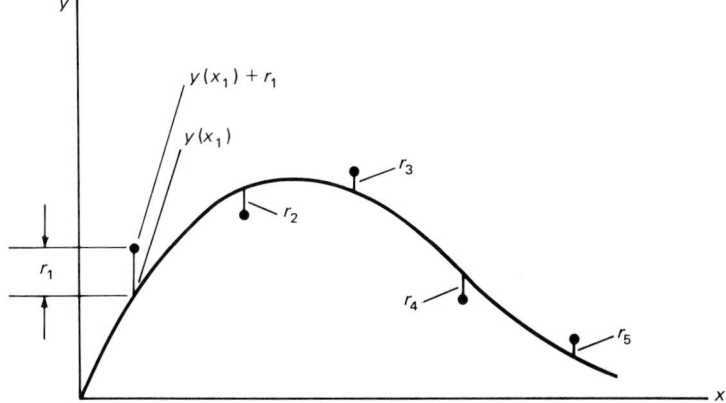

Figure 4-12   Approximating function of the form $y = k_1 x e^{-k_2 x}$

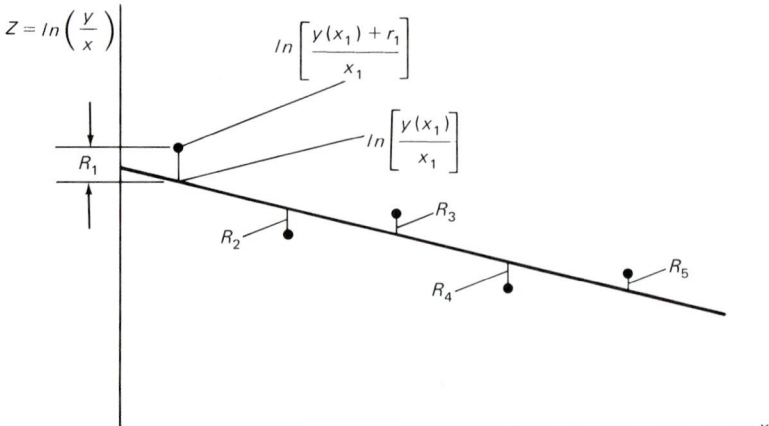

Figure 4-13 The curve of Fig. 4-12 transformed

imental data plotted in the x, y coordinate system and an approximating function of the form

$$y = k_1 x e^{-k_2 x}$$

The same curve and data points are shown in Fig. 4-13 plotted in the x, z coordinate system in which $z = \ln(y/x)$. Now, if we have errors r_i between the y_i values of the data points and the y values of the approximating curve shown in Fig. 4-12, the corresponding errors R_i in $\ln(y_i/x_i)$ are

$$R_i = \ln\left[\frac{y(x_i) + r_i}{x_i}\right] - \ln\left[\frac{y(x_i)}{x_i}\right]$$

$$= \ln\left[\frac{\dfrac{y(x_i) + r_i}{x_i}}{\dfrac{y(x_i)}{x_i}}\right] = \ln\left[1 + \frac{r_i}{y(x_i)}\right] \qquad (4\text{-}64)$$

From Eq. 4-64 and the definition of a natural logarithm,

$$e^{R_i} = 1 + \frac{r_i}{y(x_i)} \qquad (4\text{-}65)$$

The series expansion for e^{R_i} is

$$e^{R_i} = 1 + R_i + \frac{R_i^2}{2!} + \frac{R_i^3}{3!} \cdots$$

and if R_i is small,

$$e^{R_i} \cong 1 + R_i \qquad (4\text{-}66)$$

Comparing Eqs. 4-65 and 4-66, we can see that

$$R_i = \frac{r_i}{y(x_i)}$$

If we now assume that $y_i \cong y(x_i)$,

$$R_i = \frac{r_i}{y_i} \tag{4-67}$$

Thus, as was discussed in obtaining Eq. 4-53, we must minimize

$$\sum (y_i R_i)^2 \qquad (R_i = c_1 + c_2 x_i - \ln(y_i/x_i))$$

if we are to approximately minimize

$$\sum r_i^2 \qquad (r_i = k_1 x_i e^{-k_2 x_i} - y_i)$$

and give equal weight to the errors in y. Performing the minimization on the first of the above summations, we obtain an equation identical to Eq. 4-53 except that ln y_i is replaced by $\ln(y_i/x_i)$.

Summarizing, we see that to obtain a least-squares fit using an approximation function such as given by Eq. 4-60 with equal weight given to the errors in $\ln(y_i/x_i)$, Eq. 4-12 with y_i replaced by $\ln(y_i/x_i)$ is used. To obtain a least-squares fit using the same function, but with equal weight given to the errors in y, Eq. 4-53 with ln y_i replaced by $\ln(y_i/x_i)$ is used. As stated previously, in a majority of engineering applications the data could be subject to more error than represented by the differences in values obtained by minimizing $\sum R_i^2$ instead of $\sum r_i^2$, so that the distinction would be unimportant practically.

EXAMPLE 4-6

Let us now consider the use of the approximating function given by Eq. 4-60 and shown in general form in Fig. 4-11. A plot of the stress-strain data obtained from a compression test of a 6 in. by 12 in. concrete cylinder is shown in Fig. 4-14 by the 9 data points on the graph. The general form of the data plot suggests that the exponential function shown in Fig. 4-11 might be a good function to describe the nonlinear stress-strain curve of concrete. To explore this possibility, let us obtain a least-squares fit using the function

$$\sigma = k_1 \varepsilon e^{-k_2 \varepsilon} \tag{4-68}$$

in which σ is the stress in psi, and ε is the strain with units of in./in. To simplify the computation, we shall use only the 5 data points shown as solid

Figure 4-14 Stress-strain plot for concrete

black circles in Fig. 4-14. These data values are also shown in tabular form in that figure.

SOLUTION
Taking the logarithm of Eq. 4-68 to obtain a linear form as previously discussed, we obtain

$$\ln \frac{\sigma}{\varepsilon} = \ln k_1 - k_2 \varepsilon \qquad (4\text{-}69)$$

Letting $z = \ln(\sigma/\varepsilon)$, $c_1 = \ln k_1$, and $c_2 = -k_2$, Eq. 4-69 becomes

$$z = c_1 + c_2 \varepsilon \qquad (4\text{-}70)$$

As in Ex. 4-5, we will fit a curve in which equal weight is given to the errors in $\ln(\sigma/\varepsilon)$ and leave as an exercise for the reader the fitting of a curve for which equal weight is given to the errors in σ (see Prob. 4-27).

In fitting a curve for which equal weight is given to the errors in $\ln(\sigma/\varepsilon)$, the following table is formed for the summations in Eq. 4-12 in which y_i is replaced by $\ln(\sigma_i/\varepsilon_i)$ and x_i by ε_i.

ε_i	σ_i	$\ln(\sigma_i/\varepsilon_i)$	ε_i^2	$\varepsilon_i \ln(\sigma_i/\varepsilon_i)$
$500(10)^{-6}$	2250	15.320	$2.50(10)^{-7}$	$7660.0(10)^{-6}$
$1000(10)^{-6}$	3575	15.089	$10.00(10)^{-7}$	$15089.0(10)^{-6}$
$1500(10)^{-6}$	4250	14.857	$22.50(10)^{-7}$	$22285.5(10)^{-6}$
$2000(10)^{-6}$	4400	14.604	$40.00(10)^{-7}$	$29208.0(10)^{-6}$
$2375(10)^{-6}$	4200	14.385	$56.41(10)^{-7}$	$34164.4(10)^{-6}$
$7375(10)^{-6}$		74.255	$131.41(10)^{-7}$	$108,406.9(10)-6$

Using these summations, the simultaneous equations obtained are

$$5c_1 + 73.75(10)^{-4}c_2 = 74.255$$
$$73.75(10)^{-4}c_1 + 1314.1(10)^{-8}c_2 = 0.1084 \tag{4-71}$$

The solution of these simultaneous equations yields

$$c_1 = \ln k_1 = 15.585$$

$$k_1 = e^{15.585} = 5.868(10)^6$$

$$c_2 = -k_2 = -497.7$$

Using these values, the least-squares fit gives us the equation

$$\sigma = 5.868(10)^6 \varepsilon e^{-497.7\varepsilon} \tag{4-72}$$

A plot of this function in Fig. 4-14 (the dark line) shows that the function describes the stress-strain data quite well. For this reason, the exponential function of Eq. 4-68 is quite often used to analyze the flexural stresses in reinforced concrete beams.

4-6 CURVE FITTING WITH FOURIER SERIES

The application of the least-squares criterion for the "best fit" of a Fourier series, or trigonometric series, to experimental data requires that one have a basic understanding of the representation of a function, $y = f(x)$, by a Fourier series. Therefore, let us first briefly review the basic concepts of Fourier series and then illustrate the use of the matrix equation, Eq. 4-35a, for obtaining the set of simultaneous linear algebraic equations involving the undetermined Fourier coefficients.

Any single-valued function $f(x)$ that has a finite number of discontinuities may be represented by a Fourier series in the interval of $(-\pi, \pi)$, or in the interval of $(-l, l)$. For a function $f(x)$ defined in the interval of $(-l, l)$, the trigonometric form of a Fourier series is defined as

$$f(x) = \frac{a_0}{2} + \sum_{n=1}^{\infty} a_n \cos \frac{n\pi x}{l} + \sum_{n=1}^{\infty} b_n \sin \frac{n\pi x}{l} \tag{4-73}$$

in which a_n and b_n are the Fourier coefficients. For example, the function

$$f(x) = 0 \qquad 0 \le x \le l$$
$$f(x) = -x \qquad -l \le x \le 0$$

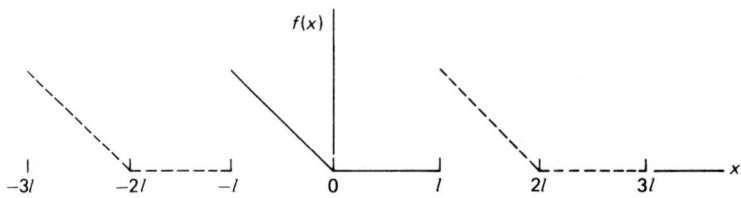

Figure 4-15 Periodic function with period of $2l$

as represented by the series of Eq. 4-73 is periodic and repeats itself as shown in Fig. 4-15. It should be noted that the period is $2l$ and that $f(x + 2l) = f(x)$.

For a given function $f(x)$, the Fourier coefficients, a_n and b_n, may be determined from the following integral equations which are stated here without proof:

$$a_n = \frac{1}{l} \int_{-l}^{l} f(x) \cos \frac{n \pi x}{l} \, dx \quad n = 0, 1, 2, 3, \ldots \qquad (4\text{-}74)$$

$$b_n = \frac{1}{l} \int_{-l}^{l} f(x) \sin \frac{n \pi x}{l} \, dx \quad n = 1, 2, 3, \ldots \qquad (4\text{-}75)$$

In many instances it is desirable to use a *half-range* series over the interval $(0, l)$. If $f(-x) = -f(x)$, the function is an *odd function,* and the cosine terms of Eq. 4-73 vanish because each of the cosine terms is an *even function.* Conversely, if $f(x) = f(-x)$, the function is an *even function,* and the sine terms of Eq. 4-73 vanish because each of the sine terms is an *odd function.* Thus,

$$f(x) = \frac{a_0}{2} + \sum_{n=1}^{\infty} a_n \cos \frac{n \pi x}{l} \qquad \text{(even)} \qquad (4\text{-}76)$$

$$f(x) = \sum_{n=1}^{\infty} b_n \sin \frac{n \pi x}{l} \qquad \text{(odd)} \qquad (4\text{-}77)$$

Now let us consider the function $f(x) = -x + 1$ defined in the interval $(0, l)$ where $l = \frac{1}{2}$. The Fourier *cosine series* represents the *even* function as shown in Fig. 4-16(a), and the Fourier *sine series* represents the *odd* function as shown in Fig. 4-16(b). In either case, the series (cosine or sine) will converge to the same value in the interval $(0, l)$, except at $x = 0$ and $x = l$. For the even function, the cosine series converges to 1 at $x = 0$ and to $\frac{1}{2}$ at $x = \frac{1}{2}$. However, the odd function is discontinuous at $x = 0$ and $x = l$, and the sine series converges to the mean value of the function at the points of discontinuity;

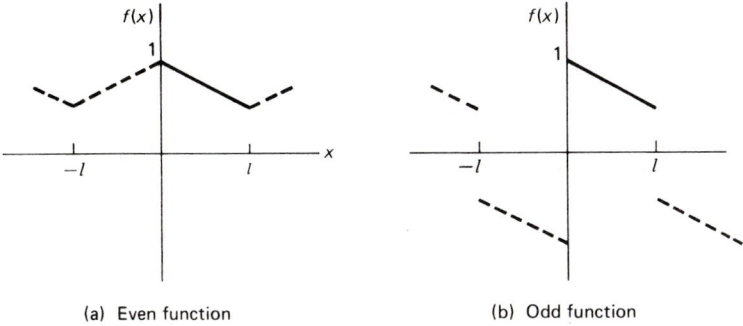

(a) Even function   (b) Odd function

Figure 4-16 Even and odd periodic functions

that is, the sine series will converge to zero at $x = 0$ and $x = l$. For half-range expansions, it can easily be shown that

$$a_n = \frac{2}{l} \int_0^l f(x) \cos \frac{n\pi x}{l} \, dx$$
$$\left. \begin{matrix} \\ n = 0, 1, 2, 3, \ldots \\ \\ \end{matrix} \right\} \text{(even)} \qquad (4\text{-}78)$$
$$b_n = 0,$$

$$b_n = \frac{2}{l} \int_0^l f(x) \sin \frac{n\pi x}{l} \, dx$$
$$\left. \begin{matrix} \\ n = 1, 2, 3, \ldots \\ \\ \end{matrix} \right\} \text{(odd)} \qquad (4\text{-}79)$$
$$a_n = 0$$

Least-Squares Procedure

In the least-squares procedure for the "best fit" of a trigonometric series to experimental data, the coefficients are not determined by the integration process indicated in Eqs. 4-74, 4-75, 4-78, and 4-79. Instead the coefficients for the first m terms of a series are determined by the procedure explained in Sec. 4-3. The number of terms, m, for a good representation of the data may not be known initially. However, a trial solution with the first 3 or 4 terms will usually indicate whether more terms are necessary. In general, the representation of data by a series improves with an increase in the number of terms in the series.

Whether we select the first m terms of Eq. 4-73, the first m terms of Eq. 4-76, or the first m terms of Eq. 4-77 depends to some extent upon the general form of the plotted data and the convergence required for a reasonable fit near the ends at $x = 0$ and $x = l$. For example, the plot in Fig. 4-17(a) clearly shows that the sine series, Eq. 4-77, is not suitable since each of the sine terms vanishes at $x = 0$ and $x = l$; that is, the sine series for any number of terms converges to zero at $x = 0$ and $x = l$, which would result in a poor fit at the ends. The cosine series, Eq. 4-76, might be suitable since the cosine terms do not vanish at $x = 0$ and $x = l$. If a trial solution of, for example, 3 terms of a

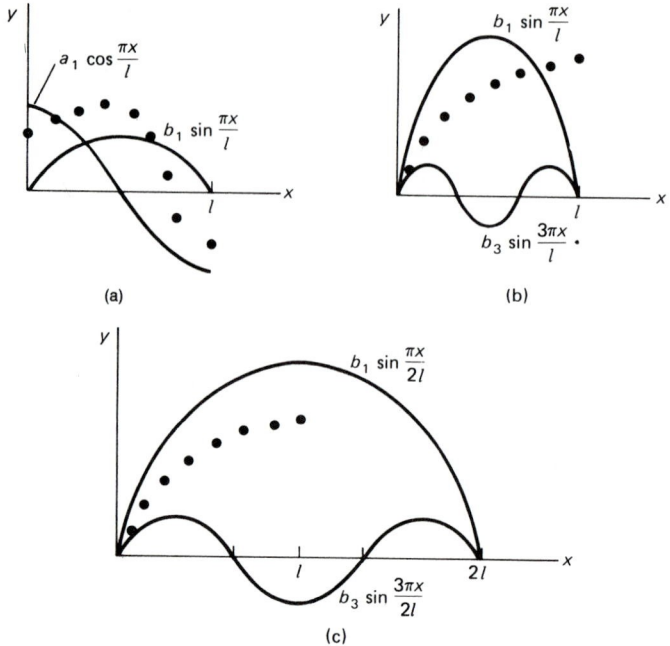

Figure 4-17 Typical data plots with trigonometric function behavior

cosine series shows that a poor representation of the data is being obtained, then a combination of cosine and sine terms of Eq. 4-73 should be used.

As another example of the selection of an appropriate series, consider the data shown in Fig. 4-17(b). In this case the data at first glance might suggest the sine series, Eq. 4-77, since an $f(x)$ fit of the data appears to go through zero. However, the sine series would converge to zero at $x = l$. The problem of convergence near the end of the plotted data can be circumvented by making the half-range equal to $2l$ (twice the value of x for the last data point) as shown in Fig. 4-17(c). Furthermore, if we consider the $f(x)$ function to be symmetrical about $x = l$, then the even-numbered coefficients must vanish; that is, b_2, b_4, and so on are equal to zero since the sin $2\pi x/2l$, sin $4\pi x/2l$, and so on are asymmetric with respect to $x = l$.

EXAMPLE 4-7

The following data represent the growth in height of a boy from the age of 11 to the age of 21.[1] It is desired to determine the best fit of a trigonometric series to the data. To simplify the computations so that they may be made

[1]Jean Demining, "Application of the Gompertz Curve to the Observed Pattern of Growth in Length of 48 Individual Boys and Girls During Adolescent Cycle of Growth," *Human Biology,* Vol. 29, No. 1, 1957.

using a pocket calculator, we will use the data denoted by the asterisks and a 3-term trigonometric series.

Elapsed Time (yr)	Growth (cm)
0 (age 11)	0
0.8	0.74
*1.4	2.25
2.0	5.25
2.4	8.25
*3.2	15.00
4.0	21.38
*4.8	26.25
5.4	28.88
6.0	30.60
7.0	32.25
*8.0	33.00
*10.0 (age 21)	35.00

SOLUTION
The data points (1.4, 2.25), (3.2, 15), (4.8, 26.25), (8.0, 33), and (10.0, 35) are first plotted as shown in Fig. 4-18. Based upon our previous discussion, we will select the sine series with only odd coefficients and with a half-range of t

$$y = 35.95 \sin \frac{\pi t}{20} - 1.2024 \sin \frac{3\pi t}{20} - 3.4690 \sin \frac{5\pi t}{20}$$

t (elapsed time, yr)

Figure 4-18   Growth-time plot

$= 20$ years so that $f(t)$ is symmetrical about $t = 10$ years as shown in the figure. Thus, for the first 3 terms we take

$$y = b_1 \sin \frac{\pi t}{20} + b_3 \sin \frac{3\pi t}{20} + b_5 \sin \frac{5\pi t}{20}$$

where y is the growth in centimeters and t is the elapsed growth time in years. For the generation of the elements of Eq. 4-35a, we note that

$$f_1(t) = \sin \frac{\pi t}{20}$$

$$f_2(t) = \sin \frac{3\pi t}{20}$$

$$f_3(t) = \sin \frac{5\pi t}{20}$$

and that $c_1 = b_1$, $c_2 = b_3$, and $c_3 = b_5$.

For $m = 3$ (number of functions), Eq. 4-35a reduces to

$$
\begin{bmatrix}
\sum [f_1(t_i)]^2 & \sum f_1(t_i)f_2(t_i) & \sum f_1(t_i)f_3(t_i) \\
\sum f_2(t_i)f_1(t_i) & \sum [f_2(t_i)]^2 & \sum f_2(t_i)f_3(t_i) \\
\sum f_3(t_i)f_1(t_i) & \sum f_3(t_i)f_2(t_i) & \sum [f_3(t_i)]^2
\end{bmatrix}
\begin{Bmatrix} b_1 \\ b_3 \\ b_5 \end{Bmatrix}
=
\begin{Bmatrix} \sum f_1(t_i)y_i \\ \sum f_2(t_i)y_i \\ \sum f_3(t_i)y_i \end{Bmatrix}
\qquad \text{(4-80)}
$$

with $i = 1, 2, \ldots, 5$ (number of data points). The values for the summations in Eq. 4-80 are obtained from the following table by summing the appropriate products and squared terms.

t_i	y_i	$f_1(t_i)$	$f_2(t_i)$	$f_3(t_i)$
1.4	2.25	0.218	0.613	0.891
3.2	15.00	0.482	0.998	0.588
4.8	26.25	0.685	0.771	-0.588
8.0	33.00	0.951	-0.588	0.000
10.0	35.00	1.000	-1.000	1.000

Having determined these summations, we obtain from Eq. 4-80

$$2.653 b_1 - 0.416 b_3 + 1.075 b_5 = 92.085$$

$$-0.416 b_1 + 3.312 b_3 - 0.320 b_5 = -17.816$$

$$1.075 b_1 - 0.320 b_3 + 2.485 b_5 = 30.390$$

The simultaneous solution of these equations yields

$$b_1 = 35.95$$

$$b_3 = -1.2024$$

$$b_5 = -3.4690$$

Thus, the best fit for a three-term sine series to the 5 data points used is

$$y = 35.95 \sin \frac{\pi t}{20} - 1.2024 \sin \frac{3\pi t}{20} - 3.4690 \sin \frac{5\pi t}{20}$$

A plot of this function, the continuous curve in Fig. 4-18, shows that it is a reasonably good representation of the 5 data points used. In addition, it should be pointed out that by taking 1 or 2 more terms of the series and using all the data points for computation of the unknown constants, a four or five-term series would give a very good representation of the growth-time data.

4-7 COMPUTER PROGRAM USING LEAST-SQUARES PROCEDURE FOR LINEAR FORMS

A least-squares fit involving n data points and m unknown constants can be done fairly easily with today's electronic pocket calculators if n is not greater than 6 or 7 and m is less than 4. However, if a large number of data points is involved and/or more than 3 simultaneous equations are to be solved, then the evaluation of the matrix elements of Eq. 4-35a or the matrix multiplications of Eq. 4-35 or Eq. 4-39 should probably be programmed for use on a digital computer. This will be done in the example which follows.

EXAMPLE 4-8

It is desired to write a computer program which will determine the coefficients c_1, c_2, and c_3 for the least-squares fit of the polynomial

$$y = c_1 + c_2 x + c_3 x^2$$

to the following data:

x	y
0.5	1.71
1.0	2.45
1.5	3.81
2.0	4.80
2.5	7.00
3.0	8.60

With some minor modifications the program we shall develop can be used to determine the c's of any linear form as expressed by Eq. 4-21 in determining a least-squares fit for a set of data. The functions $f_1(x) = 1$, $f_2(x) = x$, and $f_3(x) = x^2$ are defined by using statement functions. In a general program these statements must be modified for different linear forms. The DO loop generating the **F** matrix must also be changed if there are either more or less than three $f(x)$'s used. COMMENTS will be used in the program to call attention to statements which must be changed for different linear forms used in different problems.

The **F** matrix for m c's and n data points is

$$
\mathbf{F} = \begin{bmatrix}
f_1(x_1) & f_2(x_1) & \cdots & f_m(x_1) \\
f_1(x_2) & f_2(x_2) & \cdots & f_m(x_2) \\
\cdots\cdots\cdots\cdots\cdots\cdots\cdots \\
f_1(x_n) & f_2(x_n) & \cdots & f_m(x_n)
\end{bmatrix}
\qquad
\begin{array}{c}
\text{(4-28)} \\
\text{(repeated)}
\end{array}
$$

If we let the f functions be represented by a double-subscripted variable such as f_{ki}, in which the first subscript is the row number in the **F** matrix and the second is the column number, it can be seen that the first subscript corresponds to the subscript on x and the second to the subscript on f. Using such subscripts we see that the elements of the coefficient matrix of Eq. 4-35a can be expressed as

$$
a_{ij} = \sum_{k=1}^{n} f_{ki} f_{kj} \qquad
\begin{array}{c}
1 \le i \le m \\
1 \le j \le m
\end{array}
\tag{4-81}
$$

in which i represents the row number of the element in the **A** matrix, j represents the column number, and k is the number of data points being summed in each element. Comparing Eqs. 4-28 and 4-81, we see that the elements of the coefficient matrix of Eq. 4-35a can be generated using the elements of the **F** matrix and a triple DO loop. Advantage will be taken of the symmetry of the coefficient matrix **A** in generating its elements.

The column of constants on the right of the equal sign in Eq. 4-35a will be stored as an additional column of the coefficient matrix **A** forming the m by $m + 1$ augmented matrix **A**. The elements of this column are given by

$$
a_{i,m+1} = \sum_{k=1}^{n} f_{ki} y_k \qquad 1 \le i \le m
\tag{4-82}
$$

in which i is the row number of the augmenting column. The column elements can be readily generated using a double DO loop.

A subprogram utilizing Cholesky's method without row interchange is

CALLed to solve the simultaneous linear algebraic equations represented by Eq. 4-35a. The main program is as follows:

```
C                -LEAST SQUARES CURVE-FITTING PROGRAM-
C IN THIS PROGRAM THE ELEMENTS OF THE COEFFICIENT
C MATRIX OF EQ. 4-35A ARE GENERATED USING ELEMENTS
C OF THE F MATRIX IN A TRIPLE DO LOOP.
C THE ELEMENTS OF THE COLUMN MATRIX TO THE RIGHT
C OF THE EQUAL SIGN OF EQ. 4-35A ARE GENERATED
C USING ELEMENTS OF THE F MATRIX AND THE Y VALUES
C IN A DOUBLE DO LOOP.
C
C REPLACE THE FOLLOWING DIMENSION STATEMENT FOR
C DIFFERENT PROBLEMS INVOLVING DIFFERENT NUMBERS OF DATA
C POINTS AND DIFFERENT NUMBERS OF C VALUES.
      DIMENSION X(6), Y(6), F(6,3), A(3,4), C(3)
C
C USING STATEMENT FUNCTIONS, DEFINE THE FUNCTIONS F1(X),
C F2(X), ETC.
      F1(X)  = 1.
      F2(X)  = X
      F3(X)  = X*X
C
C USING A DATA INITIALIZATION STATEMENT, ASSIGN VALUES
C TO THE NUMBER OF C'S AND NUMBER OF DATA POINTS.
C THIS STATEMENT MUST BE CHANGED FOR EACH PROBLEM INVOLVING
C DIFFERENT M AND N VALUES.
      DATA M,N/3,6/
C
C USING A DATA INITIALIZATION STATEMENT, ASSIGN X AND Y
C VALUES OF THE DATA POINTS. THIS DATA STATEMENT
C MUST BE CHANGED FOR EACH DIFFERENT PROBLEM.
      DATA (X(I), I=1,6)/0.5,1.0,1.5,2.0,2.5,3.0/, (Y(I),
                                            I= 1,6)/1.71,
     *2.45,3.81,4.80,7.00,8.60/
C
C GENERATE THE F MATRIX. MODIFY THE STATEMENTS AS
C REQUIRED FOR DIFFERENT PROBLEMS HAVING DIFFERENT NUMBERS
C OF FUNCTIONS.
      DO 2I=1,N
      F(I,1)=F1(X(I))
      F(I,2)=F2(X(I))
    2 F(I,3)=F3(X(I))
C
C GENERATE THE LOWER TRIANGULAR ELEMENTS OF THE
C COEFFICIENT MATRIX OF EQ. 4-35A AND ASSIGN VALUES
C TO THE SYMMETRIC ELEMENTS ABOVE THE MAIN DIAGONAL.
      DO 4I=1,M
      DO 4J=1,I
      A(I,J)=0.
      DO 3K=1,N
    3 A(I,J)=A(I,J)+F(K,I)*F(K,J)
```

```
    4 A(J,I)=A(I,J)
C
C GENERATE THE ELEMENTS OF THE COLUMN MATRIX TO
C THE RIGHT OF THE EQUAL SIGN IN EQ. 4-35A.
      DO 5I=1,M
      A(I,M+1)=0.
      DO 5K=1,N
    5 A(I,M+1)=A(I,M+1)+F(K,I)*Y(K)
C
C DETERMINE THE C VALUES OF Y(X) BY SOLVING THE
C SIMULTANEOUS EQUATIONS REPRESENTED BY MATRIX EQ. 4-35A.
      MP1=M+1
      CALL CHLSKY (A,M,MP1,C)
C
C WRITE OUT THE C VALUES.
      WRITE (6,6)
    6 FORMAT ('1',4X,'C(1) THROUGH C(M)'/)
      WRITE (6,7) (I,C(I), I=1,M)
    7 FORMAT (' ',3X,'C(',I1,')=',E14.7)
      STOP
      END
```

The subroutine subprogram utilizing Cholesky's method for the solution of the simultaneous linear algebraic equations is

```
      SUBROUTINE CHLSKY (A,N,M,X)
      DIMENSION A(N,M),X(N)
C CALCULATE FIRST ROW OF UPPER UNIT TRIANGULAR MATRIX
      DO 3J=2,M
    3 A(1,J)=A(1,J)/A(1,1)
C CALCULATE OTHER ELEMENTS OF U AND L MATRICES
      DO 8I=2,N
      J=I
      DO 5 II=J,N
      SUM=0.
      JM1=J-1
      DO 4K=1,JM1
    4 SUM=SUM+A(II,K)*A(K,J)
    5 A(II,J)=A(II,J)-SUM
      IP1=I+1
      DO 7 JJ=IP1,M
      SUM=0.
      IM1=I-1
      DO 6K=1,IM1
    6 SUM=SUM+A(I,K)*A(K,JJ)
    7 A(I,JJ)=(A(I,JJ)-SUM)/A(I,I)
    8 CONTINUE
C SOLVE FOR X(I) BY BACK SUBSTITUTION
      X(N)=A(N,N+1)
      L=N-1
      DO 10 NN=1,L
      SUM=0.
      I=N-NN
      IP1=I+1
      DO 9J=IP1,N
```

```
 9  SUM=SUM+A(I,J)*X(J)
10  X(I)=A(I,M)-SUM
    RETURN
    END
```

The solution obtained is

```
 C(1) THROUGH C(M)
C(1)  =  0.1096015E 01
C(2)  =  0.8901110E 00
C(3)  =  0.5471530E 00
```

4-8 CURVE FITTING AND INTERPOLATION WITH A CUBIC SPLINE

In Sec. 4-2 it was pointed out that an $n - 1$ degree polynomial can be made to pass through n data points. If the data points are the results of an experiment, and as such subject to experimental error, the graph of the true functional relationship between the variables would not in general pass exactly through all the data points. Therefore, in fitting the data with a polynomial, a polynomial of degree *less* than $n - 1$ would usually be used as an approximating function to smooth out the approximating curve (see Fig. 4-4 and the attendant discussion). However, suppose that the data points are known to be very accurate, so that the approximating function could be expected to pass exactly through all of them. Then, the methods of App. C could be used to determine a polynomial passing exactly through all the points. However, if a large number of data points is involved, a polynomial of high degree will result, and polynomials of high degree may have extreme fluctuations between data points as shown in Fig. 4-4. In this case, the polynomial approximating function would not be a good representation of the true functional relationship between the variables even though it passed through all the points. A smoother curve yielding a better representation of the function might be obtained by passing a draftsman's *spline* through all the data points.

A draftsman's spline is a flexible elastic strip held in place by ducks (weights) which engage the spline and force it to pass through specific points. It can be bent to pass through any reasonable number of points by using a material for the spline which has sufficient flexibility. We shall determine a mathematical model of such a spline and use it to represent an approximating function through given data points which correspond to the positions of the weights.

Readers familiar with elementary beam theory should find it easy to follow the development of the cubic spline fit through its correlation with beam theory. For readers who are not, the subsequent brief correlation of the spline fit with elementary beam theory will be followed by a summary of observations drawn from this correlation pertinent to the development of the spline fit, which they may just accept.

Consider a flexible strip of material passing through the data points A, B, (x_i, y_i), (x_{i+1}, y_{i+1}), C, and through an arbitrary intermediate point (x, y) on

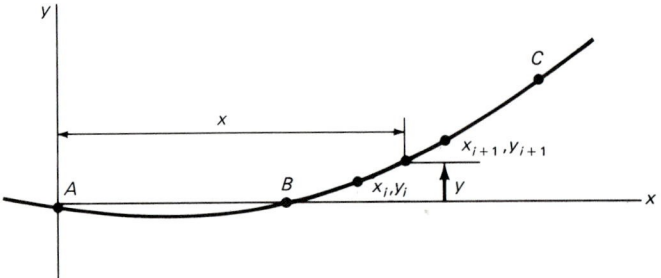

Figure 4-19 A spline passing through 5 data points

the curve as shown in Fig. 4-19. The strip is held in this position by 5 ducks at the data points just mentioned, and the ducks are connected to the spline in such a manner that they exert no moments on the spline. The deflection of the strip from the x axis (and thus its curvature) is assumed to be small for purposes of this discussion.

If we now pass an imaginary cutting plane through the spline between sections A and B and consider the portion to the left of the cut as a free body in equilibrium, we note that the bending moment M_x in the spline between points A and B is a *linear* function of x; that is,

$$M_x = P_A x$$

which is obtained by setting the sum of the moments about the right end of the free body shown in Fig. 4-20(a) equal to zero. Then, from elementary beam theory, the differential equation of the elastic curve of the strip from A to B is[2]

$$\frac{d^2y}{dx^2} = \frac{P_A x}{EI} \tag{4-83}$$

[2]See a discussion of elementary beam theory in any text on mechanics of materials, strength of materials, or mechanics of elastic bodies.

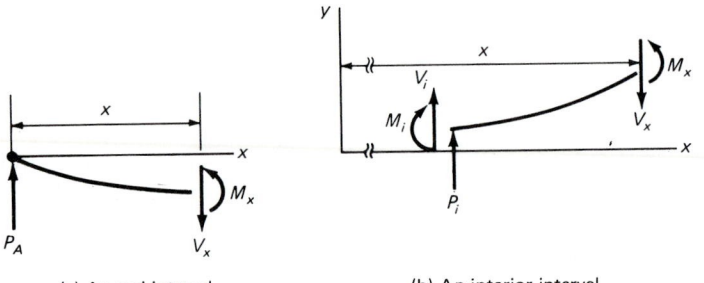

(a) An end interval   (b) An interior interval

Figure 4-20 Free bodies of spline intervals

in which E is the modulus of elasticity of the material, and I is the moment of inertia of the cross-sectional area of the spline about its neutral bending axis. The quantity P_A/EI is a constant in this instance.

Integrating Eq. 4-83, we obtain the equation of the slope of the elastic curve of the spline between points A and B as

$$y' = \frac{P_A}{2EI} x^2 + C_1 \tag{4-84}$$

in which C_1 is a constant of integration.

Integrating Eq. 4-84, we obtain the equation of the elastic curve of the spline between points A and B as

$$y = \frac{P_A}{6EI} x^3 + C_1 x + C_2 \tag{4-85}$$

From the preceding correlation with elementary beam theory, we can make the following observations:

1. The equation of the elastic curve of the spline between any 2 consecutive data points (weights) is a cubic (y is a cubic function).
2. The equation of the slope of the spline between any 2 consecutive data points is a parabola (y' is a parabolic function).
3. The equation of the bending moment in the spline between any 2 consecutive data points is a linear function (y'' is a linear function).
4. The slope of the spline is continuous. Thus, y' values obtained from the slope equations for any 2 consecutive spline intervals (defined by 3 data points) will be the same at the data point common to the 2 intervals.
5. The moments along the spline are also continuous. Thus, y'' values obtained from the moment equations for any 2 consecutive spline intervals (defined by 3 data points) will be the same at the data point common to the 2 intervals.
6. The moments (y'' values) are zero in the spline at the points of application of the end ducks.

We have made the preceding observations looking just at the spline interval between the data points A and B. However, the same observations could be made by considering any interval between data points along the spline such as shown in Fig. 4-20(b).

If Eq. 4-83 is to be an accurate mathematical model of the spline, the maximum deflection of the spline must be small. In a cubic spline fit it is assumed that the approximating function between any 2 adjacent data points is a cubic regardless of the magnitude of the curvature between the points. Thus, some difference could exist between the cubic curves obtained as the fit and the actual shape of the real spline if the curvature were extreme between the data points. However, this is a necessary assumption if the equation of y'' is to be a linear function of x.

Let us next consider a series of data points (x_i, y_i) with $i = 1, 2, 3, \ldots$ $n, n + 1$, where n is the number of data intervals, and determine the equation of the cubic for the i-th interval (the interval between x_i and x_{i+1}). Letting $i = 1, 2, 3, \ldots, n$, we will obtain a *set* of cubic equations which will constitute the mathematical model of a spline connecting the data points.

We begin with the equation of y'' for the i-th interval. Knowing that y'' varies linearly over an interval (see Fig. 4-21), we can write that

$$y'' = y_i'' + \frac{x - x_i}{x_{i+1} - x_i} (y_{i+1}'' - y_i'') \tag{4-86}$$

Letting $h_i = x_{i+1} - x_i$, multiplying y_i'' by h_i/h_i, and substituting h_i for $x_{i+1} - x_i$ in Eq. 4-86, yields

$$y'' = \frac{y_{i+1}'' (x - x_i)}{h_i} + \frac{y_i''}{h_i} (h_i - x + x_i)$$

or

$$y'' = \frac{y_{i+1}''}{h_i} (x - x_i) + \frac{y_i''}{h_i} (x_{i+1} - x) \tag{4-87}$$

in which the values of y_i'' and y_{i+1}'' are as yet unknown.

Integrating Eq. 4-87, we obtain

$$y' = \frac{y_{i+1}''}{2h_i} (x - x_i)^2 - \frac{y_i''}{2h_i} (x_{i+1} - x)^2 + C_1 \tag{4-88}$$

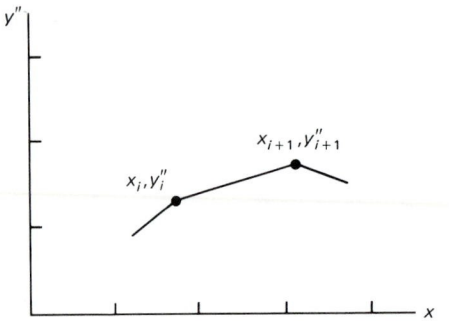

Figure 4-21 A y'' curve for the ith interval

which in turn integrates to

$$y = \frac{y''_{i+1}}{6h_i}(x - x_i)^3 + \frac{y''_i}{6h_i}(x_{i+1} - x)^3 + C_1 x + C_2 \tag{4-89}$$

Observing from Fig. 4-19 that when $x = x_i$, $y = y_i$ and, that when $x = x_{i+1}$, $y = y_{i+1}$, and remembering that $h_i = (x_{i+1} - x_i)$, we can see from Eq. 4-89 that

$$y_i = \frac{y''_i h_i^3}{6h_i} + C_1 x_i + C_2 \tag{4-90}$$

and that

$$y_{i+1} = \frac{y''_{i+1} h_i^3}{6h_i} + C_1 x_{i+1} + C_2 \tag{4-91}$$

Solving these 2 equations simultaneously for C_1 and C_2 using Cramer's rule yields

$$C_1 = \frac{y_{i+1} - y_i}{h_i} - \left[\frac{y''_{i+1} - y''_i}{6}\right] h_i$$

and $\tag{4-92}$

$$C_2 = \frac{x_{i+1} y_i}{h_i} - \frac{x_i y_{i+1}}{h_i} - (x_{i+1} y''_i - x_i y''_{i+1})\frac{h_i}{6}$$

Substituting the expressions for C_1 and C_2 into Eq. 4-89 yields

$$y = \frac{y''_{i+1}}{6h_i}(x - x_i)^3 + \frac{y''_i(x_{i+1} - x)^3}{6h_i} + \left[\frac{y_{i+1} - y_i}{h_i}\right]x - \left[\frac{(y''_{i+1} - y''_i)}{6}\right]h_i x$$

$$+ \frac{x_{i+1} y_i}{h_i} - \frac{x_i y_{i+1}}{h_i} - \left[x_{i+1} y''_i - x_i y''_{i+1}\right]\frac{h_i}{6}$$

or

$$y = \frac{y''_i}{6}\left[\frac{(x_{i+1} - x)^3}{h_i} - h_i(x_{i+1} - x)\right] + \frac{y''_{i+1}}{6}\left[\frac{(x - x_i)^3}{h_i} - h_i(x - x_i)\right]$$

$$+ y_i\left[\frac{x_{i+1} - x}{h_i}\right] + y_{i+1}\left[\frac{x - x_i}{h_i}\right] \tag{4-93}$$

Letting $i = 1, 2, 3, \ldots, n$ in Eq. 4-93, we obtain a set of n equations of the elastic curve for the n intervals of the spline. However, before we can determine y values from these equations, we must determine the y'' values in the equations which are unknown at this point.

Different conditions may be used for determining the y'' values at the end data points. One condition assumes that the values of y'' at the end data points are linear extrapolations of the y'' values at 2 adjacent points. Another, sometimes referred to as the *natural-spline fit*, assigns values of zero to y'' at each end data point, corresponding to the zero moments which exist at each end duck of the actual spline (any extensions of the spline beyond the end weights would be straight). We shall use such zero values for y'' at the ends in our subsequent discussion.

To determine the other y'' values, we utilize the fact that the slope of the spline is a continuous function as mentioned earlier; that is, at each internal data point the value of y' given by the y' equation for the interval *preceding* the data point is equal to the value of y' determined from the y' equation for the interval *following* the data point.

Substituting the expression for C_1 from Eqs. 4-92 into Eq. 4-88, we obtain the equation for the slope in the interval *following* the internal data point (x_i, y_i) as

$$y' = \frac{y''_{i+1}}{2h_i}(x - x_i)^2 - \frac{y''_i}{2h_i}(x_{i+1} - x)^2 + \frac{y_{i+1} - y_i}{h_i} - \left[\frac{y''_{i+1} - y''_i}{6}\right]h_i$$

(4-94)

For the same i value, the equation of the slope for the interval *preceding* the internal data point (x_i, y_i) is

$$y' = \frac{y''_i}{2h_{i-1}}(x - x_{i-1})^2 - \frac{y''_{i-1}}{2h_{i-1}}(x_i - x)^2 + \frac{y_i - y_{i-1}}{h_{i-1}} - \left[\frac{y''_i - y''_{i-1}}{6}\right]h_{i-1}$$

(4-95)

We next let $x = x_i$ in both of the preceding equations and equate the resulting y' values to obtain

$$\frac{y''_i}{2h_{i-1}}(x_i - x_{i-1})^2 + \frac{y_i - y_{i-1}}{h_{i-1}} - \left[\frac{y''_i - y''_{i-1}}{6}\right]h_{i-1}$$
$$= -\frac{y''_i}{2h_i}(x_{i+1} - x_i)^2 + \frac{y_{i+1} - y_i}{h_i} - \left[\frac{y''_{i+1} - y''_i}{6}\right]h_i$$

or

$$\frac{y_i''}{2} h_{i-1} + \frac{y_i - y_{i-1}}{h_{i-1}} - \left[\frac{y_i'' - y_{i-1}''}{6} \right] h_{i-1}$$

$$= -\left[\frac{y_i''}{2} \right] h_i + \frac{y_{i+1} - y_i}{h_i} - \left[\frac{y_{i+1}'' - y_i''}{6} \right] h_i$$

Collecting terms and rearranging, we obtain a more concise equation[3]

$$y_{i-1}''[h_{i-1}] + y_i''[2(h_{i-1} + h_i)] + y_{i+1}''[h_i] = 6\left[\frac{y_{i+1} - y_i}{h_i} - \frac{y_i - y_{i-1}}{h_{i-1}} \right]$$

$$(4\text{-}96)$$

With $i = 2, 3, \ldots, n$ and letting the end values y_1'' and y_{n+1}'' equal zero, we obtain a set of $n - 1$ equations containing $n - 1$ unknown y'' values of the form

$$0(h_1) + y_2''[2(h_1 + h_2)] + y_3''(h_2) = 6\left[\frac{y_3 - y_2}{h_2} - \frac{y_2 - y_1}{h_1} \right]$$

$$y_2''(h_2) + y_3''[2(h_2 + h_3)] + y_4''(h_3) = 6\left[\frac{y_4 - y_3}{h_3} - \frac{y_3 - y_2}{h_2} \right]$$

$$\cdots$$

$$(4\text{-}97)$$

$$\cdots$$

$$y_{n-1}''(h_{n-1}) + y_n''[2(h_{n-1} + h_n)] + 0(h_n) = 6\left[\frac{y_{n+1} - y_n}{h_n} - \frac{y_n - y_{n-1}}{h_{n-1}} \right]$$

The above is a tridiagonal set of simultaneous equations (see Sec. 3-2) which may be expressed by the single matrix equation

[3]The reader interested in mechanics might compare this equation to the 3-moment equation found in most mechanics of materials texts.

$$\begin{bmatrix} 2(h_1+h_2) & h_2 & 0 & 0 & \cdots & 0 & 0 \\ h_2 & 2(h_2+h_3) & h_3 & 0 & \cdots & 0 & 0 \\ 0 & h_3 & 2(h_3+h_4) & h_4 & \cdots & 0 & 0 \\ \vdots & & \vdots & & & \vdots & \vdots \\ & & & & h_{n-2} & 2(h_{n-2}+h_{n-1}) & h_{n-1} \\ 0 & 0 & 0 & 0 & \cdots & 0 & h_{n-1} & 2(h_{n-1}+h_n) \end{bmatrix} \begin{Bmatrix} y_2'' \\ y_3'' \\ y_4'' \\ \vdots \\ y_{n-1}'' \\ y_n'' \end{Bmatrix}$$

$$= 6 \begin{Bmatrix} \dfrac{y_3-y_2}{h_2} - \dfrac{y_2-y_1}{h_1} \\[2mm] \dfrac{y_4-y_3}{h_3} - \dfrac{y_3-y_2}{h_2} \\[2mm] \dfrac{y_5-y_4}{h_4} - \dfrac{y_4-y_3}{h_3} \\[2mm] \vdots \qquad \vdots \\[2mm] \dfrac{y_{n+1}-y_n}{h_n} - \dfrac{y_n-y_{n-1}}{h_{n-1}} \end{Bmatrix} \qquad (4\text{-}98)$$

in which n is the number of *data intervals*.

A computer program would then be used to solve this tridiagonal set of simultaneous equations (see the flow chart of Fig. 3-1) and the values obtained used in Eq. 4-93 to obtain the desired curves for the spline data intervals. Equation 4-98 simplifies somewhat when all the increments h_i are equal. It will be left as an exercise for the reader to determine the matrix form of Eq. 4-98 with the h_i's equal (see Prob. 4-38).

EXAMPLE 4-9

Suppose that we have obtained the data points shown in Fig. 4-22 and wish to determine a set of curves over this data interval using the spline-fit method. Remembering that $h_i = x_{i+1} - x_i$, we can compute that $h_1 = 2$, $h_2 = 3$, $h_3 = 3$, and $h_4 = 1$ from the given data values.

Substituting the appropriate h and y values into Eq. 4-98, we obtain

$$\begin{bmatrix} 10 & 3 & 0 \\ 3 & 12 & 3 \\ 0 & 3 & 8 \end{bmatrix} \begin{Bmatrix} y_2'' \\ y_3'' \\ y_4'' \end{Bmatrix} = 6 \begin{Bmatrix} (\tfrac{1}{3}-\tfrac{2}{2}) \\ (-\tfrac{3}{3}-\tfrac{1}{3}) \\ (-\tfrac{3}{1}-\tfrac{3}{3}) \end{Bmatrix} \qquad (4\text{-}99)$$

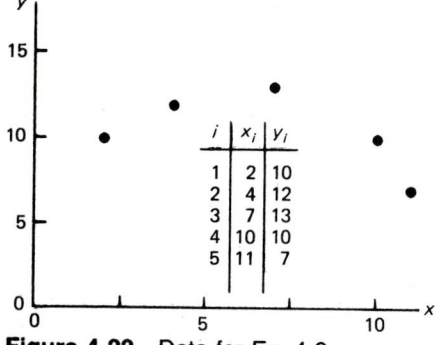

i	x_i	y_i
1	2	10
2	4	12
3	7	13
4	10	10
5	11	7

Figure 4-22   Data for Ex. 4-9

With a matrix this size we can either solve the 3 simultaneous equations using a pocket calculator, or form the augmented matrix

$$\begin{bmatrix} 10 & 3 & 0 & -4 \\ 3 & 12 & 3 & -8 \\ 0 & 3 & 8 & -12 \end{bmatrix}$$

and use a computer program based on the flow chart of Fig. 3-1 for the solution of a tridiagonal set of simultaneous equations to obtain the y'' values we need for use in Eq. 4-93.

Remembering that y_1'' and y_5'' are both zero based on our assumption of a "natural spline fit," and using one of the methods mentioned in the preceding paragraph, we obtain

$$y_1'' = 0$$

$$y_2'' = -0.3308269$$

$$y_3'' = -0.2305766$$

$$y_4'' = -1.4135332$$

$$y_5'' = 0$$

Then, using these values in Eq. 4-93 with $i = 1, 2, 3$, and 4, we can obtain the 4 cubic equations for the 4 data intervals which provide the cubic spline fit for this data.

Proceeding as just mentioned, let us determine the cubic equation (the elastic curve) of the third data interval, from $x = 7$ to $x = 10$. Letting $i = 3$, we obtain from Eq. 4-93 that

$$
y = \frac{-.2305766}{6} \left[\frac{(10 - x)^3}{3} - 3(10 - x) \right]
$$
$$
+ \frac{-1.4135332}{6} \left[\frac{(x - 7)^3}{3} - 3(x - 7) \right]
$$
$$
+ 13 \left(\frac{10 - x}{3} \right) + 10 \left(\frac{x - 7}{3} \right)
$$

which obviously can be reduced to a much simpler form for repeated use if so desired. This equation will go through the data points (7, 13) and (10, 10). If we are interested in the value of y at some point in that interval, at $x = 8$ for instance, we use this value in the preceding equation to find that

$$
y \Big|_{x=8} = 12.7563
$$

It should again be noted that a small set of simultaneous equations such as the preceding ones can be readily solved using a pocket calculator. However, when over 5 data points are involved in defining the fit, a computer solution is desirable.

It will be left as an exercise for the reader to write a computer program which, given the x_i and y_i data values, will utilize Eq. 4-98 to obtain the y'' values, use Eq. 4-93 to obtain the y values, and write out the latter for any specified x value (see Prob. 4-35).

PROBLEMS

4-1. The accompanying figure shows 5 data points in tabular form and plotted on a graph.
    a. Determine a least-squares fit to the data points using an approximation curve of the form

$$
y = c_1 + c_2 x^2
$$

    by means of a pocket calculator.
    b. What is the sum of the squares of the residuals, $\sum r_i^2$?
    c. What does the answer obtained in part b tell you about the approximation curve you obtained?

$$
\text{(partial answer: } y = 10 + 2x^2 \text{)}
$$

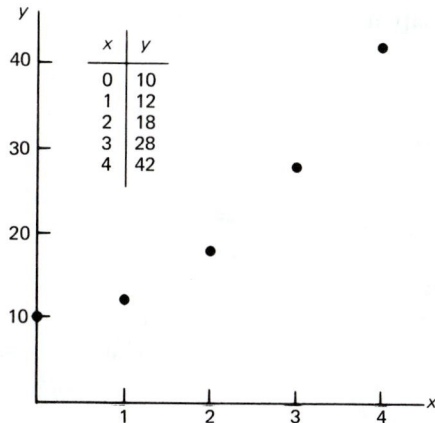

x	y
0	10
1	12
2	18
3	28
4	42

Problem 4-1

4-2 The accompanying figure shows 5 data points in tabular form and plotted on a graph.
  a. Determine a least-squares fit to the data points using an approximation equation of the form

$$y = c_1 x + c_2 x^2$$

  by means of a pocket calculator.
  b. What is the sum of the squares of the residuals, $\sum r_i^2$?
  c. What does the answer obtained in part b tell you about the approximation curve you obtained?

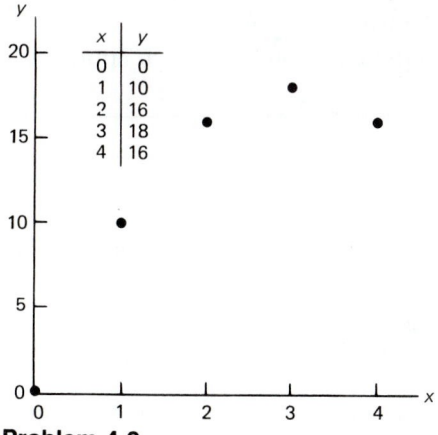

x	y
0	0
1	10
2	16
3	18
4	16

Problem 4-2

4-3. Work Prob. 4-2 using an approximation function of the form

$$y = c_1x + c_2x^2 + c_3x^3$$

by means of a pocket calculator.

4-4. In Ex. 4-2 the pure quadratic equation $y = c_1 + c_2x^2$ was used to obtain a least-squares fit to 4 data points.
   a. Obtain a least-squares fit to the same 4 data points using the approximation function $y = c_1 + c_2x + c_3x^2$ by means of a pocket calculator.
   b. Plot the function obtained in part a by determining y values at $x = 1, 2, 2.5, 3, 3.5,$ and 4, and compare with the data points.

$$\text{(answer: } y = 1.558x^2 + 1.909x + 0.368)$$

4-5. From the results of Ex. 4-2 and Prob. 4-4, determine which of the functions obtained best represents the data by determining $\sum r_i^2$ for each function.

4-6. **a.** Apply a weighting factor of 2 to the data point (1.0, 3.8) of Ex. 4-2 and obtain a least-squares fit using the function $y = c_1 + c_2x^2$ and a pocket calculator.
   b. Compare the values of c_1 and c_2 obtained in part a with the similar values obtained in Ex. 4-2.
   c. Compute $\sum r_i^2$ for the function obtained in part a and for the function of Ex. 4-2 and compare.

$$\text{(partial answer: } y = 2.09 + 1.95x^2)$$

4-7 The accompanying figure shows 6 data points plotted on a graph and also shown in tabular form. Use a pocket calculator and
   a. Determine a least-squares fit to the data points using an approximation function of the form

$$y = c_1x + c_2x^2$$

   b. Calculate the sum of the squares of the residuals, $\sum r_i^2$.
   c. Determine a least-squares fit to the same 6 data points using an approximation function of the form

$$y = c_1x + c_2x^2 + c_3x^3$$

   d. Calculate the sum of the squares of the residuals, $\sum r_i^2$, for this function and compare with the value obtained for part b. Does this comparison indicate which of the polynomials gives the better fit?

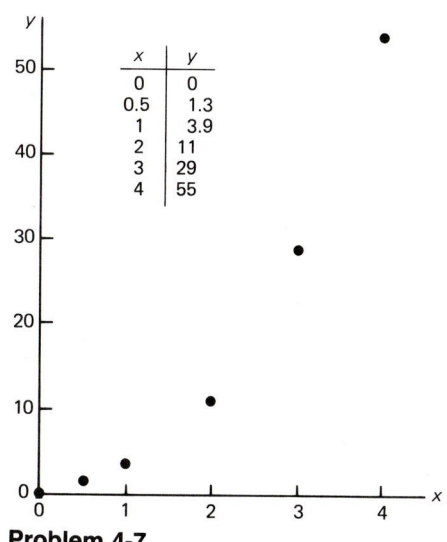

Problem 4-7

4-8. The accompanying figure shows 13 data points in tabular form and plotted on a graph which define a stress-strain curve of a material. The data values were obtained from 2 tensile tests of the material. It is desired to obtain a least-squares fit to the data using an approximating function of the form

$$\sigma = c_1 \varepsilon + c_2 \varepsilon^2$$

so that various properties of the material may be observed.
a. Determine the desired function using a pocket calculator.

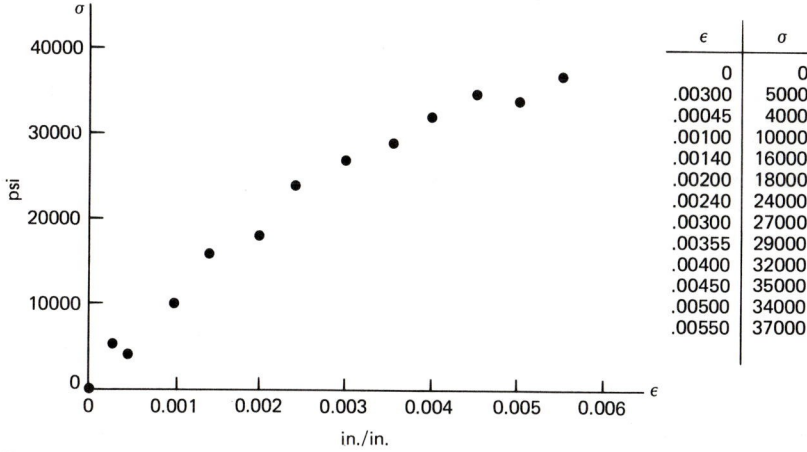

Problem 4-8

    b. From the equation of part a find the tangent modulus of the material (the derivative of the function at $\varepsilon = 0$).

    c. (Optional) Determine the yield stress of the material by sketching the curve of part a and the tangent line from part b, and then drawing a line parallel to the tangent through the point $\sigma = 0$, $\varepsilon = 0.002$ (a 0.2 percent offset).

4-9. The accompanying figure shows 20 data points in both graphical and tabular form obtained from repeated system tests. From a visual inspection of the plot of these points, 10 have been selected as best representing the relationship between v and t by the engineer in charge of the tests. These data points are specified with asterisks in the accompanying table.

    a. Make the minor modifications necessary in the computer program given in Sec. 4-7, and using the 10 asterisked data points, determine an approximating polynomial of the form

$$y = c_1 x + c_2 x^2 + c_3 x^3 + c_4 x^4$$

to fit these points.

    b. Using the modified program of part a, obtain an approximating polynomial of the same form as in part a which fits all 20 points.

    c. Plot the curves obtained in parts a and b on a common set of axes, and discuss the practice of visually selecting the most representative data points as was done in part a. Which polynomial should give the better fit to the system data shown?

t	v
.20	45*
.35	20
.35	80
.40	60
.50	135*
.60	120
.70	200*
.85	220
.85	290*
.90	300*
1.00	375*
1.10	460
1.20	400
1.20	500*
1.30	520
1.35	580
1.40	640
1.40	700*
1.55	850*
1.60	910*

Problem 4-9

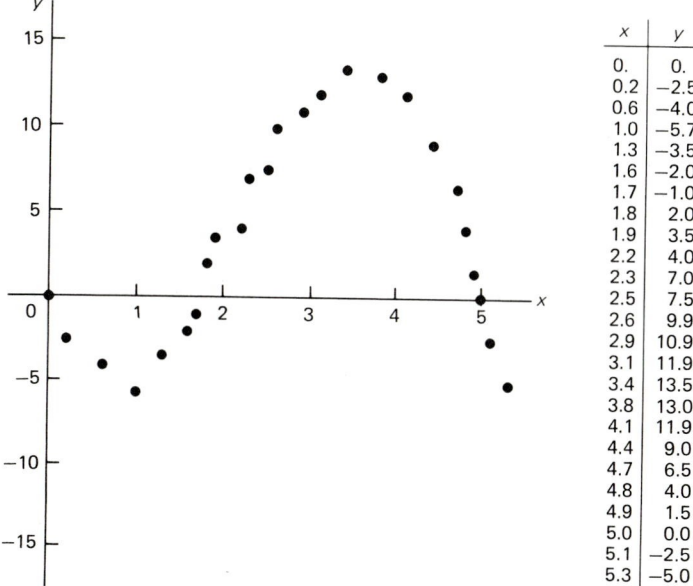

x	y
0.	0.
0.2	−2.5
0.6	−4.0
1.0	−5.7
1.3	−3.5
1.6	−2.0
1.7	−1.0
1.8	2.0
1.9	3.5
2.2	4.0
2.3	7.0
2.5	7.5
2.6	9.9
2.9	10.9
3.1	11.9
3.4	13.5
3.8	13.0
4.1	11.9
4.4	9.0
4.7	6.5
4.8	4.0
4.9	1.5
5.0	0.0
5.1	−2.5
5.3	−5.0

Problem 4-10

4-10. The accompanying figure shows 25 data points plotted on a graph and listed in tabular form. The lowest-order polynomial which we might expect to fit such values would be a cubic. Use the computer program given in Sec. 4-7, make any minor modifications in it necessary, and determine an approximating polynomial of the form

$$y = c_1 + c_2 x + c_3 x^2 + c_4 x^3$$

to fit these points.

4-11. Utilizing the computer program in Sec. 4-7 and the data points given in Ex. 4-7, determine the best fit for the growth-time curve using the polynomial

$$y = c_1 + c_2 t + c_3 t^2 + c_4 t^3$$

where $f_1(t) = 1$, $f_2(t) = t$, $f_3(t) = t^2$, $f_4(t) = t^3$. Compare the fit with the result obtained in Ex. 4-7.

4-12. Utilizing the computer program in Sec. 4-7 and the 5 data points given in Fig. 4-14, determine the best fit for the stress-strain curve using the polynomial

$$\sigma = c_1 + c_2 \varepsilon + c_3 \varepsilon^2 + c_4 \varepsilon^3$$

where $f_1(\varepsilon) = 1$, $f_2(\varepsilon) = \varepsilon$, $f_3(\varepsilon) = \varepsilon^2$, $f_4(\varepsilon) = \varepsilon^3$.

a. Compare the fit of the resulting polynomial to the given data points.

b. Determine several values between each of the data points used to check for excessive deviation in the polynomial between data points.

4-13. The accompanying figure shows 5 data points in tabular form and plotted on a graph. Determine a least-squares fit to the data using an approximation function of the form

$$y = k_1 e^{-k_2 x}$$

using a pocket calculator and giving equal weight to the errors in y.

(answer: $y = 1.97e^{-0.479x}$)

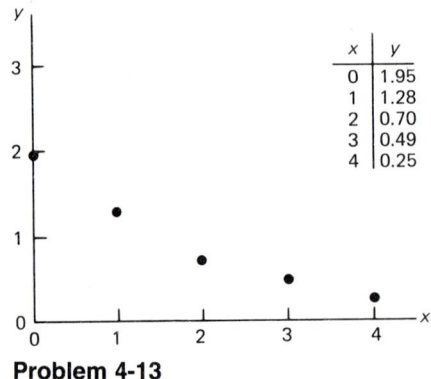

x	y
0	1.95
1	1.28
2	0.70
3	0.49
4	0.25

Problem 4-13

4-14. Refer to the data in Prob. 4-13 and determine a least-squares fit to the data using an approximation function of the form

$$y = k_1 e^{-k_2 x}$$

using a pocket calculator.

a. In determining the function, give equal weight to the errors in $\ln y$.

b. Compute $\sum(y - y_i)^2$ for both the function obtained in part a and for the function given as the answer to Prob. 4-13, and determine which of these functions gives the better fit to the data. The y's are function values, while the y_i's are corresponding data values.

(partial answer: $y = 2.024e^{-0.5068x}$)

4-15. The accompanying figure shows 5 data points in tabular form and plotted on a graph.

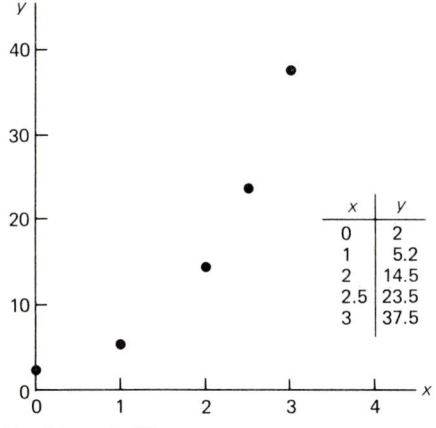

x	y
0	2
1	5.2
2	14.5
2.5	23.5
3	37.5

Problem 4-15

  a. Determine a least-squares fit to the data using an approximation function of the form

$$y = k_1 e^{k_2 x}$$

giving equal weight to the errors in ln y. Use a pocket calculator.
  b. Calculate $\sum(y - y_i)^2$ in which the y's are the function values and the y_i's are the corresponding data values.
  c. Determine a least-squares fit to the same 5 data points using an approximation function of the form

$$y = c_1 + c_2 x + c_3 x^3$$

  d. Calculate $\sum(y - y_i)^2$ for the polynomial function as you did for the exponential function in part b.
  e. Compare the values obtained in parts b and d. Does this comparison provide a true indication of which function provides a better fit to the data?

4-16. The accompanying figure shows 6 data points in both tabular form and plotted on a graph.
  a. Determine a least-squares fit to the data using an approximation function of the form

$$y = k_1 e^{k_2 x}$$

giving equal weight to the errors in y. Use a pocket calculator.
  b. Plot the curve obtained in part a using the abscissa values of the given data points to obtain points on the curve. Then superimpose the given

data points on the graph and observe the fit of the approximating curve.

c. Determine $\sum(y - y_i)^2$ for the 6 given data points where the y_i's are data values and the y's are the function values from part a.

$$\text{(answer: } y = 1.98e^{0.503x}; \sum(y - y_i)^2 = 0.01914\text{)}$$

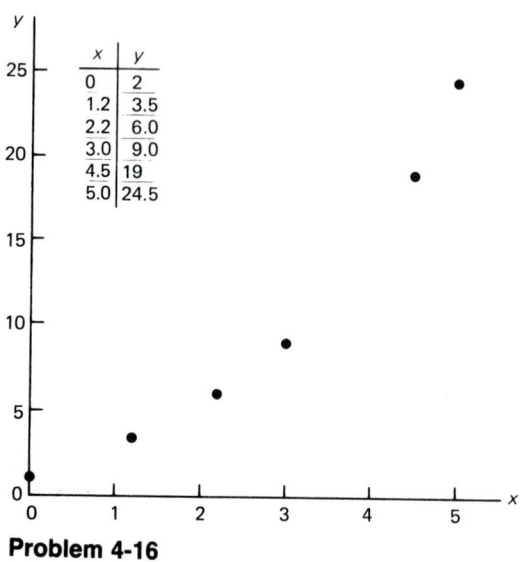

x	y
0	2
1.2	3.5
2.2	6.0
3.0	9.0
4.5	19
5.0	24.5

Problem 4-16

4-17. Work Prob. 4-16 giving equal weight to the errors in $\ln y$. Compare your answer to that given for Prob. 4-16 by comparing $\sum(y - y_i)^2$ for the 2 functions, where the y_i's are the data ordinate values and the y's are the ordinates obtained from the approximating curve at the data abscissa points.

4-18. A least-squares fit to the envelope of a free-damped vibration was obtained in Ex. 4-5. In obtaining this fit, equal weight was given to the errors in $\ln y$.

a. Using the same approximation function, obtain a least-squares fit for the envelope giving equal weight to the errors in y. Use a pocket calculator.

b. Compute $\sum(y - y_i)^2$ for the function obtained in the example and for the function of part a and determine which function gives the better least-squares fit. The y values are the function values and the y_i values are the corresponding data ordinates.

4-19. From the oscillograph record shown in the accompanying figure, determine the damping factor ξ as was done in Ex. 4-5. Select at least 4 data points, and give equal weight to the errors in ln y. Compare your answer with the answer accompanying the problem. Use a pocket calculator.

$$(\text{answer: } y = 14.59e^{-2\pi(0.0046)x})$$

Chart speed = 5 mm/sec

Problem 4-19

4-20. It is desired to determine a functional relationship between the mass density ρ of air and the altitude h above sea level for the dynamic analysis of bodies moving within the earth's atmosphere. The accompanying figure shows data plotted on the graph which is also given in tabular form.

Altitude, h, (ft)	Mass density, ρ (slugs/ft^3)
0*	0.002377
1,000	0.002308
2,000	0.002241
4,000	0.002117
6,000	0.001987
10,000*	0.001755
15,000	0.001497
20,000*	0.001267
30,000	0.000891
40,000*	0.000587
50,000	0.000364
60,000*	0.000224

$$\rho = 2580(10)^{-6}e^{-3.93(10)^{-5}h}$$

Mass density ρ, slugs/ft^3

Altitude h, ft

Problem 4-20

a. Determine a relationship between the mass density and the altitude using an approximation function of the form

$$\rho = k_1 e^{-k_2 h}$$

giving equal weight to the errors in ln ρ. Use a pocket calculator and the 5 data points signified by asterisks in the table.

b. The curve of the function for part a is shown plotted on the problem figure. Would you consider this a good fit to the data? Use the equation to interpolate values for $h = 4,000, 15,000$, and $50,000$ and compare them to the data values.

4-21. Convert the data of Prob. 4-20 to the SI system of units with ρ in kg and h in meters.

a. Using a pocket calculator and an approximation function of the form

$$\rho = k_1 e^{-k_2 h}$$

determine a fit to the data in which equal weight is given to the errors in ρ using all the data points given.

b. Convert the solution for Prob. 4-20 which is given in the figure for that problem to SI units. Then determine $\sum (\rho - \rho_i)^2$ for this function and for the function of part a. The ρ's are from the equations while the ρ_i's are the corresponding data values. Do this only for the 5 data points common to the 2 problems and observe which function gives the better fit to those 5 points.

4-22. The support of a slender hollow tube which is immersed in water is driven by an electromechanical shaker so that the motion of the support is $y = \lambda \sin \omega t$. SR-4 strain gauges mounted on the inside of the tube monitor the strain at the base of the tube. A plot of the actual strain, ε, and the support amplitude, λ, obtained as data in a test is shown in the accompanying figure along with the tabulated data.

a. Determine a least-squares fit using an approximation function of the form

$$\varepsilon = k_1 \lambda^{k_2}$$

in which equal weight is given to the errors in ln ε. Use a pocket calculator.

b. Then use the same approximating function to determine a least-squares fit in which equal weight is given to the errors in ε.

c. Does this form of approximating function do a good job of representing the form of the data? Determine ε values from the equation determined in part a and compare to the data points.

$$\text{(partial answer: } \varepsilon = 418(10)^{-6} \lambda^{0.49})$$

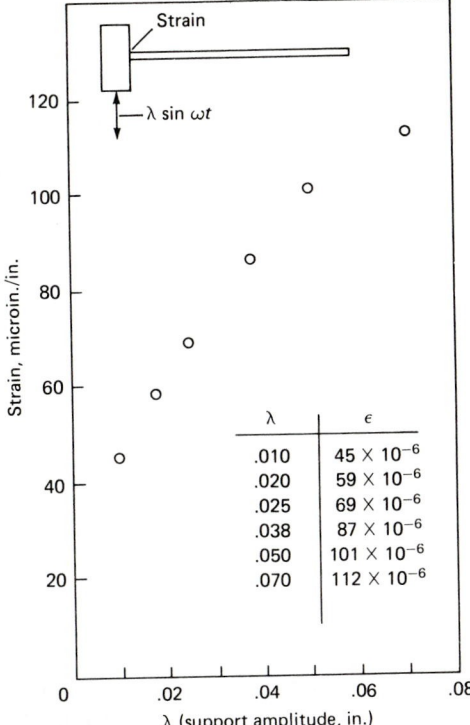

Problem 4-22

4-23. The ultimate compressive strength σ of concrete is known to decrease with an increase in the water-cement ratio, w/c. The following compressive strengths were obtained by averaging the test results of three 6 in. × 12 in. concrete cylinders for each of the w/c ratios shown:

w/c (gal/sack)	Compressive Strength (psi)
4½	7000
5	6125
5½	5237
6	4665
6½	4123
7	3840
7½	3407
8	3070
8½	2580
9	2287

The above data is shown plotted in the accompanying figure.

Problem 4-23

a. Letting $x = w/c$, determine a least-squares fit to the data using an approximation function of the form

$$\sigma = k_1 e^{-k_2 x}$$

with equal weight given to the errors in ln σ. Use a pocket calculator.

b. Compare the values from the curve obtained to the data values to see if the function provides a good fit to the data.

(answer: on curve in figure)

4-24. Write a computer program for curve fitting with an exponential function of the form

$$y = k_1 e^{-k_2 x}$$

Give equal weight to the errors in y_i by using Eq. 4-53 to obtain the two required simultaneous equations. Use Cramer's rule to solve the two equations for c_1 and c_2. Print out values of k_1 and k_2.

Use the program to obtain a least-squares fit to the data shown in Prob. 4-23. Plot the solution curve along with the given data points. Compare your solution with the solution of Prob. 4-23 in which equal weight is given to errors in ln σ_i (see Prob. Fig. 4-23 for the solution curve of Prob. 4-23). Note that when the largest y_i value (σ_i in this problem) is only a few times as large as the smallest y_i value, the difference between the two fits may be negligible.

4-25. The accompanying table shows 12 data values in tabular form and plotted on a graph.

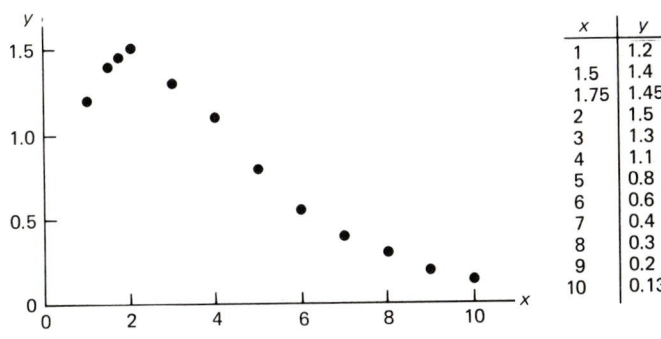

x	y
1	1.2
1.5	1.4
1.75	1.45
2	1.5
3	1.3
4	1.1
5	0.8
6	0.6
7	0.4
8	0.3
9	0.2
10	0.13

Problem 4-25

Determine a least-squares fit to the data using an approximation function of the form

$$y = k_1 x e^{-k_2 x}$$

using a pocket calculator. Give equal weight to the errors in $\ln (y_i/x_i)$

(answer: $y = 1.995 x e^{-.5014x}$)

4-26. Refer to the graph and tabularized data given in the figure accompanying Prob. 4-25 in working this problem.

  a. Write a computer program for determining a least-squares fit to the data using an approximation function of the form

$$y = k_1 x e^{-k_2 x}$$

giving equal weight to the errors in $\ln (y_i/x_i)$. Use the simultaneous equation given by Eq. 4-12 with y_i replaced by $\ln (y_i/x_i)$, and solve these equations for c_1 and c_2 using Cramer's rule. Print the values of k_1 and k_2 as output of the program. Plot the approximation function and the given data points on the same graph, and check your solution against that given for Prob. 4-25.

  b. Write a computer program to determine a least-squares fit to the data using the same function as above, but with equal weight given to the errors in y_i. Use the simultaneous equations given by Eq. 4-53 with $\ln y_i$ replaced by $\ln (y_i/x_i)$, and solve these equations for c_1 and c_2 using Cramer's rule. Plot the approximation function and the given data points on the same graph, and compare this solution to that obtained for part a.

4-27. Work Ex. 4-6 by determining an approximating curve for which equal weight is given to the errors in σ instead of to the errors in $\ln (\sigma/\varepsilon)$ as was done in the example. Use a pocket calculator.

a. Determine the equation of the approximating curve.

b. Compute $(\sigma - \sigma_i)^2$ for both the example problem and for the approximating curve you obtained in part a, and compare the two. The σ_i values are the data ordinates, and the σ values are from the approximating curve using the data abscissas.

$$\text{(partial answer: } \sigma = 5.862(10)^6 \varepsilon e^{-494.77\varepsilon})$$

4-28. Refer to Ex. 4-6 and convert the data given in Fig. 4-14 to the SI system of units.

a. Obtain a least-squares fit for the data above using an approximating function of the form

$$\sigma = k_1 \varepsilon e^{-k_2 \varepsilon}$$

with equal weight given to the errors in $\ln (\sigma/\varepsilon)$ as was done in the example.

b. Take the equation given in Ex. 4-6 and convert it directly to SI units. Compare this equation to the one obtained in part a. If there is a small difference between the equations, how would you explain this difference?

4-29. The stress-strain data obtained from a compression test of a 6 in. × 12 in. concrete cylinder is shown in the accompanying figure and in tabular form as follows:

Stress (σ)	Strain (ε)
1025 psi	$265(10)^{-6}$ in./in.
1400	400
1710	500
2080	700
2425	950
2760	1360
3005	2080 (ultimate)
2850	2450
2675	2940

Using the 5 data points referred to in the figure, obtain a least-squares fit for the function

$$\sigma = k_1 \varepsilon e^{-k_2 \varepsilon}$$

giving equal weight to the errors in $\ln (\sigma/\varepsilon)$. Use a pocket calculator.

(answer: shown on the figure)

Problem 4-29

4-30. Convert the stress-strain data given in Prob. 4-29 to the SI system of units.

a. Obtain a least-squares fit to the data using an approximation function of the form

$$\sigma = k_1 \varepsilon e^{-k_2 \varepsilon}$$

and giving equal weight to the errors in σ. Use a pocket calculator.

b. The answer shown for Prob. 4-29 on the figure was obtained using the same approximation function as used in part a but with equal weight given to the errors in $\ln(\sigma/\varepsilon)$, and in the English gravitational system of units. Convert this equation to the SI system of units.

c. Compute $\sum(\sigma - \sigma_i)^2$ for the equations obtained in parts a and b and compare to determine which gives the better fit. In this summation the σ's are obtained from the equations at the data abscissas and the σ_i's are the data ordinates.

4-31. Determine a least-squares fit of a trigonometric series for the stress-strain data of Ex. 4-6. From the plot of the data shown in Fig. 4-14, select the most suitable series from the following:

$$\sigma = \frac{a_0}{2} + a_1 \cos \frac{\pi \varepsilon}{2000} + a_2 \cos \frac{2\pi \varepsilon}{2000}$$

$$\sigma = b_1 \sin \frac{\pi \varepsilon}{4000} + b_2 \sin \frac{2\pi \varepsilon}{4000} + b_3 \sin \frac{3\pi \varepsilon}{4000}$$

$$\sigma = b_1 \sin \frac{\pi \varepsilon}{4000} + b_3 \sin \frac{3\pi \varepsilon}{4000} + b_5 \sin \frac{5\pi \varepsilon}{4000}$$

In the above terms the strain is in microinches/inch (μ) since the half-range used is 4000μ. The ultimate stress and strain for the given data are 4400 psi and 2000μ, respectively.

a. Determine the constants b_1, b_3, and b_5 for the least-squares fit mentioned above.

b. Plot the resulting series function and the given data on the same graph and observe the fit.

4-32. In Ex. 4-7 the 5 data points shown with asterisks in the table were used to determine a least-squares fit to the growth-time data for a teenage boy using a Fourier series.

a. Determine the coefficients b_1, b_3, and b_5 of the sine series used in Ex. 4-7 using the same 5 data points, but using a weighting factor of 2 for the data points (8.0, 33.0) and (10.0, 35.0).

b. Determine y for the 5 data points using in turn the equation determined in Ex. 4-7 and the equation you found in part a. Are the results obtained with the weighted data in any better agreement with the given data than the series obtained in the example?

4-33. Example 4-5 is concerned with determining a least-squares fit of an exponential approximating function to a portion of the vibration curve shown in Fig. 4-8 defined by the data points (0, 17), (16, 9), and (32, 5). Use a pocket calculator to:

a. Determine a cubic spline fit for the same portion of the vibration curve of Fig. 4-8 by determining the cubic equations for the 2 intervals defined by the 3 given data points.

b. Determine the y values for $x = 8$, $x = 20$, and $x = 26$ from both the curves obtained in part a and from the exponential function determined in Ex. 4-5. Then compare these values with each other, and with the corresponding values read from the vibration curve in Fig. 4-8.

(partial answer: $y = 2.441(10)^{-4}x^3 - 0.5625x + 17$ (for 1st interval))

4-34. Example 4-5 is concerned with determining a least-squares fit of an exponential approximating function to a portion of the vibration curve shown in Fig. 4-8 defined by the data points (0, 17), (16, 9), and (32, 5).

a. Another data point on the vibration curve is (44.5, 3). Add this data point to the 3 above, and determine a cubic spline fit for the portion of the vibration curve defined by the 4 data points by finding the cubic equations for the 3 intervals defined by the 4 data points. Use a pocket calculator.

b. Determine the y values for $x = 8$, $x = 20$, and $x = 26$ from both the curves obtained in part a and from the exponential function found in Ex. 4-5. Then compare these values with each other, and with the corresponding values read from the vibration curve in Fig. 4-8.

4-35. It is desired to obtain a cubic spline fit for the data points

x	y
0.5	1.3
1.0	3.9
2.0	11.0
3.0	29.0
4.0	55.0
4.4	66.0

    a. Write a computer program which, given the x_i and y_i data values, will utilize Eq. 4-98 to obtain the necessary y_i'' values. Utilize a subprogram for solving this tridiagonal set of simultaneous equations, following the flow chart given in Fig. 3-1 (if Prob. 3-15 has been solved, convert this program to a subprogram).

    b. Remembering that the cubic spline obtained goes through the data points, use this to check your program.

    c. Using the cubic spline for interpolation, find values of y for the following x values; 0.25, 0.75, 1.5, 2.5, 3.5, and 4.2.

    d. Obtain y values for enough specified x values so that the fitted curve from $x = 0$ to $x = 4.4$ can be plotted. (It is suggested that increments of x no larger than 0.25 be used.)

*4-36. a. Use the computer program written in Prob. 4-35 to obtain a cubic spline fit to the data points shown in Prob. 4-25. Then determine several y values in the interval $x = 2$ to $x = 3$ and place them on the curve shown with Prob. 4-25.

    b. If computer graphics facilities are available, plot the complete curve from $x = 1.0$ to $x = 10.0$. For plotting purposes, determine y values for increments of x equal to 0.02.

*4-37. Use the computer program written in Prob. 4-35 to obtain a cubic spline fit to the data points given in Prob. 4-16. Determine y values at $x = 1, 1.7, 2.6, 3.75,$ and 4.75 from both the exponential function shown as the answer to Prob. 4-16 and from the cubic spline fit. Compare these values.

*4-38. The accompanying figure shows 5 data points in tabular form and plotted on a graph. Note that the data abscissas are equally separated so that the h's computed will all be equal in the spline-fit procedure.

    a. Write the general form of Eq. 4-98 for a 3 by 3 matrix equation with the h's equal.

---

*NOTE: The program written for part a of Prob. 4-35 is used in the solution of Probs. 4-36, 4-37, 4-38, and 4-39, so it is suggested that Prob. 4-35 be assigned before any of the latter.

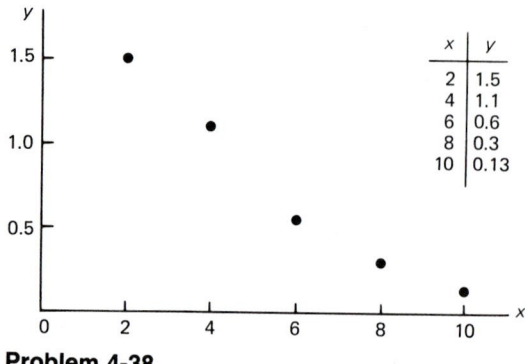

x	y
2	1.5
4	1.1
6	0.6
8	0.3
10	0.13

Problem 4-38

b. Substitute the given data values into the equation written in part a, and solve for the y'' values using a pocket calculator.
c. Determine the cubic equations for the 4 intervals of the spline.
d. From the equations written in part c determine the y values for $x = 3, 5, 7,$ and 9. Compare these values to the data values for the same abscissas given in the figure for Prob. 4-26.
e. Modify the computer program written for Prob. 4-35 to take advantage of the uniform increments for determining y values for any x values over the data range. Determine the y values for the x values given in part d, and as a check on your program also include the given data values.

*4-39. The following data points were selected from the free-damped vibration curve of Fig. 4-8 in Ex. 4-5 as points on the envelope of the curve.

x	y
0	17.0
8	12.5
16	9.0
20	7.5
32	5.0
45	3.0

Use the cubic spline fit program written for Prob. 4-35 with the required changes in DIMENSION and DATA statements to get interpolated y values for $x = 4, 10, 18,$ and 26. Compare the values obtained to corresponding values you read from the actual vibration curve in Fig. 4-8.

Chapter 5
Numerical Integration
and Differentiation

5-1 INTRODUCTION

Engineers are frequently confronted with the problem of integrating functions for which no convenient integrals are available or which cannot be integrated in terms of elementary functions. Numerical methods may be used to obtain good approximations of such integrals.

When the function to be integrated is defined in tabular form with the ordinate values being experimental measurements, an approximating function is generally determined using a curve-fitting technique, and this approximating function is then integrated analytically. However, there are instances in which raw data may plot as a fairly smooth curve with little scatter and with ordinate values obtained at equally spaced abscissa intervals. In these cases, a numerical integration method utilizing the raw data can be applied directly (see Example 5-2).

Engineers also occasionally find numerical differentiation convenient to use, although it should be pointed out that numerical differentiation is inherently much less accurate than numerical integration and is generally avoided whenever possible. However, it has been used successfully in a number of applications, and an example of such application is given later in this chapter (see Example 5-3).

Numerical integration, or numerical *quadrature* as it is often called, consists essentially of finding a close approximation to the area under a curve of a function $f(x)$ which has been determined either from experimental data or from a mathematical expression. In this chapter the direct integration methods presented include only the trapezoid rule and Simpson's rule. Their derivations in this chapter will be by the most direct methods possible. For readers interested in a more general approach to the derivation of integration formulas using interpolating polynomials, and an alternate method of deriving the formulas for the derivatives, Appendix C may be studied preceding or along with the study of Chapter 5. In Appendix C it is shown that the trapezoid and Simpson formulas are special cases of what are known as Newton-Cotes quadrature formulas. The use of Newton-Cotes and other integration formulas of order higher than Simpson's rule is seldom necessary in most engineering applications. For those cases where extremely high accuracy is required, Romberg's extrapolation method presented in this chapter will usually be found satisfactory.

5-2 INTEGRATION BY THE TRAPEZOID RULE

Consider the function $f(x)$, whose graph between $x = a$ and $x = b$ is shown in Fig. 5-1. A close approximation to the area under the curve is obtained by dividing it into n strips Δx in width and approximating the area of each strip by that of a trapezoid, as shown in the figure. Calling the ordinates y_i ($i = 1, 2, \ldots, n + 1$), the areas of the trapezoids are

$$A_1 = \Delta x \left(\frac{y_1 + y_2}{2} \right)$$

$$A_2 = \Delta x \left(\frac{y_2 + y_3}{2} \right)$$

$$\vdots \qquad \vdots$$

$$A_n = \Delta x \left(\frac{y_n + y_{n+1}}{2} \right)$$

(5-1)

The total area lying between $x = a$ and $x = b$ is given by

$$A = \int_a^b f(x)\, dx \cong A_1 + A_2 + A_3 + \cdots + A_n$$

Substituting Eq. 5-1 into this expression yields

$$A = \int_a^b f(x)\, dx \cong \frac{\Delta x}{2} (y_1 + 2y_2 + 2y_3 + \cdots + 2y_n + y_{n+1})$$

(5-2)

Figure 5-1 Approximation, by the trapezoid rule, of the area under a curve

or, letting $\Delta x = h$,

$$A = \frac{h}{2}\left(y_1 + 2\sum_{i=2}^{n} y_i + y_{n+1}\right) \tag{5-3}$$

Equation 5-2 or 5-3 is referred to as the *trapezoid* rule.

A subroutine subprogram utilizing the trapezoid rule for integrating any FORTRAN-supplied function such as sin (x), or any function defined by a function subprogram, is given below. It integrates from a lower limit of XMIN to an upper limit of XMAX, using N strips. The subprogram uses the dummy name DUMMYF for the function being integrated. This is replaced by the actual function name appearing in the argument list of the CALL statement in the calling program. The function name, because it is used as the argument of a subprogram, must appear in an EXTERNAL statement in the calling program.

```
      SUBROUTINE TRAPZ(AREA,DUMMYF,XMIN,XMAX,N)
C THIS SUBPROGRAM CALCULATES AN INTEGRAL BY THE TRAPEZOID
                                                        RULE
      H=(XMAX-XMIN)/N
      SUM=0.
      X=XMIN+H
      DO 4 I=2,N
      SUM=SUM+DUMMYF(X)
    4 X=X+H
      AREA=H/2*(DUMMYF(XMIN)+2.*SUM+DUMMYF(XMAX))
      RETURN
      END
```

Truncation Error Estimation in Integration by the Trapezoid Rule

If the function $f(x)$ can be expressed as a continuous mathematical function having continuous derivatives $f'(x)$ and $f''(x)$, the error resulting from approx-

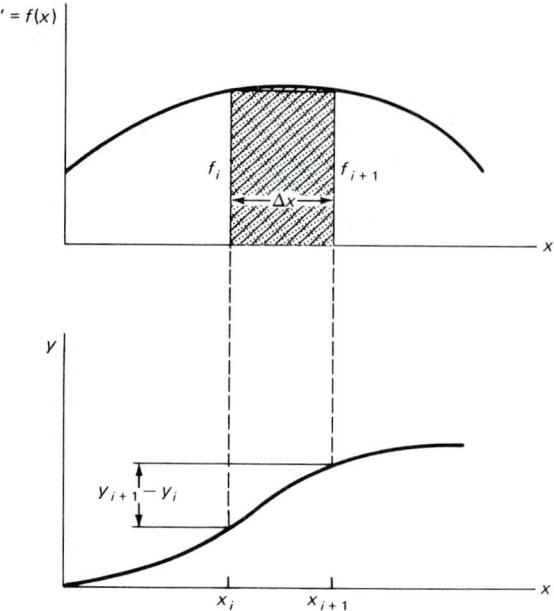

$y' = f(x)$

Figure 5-2 Assumed curves for y' and y

imating the true area in a strip under the curve of $f(x)$ between x_i and x_{i+1} by the area of a trapezoid can be shown to be

$$E_{Ti} = -\tfrac{1}{12}f''(\xi)(\Delta x)^3 \qquad x_i < \xi < x_{i+1}$$

To show this, let us consider a graph of a function $y' = f(x)$ and one of the integral of y', both plotted against the independent variable x as in Fig. 5-2. The area in the crosshatched strip under the y' curve is given by $y_{i+1} - y_i$. We will express this area as that of the shaded trapezoidal area plus a remainder. The remainder represents the per-strip error in the trapezoid rule.

Let us first expand y_{i+1} in a Taylor series about x_i, letting $\Delta x = h$,

$$y_{i+1} = y_i + y_i'h + \frac{y_i''h^2}{2!} + \frac{y_i'''h^3}{3!} + \text{higher order terms} \qquad (5\text{-}4)$$

Then the exact (crosshatched) area in the strip is

$$(y_{i+1} - y_i) = y_i'h + \frac{y_i''h^2}{2!} + \frac{y_i'''h^3}{3!} + \text{higher order terms} \qquad (5\text{-}5)$$

or

$$(y_{i+1} - y_i) = f_ih + \frac{f_i'h^2}{2!} + \frac{f_i''h^3}{3!} + \text{higher order terms} \qquad (5\text{-}6)$$

The Taylor series for f_{i+1} expanded about x_i is

$$f_{i+1} = f_i + f'_i h + \frac{f''_i h^2}{2} + \text{higher order terms}$$

from which we get

$$f'_i h = f_{i+1} - f_i - \frac{f''_i h^2}{2} - \text{higher order terms} \tag{5-7}$$

Substituting Eq. 5-7 into Eq. 5-6 yields

$$(y_{i+1} - y_i) = f_i h + \frac{[f_{i+1} - f_i - (f''_i h^2/2) - \text{higher order terms}]h}{2}$$
$$+ \frac{f''_i h^3}{3!} + \text{higher order terms} \tag{5-8}$$

or

$$\text{exact area} = \underbrace{\left(\frac{f_i + f_{i+1}}{2}\right) h}_{\text{trapezoidal area}} - \frac{1}{12} f''_i h^3 + \text{higher order terms} \tag{5-9}$$

If we define error as what must be added to the computed result to get the exact result, the per-strip truncation error of the trapezoid rule is expressed as

$$E_{Ti} = -\tfrac{1}{12} f''_i h^3 + \text{higher order terms} \tag{5-10}$$

This may be shown to be equivalent to

$$E_{Ti} = -\tfrac{1}{12} f''(\xi) h^3 \qquad x_i < \xi < x_{i+1} \tag{5-11}$$

Although this error cannot be evaluated exactly, a good estimate of its value for each strip can be obtained by assuming that f'' is fairly constant over the strip interval, and evaluating f'' at $\xi = x_i$ or at $\xi = x_{i+1/2}$.

Let us next determine an expression for the error in integrating a function by the trapezoid rule over an interval containing n strips. An error estimation can be made for each strip using Eq. 5-11, giving the total error as

$$E_T = -\tfrac{1}{12}[f''(\xi_1) + f''(\xi_2) + f''(\xi_3) + \cdots + f''(\xi_n)]h^3 \tag{5-12}$$

where ξ_1 is some x value in the first strip, ξ_2 is an x value in the second strip, and so on.

The total truncation error estimate for an integration can be made using Eq. 5-12. However, in many cases the second derivative of the function being integrated turns out to be a cumbersome expression, and this method is undesirable for such cases. A simple alternative approach based on our knowledge of the form of the error is as follows:

We define $f''(\xi)_{av}$ to be the arithmetic mean of the $f''(\xi)$ values. That is,

$$f''(\xi)_{av} = \frac{f''(\xi_1) + f''(\xi_2) + \cdots + f''(\xi_n)}{n} \tag{5-13}$$

or

$$[f''(\xi_1) + f''(\xi_2) + \cdots + f''(\xi_n)] = nf''(\xi)_{av} \tag{5-14}$$

Substituting Eq. 5-14 into Eq. 5-12, we get

$$E_T = -\tfrac{1}{12}(nf''(\xi)_{av})h^3 \tag{5-15}$$

But nh equals the total range of integration. If we are integrating from $x = a$ to $x = b$, then $nh = (b - a)$, and Eq. 5-15 becomes

$$E_T = -\tfrac{1}{12}(b - a)f''(\xi)_{av}h^2 \tag{5-16}$$

We see that $(b - a)$ is a constant and will not vary with the number of strips. The average second derivative, $f''(\xi)_{av}$, will be essentially constant so long as the number of strips does not become too small. Thus we may write that

$$E_T \cong Ch^2 \tag{5-17}$$

where C is some constant and h is any strip width. For $\Delta x = h_1$

$$E_T \cong Ch_1^2 \tag{5-18}$$

For a different strip width, $\Delta x = h_2$,

$$E_T \cong Ch_2^2 \tag{5-19}$$

Thus

$$I \cong I_{h_1} + Ch_1^2 \tag{5-20}$$

and

$$I \cong I_{h_2} + Ch_2^2 \tag{5-21}$$

where I is the exact integral value, I_{h_1} is the integral value obtained with $\Delta x = h_1$, and I_{h_2} is the integral value obtained with $\Delta x = h_2$. Subtracting Eq. 5-21 from Eq. 5-20, and solving for C, we get

$$C \cong \frac{I_{h_1} - I_{h_2}}{h_2^2 - h_1^2} \tag{5-22}$$

Then from Eq. 5-21,

$$I \cong I_{h_2} + \left[\frac{I_{h_1} - I_{h_2}}{h_2^2 - h_1^2} \right] h_2^2$$

or

$$I \cong I_{h_2} + \frac{I_{h_2} - I_{h_1}}{(h_1/h_2)^2 - 1} \tag{5-23}$$

The second term on the right side of Eq. 5-23 is the truncation error estimate for integration with $\Delta x = h_2$. Adding it to I_{h_2} will not give the exact integral value because the expression for C given by Eq. 5-22 is only approximate. However, it does give a much improved value of the integral.

Another error which is introduced in obtaining the approximate area of each strip is *roundoff error*. This arises from performing the required arithmetic operations with numerical values having a limited number of significant digits. Roundoff error can be minimized by the use of double-precision arithmetic.

From the preceding facts it can be seen that the total error over the desired interval of integration is the sum of the truncation and roundoff errors. If the total error were due only to truncation error, it could be made as small as desired by merely reducing the strip width sufficiently. For example, halving the strip width would double the number of per-strip truncation errors summed, but the expression given for the per-strip error reveals that each would be approximately one-eighth its previous size.

However, decreasing the strip width also affects the total error by increasing the total roundoff error due to the larger number of calculations in evaluating Eq. 5-3. Thus in decreasing the strip width to decrease the total error, there is an optimum point at which further decreases in strip width will cause the total error to increase rather than decrease as the roundoff error becomes dominant. The optimum strip width for a particular function is easily determined experimentally on the computer assuming that the true area under the graph of the function can be evaluated but is difficult to predetermine analytically.

5-3 ROMBERG INTEGRATION[1]

Romberg's method of integration is basically Richardson's extrapolation procedure.[2] Romberg's name is attached to the method because, according to Davis and Rabinowitz, he was the first to describe the algorithm in recursive form.[3]

We recall that the error estimate for trapezoidal integration can be expressed as

$$E_T = Ch^2 \tag{5-24}$$

in which h can take on variable values. It can be shown that, with the inclusion of higher order terms, the exact error can be expressed in the form

$$E_T = C_1h^2 + C_2h^4 + C_3h^6 + C_4h^8 + \cdots \tag{5-25}$$

For small h, the first term dominates. Equation 5-25 can also be written as

$$E_T = C_1h^2 + O(h^4) \tag{5-26}$$

where $O(h^4)$ is a quantity of "order h^4." That is, the h^4 term dominates the higher order terms as $h \to 0$. If we obtain an integral value with a particular strip width, and then halve the strip width to get a second integral value, and apply Eq. 5-23, the C_1h^2 term is removed from the error. This leaves an error $O(h^4)$, which might also be expressed as $C_2h^4 + O(h^6)$. If we now determine a third integral value by again halving the strip width, we can combine it with the second to obtain another estimate containing an error expressed by $C_2h^4 + O(h^6)$. From the two values containing errors of $C_2h^4 + O(h^6)$, we can compute (from an equation similar to Eq. 5-23) a new value in which the C_2h^4 term is removed. (A derivation parallel to that for Eq. 5-23, but using Ch^4 instead of Ch^2, gives an equation similar to Eq. 5-23 except that the exponent 2 becomes a 4.)[4] This process can continue, next removing the C_3h^6 term from the error, until the desired accuracy is obtained. An example will be given to

[1]W. Romberg, "Vereinfacte numerische Integration," *Norske Vidensk, Selskab Forhandlinger,* Bd. 28, No. 7 (1955), pp. 30–36.
[2]L. F. Richardson and J. A. Gaunt, "The Deferred Approach to the Limit," *Trans. Royal Soc., London* Vol. 226A (1927), p. 300.
[3]P. J. Davis and P. Rabinowitz, *Numerical Integration* (Waltham, Mass.: Blaisdell Publishing Company, 1967), p. 166.
[4]See the error analysis for Simpson's rule in Sec. 5-4.

clarify the procedure, but let us first convert Eq. 5-23 to a form more commonly used in Romberg integration.

$$I_{\text{improved}} = \frac{I_{h_2}\left[\left(\dfrac{h_1}{h_2}\right)^2 - 1\right] + I_{h_2} - I_{h_1}}{\left(\dfrac{h_1}{h_2}\right)^2 - 1} = \frac{I_{h_2}\left(\dfrac{h_1}{h_2}\right)^2 - I_{h_1}}{\left(\dfrac{h_1}{h_2}\right)^2 - 1} \tag{5-27}$$

If the second integration is obtained by halving the strip width, $h_1/h_2 = 2$, and Eq. 5-27 can be written as

$$I_{\text{improved}} = \frac{(2^2)I_{h_2} - I_{h_1}}{2^2 - 1} \tag{5-28}$$

or

$$I_{\text{improved}} = \frac{(2^2)(I_{\text{more accurate}}) - I_{\text{less accurate}}}{2^2 - 1} \tag{5-29}$$

Equation 5-29 is used for what is called first-order extrapolation. For second-order extrapolation, the equation becomes

$$I_{\text{improved}} = \frac{(2^4)(I_{\text{more accurate}}) - I_{\text{less accurate}}}{2^4 - 1} \tag{5-30}$$

A slight change in form is useful in writing a computer program for Romberg integration. It is

$$I_{\text{improved}} = \frac{(4^n)(I_{\text{more accurate}}) - I_{\text{less accurate}}}{4^n - 1} \tag{5-31}$$

where n is the order of the extrapolation and takes on values 1, 2, ...
A flow chart for Romberg integration is shown after the example which follows. The example should be studied prior to a study of the flow chart.

EXAMPLE 5-1

Using a pocket calculator, let us determine

$$\int_0^{\pi/2} \sin x \, dx$$

by Romberg integration. We will use up to third-order extrapolation, or until the value from the latest extrapolation completed differs from the most accurate value of the previous extrapolation by less than an epsilon value of 0.000001.

We begin by calculating trapezoid-rule results for a single strip, and for two strips, and form the following table:

Number of strips	1	2
Integral values from trapezoid rule	0.7853981634	0.948059449
First-order extrapolation value	1.002279878	

The extrapolated value shown is calculated from

$$\frac{4(0.948059449) - 0.7853981634}{4 - 1} = 1.002279878$$

Comparing 1.002279878 with 0.948059449, we find a difference whose absolute value exceeds the prescribed epsilon. Therefore, we find the integral value for four strips, and expand our table to the following:

Number of strips	1	2	4
Integral values	0.7853981634	0.948059449	0.987115801
First-order extrapolation values	1.002279878	1.000134585	
Second-order extrapolation value	0.9999915655		

The second-order extrapolation value is found from

$$\frac{4^2(1.000134585) - 1.002279878}{4^2 - 1} = 0.9999915655$$

The value 0.9999915655 differs from 1.000134585 by more than epsilon, so one more extrapolation is taken. This will be the last extrapolation regardless of the accuracy check. An integration value by the trapezoid rule with eight strips is calculated and the table expanded to

Number of strips	1	2	4	8
Integral values	0.7853981634	0.948059449	0.987115801	0.9967851719
First-order extrapolation values	1.002279878	1.000134585	1.000008296	
Second-order extrapolation values	0.9999915655	0.9999998771		
Third-order extrapolation value	1.000000009			

The third-order extrapolation value is obtained from

$$\frac{4^3(0.9999998771) - 0.9999915655}{4^3 - 1} = 1.000000009$$

This value is taken as our final answer. We note that it is an excellent result for using a maximum of only eight strips in our trapezoid integration.

In the computer, the table shown might be stored as a two-dimensional array in the form

R_{11} R_{12} R_{13} R_{14}

R_{21} R_{22} R_{23}

R_{31} R_{32}

R_{41}

in which R_{41} is the final answer.

Flow Chart for Romberg Integration

The flow chart shown in Fig. 5-3 calls for the use of the subroutine subprogram TRAPZ from Sec. 5-2 for integration by the trapezoid rule. Integration begins with N strips, and this is doubled a maximum of six times. Because of a limitation in the subprogram TRAPZ, N should not be less than two. Thus, the program may employ up to sixth-order extrapolation, unless the accuracy requirement is met sooner. The function to be integrated is defined in a function subprogram named F. Integration is from a minimum value of the independent variable A to a maximum value of B. The integral values and extrapolation values are stored in a two-dimensional array R(I,J). This flow chart does not outline the most efficient program, since the same ordinate values are calculated several times. It will be left as an exercise for the reader to write a FORTRAN program implementing the given flow chart. It is also left as an exercise to write a more efficient program by using a subprogram which calculates ordinate values instead of integral values, so that previously calculated ordinate values will not be recalculated. (See Probs. 5-21 and 5-22.)

5-4 INTEGRATION BY SIMPSON'S RULE

The trapezoid rule approximates the area under a curve by summing the areas of uniform-width trapezoids formed by connecting successive points on the curve by straight lines. Simpson's rule gives a more accurate approximation since it consists of connecting successive groups of three points on the curve by second-degree parabolas, and summing the areas under the parabolas to obtain the approximate area under the curve. For example, the area contained in the two strips under the curve of $f(x)$, in Fig. 5-4, is approximated by the crosshatched area under a parabola passing through the three points (x_i, y_i), (x_{i+1}, y_{i+1}), and (x_{i+2}, y_{i+2}).

Figure 5-3 Flow chart for Romberg integration

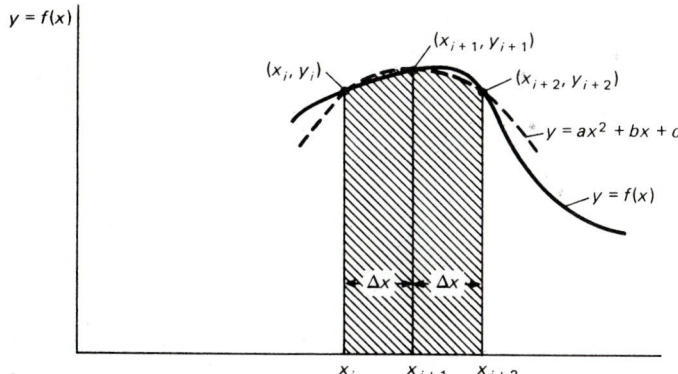

Figure 5-4 Approximation of area under a curve by use of a second-degree parabola

For convenience in deriving an expression for this area, let us assume that the two strips comprising the area under the parabola lie on opposite sides of the origin, as shown in Fig. 5-5. Such an arrangement will not compromise the generality of the derivation. The general form of the equation of the second-degree parabola connecting the three points is

$$y = ax^2 + bx + c \qquad (5\text{-}32)$$

The integration of Eq. 5-32 from $-\Delta x$ to Δx gives the area contained in the two strips shown under the parabola. Hence

$$A_{2\text{ strips}} = \int_{-\Delta x}^{\Delta x} (ax^2 + bx + c)\, dx = \left[\frac{ax^3}{3} + \frac{bx^2}{2} + cx \right]_{-\Delta x}^{\Delta x} \qquad (5\text{-}33)$$

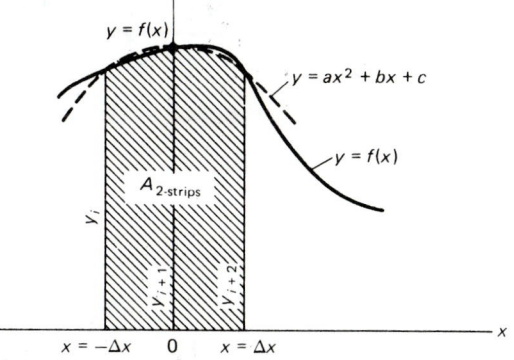

Figure 5-5 Area in two strips under a curve centered on y axis

Substituting the limits into Eq. 5-33 yields

$$A_{2 \text{ strips}} = \tfrac{2}{3}a(\Delta x)^3 + 2c(\Delta x) \tag{5-34}$$

The constants a and c can be determined from the fact that points $(-\Delta x, y_i)$, $(0, y_{i+1})$, and $(\Delta x, y_{i+2})$ must all satisfy Eq. 5-32. The substitution of these three sets of coordinates into Eq. 5-32 yields

$$y_i = a(-\Delta x)^2 + b(-\Delta x) + c$$

$$y_{i+1} = c \tag{5-35}$$

$$y_{i+2} = a(\Delta x)^2 + b(\Delta x) + c$$

Solving these equations simultaneously for the constants a, b, and c, we find that

$$a = \frac{y_i - 2y_{i+1} + y_{i+2}}{2(\Delta x)^2}$$

$$b = \frac{y_{i+2} - y_i}{2(\Delta x)} \tag{5-36}$$

$$c = y_{i+1}$$

The substitution of the first and third parts of Eq. 5-36 into Eq. 5-34 yields

$$A_{2 \text{ strips}} = \frac{\Delta x}{3}(y_i + 4y_{i+1} + y_{i+2}) \tag{5-37}$$

which gives the area in terms of the three ordinates y_i, y_{i+1}, and y_{i+2} and the width Δx of a single strip. This constitutes Simpson's rule for obtaining the approximate area contained in two equal-width strips under a curve.

If the area under a curve between two values of x is divided into n uniform strips (n even), as shown in Fig. 5-6, the application of Eq. 5-37 shows that

$$A_1 = \frac{\Delta x}{3}(y_1 + 4y_2 + y_3)$$

$$A_2 = \frac{\Delta x}{3}(y_3 + 4y_4 + y_5)$$

$$A_3 = \frac{\Delta x}{3}(y_5 + 4y_6 + y_7) \tag{5-38}$$

$$\vdots \qquad \vdots \qquad \qquad \vdots$$

$$A_{n/2} = \frac{\Delta x}{3}(y_{n-1} + 4y_n + y_{n+1})$$

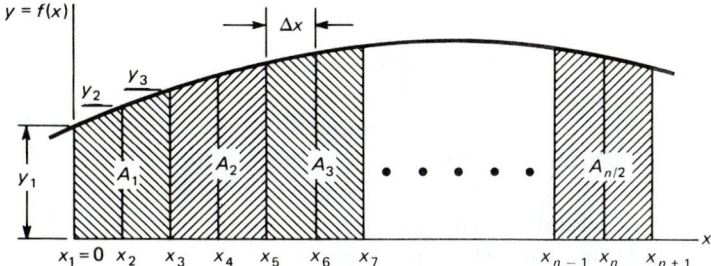

Figure 5-6 Area under curve divided into an even number of strips for approximation by Simpson's rule

Summing these areas, we can write

$$\int_{x_1=0}^{x_{n+1}} f(x) \, dx = \sum_{i=1}^{i=n/2} A_i = \frac{\Delta x}{3} \, (y_1 + 4y_2 + 2y_3 + 4y_4 + 2y_5$$

$$+ \cdots + 2y_{n-1} + 4y_n + y_{n+1})$$

or

$$\int_{x_1=0}^{x_{n+1}} f(x) \, dx = \frac{\Delta x}{3} \left(y_1 + 4 \sum_{i=2,4,6}^{i=n} y_i + 2 \sum_{i=3,5,7}^{i=n-1} y_i + y_{n+1} \right) \tag{5-39}$$

where n is even.

Equation 5-39 is called Simpson's one-third rule for obtaining the approximate area under a curve. It may be used when the area is divided into an *even* number of strips of width Δx.

A subroutine subprogram utilizing Simpson's rule for integrating any FORTRAN-supplied function such as SIN(X), or any function defined by a function subprogram, is given below. The integration is from XMIN to XMAX, using N strips. The dummy function name DUMMYF is used, and it is replaced by the actual function name when the subprogram SIMPSN is called. The function name must appear in an EXTERNAL statement in the calling program.

```
      SUBROUTINE SIMPSN (AREA, DUMMYF, XMIN, XMAX, N)
C THIS SUBPROGRAM INTEGRATES A FUNCTION BY SIMPSON'S RULE
C DUMMYF IS A DUMMY NAME FOR THE FUNCTION INTEGRATED
      H=(XMAX-XMIN)/N
      SUM=0.0
      X=XMIN+H
      DO 4 I=2,N
      IF(MOD(I,2))2,2,3
    2 SUM=SUM+4.*DUMMYF(X)
      GO TO 4
    3 SUM=SUM+2.*DUMMYF(X)
    4 X=X+H
      AREA=H/3.*(DUMMYF(XMIN)+SUM+DUMMYF(XMAX))
      RETURN
      END
```

EXAMPLE 5-2

Let us consider a U.S. Army M-14 rifle having a 0.6096 m barrel, a 7.62 mm bore, and 101.6 μm deep rifling grooves. The lead bullet used weighs 0.0956 N. The gas-pressure curve varies with the temperature of the barrel, but for practical purposes of illustration, we will use the gas-pressure data for a particular firing condition as shown in Fig. 5-7. The frictional resistance exerted on the bullet is to be considered small as compared with the propulsive force of the gas on the bullet, and the cross-sectional area of the rifling grooves is considered negligible. Our problem will be to determine the muzzle velocity of the bullet using Simpson's one-third rule.

The solution is begun by considering that the work done on the bullet while it is in the barrel is given by

$$\text{work} = \int_0^{x_\text{final}} F(x)\, dx \tag{5-40}$$

where $F(x)$ is the force of the gas acting on the bullet as a function of the displacement x. The work is thus represented by the area under the pressure-displacement curve of Fig. 5-7, multiplied by the cross-sectional area of the bore $[4.561(10)^{-5}\ \text{m}^2]$. The work done on the bullet by the gas must equal the change in kinetic energy (K.E.) of the bullet, since we are neglecting any energy loss due to frictional resistance. Therefore,

$$\int_0^{x_\text{final}} F(x)\, dx = \Delta(\text{K.E.}) = \tfrac{1}{2} m\dot{x}_\text{final}^2 - \tfrac{1}{2} m\dot{x}_\text{initial}^2 \tag{5-41}$$

Since the initial kinetic energy is zero, we may write from Eq. 5-41

$$\dot{x}_\text{final} = \sqrt{\frac{2}{m} \int_0^{x_\text{final}} F(x)\, dx} = \sqrt{\frac{2[4.56(10)^{-5}]}{0.0956/9.81} \int_0^{x_\text{final}} P(x)\, dx}$$

where $P(x)$ is the gas pressure in terms of the displacement, as given in Fig. 5-7, and

$$\int_0^{x_\text{final}} P(x)\, dx \tag{5-42}$$

is the area under the pressure-displacement curve, which we will obtain by dividing the area under the curve of Fig. 5-7 into 48 equal strips and summing

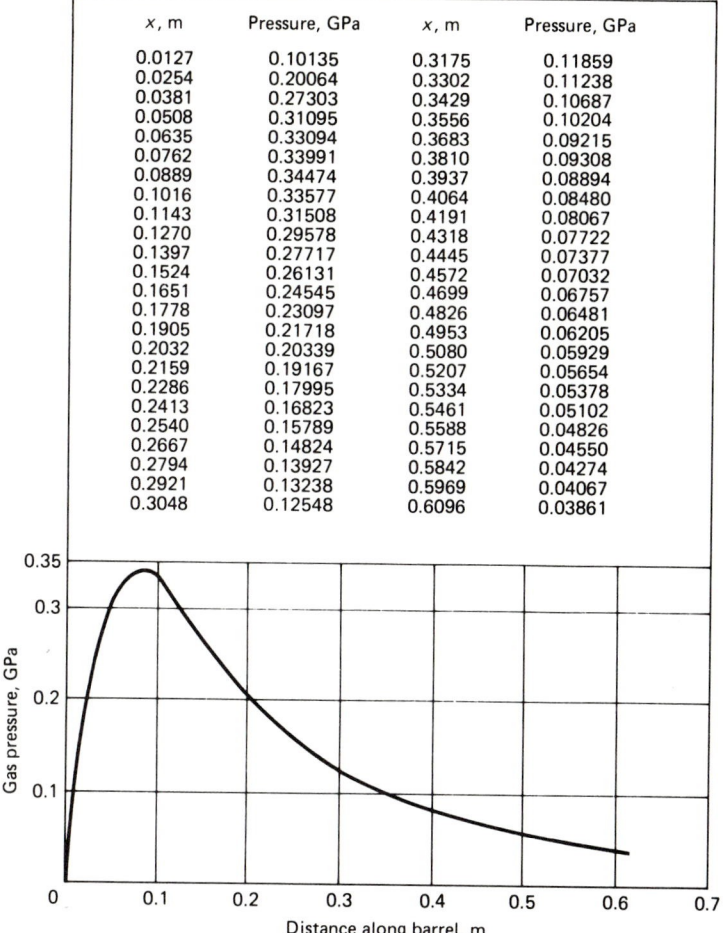

x, m	Pressure, GPa	x, m	Pressure, GPa
0.0127	0.10135	0.3175	0.11859
0.0254	0.20064	0.3302	0.11238
0.0381	0.27303	0.3429	0.10687
0.0508	0.31095	0.3556	0.10204
0.0635	0.33094	0.3683	0.09215
0.0762	0.33991	0.3810	0.09308
0.0889	0.34474	0.3937	0.08894
0.1016	0.33577	0.4064	0.08480
0.1143	0.31508	0.4191	0.08067
0.1270	0.29578	0.4318	0.07722
0.1397	0.27717	0.4445	0.07377
0.1524	0.26131	0.4572	0.07032
0.1651	0.24545	0.4699	0.06757
0.1778	0.23097	0.4826	0.06481
0.1905	0.21718	0.4953	0.06205
0.2032	0.20339	0.5080	0.05929
0.2159	0.19167	0.5207	0.05654
0.2286	0.17995	0.5334	0.05378
0.2413	0.16823	0.5461	0.05102
0.2540	0.15789	0.5588	0.04826
0.2667	0.14824	0.5715	0.04550
0.2794	0.13927	0.5842	0.04274
0.2921	0.13238	0.5969	0.04067
0.3048	0.12548	0.6096	0.03861

Figure 5-7 Gas-pressure-bullet-displacement data for the M-14 rifle for a particular firing condition

the area contained in the 24 pairs of strips by the use of Eq. 5-39. This curve has been plotted from experimental data, and we do not have a mathematical equation for it. Therefore, the subroutine subprogram previously given for integration by Simpson's rule cannot be utilized. An equation could be obtained by the curve-fitting techniques discussed in Chap. 4, but since the data shown have little scatter, an integration program will be written which utilizes the raw data.

A flow chart for the computer solution is shown in Fig. 5-8. The FORTRAN names selected to represent the variable quantities follow the flow chart.

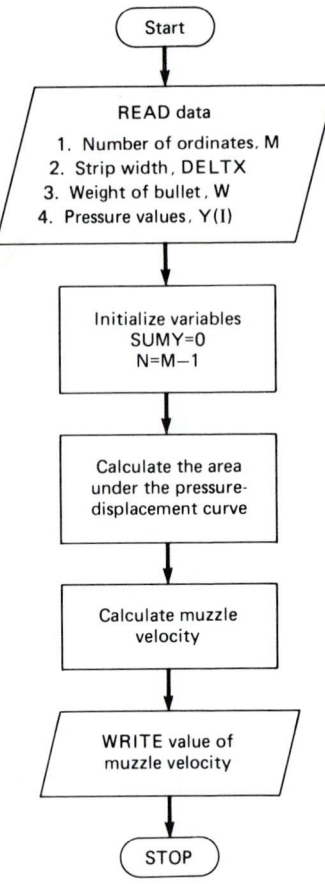

Figure 5-8 Flow chart for determining muzzle velocity of a rifle bullet, Ex. 5-2

FORTRAN Name	Quantity
N	Number of strips
M	Number of ordinates
DELTX	Width of each strip, m
W	Weight of bullet
Y(I)	Values of pressure readings, GPa
SUMY	Sum of ordinates
AREA	Area under pressure curve
XDSQ	Square of muzzle velocity
XD	Muzzle velocity, m/s
SUMEV	Sum of the even ordinates, $\displaystyle\sum_{i=2,4,6}^{i=n} y_i$
SUMOD	Sum of the odd ordinates, $\displaystyle\sum_{i=3,5,7}^{i=n-1} y_i$
K	Number of strips less 1, $(n - 1)$

The FORTRAN IV program is as follows:

```
C PROGRAM TO DETERMINE THE MUZZLE VELOCITY OF A GUN USING
                                       SIMPSON INTEGRATION
C ORDINATE VALUES OF PRESSURE CURVE GIVEN BY TABULATED DATA
        DIMENSION Y(49)
C READ IN NUMBER OF ORDINATES, STRIP WIDTH, AND WEIGHT
                                              OF BULLET
        READ (5,1) M,DELTX,W
      1 FORMAT (I2,2F10.0)
C READ IN ORDINATES OF PRESSURE-DISPLACEMENT CURVE
        READ (5,2) (Y(I),I=1,M)
      2 FORMAT(8F10.0)
        SUMEV=0.
        SUMOD=0.
        N=M-1
        K=N-1
C DETERMINE SUM OF EVEN SUBSCRIPTED ORDINATES FROM 2 TO N
        DO 4 I=2,N,2
      4 SUMEV=SUMEV+Y(I)
C DETERMINE SUM OF ODD SUBSCRIPTED ORDINATES FROM 3 TO N-1
        DO 5 I=3,K,2
      5 SUMOD=SUMOD+Y(I)
C CALCULATE THE AREA UNDER THE PRESSURE-DISPLACEMENT CURVE
        AREA=DELTX/3.*(Y(1)+4.*SUMEV+2.*SUMOD+Y(M))*1.E 09
C CALCULATE MUZZLE VELOCITY
        XDSQ=2.*0.0000456*9.81/W*AREA
        XD=SQRT(XDSQ)
C WRITE OUT THE MUZZLE VELOCITY
        WRITE(6,6)XD
      6 FORMAT('1','MUZZLE VELOCITY=',F7.2,' METERS PER
                                              SECOND')
        STOP
        END
```

The execution of the preceding program yielded this computer printout:

```
MUZZLE VELOCITY= 928.01 METERS PER SECOND
```

Truncation Error Estimation in Integration by Simpson's Rule

If the function $f(x)$ can be expressed as a continuous mathematical function having continuous derivatives, $f'(x)$ through $f^{IV}(x)$, the error resulting from approximating the true area in two strips under the graph of $f(x)$ between x_{i-1} and x_{i+1} by the area under a second-degree parabola can be shown to be

$$E_{T_i} = -\tfrac{1}{90}f^{IV}(\xi)h^5 \qquad x_{i-1} < \xi < x_{i+1} \tag{5-43}$$

where $h = \Delta x$. To show this, let us consider the graphs of $y' = f(x)$ and the integrated function y, plotted versus the independent variable x, as shown in

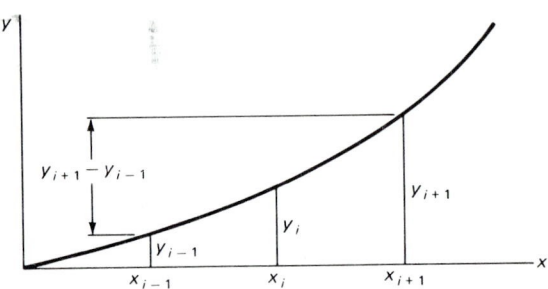

Figure 5-9 Area under a curve represented as the difference in ordinate values of the integrated function

Fig. 5-9. The crosshatched area in the two strips under the y' curve is equal to $y_{i+1} - y_{i-1}$.

Expanding y_{i+1} in a Taylor series about x_i, we obtain

$$y_{i+1} = y_i + y_i'h + \frac{y_i''h^2}{2} + \frac{y_i'''h^3}{6} + \frac{y_i^{IV}h^4}{24} + \frac{y_i^{V}h^5}{120} + \text{higher order terms}$$

(5-44)

Expanding y_{i-1} about x_i, we obtain

$$y_{i-1} = y_i - y_i'h + \frac{y_i''h^2}{2} - \frac{y_i'''h^3}{6} + \frac{y_i^{IV}h^4}{24} - \frac{y_i^{V}h^5}{120} + \text{higher order terms}$$

(5-45)

Subtracting Eq. 5-45 from Eq. 5-44, we have

$$y_{i+1} - y_{i-1} = 2y_i'h + \frac{y_i'''h^3}{3} + \frac{y_i^{V}h^5}{60} + \text{higher order terms}$$

or

$$\text{exact area} = 2f_i h + \frac{f_i'' h^3}{3} + \frac{f_i^{IV} h^5}{60} + \text{higher order terms} \qquad (5\text{-}46)$$

Now, let us expand f_{i+1} and f_{i-1} in a Taylor series about x_i.

$$f_{i+1} = f_i + f_i' h + \frac{f_i'' h^2}{2} + \frac{f_i''' h^3}{6} + \frac{f_i^{IV} h^4}{24} + \text{higher order terms} \qquad (5\text{-}47)$$

$$f_{i-1} = f_i - f_i' h + \frac{f_i'' h^2}{2} - \frac{f_i''' h^3}{6} + \frac{f_i^{IV} h^4}{24} + \text{higher order terms} \qquad (5\text{-}48)$$

Adding Eqs. 5-47 and 5-48, we obtain

$$f_{i+1} + f_{i-1} = 2f_i + f_i'' h^2 + \tfrac{1}{12} f_i^{IV} h^4 + \text{higher order terms}$$

or

$$f_i'' h^2 = f_{i+1} + f_{i-1} - 2f_i - \tfrac{1}{12} f_i^{IV} h^4 + \text{higher order terms} \qquad (5\text{-}49)$$

Substituting Eq. 5-49 into Eq. 5-46 as part of the term $f_i'' h^3/3$ gives

$$\text{exact area} = \underbrace{\frac{h}{3}[f_{i+1} + 4f_i + f_{i-1}]}_{\substack{\text{area by} \\ \text{Simpson's rule}}} - \underbrace{\frac{1}{90} f_i^{IV} h^5 + \text{higher order terms}}_{\text{truncation error}} \qquad (5\text{-}50)$$

The truncation error of Simpson's rule (the error in each two strips) is

$$E_{T_i} = -\tfrac{1}{90} f_i^{IV} h^5 + \text{higher order terms} \qquad (5\text{-}51)$$

which may be shown to be equivalent to

$$E_{T_i} = -\tfrac{1}{90} f^{IV}(\xi) h^5 \qquad x_{i-1} < \xi < x_{i+1} \qquad (5\text{-}52)$$

This *truncation error* is the quantity which must be added to the approximate area in two strips, obtained by Simpson's one-third rule, to get the true area under the curve in this interval. The truncation-error term shown cannot usually be evaluated directly. However, a good estimate of its value for each two-strip interval can be obtained by assuming that f^{IV} is fairly constant over the interval (the higher derivatives are assumed to be negligible) and evaluating f^{IV} at $\xi = x_i$. The truncation-error estimate for the total integration is obtained by summing the two-strip estimates. If the total truncation-error estimate is larger than can be tolerated, smaller two-strip intervals should be used. Considering roundoff error, which is also present, there is an optimum strip width for obtaining a minimum total error in the integration. (See the error analysis of the trapezoid method, preceding.)

In evaluating the error in the total integration by summing up the error in each two strips,

$$E_T = -\tfrac{1}{90}[f^{IV}(\xi_1) + f^{IV}(\xi_2) + \cdots + f^{IV}(\xi_{n/2})]h^5 \tag{5-53}$$

we must be able to differentiate the function being integrated four times. In many cases this leads to an excessively long expression. To avoid having to differentiate the function being integrated, let us develop a method for estimating the error, or improving the result, based on integrating twice with different strip widths, as was done for the trapezoid rule.

Equation 5-53 contains an f^{IV} evaluation for each pair of strips, or $n/2$ of them for n strips. Defining f^{IV}_{av} as the arithmetic mean of these, we have

$$f^{IV}_{av} = \frac{f^{IV}(\xi_1) + f^{IV}(\xi_2) + \cdots + f^{IV}(\xi_{n/2})}{n/2} \tag{5-54}$$

Then,

$$E_T = -\frac{1}{90}\frac{n}{2} f^{IV}_{av}h^5 \tag{5-55}$$

But $nh = (b - a)$, the interval of integration, so

$$E_T = -\tfrac{1}{180}(b - a)f^{IV}_{av}h^4 \tag{5-56}$$

Since the average fourth derivative will not vary greatly with different numbers of strips, if the number of strips is not too small, we can express the error as

$$E_T \cong Ch^4 \tag{5-57}$$

where C is a constant. For strip widths $\Delta x = h_1$ and $\Delta x = h_2$, we have

$$I \cong I_{h_1} + Ch_1^4$$
$$I \cong I_{h_2} + Ch_2^4$$

(see p. 373 for definition of I, I_{h_1}, and I_{h_2})

Subtracting gives

$$0 \cong I_{h_1} - I_{h_2} + C(h_1^4 - h_2^4)$$

or

$$C \cong \frac{I_{h_2} - I_{h_1}}{h_1^4 - h_2^4} \tag{5-58}$$

Then

$$I_{\text{improved}} = I_{h_2} + \left[\frac{I_{h_2} - I_{h_1}}{h_1^4 - h_2^4} \right] h_2^4 \tag{5-59}$$

$$= I_{h_2} + \frac{I_{h_2} - I_{h_1}}{(h_1/h_2)^4 - 1}$$

If we first run with a strip width of h_1 and then halve the interval so that $h_1/h_2 = 2$, Eq. 5-59 becomes

$$I_{\text{improved}} = I_{\text{more accurate}} + \frac{I_{\text{more accurate}} - I_{\text{less accurate}}}{15} \tag{5-60}$$

where the second term on the right is the error estimate for the more accurate integration. If we only want an improved result without separating out the truncation-error estimate, Eq. 5-60 can be put in the form

$$I_{\text{improved}} = \frac{16 I_{\text{more accurate}} - I_{\text{less accurate}}}{15} \tag{5-61}$$

Simpson's Three-Eighths Rule

In utilizing Simpson's rule for integrating a function, it might be desirable to use an odd number of strips to approximate the true area under the curve. If an odd number of strips is used, Simpson's three-eighths rule for obtaining the area contained in 3 strips under a curve can be used, in conjunction with Eq. 5-39, to find the total area. For example, if 97 strips were used, Simpson's three-eighths rule could be used to approximate the area under the curve occupied by the first 3 strips. The remaining 94 strips would then be summed, using Simpson's one-third rule. The derivation of the three-eighths rule is similar to that for the one-third rule, except that it determines the area under a *third*-degree parabola connecting four points on the given curve. The general form of the third-degree parabola is

$$y = ax^3 + bx^2 + cx + d \tag{5-62}$$

In the derivation, the constants are determined by requiring that the parabola

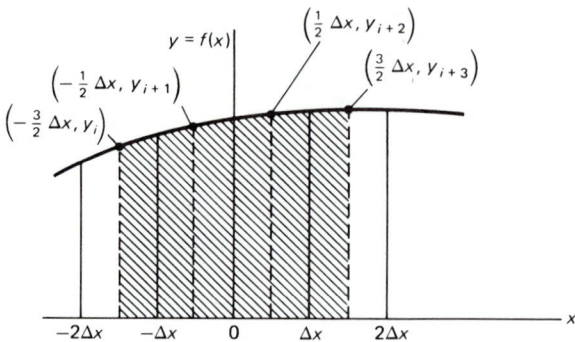

Figure 5-10 Area of three strips under a curve centered on y axis

pass through the four points indicated on the curve shown in Fig. 5-10. The range of integration is from $-3(\Delta x)/2$ to $3(\Delta x)/2$, resulting in

$$
\begin{aligned}
A_{3 \text{ strips}} &= \int_{-3(\Delta x)/2}^{3(\Delta x)/2} (ax^3 + bx^2 + cx + d)\, dx \\
&= \frac{3(\Delta x)}{8}(y_i + 3y_{i+1} + 3y_{i+2} + y_{i+3})
\end{aligned}
\tag{5-63}
$$

which is Simpson's three-eighths rule.

5-5 IMPROPER INTEGRALS

In our discussion of integration thus far, we have assumed that $f(x)$ in the integral

$$
\int_a^b f(x)\, dx
$$

is continuous for all values of x from a to b, including the end points. We have also assumed a and b to be finite. If either of the above assumptions is not true, then the integral given above is said to be an *improper integral*. Occasionally improper integrals are encountered in engineering computations, and their evaluation requires special consideration. We will discuss two different cases separately, the first in which the limits are finite but $f(x)$ is not continuous, and the second in which we have an infinite limit of integration.

Case I: Discontinuous Integrand

Problem 5-2 at the end of the chapter illustrates an example of a discontinuous integrand. One-quarter of the arc length of the lemniscate can be determined from

$$S = a \int_0^{\pi/4} \frac{d\theta}{\sqrt{\cos 2\theta}} \tag{5-64}$$

The integrand becomes infinite, however, at $\theta = \pi/4$. To solve the problem, we first break the integral into two parts

$$S = a \int_0^{\theta_1} \frac{d\theta}{\sqrt{\cos 2\theta}} + a \int_{\theta_1}^{\pi/4} \frac{d\theta}{\sqrt{\cos 2\theta}} \tag{5-65}$$

in which $(\pi/4 - \theta_1)$ is a small value. The first integral can be handled by a numerical method, and we would hope that it might be possible to obtain an estimate of the second integral. To accomplish this in this instance, let us expand the integrand in a power series about the θ value giving us difficulty, $\theta = \pi/4$. We will then attempt to integrate the series term by term and truncate the resulting series to obtain our estimate.

The Taylor series expansion for $\cos 2\theta$ about $\theta = \pi/4$ is

$$\cos 2\theta = 2\left(\frac{\pi}{4} - \theta\right) - \frac{4}{3}\left(\frac{\pi}{4} - \theta\right)^3 + \text{higher power terms}[5]$$

or

$$\cos 2\theta = 2\left(\frac{\pi}{4} - \theta\right)\left[1 - \frac{2}{3}\left(\frac{\pi}{4} - \theta\right)^2 + \text{higher power terms}\right] \tag{5-66}$$

Then,

$$\sqrt{\cos 2\theta} = \sqrt{2}\left(\frac{\pi}{4} - \theta\right)^{1/2}\left[1 - \frac{2}{3}\left(\frac{\pi}{4} - \theta\right)^2 + \text{higher power terms}\right]^{1/2} \tag{5-67}$$

From the rules governing multiplication of infinite power series, we can easily verify that

$$\left[1 - \frac{2}{3}\left(\frac{\pi}{4} - \theta\right)^2 + \text{higher power terms}\right]^{1/2}$$
$$= \left[1 - \frac{1}{3}\left(\frac{\pi}{4} - \theta\right)^2 + \text{higher power terms}\right]$$

[5]Terms containing higher powers of $(\pi/4 - \theta)$.

Thus,

$$\sqrt{\cos 2\theta} = \sqrt{2}\left(\frac{\pi}{4} - \theta\right)^{1/2}\left[1 - \frac{1}{3}\left(\frac{\pi}{4} - \theta\right)^2 + \text{ higher power terms}\right]$$

(5-68)

Our integrand, $1/\sqrt{\cos 2\theta}$, becomes

$$\frac{1}{\sqrt{\cos 2\theta}} = \frac{1}{\sqrt{2}}\left(\frac{\pi}{4} - \theta\right)^{-1/2}\left[1 - \frac{1}{3}\left(\frac{\pi}{4} - \theta\right)^2 + \text{ higher power terms}\right]^{-1}$$

From the rules for division of infinite power series, we can verify that

$$\left[1 - \frac{1}{3}\left(\frac{\pi}{4} - \theta\right)^2 + \text{ higher power terms}\right]^{-1}$$

$$= \left[1 + \frac{1}{3}\left(\frac{\pi}{4} - \theta\right)^2 + \text{ higher power terms}\right]$$

Thus,

$$a\int_{\theta_1}^{\pi/4} \frac{d\theta}{\sqrt{\cos 2\theta}} = \frac{a}{\sqrt{2}}\int_{\theta_1}^{\pi/4}\left[\left(\frac{\pi}{4} - \theta\right)^{-1/2} + \frac{1}{3}\left(\frac{\pi}{4} - \theta\right)^{3/2}\right.$$

$$\left. + \text{ higher power terms}\right] d\theta$$

$$= \frac{a}{\sqrt{2}}\left[-2\left(\frac{\pi}{4} - \theta\right)^{1/2} - \left(\frac{2}{5}\right)\left(\frac{1}{3}\right)\left(\frac{\pi}{4} - \theta\right)^{5/2}\right.$$

$$\left. + \text{ higher power terms}\right]_{\theta_1}^{\pi/4}$$

$$= \sqrt{2}a\left(\frac{\pi}{4} - \theta_1\right)^{1/2} + \frac{\sqrt{2}}{5}a\left(\frac{1}{3}\right)\left(\frac{\pi}{4} - \theta_1\right)^{5/2}$$

$$+ \text{ higher power terms}$$

Since the quantity $(\pi/4 - \theta_1)$ is small, we can neglect all but the first term of the series for our estimate of

$$a\int_{\theta_1}^{\pi/4} \frac{d\theta}{\sqrt{\cos 2\theta}}$$

If we take θ_1 as 44.5 deg (0.77667 radian), the estimated value of this integral is 0.13211a.

Another approach to this problem would be to approximate the length of the lemniscate omitted in integrating from 0 to 44.5 deg instead of to 45 deg, with the chord ρ at 44.5 deg. This gives us

$$\rho = a \sqrt{\cos 2\theta} = 0.13211a$$

as before.

Still another approach that could be used on this problem would be to note that as θ_1 gets closer and closer to 45 deg, the omitted length becomes very small. Thus, for a satisfactory solution to this problem, we could truncate the interval, integrating from 0 to, say, 44.9 deg by a numerical method. In general, truncating the interval is an unsafe practice, but in this instance we can see even without an estimate that we are omitting very little of the correct length.

If the singularity occurs in the interior of the integration interval, rather than at an end point, the interval must be broken into two parts and each handled as a problem where the discontinuity occurs at an end point of the interval.

Davis and Rabinowitz discuss other techniques for handling improper integrals of this type, such as a change of variable, subtracting out the discontinuity, ignoring the discontinuity, and the use of integration by parts.[6]

Case II: Infinite Limit of Integration

This type of problem can often be handled by a change of variable to make the infinite limit become a zero limit for the new variable. For example, if we have the integral

$$\int_1^\infty \frac{dx}{1 + x^2 + x^3}$$

we can make the upper limit zero by the substitution $x = t^n$ where $n \leq -1$. Taking $n = -1$, we have $dx = -t^{-2}\, dt$, and the integral becomes

$$-\int_1^0 \frac{dt}{t^2[1 + (1/t^2) + (1/t^3)]} = \int_0^1 \frac{t\, dt}{t^3 + t + 1}$$

which is a proper integral. If the transformation leads to case I, which was discussed earlier, in which an improper integral is obtained, the problem can then be approached by the methods discussed there.

[6]P. J. Davis and P. Rabinowitz, *Numerical Integration* (Waltham, Mass.: Blaisdell Publishing Co., 1967), pp. 71–80.

5-6 NUMERICAL DIFFERENTIATION

We will now direct our attention to ways of numerically differentiating functions which are defined only by tabulated data or by experimentally determined curves. Tabulated experimental data are generally not used directly in numerical differentiation because the scatter would cause serious accuracy problems. Whenever possible, an analytical expression for a smooth curve which fits the data should be determined (using techniques given in Chap. 4 on curve fitting). Analytical differentiation can then be used, or numerical differentiation with ordinate values obtained from the fitted curve. We will be interested here only in numerical differentiation. The method we shall discuss utilizes Taylor-series expansions. The Taylor series for a function $y = f(x)$ at $(x_i + h)$ expanded about x_i is

$$y(x_i + h) = y_i + y_i'h + \frac{y_i''h^2}{2!} + \frac{y_i'''h^3}{3!} + \cdots \tag{5-69}$$

where $h = \Delta x$ and y_i is the ordinate corresponding to x_i and $(x_i + h)$ is in the region of convergence. The function at $(x_i - h)$ is similarly given by

$$y(x_i - h) = y_i - y_i'h + \frac{y_i''h^2}{2!} - \frac{y_i'''h^3}{3!} + \cdots \tag{5-70}$$

Subtracting Eq. 5-70 from Eq. 5-69, we obtain

$$y_i' = \frac{y(x_i + h) - y(x_i - h)}{2h} - \left(\frac{1}{6} y_i'''h^2 + \cdots\right) \tag{5-71}$$

Looking at Fig. 5-11, we see that if we designate equally spaced points to the right of x_i as x_{i+1}, x_{i+2}, and so on, and those to the left of x_i as x_{i-1}, x_{i-2}, and identify the corresponding ordinates as y_{i+1}, y_{i+2}, y_{i-1}, and y_{i-2}, respectively, Eq. 5-71 can be written in the form

$$y_i' = \frac{y_{i+1} - y_{i-1}}{2h} \tag{5-72}$$

with error of order h^2. Equation 5-72 is called the *central-difference* approximation of y' at x_i, with errors of order h^2. Graphically, the approximation represents the slope of the dashed line in Fig. 5-11. The actual derivative is represented by the slope of the solid line drawn tangent to the curve at x_i.

If we add Eqs. 5-69 and 5-70 and use the notation previously described, we may write the following expression for the second derivative:

$$y_i'' = \frac{y_{i+1} - 2y_i + y_{i-1}}{h^2} - \left(\frac{1}{12} y_i^{IV}h^2 + \cdots\right) \tag{5-73}$$

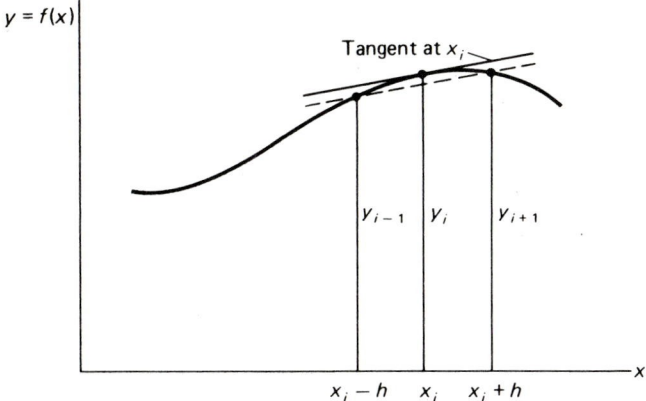

Figure 5-11 Approximation of the derivative at x_i

The approximate expression using only the first term to the right of the equal sign is the *central-difference* approximation of the second derivative of the function at x_i, with error of order h^2. As with the first derivative, approximations with error of higher order can also be derived. The approximate expression may be interpreted graphically as the slope of the line tangent to the curve at $x_{i+1/2}$ minus the slope of the line tangent to the curve at $x_{i-1/2}$ divided by h, where the slopes of the tangent lines are approximated by the expressions,

$$y'_{i+1/2} = \frac{y_{i+1} - y_i}{h}$$

$$y'_{i-1/2} = \frac{y_i - y_{i-1}}{h}$$

That is,

$$y''_i = \frac{\dfrac{y_{i+1} - y_i}{h} - \dfrac{y_i - y_{i-1}}{h}}{h} = \frac{y_{i+1} - 2y_i + y_{i-1}}{h^2}$$

To obtain an expression for the third derivative, we use *four* terms on the right side of each of Eqs. 5-69 and 5-70. Subtracting Eq. 5-70 from Eq. 5-69 yields

$$y_{i+1} - y_{i-1} = 2y'_i h + \frac{2y'''_i h^3}{3!} \qquad (5\text{-}74)$$

If we expand the Taylor series about x_i to obtain expressions for $y = f(x)$ at $(x_i + 2h)$ and $(x_i - 2h)$, respectively, we obtain

$$y(x_i + 2h) = y_i + y_i'(2h) + \frac{y_i''(2h)^2}{2!} + \frac{y_i'''(2h)^3}{3!} + \cdots \qquad (5\text{-}75)$$

$$y(x_i - 2h) = y_i - y_i'(2h) + \frac{y_i''(2h)^2}{2!} - \frac{y_i'''(2h)^3}{3!} + \cdots \qquad (5\text{-}76)$$

Subtracting Eq. 5-76 from Eq. 5-75, and using just the four terms of each expansion shown, gives

$$y_{i+2} - y_{i-2} = 4y_i'h + \tfrac{8}{3}y_i'''h^3 \qquad (5\text{-}77)$$

The simultaneous solution of Eqs. 5-74 and 5-77 for the third derivative yields

$$y_i''' = \frac{y_{i+2} - 2y_{i+1} + 2y_{i-1} - y_{i-2}}{2h^3} \qquad (5\text{-}78)$$

Equation 5-78 gives the first central-difference expression for the third derivative of y at x_i. By retaining two additional terms in the Taylor series expansions, we find that the error in this approximate expression is of order h^2.

Successively higher derivatives can be obtained by this method, but, since they require the solution of increasingly larger numbers of simultaneous equations, the process becomes quite tedious. The same technique may also be used to find more accurate expressions for the derivatives by using additional terms in the Taylor-series expansion. However, the derivations of these more accurate expressions, particularly for derivatives higher than the second, become very laborious because of the numbers of simultaneous equations which must be solved. Derivations of the more accurate expressions are not given here, but such expressions for several derivatives are included in the summary which follows this discussion. Derivations for the higher derivatives are accomplished with much greater facility and far less labor by using *difference*, *averaging*, and *derivative* operators. Such a method is outside the scope of this text, but it can be found in various books concerned with numerical analysis.[7]

[7]M. G. Salvadori and M. L. Baron, *Numerical Methods in Engineering* (Englewood Cliffs, N.J.: Prentice-Hall, Inc., 1961).

It has been shown that the central-difference expressions for the various derivatives involve values of the function on both sides of the x value at which the derivative of the function is desired. By utilizing the appropriate Taylor-series expansions, one can easily obtain expressions for the derivatives which are entirely in terms of values of the function at x_i and points to the right of x_i. These are known as *forward-finite-difference* expressions. In a similar manner, derivative expressions which are entirely in terms of values of the function at x_i and points to the *left* of x_i can be found. These are known as *backward-finite-difference* expressions. In numerical differentiation, forward-difference expressions are used when data to the left of a point at which a derivative is desired are not available, and backward-difference expressions are used when data to the right of the desired point are not available. Central-difference expressions, however, are more accurate than either forward- or backward-difference expressions. This can be seen by noting the order of the error in the summary of the differentiation formulas which follows.

Central-Difference Expressions with Error of Order h^2

$$y_i' = \frac{y_{i+1} - y_{i-1}}{2h}$$

$$y_i'' = \frac{y_{i+1} - 2y_i + y_{i-1}}{h^2}$$

$$y_i''' = \frac{y_{i+2} - 2y_{i+1} + 2y_{i-1} - y_{i-2}}{2h^3}$$

$$y_i'''' = \frac{y_{i+2} - 4y_{i+1} + 6y_i - 4y_{i-1} + y_{i-2}}{h^4}$$

(5-79)

Central-Difference Expressions with Error of Order h^4

$$y_i' = \frac{-y_{i+2} + 8y_{i+1} - 8y_{i-1} + y_{i-2}}{12h}$$

$$y_i'' = \frac{-y_{i+2} + 16y_{i+1} - 30y_i + 16y_{i-1} - y_{i-2}}{12h^2}$$

$$y_i''' = \frac{-y_{i+3} + 8y_{i+2} - 13y_{i+1} + 13y_{i-1} - 8y_{i-2} + y_{i-3}}{8h^3}$$

$$y_i'''' = \frac{-y_{i+3} + 12y_{i+2} - 39y_{i+1} + 56y_i - 39y_{i-1} + 12y_{i-2} - y_{i-3}}{6h^4}$$

(5-80)

Forward-Difference Expressions with Error of Order *h*

$$y_i' = \frac{y_{i+1} - y_i}{h}$$

$$y_i'' = \frac{y_{i+2} - 2y_{i+1} + y_i}{h^2}$$

$$y_i''' = \frac{y_{i+3} - 3y_{i+2} + 3y_{i+1} - y_i}{h^3}$$

$$y_i'''' = \frac{y_{i+4} - 4y_{i+3} + 6y_{i+2} - 4y_{i+1} + y_i}{h^4}$$

(5-81)

Forward-Difference Expressions with Error of Order *h²*

$$y_i' = \frac{-y_{i+2} + 4y_{i+1} - 3y_i}{2h}$$

$$y_i'' = \frac{-y_{i+3} + 4y_{i+2} - 5y_{i+1} + 2y_i}{h^2}$$

$$y_i''' = \frac{-3y_{i+4} + 14y_{i+3} - 24y_{i+2} + 18y_{i+1} - 5y_i}{2h^3}$$

$$y_i'''' = \frac{-2y_{i+5} + 11y_{i+4} - 24y_{i+3} + 26y_{i+2} - 14y_{i+1} + 3y_i}{h^4}$$

(5-82)

Backward-Difference Expressions with Error of Order *h*

$$y_i' = \frac{y_i - y_{i-1}}{h}$$

$$y_i'' = \frac{y_i - 2y_{i-1} + y_{i-2}}{h^2}$$

$$y_i''' = \frac{y_i - 3y_{i-1} + 3y_{i-2} - y_{i-3}}{h^3}$$

$$y_i'''' = \frac{y_i - 4y_{i-1} + 6y_{i-2} - 4y_{i-3} + y_{i-4}}{h^4}$$

(5-83)

Backward-Difference Expressions with Error of Order h^2

$$y_i' = \frac{3y_i - 4y_{i-1} + y_{i-2}}{2h}$$

$$y_i'' = \frac{2y_i - 5y_{i-1} + 4y_{i-2} - y_{i-3}}{h^2}$$

(5-84)

$$y_i''' = \frac{5y_i - 18y_{i-1} + 24y_{i-2} - 14y_{i-3} + 3y_{i-4}}{2h^3}$$

$$y_i'''' = \frac{3y_i - 14y_{i-1} + 26y_{i-2} - 24y_{i-3} + 11y_{i-4} - 2y_{i-5}}{h^4}$$

EXAMPLE 5-3

In Ex. 2-4 the Newton-Raphson method was used to determine the output lever angles of a crank-and-lever four-bar linkage system for each 5 deg of rotation of the input crank. Now we will determine the angular velocity and the angular acceleration of the output lever of the same type of mechanism for each 5 deg of rotation of the input crank, with the latter rotating at a uniform angular velocity of 100 rad/s.

We can determine the output lever positions ϕ, corresponding to each 5 deg of crank rotation θ, by utilizing Freudenstein's equation and the Newton-Raphson method, as was done in Ex. 2-4. Such a set of values, in effect, gives us a series of points on the ϕ versus θ curve, and the ϕ values are stored in memory to provide data for the differentiation processes which follow. The slope of the ϕ-θ curve may be related to the angular velocity of the output lever $d\phi/dt$ if we realize that, with the crank rotating at a constant ω, its angular position is given by

$$\theta = \omega t$$

so that

$$\frac{d\phi}{d\theta} = \frac{1}{\omega}\frac{d\phi}{dt}$$

The angular acceleration of the output lever $d^2\phi/dt^2$ may be related to this curve by realizing that since

$$\frac{d\phi}{d\theta} = \frac{1}{\omega}\frac{d\phi}{dt}$$

it follows that

$$\frac{d^2\phi}{d\theta^2} = \frac{1}{\omega}\left(\frac{d^2\phi}{d\theta\,dt}\right)$$

But, since $d\theta = \omega\,dt$,

$$\frac{d^2\phi}{d\theta^2} = \frac{1}{\omega^2}\left(\frac{d^2\phi}{dt^2}\right)$$

Thus, in performing the numerical differentiation indicated by Eqs. 5-72 and 5-73, using the ϕ values stored in memory (where θ is the independent variable), we multiply these expressions by ω and ω^2, respectively, to obtain the desired angular-velocity and acceleration values. A flow chart is shown in Fig. 5-12.

In the program which follows, the input crank angles and corresponding lever angles will be stored in memory in terms of degrees and will be printed out along with the angular-velocity and acceleration values. Subscripted variables are used for preserving these values in memory. The variable names used in the FORTRAN program are as follows:

FORTRAN Name	Quantity	Given Value
A	Length of crank a, in.	1
B	Length of crank b, in.	2
C	Length of crank c, in.	2
D	Length of crank d, in.	2
EPSI	Accuracy-check value ε, radians	0.00001
M	Number of positions of crank for which lever angle is determined	73
DELTH	Increment of crank angle $\Delta\theta$, deg	5
DELX	Increment of crank angle $\Delta\theta$, radians	
PHEST	Estimated value of ϕ corresponding to θ_{min}, deg	41
TH	Crank angle θ, deg	$\theta_0 = 0$
THMX	Maximum value of crank angle θ, deg	360
X	Crank angle θ, radians	
XMAX	Maximum value of crank angle θ, radians	
R1	d/c	
Y1	Improved value of output angle ϕ, for a given crank angle θ, radians	
OMEGA	Angular velocity of crank ω, rad/s	100
I	Subscript	
N	Subscript	
K	Number of crank positions less 1	
PHE(I)	Output-lever-angle values stored in memory, deg	

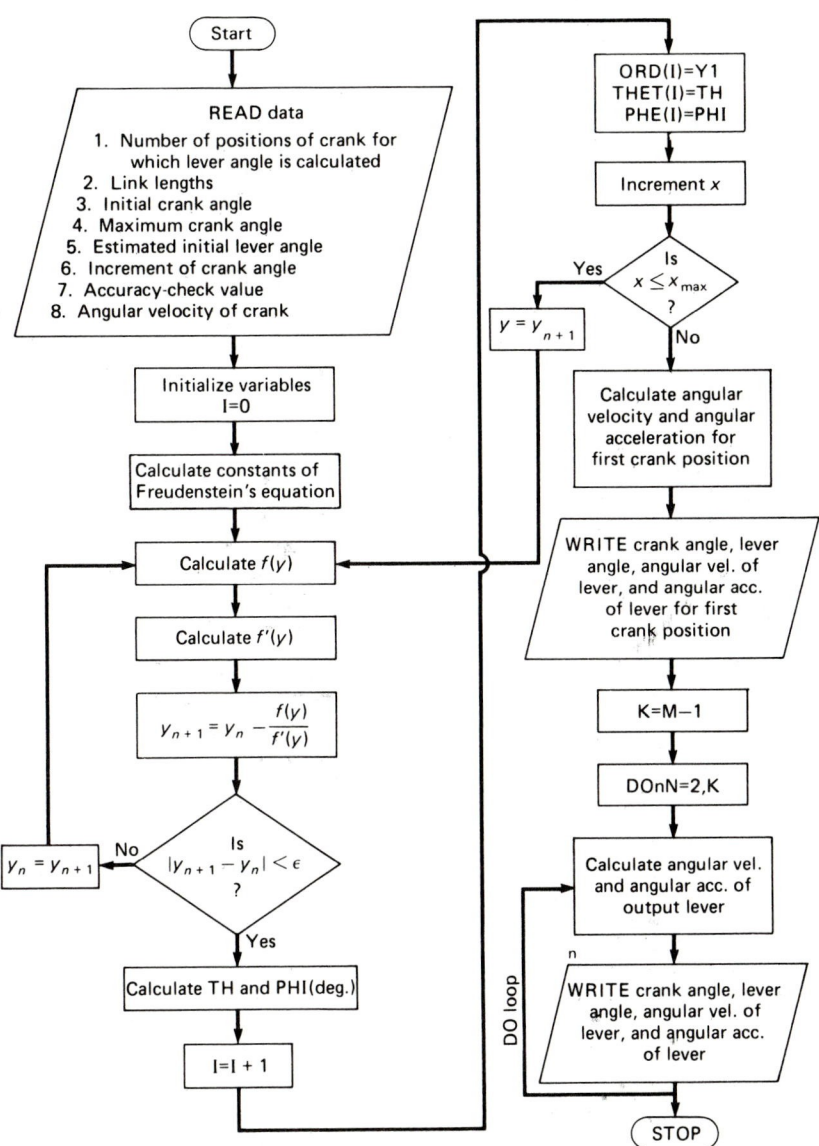

Figure 5-12 Flow chart for Ex. 5-3

FORTRAN Name	Quantity	Given Value
ORD(I)	Output-lever-angle values stored in memory, radians	
THET(I)	Crank-angle values stored in memory, deg	
ANG V	Angular velocity of output lever, rad/s	
ANG A	Angular acceleration of output lever, rad/s^2	

The FORTRAN program is as follows:

```
C THIS PROGRAM DETERMINES ANGULAR POSITION, VELOCITY, AND
                                                   ACCELERATION
C OF THE ROCKER LINK OF A CRANK AND ROCKER MECHANISM
C THE NEWTON-RAPHSON METHOD IS USED WITH FREUDENSTEINS
                                                       EQUATION
C TO DETERMINE THE ANGULAR POSITION OF THE ROCKER LINK
C ANGULAR VELOCITY AND ACCELERATION ARE DETERMINED BY
                                        NUMERICAL DIFFERENTIATION
      DIMENSION ORD(73),THET(73),PHE(73)
      WRITE(6,1)
    1 FORMAT('1','CRANK AND ROCKER KINEMATIC ANALYSIS'/)
      READ(5,2)M
    2 FORMAT(I3)
      READ(5,3)A,B,C,D,TH,THMAX,PHEST,DELTH,EPSI,OMEGA
    3 FORMAT(8F10.0)
      WRITE(6,4)A,B,C,D
    4 FORMAT(' ','A = ',F6.3,1X,'B = ',F6.3,1X,'C = ',F6.3,1X,
                                                'D = ',F6.3/)
      WRITE(6,5)OMEGA
    5 FORMAT(' ','ANG VEL OF CRANK = ',F5.0,' RAD PER SEC'//)
      WRITE(6,6)
    6 FORMAT(' ',3X,'THETA',4X,'PHI',4X,'ANG V',4X,'ANG
                                                       A'//)
      DELX=DELTH*.01745329
      XMAX=THMAX*.01745329
      I=0
      R1=D/C
      R2=D/A
      R3=(D*D+A*A-B*B+C*C)/(2.*C*A)
      X=TH*.01745329
      Y=PHEST*.01745329
    7 FOFY=R1*COS(X)-R2*COS(Y)+R3-COS(X-Y)
      DFOFY=R2*SIN(Y)-SIN(X-Y)
      Y1=Y-FOFY/DFOFY
      IF(ABS(Y1-Y)-EPSI)9,9,8
    8 Y=Y1
      GO TO 7
    9 TH=X/.01745329
      PHI=Y1/.01745329
      I=I+1
      ORD(I)=Y1
      THET(I)=TH
      PHE(I)=PHI
      X=X+DELX
      IF(X-XMAX)10,10,11
   10 Y=Y1
      GO TO 7
   11 ANG V=(ORD(2)-ORD(M-1))/(2.*DELX)*OMEGA
      ANG A=(ORD(2)-2.*ORD(1)+ORD(M-1))/(DELX*DELX)*OMEGA**2
      WRITE(6,12) THET(1),PHE(1),ANG V,ANG A
```

```
12 FORMAT(' ',3X,F5.1,3X,F5.2,2X,F6.1,2X,F7.0)
   K=M=1
   DO 13 N=2,K
   ANG V=(ORD(N+1)-ORD(N-1))/(2.*DELX)*OMEGA
   ANG A=(ORD(N+1)-2.*ORD(N)+ORD(N-1))/(DELX*DELX)
                                            *OMEGA**2
13 WRITE(6,12) THET(N),PHE(N),ANG V,ANG A
   STOP
   END
```

The computer printout of the results of the calculation is as follows:

CRANK AND ROCKER KINEMATIC ANALYSIS A= 1.000 B= 2.000
C= 2.000 D= 2.000 ANG VEL OF CRANK = 100. RAD PER SEC

THETA	PHI	ANG V	ANG A	THETA	PHI	ANG V	ANG A
0.0	41.41	33.3	2506.	100.0	87.09	42.8	-2882.
5.0	43.13	35.5	2442.	105.0	89.17	40.0	-3530.
10.0	44.96	37.6	2343.	110.0	91.09	36.6	-4280.
15.0	46.89	39.6	2220.	115.0	92.83	32.5	-5148.
20.0	48.92	41.4	2078.	120.0	94.34	27.6	-6156.
25.0	51.03	43.2	1913.	125.0	95.59	21.7	-7323.
30.0	52.23	44.8	1731.	130.0	96.51	14.7	-8662.
35.0	55.51	46.2	1530.	135.0	97.06	6.5	-10174.
40.0	57.85	47.4	1319.	140.0	97.16	-3.1	-11822.
45.0	60.25	48.5	1087.	145.0	96.75	-14.2	-13529.
50.0	62.70	49.3	847.	150.0	95.75	-26.7	-15126.
55.0	65.19	50.0	589.	155.0	94.08	-40.4	-16346.
60.0	67.70	50.4	319.	160.0	91.71	-54.9	-16803.
65.0	70.22	50.5	28.	165.0	88.60	-69.2	-16069.
70.0	72.75	50.4	-278.	170.0	84.79	-82.2	-13807.
75.0	75.26	50.0	-611.	175.0	80.37	-92.6	-10017.
80.0	77.75	49.3	-974.	180.0	75.52	-99.2	-5142.
85.0	80.19	48.3	-1373.	185.0	70.45	-101.5	-21.
90.0	82.58	46.9	-1817.	190.0	65.37	-99.6	4469.
95.0	84.88	45.1	-2314.	195.0	60.49	-94.2	7738.

THETA	PHI	ANG V	ANG A	THETA	PHI	ANG V	ANG A
200.0	55.95	-86.6	9638.	280.0	29.00	-2.1	2677.
205.0	51.83	-77.9	10353.	285.0	28.96	0.2	2576.
210.0	48.16	-68.9	10239.	290.0	29.02	2.4	2506.
215.0	44.93	-60.3	9618.	295.0	29.20	4.6	2465.
220.0	42.13	-52.3	8764.	300.0	29.48	6.7	2442.
225.0	39.71	-45.0	7835.	305.0	29.87	8.9	2440.
230.0	37.63	-38.6	6942.	310.0	30.37	11.0	2451.
235.0	35.85	-32.9	6128.	315.0	30.98	13.2	2476.
240.0	34.34	-27.8	5412.	320.0	31.69	15.3	2505.
245.0	33.07	-23.4	4802.	325.0	32.51	17.5	2538.
250.0	32.00	-19.4	4288.	330.0	33.44	19.8	2569.
255.0	31.13	-15.9	3857.	335.0	34.48	22.0	2596.
260.0	30.42	-12.6	3509.	340.0	35.64	24.3	2613.
265.0	29.86	-9.7	3220.	345.0	36.91	26.6	2616.
270.0	29.45	-7.0	2994.	350.0	38.30	28.8	2604.
275.0	29.16	-4.5	2813.	355.0	39.80	31.1	2572.

These results were compared with results obtained by a purely analytical method and found to compare very well. At the peak angular acceleration, the results obtained by numerical differentiation varied from the analytical result by approximately 0.6 percent.

PROBLEMS

5-1. Consider integration by the trapezoidal rule of the functions shown in (a) and (b) of the accompanying illustration. By inspection of a typical strip, determine whether the truncation error E_{T_i} per strip is positive or negative for each function. Is your answer obtained by inspection consistent with a consideration of Eq. 5-11?

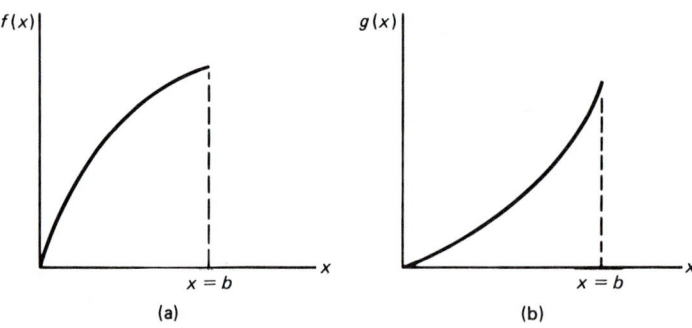

(a)   (b)

Problem 5-1

5-2. Use a pocket calculator to determine the approximate area under the curve $f(x) = \sin x$ between $x = 0$ and $x = \pi/2$ by the trapezoid rule for $h = 30$ deg, and $h = 15$ deg. Compare your results with the exact integral. Also determine from your results an improved value for the approximate area by using Eq. 5-23.

5-3. **a.** Use a pocket calculator to determine the approximate area under the curve $y = 1 + x^2$ between $x = 0$ and $x = 4$ by the trapezoid rule with $h = 1$. Compare your answer with that obtained from an integration by calculus.

  b. Determine the approximate area by Romberg's method for a second order extrapolation (4 strips) and compare the result with that obtained in part a.

  (answer: 26.0 by trapezoid, 25.333 by Romberg)

5-4. **a.** Use a pocket calculator to determine the approximate area under the curve $y = 2 - x^2$ between $x = 0$ and $x = 4$ by the trapezoid rule with $h = 1$. Compare your answer with that obtained by calculus.

b. Determine the approximate area by Romberg's method for a second order extrapolation (4 strips) and compare the result with that obtained in part a.

5-5. Use a pocket calculator to determine the approximate area under the curve $y = 10 - x^3$ between $x = 0$ and $x = 4$ by Simpson's rule with 4 strips $(n = 4)$. Compare your answer with that obtained by calculus and explain why the result from Simpson's rule is exact in this case.

5-6. The arc length BP of an ellipse is given by

$$BP = a \int_0^\phi \sqrt{1 - \left(\frac{a^2 - b^2}{a^2}\right) \sin^2 \phi} \, d\phi$$

where a and b are, respectively, the semimajor and semiminor axes of the ellipse, and ϕ is the angle shown in the accompanying figure. It has been proved that the preceding integral cannot be evaluated in finite form in terms of elementary functions of ϕ.

Write a general FORTRAN program for determining, by the trapezoid rule, the arc length of an ellipse corresponding to any desired angle ϕ. Then use the program, with appropriate data input, to determine the circumference of an ellipse whose equation is given by $4x^2 + 9y^2 = 36$.

(partial answer: arc length $= 15.86531$ with $\phi = 90°$)

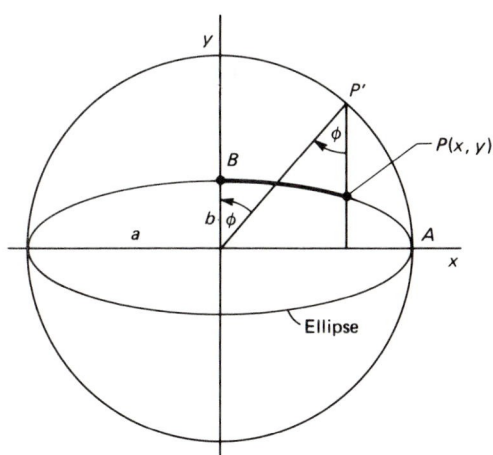

Problem 5-6

5-7. The equation of the lemniscate shown in the accompanying figure is

$$\rho^2 = a^2 \cos 2\theta$$

An element of arc length ds is equal to $\sqrt{(d\rho)^2 + (\rho\,d\theta)^2}$ from which

$$ds = \frac{a\,d\theta}{\sqrt{\cos 2\theta}}$$

and

$$s = \int_0^\theta \frac{a\,d\theta}{\sqrt{\cos 2\theta}}$$

Write a FORTRAN program for determining the total arc length of the lemniscate by use of the trapezoid rule. (See Sec. 5-5 for a discussion of this problem.)

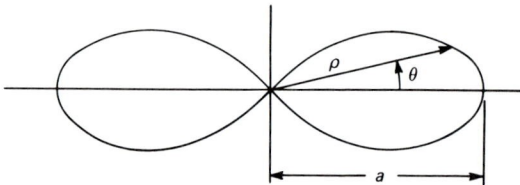

Problem 5-7

5-8. A particle P of mass m is attracted toward a fixed point C by a force that varies inversely as the distance between them. It is desired to determine the time required for the particle to reach point C when starting from rest at a distance r from C.

Applying Newton's second law to the particle, we obtain the following equation of motion:

$$\frac{d^2x}{dt^2} = -\frac{k}{mx}$$

Problem 5-8

The initial conditions are

$$t = 0 \begin{vmatrix} \dfrac{dx}{dt} = 0 \\[2mm] x = r \end{vmatrix}$$

Letting $v = dx/dt$, it can be seen that

$$\frac{dv}{dt} = \frac{d^2x}{dt^2} = \left(\frac{dv}{dx}\right)\left(\frac{dx}{dt}\right) = v\frac{dv}{dx}$$

Substituting the latter expression into the equation of motion yields

$$v\,dv = -\frac{k}{mx}\,dx$$

Integrating this equation, we obtain

$$\frac{v^2}{2} = -\frac{k}{m}\ln x + C$$

Application of the given initial conditions shows that

$$C = \frac{k}{m}\ln r$$

Substituting this expression for the constant of integration and the relation $v^2 = (dx/dt)^2$ into the equation resulting from the integration, we find that

$$t = -\frac{1}{\sqrt{2k/m}}\int_r^0 \frac{dx}{\sqrt{\ln (r/x)}}$$

Write a FORTRAN program for evaluating the integral by the trapezoid rule.

5-9. The system of the accompanying illustration is released from rest in the position shown. Each of the cylinders A and B weighs 32.2 lb, and C weighs 16.1 lb. The cord attached to C winds around cylinder B as cylinder B rotates about its pivot axis O. A rod of negligible weight is attached to cylinders A and B.

    a. Noting that the centroidal mass moment of inertia for each cylinder is $\bar{I}_A = \bar{I}_B = 0.125$ lb-ft-sec^2, show that the equation of motion of the system is

$$\frac{d\dot\theta}{dt} = \frac{64.4\cos\theta - 8.05}{4.375}$$

where θ is the angular displacement of the light rod and cylinders.

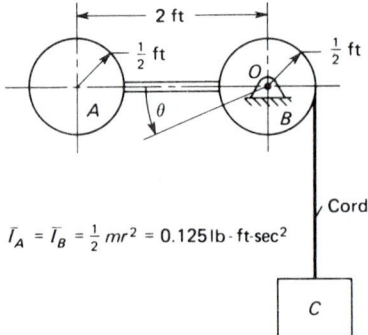

$$\bar{I}_A = \bar{I}_B = \frac{1}{2}mr^2 = 0.125\,\text{lb-ft-sec}^2$$

Problem 5-9

b. From the equation of motion, formulate the integral which may be used to find the time t for the system to rotate through the angle θ.

c. Using the integral of part b, write a FORTRAN program for obtaining the t versus θ values for one-half of a cycle of motion. Use either the trapezoid rule or Simpson's rule.

(partial answer: $t = 0.8044662$ sec with $\theta = 151°$)

5-10. Work Prob. 5-9 where the 2-ft distance is to be taken as 0.5 m, and the diameter of cylinders A and B is 0.15 m. The weights and mass moments of inertia are

$$W_A = W_B = 100 \text{ N}$$

$$W_C = 50 \text{ N}$$

$$\bar{I}_A = \bar{I}_B = 0.15 \text{ kg-m}^2$$

5-11. An Alnico magnet A exerts a force on a steel block of weight W that is inversely proportional to the square of the distance between the mass centers of the magnet and the block. If the coefficient of friction between the block and the fixed surface is f, the equation of motion of the block is found to be

$$\frac{d\dot{x}}{dt} = -\frac{kg}{Wx^2} + fg$$

where k is a constant, and g is the acceleration of gravity.

a. Considering that the block is released from rest with an initial displacement of x_0, show that the expression for the velocity is

$$\dot{x} = \sqrt{\frac{2kg}{W}\left(\frac{1}{x} - \frac{1}{x_0}\right) + 2fg(x - x_0)}$$

b. Formulate the integral for calculating the time t for different values of x.

c. Write a FORTRAN program for obtaining the t versus x values. Use either the trapezoid rule or Simpson's rule. For a computer solution, take $f = 0.2$, $k = 1000$ lb-in.^{2}, $g = 386$ in./sec^2, $W = 10$ lb, and $x_0 = 12$ in.

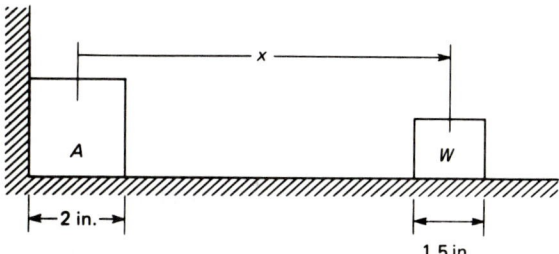

Problem 5-11

5-12. Referring to Prob. 5-11, write a FORTRAN program for obtaining the t versus x values for coefficient-of-friction values of 0.1, 0.2, 0.3, 0.4, and 0.5. Use Simpson's rule.

5-13. Work Prob. 5-11 by converting the system data of the problem to the SI system of units.

5-14. A particle of mass m is released from rest at the edge of a hemispherical bowl such as the one shown in the accompanying figure. The particle then slides down the inside surface of the bowl which is assumed frictionless. It is desired to find the time required for the particle to reach the bottom of the bowl.

Applying Newton's second law in the tangential direction, write the differential equation of motion of the mass with θ as the dependent variable. Using Prob. 5-8 as a reference, determine the integral which may be evaluated to find the required time for the mass to slide to the bottom of the bowl.

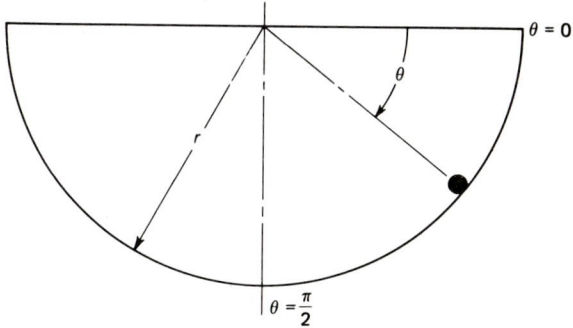

Problem 5-14

Write a FORTRAN program for evaluating the integral determined. Use the trapezoid rule.

5-15. Write a FORTRAN program for determining the arc length of an ellipse, corresponding to any angle ϕ, by the use of Simpson's rule. Refer to Prob. 5-6 and its accompanying figure for the necessary problem information.

5-16. Write a FORTRAN program for determining the total arc length of a lemniscate by the use of Simpson's rule. Refer to Prob. 5-7 and its accompanying figure for the necessary problem information.

5-17. Write a FORTRAN program for evaluating the integral of Prob. 5-8 by Simpson's rule.

5-18. The functions $f(x) = 1/(1 + x^2)$ and $g(x) = 1/(1 + e^{-x} + x^2)$ are shown graphically in the accompanying illustration. The evaluation

$$\int_0^\infty \frac{dx}{1 + x^2} = \frac{\pi}{2}$$

may be obtained by the direct integration of $f(x)$. Thus the integral

$$\int_0^\infty g(x)\,dx$$

may be evaluated by considering that

$$\int_0^\infty \frac{dx}{1 + e^{-x} + x^2} = \frac{\pi}{2} - A$$

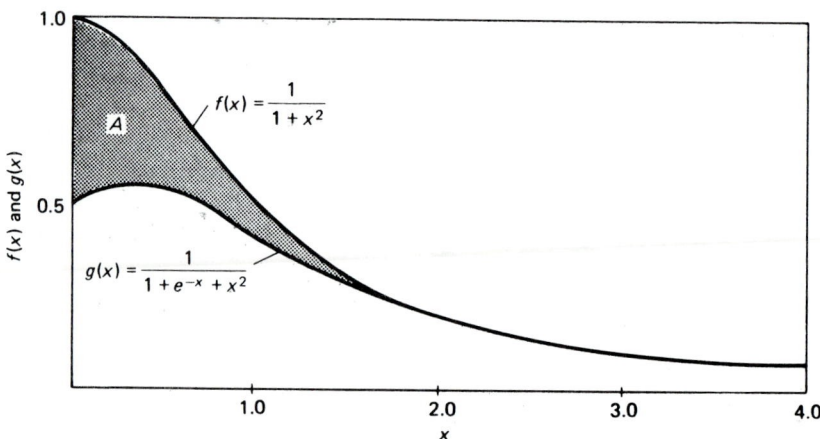

Problem 5-18

where A is the area (see shaded area in accompanying illustration) between $f(x)$ and $g(x)$ from zero to infinity. Since $f(x)$ and $g(x)$ approach each other rapidly for finite values of x, as shown in the figure, the area A may be evaluated quite accurately by using either the trapezoid rule or Simpson's rule, with integration over a finite range. Write a FORTRAN program for evaluating the area A and obtain the value of the integral

$$\int_0^\infty g(x)\, dx$$

by utilizing the relationship

$$\int_0^\infty g(x)\, dx = \frac{\pi}{2} - A$$

(answer: integral value $= 1.268012$)

5-19. A satellite, having unequal principal moments of inertia, is subjected to a gravity-stabilizing torque which tends to align the axis of the minimum moment of inertia with the radius vector connecting the mass centers of the earth and the satellite. For the satellite shown in the accompanying figure, the minimum moment of inertia is about the x axis, and the

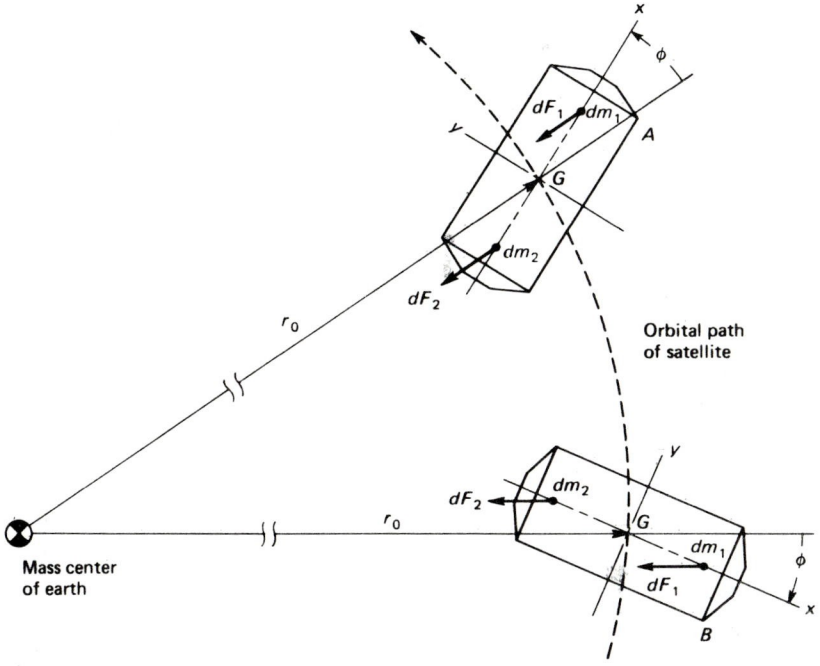

Problem 5-19

gravity torque tends to align this axis with the radius vector r_0. However, since the inertia of the satellite causes it to overshoot the equilibrium position, thus introducing a torque in the opposite direction, the satellite oscillates very slowly as it moves on its orbital path.

The gravity torque can be visualized, in a qualitative sense, by considering the differential gravity forces dF_1 and dF_2, which are shown acting on the differential masses dm_1 and dm_2, respectively. If these differential masses are equidistant from the mass center G of the satellite, then $dF_2 > dF_1$, since dm_2 is closer to the mass center of the earth than is dm_1. Thus, in position A the differential gravity torque due to dF_1 and dF_2 is clockwise. Similarly, in position B the differential gravity torque is counterclockwise. By integrating over the mass of the satellite, the differential equation of motion, describing the oscillation of a satellite moving in a circular orbit, is found to be

$$\frac{d\phi}{dt} + \frac{3}{2}\frac{R^2 g}{r_0^3}\left(\frac{I_y - I_x}{I_z}\right)\sin 2\phi = 0$$

where

$$
\begin{aligned}
R &= \text{radius of earth, } 20.9(10)^6 \text{ ft} \\
g &= \text{acceleration of gravity at earth's surface, } 32.2 \text{ ft/sec}^2 \\
R^2 g &= 1.407(10)^{16} \text{ ft}^3/\text{sec}^2 \\
r_0 &= \text{radius of circular orbital path} \\
I_x, I_y, \text{ and } I_z &= \text{principal moments of inertia } (I_x \text{ is minimum}) \\
\phi &= \text{angular displacement measured from line connecting} \\
&\quad \text{mass centers of earth and satellite}
\end{aligned}
$$

To obtain the period of oscillation τ, the differential equation of motion in ϕ can be transformed to the elliptic integral

$$\tau = \frac{4}{C\sqrt{2}}\int_0^{\pi/2}\frac{d\beta}{\sqrt{1 - \sin^2\phi_0 \sin^2\beta}}$$

where

$$C = \sqrt{\frac{3}{2}\frac{R^2 g}{r_0^3}\left(\frac{I_y - I_x}{I_z}\right)}$$

$\phi_0 = $ amplitude of oscillation

and the relationship

$$\sin\phi = \sin\phi_0 \sin\beta$$

introduces the dummy variable appearing in the equation for τ.

Write a FORTRAN program for obtaining the period of oscillation by integrating the given elliptic integral, by either the trapezoid rule or by Simpson's rule, with the following data:

$$r_0 = 1.1R$$

$$I_y = I_z$$

$$I_x = 0.5I_y$$

$$\phi_0 = 10, 20, 30, 40, 50, 60, 70, 80, \text{ and } 85 \text{ deg}$$

Using the computer results, plot the period τ as a function of ϕ_0. Compute the period τ for the above conditions, utilizing a table of values for elliptic integrals, and compare with the computer results.

(partial answer: $\tau = 5875.668$ sec with $\phi_0 = 50°$)

5-20. Refer to Prob. 5-19 and work it using the SI system of units where

$$R = 6.3703(10)^6 \; m$$

$$g = 9.91 \; m/\text{sec}^2$$

$$R^2g = 3.98(10)^{14} \; m^3/\text{sec}^2$$

5-21. Write a computer program for integrating any function defined by a function subprogram using Romberg integration. (Follow the flow chart given in Fig. 5-3 of the text.)

5-22. Improve the Romberg integration program of Prob. 5-21 by using a subprogram which calculates function ordinates rather than performing the complete trapezoidal integration. The trapezoidal integration will be a part of the Romberg program. Ordinate values which have been calculated once should not be recalculated when the number of strips is doubled. Their sum should be retained as the value of a variable.

5-23. In the slider-crank mechanism shown in part a of the accompanying figure, the slider B is driven by a Scotch-yoke mechanism shown in part b which gives it simple harmonic motion. Its displacement x is given by

$$x = R(1 - \cos \omega t)$$

where

ωt = crank angle of Scotch-yoke mechanism (see figure)

R = crank lengths of slider-crank and Scotch-yoke mechanisms

(a)

(b)

Problem 5-23

From geometry, x may be related to the crank angle θ by the formula

$$
\begin{aligned}
x &= R + L - R\cos\theta - L\cos\phi \\
&= R(1 - \cos\theta) + L(1 - \cos\phi) \\
&= R(1 - \cos\theta) + L(1 - \sqrt{1 - \sin^2\phi}) \\
&= R(1 - \cos\theta) + L[1 - \sqrt{1 - (R/L)^2 \sin^2\theta}]
\end{aligned}
$$

where θ, ϕ, and L are shown in the figure.

Using the following data, determine the values of θ corresponding to values of ωt from 0 to 175 deg (use 5-deg increments), using the Newton-Raphson method. Then determine the values of $d\theta/d\,(\omega t)$ and $d^2\theta/d\,(\omega t)^2$ by numerical differentiation.

$R = 4$ in.

$L = 6$ in.

(partial answer: for $\omega t = 60°$, $d\theta/d(\omega t) = 0.7827653$, $d^2\theta/d(\omega t)^2 = -0.03352227$)

5-24. The computer program shown in Ex. 5-3 was used for determining the angular velocity and acceleration of the output lever of a crank-and-lever mechanism using the first two numerical differentiation formulas of Eq. 5-79. Modify this program to utilize the first two differentiation formulas of Eq. 5-80, so that more accurate results may be obtained. Compare the solution obtained with the solution given in Ex. 5-3.

5-25. An automatic washer transmission uses the linkage shown in the accompanying figure to convert rotary motion from the drive motor to a large oscillating output of the agitator shaft G. The 79-tooth helical gear is driven by the 12-tooth helical pinion which rotates at a constant speed of 435 rpm. Links 2, 4, and 6 rotate or oscillate about fixed axes. Links 2, 3, and 4 (DA, AB, and BC) along with the fixed base constitute a four-bar linkage. Links 4, 5, and 6 (CE, EF, and FG) along with the fixed base constitute a second four-bar linkage in series with the first. Angle ϕ may be found for any angle θ using Freudenstein's equation and the Newton-Raphson root-finding technique as in Exs. 2-4 and 5-3. Angle α is equal to angle ϕ plus a constant. With angle α known, the corresponding angle β may be found, again using Freudenstein's equation and the Newton-Raphson method.

Write a FORTRAN program which determines and stores values of angle β for every degree of angle θ. Using these stored values of β and numerical differentiation, determine the angular velocity and angular acceleration of link 6 for every 5 deg of angle θ. Use Ex. 5-3 as a guide. For the numerical differentiation, use a $\Delta\theta$ value of 1 deg (or the corresponding value in radians). Print out values of θ and β in degrees and the angular velocity and angular acceleration of link 6 for every 5 deg of angle θ.

79-tooth helical gear

12-tooth helical pinion

Automatic washer drive

Link lengths
DA = 1.94 in.
AB = 6.86 in.
CB = 2.36 in.
EF = 1.87 in.
GF = 1.26 in.
DC = 7.00 in.
CG = 1.25 in.
CE = 2.39 in.

Problem 5-25

Chapter 6
Numerical Integration of Ordinary Differential Equations: Initial-Value Problems

6-1 INTRODUCTION

Initial-value problems are problems in which the values of the dependent variable and the necessary derivatives are known at the point at which integration begins. Such a large number of integration methods are available to handle problems of this type that an engineer may have difficulty in deciding which to use. In this chapter the most widely used methods are presented in some detail, and a summary is included to aid the reader in selecting one of these methods for a particular application.

The methods discussed will vary in complexity, since, in general, the greater the accuracy of a method, the greater is its complexity. Included are Euler's, modified Euler, Runge-Kutta, Milne's, and Hamming's methods. The error analysis of each of these methods is explained in detail.

This chapter will be concerned primarily with the solution of first-order differential equations and of sets of simultaneous first-order differential equations, since, as will be seen later, an nth-order differential equation may be solved by transforming it to a set of n simultaneous first-order differential equations. Several examples will be given in which the methods developed for solving first-order differential equations are extended to solve equations of higher order.

Figure 6-1   Cantilever beam with intensity of loading indicated by length of arrows

6-2 DIRECT NUMERICAL-INTEGRATION METHOD

Let us consider the cantilever beam shown in Fig. 6-1. The intensity of loading is some function of the displacement x along the beam, x being measured positively from the left end of the beam. The bending moment M along the beam will also be some function of x, and the M/EI diagram will have the general form shown in Fig. 6-2.

The differential equation of the elastic curve of a beam with a uniform cross section is

$$\frac{d^2y}{dx^2} = \frac{M(x)}{EI} \tag{6-1}$$

where E and I are the modulus of elasticity and the moment of inertia of the cross section, respectively. The initial conditions for the cantilever beam are

$$x = 0 \left| \begin{array}{l} y = 0 \\ y' = 0 \end{array} \right.$$

The numerical solution of Eq. 6-1 presents no particular difficulty. Its solution involves the determination of the deflection y for a series of equally spaced x values and is accomplished by two successive integrations. The curve of y' (the slope of the elastic curve) versus x may easily be obtained, since the value of y' is known at $x = 0$, and the change in y' from x_i to x_{i+1} is represented by the area under the M/EI curve between the given x values. The general form

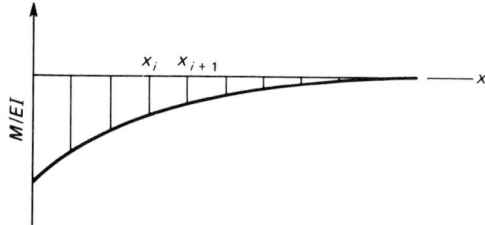

Figure 6-2   Typical M/EI diagram of a cantilever beam

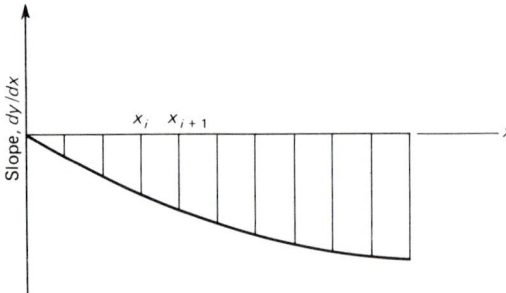

Figure 6-3 Typical slope curve of a cantilever beam

of the y' versus x curve is shown in Fig. 6-3. The y versus x curve, which is known as the elastic curve of the beam, is obtained in a similar manner, since the value of y is known at $x = 0$, and the change in y over an x interval is given by the corresponding area under the y' versus x curve. Either the trapezoid rule or Simpson's rule can be used for determining the areas mentioned. The general form of the elastic curve of a cantilever beam is shown in Fig. 6-4.

It should now be apparent that the numerical solution of a differential equation, in which the curve of the highest-order derivative is known, may be obtained by direct numerical integration, provided the necessary initial conditions are known. Denoting $y^n = d^n y/dx^n$, we may generalize that all nth-order differential equations of the form

$$y^n = f(x) \tag{6-2}$$

with the initial conditions

$$x = x_0 \begin{vmatrix} y &=& y_0 \\ y' &=& y_0' \\ \vdots & & \vdots \\ y^{n-1} &=& y_0^{n-1} \end{vmatrix}$$

can be solved in the manner discussed.

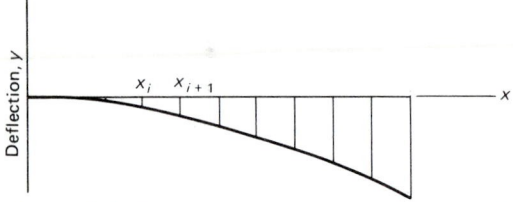

Figure 6-4 Typical deflection curve of a cantilever beam

6-3 EULER'S METHOD (THE EULER-CAUCHY METHOD)

The expression

$$y^n = f(x, y, y', y'', \ldots, y^{n-1}) \tag{6-3}$$

is a more general form of an nth-order differential equation than the one described in the preceding paragraphs. In such a differential equation the highest order (the nth) derivative is not merely a function of the independent variable but is also a function of the dependent variable, whose values we are seeking, and the derivatives of order less than n. *Direct* integration of such a differential equation, using the trapezoid rule or Simpson's rule, is not possible. To illustrate a simple method of obtaining an approximate solution of a differential equation of this type, let us consider the first-order equation

$$y' = f(x, y) \tag{6-4}$$

with the initial condition of $y = 0$ when $x = 0$. We wish to obtain the y versus x curve, which suggests using the area under the y' versus x curve. However, the latter curve is unknown, since y' is a function of y. To illustrate, let us assume that these curves have the general form of those shown in Fig. 6-5.

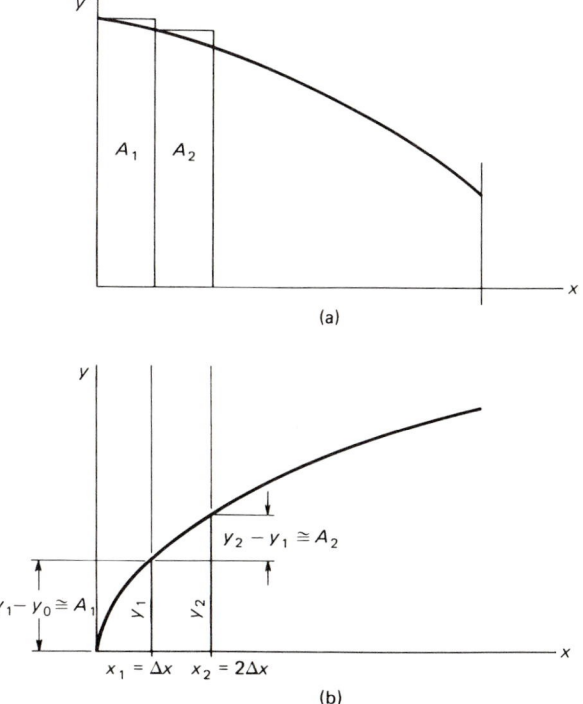

(a)

(b)

Figure 6-5 Assumed curves of y' and y versus x satisfying $y' = f(x,y)$

Since the initial value of y is known, we can determine the initial value of y' from the given differential equation. The change in y from $x = 0$ to $x = \Delta x$ is represented by the area under the y' curve between the given values of x. An approximate value of this area can be obtained by assuming that it is equal to the rectangular area A_1, shown in Fig. 6-5(a). Letting $\Delta x = h$, this area may be expressed as

$$A_1 = y_1 - y_0 = y_0'h$$

from which

$$y_1 = y_0 + y_0'h \tag{6-5}$$

Having determined a close approximation of the value of y_1 by the use of Eq. 6-5 (by using small h values), we can get a good approximation of y_1' from the given differential equation, since

$$y_1' = f(x_1, y_1)$$

Then, since $y_2 - y_1$ is approximately equal to the area under the y' curve from x_1 to x_2, as shown by the rectangular area A_2 in Fig. 6-5,

$$y_2 = y_1 + y_1'h \tag{6-6}$$

Proceeding as before, y_2' may next be determined from the differential equation, by using the value of y_2 obtained from Eq. 6-6 and a value of $x_2 = 2h$. The subsequent y_i and y_i' values are found in a similar manner. Equations 6-5 and 6-6 may be expressed, in general form, as

$$y_{i+1} = y_i + y_i'h \tag{6-7}$$

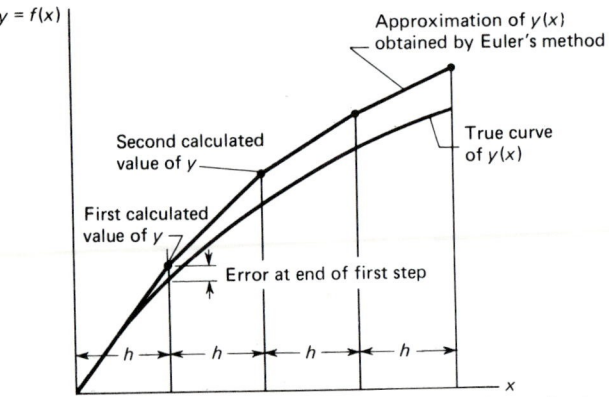

Figure 6-6 Comparison of solution by Euler's method with true solution

Equation 6-7 is known as Euler's forward-integration equation. Euler's method is called a "self-starting" method, since it requires a value of the dependent variable at only one point to start the procedure.

A graphical representation of a portion of the function $y(x)$, as obtained by Euler's method, is shown in Fig. 6-6. Let us assume the initial condition of $y = 0$ at $x = 0$. With a known initial value of y, the initial slope of the curve can be determined from the differential equation. The first calculated y value, indicated in Fig. 6-6, can then be obtained from Euler's equation (Eq. 6-7). It can be seen from the figure that Euler's method, in effect, approximates the function $y(x)$ over the first-step interval by a straight line. The substitution of this calculated value of y into the differential equation then gives an approximation of the slope of the curve at $x = h$. A second application of Euler's equation yields a second calculated value of y, as shown in the figure, which is, in turn, substituted into the differential equation to obtain an approximation of the slope at $x = 2h$. This process is repeated over the desired range of integration, so that the true $y(x)$ curve is approximated by a series of straight-line segments.

Error Estimation for Euler's Method

Euler's formula is simply a truncated Taylor series in which terms containing h^2 and higher powers are neglected. The Taylor series for y_{i+1} expanded about x_i with the Lagrangian form of the remainder is

$$y_{i+1} = y_i + y_i'h + \frac{y''(\xi)h^2}{2}, \qquad x_i < \xi < x_{i+1} \tag{6-8}$$

The last term of Eq. 6-8 is the *truncation-error term* of Euler's method. Assuming that y'' is fairly constant over the ith-step interval, so that the higher derivative terms are negligible, an estimate of the truncation error E_T in the ith step can be obtained from

$$E_{T_i} \cong \frac{y_i''h^2}{2} \tag{6-9}$$

where y'' is evaluated at $\xi = x_i$. If a truncation-error analysis is made at each step, Eq. 6-9 may be used to estimate the truncation error at each step for comparison with some selected set of limiting values. If the estimate exceeds the bound of the maximum specified error, the step size can be reduced and the numerical process continued. On the other hand, if the estimate is smaller than the minimum limit, the step size can be increased and the numerical process continued. In either case the final value of y, calculated by using the old step size, is used as the initial value of y for the subsequent interval of integration using the new step size.

In an instance in which the differentiation of

$$y' = f(x, y) \tag{6-10}$$

to obtain y'' for use in estimating the per-step truncation error of Euler's method leads to a rather complicated function, a more practical approach can be made by using a constant step size h to obtain a solution, and then obtaining another solution using a smaller step size, say, $h/2$. If the two solutions yield results which are in good agreement throughout—to four figures, for example—it is fairly safe to assume that both are reasonably accurate to four figures, and that the one with the smaller step size has greater than four-figure accuracy. If the two solutions are not in good agreement throughout, one using a still smaller step size should be obtained for comparison with the solution obtained with the next higher step size, and so forth. If the initial step size chosen happened to be too small, so that roundoff error dominated, it would be necessary to follow the above procedure, but increase the step size each time. The programmer who does not wish to complicate his program by incorporating a variable step size over the range of integration will find the procedure just discussed a practical means of checking the accuracy of a solution obtained by any of the integration methods described in this chapter.

EXAMPLE 6-1

The rattrap shown in Fig. 6-7 consists of a movable jaw, trip arm, torsion spring, and trip pan. Upon release of the trip arm owing to a slight disturbance

Figure 6-7 Rattrap shown in open position

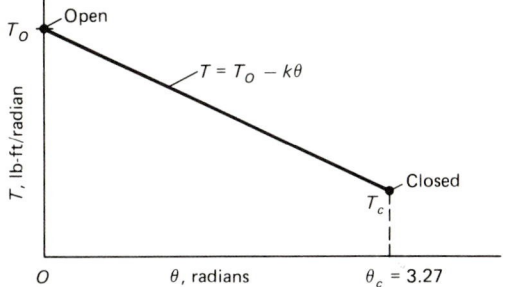

Figure 6-8 Torque-displacement characteristic of torsion spring

of the trip pan, the torque of the torsion spring closes the rotating jaw and kills the rodent.

The manufacturer has received complaints about the performance of the trap with respect to the closure time of the jaw and the impact force of the jaw on the rodent. To analyze the trap, it is desired to obtain data for drawing θ-t, ω-t, and ω-θ curves for the jaw of the trap.

The data for the trap are $A = 1.125$ in., $B = 0.5$ in., $R = 3.75$ in., and $I_O = 0.0006$ lb-ft-sec^2 (mass moment of inertia of the jaw about the pivot axis).

The torque-displacement characteristic of the linear torsion spring is shown in Fig. 6-8. When closed, the jaw exerts a force against the base which has a component perpendicular to the jaw of 2 lb, and a force of 9 lb is required to hold the jaw in the open position. From the given information, we find that

$\theta_k = 2.97$ radians or 170.4 deg (angular displacement of jaw upon contact with rat)

$\theta_c = 3.27$ radians or 187.7 deg (angular displacement of jaw in the closed position)

$T_O = 9(3.75)/12 = 2.81$ lb-ft (torque of spring in open position; $\theta = 0$)

$T_c = 2(3.75)/12 = 0.625$ lb-ft (torque of spring in closed position)

Upon release, the jaw is subjected to the torque T of the spring, as shown in Fig. 6-9. From elementary dynamics we know that the external torque T about point O equals $I_O\ddot{\theta}$. Taking θ and $\ddot{\theta}$ positive, as shown in the figure, the differential equation of motion is

$$\ddot{\theta} + \frac{k\theta}{I_O} = \frac{T_O}{I_O} \tag{6-11}$$

Figure 6-9 Movable jaw after release

Referring to Fig. 6-8, it can be seen that the torsional spring constant may be expressed as

$$k = \frac{T_O - T_c}{\theta_c} = \frac{2.81 - 0.625}{3.27} = 0.669 \text{ lb-ft/radian} \tag{6-12}$$

Using the relationship given in Eq. 6-12, we may rewrite Eq. 6-11 as

$$\ddot{\theta} + \frac{k\theta}{I_O} = \frac{T_c + k\theta_c}{I_O} \tag{6-13}$$

In this example we will use Euler's forward-integration method to obtain the desired data for drawing θ-t, ω-t, and ω-θ curves for the trap jaw. We will also compare the data obtained for the θ-t curve by Euler's method with corresponding values determined from an analytical solution of Eq. 6-11.

Inspection of Eq. 6-13 reveals that we are considering a second-order differential equation of the form

$$\ddot{\theta} = f(\theta) \tag{6-14}$$

whereas the discussion thus far has dealt only with first-order differential equations. However, we can make the discussion pertinent to the solution of second-order equations, since the latter may be reduced to a set of two first-order equations which can be solved simultaneously. Realizing that

$$\dot{\theta} = \omega$$

and

$$\ddot{\theta} = \dot{\omega}$$

Eq. 6-13 can be reduced to the two first-order differential equations

$$\dot{\theta} = \omega \tag{a}$$
$$\tag{6-15}$$
$$\dot{\omega} + \frac{k\theta}{I_O} = \frac{T_c + k\theta_c}{I_O} \tag{b}$$

which can be solved simultaneously to obtain the desired data of the problem.

Using Euler's forward-integration equation (Eq. 6-7) with Eq. 6-15b, we can write

$$\omega_{i+1} = \omega_i + \dot{\omega}_i(\Delta t) \tag{6-16}$$

in which the term $\dot{\omega}_i(\Delta t)$ approximates the area in one strip under the $\dot{\omega}$-t curve. This approximate area is shown as the crosshatched area A_1 in Fig. 6-10(a). We next apply Euler's equation to Eq. 6-15a and obtain

$$\theta_{i+1} = \theta_i + \omega_i(\Delta t) \tag{6-17}$$

Let us now write Eqs. 6-15b, 6-16, and 6-17 as a set, so that we may examine their interdependence, writing Eq. 6-15b in the subscripted form in which it will be used in the numerical process.

$$\dot{\omega}_i = \left(\frac{T_c + k\theta_c}{I_O}\right) - \frac{k\theta_i}{I_O}$$

$$\omega_{i+1} = \omega_i + \dot{\omega}_i(\Delta t) \tag{6-18}$$

$$\theta_{i+1} = \theta_i + \omega_i(\Delta t)$$

Selecting a value for Δt and remembering that the initial conditions are $\theta = \omega = 0$ when $t = 0$, we see that $\dot{\omega}_0$, ω_1, and θ_1 can be evaluated from Eq.

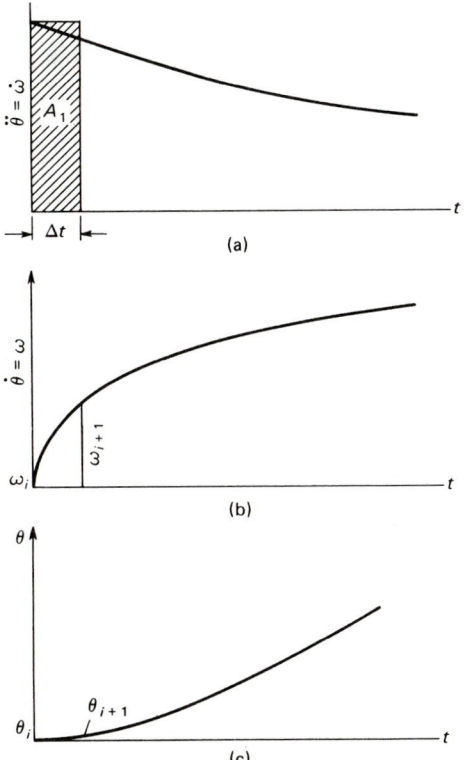

Figure 6-10 Dynamic-characteristic curves for the rattrap jaw of Ex. 6-1

6-18. In doing this, the first-step results will contain the inherent errors of Euler's method. For example, we obtain the obviously incorrect value of $\theta_1 = 0$. If Δt is very small, this error will not be serious but it is apparent that the trapezoidal approximation to the area under the ω-t curve in the first step would give a much better value of θ_1. Use of a trapezoidal approximation will also improve the accuracy in all subsequent steps. Since ω_i and ω_{i+1} are both known before we are ready to calculate θ_{i+1}, we can use the trapezoid rule to obtain θ_{i+1}, as follows:

$$\theta_{i+1} = \theta_i + \left(\frac{\omega_i + \omega_{i+1}}{2}\right)\Delta t \tag{6-19}$$

It can be seen that the following value will be obtained for θ_1

$$\theta_1 = \frac{\omega_1(\Delta t)}{2}$$

which is a closer approximation of the value of θ at the end of the first Δt interval.

Hence we will program the problem for a solution on the computer, using the following set of equations:

$$\dot{\omega}_i = \left(\frac{T_c + k\theta_c}{I_O}\right) - \frac{k\theta_i}{I_O}$$

$$\omega_{i+1} = \omega_i + \dot{\omega}_i(\Delta t) \tag{6-20}$$

$$\theta_{i+1} = \theta_i + \left(\frac{\omega_i + \omega_{i+1}}{2}\right)\Delta t$$

where we are using Euler's forward-integration equation to solve Eq. 6-15b and the trapezoid rule to solve Eq. 6-15a.

This program is to be run on a pure binary computer, and we note that the time increment shown below, 0.0001 sec, cannot be expressed precisely in pure binary form, so that the 10 time increments will not add up exactly to the print increment of 0.001 sec. For a printout in this program, the time only need be within a small epsilon value (EPSI) of the print time. See the discussion following the listing of FORTRAN variable names in Ex. 6-4 regarding this problem on a pure binary computer.

The flow chart for the computer solution is shown in Fig. 6-11. The variable names selected for the program are as follows:

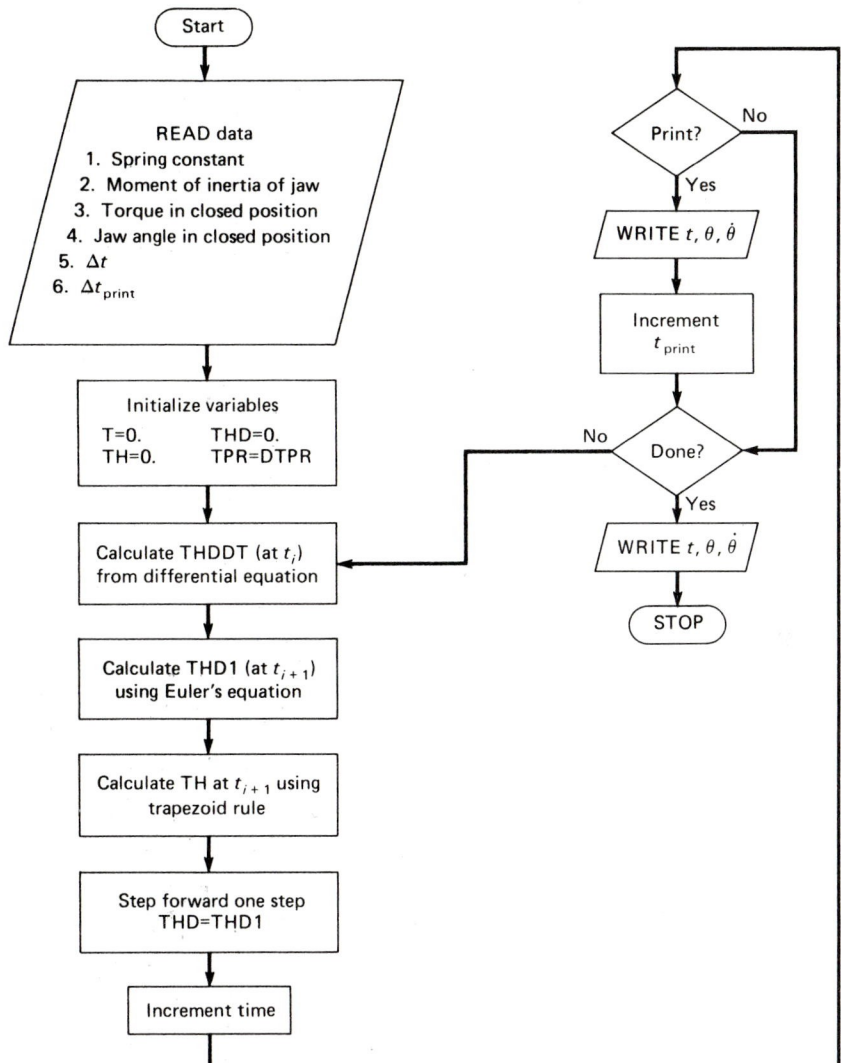

Figure 6-11   Flow chart for numerical solution of rattrap problem of Ex. 6-1

FORTRAN Name	Quantity	Numerical Value Used in Solution
SK	Spring constant k, lb-ft/radian	0.669
I	Moment of inertia I_0, lb-ft-sec^2	0.0006
TORCL	Torque closed position T_c, lb-ft	0.625
THCL	Jaw angle θ in closed position θ_c, radians	3.270
DELT	Time increment Δt, sec	0.0001
DTPR	Print increment, Δt_{print}, sec	0.0010

FORTRAN **Name**	**Quantity**	**Numerical Value** **Used in Solution**
T	Time t, sec	
TH	Jaw angle θ_i	
THD	Jaw angular velocity $\dot{\theta}_i$	
THDDT	Jaw angular acceleration $\ddot{\theta}_i$	
THD1	Jaw angular velocity one station ahead of THD, $\dot{\theta}_{i+1}$	
TPR	Time value at each printout	
EPSI	A small value used to assure a printout when T is supposed to exactly equal TPR but does not	0.00003

The FORTRAN IV program for the problem is as follows:

```
      REAL I
      WRITE (6,10)
   10 FORMAT ('1', 1X, 'DYNAMIC CHARACTERISTICS OF A RATTRAP')
      WRITE (6,1)
    1 FORMAT ('0',5X,' TIME' ,6X, 'THETA' ,6X, 'ANG V' ,//)
      READ (5,2) SK,I,TORCL,THCL,DELT,DTPR,EPSI
    2 FORMAT(7F10.0)
      T=0.
      TH=0.
      THD=0.
      TPR=DTPR
    3 THDDT=(TORCL+SK*THCL)/I-SK*TH/I
      THD1=THD+THDDT*DELT
      TH=TH+(THD+THD1)/2.*DELT
      THD=THD1
      T=T+DELT
      IF(ABS(T-TPR)-EPSI) 4,4,6
    4 WRITE(6,5) T,TH,THD
      TPR=TPR+DTPR
    5 FORMAT(' ',5X,F7.4,4X,F6.3,4X,F7.2)
    6 IF(TH-THCL) 3,7,7
    7 WRITE(6,5) T,TH,THD
      STOP
      END
```

The results obtained from the computer solution are given by the following printout:

```
DYNAMIC CHARACTERISTICS OF A RATTRAP
TIME          THETA        ANG V
0.0010        0.002         4.69
0.0020        0.009         9.37
```

DYNAMIC CHARACTERISTICS OF A RATTRAP

TIME	THETA	ANG V
0.0030	0.021	14.04
0.0040	0.037	18.70
0.0050	0.058	23.33
0.0060	0.084	27.94
0.0070	0.114	32.52
0.0080	0.149	37.07
0.0090	0.188	41.57
0.0100	0.232	46.02
0.0110	0.280	50.43
0.0120	0.333	54.78
0.0130	0.390	59.06
0.0140	0.451	63.29
0.0150	0.517	67.44
0.0160	0.586	71.52
0.0170	0.660	75.51
0.0180	0.737	79.43
0.0190	0.818	83.25
0.0200	0.904	86.99
0.0210	0.992	90.62
0.0220	1.085	94.16
0.0230	1.181	97.59
0.0240	1.280	100.91
0.0250	1.382	104.12
0.0260	1.488	107.21
0.0270	1.597	110.19
0.0280	1.708	113.04
0.0290	1.823	115.76
0.0300	1.940	118.36
0.0310	2.059	120.83
0.0320	2.181	123.16
0.0330	2.306	125.35
0.0340	2.432	127.40
0.0350	2.560	129.31
0.0360	2.691	131.08
0.0370	2.823	132.70
0.0380	2.956	134.18
0.0390	3.091	135.50
0.0400	3.227	136.67
0.0404	3.282	137.10

To check the accuracy of the numerical method used, the angular displacements were solved on the computer, using the equation

$$\theta = \frac{T_c + k\theta_c}{k}\left(1 - \cos\sqrt{\frac{k}{I_O}}\,t\right)$$

which is the analytical solution of Eq. 6-13. To save space, the complete printout for the latter solution is not shown, but some of the results are reproduced below, to afford a comparison with the numerical solution.

Time	Theta (Numerical)	Theta (Analytical)
0.0010	0.002	0.002
0.0050	0.058	0.058
0.0100	0.232	0.232
0.0200	0.904	0.903
0.0250	1.382	1.382
0.0300	1.940	1.939
0.0400	3.227	3.225
0.0404	3.282	3.279

It is apparent that the numerically obtained values compare quite closely with those determined analytically.

6-4 MODIFIED EULER METHODS

The Self-Starting Modification

This is a self-starting method of the predictor-corrector type, having greater accuracy than Euler's method. It is known by a variety of names, the Euler-trapezoidal method, the Euler predictor-corrector method, the improved Euler method, and Heun's method. Some European authors refer to it as the Euler-Cauchy method, which the Euler method discussed in the preceding section is also sometimes called. We will call it the *self-starting modified Euler method* to differentiate it from another modification which is not self-starting.

We again consider a first-order differential equation of the form

$$y' = f(x, y) \tag{6-21}$$

where the value of y is known when $x = 0$. Let us assume that the curves of y' and y versus x are those shown in Fig. 6-12. If we substiture the known initial value of y into Eq. 6-21, we obtain the value of y' at $x = 0$. Next, a *predicted* value of y at $x = \Delta x$ is found by using Euler's equation

$$P(y_1) = y_0 + y_0'h \tag{6-22}$$

where $P(y_1)$ is the predicted value of y_1 and $h = \Delta x$. In using Eq. 6-22 to obtain the predicted value of y_1, the term $y_0'h$ is the rectangular area A_1 shown in Fig. 6-12(a). This area is obviously larger than the true area under the given curve, so the predicted value of y_1 obtained is too large by some small amount. However, if the predicted value of y_1 is substituted into the given differential equation (Eq. 6-21) along with $x = h$, an approximate value of y_1' may be

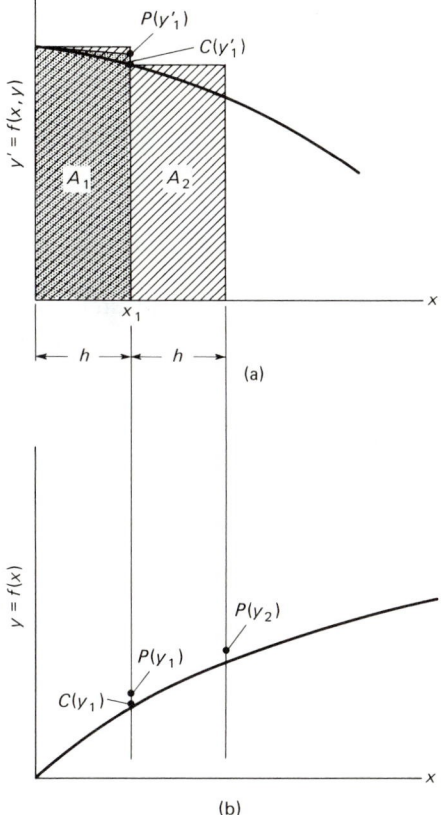

Figure 6-12 The y' and y versus x curves satisfying $y' = f(x,y)$

obtained. Since this value of y_1' is based on the predicted value of y_1, $P(y_1)$, we will use the notation $P(y_1')$ to represent it. Then, using the shaded *trapezoidal* area shown in Fig. 6-12(a) as the approximation of the true area under the y' curve, a corrected value of y_1, which we will denote by $C(y_1)$, can be determined as

$$C(y_1) = y_0 + \left(\frac{y_0' + P(y_1')}{2}\right)h \qquad (6\text{-}23)$$

Equation 6-23 is thus known as the *corrector* equation. The corrected value of y_1 is next substituted into Eq. 6-21 to obtain a corrected value of y_1'. The latter value is denoted by $C(y_1')$, as indicated in Fig. 6-12(a). The iteration process continues, by using $C(y_1')$ in place of $P(y_1')$ in Eq. 6-23, to obtain a still better value of y_1, and then using this improved value in Eq. 6-21 to get a further improved value of y_1'. The process is repeated until successive values of y_1 differ by less than some prescribed epsilon value selected to specify the accuracy desired.

With the desired value of y_1 obtained, we are ready to move ahead one step to determine the value of y_2. This begins by using the predictor equation

$$P(y_2) = y_1 + y_1' h \tag{6-24}$$

where $P(y_2)$ is the first predicted value of y_2, and y_1 and y_1' are the most accurate values obtained for these quantities in the preceding iteration. The iterative process described for determining an accurate value of y_1 is then repeated, and so on.

The general form of Eqs. 6-22 and 6-23, for application at any step, is

(Predictor) $\qquad P(y_{i+1}) = y_i + y_1' h \qquad$ (a)

$$\tag{6-25}$$

(Corrector) $\qquad C(y_{i+1}) = y_i + \left[\dfrac{y_i' + P(y_{i+1}')}{2} \right] h \qquad$ (b)

Error Analysis of the Self-Starting Modified Euler Method

Since the corrector equation of this method is based on using a trapezoidal area to represent the true area in one strip under the y' versus x curve, the per-step truncation error of this method is the same as the truncation error of the trapezoid rule, and is

$$E_{TC_i} = -\tfrac{1}{12} y'''(\xi) h^3 \qquad x_i < \xi < x_{i+1} \tag{6-26}$$

with order of h^3. Assuming that y''' is fairly constant over the ith step so that the higher derivatives are negligible, we can evaluate y''' at $\xi = x_i$ and obtain an estimate of the truncation error in computing y_{i+1} as

$$E_{TC_i} = -\tfrac{1}{12} y_i''' h^3 \tag{6-27}$$

As discussed under Euler's method, the error estimate given by Eq. 6-27 can be used for comparison with some selected set of limiting values to adjust the step size, when necessary, during the integration process.

If y''' is a rather complicated function, the determination of the truncation error at each step may become quite cumbersome if one uses the method just described. One alternative method of obtaining a solution having some desired degree of accuracy is to run separate solutions, each with a different step size, and compare the solutions obtained, decreasing (or possibly increasing) the step size at each run until consecutive solutions are in good agreement.

Another alternative is to base adjustment of the step size on a truncation-error estimate by Richardson's method,[1] in which two solutions, each with a

---

[1] L. F. Richardson and J. A. Gaunt, "The Deferred Approach to the Limit," *Trans. Roy. Soc. London*, Vol. 226A (1927), p. 300.

different step size, are run simultaneously. A truncation-error estimate is obtained at each step in terms of the two y values obtained at that step. To develop this way of estimating the per-step truncation error for an rth-order method, consider that

$$C_1(h)^{r+1} = \text{the per-step truncation error in an } r\text{th-order method (a method having a per-step truncation error of order } r+1) \text{ using a step size of } h$$

$$C_2\left(\frac{h}{2}\right)^{r+1} = \text{the per-step truncation error in the same } r\text{th-order method using a step size of } h/2 \quad^2$$

$$y^{(1)} = \text{the } y \text{ value obtained at } x_{i+1} \text{ using a step size of } h \text{ in stepping forward from } x_i$$

$$y^{(2)} = \text{the } y \text{ value obtained at } x_{i+1} \text{ using two steps of size } h/2 \text{ in stepping forward from } x_i$$

$$Y = \text{the true value of } y \text{ at } x_{i+1}$$

Isolating the truncation error of the step from the effects of previous error in the solution, in accordance with the definition given for per-step truncation error, and assuming that roundoff error in the step calculations is negligible, we can write

$$Y - y^{(1)} = C_1(h)^{r+1} \tag{6-28}$$

$$Y - y^{(2)} \cong 2C_2\left(\frac{h}{2}\right)^{r+1} \tag{6-29}$$

If the derivative y^{r+1} is fairly constant over the interval h, we may assume that $C_1 \cong C_2$. Subtracting Eq. 6-29 from Eq. 6-28 yields

$$\frac{y^{(2)} - y^{(1)}}{2^r - 1} \cong 2C_2\left(\frac{h}{2}\right)^{r+1} \tag{6-30}$$

Comparing Eqs. 6-30 and 6-29, it can be seen that the approximate truncation error in obtaining y at x_{i+1}, using two steps of size $h/2$ in stepping forward from x_i is given by

$$E_T \cong \frac{y^{(2)} - y^{(1)}}{2^r - 1} \tag{6-31}$$

^{2}
$$C_1 = cy^{r+1}(\xi_1) \qquad C_2 = cy^{r+1}(\xi_2) \qquad \begin{array}{c} x_i < \xi_1 < x_{i+1} \\ x_i < \xi_2 < x_{i+1/2} \end{array}$$

For the modified Euler methods ($r = 2$), Eq. 6-31 becomes

$$E_T \cong \frac{y^{(2)} - y^{(1)}}{3} \tag{6-32}$$

An estimate of the per-step truncation error in the corrector equation of some predictor-corrector methods can also be determined, at each step, in terms of the predicted y value and the final corrected y value. When both the predictor equation and the corrector equation of a method have the same order of truncation error, it is relatively easy to obtain a truncation-error estimate at each step, in such terms, since the estimate can essentially be obtained as the by-product of calculations required in the predictor-corrector process.

The Non-Self-Starting Modified Euler Method

In the self-starting modified Euler method, the predictor equation has a truncation error of order h^2 (Eq. 6-9) whereas the corrector equation has a truncation error of order h^3 (Eq. 6-26). A truncation-error estimate at each step in terms of the predicted y value and final corrected y value is not possible. When an error estimate is to be made at each step in terms of these quantities, the non-self-starting modified Euler method should be used, since, as we will see, the predictor and corrector equations have truncation errors of the same order. The predictor equation of this method is

$$P(y_{i+1}) = y_{i-1} + 2y_i'h \tag{6-33}$$

The area in two strips under the y' versus x curve from x_{i-1} to x_{i+1} is approximated by the crosshatched area shown in Fig. 6-13. The corrector equation is the same as for the self-starting modified Euler method as given by Eq. 6-25b. Thus the complete set to be used in this method is

$$
\left.
\begin{array}{lll}
\text{(Predictor)} & P(y_{i+1}) = y_{i-1} + 2y_i'h & \text{(a)} \\[2mm]
\text{(Differential equation)} & P(y_{i+1}') = f[x_{i+1}, P(y_{i+1})] & \text{(b)} \\[2mm]
\text{(Corrector)} & C(y_{i+1}) = y_i + \dfrac{h}{2}[y_i' + P(y_{i+1}')] & \text{(c)}
\end{array}
\right\} \quad \text{(6-34)}
$$

Although we will be able to derive a way of easily estimating the per-step truncation error using this method, the convenient self-starting feature of the previously described modified Euler method is lost. In addition to the usual initial value of y required for solving a first-order differential equation, one additional value of y must be known to get the method started. Integration by this method is usually started by applying Eq. 6-25a and Eq. 6-25b for the first step, and then switching to the set given by Eq. 6-34. The additional

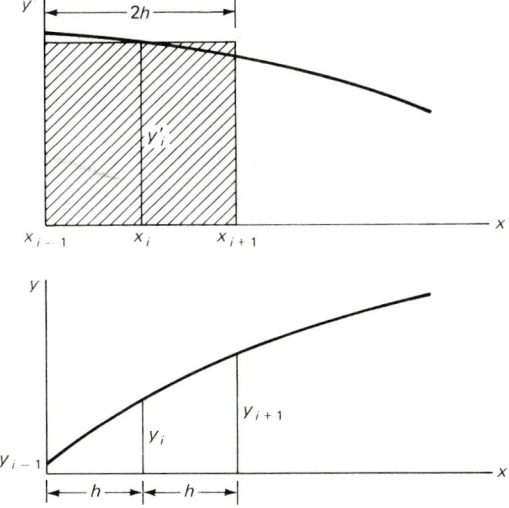

Figure 6-13   The area in two strips under the y' versus x curve approximated by a rectangular area (the non-self-starting modified Euler method)

required starting value can often be obtained quite easily with the use of a pocket calculator, but it can be calculated as part of the computer program if desired.

Error Analysis of the Non-Self-Starting Modified Euler Method

Since the corrector equation of this method is the same as that of the self-starting modification, the per-step truncation error is the same; it is

$$E_{TC_i} = -\tfrac{1}{12}y'''(\xi)h^3 \qquad x_i < \xi < x_{i+1} \tag{6-35}$$

However, as previously mentioned, y''' may turn out to be a complicated function, making the use of Eq. 6-35 quite cumbersome. Therefore, we will develop a technique for estimating the per-step truncation error in terms of the predicted and final corrected values of y at each step. This is possible because the predictor and corrector equations have errors of the same order.

First, examining the per-step truncation error of the predictor equation, we expand y_{i+1} in a Taylor series about x_i to obtain

$$y_{i+1} = y_i + y_i'h + \frac{y_i''h^2}{2!} + \frac{y'''(\xi_1)h^3}{3!}, \qquad x_i < \xi_1 < x_{i+1} \tag{6-36}$$

Similarly, expanding y_{i-1} about x_i yields

$$y_{i-1} = y_i - y_i'h + \frac{y_i''h^2}{2!} - \frac{y'''(\xi_2)h^3}{3!}, \qquad x_{i-1} < \xi_2 < x_i \tag{6-37}$$

Subtracting Eq. 6-37 from Eq. 6-36 gives

$$y_{i+1} - y_{i-1} = 2y_i'h + \frac{2y'''(\xi_3)h^3}{3!}, \qquad x_{i-1} < \xi_3 < x_{i+1} \tag{6-38}$$

Comparing Eq. 6-38 with Eq. 6-34a, we can write Eq. 6-38 as

$$y_{i+1} = \underbrace{y_{i-1} + 2y_i'h}_{\substack{\text{predictor} \\ \text{equation}}} + \underbrace{\frac{2y'''(\xi_3)h^3}{3!}}_{\substack{\text{truncation} \\ \text{error}}} \tag{6-39}$$

to see that the per-step truncation error of the predictor equation

$$E_{TP_i} = \frac{y'''(\xi_3)h^3}{3} \tag{6-40}$$

is of order h^3. This is of the same order as the per-step truncation error of the corrector equation given by Eq. 6-26.

Knowing the per-step truncation errors of both the predictor and the corrector equations, consider that

$$P\left(\frac{1}{y}\right) = \text{the predicted } y \text{ value obtained at } x_{i+1} \text{ in the integration process in the first and only application of the predictor equation at that step}$$

$$C\left(\frac{n}{y}\right) = \text{the corrected } y \text{ value obtained at } x_{i+1} \text{ in the } n\text{th (final) application of the corrector equation at that step}$$

$$Y = \text{the true value of } y \text{ at } x_{i+1}$$

Isolating the truncation error of the ith step from the effects of previous errors, in accordance with the definition given of per-step truncation error, and assuming that roundoff error is negligible in the calculations of the step, we can write

(Predictor) $\qquad Y = P\left(\dfrac{1}{y}\right) + \dfrac{1}{3} y'''(\xi_3)h^3 \qquad x_{i-1} < \xi_3 < x_{i+1}$ $\qquad$ (6-41)

(Corrector) $\qquad Y = C\left(\dfrac{n}{y}\right) - \dfrac{1}{12} y'''(\eta)h^3 \qquad x_i < \eta < x_{i+1}$ $\qquad$ (6-42)

Subtracting Eq. 6-41 from Eq. 6-42, we obtain

$$0 = C\left(\frac{n}{y}\right) - P\left(\frac{1}{y}\right) - \frac{5}{12} y'''(\eta_1)h^3 \qquad x_{i-1} < \eta_1 < x_{i+1} \tag{6-43}$$

Comparing Eqs. 6-43 and 6-26, we can write an estimate of the per-step truncation error of the corrector equation, in terms of the predicted y value and the final corrected y value, as

$$E_{TC} \cong -\frac{1}{5}\left[C\binom{n}{y} - P\binom{1}{y} \right]$$

(6-44)

EXAMPLE 6-2

This example will illustrate the self-starting modified method applied to two simultaneous second-order differential equations.

When a paratrooper jumps from an aircraft which is in straight and level flight, he has an initial velocity equal to that of the aircraft, and he is a freely falling body during the time interval before opening his parachute. The velocity of the paratrooper during this free-fall interval may be described by a set of rectangular components, as shown in Fig. 6-14.

The decelerating force to which the paratrooper is subjected when the parachute opens is essentially proportional to the square of his free-fall velocity at the time the chute opens. With slow-flying aircraft, this decelerating force is not excessive. The paratrooper jumps, and a relatively short static line, attached to both the rip cord of the chute and the aircraft, opens the chute after a short free fall which is just sufficient to clear the aircraft. However, aircraft dropping paratroopers while flying at slow speeds present ideal targets for enemy ground fire. Therefore, it is desirable to drop the paratroopers from faster-flying aircraft. Since the impact force on the paratrooper increases approximately as the *square* of the velocity at the time the chute opens, it is desirable to open the chute at the instant when the free-fall velocity is at a minimum.

It is a well-known fact that a body falling freely in a resisting medium, if allowed to fall far enough, will eventually reach a limiting or *terminal* velocity.

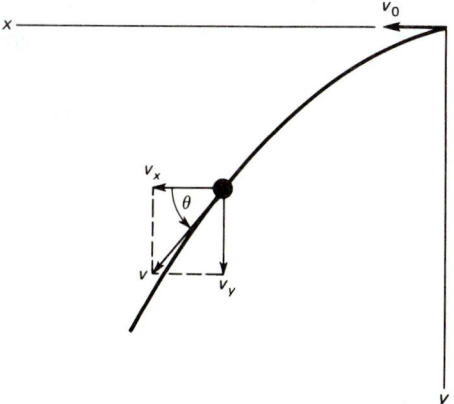

Figure 6-14   Coordinate system of paratrooper problem

This limiting velocity is reached when the resistive force, or drag due to the fluid medium, just balances the weight of the falling body. It has been claimed that, for any horizontal launching speed, the velocity of the paratrooper falling freely will pass through a *minimum* value *less* than either the *launching* or the *terminal* velocity.

In general, the drag force D on a body, owing to air resistance, is proportional to the projected area of the body normal to the direction of motion, the air density, and approximately the square of the velocity. Usually, the drag force D is expressed in the form

$$D = \frac{C\gamma A v^2}{2} \tag{6-45}$$

where

γ = mass density of the fluid medium, lb-sec^2/ft^4

A = projected area of the body normal to the direction of motion, ft^2

C = drag coefficient, dimensionless

v = velocity, ft/sec

If we assume that the projected area A of the paratrooper is essentially constant, that the drag coefficient C is constant over the range of velocities encountered, and that the mass density γ of the air is a constant, then the quantity $C\gamma A$ may be considered as a constant, so that

$$\frac{C\gamma A}{2} = \text{constant} = K$$

and, from Eq. 6-45,

$$D = Kv^2 \tag{6-46}$$

Referring to Fig. 6-14 and considering Newton's second law, the equations of motion in rectangular coordinates are readily found to be

(x direction) $$\frac{W}{g}\frac{dv_x}{dt} = -Kv^2 \cos\theta \tag{6-47}$$

and

(y direction) $$\frac{W}{g}\frac{dv_y}{dt} = W - Kv^2 \sin\theta \tag{6-48}$$

where

v_x = horizontal component of velocity, ft/sec

v_y = vertical component of velocity, ft/sec

$v = \sqrt{v_x^2 + v_y^2}$ = resultant velocity, ft/sec

W = weight of paratrooper and equipment, lb

g = acceleration of gravity = 32.2 ft/sec^2

K = coefficient of aerodynamic resistance, lb-sec^2/ft^2

Noting that $\cos \theta = v_x/v$ and that $\sin \theta = v_y/v$, Eqs. 6-47 and 6-48 may be written in the form

$$\frac{W}{g} \frac{dv_x}{dt} = -Kvv_x \tag{6-49}$$

$$\frac{W}{g} \frac{dv_y}{dt} = W - Kvv_y \tag{6-50}$$

Substituting

$$v = \sqrt{v_x^2 + v_y^2}$$

in Eqs. 6-49 and 6-50, expressing the time-dependent variables in Newtonian notation, and rearranging algebraically, we obtain the equations of motion in a form convenient for solution by numerical integration. They are

$$(x \text{ direction}) \quad \ddot{x} = -\frac{Kg}{W} \sqrt{\dot{x}^2 + \dot{y}^2} \, \dot{x} \tag{6-51}$$

and

$$(y \text{ direction}) \quad \ddot{y} = g - \frac{Kg}{W} \sqrt{\dot{x}^2 + \dot{y}^2} \, \dot{y} \tag{6-52}$$

where

$\dot{x}$ = horizontal component of velocity, ft/sec

$\dot{y}$ = vertical component of velocity, ft/sec

K = coefficient of aerodynamic resistance, lb-sec^2/ft^2

g = acceleration of gravity, ft/sec^2

W = weight of paratrooper and equipment, lb

The coefficient of aerodynamic resistance K can be determined from the fact that the average terminal velocity reached by paratroopers falling with unopened parachutes has been found to be approximately 160 ft/sec at low altitudes. Applying the equation of equilibrium in the vertical direction to a body falling at terminal velocity gives

$$W = K(V_t)^2$$

or

$$K = \frac{W}{V_t^2} \tag{6-53}$$

where V_t is the terminal velocity, in feet per second, and W is the weight of the body. Substituting this expression for K into Eqs. 6-51 and 6-52, we obtain

$$\ddot{x} = \frac{g}{V_t^2} \sqrt{\dot{x}^2 + \dot{y}^2}\, \dot{y} \tag{6-54}$$

and

$$\ddot{y} = g - \frac{g}{V_t^2} \sqrt{\dot{x}^2 + \dot{y}^2}\, \dot{y} \tag{6-55}$$

With the origin of the x-y coordinate system located at the point of launch, as shown in Fig. 6-15, the initial conditions are

$$t = 0 \begin{vmatrix} x = 0 \\ \dot{x} = 440 \text{ ft/sec} \\ y = 0 \\ \dot{y} = 0 \end{vmatrix}$$

Figure 6-15 Trajectory of paratrooper

The objective of our analysis will be to determine (1) the data necessary to plot the x-t, y-t, $\dot{x}$-t, $\dot{y}$-t, and V-t curves for a paratrooper launched horizontally with a velocity of 300 mph and (2) the optimum time for opening the parachute after a period of free fall (the time when the velocity of the paratrooper is minimum).

In applying Euler's self-starting modified method to the simultaneous solution of Eqs. 6-54 and 6-55 for values of $\dot{x}$ and $\dot{y}$, the reader should realize that we are, in effect, solving the following two *first-order* differential equations

$$\dot{v}_x = -\frac{g}{V_t^2} \sqrt{v_x^2 + v_y^2}\, v_x \tag{6-56}$$

and

$$\dot{v}_y = g - \frac{g}{V_t^2} \sqrt{v_x^2 + v_y^2}\, v_y \tag{6-57}$$

for v_x and v_y, where the reduction was accomplished by the relations

$$v_x = \dot{x} \qquad v_y = \dot{y}$$
$$\dot{v}_x = \ddot{x} \qquad \dot{v}_y = \ddot{y}$$

However, in applying the predictor-corrector equations (Eq. 6-25), we will use the notation of Eqs. 6-54 and 6-55. After obtaining the desired values of $\dot{x}$ and $\dot{y}$ in each step, we will use these values with the trapezoid rule to solve the equations

$$\frac{dx}{dt} = \dot{x} \tag{6-58}$$

and

$$\frac{dy}{dt} = \dot{y} \tag{6-59}$$

to obtain values of the displacements x and y. Since x and y do not appear in explicit form in Eqs. 6-54 and 6-55, their solutions need not be obtained simultaneously with those of Eqs. 6-58 and 6-59. However, these equations will be solved simultaneously in the computer solution accompanying this example, to avoid the necessity of storing the calculated $\dot{x}$ and $\dot{y}$ values in memory for subsequent use in obtaining the desired x and y values.

The predictor-corrector equations, in a form applicable to the solution of Eqs. 6-54 and 6-55 for values of $\dot{x}$ and $\dot{y}$, are

$$P(\dot{x}_{i+1}) = \dot{x}_i + \ddot{x}_i(\Delta t) \qquad \text{(a)}$$

$$C(\dot{x}_{i+1}) = \dot{x}_i + \left[\frac{\ddot{x}_i + P(\ddot{x}_{i+1})}{2}\right]\Delta t \qquad \text{(b)}$$

$$P(\dot{y}_{i+1}) = \dot{y}_i + \ddot{y}_i(\Delta t) \qquad \text{(c)}$$

$$C(\dot{y}_{i+1}) = \dot{y}_i + \left[\frac{\ddot{y}_i + P(\ddot{y}_{i+1})}{2}\right]\Delta t \qquad \text{(d)}$$

$$(6\text{-}60)$$

The equations for solving the x and y values by the trapezoid rule are

$$x_{i+1} = x_i + \left(\frac{\dot{x}_i + \dot{x}_{i+1}}{2}\right)\Delta t$$

$$y_{i+1} = y_i + \left(\frac{\dot{y}_i + \dot{y}_{i+1}}{2}\right)\Delta t$$

$$(6\text{-}61)$$

The initial conditions supply us with values of x, y, $\dot{x}$, and $\dot{y}$ for $t = 0$, and we can determine values of $\ddot{x}$ and $\ddot{y}$ when $t = 0$ by substituting appropriate values in Eqs. 6-54 and 6-55. We next obtain predicted values of $\dot{x}_1$ and $\dot{y}_1$, using the predictor equations (Eq. 6-60a and c). In obtaining these predicted values, the true areas under the curves of $\ddot{x}$ and $\ddot{y}$ are approximated by the *rectangular crosshatched* areas shown in Fig. 6-16(a) and (d). The predicted values $P(\dot{x}_1)$ and $P(\dot{y}_1)$ are shown in Fig. 6-16(b) and (e). We next substitute $P(\dot{x}_1)$ and $P(\dot{y}_1)$ into Eqs. 6-54 and 6-55 to obtain approximate values of $\ddot{x}_1$ and $\ddot{y}_1$, which are shown as $P(\ddot{x}_1)$ and $P(\ddot{y}_1)$ in Fig. 6-16(a) and (d). Then, using the corrector equations (Eq. 6-60b and d), corrected values of $\dot{x}_1$ and $\dot{y}_1$ are obtained. These values, designated as $C(\dot{x}_1)$ and $C(\dot{y}_1)$, are shown in Fig. 6-16(b) and (e). The corrector equation approximates the true areas under the $\ddot{x}$ and $\ddot{y}$ curves by the *shaded trapezoidal* areas shown in Fig. 6-16(a) and (d). The corrected values of $\dot{x}_1$ and $\dot{y}_1$ are next substituted into Eqs. 6-54 and 6-55 to obtain improved values of $\ddot{x}_1$ and $\ddot{y}_1$ which are, in turn, used in Eq. 6-60b and d to obtain still better values of $\dot{x}_1$ and $\dot{y}_1$. The process continues until successive values of $\dot{x}_1$ and $\dot{y}_1$, respectively, vary by less than some preassigned epsilon value specifying the accuracy desired. At this point we proceed with the determination of the values of x_1 and y_1, using Eq. 6-61, which approximates the true area under the $\dot{x}$ and $\dot{y}$ curves by the crosshatched areas shown in Fig. 6-16(b) and (e).

In the computer program, shown later, the total velocity of the paratrooper is calculated at each step and compared with the velocity at the previous station to determine the lowest velocity calculated. As stated at the beginning of the problem, the time at which the lowest velocity is reached is considered the optimum parachute-opening time.

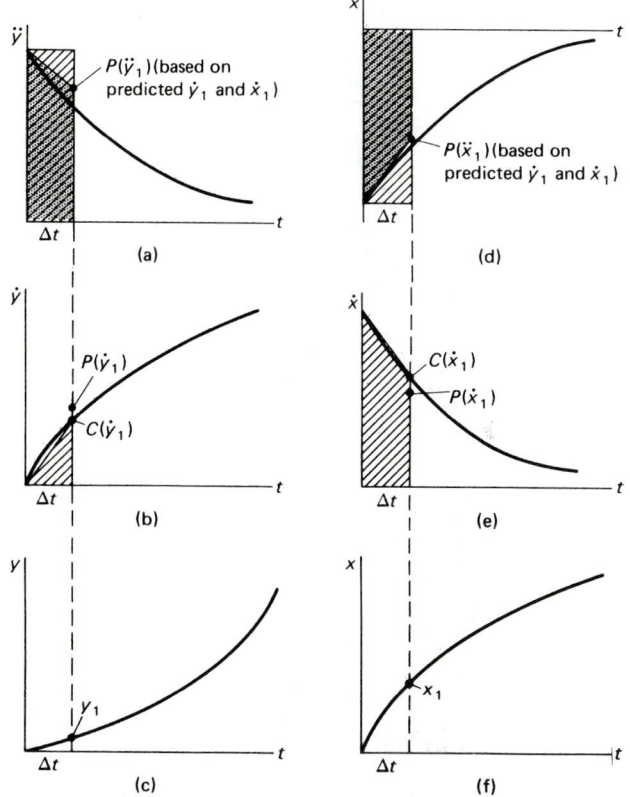

Figure 6-16 General shape of dynamic-characteristic curves for the paratrooper of Ex. 6-2

The flow chart is shown in Fig. 6-17. The variable names and the quantities which they represent in the FORTRAN program are as follows:

Variable Name	Quantity	Value Used in Problem
TERM	Terminal velocity, ft/sec	160
XD	Velocity in x direction $\dot{x}_i$, ft/sec	440 (initial)
DELT	Time increment Δt, sec	0.1
DTPR	Print increment Δt_{print}, sec	0.5
EPSI	Accuracy-check value, ft/sec	0.0001
TMAX	Maximum time value, sec	20
TPR	Time at which a print occurs, sec	
N	Integer variable used in program control	
T	Time, sec	
G	Acceleration of gravity, ft/sec^2	32.17
X	Displacement in x direction, ft	
Y	Displacement in y direction, ft	

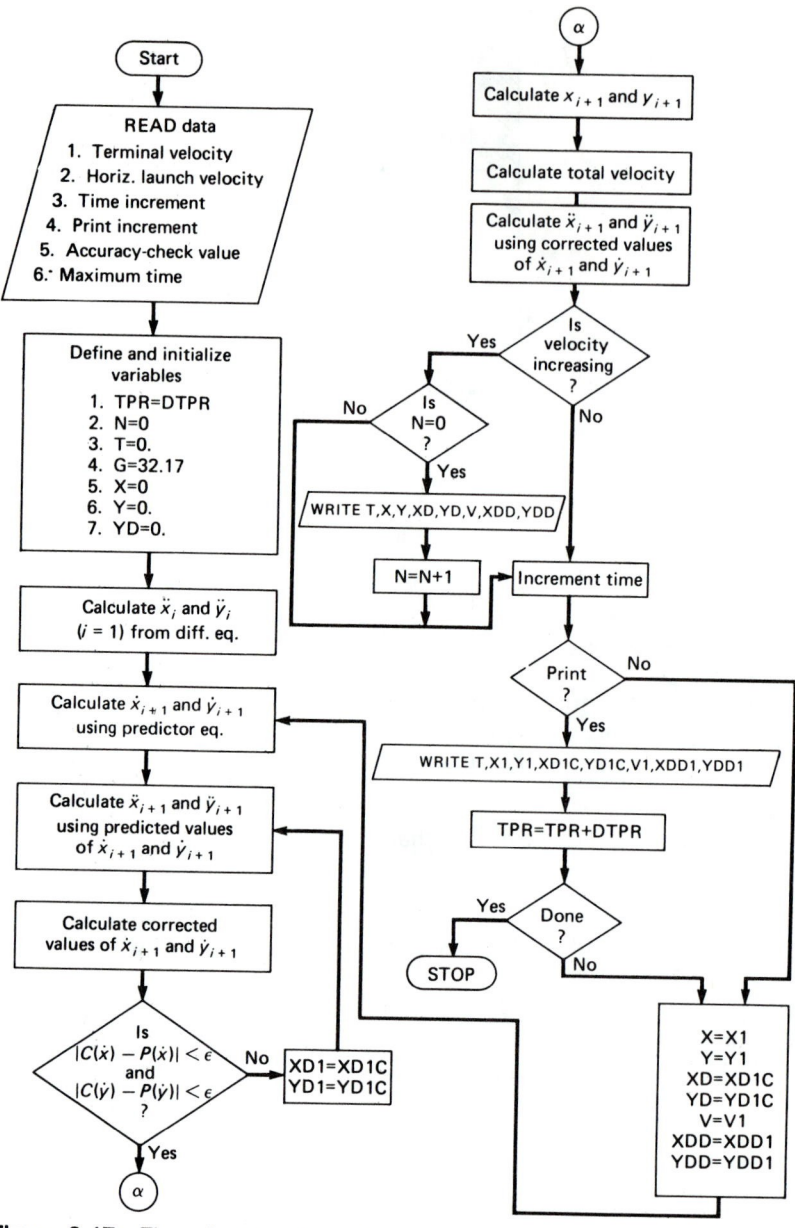

Figure 6-17 Flow chart for Ex. 6-2

Variable Name	Quantity	Value Used in Problem
YD	Vertical component of velocity, $\dot{y}_i$, ft/sec	
V	Total velocity, ft/sec	
XDD	Acceleration in x direction $\ddot{x}_i$, ft/sec^2	
YDD	Acceleration in y direction $\ddot{y}_i$, ft/sec^2	
XD1	Velocity in x direction one station ahead of t_i, $\dot{x}_{i+1}$, ft/sec	
YD1	Velocity in y direction one station ahead of t_i, $\dot{y}_{i+1}$, ft/sec	
V1	Total velocity one station ahead of t_i, ft/sec	
XDD1	Acceleration in x direction one station ahead of t_i, $\ddot{x}_{i+1}$, ft/sec^2	
YDD1	Acceleration in y direction one station ahead of t_i, $\ddot{y}_{i+1}$, ft/sec^2	
YD1C	Corrected value of y_{i+1}, ft/sec	
DIFXD	Difference in successive calculated values of $\dot{x}_{i+1}$ at a particular station, ft/sec	
DIFYD	Difference in successive calculated values of $\dot{y}_{i+1}$ at a particular station, ft/sec	
X1	Displacement in x direction one station ahead of t_i, x_{i+1}, ft	
Y1	Displacement in y direction one station ahead of t_i, y_{i+1}, ft	

The FORTRAN program follows.

```
C DYNAMIC CHARACTERISTICS OF FREE FALL OF A PARATROOPER
      READ(5,1) TERM,XD,DELT,DTPR,EPSI,TMAX
    1 FORMAT(6F10.0)
      WRITE(6,2) XD
    2 FORMAT('1','HORIZONTAL LAUNCH VELOCITY=',
                                    F7.2,' FT/SEC'//)
      WRITE(6,3)
    3 FORMAT(' ',2X,'T',6X,'X',7X,'Y',6X,'VX',6X,'VY',6X,'V'/)
      TPR=DTPR
      N=0
      T=0.
      G=32.17
      X=0.
      Y=0.
      YD=0.
      V=XD
      XDD=-G/TERM**2*V*XD
      YDD=G-G/TERM**2*V*YD
```

```
4 XD1 = XD + XDD*DELT
  YD1 = YD + YDD*DELT
5 V1 = SQRT(XD1**2 + YD1**2)
  XDD1 = -G/TERM**2*V1*XD1
  YDD1 = G-G/TERM**2*V1*YD1
  XD1C = XD + (XDD + XDD1)/2.*DELT
  YD1C = YD + (YDD + YDD1)/2.*DELT
  DIFXD = XD1C-XD1
  DIFYD = YD1C-YD1
  IF(ABS(DIFXD)-EPSI) 6,7,7
6 IF(ABS(DIFYD)-EPSI) 8,7,7
7 XD1 = XD1C
  YD1 = YD1C
  GO TO 5
8 X1 = X + (XD + XD1C)/2.*DELT
  Y1 = Y + (YD + YD1C)/2.*DELT
  V1 = SQRT(XD1C**2 + YD1C**2)
  XDD1 = -G/TERM**2*V1*XD1C
  YDD1 = G-G/TERM**2*V1*YD1C
  IF(V1-V) 12,12,9
9 IF(N) 12,10,12
10 WRITE(6,11) T,X,Y,XD,YD,V
11 FORMAT(' ',F4.1,4F8.1,F7.1)
  N = N+1
12 T = T+DELT
  IF(ABS(T-TPR)-.03) 13,13,16
13 WRITE(6,11) T,X1,Y1,XD1C,YD1C,V1
  TPR = TPR+DTPR
  IF(ABS(T-TMAX)-.03) 15,15,16
15 STOP
16 X = X1
  Y = Y1
  XD = XD1C
  YD = YD1C
  V = V1
  XDD = XDD1
  YDD = YDD1
  GO TO 4
  END
```

The results of the computer calculations are shown in the following print-out, where the column headings VX and VY denote the velocity components XD and YD, respectively.

```
HORIZONTAL LAUNCH VELOCITY = 440.00 FT/SEC
```

T	X	Y	VX	VY	V
0.5	194.3	3.7	344.6	14.3	344.9
1.0	350.3	14.0	283.1	26.4	284.3
1.5	480.5	29.9	240.1	37.3	242.9
2.0	592.2	51.1	208.1	47.3	213.4
2.5	689.8	77.2	183.3	56.8	191.9
3.0	776.3	107.9	163.3	65.8	176.1

T	X	Y	VX	VY	V
3.5	853.6	142.9	146.8	74.4	164.5
4.0	923.4	182.2	132.7	82.6	156.3
4.5	986.7	225.5	120.5	90.4	150.6
5.0	1044.2	272.5	109.8	97.7	146.9
5.5	1096.6	323.1	100.2	104.5	144.7
6.0	1144.5	376.9	91.5	110.8	143.7
6.4	1179.8	422.2	85.1	115.5	143.5
6.5	1188.2	433.8	83.6	116.6	143.5
7.0	1228.2	493.5	76.4	122.0	143.9
7.5	1264.7	555.7	69.8	126.8	144.7
8.0	1298.1	620.1	63.7	131.1	145.7
8.5	1328.5	686.7	58.1	134.9	146.9
9.0	1356.2	755.0	52.9	138.4	148.1
9.5	1381.5	825.0	48.2	141.4	149.4
10.0	1404.5	896.3	43.9	144.0	150.5
10.5	1425.4	968.9	39.9	146.3	151.6
11.0	1444.5	1042.6	36.3	148.3	152.7
11.5	1461.8	1117.2	32.9	150.0	153.6
12.0	1477.5	1192.6	29.9	151.5	154.4
12.5	1491.7	1268.6	27.1	152.8	155.2
13.0	1504.6	1345.3	24.6	153.9	155.9
13.5	1516.3	1422.5	22.3	154.8	156.4
14.0	1527.0	1500.1	20.2	155.6	156.9
14.5	1536.6	1578.1	18.3	156.3	157.4
15.0	1545.3	1656.4	16.6	156.9	157.8
15.5	1553.2	1735.0	15.0	157.4	158.1
16.0	1560.4	1813.8	13.6	157.8	158.4
16.5	1566.8	1892.8	12.3	158.2	158.6
17.0	1572.7	1972.0	11.1	158.4	158.8
17.5	1578.0	2051.2	10.1	158.7	159.0
18.0	1582.8	2130.6	9.1	158.9	159.2
18.5	1587.1	2210.1	8.3	159.1	159.3
19.0	1591.0	2289.7	7.5	159.2	159.4
19.5	1594.6	2369.4	6.8	159.4	159.5
20.0	1597.8	2449.1	6.1	159.5	159.6

The computer results show that a minimum velocity of 143.5 ft/sec is reached when $t = 6.4$ sec, which indicates the optimum time to open the parachute. The velocity data are plotted in Fig. 6-18.

6-5 RUNGE-KUTTA METHODS

A Runge-Kutta method is one which employs a recurrence formula of the form

$$y_{i+1} = y_i + a_1 k_1 + a_2 k_2 + a_3 k_3 + \cdots + a_n k_n \tag{6-62}$$

to calculate successive values of the dependent variable y of the differential equation

$$\frac{dy}{dx} = y' = f(x, y) \tag{6-63}$$

Figure 6-18 Total velocity of paratrooper

where

$$k_1 = (h)f(x_i, y_i)$$

$$k_2 = (h)f(x_i + p_1 h, y_i + q_{11}k_1) \tag{6-64}$$

$$k_3 = (h)f(x_i + p_2 h, y_i + q_{21}k_1 + q_{22}k_2)$$

$$\dotfill$$

$$k_n = (h)f(x_i + p_{n-1}h, y_i + q_{n-1,1}k_1 + q_{n-1,2}k_2 + \cdots + q_{n-1,n-1}k_{n-1})$$

The above Runge-Kutta equations can be written more compactly as

$$y_{i+1} = y_i + \sum_{j=1}^{n} a_j k_j \tag{6-65}$$

where

$$k_j = hf(x_i + p_{j-1}h, y_i + \sum_{l=1}^{j-1} q_{j-1,l}k_l) \qquad (j = 1, 2, \dots, n) \tag{6-66}$$

in which, by definition,

$$p_0 = 0 \quad \text{and} \quad \sum_{l=1}^{j-1} q_{j-1,l} k_l = 0 \quad \text{for} \quad j = 1$$

The a's, p's, and q's must assume values such that Eq. 6-62 accurately yields successive values of y. As will be shown later, these values are determined by making Eq. 6-62 equivalent to a certain specified number of terms of a Taylor-series expansion of y about x_i.

If we let m be the order of the Runge-Kutta method, with n the number of function evaluations per step (number of k values), there is a particular maximum value of m for each n. For n values up to 7, we have

$$1 \leq n \leq 4, \; m_{\text{max}} = n$$

$$n = 5, \; m_{\text{max}} = 4$$

$$n = 6, \; m_{\text{max}} = 5$$

$$n = 7, \; m_{\text{max}} = 6$$

Various Runge-Kutta methods are classified as (m, n) methods. A $(5, 6)$ method, for example, would be a fifth-order method requiring six function evaluations per step.

Runge-Kutta methods are called *single-step* methods, since they require only knowledge of y_i to determine y_{i+1}. Thus these methods are *self-starting*. It is theoretically possible to develop methods of any order, but the developments get increasingly complex with increasing order. Runge-Kutta methods were among the earliest methods employed in the numerical solution of differential equations, and they are still widely used. As with any method, they possess certain advantages and disadvantages which must be weighed in considering their suitability for a particular application. The principal advantage of the Runge-Kutta methods is their self-starting feature and consequent ease of programming. One disadvantage is the requirement that the function $f(x, y)$ must be evaluated for several slightly different values of x and y in every step of the solution (in every incrementation of x by h). This repeated determination of $f(x, y)$ may result in a less efficient method with respect to computing time than other methods of comparable accuracy in which previously determined values of the dependent variable are used in subsequent steps. Methods of the latter type mentioned are called multiple-step methods, and Hamming's and Milne's methods are examples of such. They are discussed later in this chapter. Another disadvantage of Runge-Kutta methods is that it is more difficult to estimate the per-step error for higher order solutions than for solutions obtained by some of the multiple-step methods.

Before illustrating the general procedure for developing a Runge-Kutta method, let us review (1) the definition of a *total differential* and (2) the expansion of a function of two variables in a *Taylor series*, since both will be pertinent to the development.

1. If $y' = f(x, y)$, the total differential dy' is

$$dy' = \frac{\partial f}{\partial x} dx + \frac{\partial f}{\partial y} dy$$

Upon dividing by dx, we obtain

$$\frac{dy'}{dx} = \frac{\partial f}{\partial x} + \frac{\partial f}{\partial y} \frac{dy}{dx} \tag{6-67}$$

Differentiating again with respect to x yields

$$\frac{d^2 y'}{dx^2} = \frac{\partial[(\partial f/\partial x) + (\partial f/\partial y)(dy/dx)]}{\partial x} + \frac{\partial[(\partial f/\partial x) + (\partial f/\partial y)(dy/dx)]}{\partial y} \left(\frac{dy}{dx}\right) \tag{6-68}$$

Higher derivatives of y' may be determined in a similar manner.

2. Consider some general function of two variables such as $z = f(x, y)$. Such a function may be expanded about a point x_i, y_i in a Taylor series for functions of two variables, as follows:

$$z(x_i + l, y_i + j) = f(x_i, y_i) + l\left[\frac{\partial f}{\partial x}(x_i, y_i)\right] + j\left[\frac{\partial f}{\partial y}(x_i, y_i)\right]$$
$$+ \frac{1}{2!}\left\{l^2\left[\frac{\partial^2 f}{\partial x^2}(x_i, y_i)\right] + 2lj\left[\frac{\partial^2 f}{\partial x \partial y}(x_i, y_i)\right] + j^2\left[\frac{\partial^2 f}{\partial y^2}(x_i, y_i)\right]\right\} + \cdots \tag{6-69}$$

where l and j are increments of x and y, respectively.

We are now ready to proceed with the development of a *second-order* Runge-Kutta method ($n = 2$ in Eq. 6-62). Equation 6-62 becomes

$$y_{i+1} = y_i + a_1 k_1 + a_2 k_2 \tag{6-70}$$

in which

$$\left.\begin{array}{l} k_1 = (h)f(x_i, y_i) \\ k_2 = (h)f(x_i + p_1 h, y_i + q_{11}k_1) \end{array}\right\} \tag{6-71}$$

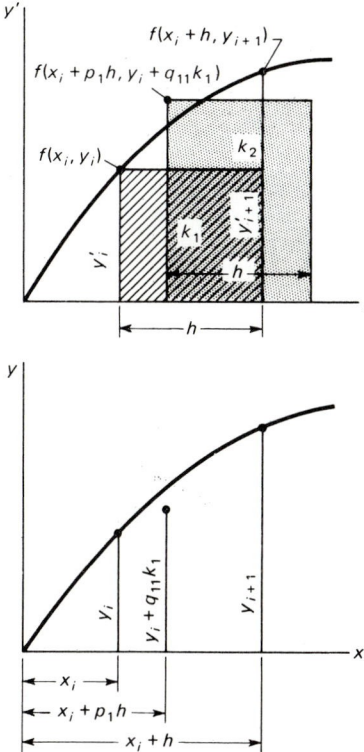

Figure 6-19 Graphical interpretation of k functions

Our problem is to determine values for a_1, a_2, p_1, and q_{11}, so that Eq. 6-70 yields an accurate value of y_{i+1}. A graphical interpretation of the k functions is illustrated in Fig. 6-19. The crosshatched area represents k_1, and k_2 is represented by the shaded area. (There would be similar rectangular areas for each k function of Eq. 6-62 for higher order Runge-Kutta equations.) For the second-order method being discussed, Eq. 6-62 could be written as

$$y_{i+1} = y_i + a_1 \text{ (crosshatched area)} + a_2 \text{ (shaded area)}$$

It should be evident that the size of the shaded area representing k_2 depends upon the values determined for p_1 and q_{11}.

We shall determine values for a_1, a_2, p_1, and q_{11} by making Eq. 6-70 equivalent to a truncated Taylor-series expansion of y about x_i. As the first step, let us expand y_{i+1} about x_i. We obtain

$$y_{i+1} = y_i + hy_i' + \frac{h^2}{2!} y_i'' + \cdots \tag{6-72}$$

Remembering that the given differential equation is $y' = f(x, y)$, we write

$$y_i' = f(x_i, y_i) \tag{6-73}$$

From Eq. 6-67 it can be seen that

$$y_i'' = \frac{\partial f}{\partial x}(x_i, y_i) + \left[\frac{\partial f}{\partial y}(x_i, y_i)\right]\left[f(x_i, y_i)\right] \tag{6-74}$$

Substituting Eqs. 6-73 and 6-74 into Eq. 6-72, we obtain the expansion in the following form:

$$y_{i+1} = y_i + (h)f(x_i, y_i)$$
$$+ \frac{h^2}{2!}\left\{\frac{\partial f}{\partial x}(x_i, y_i) + \left[\frac{\partial f}{\partial y}(x_i, y_i)\right]\left[f(x_i, y_i)\right]\right\} + \frac{h^3}{3!}\left\{\cdots\right\} + \cdots \tag{6-75}$$

Looking at Eqs. 6-70, 6-71, and 6-75, we see that k_2 must be expressed in terms of $f(x_i, y_i)$, $\partial f/\partial x(x_i, y_i)$, and $\partial f/\partial y(x_i, y_i)$ if Eqs. 6-70 and 6-75 are to contain similar terms. This can be accomplished by expanding k_2 in a Taylor series for functions of two variables about x_i, y_i. Using the first three terms of Eq. 6-69 and realizing that $l = p_1 h$ and $j = q_{11}k_1$ (see Eq. 6-71), we may write

$$k_2 = h\left\{f(x_i, y_i) + p_1h\left[\frac{\partial f}{\partial x}(x_i, y_i)\right] + q_{11}k_1\left[\frac{\partial f}{\partial y}(x_i, y_i)\right]\right\} \tag{6-76}$$

Substituting the first of Eq. 6-71 and Eq. 6-76 into Eq. 6-70, we obtain

$$y_{i+1} = y_i + a_1(h)f(x_i, y_i) + a_2(h)f(x_i, y_i)$$
$$+ a_2h^2\left\{p_1\frac{\partial f}{\partial x}(x_i, y_i) + q_{11}\left[\frac{\partial f}{\partial y}(x_i, y_i)\right]\left[f(x_i, y_i)\right]\right\} \tag{6-77}$$

Equating coefficients of similar terms in Eqs. 6-75 and 6-77, we obtain the following three independent equations:

$$a_1 + a_2 = 1$$
$$a_2p_1 = \tfrac{1}{2} \tag{6-78}$$
$$a_2q_{11} = \tfrac{1}{2}$$

which contain four unknowns. By arbitrarily assigning a value to one unknown and then solving for the other three, we can obtain as many different sets of values as we desire and, in turn, as many different sets of Eqs. 6-70 and 6-71 as desired.

A solution obtained by the use of Eq. 6-70 in a step-by-step integration will have a per-step truncation error of order h^3, since terms containing h^3 and higher powers of h were neglected in the development. Thus, this is known as a *second-order* Runge-Kutta method.

If a particular second-order method is defined by letting $a_1 = \frac{1}{2}$ in Eq. 6-78, then

$$a_2 = \tfrac{1}{2}$$

$$p_1 = 1$$

$$q_{11} = 1$$

Equations 6-70 and 6-71 then become

$$y_{i+1} = y_i + \tfrac{1}{2}(k_1 + k_2) \qquad \text{(a)}$$

with

$$\left. \begin{array}{l} k_1 = (h)f(x_i,\, y_i) \\ k_2 = (h)f(x_i + h,\, y_i + k_1) \end{array} \right\} \qquad \text{(b)}$$

$$(6\text{-}79)$$

This set of equations may be used to solve first-order differential equations with an accuracy comparable to that of Euler's modified methods. In fact, if Eq. 6-79b is substituted into Eq. 6-79a, the resulting equation

$$y_{i+1} = y_i + \tfrac{1}{2}\{(h)f(x_i,\, y_i) + (h)f[x_i + h,\, y_i + (h)f(x_i,\, y_i)]\} \qquad (6\text{-}80)$$

is exactly equivalent to Euler's self-starting modified method with the iteration at each step omitted. This may be verified by examining the graphical representation of the equation in Fig. 6-20.

Because the second-order Runge-Kutta method has only the order of accuracy of Euler's modified methods, let us consider Runge-Kutta methods with higher orders of accuracy. Since the development of such methods rapidly increases in complexity with an increase in accuracy, and since the general procedure has just been demonstrated for a second-order method, the developments will not be given for higher orders. For example, in developing a third-order method, all Taylor-series terms containing h^3 must be retained; in developing a fourth-order method, all h^4 terms must be retained, and so forth.

If $n = 3$, in Eq. 6-62, and a procedure similar to the one previously outlined is followed, the equating of coefficients of terms containing h, h^2, and h^3 will yield a set of equations with six constraints on the parameters. With eight parameters involved, two of them can be assigned values arbitrarily. With a particular choice of values for two such parameters, the following *third-order* (3,3) Runge-Kutta formula can be obtained:

$$y_{i+1} = y_i + \tfrac{1}{6}(k_1 + 4k_2 + k_3) \qquad (6\text{-}81)$$

in which

Figure 6-20 Graphical representation of a second order Runge-Kutta method

$$
\left.
\begin{aligned}
k_1 &= (h)f(x_i,\, y_i) \\[4pt]
k_2 &= (h)f\!\left(x_i + \frac{h}{2},\, y_i + \frac{k_1}{2} \right) \\[4pt]
k_3 &= (h)f(x_i + h,\, y_i - k_1 + 2k_2)
\end{aligned}
\right\}
\qquad (6\text{-}82)
$$

Since terms containing h^4 are neglected, the error is said to be of order h^4.

A well-known fourth-order (4, 4) Runge-Kutta method, often referred to as the *classic* form, resulting from taking n equal to 4 in Eq. 6-62, equating terms through and including those containing h^4, and selecting a particular set of two arbitrary parameter values, is expressed as follows:[3]

$$
y_{i+1} = y_i + \tfrac{1}{6}(k_1 + 2k_2 + 2k_3 + k_4) \qquad (6\text{-}83)
$$

in which

$$
\left.
\begin{aligned}
k_1 &= (h)f(x_i,\, y_i) \\[6pt]
k_2 &= (h)f\!\left(x_i + \frac{h}{2},\, y_i + \frac{k_1}{2} \right) \\[6pt]
k_3 &= (h)f\!\left(x_i + \frac{h}{2},\, y_i + \frac{k_2}{2} \right) \\[6pt]
k_4 &= (h)f(x_i + h,\, y_i + k_3)
\end{aligned}
\right\}
\qquad (6\text{-}84)
$$

[3]The interested reader will find a complete derivation in *Mathematical Methods for Digital Computers*, eds. Anthony Ralston and Herbert S. Wilf (New York: John Wiley & Sons, Inc., 1960).

In this method the per-step error is of order h^5.

Another fourth-order (4, 4) method known as the Gil form,[4] which minimizes roundoff error, is

$$y_{i+1} = y_i + \tfrac{1}{6}[k_1 + (2 - \sqrt{2})k_2 + (2 + \sqrt{2})k_3 + k_4] \tag{6-85}$$

where

$$k_1 = (h)f(x_i, y_i)$$

$$k_2 = (h)f\left(x_i + \frac{h}{2}, y_i + \frac{k_1}{2}\right)$$

$$k_3 = (h)f\left[x_i + \frac{h}{2}, y_i + (\sqrt{2} - 1)\frac{k_1}{2} + (2 - \sqrt{2})\frac{k_2}{2}\right] \tag{6-86}$$

$$k_4 = (h)f\left[x_i + h, y_i - \sqrt{2}\frac{k_2}{2} + \left(1 + \frac{\sqrt{2}}{2}\right)k_3\right]$$

When the order of the method is 3 or 4, there are two arbitrary parameters to be chosen in the derivation of the various Runge-Kutta forms. When the order is 5 or more ($m = 5$), there are five or more arbitrary parameters, leading to a very large number of different forms. Fifth-order methods have been found by numerical experiments to generally be highly desirable where quite high accuracy is required. A (5, 6) method by Butcher[5] has been found to be particularly desirable. The equations of this method are

$$y_{i+1} = y_i + \tfrac{1}{90}(7k_1 + 32k_3 + 12k_4 + 32k_5 + 7k_6) \tag{6-87}$$

where

$$k_1 = (h)f(x_i, y_i)$$

$$k_2 = (h)f\left(x_i + \frac{h}{4}, y_i + \frac{k_1}{4}\right)$$

$$k_3 = (h)f\left(x_i + \frac{h}{4}, y_i + \frac{k_1}{8} + \frac{k_2}{8}\right)$$

$$k_4 = (h)f\left(x_i + \frac{h}{2}, y_i - \frac{k_2}{2} + k_3\right) \tag{6-88}$$

$$k_5 = (h)f(x_i + \tfrac{3}{4}h, y_i + \tfrac{3}{16}k_1 + \tfrac{9}{16}k_4)$$

$$k_6 = (h)f(x_i + h, y_i - \tfrac{3}{7}k_1 + \tfrac{2}{7}k_2 + \tfrac{12}{7}k_3 - \tfrac{12}{7}k_4 + \tfrac{8}{7}k_5)$$

---

[4] S. Gil, "A Process for the Step-by-Step Integration of Differential Equations in an Automatic Digital Computing Machine," *Proc. Cambridge Philos. Soc.*, Vol. 47 (1951), pp. 96–108.

[5] J. C. Butcher, "On Runge-Kutta Processes of Higher Order," *J. Australian Math. Soc.*, Vol. 4 (1964), p. 179.

Numerical experiments by Waters[6] led to the conclusion that the above method was "best" of many methods tried on a system of 64 first-order differential equations in terms of accuracy and minimum computing time. The authors have found similar favorable results for this Butcher (5, 6) method in applying various fourth-, fifth-, and sixth-order methods to the orbit problem given at the end of this chapter (Prob. 6-34).

Error Analysis of Runge-Kutta Methods

One of the disadvantages of the higher order Runge-Kutta methods mentioned earlier is the difficulty encountered in estimating the per-step truncation error. An expression for the approximate per-step truncation error is given by Romonelli, but it is difficult to apply.[7] Richardson's method is, perhaps, the most practical one available. Richardson's expression for the fourth-order Runge-Kutta method (Eq. 6-31 with $r = 4$) is

$$E_T \cong \frac{y^{(2)} - y^{(1)}}{15} \tag{6-89}$$

Collatz has suggested that, in using the fourth-order method, the step size used may be based upon the relationship

$$\left| \frac{k_2 - k_3}{k_1 - k_2} \right|$$

where the expressions for the k's are as given by Eq. 6-84.[8] When this quantity exceeds a few hundredths, the step size should be decreased accordingly.

The engineer who is unfamiliar with the intricacies of error analysis will find that a practical method of ensuring the use of a suitable step size in a Runge-Kutta method is to run several trial solutions, with different step sizes in each one, until consecutive solutions are obtained in which the results are in good agreement throughout. (This procedure was discussed in Sec. 6-3 in regard to the error analysis of Euler's method.)

Having discussed the general method of developing Runge-Kutta formulas and having shown several specific different-order Runge-Kutta equations, let us illustrate the use of the classic third-order method in solving a first-order differential equation.

[6]J. Waters, "Methods of Numerical Integration Applied to a System Having Trivial Function Evaluations," *Commun. Ass. Comp. Mach.*, Vol. 9 (1966), p. 293.

[7]Anthony Ralston and Herbert S. Wilf, eds., *Mathematical Methods for Digital Computers* (New York: John Wiley & Sons, Inc., 1960), p. 116.

[8]L. Collatz, *Numerische Behandlung von Differentialgleichungen* (Berlin: Springer-Verlag, 1950), p. 34.

EXAMPLE 6-3

The circuit shown in Fig. 6-21 contains a source of emf, an inductance, and a resistor, the magnitude of the latter varying with its temperature. Since the temperature of the resistor increases with increasing current in the circuit, the resistance is a function of the current. In the range of current flow i for this problem, the resistance can be expressed as $R = a + bi^2$. Switch S is closed at time $t = 0$, and the current flow is desired as a function of time for $t > 0$.

Applying Kirchhoff's voltage law (the algebraic sum of all voltage changes around a closed circuit is equal to zero) to the circuit loop, the following differential equation is obtained:

$$E - L\frac{di}{dt} - (a + bi^2)i = 0 \qquad (6\text{-}90)$$

Equation 6-90 may be rearranged algebraically so that

$$\frac{di}{dt} = \frac{E}{L} - \frac{b}{L}i^3 - \frac{a}{L}i \qquad (\text{when } t = 0,\ i = 0) \qquad (6\text{-}91)$$

Let us now write a FORTRAN program for determining $i(t)$, using Eqs. 6-81 and 6-82. The program will be kept general, so that various parameter values may be used for investigating different circuit combinations. We will assume that the parameter values for this particular example are

E = 200 volts
L = 3 henries
a = 100 ohms
b = 50 ohms/amp^2

The FORTRAN names used and the quantities which they represent are as follows:

$R = a + bi^2$

Figure 6-21   Circuit diagram for Ex. 6-3

FORTRAN Name	Quantity	Numerical Values Used as Data
AMP	Current, amps	Initially zero
A	Constant part of resistance, ohms	100
B	Coefficient of i^2 in resistance expression, ohms/amp^2	50
HENRY	Inductance, henries	3
E	Emf, volts	200
C	B/henry	
D	A/henry	
AK1, AK2, AK3	k_1, k_2, and k_3 [9]	
T	Time, sec	
TPR	Print time, sec	
DELT	Increment of time, sec	0.001
DTPR	Increment of print time, sec	0.002
TMAX	Maximum time, sec	0.05
DIDT	Statement function name for di/dt of Eq. 6-91, with AMP being the argument	

The flow chart for the problem is shown in Fig. 6-22. The FORTRAN IV program, written from the outline provided by the flow chart, is as follows:

```
  DIDT(AMP)=E/HENRY-C*AMP**3-D*AMP
  WRITE(6,1)
1 FORMAT(1H1,'CURRENT IN A RESISTANCE-INDUCTANCE CIRCUIT'//)
  WRITE(6,2)
2 FORMAT(11X,'TIME',11X,'CURRENT'//)
  READ(5,3)T,DELT,DTPR,AMP,E,HENRY,A,B,TMAX
3 FORMAT(9F8.0)
  TPR=DTPR
  C=B/HENRY
  D=A/HENRY
4 AK1=DELT*DIDT(AMP)
  AK2=DELT*DIDT(AMP+AK1/2.)
  AK3=DELT*DIDT(AMP-AK1+2.*AK2)
  AMP=AMP+(AK1+4.*AK2+AK3)/6.
  T=T+DELT
  IF(ABS(T-TPR)-.0001)5,5,4
5 WRITE(6,6)T,AMP
6 FORMAT(1H ,10X,F5.3,12X,F6.4)
  TPR=TPR+DTPR
  IF(ABS(T-TMAX)-.0001)7,7,4
7 STOP
  END
```

The data output obtained from the computer solution is

[9]Since the independent variable t does not appear explicitly in Eq. 6-91, it is not necessary to provide incremented values of time to calculate k values within each step.

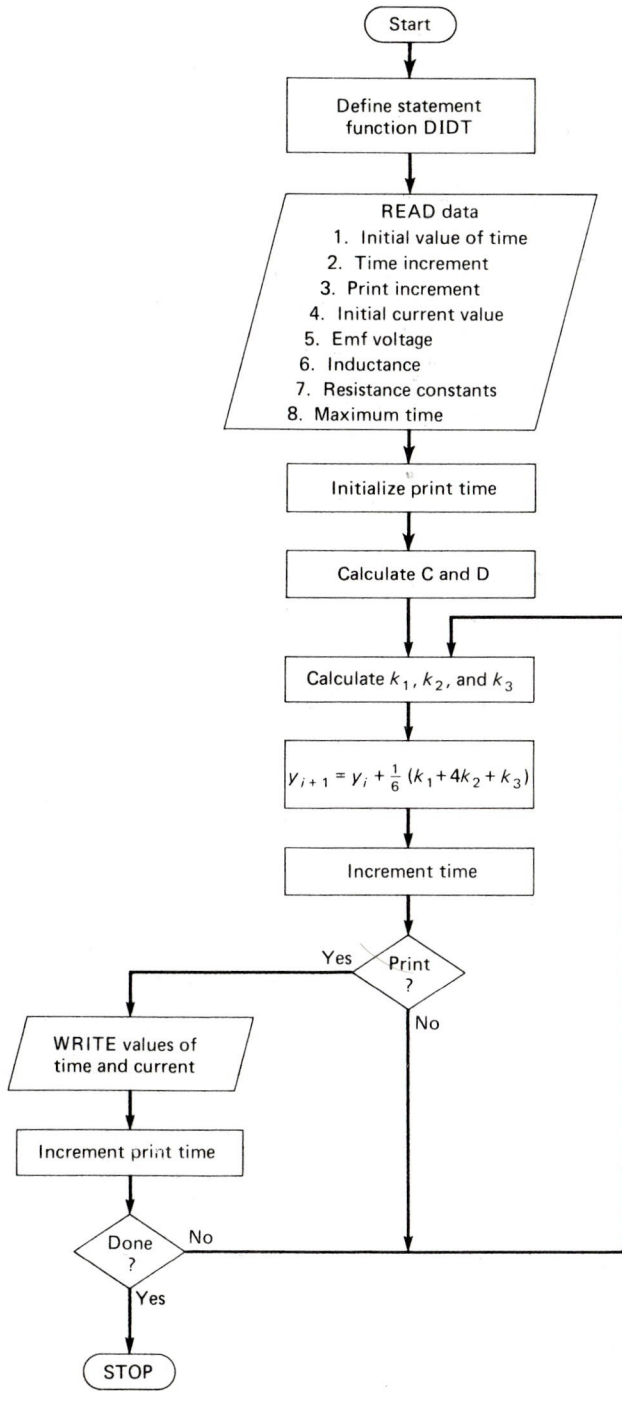

Figure 6-22 Flow chart for Ex. 6-3

CURRENT IN A RESISTANCE–INDUCTANCE CIRCUIT

TIME	CURRENT
0.002	0.1290
0.004	0.2494
0.006	0.3613
0.008	0.4647
0.010	0.5593
0.012	0.6451
0.014	0.7221
0.016	0.7905
0.018	0.8506
0.020	0.9029
0.022	0.9480
0.024	0.9866
0.026	1.0193
0.028	1.0470
0.030	1.0701
0.032	1.0894
0.034	1.1055
0.036	1.1188
0.038	1.1298
0.040	1.1388
0.042	1.1462
0.044	1.1523
0.046	1.1573
0.048	1.1614
0.050	1.1647

The data are represented graphically by the curve of Fig. 6-23, illustrating the current buildup in the circuit with time.

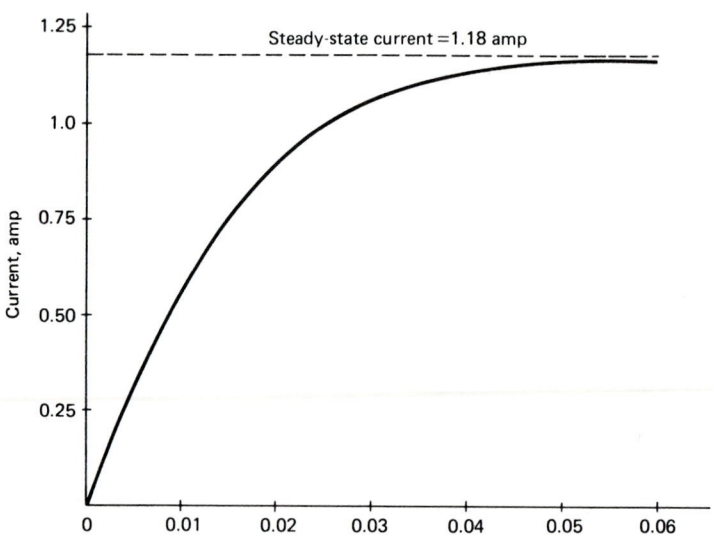

Figure 6-23 Graphical display of data for Ex. 6-3

6-6 SOLUTION OF SIMULTANEOUS ORDINARY DIFFERENTIAL EQUATIONS BY RUNGE-KUTTA METHODS

It is frequently necessary to solve sets of simultaneous first-order differential equations in analyzing engineering systems. Such equations occur quite frequently in obtaining solutions of higher order differential equations which are transformed to sets of first-order differential equations as part of the solution process. Runge-Kutta methods are well suited for the solution of such equations, and their application will be discussed here.

Let us first consider the solution of two simultaneous first-order differential equations of the form

$$\frac{dy}{dx} = f[x, y(x), u(x)]$$

$$\frac{du}{dx} = F[x, y(x), u(x)]$$

(6-92)

where the initial values ($y = y_0$, $u = u_0$, when $x = x_0$) are known. Runge-Kutta formulas can be used to solve Eq. 6-92. Using the classic fourth-order method already described (Eqs. 6-83 and 6-84), for example, the following *sets* of equations would be used:

$$y_{i+1} = y_i + \tfrac{1}{6}(k_1 + 2k_2 + 2k_3 + k_4)$$

(6-93)

where

$$k_1 = (h)f(x_i, y_i, u_i)$$

$$k_2 = (h)f\left(x_i + \frac{h}{2}, y_i + \frac{k_1}{2}, u_i + \frac{q_1}{2}\right)$$

$$k_3 = (h)f\left(x_i + \frac{h}{2}, y_i + \frac{k_2}{2}, u_i + \frac{q_2}{2}\right)$$

$$k_4 = (h)f(x_i + h, y_i + k_3, u_i + q_3)$$

(6-94)

and

$$u_{i+1} = u_i + \tfrac{1}{6}(q_1 + 2q_2 + 2q_3 + q_4)$$

(6-95)

where

$$q_1 = (h)F(x_i, y_i, u_i)$$

$$q_2 = (h)F\left(x_i + \frac{h}{2}, y_i + \frac{k_1}{2}, u_i + \frac{q_1}{2}\right)$$

$$q_3 = (h)F\left(x_i + \frac{h}{2}, y_i + \frac{k_2}{2}, u_i + \frac{q_2}{2}\right)$$

$$q_4 = (h)F(x_i + h, y_i + k_3, u_i + q_3)$$

(6-96)

Note that in the expressions for the k's and q's, y_i is incremented by a parameter times a k value, since k's are used in the recurrence formula for y values. Also, u_i is incremented by a parameter times a q value, since q's are used in the recurrence formula for u values. Also note that function $f(x, y, u)$ is used for calculating k values, since it is equal to dy/dx, and k's are used in the recurrence formula for y. The function $F(x, y, u)$ is used for calculating q values, since it is equal to du/dx, and q's are used in the recurrence formula for u values. This same general pattern holds for any number of simultaneous equations.

The solution of Eq. 6-92 begins by substituting the initial values of y and u, which must be known, into the given differential equations to obtain initial values of the functions f and F. Values of k_1 and q_1 are next obtained by multiplying the initial values of f and F, respectively, by h, as indicated in Eqs. 6-94 and 6-96 where $h = \Delta x$, the step increment. With values of k_1 and q_1 known, k_2 and q_2 are next evaluated, then k_3 and q_3, and finally k_4 and q_4. Then the recurrence formulas (Eqs. 6-93 and 6-95) are used to obtain values of y and u at $x = x_i + h$ (y_{i+1} and u_{i+1}). These new values of y and u are then used as beginning values in starting the procedure (just described) over again, to obtain values of y_{i+2} and u_{i+2} at $x = x_i + 2h$, and so on, until the desired range of integration has been covered.

Any number of simultaneous first-order differential equations may be solved by merely using a set of equations such as those shown for each dependent variable appearing in the set of simultaneous differential equations.

An nth-order differential equation can be solved by transforming the equation to a set of n simultaneous first-order differential equations and applying n Runge-Kutta formulas, as discussed in the preceding paragraphs. The procedure can be simplified by combining equations, as will be shown in the following paragraphs.

Consider the second-order differential equation

$$\frac{d^2x}{dt^2} = f\left(t, x, \frac{dx}{dt}\right) \tag{6-97}$$

Letting $v = dx/dt$, Eq. 6-97 can be transformed to the two first-order differential equations

$$\left. \begin{aligned} \frac{dv}{dt} &= f(t, x, v) \\[2ex] \frac{dx}{dt} &= v \end{aligned} \right\} \tag{6-98}$$

Referring to Eqs. 6-93 through 6-96, the following two fourth-order Runge-Kutta formulas could be used to solve Eq. 6-98:

$$v_{i+1} = v_i + \tfrac{1}{6}(k_1 + 2k_2 + 2k_3 + k_4) \tag{6-99}$$

where

$$k_1 = (h)f(t_i, x_i, v_i)$$

$$k_2 = (h)f\left(t_i + \frac{h}{2}, x_i + \frac{q_1}{2}, v_i + \frac{k_1}{2}\right)$$

$$k_3 = (h)f\left(t_i + \frac{h}{2}, x_i + \frac{q_2}{2}, v_i + \frac{k_2}{2}\right)$$

$$k_4 = (h)f(t_i + h, x_i + q_3, v_i + k_3)$$

(6-100)

and

$$x_{i+1} = x_i + \tfrac{1}{6}(q_1 + 2q_2 + 2q_3 + q_4)$$

(6-101)

where

$$q_1 = hF(v_i) = h(v_i)$$

$$q_2 = hF\left(v_i + \frac{k_1}{2}\right) = h\left(v_i + \frac{k_1}{2}\right)$$

$$q_3 = hF\left(v_i + \frac{k_2}{2}\right) = h\left(v_i + \frac{k_2}{2}\right)$$

$$q_4 = hF(v_i + k_3) = h(v_i + k_3)$$

(6-102)

However, we may obtain a more compact set of equations by substituting the expressions for the q's into both the expressions for the k's and the recurrence formula of Eq. 6-101. Performing these substitutions yields

$$x_{i+1} = x_i + hv_i + \frac{h}{6}(k_1 + k_2 + k_3)$$

$$v_{i+1} = v_i + \tfrac{1}{6}(k_1 + 2k_2 + 2k_3 + k_4)$$

(6-103)

where

$$k_1 = (h)f(t_i, x_i, v_i)$$

$$k_2 = (h)f\left[t_i + \frac{h}{2}, x_i + \frac{h}{2}v_i, v_i + \frac{k_1}{2}\right]$$

$$k_3 = (h)f\left[t_i + \frac{h}{2}, x_i + \frac{h}{2}v_i + \frac{h}{4}k_1, v_i + \frac{k_2}{2}\right]$$

$$k_4 = (h)f\left[t_i + h, x_i + hv_i + \frac{h}{2}k_2, v_i + k_3\right]$$

(6-104)

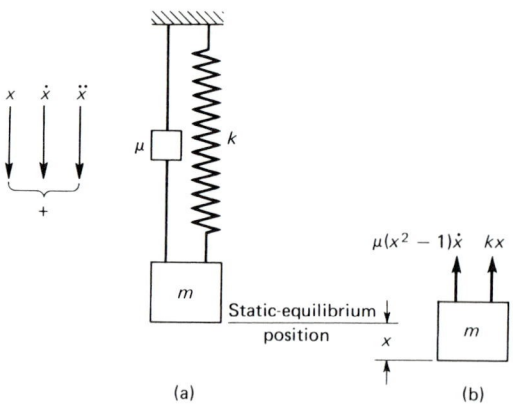

Figure 6-24 System of Ex. 6-4

EXAMPLE 6-4

To illustrate the application of Eqs. 6-103 and 6-104 in solving a second-order differential equation, consider the vibrating system shown in Fig. 6-24(a). A unit mass is attached to a spring having a spring constant of 1 lb/ft, and also to a damping device that exerts a force on the mass which depends upon both the displacement and the velocity of the mass. The damping force may be expressed mathematically as

$$F_d = \mu(x^2 - 1)\dot{x} \tag{6-105}$$

where μ is a damping coefficient. It is desired to obtain x-t and $\dot{x}$-t curves for studying the displacement and velocity characteristics of the system.

A free-body diagram of the mass is shown in Fig. 6-24(b). The gravity force acting on such a system is customarily not shown on the free body, since the amplitude of vibration x is measured from the static-equilibrium position of the mass, in which position the gravity force is equal to the spring force, and these forces cancel from the resulting differential equation.

Noting the positive direction assumed for x, $\dot{x}$, and $\ddot{x}$, as shown in the figure, and the positive displacement used in determining the free-body diagram, the application of Newton's second law yields

$$-kx - \mu(x^2 - 1)\dot{x} = m\ddot{x}$$

or, more simply,

$$\ddot{x} + \mu(x^2 - 1)\dot{x} + x = 0 \tag{6-106}$$

since $m = k = 1$.

Equation 6-106 is a classical nonlinear differential equation known as *Van der Pol's equation*. Although the mechanical system from which Eq. 6-106 was derived is a hypothetical one, this equation does actually represent the behavior of a certain type of electronic oscillator.[10]

The reader who is familiar with vibration theory will recognize that if $|x| > 1$, the second term of Eq. 6-106 is a *positive-damping* term which represents a loss of energy from the system. Conversely, if $|x| < 1$ this term is a *negative-damping* term which represents an addition of energy to the system. Thus if we were initially to displace the mass less than 1 ft and then release it, the resulting vibrations would increase in amplitude until they reached some magnitude exceeding 1 ft, at which time energy would be removed from the system during the portion of each cycle in which $|x| > 1$. The buildup in amplitude would thus be limited, and it would seem reasonable to expect the amplitude of vibration to reach some stable state after some interval of time.

To program Eq. 6-106 for solution on the computer, we note that

$$\left. \begin{aligned} \dot{x} &= \frac{dx}{dt} \\[2em] \text{so that} & \\[2em] \ddot{x} &= \frac{d\dot{x}}{dt} \end{aligned} \right\} \qquad (6\text{-}107)$$

Utilizing these relationships, Eq. 6-106 may be transformed to the first-order differential equations

$$\left. \begin{aligned} \frac{d\dot{x}}{dt} &= -\mu(x^2 - 1)\dot{x} - x \qquad \text{(a)} \\[1.5em] \frac{dx}{dt} &= \dot{x} \qquad\qquad\qquad\quad \text{(b)} \end{aligned} \right\} \qquad (6\text{-}108)$$

Referring to Eqs. 6-103 and 6-104, and noting that the variable t does not appear explicitly in Eq. 6-108, we may write the fourth-order Runge-Kutta formulas

$$x_{i+1} = x_i + (h)\dot{x}_i + \frac{h}{6}(k_1 + k_2 + k_3) \qquad (6\text{-}109)$$

$$\dot{x}_{i+1} = \dot{x}_i + \tfrac{1}{6}(k_1 + 2k_2 + 2k_3 + k_4)$$

[10]N. Minorsky, *Introduction to Nonlinear Mechanics* (Ann Arbor, Mich.: J. W. Edwards, Publisher, Inc., 1947), p. 293.

where

$$k_1 = (h)f(x_i, \dot{x}_i)$$

$$k_2 = (h)f\left[x_i + \frac{h}{2}\dot{x}_i, \dot{x}_i + \frac{k_1}{2}\right]$$

$$k_3 = (h)f\left[x_i + \frac{h}{2}\dot{x}_i + \frac{h}{4}k_1, \dot{x}_i + \frac{k_2}{2}\right] \qquad (6\text{-}110)$$

$$k_4 = (h)f\left[x_i + (h)\dot{x}_i + \frac{h}{2}k_2, \dot{x}_i + k_3\right]$$

The numerical solution begins with the substitution of the initial values of x and $\dot{x}$ into Eq. 6-108a to obtain a value of this function for use in determining k_1. The successive k values are then determined for use in the recurrence formulas shown to obtain values of x_{i+1} and $\dot{x}_{i+1}$. The latter values obtained are then used in Eqs. 6-108a and 6-110 to obtain new k values for substitution into Eq. 6-109 to obtain values of x_{i+2} and $\dot{x}_{i+2}$, and so on. An outline of the procedure is shown in the flow chart of Fig. 6-25. The initial values used are

$$t = 0 \begin{vmatrix} x = 0.75 \text{ ft} \\ \dot{x} = 0 \end{vmatrix}$$

The FORTRAN variable names used in the source program and the quantities which they represent are as follows:

FORTRAN Name	Quantity	Values Used in Problem
COEFF	Damping coefficient, lb-sec/ft^3	4.0
X	Displacement of mass from static-equilibrium position, ft	$x_0 = 0.75$
XD	Velocity of mass, ft/sec	$x_0 = 0.0$
H	Time increment, sec	0.05
DTPR	Print increment, sec	0.10
TMAX	Time interval for which solution is desired, sec	20.0
T	Time, sec	
TPR	Print time, sec	
AK1, AK2, AK3, AK4	Quantities k_1, k_2, k_3, and k_4 of Runge-Kutta formulas	

The FORTRAN IV computer program used to implement the procedures outlined by the flow chart is shown below. The time increment has been chosen

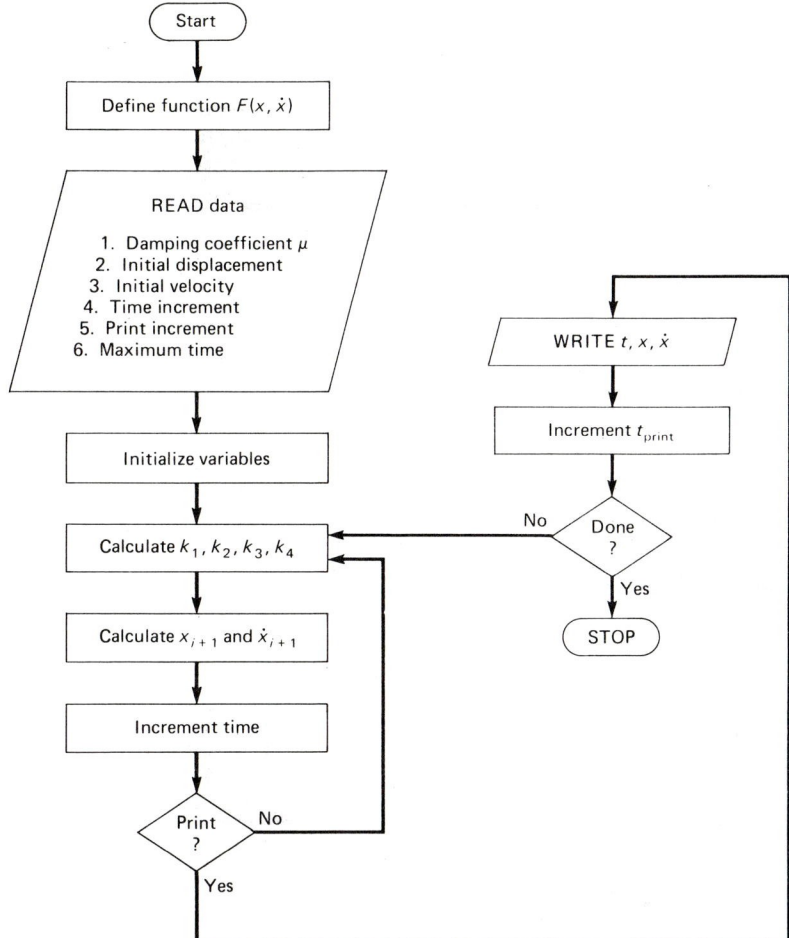

Figure 6-25   Flow chart for Ex. 6-4

as 0.05 sec. Since the program was run on a pure binary computer, and this quantity cannot be expressed exactly in pure binary form, some small roundoff error is to be expected in the time. For example, 20 time increments of 0.05 sec will not add up to exactly 1.0 sec. As a result, print times will not be exact integer multiples of the time increments as they would be if no roundoff error were present. To obtain printout at the times specified in the program, it is required that the time be within one-tenth of a step of the print time. This is accomplished with the statement

```
IF(ABS(T-TPR)-.005)4,4,3
```

in the program.

To avoid roundoff error altogether in the time, the time increment should be expressed in whole numbers or in a form exactly expressible in pure binary form such as $1/2^n$, where n is an integer. For example, in the problem which follows, time could be incremented and kept track of in milliseconds with no roundoff error introduced. The time in milliseconds could then be converted to time in seconds prior to printing out a time value, if time in seconds were desired.

```
C SOLUTION OF VAN DER POLS NONLINEAR DIFFERENTIAL EQUATION
                                                           USING
C THE CLASSICAL FOURTH-ORDER RUNGE-KUTTA METHOD
      F(X,XD)=-COEFF*(X*X-1.)*XD-X
      WRITE(6,1)
    1 FORMAT(1H1,26H  TIME  DISPL  VELOCITY/)
      READ(5,2)COEFF,X,XD,H,DTPR,TMAX
    2 FORMAT(6F10.0)
      T=0
      TPR=DTPR
    3 AK1=H*F(X,XD)
      AK2=H*F(X+H/2.*XD,XD+AK1/2.)
      AK3=H*F(X+H/2.*(XD+AK1/2.),XD+AK2/2.)
      AK4=H*F(X+H*(XD+AK2/2.),XD+AK3)
      X=X+H*(XD+(AK1+AK2+AK3)/6.)
      XD=XD+(AK1+2.*AK2+2.*AK3+AK4)/6.
      T=T+H
      IF(ABS(T-TPR)-.005)4,4,3
    4 WRITE(6,5)T,X,XD
    5 FORMAT(1H ,F6.2,3X,F6.3,4X,F7.3)
      TPR=TPR+DTPR
      IF(ABS(T-TMAX)-.005)6,6,3
    6 STOP
      END
```

Since 200 data printouts were obtained over the integration interval of 20 sec, the computer printout is not shown, owing to space considerations. Instead, the data obtained are plotted in graphical form in Figs. 6-26 and 6-27. Note that the vibration becomes essentially periodic and reaches a stable state in the 20-sec interval considered.

6-7 MILNE'S METHOD

As the step-by-step numerical integration of a differential equation progresses, the solution being obtained may tend to depart more and more from the true answer, owing to cumulative *per-step* error. If the solution must be obtained by using a relatively large number of steps, it is very important that the per-step error be kept small. The per-step error, using Euler's method, is of order h^2. The modified Euler methods have a per-step error of order h^3. It can be shown that Milne's method has a per-step error of order h^5. Thus, Milne's method is considerably more accurate than either Euler's method or the modified Euler methods, when a relatively large number of steps is involved. However, Milne's method does have the disadvantage of not being self-starting, though, as we will see later, this is not a serious disadvantage.

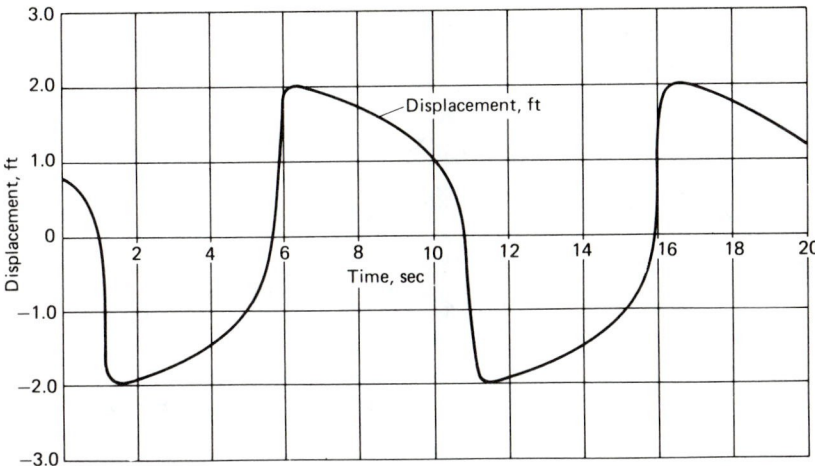

Figure 6-26   Displacement-time data for Ex. 6-4

The development of Milne's method begins by dividing the area under a given portion of a curve $y = f(x)$ into four h-width strips, as shown in Fig. 6-28. The true area under this portion of the curve is then approximated by considering the area of these four strips under a second-degree parabola having three coordinates in common with the actual curve, as indicated by the dashed line in Fig. 6-28. The crosshatched area is the approximate area obtained. To determine an expression for this crosshatched area in terms of h and the appropriate y ordinates, it is convenient to consider the four strips as centered on the y axis, as shown in Fig. 6-29. This arrangement does not compromise the generality of the results obtained, and it has the advantage of simplifying the intermediate expressions involved in determining the desired form of the

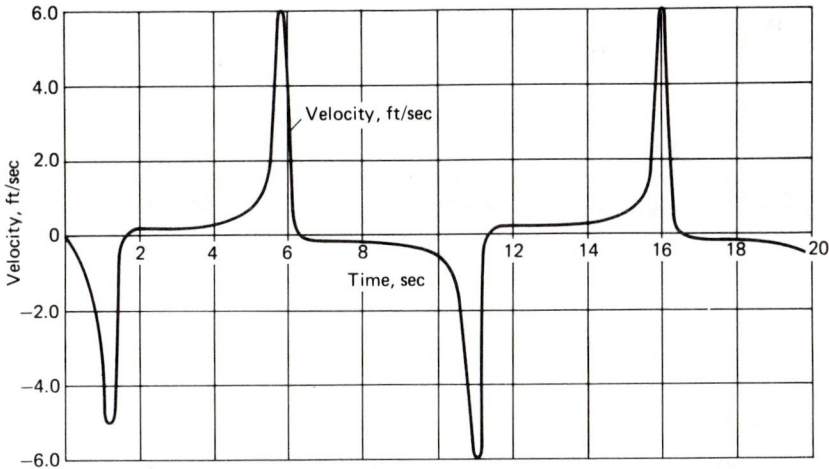

Figure 6-27   Velocity-time data for Ex. 6-4

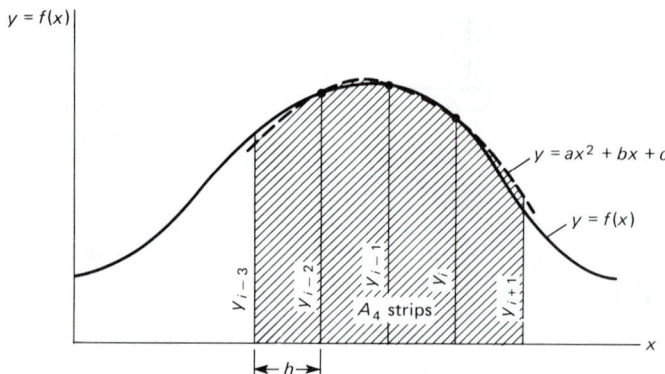

Figure 6-28 Area in four strips under a curve approximated by area under a second-degree parabola

expression for the area of four such strips. The crosshatched area of Fig. 6-29 is given by

$$A_{4 \text{ strips}} = \int_{-2h}^{2h} (ax^2 + bx + c) \, dx \tag{6-111}$$

Integrating Eq. 6-111 and substituting the limits gives

$$A_{4 \text{ strips}} = \tfrac{16}{3} ah^3 + 4ch \tag{6-112}$$

The constants a and c are determined in the manner explained on page 380. The appropriate expressions are

$$a = \frac{y_i - 2y_{i-1} + y_{i-2}}{2h^2}$$
$$c = y_{i-1} \tag{6-113}$$

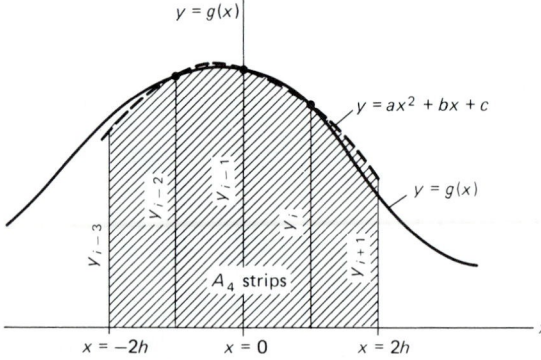

Figure 6-29 Area of four strips centered on y axis

Substituting Eq. 6-113 into Eq. 6-112 yields, for the area of the four strips in terms of h and the y ordinates shown,

$$A_{4 \text{ strips}} = \tfrac{4}{3}h[2y_i - y_{i-1} + 2y_{i-2}] \tag{6-114}$$

This expression will be used later as part of the predictor equation.

Let us consider the application of Milne's method in integrating a first-order differential equation of the form

$$y' = f(x, y) \tag{6-115}$$

where the value of y is known for $x = 0$. This technique consists, basically, of obtaining approximate values of y by the use of a *predictor* equation and then correcting these values by the iterative use of a corrector equation. Milne's predictor equation

$$P(y_{i+1}) = y_{i-3} + \tfrac{4}{3}h[2y'_i - y'_{i-1} + 2y'_{i-2}] \tag{6-116}$$

utilizes the area of four strips under a parabolic approximation of a curve (see Eq. 6-114) to provide a predicted value for the successive y ordinates. Milne's *corrector* equation

$$C(y_{i+1}) = y_{i-1} + \frac{h}{3}[y'_{i-1} + 4y'_i + P(y'_{i+1})] \tag{6-117}$$

provides corrected y values by using Simpson's rule for determining the area of two strips under a curve (see p. 380).

Assuming that the resulting y and y' curves of Eq. 6-115 have the general form of the curves shown in Fig. 6-30, the first step is to obtain a predicted value of y_4. Utilizing Eq. 6-116 with $i = 3$,

$$P(y_4) = y_0 + \tfrac{4}{3}h[2y'_3 - y'_2 + 2y'_1] \tag{6-118}$$

The predicted value obtained is then substituted into the given differential equation (Eq. 6-115) along with the appropriate x value to obtain a predicted value of y'_4, which is designated as $P(y'_4)$. This value is then used in Eq. 6-117 to obtain a corrected value of y_4 as

$$C(y_4) = y_2 + \frac{h}{3}[y'_2 + 4y'_3 + P(y'_4)] \tag{6-119}$$

The three steps just outlined are the first steps in the application of Milne's method. However, inspection of Eqs. 6-118 and 6-119 reveals that, before $P(y_4)$ and $C(y_4)$ can be obtained, starting values must be determined, in some

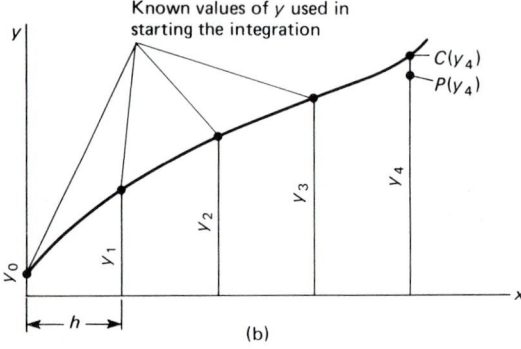

Figure 6-30 Graphical illustration of integration by Milne's method

manner, for y_1', y_2', y_3', and y_2. Furthermore, in stepping forward to obtain values of $P(y_5)$ and $C(y_5)$, starting values must also be known for y_1 and y_3.

The required starting values of y can be determined by the use of the following Taylor-series expansions:

$$y_1 = y_0 + y_0'h + \frac{y_0''h^2}{2!} + \frac{y_0'''h^3}{3!} + \cdots$$

$$y_2 = y_0 + y_0'[2h] + \frac{y_0''[2h]^2}{2!} + \frac{y_0'''[2h]^3}{3!} + \cdots \qquad (6\text{-}120)$$

$$y_3 = y_0 + y_0'[3h] + \frac{y_0''[3h]^2}{2!} + \frac{y_0'''[3h]^3}{3!} + \cdots$$

The numerical values of each of the derivatives, y_0', y_0'', y_0''', and so on, which are required to evaluate Eq. 6-120, are obtained by substituting $x = 0$ and $y = y_0$ into Eq. 6-115 and its derivatives y'', y''', and so forth. Having determined y_1, y_2, and y_3 from Eq. 6-120, the required values of y_1', y_2', and y_3' are next obtained by substituting the corresponding x and y values into Eq. 6-115.

The number of terms used in each Taylor series should include terms up to and including h^4 or the last term which yields a numerical value compatible with the digit capacity allowed by the computer being used, whichever number of terms is the least.

Another way of starting Milne's method is to determine the required value of each of the ordinates y_1, y_2, and y_3 by the use of a Runge-Kutta formula. A value of each of the ordinates y_1', y_2', and y_3' may then be obtained, as before, by substituting the appropriate x and y values into Eq. 6-115. The fourth-order Runge-Kutta formula frequently used is

$$y_{i+1} = y_i + \tfrac{1}{6}(k_1 + 2k_2 + 2k_3 + k_4) \tag{6-121}$$

where the respective k values are determined by substituting appropriate values into Eq. 6-115, as follows:

$$k_1 = (h)f(x_i, y_i)$$

$$k_2 = (h)f\left(x_i + \frac{h}{2}, y_i + \frac{k_1}{2}\right)$$

$$k_3 = (h)f\left(x_i + \frac{h}{2}, y_i + \frac{k_2}{2}\right)$$

$$k_4 = (h)f(x_i + h, y_i + k_3)$$

The solution of Eq. 6-115 could be obtained in its entirety using only the Runge-Kutta method, and with the same degree of accuracy as Milne's method, since both have a per-step error of the order of h^5. However, Milne's method is considered to be more efficient (less machine time) than the Runge-Kutta method, and estimation of the per-step error is easier using Milne's method. It is often used for these reasons, even though the Runge-Kutta method has the advantage of being self-starting. Because the Runge-Kutta method is self-starting and has the same degree of accuracy as Milne's method, it is frequently used to start the latter method, as just described. In using either the Taylor series or the Runge-Kutta method for starting Milne's procedure, the required starting values may be obtained manually or by using a calculator. However, if it is desired to use the computer to obtain the starting values so that the program is self-contained, it is generally easier to use the Runge-Kutta method, since higher derivatives of the given differential equation are not required by this method. If the derivatives of the given differential equation become increasingly complex with each successive differentiation, the Runge-Kutta procedure should be utilized for obtaining starting values, whether done manually, by calculator, or by computer.

With the starting procedure established, the following equations provide an outline of the subsequent steps involved,

(Predictor)

$$P(y_{i+1}) = y_{i-3} + \tfrac{4}{3}h[2y'_i - y'_{i-1} + 2y'_{i-2}] \qquad \text{(a)}$$

(Differential equation)

$$P(y'_{i+1}) = f[x_{i+1}, P(y_{i+1})] \qquad \text{(b)}$$

(Corrector)

$$C(y_{i+1}) = y_{i-1} + \frac{h}{3}[y'_{i-1} + 4y'_i + P(y'_{i+1})] \qquad \text{(c)}$$

(6-122)

(Differential equation)

$$C(y'_{i+1}) = f[x_{i+1}, C(y_{i+1})] \qquad \text{(d)}$$

(Iterating corrector)

$$C(y_{i+1}) = y_{i-1} + \frac{h}{3}[y'_{i-1} + 4y'_i + C(y'_{i+1})] \qquad \text{(e)}$$

where Eq. 6-122b and d indicate the forms in which the given differential equation is used. Assuming that the starting values (shown in Fig. 6-30) have been determined, the first step is to obtain a predicted value of y_4, using Eq. 6-122a. This equation predicts the value of y_4 by adding the value of y_0 to the value of the crosshatched area shown under the parabola in Fig. 6-30(a). Since this area is indicated as less than the true area, $P(y_4)$ will be smaller than the true value of y_4, as shown in Fig. 6-30(b). The next step is to substitute $x_4 = 4h$ and $P(y_4)$ into the given differential equation, as indicated by Eq. 6-122b to obtain a predicted value of y'_4, which is shown as $P(y'_4)$ in Fig. 6-30(a). This predicted value of y'_4 is then used in the corrector equation (Eq. 6-122c) to obtain a *corrected* value of y_4, which is shown as $C(y_4)$ in Fig. 6-30(b). This corrected value of y_4 is obtained as the sum of y_2 and the shaded area under the curve in Fig. 6-30(a), which area is found from Simpson's rule for the area of two strips. The corrected value of y_4 is next substituted into Eq. 6-122d to obtain an improved value of y'_4, which is shown as $C(y'_4)$ in Fig. 6-30(a). The latter value is then used in Eq. 6-122e to obtain a further improved value of y_4, which is, in turn, substituted back into Eq. 6-122d to obtain a further improved value of y'_4, and so on. The iteration process involving Eq. 6-122d and e then continues until successive values of y_4 differ by less than the value of some desired epsilon. With y_4 determined to the desired accuracy, the method steps forward one h increment, and the above process is repeated to obtain y_5, and so on. In programming the problem, it is not actually necessary to write Eq. 6-122e as a separate FORTRAN statement, since the program can be written so that Eq. 6-122c performs the function of Eq. 6-122e in the iteration process of each step.

Relieving the Instability of Milne's Method

As is pointed out in Sec. 6-8, Milne's method is *unstable*. This instability does not appear in the solution of many problems, but in those in which it does the effects can be disastrous. Since stability is discussed in Sec. 6-8, we will simply show in this section the method given by Milne and Reynolds[11] for damping out the extraneous oscillations which sometimes appear in Milne's method after a sufficient number of steps.

The corrector equation of Milne's method is based on Simpson's one-third rule (Eq. 6-117). It is this equation which under certain conditions can produce an error which fluctuates in sign and grows exponentially. The following procedure is shown by Milne and Reynolds as a procedure to damp out such oscillations.

After a finite number of steps, k, $y_{i+1} = y_k$ is recomputed using Simpson's three-eighths rule,

$$y_k = y_{k-3} + \frac{3h}{8} (y'_k + 3y'_{k-1} + 3y'_{k-2} + y'_{k-3})$$

Then a new $C(y_k)$ is calculated to replace the original $C(y_k)$ as follows:

$$C(y_k)_{new} = \frac{C(y_k)_{old} + y_k}{2}$$

The maximum value of k that will keep the solution stable depends on the step size h. In problems in which stabilizing is required, some experimenting may be required to determine a suitable k. Milne and Reynolds show an example in which stabilizing is carried out every 50 steps. They say that if instability is not removed for k as small as 10, it may be worthwhile to reduce the step size h. Their rough rule of thumb states that cutting h in half permits the doubling of k.

Error Estimation in Milne's Method

Milne's method is a predictor-corrector type, and we will be interested in a means of estimating its per-step truncation error. To investigate this error, let us again assume that we are integrating the differential equation

$$y' = g[x, y(x)] \tag{6-123}$$

[11]See W. E. Milne and R. R. Reynolds, "Stability of a Numerical Solution of Differential Equations," *J. Assoc. Computing Machinery*, Vol. 6, No. 2 (April 1959), pp. 196–203, and "Stability of a Numerical Solution of Differential Equations—Part II," *J. Assoc. Computing Machinery*, Vol. 7, No. 1 (Jan. 1960), pp. 46–56.

with the initial condition of $y = 0$ at $x = a$. Since y is a function of x, y' is actually some unknown function of x alone, which we will call $f(x)$. We will further assume that the graphs of $f(x)$ and y appear in the general form given in Fig. 6-31.

In Milne's method the approximate area under the $f(x)$ curve from x_{i-3} to x_{i+1} (the shaded area of Fig. 6-31) is added to y_{i-3} to obtain a predicted value of y_{i+1}. To determine an estimate of the per-step truncation error in the predictor equation, we obtain an exact expression for the area in the four strips (the crosshatched area in Fig. 6-31) and compare this expression with the expression for the approximate area used in the predictor equation.

The area under the graph of $f(x)$ from $x = a$ to any x value in Fig. 6-31 is a function of x and is equal to the value of y at the x value. That is,

$$y(x) = \int_a^x f(x)\,dx$$

from which

$$y_i' = f_i$$
$$y_i'' = f_i'$$

$$\vdots \qquad \vdots$$

$$\text{(6-124)}$$

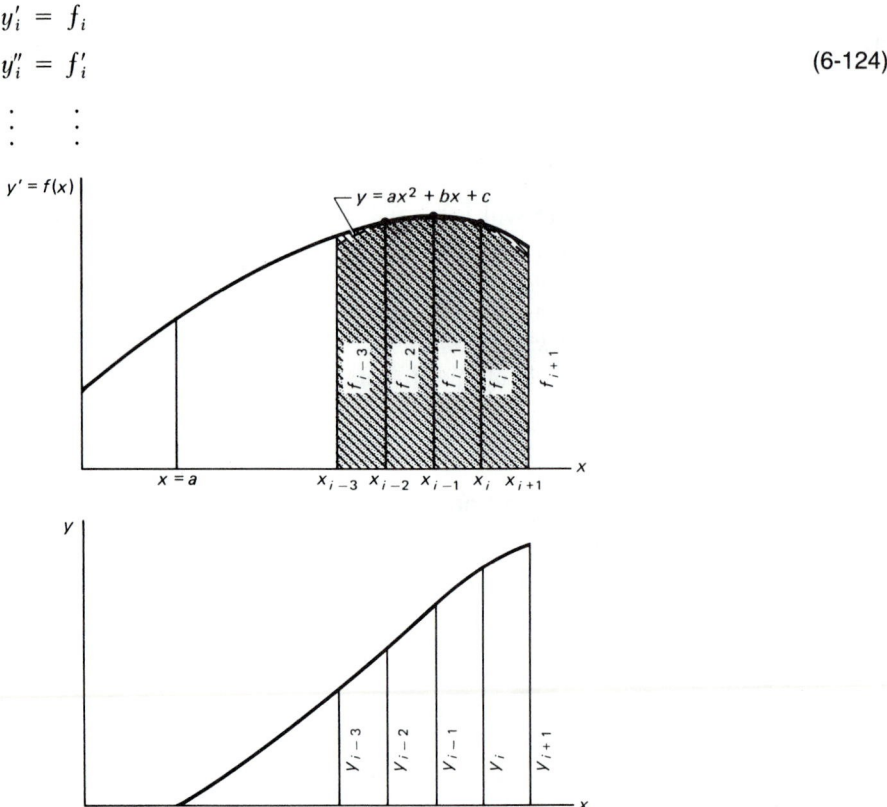

Figure 6-31 Assumed curves for $f(x)$ and y

To determine an exact expression for the area of the four strips shown in Fig. 6-31, we first expand y_{i+1} in a Taylor series about x_{i-1}. This expansion is

$$y_{i+1} = y_{i-1} + y'_{i-1}(2h)$$

$$+ \frac{y''_{i-1}(2h)^2}{2!} + \frac{y'''_{i-1}(2h)^3}{3!} + \frac{y^{IV}_{i-1}(2h)^4}{4!} + \frac{y^{V}(\xi_1)(2h)^5}{5!}$$

or

$$y_{i+1} - y_{i-1} = 2y'_{i-1}h + 2y''_{i-1}h^2 + \tfrac{4}{3}y'''_{i-1}h^3 + \tfrac{2}{3}y^{IV}_{i-1}h^4 + \tfrac{4}{15}y^{V}(\xi_1)h^5,$$

$$x_{i-1} < \xi_1 < x_{i+1} \qquad (6\text{-}125)$$

Similarly, expanding y_{i-3} about x_{i-1} yields

$$y_{i-3} - y_{i-1} = -2y'_{i-1}h + 2y''_{i-1}h^2 - \tfrac{4}{3}y'''_{i-1}h^3 + \tfrac{2}{3}y^{IV}_{i-1}h^4 - \tfrac{4}{15}y^{V}(\xi_2)h^5,$$

$$x_{i-3} < \xi_2 < x_{i+1} \qquad (6\text{-}126)$$

Subtracting Eq. 6-126 from Eq. 6-125 yields

$$y_{i+1} - y_{i-3} = 4y'_{i-1}h + \tfrac{8}{3}y'''_{i-1}h^3 + \tfrac{8}{15}y^{V}(\xi_3)h^5, \qquad x_{i-3} < \xi_3 < x_{i+1}$$

$$(6\text{-}127)$$

which is an exact expression for the area of the four strips composing the crosshatched area of Fig. 6-31.

Substituting the relationships of Eq. 6-124 into Eq. 6-127, we can express the exact area as

$$y_{i+1} - y_{i-3} = 4f_{i-1}h + \tfrac{8}{3}f''_{i-1}h^3 + \tfrac{8}{15}f^{IV}(\xi_3)h^5, \qquad x_{i-3} < \xi_3 < x_{i+1}$$

$$(6\text{-}128)$$

To put Eq. 6-128 in a form in which we can compare it with Milne's predictor equation, we must express $f''_{i-1}h^2$ in terms of f_i, f_{i-1}, and f_{i-2}. Using a Taylor series, we expand f_i and f_{i-2} about x_{i-1} as

$$f_i = f_{i-1} + f'_{i-1}h + \frac{f''_{i-1}h^2}{2!} + \frac{f'''_{i-1}h^3}{3!} + \frac{f^{IV}(\xi_4)h^4}{4!}, \qquad x_{i-1} < \xi_4 < x_i$$

$$(6\text{-}129)$$

and

$$f_{i-2} = f_{i-1} - f'_{i-1}h + \frac{f''_{i-1}h^2}{2!} - \frac{f'''_{i-1}h^3}{3!} + \frac{f^{IV}(\xi_5)h^4}{4!},$$

$$x_{i-2} < \xi_5 < x_{i-1} \qquad (6\text{-}130)$$

Adding Eqs. 6-129 and 6-130 gives

$$f_i + f_{i-2} = 2f_{i-1} + f''_{i-1}h^2 + \tfrac{1}{12}f^{\text{IV}}(\xi_6)h^4$$

from which

$$f''_{i-1}h^2 = (f_i - 2f_{i-1} + f_{i-2}) - \tfrac{1}{12}f^{\text{IV}}(\xi_6)h^4, \qquad x_{i-2} < \xi_6 < x_i$$

$$(6\text{-}131)$$

Then, substituting Eq. 6-131 into Eq. 6-128, we obtain

$$y_{i+1} - y_{i-3} = \underbrace{\frac{4h}{3}(2f_i - f_{i-1} + 2f_{i-2})}_{\text{Milne's predictor equation}} + \underbrace{\frac{14}{45}f^{\text{IV}}(\xi_7)h^5,}_{\text{truncation error}}$$

$$x_{i-3} < \xi_7 < x_{i+1} \qquad (6\text{-}132)$$

Equation 6-132 reveals that the per-step truncation error of Milne's predictor equation is given by

$$E_{TP} = \tfrac{14}{45}f^{\text{IV}}(\eta)h^5 = \tfrac{14}{45}y^{\text{V}}(\eta)h^5, \qquad x_{i-3} < \eta < x_{i+1} \qquad (6\text{-}133)$$

The per-step truncation error of Milne's corrector equation is the truncation error of Simpson's one-third rule, which has been shown to be

$$E_{TC} = -\tfrac{1}{90}f^{\text{IV}}(\xi)h^5 = -\tfrac{1}{90}y^{\text{V}}(\xi)h^4, \qquad x_{i-1} < \xi < x_{i+1}$$

An estimate of the per-step truncation error of Milne's corrector equation can be obtained in terms of the predicted and corrected y values at a given step from

$$E_{TC} \cong -\frac{1}{29}\left[C\binom{n}{y} - P\binom{1}{y}\right] \qquad (6\text{-}134)$$

where

$$P\binom{1}{y} = \text{the predicted value of } y \text{ at } x_{i+1}$$

$$C\binom{n}{y} = \text{the corrected value of } y \text{ obtained in the } n\text{th (final) iteration at } x_{i+1}$$

Equation 6-134 is developed in a manner similar to that of Eq. 6-44, as discussed under the error analysis of the non-self-starting modified Euler method.

EXAMPLE 6-5

A small rocket having an initial weight of 3000 lb, including 2400 lb of fuel, is fired vertically upward. The rocket burns fuel at a constant rate of 40 lb/sec, which provides a thrust of 7000 lb. Instruments are carried by the rocket to record data from which acceleration-time, velocity-time, and displacement-time curves can be obtained.

We wish to provide a theoretical analysis of the rocket flight which will yield data enabling us to plot the same curves obtained from the data recorded by the rocket instruments. A comparison of these sets of data can then be used to check the validity of the mathematical model used in the theoretical analysis. Such a check is desirable, since the model is conditioned by certain necessary simplifying assumptions, as follows: (1) the drag force is proportional to the square of the velocity ($D = Kv^2$), and (2) the coefficient of aerodynamic resistance K has an average value of 0.008 lb-sec²/ft².

A free-body diagram of the rocket appears in Fig. 6-32. The forces acting on the rocket are

T = thrust force, 7000 lb

W = total weight of rocket, fuel, and equipment at time t, $(3000 - 40t)$

D = drag, $0.008\dot{y}^2$ lb

Assuming y to be positive upward, as shown in the figure, we use Newton's second law to obtain the second-order nonlinear differential equation

$$\ddot{y} = \frac{gT}{W} - g - \frac{K\dot{y}^2 g}{W} \tag{6-135}$$

which has variable coefficients. The initial conditions of the problem are

$$t = 0 \begin{vmatrix} y = 0 \\ \dot{y} = 0 \end{vmatrix}$$

The solution of Eq. 6-135 will illustrate the application of Milne's method for obtaining the solution of a second-order differential equation. The required starting values of y, $\dot{y}$, and $\ddot{y}$, shown below, were obtained from the initial conditions, Taylor-series expansions, and the use of Eq. 6-135 by the procedure outlined in the preceding discussion.

$y_0 = 0.0$ ft	$\dot{y}_0 = 0.0$ ft/sec	
$y_1 = 0.2146$ ft	$\dot{y}_1 = 4.294$ ft/sec	$\ddot{y}_1 = 42.99$ ft/sec²
$y_2 = 0.8591$ ft	$\dot{y}_2 = 8.598$ ft/sec	$\ddot{y}_2 = 43.08$ ft/sec²
$y_3 = 1.935$ ft	$\dot{y}_3 = 12.911$ ft/sec	$\ddot{y}_3 = 43.18$ ft/sec²

$K\dot{y}^2$

$W = 3000 - 40t$

$+ y$

T

Figure 6-32 Free-body diagram of rocket of Ex. 6-5

In obtaining these values, a value of $\Delta t = 0.1$ was used, and the highest derivative used in the Taylor-series expansions was y^{IV}.

Remember that if the computer program is to be run a number of times, using different data in each run, the calculation of the starting values should be included in the program, so that their calculation becomes part of the computing process. As mentioned previously, the Runge-Kutta equation is more easily programmed for the calculation of starting values than are Taylor-series expansions. The Runge-Kutta formula (Eq. 6-121) can be used to determine starting values for the solution of a first-order differential equation. However, in applying the Runge-Kutta method to the solution of a second-order differential equation of the form $\ddot{y} = f(\dot{y}, y, t)$, as in this example, two formulas are required as discussed in Sec. 6-6. Although many variations of Runge-Kutta formulas exist, Eqs. 6-103 and 6-104 with y as a dependent variable instead of x will be found suitable for the determination of the required starting values. As in the formulas given for solving first-order differential equations, the error in these formulas is of order h^5.

We will make use of Eq. 6-122 in the following form:

(Predictor)

$$P(\dot{y}_{i+1}) = \dot{y}_{i-3} + \tfrac{4}{3}h[2\ddot{y}_i - \ddot{y}_{i-1} + 2\ddot{y}_{i-2}] \qquad \text{(a)}$$

(Differential equation)

$$P(\ddot{y}_{i+1}) = f[t_{i+1}, P(\dot{y}_{i+1})] \qquad \text{(b)}$$

(Corrector)

$$C(\dot{y}_{i+1}) = \dot{y}_{i-1} + \frac{h}{3}[\ddot{y}_{i-1} + 4\ddot{y}_i + P(\ddot{y}_{i+1})] \qquad \text{(c)}$$

(6-136)

(Differential equation)

$$C(\ddot{y}_{i+1}) = f[t_{i+1}, C(\dot{y}_{i+1})] \qquad \text{(d)}$$

(Iterating corrector)

$$C(\dot{y}_{i+1}) = \dot{y}_{i-1} + \frac{h}{3}[\ddot{y}_{i-1} + 4\ddot{y}_i + C(\ddot{y}_{i+1})] \qquad \text{(e)}$$

The dynamic-characteristics curves of the rocket for t near zero are sketched in Fig. 6-33. A predicted value of $\dot{y}_4$ is the first value obtained. It is determined from Eq. 6-136a, with $i = 3$, as

$$P(\dot{y}_4) = \dot{y}_0 + \tfrac{4}{3}h[2\ddot{y}_3 - \ddot{y}_2 + 2\ddot{y}_1]$$

where the second term on the right side is the crosshatched area under the parabola in Fig. 6-33(a). A predicted value of $\ddot{y}_4$ is next obtained by substituting $t_4 = 4h$ and the predicted value of $\dot{y}_4$ into Eq. 6-135, as indicated by Eq. 6-136b. This predicted value of $\ddot{y}_4$ is then substituted into Eq. 6-136c to obtain a corrected value of $\dot{y}_4$. The second term on the right side of Eq. 6-136c is the shaded area shown in Fig. 6-33(a). The corrected value $C(\dot{y}_4)$ is next substituted, along with $t_4 = 4h$, into Eq. 6-135 to obtain a corrected value of $\ddot{y}_4$, as indicated by Eq. 6-136d. This corrected value of $\ddot{y}_4$ is then substituted into Eq. 6-136e to obtain a further improved value of $\dot{y}_4$. This value is then substituted into Eq. 6-135 to obtain a further improved value of $\ddot{y}_4$, which is, in turn, substituted back into Eq. 6-136e to obtain an even-more-accurate value of $\dot{y}_4$. The iterative process involving Eq. 6-136d and e continues until successive values of $\dot{y}_4$ vary by less than some value epsilon chosen to specify the accuracy desired. In programming the problem, it is not actually necessary to

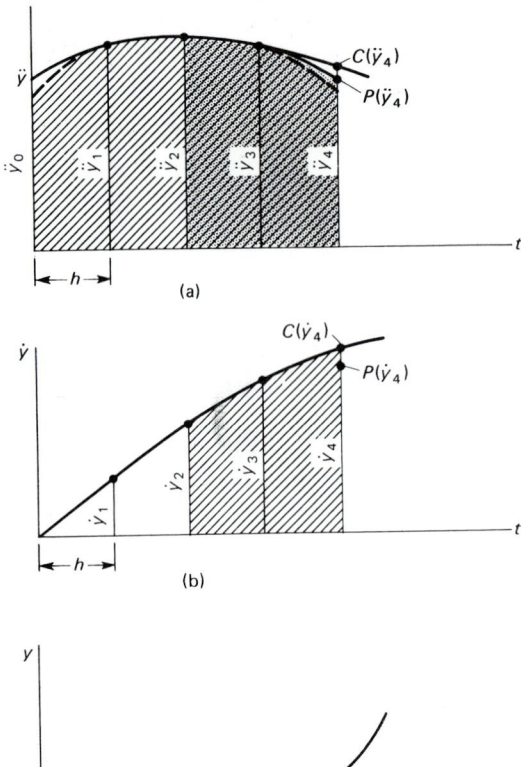

Figure 6-33 General characteristic curves for rocket of Ex. 6-5

write Eq. 6-136e as a separate FORTRAN statement, since the program can be written so that Eq. 6-136c performs the function of Eq. 6-136e in the iteration process of each step (see the FORTRAN program of this example).

Since the given differential equation (Eq. 6-135) does not contain y in explicit form, it is not necessary to calculate a value of y_4 until $\dot{y}_4$ has been determined with the accuracy desired.[12] The value of y_4 is then calculated, using Milne's corrector equation (Simpson's rule), as

$$y_4 = y_2 + \frac{h}{3}[\dot{y}_2 + 4\dot{y}_3 + \dot{y}_4]$$

[12]See brief discussion of the procedure for using Milne's method when y appears in explicit form in the differential equation following data shown at the end of this example.

where the second term on the right is the crosshatched area shown in Fig. 6-33b. After obtaining y_4, we move forward one step and repeat the process to determine values of $\dot{y}_5$ and y_5, and so on. This is continued until a time is reached corresponding to burnout (60 sec).

The flow chart for programming this problem is given in Fig. 6-34. The variable names, quantities, and values used are as follows:

Variable Name	Quantity	Value
W1	Total initial weight of rocket, lb	3000
WF	Initial weight of fuel, lb	2400
TH	Thrust, lb	7000
FR	Fuel-consumption rate, lb/sec	40
DK	Coefficient of aerodynamic resistance, lb-sec^2/ft^2	0.008
G	Acceleration of gravity, ft/sec^2	32.17
DELT	Time increment, sec	0.1
DTPR	Print increment, sec	2.0
EPSI	Accuracy-check value, ft/sec	0.0001
Y	Displacement value at station $i - 3$, ft	(Initial) 0.0000
Y1	Displacement at station $i - 2$, ft	(Initial) 0.2146
Y2	Displacement at station $i - 1$, ft	(Initial) 0.8591
Y3	Displacement at station i, ft	(Initial) 1.9350
YD	Velocity value at station $i - 3$, ft/sec	(Initial) 0.0000
YD1	Velocity at station $i - 2$, ft/sec	(Initial) 4.294
YD2	Velocity at station $i - 1$, ft/sec	(Initial) 8.598
YD3	Velocity at station i, ft/sec	(Initial) 12.911
YDD1	Acceleration at station $i - 2$, ft/sec^2	(Initial) 42.99
YDD2	Acceleration at station $i - 1$, ft/sec^2	(Initial) 43.08
YDD3	Acceleration at station i, ft/sec^2	(Initial) 43.18
T	Time, sec	
TMAX	Time at burnout, sec	60
TPR	Time at which printout occurs, sec	
W	Weight of rocket, fuel, and equipment at time t, lb	
YD4P	Predicted value of velocity, ft/sec	
YDD4	Acceleration of rocket, ft/sec^2	
YD4C	Corrected value of velocity, ft/sec	
Y4	Displacement at station $i + 1$, ft	

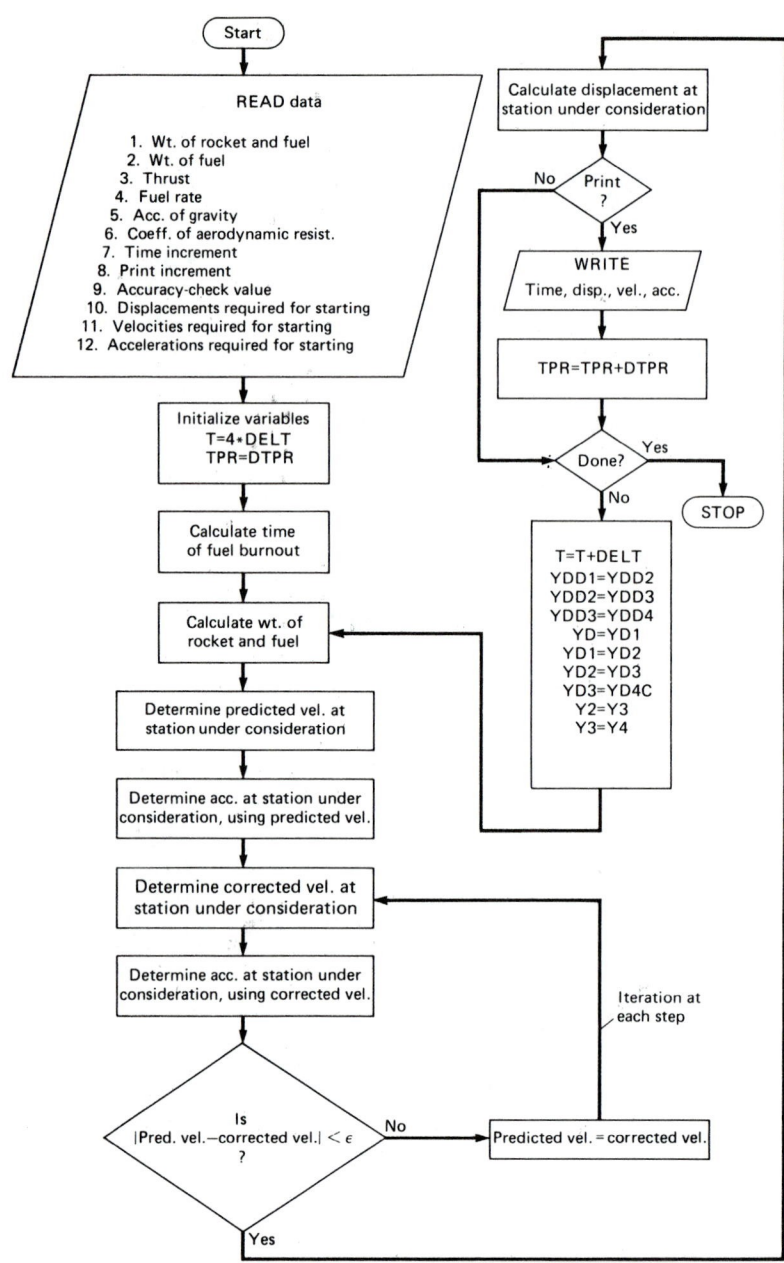

Figure 6-34 Flow chart for Ex. 6-5

The FORTRAN IV program follows. Note that all parts of Eq. 6-136 do not appear explicitly in the program. Since Eq. 6-136c is used only once in a particular sequence and is then replaced by Eq. 6-136e, the program utilizes statement 6 to fulfill the function of both Eqs. 6-136c and e.

```
C       DYNAMIC CHARACTERISTICS OF A ROCKET
C       NUMERICAL INTEGRATION BY MILNE METHOD
        READ(5,1)W1,WF,TH,FR,G,DK,H,DTPR,EPSI
   1 FORMAT(11F5.0)
        READ(5,1)Y,Y1,Y2,Y3,YD,YD1,YD2,YD3,YDD1,YDD2,YDD3
        WRITE(6,2)
   2 FORMAT(1H1,5X,1HW,8X,1HF,7X,2HTH,7X,1HR,7X,1HG,7X,
       *1HK,5X,2H H,4X,3HDTP,5X,3HEPS/)
        WRITE(6,3)W1,WF,TH,FR,G,DK,H,DTPR,EPSI
   3 FORMAT(2F9.1,F8.0,2F8.2,F8.4,2F6.2,F9.5///)
        WRITE(6,4)
   4 FORMAT(7H    TIME,6X,6HDISPL.,6X,4HVEL.,7X,4HACC./)
        T=4.*H
        TMAX=WF/FR
        TPR=DTPR
   5 W=W1-FR*T
        YD4P=YD+4./3.*(2.*YDD1-YDD2+2.*YDD3)*H
        YDD4=G*TH/W-G-DK*G/W*(YD4P**2)
   6 YD4C=YD2+H/3.*(YDD2+4.*YDD3+YDD4)
        YDD4=G*TH/W-G-DK*G/W*(YD4C**2)
        IF(ABS(YD4C-YD4P)-EPSI)8,8,7
   7 YD4P=YD4C
        GO TO 6
   8 Y4=Y2+H/3.*(YD2+4.*YD3+YD4C)
        IF(ABS(T-TPR)-.01)9,9,11
   9 WRITE(6,10)T,Y4,YD4C,YDD4
  10 FORMAT(1H ,F7.2,F12.1,F11.2,F10.2)
        TPR=TPR+DTPR
  11 IF(ABS(T-TMAX)-.01) 12,12,13
  12 STOP
  13 T=T+H
        YDD1=YDD2
        YDD2=YDD3
        YDD3=YDD4
        YD=YD1
        YD1=YD2
        YD2=YD3
        YD3=YD4C
        Y2=Y3
        Y3=Y4
        GO TO 5
        END
```

The computer printout is shown in tabular form. The desired dynamic-characteristic curves, as plotted from the data printout, are given in Fig. 6-35. These curves are available for comparison with the corresponding curves obtained from the instruments carried by the rocket.

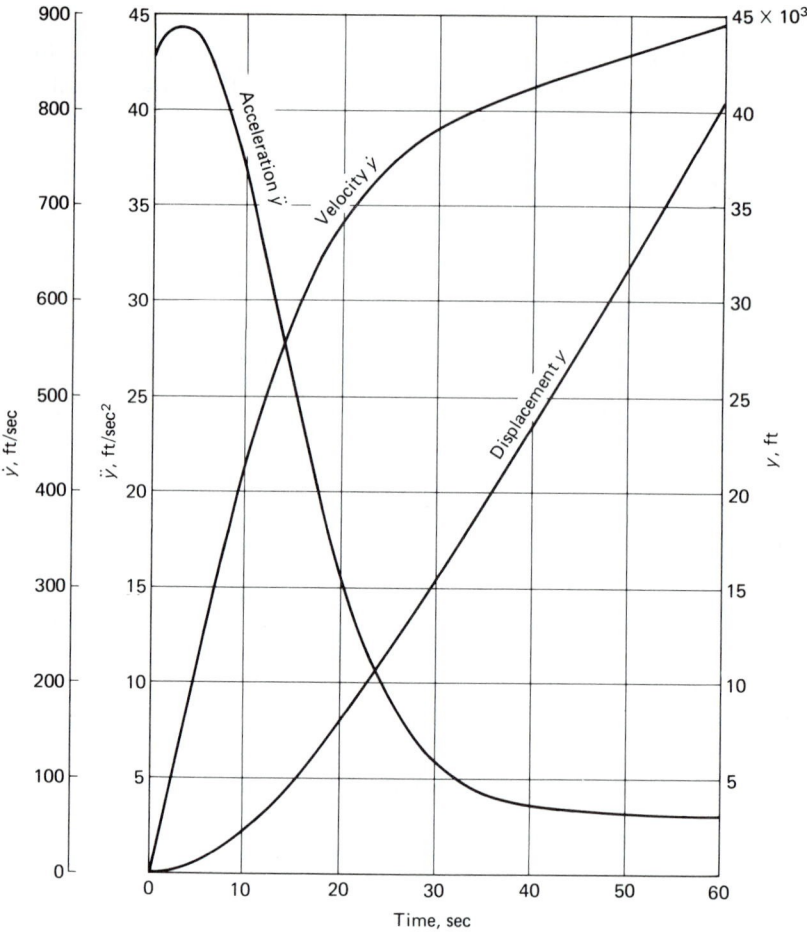

Figure 6-35 Dynamic-characteristic curves of the rocket of Ex. 6-5

W	F	TH	R	G	K	H	DTP	EPS
3000.0	2400.0	7000.	40.00	32.17	0.0080	0.10	2.00	0.00100

TIME	DISPL.	VEL.	ACC.
2.00	86.9	87.38	44.28
4.00	350.5	176.20	44.31
6.00	790.8	263.68	42.94
8.00	1402.5	347.09	40.29
10.00	2174.9	424.15	36.63
12.00	3093.7	493.20	32.35
14.00	4141.8	553.38	27.82
16.00	5301.2	604.55	23.39
18.00	6554.3	647.19	19.32
20.00	7884.8	682.17	15.75
22.00	9278.5	710.57	12.76
24.00	10723.5	733.57	10.33
26.00	12209.9	752.24	8.42

TIME	DISPL.	VEL.	ACC.
28.00	13730.1	767.55	6.96
30.00	15278.3	780.33	5.87
32.00	16850.2	791.24	5.08
34.00	18442.4	800.79	4.51
36.00	20052.6	809.38	4.11
38.00	21679.4	817.30	3.83
40.00	23321.5	824.75	3.64
42.00	24978.1	831.88	3.50
44.00	26648.8	838.78	3.41
46.00	28333.1	845.53	3.34
48.00	30030.8	852.16	3.29
50.00	31741.6	858.70	3.25
52.00	33465.5	865.16	3.21
54.00	35202.1	871.55	3.18
56.00	36951.6	877.89	3.15
58.00	38713.6	884.17	3.11
60.00	40488.1	890.39	3.08

If y had appeared explicitly in Eq. 6-135, then Eqs. 6-137a and c below would have to be used *following* Eqs. 6-136a and c, and Eqs. 6-137b and d below would *replace* Eqs. 6-136b and d.

(Predictor for y)

$$P(y_{i+1}) = y_{i-1} + \frac{h}{3}\left[\dot{y}_{i-1} + 4\dot{y}_i + P(\dot{y}_{i+1})\right] \qquad \text{(a)}$$

(Differential equation)

$$P(\ddot{y}_{i+1}) = f[t_{i+1}, P(y_{i+1}), P(\dot{y}_{i+1})] \qquad \text{(b)}$$

(6-137)

(Iterating corrector for y)

$$C(y_{i+1}) = y_{i-1} + \frac{h}{3}\left[\dot{y}_{i-1} + 4\dot{y}_i + C(\dot{y}_{i+1})\right] \qquad \text{(c)}$$

(Differential equation)

$$C(\ddot{y}_{i+1}) = f[t_{i+1}, C(y_{i+1}), C(\dot{y}_{i+1})] \qquad \text{(d)}$$

6-8 HAMMING'S METHOD

The various numerical methods for solving differential equations discussed thus far in this chapter have had different per-step truncation errors, varying from order h^2 for Euler's method to order h^5 for Milne's method and the fourth-order Runge-Kutta method. The per-step truncation error of a method is often referred to as a *local* error since it is an error introduced by the step in the integrating procedure. Roundoff error is also considered as a local error since it too is an error introduced by the step. However, the *total* error existing in the solution during any particular step (the difference between the true value at that point and the numerically calculated value) depends not only upon the magnitude of the local errors introduced by that step but also upon the propagation characteristics of local errors introduced in preceding steps, for local errors may tend to grow during subsequent steps, and, when a great many steps are involved in an integration, the total error may be appreciable.

In problems where the range of integration is considerable, the numerical method employed must be *stable* and/or *relatively stable* to obtain an accurate solution.[13] A numerical method is defined as stable if, in the process of integrating a differential equation such as

$$y' = f(x, y) \tag{6-138}$$

where $\partial f/\partial y < 0$, the difference between the true solution and the numerical solution (the total error) tends to *decrease* in magnitude as the integration progresses. The stability of a method is not defined when considering the integration of a differential equation such as Eq. 6-138 where $\partial f/\partial y > 0$. The solution of such an equation will increase in an exponential manner, and the total error will generally increase in the same way. In solving such a differential equation over an extended range of integration, a method should be used which is *relatively stable*. A method is defined as relatively stable if the *rate of growth* of the total error during the process of integration is *less* than that of the solution. This may be expressed mathematically by stating that if the solution has the general form of

$$y = Ae^x$$

then the total error caused by the numerical method must be of the general form of

$$\varepsilon = Be^{mx}$$

with $m < 1$ for the method to be considered relatively stable.

The relative stability of a method is also important when used to solve a differential equation such as Eq. 6-138 for which $\partial f/\partial y < 0$ if the solution approaches zero asymptotically, for, if an accurate solution is desired involving a value of y very close to zero, the *rate of diminution* of the total error must be *greater* than that of the solution. Expressed mathematically, if the solution has the form of

$$y = Ae^{-x}$$

then the total error caused by the method must be of the general form of

$$\varepsilon = Be^{-mx}$$

with $m > 1$ for the method to be considered relatively stable.

[13]Richard W. Hamming, *Numerical Methods for Scientists and Engineers* (New York: McGraw-Hill Book Company, 1962), p. 191. Anthony Ralston and Herbert S. Wilf, eds., *Mathematical Methods for Digital Computers* (New York: John Wiley & Sons, 1960), p. 103.

Figure 6-36 Curve of $d\dot{y}/dt$ versus $\dot{y}$ for rocket of Ex. 6-5

Figure 6-35, accompanying the rocket problem of Ex. 6-5, provides the data necessary to plot a curve of $d\dot{y}/dt$ versus $\dot{y}$, as shown in Fig. 6-36. It can be seen, from this latter figure, that $\partial f/\partial \dot{y} < 0$ for most of the range of $\dot{y}$ under consideration. Therefore, if a stable numerical method is used to integrate

$$\frac{d\dot{y}}{dt} = f(\dot{y}, t)$$

there should be no danger of the total error growing to serious proportions, even though the integration might involve a large number of steps over an extended range of integration.

The curve of $\dot{y}$ versus y for the same problem is shown in Fig. 6-37. In this instance it can be seen that $\partial f/\partial y > 0$. Therefore, in the integration of

$$\dot{y} = f(y, t)$$

the stability of the method employed is not defined, as discussed previously. The solution y increases with time in a general exponential manner, as shown in Fig. 6-38. Here the use of a relatively stable method will ensure that the rate of growth of the total error is no greater than the rate of growth of the solution, even though both grow in an exponential manner.

The propagation of errors during an integration is not a serious obstacle in the solution of many practical engineering problems. Since we are often not interested in solutions requiring extended ranges of integration, the use of relatively small h values will provide sufficiently accurate answers, regardless of the stability or relative-stability characteristics of the numerical method employed. For example, the solutions provided by Milne's method (which is neither stable nor relatively stable) in Ex. 6-5 agree very closely with the

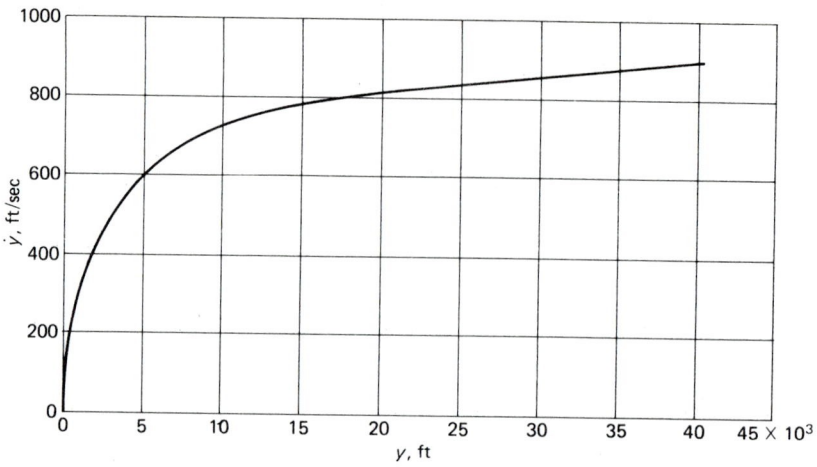

Figure 6-37 Curve of $\dot{y}$ versus y for the rocket of Ex. 6-5

corresponding solutions provided by Hamming's method (which is both stable and relatively stable) in Ex. 6-6 which appears later in this section. However, if solutions were desired over a much longer range of integration than is required in these examples, Milne's method would not provide the same degree of accuracy as would Hamming's method, because Milne's method is unstable, and the total error would grow to proportions capable of introducing serious error during the latter stages of the integration; the discrepancy between the solutions would become more and more pronounced as the range of integration was arbitrarily extended. In certain types of equations, such as Van der Pol's equation, for example, instability leads to serious errors in the solution, even over a relatively short range of integration (see Prob. 6-17).

Hamming's method, as mentioned above, is both stable and relatively stable. This method uses the same predictor equation as does Milne's method; that is,

$$P(y_{i+1}), = y_{i-3} + \frac{4h}{3}[2y'_i - y'_{i-1} + 2y'_{i-2}] \tag{6-139}$$

where $P(y_{i+1})$, as before, indicates a predicted value of y_{i+1}. To derive Hamming's corrector equation, a generalized corrector equation of the form shown below is considered:

$$y_{i+1} = a_i y_i + a_{i-1} y_{i-1} + a_{i-2} y_{i-2} + h(b_{i+1} y'_{i+1} + b_i y'_i + b_{i-1} y'_{i-1}) \tag{6-140}$$

If appropriate Taylor-series expansions for y_{i-2}, y_{i-1}, y_{i+1}, y'_{i-1}, and y'_{i+1} are substituted into Eq. 6-140, the following equation is obtained:

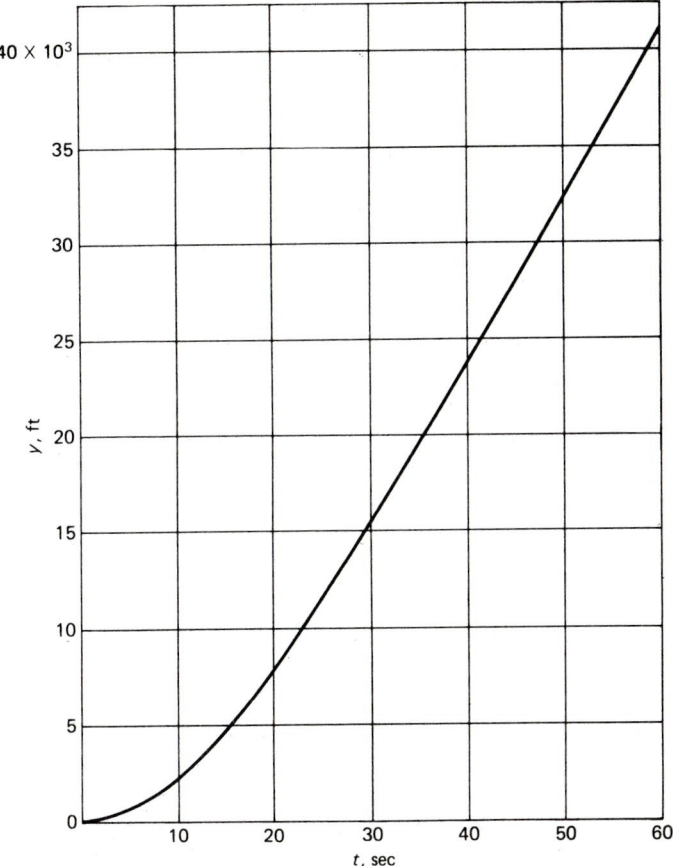

Figure 6-38 Displacement y versus t for rocket of Ex. 6-5

$$\left[y_i + y_i'h + \frac{y_i''h^2}{2!} + \frac{y_i'''h^3}{3!} + \frac{y_i''''h^4}{4!} + \cdots \right]$$

$$= a_i y_i + a_{i-1}\left[y_i + y_i'(-h) + \frac{y_i''(-h)^2}{2!} + \frac{y_i'''(-h)^3}{3!} + \frac{y_i^{IV}(-h)^4}{4!} + \cdots \right]$$

$$+ a_{i-2}\left[y_i + y_i'(-2h) + \frac{y_i''(-2h)^2}{2!} + \frac{y_i'''(-2h)^3}{3!} + \frac{y_i^{IV}(-2h)^4}{4!} + \cdots \right]$$

$$+ hb_{i+1}\left[y_i' + y_i''h + \frac{y_i'''h^2}{2!} + \frac{y_i^{IV}h^3}{3!} + \cdots \right] + hb_i y_i'$$

$$+ hb_{i-1}\left[y_i' + y_i''(-h) + \frac{y_i'''(-h)^2}{2!} + \frac{y_i^{IV}(-h)^3}{3!} + \cdots \right]$$

$$(6\text{-}141)$$

where the bracketed terms are the series expansions. Equating coefficients of y_i, y_i', y_i'', y_i''', and y_i^{IV}, respectively, on each side of Eq. 6-141 yields the following relationships:

$$
\begin{aligned}
a_i + a_{i-1} + a_{i-2} &= 1 \quad &\text{(a)} \\
-a_{i-1} - 2a_{i-2} + b_{i+1} + b_i + b_{i-1} &= 1 \quad &\text{(b)} \\
+\tfrac{1}{2}a_{i-1} + 2a_{i-2} + b_{i+1} - b_{i-1} &= \tfrac{1}{2} \quad &\text{(c)} \\
-\tfrac{1}{6}a_{i-1} - \tfrac{4}{3}a_{i-2} + \tfrac{1}{2}b_{i+1} + \tfrac{1}{2}b_{i-1} &= \tfrac{1}{6} \quad &\text{(d)} \\
+\tfrac{1}{24}a_{i-1} + \tfrac{2}{3}a_{i-2} + \tfrac{1}{6}b_{i+1} - \tfrac{1}{6}b_{i-1} &= \tfrac{1}{24} \quad &\text{(e)}
\end{aligned}
$$

(6-142)

The five equations shown above contain six unknowns. A sixth equation necessary for determining the six unknowns could be obtained by adding one additional term to each of the Taylor-series expansions used in obtaining Eq. 6-142 and equating the coefficients of y_i^V. However, Hamming[14] found that the use of $a_{i-1} = 0$ led to a corrector equation that was both stable and relatively stable when certain conditions were imposed upon the magnitude of h. Using a value of $a_{i-1} = 0$, the parts of Eq. 6-142 can be solved simultaneously to yield the following values:

$$
\begin{aligned}
a_i &= \tfrac{9}{8} & b_{i+1} &= \tfrac{3}{8} \\
a_{i-2} &= -\tfrac{1}{8} & b_i &= \tfrac{3}{4} \\
& & b_{i-1} &= -\tfrac{3}{8}
\end{aligned}
$$

Substituting these values into Eq. 6-140 yields Hamming's corrector equation

$$
C(y_{i+1}) = \tfrac{1}{8}\{9y_i - y_{i-2} + 3h[P(y_{i+1}') + 2y_i' - y_{i-1}']\}
\tag{6-143}
$$

where $C(y_{i+1})$ denotes a corrected value of y_{i+1}. Hamming's corrector equation is both stable and relatively stable for solving differential equations with $\partial f/\partial y < 0$ when

$$
h < \frac{0.75}{|\partial f/\partial y|}
$$

and the corrector equation is used to iterate to convergence. The corrector equation is relatively stable for solving differential equations in which $\partial f/\partial y > 0$ when

$$
h < \frac{0.4}{\partial f/\partial y}
$$

[14]Richard W. Hamming, "Stable Predictor-Corrector Methods for Ordinary Differential Equations," *J. Assoc. Computing Machinery*, Vol. 6, No. 1 (1959), pp. 37–47.

and the corrector equation is used to iterate to convergence. To keep the per-step error small, h would normally be less than either of the h values specified above. The per-step error of Hamming's method is of order h^5, which is of the same order as Milne's method.

One form of Hamming's method consists of using Eq. 6-139 as a predictor equation and then using the given differential equation in conjunction with Hamming's corrector equation (Eq. 6-143) to iterate to convergence, as was done in Milne's method. An alternate procedure, suggested by Hamming, saves iteration time on the computer. A study of the truncation errors of Eqs. 6-139 and 6-143 indicates that most of the error in the predicted value of y_{i+1} can be eliminated by the use of the following *modifier* equation:

$$M(y_{i+1}) = P(y_{i+1}) - \tfrac{112}{121}[P(y_i) - C(y_i)] \qquad\qquad (6\text{-}144)$$

where $M(y_{i+1})$ indicates a modified value of y_{i+1} and the other symbols indicate predicted and corrected values, as before. This modified value of y_{i+1} is next substituted into the given differential equation to obtain a modified value of y'_{i+1} which is designated as $M(y'_{i+1})$. This modified value is then used in the corrector equation

$$C(y_{i+1}) = \tfrac{1}{8}\{9y_i - y_{i-2} + 3h[M(y'_{i+1}) + 2y'_i - y'_{i-1}]\} \qquad\qquad (6\text{-}145)$$

to obtain a corrected value of y_{i+1}, as shown. The study made of the truncation errors of Eqs. 6-139 and 6-143 also reveals that most of the error in the corrected value of y_{i+1} can be eliminated by using the equation

$$F(y_{i+1}) = C(y_{i+1}) + \tfrac{9}{121}[P(y_{i+1}) - C(y_{i+1})] \qquad\qquad (6\text{-}146)$$

where $F(y_{i+1})$ indicates the final value of y_{i+1}. Thus, in place of iterating the corrector equation to convergence at each step, Eqs. 6-139, 6-144, 6-145, and 6-146 are used just once (in that sequence) for each step. These equations are grouped here for the sake of convenience and are shown in the order in which they are used:

(Predictor)

$$P(y_{i+1}) = y_{i-3} + \frac{4h}{3}[2y'_i - y'_{i-1} + 2y'_{i-2}] \qquad\qquad (a)$$

(Modifier)

$$M(y_{i+1}) = P(y_{i+1}) - \tfrac{112}{121}[P(y_i) - C(y_i)] \qquad\qquad (b)$$

$$(6\text{-}147)$$

(Corrector)

$$C(y_{i+1}) = \tfrac{1}{8}\{9y_i - y_{i-2} + 3h[M(y'_{i+1}) + 2y'_i - y'_{i-1}]\} \qquad \text{(c)}$$

(Final value)

$$F(y_{i+1}) = C(y_{i+1}) + \tfrac{9}{121}[P(y_{i+1}) - C(y_{i+1})] \qquad \text{(d)}$$

When the procedure involving Eq. 6-147 is employed instead of the iteration procedure, a different condition must be imposed upon the magnitude of h to ensure stability and relative stability. In this case (with $\partial f/\partial y < 0$) the condition is

$$h < \frac{0.65}{|\partial f/\partial y|}$$

Hamming's method, as well as other predictor-corrector methods, can be further refined to save machine time by varying the magnitude of h during the progress of the integration. A change in the magnitude of h is dictated by the relationship existing between the magnitudes of the predicted and corrected values of y_{i+1} calculated. If $[P(y_{i+1}) - C(y_{i+1})]$ is less than some prescribed value, h is doubled; if the same expression is larger than some other prescribed value, h is halved. For a further discussion of adjusting step size, based on a truncation-error analysis at each step, see Sec. 6-9.

Error Estimation for Hamming's Method

The predictor equation used in Hamming's method is the same as the predictor equation of Milne's method, so the per-step truncation error in a predicted value is given by

$$E_{TP} = \tfrac{14}{45}f^{IV}(\eta)h^5 = \tfrac{14}{45}y^V(\eta)h^5, \qquad x_{i-3} < \eta < x_{i+1} \qquad \text{(6-148)}$$

as developed earlier (Eq. 6-133).

To obtain the per-step truncation error of Hamming's corrector equation, let us return for a moment to the development of Hamming's method and read particularly the text from Eqs. 6-140 to 6-143. From that discussion it can be seen that the left and right sides of Eq. 6-141 have been made equal by the a and b values determined from Eq. 6-142 (with $a_{i-1} = 0$). It can also be seen that the left side of Eq. 6-141 is only an approximate expression for y_{i+1}, since y_{i+1} is expressed as a truncated Taylor series. If we add the remaining Taylor-series terms of the expansion of y_{i+1} (in a Lagrangian-remainder form) to both sides of Eq. 6-141 and insert Hamming's a and b values, we can obtain an expression for the *true* value of y_{i+1} as

$$(y_{i+1})_{\text{true}} = \left[y_i + y_i'h + \frac{y_i''h^2}{2!} + \frac{y_i'''h^3}{3!} + \frac{y_i^{IV}h^4}{4!} + \frac{y^V(\xi_i)h^5}{5!} \right]$$

$$= \frac{9}{8} y_i - \frac{1}{8} \left[y_i + y_i'(-2h) + \frac{y_i''(-2h)^2}{2!} \right.$$

$$\left. + \frac{y_i'''(-2h)^3}{3!} + \frac{y_i^{IV}(-2h)^4}{4!} \right]$$

$$+ \frac{3h}{8} \left[y_i' + y_i''h + \frac{y_i'''h^2}{2!} + \frac{y_i^{IV}h^3}{3!} \right] + \frac{3h}{4} y_i'$$

$$- \frac{3h}{8} \left[y_i' + y_i''(-h) + \frac{y_i'''(-h)^2}{2!} + \frac{y_i^{IV}(-h)^3}{3!} \right] + \frac{y^V(\xi_1)h^5}{5!}$$

(6-149)

Now let us examine the expression for y_{i+1} which is obtained by using Hamming's corrector equation (Eq. 6-143). Considering only the truncation error of the step by assuming the solution to be correct up to the step considered, all the y and y' values shown on the right side of the equation will be *true* values. Therefore, substituting a complete Taylor series (in Lagrangian-remainder form) for y_{i-2}, y_{i-1}', and y_{i+1}' in Eq. 6-143, we obtain

$$(y_{i+1})_{\text{Hamming}} = \frac{9}{8} y_i - \frac{1}{8} \left[y_i + y_i'(-2h) + \frac{y_i''(-2h)^2}{2!} + \frac{y_i'''(-2h)^3}{3!} \right.$$

$$\left. + \frac{y_i^{IV}(-2h)^4}{4!} + \frac{y^V(\xi_2)(-2h)^5}{5!} \right]$$

$$+ \frac{3h}{8} \left[y_i' + y_i''h + \frac{y_i'''h^2}{2!} + \frac{y_i^{IV}h^3}{3!} + \frac{y^V(\xi_3)h^4}{4!} \right] + \frac{3h}{4} y_i'$$

$$- \frac{3h}{8} \left[y_i' + y_i''(-h) + \frac{y_i'''(-h)^2}{2!} + \frac{y_i^{IV}(-h)^3}{3!} + \frac{y^V(\xi_4)(-h)^4}{4!} \right]$$

(6-150)

Comparing the expression for the true value of y_{i+1} (given by Eq. 6-149) with the expression for y_{i+1} from Hamming's corrector equation (given by Eq. 6-150), it is apparent that Hamming's corrector equation does not yield a true value of y_{i+1}. The difference between these expressions is the per-step truncation error of Hamming's corrector equation. Subtracting Eq. 6-150 from Eq. 6-149, we obtain

$$E_{TC} = (y_{i+1})_{\text{true}} - (y_{i+1})_{\text{Hamming}}$$

$$= \frac{1}{8} \frac{y^V(\xi_2)(-2h)^5}{5!} - \frac{3}{8} \frac{y^V(\xi_3)h^5}{4!} + \frac{3}{8} \frac{y^V(\xi_4)h^5}{4!} + \frac{y^V(\xi_1)h^5}{5!} \qquad \text{(6-151)}$$

Assuming that y^V is nearly constant in the interval from x_{i-2} to x_{i+1}, Eq. 6-151 reduces to

$$E_{TC} = -\tfrac{1}{40}y^V(\eta)h^5, \qquad x_{i-2} < \eta < x_{i+1} \tag{6-152}$$

Thus, Hamming's corrector equation for a true value of y_{i+1} may be written as

$$y_{i+1} = \tfrac{1}{8}[9y_i - y_{i-2} + 3h(y'_{i+1} + 2y'_i - y'_{i-1})] - \tfrac{1}{40}y^V(\eta)h^5 \tag{6-153}$$

As discussed before, an estimate of the per-step truncation error can be obtained from Eq. 6-152 by assuming that y^V is fairly constant over the interval and evaluating the truncation-error term at $\eta = x_i$, although the estimate is generally not made in this manner, owing to the difficulty of obtaining y^V.

A more practical approach can be made by obtaining an estimate of the per-step truncation error in terms of the predicted and corrected values of y at each step. Consider that

$$P\!\left(\dfrac{1}{y}\right) = \text{the predicted value of } y \text{ obtained at } x_{i+1} \text{ in the integration process}$$

$$C\!\left(\dfrac{n}{y}\right) = \begin{array}{l}\text{the corrected value of } y \text{ obtained at } x_{i+1} \text{ in the } n\text{th (final) iteration} \\ \text{at that step}\end{array}$$

$$Y = \text{the true value of } y \text{ at } x_{i+1}$$

Isolating the truncation error of the ith step from the effects of previous errors, in accordance with the definition given for per-step truncation error, and assuming that roundoff error in the calculations of the step is negligible, we can write

$$Y = P\!\left(\dfrac{1}{y}\right) + \dfrac{14}{45}\,y^V(\eta_1)h^5, \qquad x_{i-3} < \eta_1 < x_{i+1} \tag{6-154}$$

$$Y = C\!\left(\dfrac{n}{y}\right) - \dfrac{1}{40}\,y^V(\eta_2)h^5, \qquad x_{i-2} < \eta_2 < x_{i+1} \tag{6-155}$$

Subtracting Eq. 6-154 from Eq. 6-155 yields

$$0 = C\!\left(\dfrac{n}{y}\right) - P\!\left(\dfrac{1}{y}\right) - \dfrac{121}{360}\,y^V(\eta_3)h^5, \qquad x_{i-3} < \eta_3 < x_{i+1}$$

or

$$C\!\left(\dfrac{n}{y}\right) - P\!\left(\dfrac{1}{y}\right) = \left(\dfrac{121}{9}\right)\!\left(\dfrac{1}{40}\right)y^V(\eta_3)h^5 \tag{6-156}$$

Comparing Eqs. 6-152 and 6-156, it can be seen that an estimate of the per-step truncation error, in the final application of Hamming's corrector equation, is

$$E_{TC} \cong -\frac{9}{121}\left[C\left(\begin{matrix} n \\ y \end{matrix}\right) - P\left(\begin{matrix} 1 \\ y \end{matrix}\right) \right] \qquad (6\text{-}157)$$

EXAMPLE 6-6

Let us use Hamming's method to solve the rocket problem of Ex. 6-5. The reader should reread the first three paragraphs of Ex. 6-5 for a discussion of the problem and the assumptions involved in deriving the following differential equation of motion of the rocket:

$$\ddot{y} = \frac{gT}{W} - g - \frac{K\dot{y}^2 g}{W} \qquad (6\text{-}158)$$

where

y = displacement of rocket, ft
$\dot{y}$ = velocity of rocket, ft/sec
$\ddot{y}$ = acceleration of rocket, ft/sec^2
T = thrust force, 7000 lb
W = total weight of rocket, fuel, and equipment at time t, $(3000 - 40t)$ lb
K = coefficient of aerodynamic resistance, 0.008 lb-sec^2/ft^2
g = acceleration of gravity, 32.17 ft/sec^2

The initial conditions of the problem, as before, are

$$t = 0 \left| \begin{matrix} y = 0 \\ \dot{y} = 0 \end{matrix} \right.$$

The same starting values used in solving the problem by Milne's method are required here. They are repeated for convenience:

$y_0 = 0.0$ ft $\qquad \dot{y}_0 = 0.0$ ft/sec

$y_1 = 0.2146$ ft $\qquad \dot{y}_1 = 4.294$ ft/sec $\qquad \ddot{y}_1 = 42.99$ ft/sec^2

$y_2 = 0.8591$ ft $\qquad \dot{y}_2 = 8.598$ ft/sec $\qquad \ddot{y}_2 = 43.08$ ft/sec^2

$y_3 = 1.935$ ft $\qquad \dot{y}_3 = 12.911$ ft/sec $\qquad \ddot{y}_3 = 43.18$ ft/sec^2

In using Hamming's noniterative method to solve a second-order differential equation such as Eq. 6-158, in which y is not present in explicit form, we use Eq. 6-147 in the following form:

(Predictor)

$$P(\dot{y}_{i+1}) = \dot{y}_{i-3} + \frac{4h}{3}[2\ddot{y}_i - \ddot{y}_{i-1} + 2\ddot{y}_{i-2}] \qquad \text{(a)}$$

(Modifier)

$$M(\dot{y}_{i+1}) = P(\dot{y}_{i+1}) - \tfrac{112}{121}[P(\dot{y}_i) - C(\dot{y}_i)] \qquad \text{(b)}$$

(Differential equation)

$$M(\ddot{y}_{i+1}) = f[t_{i+1}, M(\dot{y}_{i+1})] \qquad \text{(c)}$$

(6-159)

(Corrector)

$$C(\dot{y}_{i+1}) = \tfrac{1}{8}\{9\dot{y}_i - \dot{y}_{i-2} + 3h[M(\ddot{y}_{i+1}) + 2\ddot{y}_i - \ddot{y}_{i-1}]\} \qquad \text{(d)}$$

(Final value of $\dot{y}$)

$$F(\dot{y}_{i+1}) = C(\dot{y}_{i+1}) + \tfrac{9}{121}[P(\dot{y}_{i+1}) - C(\dot{y}_{i+1})] \qquad \text{(e)}$$

(Final value of $\ddot{y}$)

$$F(\ddot{y}_{i+1}) = f[t_{i+1}, F(\dot{y}_{i+1})] \qquad \text{(f)}$$

where Eq. 6-159c indicates the substitution of the modified value of $\dot{y}_{i+1}$ and the corresponding time value into the given differential equation to obtain the modified value of $\ddot{y}_{i+1}$ required in Eq. 6-159d. Since y does not appear explicitly in the differential equation being solved, y_{i+1} values are not required in determining $M(\ddot{y}_{i+1})$ values. Thus, final $\dot{y}_{i+1}$ values can be obtained without determining the corresponding y_{i+1} values. If displacement values are desired, they may be determined from Hamming's corrector equation as the final step in each cycle of calculation. This equation is

$$y_{i+1} = \tfrac{1}{8}\{9y_i - y_{i-2} + 3h[F(\dot{y}_{i+1}) + 2\dot{y}_i - \dot{y}_{i-1}]\} \qquad \text{(6-160)}$$

where the final value of $\dot{y}_{i+1}$ is used in place of the modified value to obtain the most accurate value of y_{i+1} possible. It may be noted, in the program which follows, that in the *first cycle* of Eq. 6-159 the starting value of $\dot{y}_i$ is used for both $P(\dot{y}_i)$ and $C(\dot{y}_i)$ in Eq. 6-159b.

If the differential equation to be solved contains y in explicit form, Eqs. 6-159 and 6-160 are not sufficient for obtaining a solution. A brief discussion of this case, with the necessary equations, is given at the conclusion of this example.

A computer solution of Eq. 6-158 designed to yield the data necessary to plot curves of the displacement velocity, and acceleration of the rocket is outlined in the flow chart shown in Fig. 6-39. Note that the previously deter-

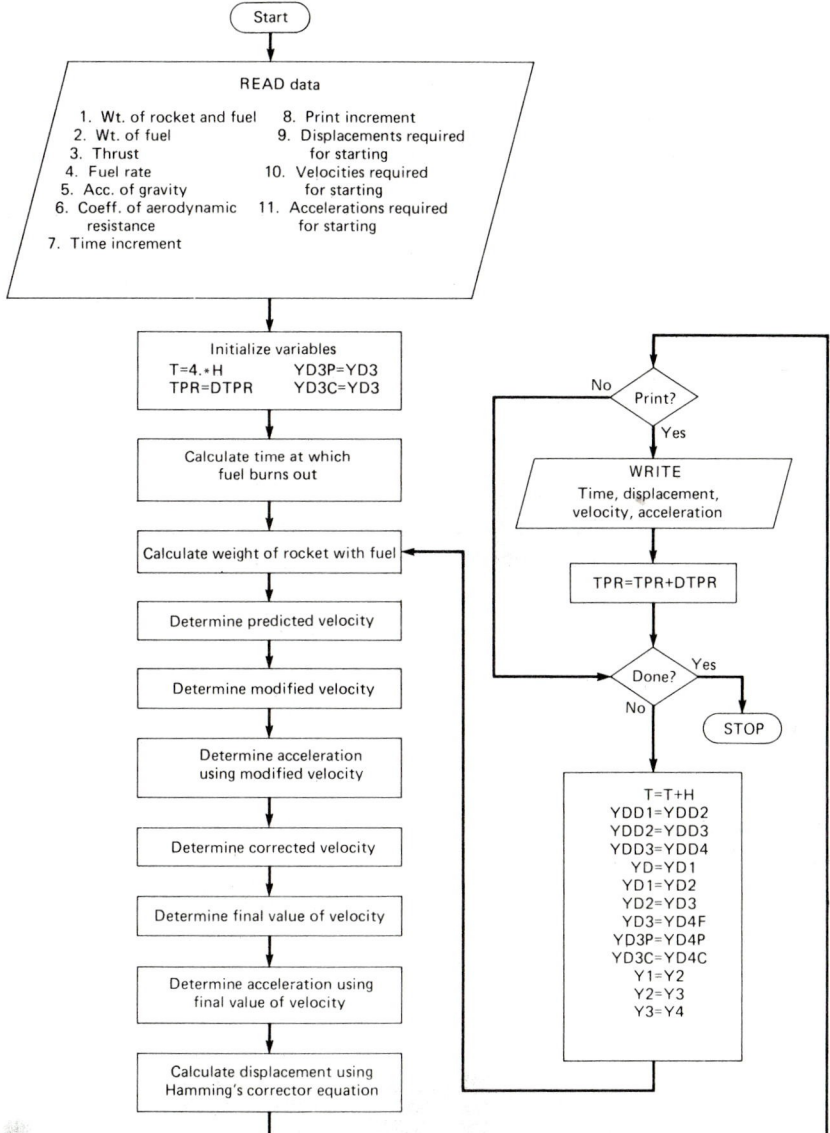

Figure 6-39 Flow chart for solution of rocket problem by Hamming's method

mined starting values are read in as data and that Hamming's method utilizing Eqs. 6-159 and 6-160 is the method programmed. The variable names used in the program are as follows:

FORTRAN Name	Quantity	Value Used
W1	Initial weight of rocket, fuel, and equipment	3000 lb
WF	Initial weight of fuel	2400 lb
TH	Thrust	7000 lb
FR	Rate of fuel consumption	40 lb/sec
G	Acceleration of gravity	32.17 ft/sec^2
DK	Coefficient of aerodynamic resistance	0.008 lb-sec^2/ft^2
DELT	Time increment	0.1 sec
DTPR	Print increment	2.0 sec
Y, Y1, Y2, Y3	Successive values of displacement	(See starting values)
YD, YD1, YD2, YD3	Successive values of velocity	(See starting values)
YDD1, YDD2, YDD3	Successive values of acceleration	(See starting values)
T	Time, sec	
TMAX	Time at which fuel burnout occurs	
TPR	Time at which printout occurs, sec	
YD4P	Predicted value of $\dot{y}$ at time considered, ft/sec	
YD4M	Modified value of $\dot{y}$ at time considered, ft/sec	
W	Weight of rocket, fuel, and equipment at time t, lb	
YD4C	Corrected value of $\dot{y}$ at time considered, ft/sec	
YD4F	Final value of $\dot{y}$ at time considered, ft/sec	
YDD4	Acceleration at time considered, ft/sec^2	
Y4	Displacement at time considered, ft	
YD3P	Predicted value of $\dot{y}$ one time increment preceding time considered, ft/sec	
YD3C	Corrected value of $\dot{y}$ one time increment preceding time considered, ft/sec	

The computer program used is as follows:

```
C     DYNAMIC CHARACTERISTICS OF A ROCKET
C     NUMERICAL INTEGRATION BY HAMMING METHOD
      READ (5,1)W1,WF,TH,FR,G,DK,H,DTPR
    1 FORMAT(11F5.0)
      READ(5,1)Y,Y1,Y2,Y3,YD,YD1,YD2,YD3,YDD1,YDD2,YDD3
      WRITE(6,2)
    2 FORMAT(1H1,5X,1HW,8X,1HF,7X,2HTH,7X,1HR,7X,1HG,7X,
     *1HK,5X,2H H,4X,3HDTP/)
      WRITE(6,3)W1,WF,TH,FR,G,DK,H,DTPR
    3 FORMAT(2F9.1,F8.0,2F8.2,F8.4,2F6.2///)
      WRITE(6,4)
    4 FORMAT(7H    TIME,6X,6HDISPL.,6X,4HVEL.,7X,4HACC./)
      T=4.*H
      TMAX=WF/FR
      TPR=DTPR
      YD3P=YD3
      YD3C=YD3
    5 W=W1-FR*T
      YD4P=YD+4./3.*(2.*YDD1-YDD2+2.*YDD3)*H
      YD4M=YD4P-112./121.*(YD3P-YD3C)
      YDD4=G*TH/W-G-DK*G/W*(YD4M**2)
      YD4C=.125*(9.*YD3-YD1+3.*H*(YDD4+2.*YDD3-YDD2))
      YD4F=YD4C+9./121.*(YD4P-YD4C)
      YDD4=G*TH/W-G-DK*G/W*(YD4F**2)
      Y4=.125*(9.*Y3-Y1+3.*H*(YD4F+2.*YD3-YD2))
      IF(ABS(T-TPR)-.01)6,6,8
    6 WRITE(6,7)T,Y4,YD4F,YDD4
    7 FORMAT(1H ,F7.2,F12.1,F11.2,F10.2)
      TPR=TPR+DTPR
    8 IF(ABS(T-TMAX)-.01)9,9,10
    9 STOP
   10 T=T+H
      YDD1=YDD2
      YDD2=YDD3
      YDD3=YDD4
      YD=YD1
      YD1=YD2
      YD2=YD3
      YD3=YD4F
      YD3P=YD4P
      YD3C=YD4C
      Y1=Y2
      Y2=Y3
      Y3=Y4
      GO TO 5
      END
```

The computer results are shown in the following tabular form:

W	F	TH	R	G	K	H	DTP
3000.0	2400.0	7000.	40.00	32.17	0.0080	0.10	2.00

TIME	DISPL.	VEL.	ACC.
2.00	86.9	87.38	44.28
4.00	350.5	176.20	44.31
6.00	790.8	263.67	42.94
8.00	1402.4	347.09	40.29
10.00	2174.9	424.15	36.63
12.00	3093.6	493.20	32.35
14.00	4141.7	553.36	27.82
16.00	5301.0	604.53	23.40
18.00	6554.0	647.15	19.32
20.00	7884.3	682.13	15.76
22.00	9277.8	710.54	12.76
24.00	10722.4	733.53	10.34
26.00	12208.4	752.20	8.43
28.00	13728.3	767.51	6.97
30.00	15276.2	780.29	5.88
32.00	16847.7	791.20	5.09
34.00	18439.6	800.76	4.52
36.00	20049.5	809.35	4.12
38.00	21675.9	817.27	3.84
40.00	23317.7	824.72	3.64
42.00	24974.0	831.85	3.51
44.00	26644.3	838.76	3.42
46.00	28328.3	845.51	3.35
48.00	30025.7	852.14	3.30
50.00	31736.3	858.68	3.26
52.00	33459.8	865.14	3.22
54.00	35196.2	871.53	3.19
56.00	36945.4	877.87	3.16
58.00	38707.0	884.14	3.13
60.00	40481.2	890.36	3.10

A comparison of the results shown with those obtained by Milne's method in Ex. 6-5 reveals that they are nearly identical. As explained previously, the results obtained by these methods are very similar when the range of integration required is not extended and the stability or relative stability of the numerical method employed is not a critical factor in obtaining an accurate solution.

As stated before, Eq. 6-159 must be modified to obtain the solution of a second-order differential equation if y appears in explicit form in the equation. The following equations, shown in correct sequence, would then be applicable:

(Predictor for $\dot{y}$)

$$P(\dot{y}_{i+1}) = \dot{y}_{i-3} + \frac{4h}{3}[2\ddot{y}_i - \ddot{y}_{i-1} + 2\ddot{y}_{i-2}] \qquad (a)$$

(Modifier for $\dot{y}$)

$$M(\dot{y}_{i+1}) = P(\dot{y}_{i+1}) - \tfrac{112}{121}[P(\dot{y}_i) - C(\dot{y}_i)] \qquad \text{(b)}$$

(Predictor for y)

$$P(y_{i+1}) = \tfrac{1}{8}\{9y_i - y_{i-2} + 3h[M(\dot{y}_{i+1}) + 2\dot{y}_i - \dot{y}_{i-1}]\} \qquad \text{(c)}$$

(Differential equation)

$$M(\ddot{y}_{i+1}) = f[(t_{i+1}, P(y_{i+1}), M(\dot{y}_{i+1})] \qquad \text{(d)}$$

(Corrector for $\dot{y}$)

$$C(\dot{y}_{i+1}) = \tfrac{1}{8}\{9\dot{y}_i - \dot{y}_{i-2} + 3h[M(\ddot{y}_{i+1}) + 2\ddot{y}_i - \ddot{y}_{i-1}]\} \qquad \text{(e)}$$

(Final value of $\dot{y}$)

$$F(\dot{y}_{i+1}) = C(\dot{y}_{i+1}) + \tfrac{9}{121}[P(\dot{y}_{i+1}) - C(\dot{y}_{i+1})] \qquad \text{(f)}$$

(Final value of y)

$$F(y_{i+1}) = \tfrac{1}{8}\{9y_i - y_{i-2} + 3h[F(\dot{y}_{i+1}) + 2\dot{y}_i - \dot{y}_{i-1}]\} \qquad \text{(g)}$$

(Final value of $\ddot{y}$)

$$F(\ddot{y}_{i+1}) = f[t_{i+1}, F(y_{i+1}), F(\dot{y}_{i+1})] \qquad \text{(h)}$$

$$(6\text{-}161)$$

Note that Eq. 6-161c, which is used as a predictor equation for y_{i+1}, is Hamming's corrector equation. An equation of the form of Eq. 6-161a could be used to obtain this predicted value, but, since $M(\dot{y}_{i+1})$ is known at this point, Eq. 6-161c can be used to obtain a better predicted value. Equation 6-161c provides a y_{i+1} value to substitute into the given differential equation in obtaining a modified value of $\ddot{y}_{i+1}$, as indicated by Eq. 6-161d. The final value of y_{i+1} is again determined by Hamming's corrector equation, as discussed in explaining Eq. 6-160.

6-9 ERROR IN THE NUMERICAL SOLUTIONS OF DIFFERENTIAL EQUATIONS

The use of numerical methods for solving differential equations generally yields "solutions" which differ from the true solutions. The difference between the numerical solution and the true solution, at any given step is known as the *total* error at that step. If the numerical solution is to be of practical value, the total error obviously must be kept within reasonable limits over the desired solution interval. The primary purpose of error analysis is to provide a means of controlling this error. The total error at any step results from the following conditions:

1. A roundoff error is introduced in the integration process at a given step by performing the arithmetic operations of that step with numerical values having a limited number of significant digits. This is known as *per-step roundoff error*.
2. A truncation error is introduced in the integration process at a given step by the use of approximate formulas in the calculations of that step. For example, the corrector formula of the modified Euler method has a truncation error of order h^3, which means that series terms containing h^3 and higher powers are neglected in using a trapezoidal area to approximate the true area of one strip under the curve of the function being integrated. This is known as *per-step truncation error*.
3. An error is present at a given step because of errors introduced in preceding steps.

With perhaps eight significant digits used in the calculations, the roundoff error introduced at each step for any of the integration methods we have discussed is very small. However, if an *unstable* method is used and if the integration involves a large number of steps, the cumulative effect of the per-step roundoff errors and their magnification in calculating subsequent steps can lead to serious total error. The use of double-precision arithmetic, which is possible on most computers, is an effective means of controlling total error due to roundoff.

Obviously, the truncation error at each step is minimum in methods which employ formulas having truncation errors of high order. This error can be reduced, in any method, by reducing the step size. However, in reducing the per-step truncation error by decreasing the step size, a limit is reached at which further reduction in step size increases the total number of steps to a point where roundoff error becomes dominant, and the total error will increase with further reduction in step size. As with roundoff error, the cumulative effect of small per-step truncation errors and their magnification in calculating subsequent steps can lead to serious total error. The use of a *stable* method such as Hamming's, under certain conditions, ensures that an error introduced at a particular step will not be magnified in subsequent ones. Although unstable methods give no such guarantee, we have seen that they can be used quite satisfactorily if an excessive number of steps is not required.

Since the total error in a numerical-integration process depends on the step size used, the analyst is faced with the problem of selecting a step size to maintain the total error less than some specified bound. On the other hand, there is no point in making the solution more accurate than the data justify by choosing too small a step size, since this unnecessarily uses expensive machine time. Furthermore, as previously stated, there is a limit to the increase in accuracy which can be obtained by decreasing the step size, owing to the presence of roundoff error. On what basis, then, can the step size be selected? To answer this question let us further examine, with respect to step size, the effect of each of the per-step errors discussed on the total error.

Roundoff error is generally present to some degree in each step of a numerical-integration process. Since its magnitude in each step depends primarily upon the digital capacity of the computer being used, the per-step roundoff error is essentially independent of the step size used. The total error due to roundoff increases with the number of steps.

Truncation error also appears in each step of the numerical process. Unlike roundoff error, the per-step truncation error is a function of the step size, since it varies as the order of error, h^n, of the method being used. Thus, the only means of controlling the overall per-step error of a method at a given step is by controlling the truncation error at that step. The total error is decreased as the per-step truncation error is decreased up to the point where the increasing number of steps and the presence of roundoff error causes an increase in the total error. Thus, the total error can be kept to a minimum by maintaining the per-step truncation error within some appropriate limiting values or bounds. However, bounds are not always selected on the basis of optimum accuracy; they may be chosen to minimize the machine time required for a solution. This would be true in a case where the optimum accuracy would exceed the justifiable accuracy, as previously mentioned.

In initially selecting a step size for a method, the per-step truncation error, which, it is felt, can be tolerated with respect to the number of steps anticipated in the process, is defined by a set of limiting values as discussed in the preceding paragraph. The best possible estimate is then made of the general magnitude of the derivative function appearing in the truncation-error term of the method, and a step size is calculated to make the per-step truncation error fall within the defined limits. After some experience with different methods for various types of problems, the initial step size can usually be selected with little difficulty.

If the derivative in the truncation-error term of a method is of high order, an estimate of its value may be difficult to determine, and the initial step size chosen may need to be adjusted on the basis of results obtained in the numerical process. A truncation-error analysis can often be made at each step of a numerical process, and the results can be used to adjust the step size at that point, if necessary, for subsequent calculations. Such per-step truncation-error analyses have been discussed for each of the integration methods considered in this chapter. The use of such an analysis in adjusting the step size is discussed in the subsection on the error estimation of Euler's method (Sec. 6-3).

6-10 SELECTING A NUMERICAL-INTEGRATION METHOD

Having discussed several different numerical methods of integrating differential equations and the error analysis of each of these methods, we are now in a position to compare the methods from the standpoint of selecting the best one for a particular application.

1. When it is obvious that the range of integration of a problem is relatively short, relatively small step sizes can be used without excessive computing time, and there is little reason to analyze the truncation error at each step, or to complicate the solution by using one of the more accurate methods. Stability is also unlikely to be a problem over a short range of integration, so a simple self-starting method such as Euler's should be satisfactory.
2. When it is obvious that the range of integration of a problem is long enough to involve a large number of steps, as in a vibration problem where the motion is to be studied over a substantial number of oscillations, a method having a small per-step truncation error (such as Milne's or Hamming's) should be used in order to minimize the cumulative error. A per-step truncation-error analysis could be made at each step to minimize the computing time required, while at the same time attaining the desired accuracy, by controlling the step size. If stability is a problem, either Hamming's method should be used in preference to Milne's, or the stabilizing technique of Milne and Reynolds should be used with Milne's method. Starting values, in either case, could be determined by using a fourth-order Runge-Kutta method.
3. When a small per-step truncation error is desired, and computing time is not important enough to require a per-step truncation-error analysis, the classic fourth-order Runge-Kutta method is a convenient one to use. It is self-starting, stability is usually not a problem, and the equations are easy to program. If double-precision arithmetic is not available, or if for some other reason roundoff error must be minimized, Gill's fourth-order Runge-Kutta method may be used. For problems in which very high accuracy must be maintained, as, for example, in the orbit problems at the end of this chapter (Probs. 6-34 and 6-35), Butcher's fifth-order Runge-Kutta method has been found highly desirable.
4. When a problem involves some intermediate range of integration wherein the accumulation of error and computing time must be considered, but neither is a critical factor, the self-starting modified Euler method or a third-order Runge-Kutta method should prove satisfactory. If a per-step error estimate is desired for purposes of controlling step size, the non-self-starting modification of Euler's method should be used.

There are many numerical methods, other than those covered in this chapter, for solving differential equations, including techniques especially fitted for certain types or orders of differential equations. However, one of the methods described here should be suitable for most engineering problems of the initial-value type.

PROBLEMS

6-1. Utilizing the relationship from elementary beam theory that

$$EI \frac{d^2y}{dx^2} = M$$

write the moment equation for the beam shown in the accompanying figure and write a program for determining the elastic curve of the beam.

Problem 6-1

6-2. Utilizing the relationship from elementary beam theory that

$$EI \frac{d^2y}{dx^2} = M$$

write the necessary moment equations and a program for determining the elastic curve of the beam shown in the accompanying figure.

Problem 6-2

6-3. The linear-lag behavior of many components in a control system may be described by the differential equation

$$\frac{dy}{dt} + \frac{y}{\tau} = \frac{Af(t)}{\tau}$$

where y = variable output of the component

$f(t)$ = variable input to the component

A = gain factor

τ = time constant

a. If the input is the ramp function $f(t) = t$, show that the solution to the differential equation is

$$y = A\tau(e^{-t/\tau} - 1) + At$$

when $y = 0$ at $t = 0$.

b. Given that $A = 10$ and $\tau = 1$, determine the output y at $t = 1$ sec by Euler's forward-integration equation. Use a pocket calculator with $\Delta t = 0.25$ and carry the integration to 6 decimal digits. Compare the numerical integration result with that from the analytical solution.

c. Do the same as in part b except use the self-starting modified Euler method. Carry out iterations until no change occurs in the 3rd decimal digit.

(partial answer: part b, $y = 3.164063$; part c, $y = 3.659$)

6-4. Solve part b of Prob. 6-3 by using the third order Runge-Kutta method instead of Euler's forward-integration equation.

6-5. A capacitance C has been added to the circuit shown in Ex. 6-3 so that

$$\frac{di}{dt} + \frac{Ri}{L} + \frac{1}{C}\int i\,dt = \frac{E}{L}$$

where the resistance $R = a + bi^2$. Noting that the current i in terms of the charge q in coulombs is $i = dq/dt$, the differential equation may be written as

$$\ddot{q} + \frac{a\dot{q}}{L} + \frac{b\dot{q}^3}{L} + \frac{q}{LC} = \frac{E}{L}$$

Problem 6-5

Write a computer program using the fourth-order Runge-Kutta method to obtain a solution for the charge q and current i. The parameter values are

E = 200 volts
L = 3 henries
a = 100 ohms
b = 50 ohms/amp
C = 8.4×10^{-7} farads

For oscillating systems such as this circuit, the accuracy of a numerical integration depends upon the ratio of $\Delta t/\tau$ where $\tau = 2\pi\sqrt{LC}$ is the natural undamped period of oscillation. To study the effect of $\Delta t/\tau$, take the limit of integration over one period, τ, and obtain solutions for the following Δt increments of integration:

$\Delta t/\tau = 0.1$
$\Delta t/\tau = 0.04$
$\Delta t/\tau = 0.02$

(partial answer: for $t = 0.002$ and $\Delta t/\tau = 0.02$, $i = 0.0975$ amps, $q = 0.1141215(10)^{-3}$ coulombs)

6-6. A spherical water tank of radius R is drained through a circular orifice of radius r at the bottom of the tank. An air hole at the top of the tank allows atmospheric pressure to exist in the empty portion of the tank. It is desired to determine the curve of the water height h versus time, so that the time to drain the tank to any level from any other level may be determined.

Problem 6-6

The volume of the water in the tank for any height h is

$$V = \tfrac{1}{3}\pi h^2(3R - h) \tag{a}$$

The rate of change of volume of water in the tank is

$$\frac{dV}{dt} = -Av \tag{b}$$

where A is the area of the orifice and v is the velocity of the water flowing through the orifice. Equation b may be rewritten as

$$\frac{dV}{dt} = -\pi r^2\sqrt{2gh} \tag{c}$$

where g is the acceleration of gravity.

Differentiation of Eq. a will also yield an expression for dV/dt, which is

$$\frac{dV}{dt} = (2\pi hR - \pi h^2)\frac{dh}{dt} \tag{d}$$

Combining Eqs. c and d and solving for dh/dt yields the differential equation

$$\frac{dh}{dt} = \frac{-r^2\sqrt{2gh}}{2hR - h^2} \tag{e}$$

The data values for the problems are

$R = 10$ ft
$r = 0.125$ ft
$g = 115,812$ ft/min^2
$h_0 = 19.875$ ft (note that if tank is full initially, the denominator of Eq. e is zero)
$\Delta t = 0.125$ min

Solve the first-order differential equation by the method assigned. Stop execution of the program when the tank is nearly empty. You may want to decrease the time increment when the water height gets below a certain level. If you do not program the problem to stop when some small h value is reached, execution will automatically stop when the value of h goes negative.

6-7. Solve Prob. 6-6 in which the data values are

$$R = 3.5 \text{ m}$$
$$r = 40 \text{ mm}$$
$$g = 9.81 \text{ m/s}^2$$
$$h_0 = 6.9 \text{ m}$$
$$\Delta t = 7.5 \text{ s}$$

6-8. An arrow (assumed to be a long slender cylinder) is fired vertically upward so that it is subjected to a drag force D as shown on the figure and the gravity force shown. The drag force for a long slender cylinder moving in a fluid medium with a velocity v may be taken as

$$D = \frac{C\gamma A v^2}{2}$$

where

γ = mass per unit volume of fluid medium

A = cross-sectional area of cylinder

C = drag coefficient (approximately equal to 1 for a cylinder in coaxial flow for a Reynolds number in the region $10^3 < R < 10^5$)

$D = k\dot{y}^2$

Problem 6-8

Assuming a constant value of $C = 1$, the differential equation of motion for the arrow during vertical flight upward is found to be

$$\frac{d\dot{y}}{dt} + \frac{K}{m}\dot{y}^2 = -g$$

or

$$\frac{dv}{dt} + \frac{K}{m}v^2 = -g$$

where

$\dot{y} = v$
$K = \gamma A/2$ (coefficient of aerodynamic resistance)
$g =$ acceleration of gravity (32.2 ft/sec^2)
$m =$ mass of arrow (W/g)

The data values for the problem are

$\gamma = 0.00237$ lb-sec^2/ft^4
$A = 7(10)^{-4}$ ft^2
$W = 0.0573$ lb

Write a program to solve the first-order differential equation by the method assigned, and determine the time t_f to reach the maximum height h for an initial velocity of 200 ft/sec.

(answer: $t_f \cong 5.31$ sec)

6-9. Refer to Prob. 6-8 and work it using the following data:

$\gamma = 1.22$ n·sec^2/m^4
$A = 0.65(10)^{-4}$ m^2
$m = 0.026$ kg
$g = 9.81$ m/sec^2

6-10. *The Northwestern Natural Gas Co. has just discovered a new gas well, and they want to study the economics of connecting this well into their existing distribution system. Their geologists estimate that the well contains 8500 tons of natural gas at a pressure of 900 psia. The point at which they want to connect the well with the distribution system is at 400 psia,

*Based on an IBM short-course problem.

so with a direct connection the latter pressure is the discharge pressure P_d which the new well will initially sense.

The discharge Q in tons/day through the outlet pipe from the well may be approximated by

$$Q = C(P^2 - P_d^2)^{0.8}$$

where

$$C = 1.11151(10)^{-4}$$
$$P = \text{internal pressure of gas in well, psia}$$
$$P_d = \text{discharge pressure, psia}$$

The rate of change of pressure in the gas well is assumed to be directly proportional to the discharge Q. That is,

$$\frac{dP}{dt} = -kQ \qquad \left(\text{where } k = \frac{900 \text{ psia}}{8500 \text{ tons}} \right)$$

Substituting the expression for Q into the latter equation, we obtain the first-order differential equation

$$\frac{dP}{dt} = -kC(P^2 - P_d^2)^{0.8}$$

with the initial condition that when $t = 0$, $P = 900$ psia.

As the gas pool is depleted, the pressure in the well will drop, and the discharge Q will diminish. When production drops below 2 tons/day, a constant pressure differential compressor is to be added to the system

Problem 6-10

as shown in the figure. The compressor will be used to boost the pressure by 100 psia so that the discharge pressure sensed by the pipe from the well will change from 400 to 300 psia. It is planned that production will continue with this compressor until the discharge again falls below 2 tons/day. At this time a second compressor will be added which can boost the pressure an additional 100 psia, so that the pipe from the well will sense a pressure of 200 psia instead of 300 psia. Production is to continue with the two compressors in the system until the discharge falls below 1 ton/day, below which production is assumed unfeasible.

Determine the complete pressure-time curve for the well using the integration method assigned. Use $\Delta t = 0.5$ day. Also determine the total cumulative recovery of tons of natural gas by using trapezoidal integration of the $Q - t$ relationship.

(partial answer: for $t = 30$ days, $P = 884$ psia, recovery $= 146.5$ tons)

6-11. Using the data of Prob. 6-10, evaluate an alternative plan using two 75 psia pressure differential compressors instead of the 100 psia compressors. Such a plan would result in an initially smaller investment by the company. Compare the total cumulative recovery with that obtained in Prob. 6-10.

6-12. A small rocket with an initial weight of 3000 lb, including 2400 lb of fuel, is fired vertically upward. The rocket burns fuel at the rate of 40 lb/sec, which develops a thrust T of 7000 lb. Considering that the drag force D

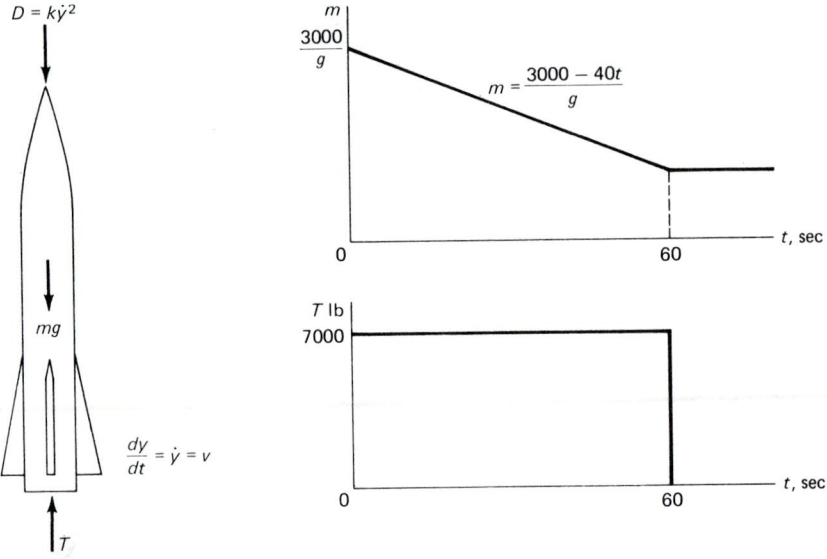

Problem 6-12

is proportional to the square of the velocity $\dot{y}$, the differential equation of motion from Newton's second law is found to be

$$\frac{d\dot{y}}{dt} + \frac{K}{m}\dot{y}^2 = \frac{T}{m} - g$$

or

$$\frac{dv}{dt} + \frac{K}{m}v^2 = \frac{T}{m} - g$$

where

$$m = \frac{3000 - 40t}{g} \qquad 0 < t \le 60$$

$$T = 7000 \text{ lb} \qquad 0 < t \le 60$$

Noting that the mass m and thrust T vary with time as shown, write a program to determine:

a. The velocity as a function of time.
b. The time required to reach the maximum height h when $v = 0$.

Assume that $g = 32.2$ ft/sec^2 and is constant, and that the coefficient of aerodynamic resistance is $K = 8(10)^{-3}$ lb-sec^2/ft^2.

Note that the velocity values obtained from the solution of the first-order differential equation can be compared with the values obtained in Ex. 6-5 in which the second-order differential equation for the rocket was used.

(partial answer: part b, $t \cong 71$ sec)

6-13. *A water conservation district has dammed a stream to create a small reservoir for irrigation and flood control. The rated capacity of the reservoir is 4000 acre-ft. When the total storage exceeds that amount, discharge is automatically initiated through the spillway of the dam. Since past records show that very heavy rainstorms occur on the average of about once in every 10 years, it is desired to determine the effectiveness of the reservoir if heavy flooding should occur. Weather data further reveal that a typical heavy rainstorm could be expected to cause an inflow into the reservoir in excess of normal flow for approximately 30 hours as shown in the following table:

*Based on an IBM short-course problem.

Time (hr)	Inflow (acre-ft/hr)	Time (hr)	Inflow (acre-ft/hr)
0	10	10	35
1	35	11	31
2	61	12	28
3	69	13	25
4	70	14	21
5	66	15	20
6	60	20	12
7	54	25	11
8	48	30	10
9	42		

Using curve-fitting techniques as discussed in Chap. 4, the inflow I in acre-ft/hr may be expressed as a function of time by the equation

$$I = 41.91te^{-0.273t} + 10$$

The differential equation

$$\frac{dV}{dt} = I - D$$

can be solved to obtain the volume of water in the reservoir as a function of time, and involves the inflow I and the discharge D as shown. In this equation

$$D = CK(V - V_d)^{1.5} \qquad \text{if } V > V_d$$

$$D = 0 \qquad\qquad\qquad \text{if } V \leq V_d$$

where V_d is the rated capacity of the reservoir (4000 acre-ft in this problem). The constant $K = 0.02$, and the discharge coefficient C is a function of the discharge D. Calibration tests of the gated spillway show that this function may be approximated as follows:

$$0 < D < 25 \qquad C = 0.8$$
$$25 \leq D < 50 \qquad C = 0.85$$
$$50 \leq D < 75 \qquad C = 0.95$$
$$75 \leq D \qquad\quad C = 1.00$$

Using the self-starting modified Euler method, obtain the data from which plots of reservoir volume versus time and discharge versus time may be drawn. Use $\Delta t = 0.1$ hr, and study the flow for a period of 30 hr, starting at the beginning of the storm. Assume that the reservoir holds 3900 acre-ft of water when the storm begins.

(partial answer: for $t = 3$ hrs, $D = 4.1$ acre-ft/hr, $V = 4040$ acre feet)

6-14. The differential equation of motion of the spring-and-mass system shown is

$$\ddot{x} + p^2 x = 0$$

where $p^2 = k/m$. If the weight of the mass is 10 lb, the spring constant $k = 1.5$ lb/in., and the initial values are

$$t = 0 \begin{vmatrix} x = 5 \text{ in.} \\ \dot{x} = 0 \end{vmatrix}$$

write a program for determining the x-t curve for one cycle of motion (frequency $= p/2\pi$ Hz).

$$\ddot{x} + p^2 x = 0$$

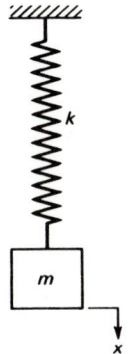

Problem 6-14

6-15. The differential equation of motion of the viscously damped spring-and-mass system shown in the accompanying figure is

$$\ddot{x} + 2n\dot{x} + p^2 x = 0$$

where $p^2 = k/m$, and $2n = c/m$. If the weight of the block is 15 lb, the

Problem 6-15

spring constant $k = 2$ lb/in., and the initial values are

$$t = 0 \begin{vmatrix} x = 5 \text{ in.} \\ \dot{x} = 0 \end{vmatrix}$$

a. Write a program for determining the x-t and $\dot{x}$-t curves for three cycles of motion for each of the following damping ratios: $n/p = 0.05$, 0.10, 0.25, and 1.0 (frequency $= \sqrt{p^2 - n^2}/2\pi$ Hz).
b. Modify the program written for part a so that only the peak values of motion (the amplitude of each successive half-cycle) are printed out as data.

(partial answer: for $n/p = 0.25$ and $t = 0.52$ sec, $x = -1.984157$ in., $\dot{x} = 6.608121$ in./sec)

6-16. Solve Prob. 6-15 with the problem data as follows:

$$k = 250 \text{ N/m}$$
$$m = 5.2 \text{ kg}$$

with the initial conditions

$$t = 0 \begin{vmatrix} x = 0 \\ \dot{x} = 0.2 \text{ m/s} \end{vmatrix}$$

6-17. The permanent magnet A exerts a force on the weight W that is inversely proportional to the square of the distance x between the mass center of W and the mass center of the magnet. If the coefficient of friction between W and the flat surface is f, show that the differential equation of motion of W is

$$\frac{d^2x}{dt^2} + \frac{k}{mx^2} - fg = 0$$

Write a FORTRAN program for obtaining the acceleration $\ddot{x}$, the velocity $\dot{x}$, and the displacement x in terms of time t. Consider that the weight W is released from rest with an initial value of $x_0 = 12$ in. As additional data, it is given that $k/m = 7200$ sec^{-2}, $f = 0.1$, and $g = 386$ in./sec^2. It is suggested that the solution be obtained by using Euler's method.

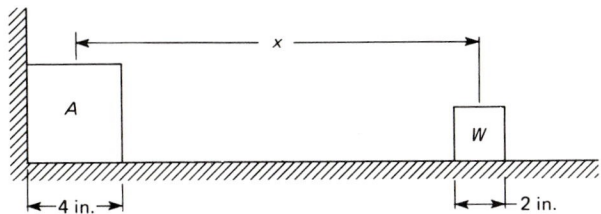

Problem 6-17

6-18. Solve Prob. 6-17 by converting the problem data given in that problem to the SI system of units for input data to your program.

6-19. A particle of mass m is released from rest at the edge of a hemispherical bowl, as shown in the accompanying figure, and slides down the inside surface of the bowl. If the coefficient of friction between the particle and the surface of the bowl is f, determine the differential *equations* of motion of the particle in the tangential direction. Note that since friction always opposes motion, different equations define the motion when $\dot{\theta}$ is positive and when $\dot{\theta}$ is negative.

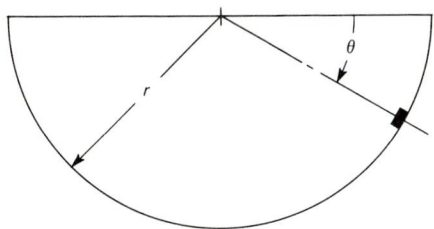

Problem 6-19

Write a FORTRAN program for determining the θ-t and $\dot{\theta}$-t curves for the period of time necessary for the particle to return to rest on the side from which it was released. Draw the θ-t and $\dot{\theta}$-t curves for a bowl with $r = 1.0$ ft and $f = 0.20$. Use the self-starting modified Euler method.

6-20. The accompanying figure shows a projectile of weight W in motion in a coordinate system whose origin is at the point from which the projectile was fired. Assuming that the acceleration of gravity is constant and that the air resistance is proportional to the square of the *total* velocity, derive the differential equations of motion for the projectile (in the x and y directions) and write a FORTRAN program for determining the x-t, y-t, $\dot{x}$-t, $\dot{y}$-t, $\ddot{x}$-t, and $\ddot{y}$-t curves from the time of firing until the projectile strikes the ground. Use the self-starting modified Euler method.

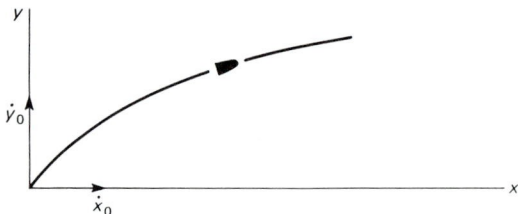

Problem 6-20

6-21. Section 6-7 includes an explanation of Milne's method of numerically integrating ordinary differential equations. Also included is a discussion concerned with using the fourth-order Runge-Kutta method to obtain starting values for the numerical process, by means of the computer. In Ex. 6-5 a program is shown in which the starting values were precalculated manually and entered into the program as data input.

Revise the program shown by adding the program steps necessary to have the computer calculate the necessary starting values for the problem, in Ex. 6-5, by using the appropriate Runge-Kutta formulas.

6-22. Work the problem of Ex. 6-3 using Euler's method and compare results with the more accurate values obtained by the third-order Runge-Kutta method used in that example.

6-23. Rewrite the FORTRAN source program of Ex. 6-4, using fourth-order Runge-Kutta formulas for obtaining starting values before switching over to Milne's method. Does instability appear in the solution? If so, use

Hamming's corrector equation in place of Milne's, and rerun the problem.

6-24. A system is released from rest in the position shown in part a of the accompanying figure. Each of the two cylinders shown weighs 32.2 lb and has a centroidal mass-moment-of-inertia of 0.125 ft-lb-sec². Body C weighs 16.1 lb. The free-body diagram for dynamic equilibrium is shown in part b. Determine the differential equation of motion of the system, and write a program for solving the resulting differential equation to obtain $\dot{\theta}$-t and θ-t curves over a 2-sec interval after the system is released from rest.

(partial answer: for $t = 0.6$ sec, $\theta = 1.9448$ rad, $\dot{\theta} = 4.4996$ rad/sec)

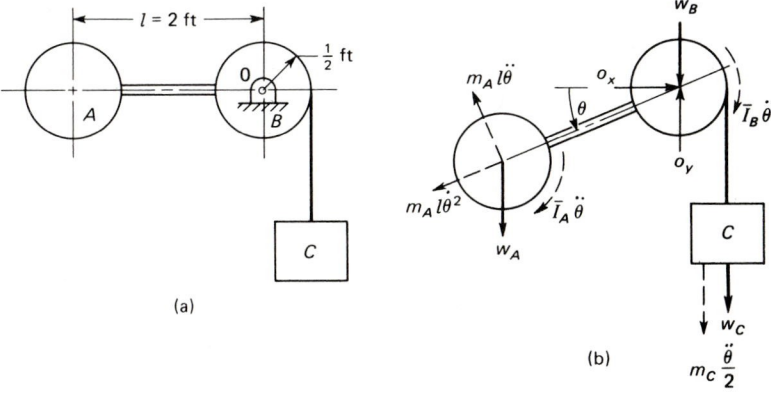

(a)

(b)

Problem 6-24

6-25. Refer to Prob. 6-24 and solve the problem if each of the 2 cylinders shown has a mass of 14.6 kg and a centroidal mass-moment-of-inertia of 0.1695 N·m·sec², and body C weighs 71.62 N.

6-26. The circuit shown in the accompanying figure consists of a coil wound around an iron core, a resistance R, a switch SW, and a voltage source E. The magnetization curve may be obtained from the equation

$$Ni = 0.5\phi + 0.003\phi^3$$

where

N = number of turns of coil
ϕ = flux in the core, kilolines
i = current, amp

Problem 6-26

From Kirchhoff's law, the impressed voltage E is

$$E = Ri + L\frac{di}{dt} = Ri + N\frac{d\phi}{dt}(10)^{-5}$$

where

L = self-inductance, henries
R = resistance, ohms
t = time, sec

If $N = 100$ turns and $R = 500$ ohms, show that the differential equation for the flux is

$$\frac{d\phi}{dT} = E - 2.5\phi - 0.015\phi^3$$

where T is in *milliseconds*. Determine solutions of this differential equation for (a) $E = 20$ volts and (b) $E = 40$ volts.

(partial answer: for $E = 20$ volts and $t = 5$ sec, $\phi = 6.415584$ kilolines)

6-27. In the accompanying figure a rocket is anchored to a very rigid abutment by an elastic supporting structure of stiffness k lb/ft. The pertinent data for a static firing test are as follows:

m_0 = initial mass = 100 slugs
t_0 = burnout time = 100 sec
m_{bo} = mass at burnout = 0.1 m_0 = 10 slugs
m' = constant rate at which fuel is burned = 0.9 slug/sec
u = velocity of jet stream relative to rocket = 8000 ft/sec
T = constant thrust = $m'u$ = 7200 lb
m = mass of rocket for $0 \le t \le 100$ sec

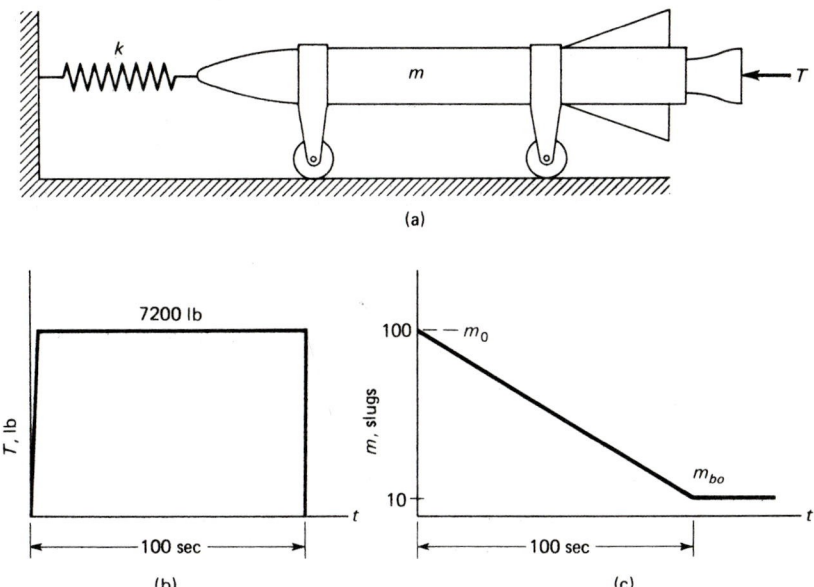

(a)

7200 lb

T, lb

100 sec

(b)

100 --- m_0

m, slugs

10

m_{bo}

100 sec

(c)

Problem 6-27

Considering that the thrust T reaches its maximum value in a few milliseconds, the differential equation of motion of the rocket is $m\ddot{x} + kx = T$ where $m = m_0 - m't$. Thus, the mathematical model of the system is a differential equation with a variable coefficient.

Program the equation to the computer and determine the maximum acceleration $\ddot{x}$ and the maximum displacement x for k/m_0 equal to 2000, 4000, 6000, 8000, and 10,000.

6-28. The decay of the unstable isotope ^{135}Te, with atomic weight of 135, results in the chemical-kinetics process

$$(^{135}\text{Te})^{k_1} \to (^{135}\text{I})^{k_2} \to (^{135}\text{Xe})^{k_3} \to (^{135}\text{Cs})^{k_4} \to \text{Ba}$$

where

Element	Half-life
Te = tellurium	2 min
I = iodine	6.7 hr
Xe = xenon	9.2 hr
Cs = cesium	$2(10)^4$ yr
Ba = barium	Stable

The set of simultaneous equations representing the transformations of the unstable isotopes to an end result of stable barium are

$$\frac{d(\text{Te})}{dt} = -k_1(\text{Te})$$

$$\frac{d(\text{I})}{dt} = k_1(\text{Te}) - k_2(\text{I})$$

$$\frac{d(\text{Xe})}{dt} = k_2(\text{I}) - k_3(\text{Xe})$$

$$\frac{d(\text{Cs})}{dt} = k_3(\text{Xe}) - k_4(\text{Cs})$$

$$\frac{d(\text{Ba})}{dt} = k_4(\text{Cs})$$

The reaction rate k for each unstable isotope can be determined from its half-life, as shown following for the isotope tellurium:

$$\int_1^{1/2} \frac{d(\text{Te})}{\text{Te}} = -k_1 \int_0^{120\text{sec}} dt$$

Write a computer program for determining the amount of each element present (a) at 5-sec intervals for the first 2 min, (b) at 1000-sec intervals for the next 9 hr, and (c) at $(10)^{10}$-sec intervals for the next 100 intervals. (*Hint:* Use the Runge-Kutta method and change the time increments for the different time intervals given above.)

6-29. A narrow ring of radius $R = 0.1$ m has a positive charge of $q = 8.00(10)^{-18}$ coulomb uniformly distributed over its circumference. The resultant electric-field strength at a distance x from the ring along the axis shown in the accompanying figure is given by

$$E = \frac{q \cos \alpha}{4\pi\varepsilon_0 s^2}$$

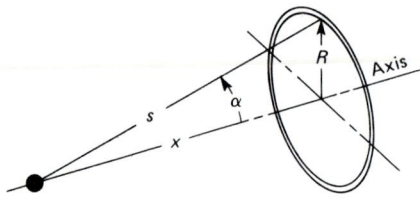

Problem 6-29

where s and α are as defined in the figure. If $\varepsilon_0 = 8.85(10)^{-12}$ coulomb^2/newton-m^2, determine the differential equation of motion of an electron released from rest at a position x_0 along the axis of the ring.

Write a FORTRAN program for determining the x-t and $\dot{x}$-t curves for one cycle of motion of the electron, using Euler's method. The mass of an electron is approximately $9.11(10)^{-31}$ kg, and the charge on an electron is $1.6(10)^{-19}$ coulomb. The electron is released from rest at a distance $x_0 = 0.2$ m from the plane of the ring.

(partial answer: for $t = 4.5$ ms, $x = -0.1925184$ m, $\dot{x} = -92.57411$ m/s)

6-30. An "infinitely long straight wire" has a uniform positive charge of $\lambda = 2.56(10)^{-17}$ coulomb/m. The resultant electric-field strength at a point a distance r from the wire is given by

$$E = \frac{\lambda}{2\pi\varepsilon_0 r}$$

where $\varepsilon_0 = 8.85(10)^{-12}$ coulomb^2/newton-m^2. The charge on an electron is $1.6(10)^{-19}$ coulomb. Determine the differential equation of motion of an electron released from rest near the wire.

Write a FORTRAN program for determining the r-t and $\dot{r}$-t curves for one cycle of motion of the electron, using Euler's method. The electron is released from rest at a distance $r_0 = 0.1$ m from the wire. Assume that there is a very small hole in the wire through which the electron can pass. The mass of an electron is approximately $9.11(10)^{-31}$ kg.

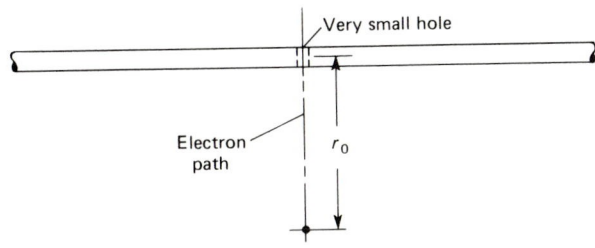

Problem 6-30

6-31. Neglecting the mass of the slender rod, the differential equation of motion of the pendulum shown in the accompanying figure is

$$\ddot{\theta} + \frac{g}{l} \sin \theta = 0$$

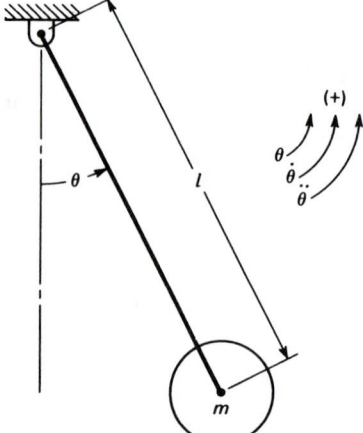

Problem 6-31

Using the initial values

$$t = 0 \left|\begin{array}{l} \theta = \pi/4 \\ \dot{\theta} = 0 \end{array}\right.$$

write a program for determining the θ-t curve for one period of oscillation for each of the following rod lengths: 40 in., 30 in., and 10 in. (frequency $\cong \sqrt{g/4l\pi^2}$ Hz).

6-32. Two tanks with cross-sectional areas of A_1 and A_2 are connected together with a pipe of length l and area A_0. The tanks and connecting pipe are filled with a fluid having a mass density of γ lb-sec²/ft⁴. The initial height of the fluid is h in each tank. It is desired to study the dynamic behavior of the two-tank system when a uniform pressure p is suddenly applied to the fluid surface of tank 2. The pressure p is described by the function

$$p = p_0 f(t)$$

where

$$f(t) = 1 \qquad 0 < t < t_0$$
$$f(t) = 0 \qquad t > t_0$$

Due to the blast pressure, the fluid in tank 1 will experience an upward displacement of x_1 and the fluid in tank 2 will experience a downward displacement of x_2. If x_1 and x_2 are not small in comparison to h, the

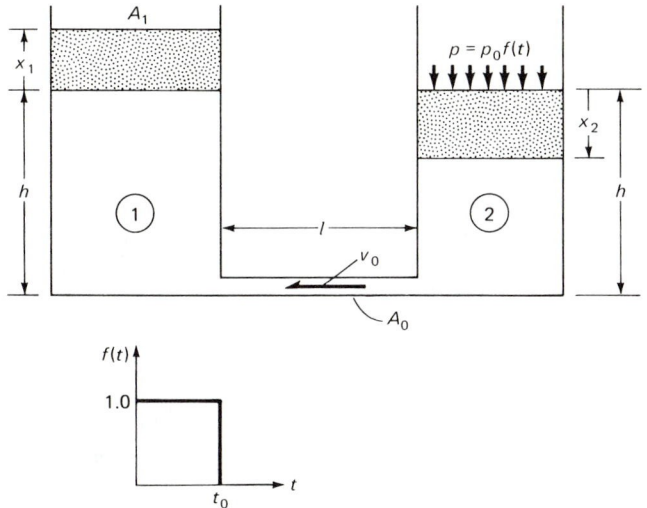

Problem 6-32

nonlinear differential equation for the system, in terms of x_1 (neglecting friction) is

$$\ddot{x}_1 + \frac{[1 - (A_1/A_2)^2]}{2D}\dot{x}_1^2 + g\frac{[1 + A_1/A_2]}{D}x_1 = \frac{p_0 f(t)}{\gamma D}$$

where

$$D = h[1 + A_1/A_2] + [1 - (A_1/A_2)^2]x_1 + \frac{lA_1}{A_0}$$

$g = 32.2$ ft/sec² (acceleration of gravity)

This nonlinear differential equation can be derived by considering the kinetic energy T and potential energy V of the system as noted in Prob. 9-16 of Chap. 9.

Write a computer program using the fourth-order Runge-Kutta method for the following parameters to obtain x_1 and $\dot{x}_1$:

$A_1/A_2 = 0.25, 2.0, 5.0$

$h = 10$ ft, $l = 1$ ft, $A_1/A_0 = 10$

$p_0/\gamma = 100$ ft²/sec², $t_0 = 2$ sec

If graphic capabilities are available obtain a computer plot of x_1.

(partial answer: for $A_1/A_2 = 0.25$ at $t = 1$ sec, $x_1 = 1.867$ ft, $\dot{x}_1 = 3.1$ ft/sec)

6-33. A study is to be made of the trajectory of a pilot ejected from an airplane at various altitudes and various airplane velocities (based on a problem from an IBM CSMP short course). It is important that the ejected pilot and seat mechanism clear the vertical stabilizer by a safe margin.

Let the origin of a fixed x'-y' coordinate system be at the center of mass of the pilot and seat ejection mechanism at the instant ejection begins. In part a of the accompanying figure, the forces which act on the pilot and seat mechanism are shown at some time t after ejection has occurred.

Applying Newton's second law along a tangent to the trajectory, with the direction of the velocity taken as the positive direction, we obtain

$$-D - W \sin \theta = \dot{V} M \tag{1}$$

in which D is the drag force, W is the weight of the pilot and seat, $\dot{V}$ is the tangential acceleration, and M is the mass of the pilot and seat. The drag force D is given by

$$\tfrac{1}{2}\gamma C_D S V^2$$

where γ is the mass density of the air, C_D is the drag coefficient, and S is the projected area of the pilot and seat normal to the direction of motion. The air density γ will vary with the altitude.

Applying Newton's second law in the normal direction and taking the direction toward the center of curvature as the positive direction, we obtain

$$W \cos \theta = \frac{MV^2}{\rho} \tag{2}$$

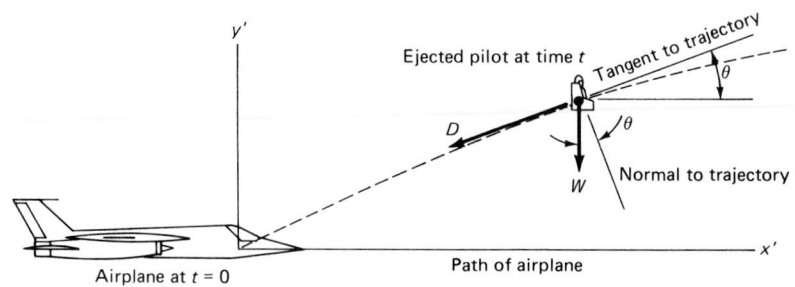

Problem 6-33(a)

in which V is the velocity of the pilot and seat and ρ is the radius of curvature of the trajectory. The quantity V^2/ρ is the acceleration in the normal direction.

Replacing one of the V's in Eq. 2 by $-\rho\dot\theta$ ($V = -\rho\dot\theta$ since V is positive for a decreasing angle θ), we obtain

$$W \cos \theta = -M\dot\theta V \tag{3}$$

Dividing Eqs. 1 and 3 through by M, and replacing W/M with g, we obtain

$$\frac{dV}{dt} = -\frac{\frac{1}{2}\gamma C_D S V^2}{M} - g \sin \theta \tag{4}$$

and

$$\frac{d\theta}{dt} = \frac{-g \cos \theta}{V} \tag{5}$$

Now let us consider the trajectory of the pilot and seat relative to the airplane as shown in part b of the accompanying figure. Let the x-y coordinate system shown move with the airplane in horizontal flight. The y displacement of the pilot and seat may be obtained at any time t by integrating

$$\frac{dy}{dt} = V \sin \theta \tag{6}$$

The x displacement may be obtained by integrating

$$\frac{dx}{dt} = V \cos \theta - V_a \tag{7}$$

in which V_a is the velocity of the airplane.

Airplane and pilot at time t

Problem 6-33(b)

Equations 4, 5, 6, and 7 constitute a set of four first-order differential equations to be solved simultaneously. It should be noted, however, that Eqs. 4 and 5 are valid only after the seat has cleared the rails ($y > 4$ ft for this problem). Prior to that time

$$\frac{dV}{dt} = 0 \tag{8}$$

and

$$\frac{d\theta}{dt} = 0 \tag{9}$$

are assumed to hold. We are assuming that the pilot and seat reach the ejection velocity relative to the plane, V_e, in a very short time, and that this relative velocity remains constant until the seat clears the rails.

Write a computer program using the fourth-order Runge-Kutta method to solve the set of four first-order differential equations (Eqs. 4, 5, 6, and 7) to determine the conditions for safe ejections in terms of airplane velocity V_a and altitude.

The initial conditions are

$$t = 0 \begin{vmatrix} x = 0 \\ y = 0 \\ V = [(V_a - V_e \sin \theta_e)^2 + (V_e \cos \theta_e)^2]^{1/2} \\ \theta = \tan^{-1} \dfrac{V_e \cos \theta_e}{V_a - V_e \sin \theta_e} \end{vmatrix} \tag{10}$$

The angle θ_e is shown in part c of the accompanying figure.

The trajectory study should include velocities, V_a, ranging from 100 to 1000 ft/sec in increments of 100 ft/sec, and altitudes ranging from sea

Problem 6-33(c)

level to 60,000 ft in increments of 1000 ft, and determining the maximum velocity at each altitude for a safe ejection. A safe ejection will be considered one in which y is greater than 20 ft when x equals minus 30 ft. This will result in the center of mass of the pilot and seat passing more than 8 ft above the top of the vertical stabilizer (see part b of the accompanying figure).

The following data values are to be used:

M = mass of pilot and seat, 7.0 slugs

V_e = ejection velocity relative to plane, 40.0 ft/sec

C_D = drag coefficient, 1.0 (dimensionless)

θ_e = angle of ejection, 15.0 deg

S = projected area, pilot and seat, 10.0 ft^2

g = acceleration of gravity, 32.2 ft/sec^2

The mass density of the air at various altitudes is as follows:

Altitude (ft)	γ(lb-sec^2/ft^4)
0	0.002377
1,000	0.002308
2,000	0.002241
4,000	0.002117
6,000	0.001987
10,000	0.001755
15,000	0.001497
20,000	0.001267
30,000	0.000891
40,000	0.000587
50,000	0.000364
60,000	0.000234

Problem 6-33(d)

Begin the study at sea level and a velocity of 100 ft/sec. Use a t_{max} of 3.0 sec, $\Delta t = .01$ sec, and a condition which will stop the integration when x becomes algebraically less than -30. Thus, when $x \cong -30$ ft, integration will cease. The y value should be checked to see if it is greater than 20.0 ft, which indicates a safe ejection. If a safe ejection is indicated, write out the altitude, velocity of the airplane, and the y value. If an ejection is safe at some particular altitude and velocity, it will be safe at all altitudes higher than that altitude for all velocities up to that velocity because of the decreasing drag force with higher altitudes. Therefore, after a safe ejection at a given altitude and velocity is indicated, the velocity should be increased by 100 ft/sec for a rerun. Eventually an unsafe ejection condition will occur. When it does, the altitude of the airplane should be incremented by 1000 ft with the velocity unchanged. This continues until a safe ejection again occurs, and the velocity is then incremented as explained earlier. Reruns are made until either the incremented altitude exceeds 60,000 ft or the incremented velocity exceeds 1000 ft/sec. With the data obtained, the altitude-velocity region shown in part d of the accompanying figure can be separated into safe and unsafe parts. With the technique outlined, it will not be necessary to run for all combinations of altitude and velocity.

6-34. The accompanying figure shows the earth with mass m_e, the moon with mass m_m, and a satellite with mass m. The satellite is small compared to the earth and the moon ($m \ll m_e$, $m \ll m_m$). The three masses are assumed to attract each other according to the inverse square law, but the influence of the satellite on the motion of the earth and the moon is

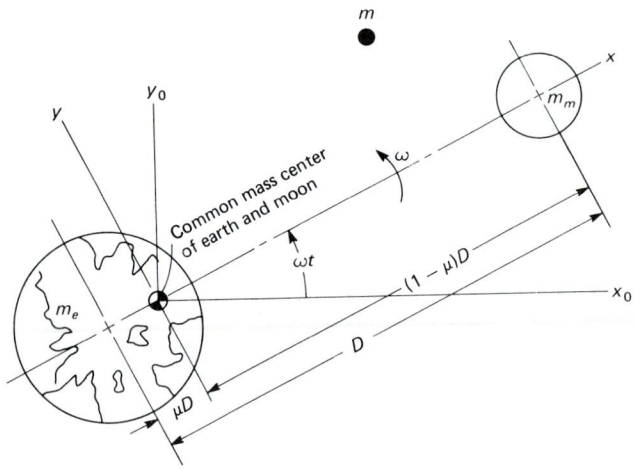

Problem 6-34

considered to be negligible. The analysis of such a system is referred to as the restricted three-body problem.

The earth and the moon revolve about their common center of mass, which is located inside the earth as shown in the figure. The distance D between the mass center of the earth and that of the moon is assumed to be constant. The motion of the satellite is such that it lies in the plane of revolution of the earth and the moon.

The x_0-y_0 coordinate system shown is nonrotating, and its acceleration is assumed as negligible (Newton's second law is valid in this reference frame). Transforming the equation of motion of the satellite in the x_0 direction in the nonrotating set of axes to the rotating x-y coordinate system results in two equations of motion in the latter coordinate system. If the distance D between the mass centers of the earth and moon is chosen as unity, and the unit of time is chosen such that the angular velocity ω of the rotating x-y reference frame is unity ($\tau = 2\pi$), the equations of motion of the satellite in terms of the x-y coordinate system are

$$\ddot{x} = x + 2\dot{y} - \mu' \frac{x + \mu}{[(x + \mu)^2 + y^2]^{3/2}} - \mu \frac{x - \mu'}{[(x - \mu')^2 + y^2]^{3/2}}$$

$$\ddot{y} = y - 2\dot{x} - \mu' \frac{y}{[(x + \mu)^2 + y^2]^{3/2}} - \mu \frac{y}{[(x - \mu')^2 + y^2]^{3/2}}$$

where

$$\mu = \frac{m_m}{m_e + m_m}$$

$$\mu' = 1 - \mu$$

These equations may be solved numerically to obtain the x and y coordinates of the satellite for various values of the independent variable time. It is known that closed periodic orbits exist in the rotating x-y coordinate system.

Write a FORTRAN program for solving these equations simultaneously, using the fourth-order Runge-Kutta method. Using the following initial conditions and parameters, determine the path of the satellite in the x-y system:*

---

*These initial conditions result in a closed periodic orbit. See NASA Contractor Report CR-61139, "Study of the Methods for the Numerical Solution of Ordinary Differential Equations," prepared by O. B. Francis, Jr. et al. for the NASA-George C. Marshall Space Flight Center, June 7, 1966.

$$t = 0 \begin{cases} x = 0.9940000000000000 \\ y = 0.0000000000000000 \\ \dot{x} = 0.0000000000000000 \\ \dot{y} = -2.1138987966945027 \end{cases}$$

$$\mu = 0.0122774710000000$$

$$\tau = 5.4367954392601900 \text{ time units}$$

Use the radius of curvature of the satellite's path in the x-y system to control the time increment in the computer program. If $\rho < 0.1$, use $\Delta t = 1/2^{13}$; if $0.1 \le \rho < 0.7$, use $\Delta t = 1/2^{10}$; if $0.7 \le \rho < 2.0$, use $\Delta t = 1/2^{7}$; and if $\rho \ge 2.0$, use $\Delta t = 1/2^{6}$. The given time increments are expressible exactly in binary form so that cumulative roundoff error in summing the time increments is avoided using a binary computer.

6-35. Using the computer program written for Prob. 6-34 and the following initial conditions and parameters, determine the path of the satellite in the rotating x-y coordinate system:

$$t = 0 \begin{cases} x = 0.9940000000000000 \\ y = 0.0000000000000000 \\ \dot{x} = 0.0000000000000000 \\ \dot{y} = -2.0317326295573368 \end{cases}$$

$$\mu = 0.0122774710000000$$

$$\tau = 11.1243403372660851 \text{ time units}$$

Use the same time increments as suggested in Prob. 6-34.

Chapter 7
Ordinary Differential Equations: Boundary-Value Problems

7-1 INTRODUCTION

Problems in which the conditions to be satisfied by the solution or its derivatives are given at the point where the integration is to begin are usually referred to as *initial-value* problems, as explained in Chap. 6. We will now consider problems in which conditions are specified at both ends of the interval over which the integration is to occur. Ones of this type are known as *boundary-value* problems. Since these involve a minimum of two boundary conditions, we will obviously be considering differential equations of the second order or higher.

The numerical solution of boundary-value problems is somewhat more difficult than that of initial-value problems. Two elementary methods are used to solve engineering problems of this type: one consists of a trial-and-error procedure; the other requires the simultaneous solution of a set of algebraic equations.

7-2 TRIAL-AND-ERROR METHOD

A trial-and-error method can be used to solve both linear and nonlinear differential equations of the second order or higher. The technique involves the assumption or approximate calculation of the initial values of the problem which are unknown. This, in effect, reduces the problem to an initial-value problem for which trial solutions can be obtained by using one of the integration methods discussed in Chap. 6. After a trial solution is obtained, the known boundary values at the end of the integration interval are compared with the corresponding values provided by the trial solution. If the solution values at this point do not agree with the known boundary values, new initial-condition values must be approximated and another trial solution made. This procedure continues until a trial solution is obtained which satisfies the known final boundary values.

It should be apparent that if it becomes necessary to approximate several different initial values, the number of trial solutions required could become very large. For this reason the trial-and-error approach is usually applied only to the solution of problems in which just one initial value is unknown. For example, if we consider the equation

$$y'' = f(x, y, y') \tag{7-1}$$

with the boundary conditions

$$x = a \begin{vmatrix} y = y_a \\ y' = ? \end{vmatrix} \qquad x = b \begin{vmatrix} y = y_b \end{vmatrix}$$

we can assume a value for y' at $x = a$ and integrate as we normally would to obtain the solution of a second-order initial-value problem, using a method applicable to that type of problem. If the value of y at $x = b$, provided by the trial solution, is larger than the known boundary value at this point, a new initial value of y' is chosen which is smaller than the original approximate value used, and another trial solution is made. If the resulting value of y at $x = b$ is smaller than y_b, a larger initial value is chosen for y', and another trial solution is made. This procedure continues until a solution is obtained in which the calculated value of y at $x = b$ is approximately equal to the boundary value at that point, within some prescribed limit of accuracy.

In general, the relationship between the initial trial values of y' and the resulting final values of y obtained from the trial y' values is not a linear one. However, linear interpolation is sometimes used to determine approximate initial values. In this procedure successive approximate values of y_a' and the corresponding values of y obtained at $x = b$ are used along with the known boundary value of y at $x = b$ to obtain a new value of y_a' for a subsequent trial solution.

A bisection method, similar to the bisection technique employed for finding roots of functions (Sec. 2-3), is frequently used and is somewhat easier to apply than linear interpolation. In this procedure, two trial values of y' at $x = a$ are selected which are quite sure to bracket the correct value of y_a'. Let these selected trial values be y'_{a_1} and y'_{a_2}. We then use

$$y'_a = 0.5(y'_{a_1} + y'_{a_2})$$

in an integration procedure to determine y at $x = b$ for this y'_a value. From the y_b value obtained, it can usually be determined whether the correct y'_a value is between y'_{a_1} and y'_a or between y'_a and y'_{a_2} by checking whether the value of y_b obtained is larger or smaller than the correct value known for y_b from the boundary condition. Suppose it is between y'_{a_1} and y'_a. In this case y'_a is renamed y'_{a_2}, and a new y'_a is calculated from

$$y'_a = 0.5(y'_{a_1} + y'_{a_2})$$

Integration is then performed using the new y'_a to find a new y_b. The latter value is then again compared to the known correct y_b value to determine if the correct y'_a value is between y'_{a_1} and y'_a or between y'_a and y'_{a_2}. Suppose that this time the correct value is between y'_a and y'_{a_2}. In this case y'_a is renamed y'_{a_1}, and a new y'_a is calculated as before. The procedure continues until the y value at $x = b$ is sufficiently close to the known boundary value. The bisection technique is illustrated and further explained in the example which follows. In this example the second known boundary value is that of the first derivative at the second boundary.

EXAMPLE 7-1

Let us consider the problem of dissipating heat in space. In many engineering applications, heat must be dissipated from bodies. We are all aware of common examples of heat dissipation—from combustion engines, air-conditioning units, bearing surfaces, and so on. Often, heat is dissipated from a body by the simultaneous action of conductive and convective heat transfer to a fluid medium surrounding the body, and by thermal radiation. The dissipation of heat from a body deep in outer space is limited to thermal radiation, because of the negligible amount of atmosphere encountered there. Therefore, the thermal-radiation characteristics of materials and the geometries of radiating surfaces become very important in considering heat dissipation in such an environment.

In the power plant of a space station, for example, heat must be dissipated to maintain the plant at a normal operating temperature. If a working fluid is utilized to transfer heat from the power plant through coolant tubes which are exposed to surrounding space, and is then recycled through the power plant, the fluid must lose some heat during the cycle. Assuming that the material composing the coolant tubes is an excellent conductor, the amount of heat dissipated from the space station will depend primarily on the thermal-radiation characteristics of the tubing. Since the rate of heat transfer by thermal

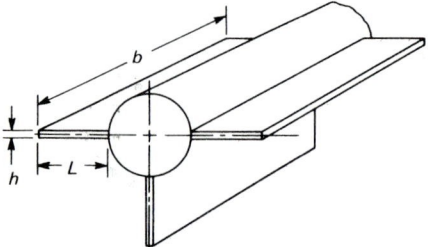

Figure 7-1   Heat-dissipating system

radiation is a function, among others, of the area of the radiating surface, the addition of area to the coolant tubing, in the form of numerous small fins, facilitates heat dissipation and reduces the amount of tubing required. Figure 7-1 is a simplified sketch of a section of coolant tubing with several such fins attached.

We will be concerned with analyzing temperature distributions along fins with various geometries. With a constant operating temperature for the power plant, the problem is one of *steady* heat flow with the system in thermal equilibrium. Since the dissipation of heat by the fin being considered involves both conduction along the fin and radiation from the fin surface, a brief review of the basic principles of each type of heat transfer is in order before proceeding to the development of the differential equation defining the temperature distribution along such a fin.

Conduction

Fourier's law of conduction states that the instantaneous rate of heat flow is proportional to the area A through which the heat flows at right angles, and to the temperature gradient along the flow axis. It is formulated as

$$\frac{\partial Q}{\partial \phi} = -kA \frac{\partial T}{\partial x} \tag{7-2}$$

where ϕ is time, A is area, $\partial T/\partial x$ is the temperature gradient and is negative when heat flow is in the positive x direction, and k is a proportionality factor which is a function of the physical properties of the conductor and is referred to as the *thermal conductivity* of the conductor. Since the temperature at any given location in a conductor does not vary with time for steady-state conduction, it follows that the temperature gradient and, consequently, the rate of heat flow are likewise independent of time. Hence the instantaneous rate of heat flow $\partial Q/\partial \phi$ becomes a constant rate of heat flow and is usually designated as q_c. Equation 7-2 then becomes, for steady heat flow,

$$q_c = -kA \frac{dT}{dx} \tag{7-3}$$

Equation 7-3, with the appropriate parameter values, will define the rate of heat transfer by conduction along the fin to be considered in our analysis.

Thermal Radiation

When a body is heated, radiant energy is emitted by the body at a rate and of a quality dependent on the temperature of the body. The *emissive power* W of a surface actually varies not only with the temperature but also with the roughness of the surface and, if the surface is metal, with the degree of surface oxidation. The quality of radiation is measured by its distribution in the spectrum, and is a function of the wavelength of emission and the temperature at which emission occurs. A surface which emits radiant energy will also absorb incident radiation. The fraction of the total incident radiation present which a surface is capable of absorbing is called the *absorptivity* of the surface; it is designated by α.

Consider two small surfaces, of area A_1 and A_2, in a large enclosure which is perfectly insulated from any external heat transfer. When the surfaces reach a state of thermal equilibrium, they will emit radiation at the respective rates $A_1 W_1$ and $A_2 W_2$ throughout the portion of the hemisphere above each element of surface. If the incident radiation impinging on the surfaces, owing to the radiation of the enclosure, is designated as I, and the surfaces have respective absorptivities of α_1 and α_2, they will absorb the incident radiation in that proportion, and an energy balance will show that

$$\alpha_1 I A_1 = A_1 W_1 \quad \text{and} \quad \alpha_2 I A_2 = A_2 W_2 \tag{7-4}$$

from which

$$\frac{W_1}{\alpha_1} = \frac{W_2}{\alpha_2} = \frac{W_3}{\alpha_3} = \cdots \frac{W_n}{\alpha_n} \tag{7-5}$$

The above generalization—that, at thermal equilibrium, the ratio of the emissive power of a surface to its absorptivity is the same for all bodies—is known as Kirchhoff's law. Since α is the fraction of incident radiation absorbed and cannot exceed unity, Eq. 7-4 shows that an upper limit exists on the emissive power of a body. This upper limit is usually denoted as W_B, and any surface having this upper-limiting emissive power is called a *perfect radiator*. Since such a surface must also have perfect absorptivity (α = unity), it will have zero reflectivity, and is thus commonly referred to as a *black body*.

The ratio of the emissive power of an actual surface (commonly called a *gray body*) to that of a black body is called the *emissivity* of the surface and is denoted by ε. Since the emissivity of an actual body is, in general, $W_n = W_B \varepsilon_n$, Eq. 7-5 may be rewritten as

$$\frac{W_B \varepsilon_1}{\alpha_1} = \frac{W_B \varepsilon_2}{\alpha_2} = \frac{W_B \varepsilon_3}{\alpha_3} = \cdots = \frac{W_B}{\alpha_B} \tag{7-6}$$

where W_B/α_B is the ratio for a black body. Since α_B is unity for a black body, Eq. 7-6 may be reduced to

$$\frac{\varepsilon_1}{\alpha_1} = \frac{\varepsilon_2}{\alpha_2} = \frac{\varepsilon_3}{\alpha_3} = \cdots = \text{unity} \tag{7-7}$$

Thus, Kirchhoff's law may be restated to say that, at thermal equilibrium, the emissivity and absorptivity of a body are the same. Actually, this law is valid only when the body is receiving radiation from surroundings at its own temperature, since the emissivity of a body at temperature T_1 is not the same as its absorptivity when it is absorbing radiation from some other body at temperature T_2. However, owing to the high values of emissivity of most surfaces which are of engineering importance, and because of the small change of their emissivities with temperature, the emissivity and absorptivity of a body may be considered equal without introducing serious error. The emissivity value normally used is the value associated with the higher temperature.

Other factors involved in the transfer of heat by thermal radiation include the shape and relative positions of the heat-interchanging surfaces. Although the *intensity of radiation* of black bodies is independent of these factors, this is not true for actual bodies. For the latter, the intensity varies with the angle between the normals to the two surfaces. Two values of emissivity are therefore usually considered—*hemispherical* emissivity and *normal* emissivity. For non-metals, the hemispherical emissivity is substantially the same as the normal emissivity. Fortunately, for most surfaces used in engineering, the values of normal emissivity may be used for hemispherical-emission conditions without introducing appreciable error.

The preceding discussion is a good example of the rational idealization which occurs in describing physical phenomena by representative mathematical models.

Since the total emissive power of a black body depends only on its temperature, the second law of thermodynamics may be utilized to prove a proportionality between emissive power and the fourth power of the absolute temperature. This relation, the Stefan-Boltzmann law, is

$$W_B = \sigma T^4 \tag{7-8}$$

where σ is the Stefan-Boltzmann constant.

The net rate of loss of energy by radiation from a body at temperature T_1 in black surroundings at temperature T_2 is given by

$$q_r = \sigma A_r(\varepsilon_1 T_1^4 - \alpha_{1,2} T_2^4) \tag{7-9}$$

where A_r is the area of the radiating surface, ε_1 is the emissivity of the radiating body at temperature T_1, and T_1 and T_2 are the temperatures of the radiating

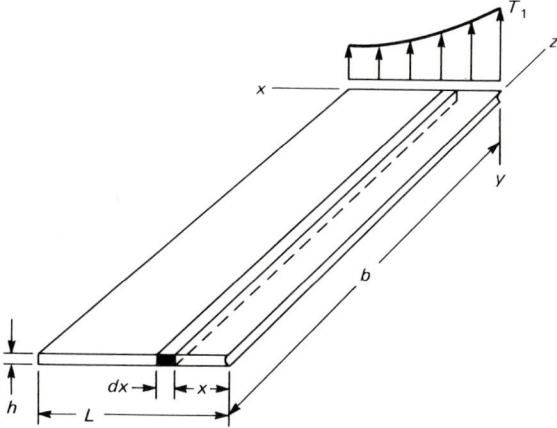

Figure 7-2 Geometry of radiating fin

and receiving bodies, respectively, measured in degrees Rankine (°R). The subscripts of the absorptivity factor $\alpha_{1,2}$ refer to the value of the absorptivity with different emitter and receiver temperatures T_1 and T_2. Referring to the previous discussion of the relationship between ε_1 and $\alpha_{1,2}$ for engineering applications, we may rewrite Eq. 7-9 as

$$q_r = \sigma A_r \varepsilon_1 (T_1^4 - T_2^4) \tag{7-10}$$

since $\varepsilon_1 \cong \alpha_{1,2}$.

  With the preceding information as a background, let us consider the development of the differential equation defining the thermal-equilibrium state of one of the fins of Fig. 7-1. Such a fin is shown in Fig. 7-2, with the geometry defined. The parameters with which we will be concerned are as follows:

T_1 = absolute Fahrenheit temperature at any position along the fin, °R

T_2 = absolute Fahrenheit temperature of surrounding space, 0°R

σ = Stefan-Boltzmann constant, $0.173(10)^{-8}$ Btu/(ft)²(hr)(°R)⁴

ε_1 = emissivity of fin, 0.8

b = width of fin in z direction, 0.5 ft

h = thickness of fin, $0.005 \le h \le 0.01$ ft

k = thermal conductivity of fin, 25 Btu/(hr)(ft)(°R)

$(T_1)_0$ = constant temperature of fin at root end ($x = 0$), 2000°R

L = length of fin, 0.25 ft

  Since the root end of the fin, $x = 0$, is exposed to a constant heat source such that its temperature is a constant 2000°R, the fin will be in thermal equilibrium when the net heat loss per hour due to radiation is equal to the heat per hour flowing into the fin from the coolant tube to which the fin is attached. Since a temperature gradient must exist in order that heat can be conducted along the fin, the temperature T_1 will be different at each x coordinate along the fin. Because the radiation of heat is a function of the temperature T_1 of the radiating surface, the radiation of each differential area along the fin in the x direction will be different. With the fin as a whole in thermal equilibrium, each element of the fin must also be in thermal equilibrium. Therefore, the difference between the amount of heat flowing into and out of each differential element (per unit of time) must equal the heat dissipated (per unit of time) by the radiating surfaces of the element. Referring to Fig. 7-2, an element is selected which has a cross-sectional area bh, an effective radiating surface of $2b\ dx$, and a length of dx. Neglecting any radiation from the very small perimetrical surfaces of the fin and the curvature of the root area of the fin, we may write, from Eqs. 7-3 and 7-10,

$$\left[-kbh\left(\frac{dT_1}{dx}\right)_x\right] - \left[-kbh\left(\frac{dT_1}{dx}\right)_{x+dx}\right] = \sigma\varepsilon_1(2b\ dx)(T_1^4 - T_2^4)$$

from which

$$kbh\left[\frac{(dT_1/dx)_{x+dx} - (dT_1/dx)_x}{dx}\right] = 2\sigma\varepsilon_1 b(T_1^4 - T_2^4)$$

or

$$\frac{d^2T_1}{dx^2} = \frac{2\sigma\varepsilon_1}{kh}(T_1^4 - T_2^4) \qquad\qquad (7\text{-}11)$$

Equation 7-11 is the differential equation defining the thermal-equilibrium state of the fin, the solution of which will yield the temperature distribution along the fin.

The pertinent boundary values are

$$x = 0 \left|\begin{array}{l} T_1 = 2000°\mathrm{R} \\ \dfrac{dT_1}{dx} = ? \end{array}\right. \qquad x = L \left|\dfrac{dT_1}{dx} = 0\right. \qquad (7\text{-}12)$$

To illustrate the trial-and-error solution of Eq. 7-11, we will use the self-starting modified Euler method which was discussed in Sec. 6-4. The equations outlining this method are as follows:

(Predictor for T')

$$P(T'_{i+1}) = T'_i + T''_i(\Delta x) \qquad \text{(a)}$$

(Predictor for T)

$$P(T_{i+1}) = T_i + \left[\frac{T'_i + P(T'_{i+1})}{2}\right](\Delta x) \qquad \text{(b)}$$

(Differential equation)

$$P(T''_{i+1}) = f[P(T_{i+1})] \qquad \text{(c)}$$

(Corrector for T')

$$C(T'_{i+1}) = T'_i + \left[\frac{T''_i + P(T''_{i+1})}{2}\right](\Delta x) \qquad \text{(d)}$$

(Corrector for T)

$$C(T_{i+1}) = T_i + \left[\frac{T'_i + C(T'_{i+1})}{2}\right](\Delta x) \qquad \text{(e)}$$

(Differential equation)

$$C(T''_{i+1}) = f[C(T_{i+1})] \qquad \text{(f)}$$

(7-13)

where $P(T'_{i+1})$, $C(T'_{i+1})$, and $P(T_{i+1})$, $C(T_{i+1})$ are predicted and corrected values of the temperature gradients and temperatures, respectively. Note that T_1 is designated merely as T in Eq. 7-13 to facilitate the subscripting used. The symbols $P(T''_{i+1})$ and $C(T''_{i+1})$ indicate predicted and corrected values of (T''_{i+1}) which are obtained by substituting the appropriate T values into the given differential equation as indicated by Eq. 7-13c and f.

Inspection of Eq. 7-13a reveals that we cannot start the numerical integrating process until we have obtained an initial value of T'_i. The steps of a trial-and-error procedure employing bisection for arriving at a correct T'_i are listed below. It is suggested that the steps shown be studied in conjunction with the flow chart shown in Fig. 7-4.

1. Two initial values of T' are chosen, one of them being a very small negative value or zero and the other a very large negative value (T' is known to be negative at the root of the fin, $x = 0$) such that the correct initial value of T' is quite sure to be between the two values selected. In the program shown later, the name LOW is used for the small value and HIGH for the large value.
2. The T' value used for the first trial is the average of the two values discussed above (the T' interval is bisected). That is,

$$T' = 0.5(\text{HIGH} + \text{LOW}) \qquad (7\text{-}14)$$

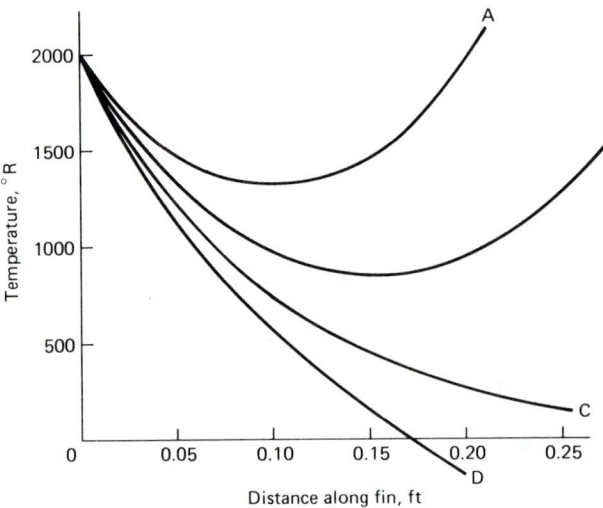

Figure 7-3 Temperature curves for various assumed initial temperature gradients

3. Equation 7-13 is then used to integrate over the desired interval from $x = 0$ to $x = L$, using the T' value in step 2 as a starting value. Equation 7-11 is very sensitive with respect to the initial value of T'. For example, if T' is chosen as just a very little smaller negative value than the correct value, the T values can become very large before the integration interval is completed, even resulting in overflow in the computer. This is shown in curve A of Fig. 7-3 where the T curve heads for a large value before the end of the fin is reached. Conversely, if T' is chosen as just a very little larger negative value than the correct one, the T curve will go negative before the end of the fin is reached, as shown by curve D of Fig. 7-3. Physically it is known that T can never exceed the initial value of 2000°R, nor can it ever be less than 0°R. Therefore, if T exceeds 2000°R at any time during the integration, the integration is terminated. Since this indicates that T is becoming too large, the initial T' was too small. The correct initial T' value is then known to have a value between the T' value tried and HIGH. Therefore, the T' previously tried is assigned to the name LOW, and a new trial T' value equal to the average of LOW and HIGH is calculated, and the T values checked using this trial value to see if the values follow a curve like A or D. If they again result in a curve like A, the process just described is repeated. If the new trial value results in T values which go negative as in curve D, the integration is again terminated. This means that the initial T' value is too high, and that the correct T' value thus lies between the T' value used and LOW. Therefore, the T' previously tried is assigned to the name HIGH, and a new trial value of T' is calculated which is equal to the average of LOW and HIGH.

4. The trial runs of part 3 continue until an integration is completed, which means that a positive value of T which is less than 2000°R has been obtained at $x = L$, the end of the fin. The first integration completed could have the form of either curve B or curve C in Fig. 7-3. If, by chance, the T' value used in the run which resulted in a completed integration were the correct T' value, the value of T' would be zero at $x = L$, the T curve would appear as one of the curves in Fig. 7-5, and a solution would have been obtained. However, the results of the first completed integration will generally be one of the curves B or C in Fig. 7-3. In the first case, with the final T' value positive, we know that a larger negative initial T' value must be used for the next integration. Therefore, the previously used T' value is assigned to the name LOW, and a new T' value is calculated as the average of LOW and HIGH for the next run. If the final T' value is negative, we know that a smaller negative initial T' value must be used. Therefore, the previously used T' value is assigned to the name HIGH, and a new T' value is calculated as the average of LOW and HIGH for the next run.
5. The integration trials of part 4 continue until the final T' value is sufficiently close to zero. One final integration is then performed in which T and T' values are printed at selected increments of x.

In discussing the use of the self-starting modified Euler method in Sec. 6-4, iteration was used at each integration step until two successive corrected values of the dependent variable differed by less than a small prescribed value. However, in this problem in which the complete integration may have to be performed several times because of the trial-and-error nature of the solution, we will make a small sacrifice in accuracy to save computing time by not iterating at each integration step.

The flow chart for the solution of this example is shown in Fig. 7-4. The variable names associated with the problem quantities in the computer program are as follows:

FORTRAN

Name	Quantity	Problem Value
LOW	An initial temperature gradient value which is quite certain to be smaller than the correct temperature gradient T' (first value of LOW shown)	-0.010°R/ft
HIGH	An initial temperature gradient value which is quite certain to be larger than the correct temperature gradient T' (first value of HIGH shown)	$-40,000$°R/ft
EMISS	Emissivity of fin	0.8
C	Thermal conductivity of fin	25 Btu/(hr)(ft)(°R)

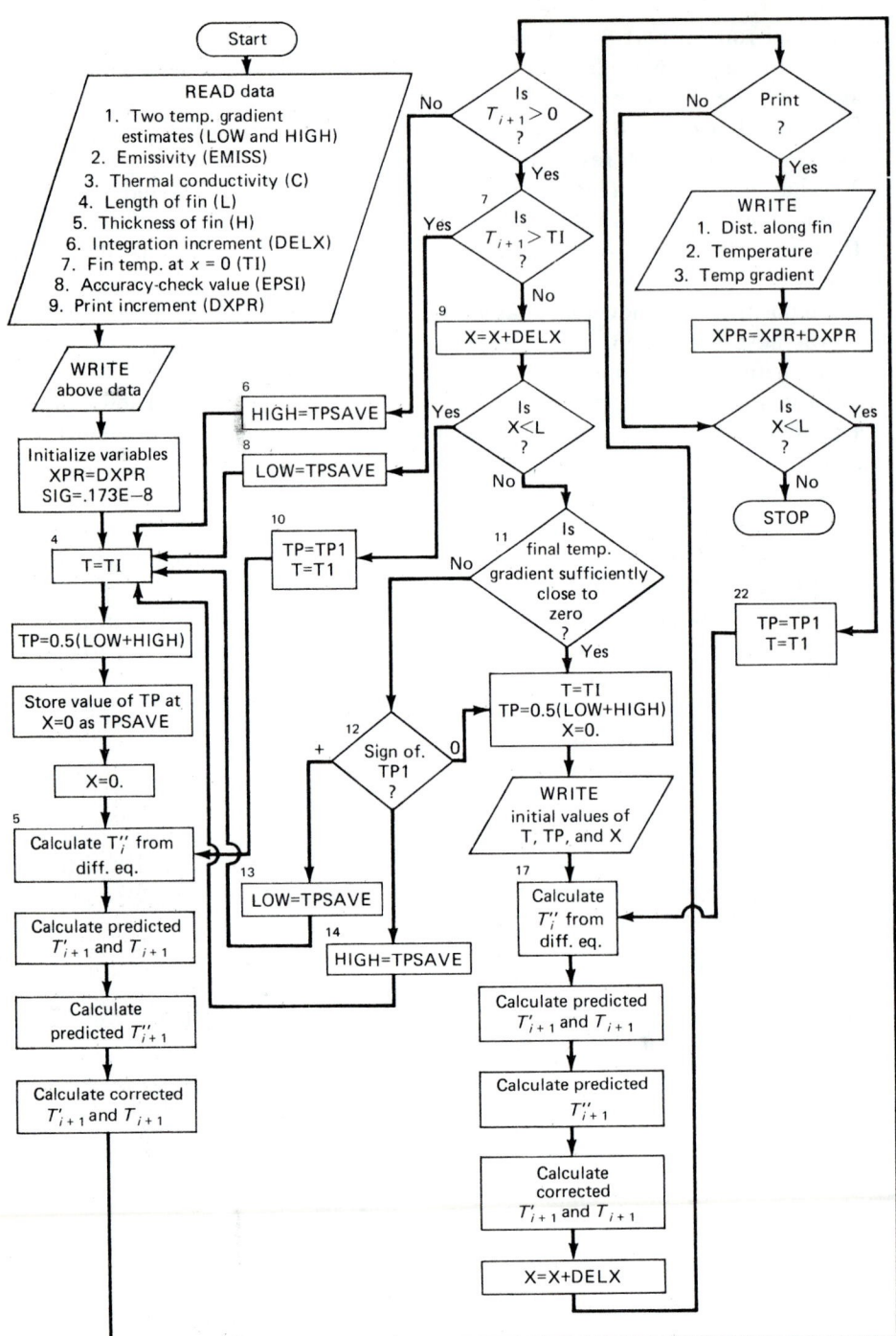

Figure 7-4 Flow chart for Ex. 7-1

FORTRAN

Name	Quantity	Problem Value
L	Length of fin	0.25 ft
H	Thickness of fin	0.005 ft
DELX	Increment of distance along fin	0.005 ft
TI	Known temperature of fin at $x = 0$	2000°R
EPSI	Accuracy-check value for final T'	1°R/ft
TPSAVE	Each initial value of T' used is stored under the name TPSAVE, and this value is later assigned to either HIGH or LOW	
XPR	x value at which a printout occurs	ft
DXPR	Increments of x used for printout	0.01 ft
X	Variable distance along fin	ft
SIG	Stefan-Boltzmann constant	$0.173(10)^{-8}$ Btu/(ft)^2(hr)(°R)^4
T	Temperature at points along fin length	°R
Tl	Temperature one station in advance of that at which temperature is T	°R
TP	Temperature gradient at points along fin length	°R/ft
TP1	Temperature gradient one station in advance of that at which gradient is TP	°R/ft
TDP	Second derivative of temperature with respect to x, (T'')	°R/ft^2
TDP1	Second derivative of temperature, with respect to x, one station in advance of that at which TDP applies	°R/ft^2

The FORTRAN IV source program used to implement the flow chart is as follows:

```
C TEMPERATURE DISTRIBUTION ALONG A RADIATING FIN
      REAL LOW,L
      READ(5,1)LOW,HIGH,EMISS,C,L,H,DELX,TI,ESPI,DXPR
    1 FORMAT(10F7.0)
      WRITE(6,2)
    2 FORMAT(1H1, ' LOW ' ,3X,'HIGH     EMISS',4X, 'C',4X, 'L' ,5X,
                                                    'H' ,4X,
     *'DELX' ,4X, 'TI' ,4X, 'EPSI' ,3X, 'DXPR'/)
      WRITE(6,3)LOW,HIGH,EMISS,C,L,H,DELX,TI,EPSI,DXPR
    3 FORMAT(1H ,F5.3,F9.0,F4.1,F6.1,F5.2,F6.3,F7.3,F8.0,
                                              F6.1,F7.3)
      XPR=DXPR
      SIG=.173E-8
```

```
  4 T=TI
    TP=0.5*(LOW+HIGH)
    TPSAVE=TP
    X=0.
  5 TDP=2.*SIG*EMISS*T**4/(C*H)
    TP1=TP+TDP*DELX
    T1=T+(TP+TP1)/2.*DELX
    TDP1=2.*SIG*EMISS*T1**4/(C*H)
    TP1=TP+(TDP+TDP1)/2.*DELX
    T1=T+(TP+TP1)/2.*DELX
    IF(T1)6,6,7
  6 HIGH=TPSAVE
    GO TO 4
  7 IF(T1-TI)9,9,8
  8 LOW=TPSAVE
    GO TO 4
  9 X=X+DELX
    IF(ABS(X-L)-.001)11,11,10
 10 TP=TP1
    T=T1
    GO TO 5
 11 IF(ABS(TP1)-EPSI)15,15,12
 12 IF(TP1)14,15,13
 13 LOW=TPSAVE
    GO TO 4
 14 HIGH=TPSAVE
    GO TO 4
 15 WRITE(6,16)
 16 FORMAT(1H0,15HDISPL ALONG FIN,6X,11HTEMPERATURE,7X,
   *13HTEMP GRADIENT/)
    T=TI
    TP=0.5*(LOW+HIGH)
    X=0.
    WRITE(6,19)X,T,TP
 17 TDP=2.*SIG*EMISS*T**4/(C*H)
    TP1=TP+TDP*DELX
    T1=T+(TP+TP1)/2.*DELX
    TDP1=2.*SIG*EMISS*T1**4/(C*H)
    TP1=TP+(TDP+TDP1)/2.*DELX
    T1=T+(TP+TP1)/2.*DELX
    X=X+DELX
    IF(ABS(X-XPR)-.001)18,18,20
 18 WRITE(6,19)X,T1,TP1
 19 FORMAT(1H ,4X,F6.3,13X,F7.0,13X,F9.0)
    XPR=XPR+DXPR
 20 IF(ABS(X-L)-.001)21,21,22
 21 STOP
 22 TP=TP1
    T=T1
    GO TO 17
    END
```

Figure 7-5 Temperature distribution along radiating fin

A graphical plot of the results given by the computer printout (to follow) is shown in Fig. 7-5, along with similar curves for two other fin thicknesses for which the tabular data are not shown.

LOW	HIGH	EMISS	C	L	H	DELX	TI	EPSI	DXPR
−.010	−40000.	0.8	25.0	0.25	0.005	0.005	2000.	1.0	0.010

DISPL ALONG FIN	TEMPERATURE	TEMP GRADIENT
0.0	2000.	−16639.
0.010	1849.	−13598.
0.020	1725.	−11336.
0.030	1621.	−9601.
0.040	1532.	−8234.
0.050	1455.	−7132.
0.060	1388.	−6227.
0.070	1330.	−5472.
0.080	1278.	−4831.
0.090	1233.	−4280.
0.100	1193.	−3801.
0.110	1157.	−3380.
0.120	1125.	−3005.
0.130	1097.	−2668.
0.140	1071.	−2362.
0.150	1049.	−2082.
0.160	1030.	−1824.
0.170	1013.	−1583.
0.180	998.	−1357.
0.190	985.	−1143.
0.200	975.	−939.
0.210	967.	−742.
0.220	960.	−552.
0.230	956.	−365.
0.240	953.	−182.
0.250	952.	0.

7-3 SIMULTANEOUS-EQUATION METHOD

We will now examine a method of solving ordinary differential equations of the boundary-value type which involves the solution of simultaneous algebraic

Figure 7-6 Simply supported beam of Ex. 7-2. (a) Beam loading and dimensions of shaft (b) Stations along beam

equations. In this process, the differential equation to be solved is first put into finite-difference form. If the interval over which the integration is desired is then divided into equal increments, the finite-difference equation used to approximate the given differential equation must be satisfied at *each* of the stations dividing the interval. The finite-difference equation has the form of an algebraic equation at each station, and if n stations are used we obtain a set of $n - 2$ algebraic equations which can be solved simultaneously to obtain a desired solution. Such a set of equations can be solved by any of the applicable methods discussed in Chap. 3.

This approach to the solution of boundary-value problems is usually reserved for linear differential equations, since the resulting algebraic equations are also linear and are more easily solved than those resulting from nonlinear differential equations. The procedure involved is illustrated by the following example.

EXAMPLE 7-2

Let us determine the elastic curve of the nonuniform shaft described in Fig. 7-6(a).[1] From mechanics of materials, we know that the equation defining the elastic curve (the deflection of the beam at any point) can be obtained by two

---

[1] Merl D. Creech, Robert L. Ammons, and James I. McPherson, "Deflections of Complex Beams," *Prod. Eng.*, Aug. 14, 1961, pp. 47–49.

successive integrations beginning with the integration of the differential equation

$$\frac{d^2y}{dx^2} = \frac{M}{EI} \tag{7-15}$$

where

$y =$ beam deflection at any point, in.

$x =$ variable distance along the beam, in.

$M =$ internal bending moment at any point along the beam, lb-in.

$E =$ modulus of elasticity, $lb/in.^2$

$I =$ area moment of inertia of beam cross section, $in.^4$

In general, the expression M/EI is a function of the variable distance x along the beam. When this relationship can be easily expressed by a single continuous expression over the length of the beam (the desired range of integration), the *integration* method, mentioned above, provides a convenient means of analytically determining the elastic curve of the beam. However, when M/EI cannot be represented by a single elementary function over the desired range of x, an analytical solution becomes somewhat involved. For example, the determination of an analytical solution yielding the elastic curve of the shaft in Fig. 7-6(a), by the integration method, would require the solution of five differential equations, since five different expressions would be required to define M/EI over the length of the shaft, because of the abrupt changes in cross section and the loading shown. The two integrations required would thus involve ten equations and ten attendant constants of integration. Although a solution could be obtained, the process would be rather tedious. The *moment-area* method or *Castigliano's* method could also be used but would be equally tedious for solving a beam or shaft problem of this type.

The reduction of Eq. 7-15 to finite-difference form, with the resulting set of simultaneous linear algebraic equations, provides a convenient method of programming the problem to the digital computer. Using the central-difference expression with error of order h^2 for d^2y/dx^2 (see Eq. 5-79), Eq. 7-15 becomes

$$\frac{y_{i+1} - 2y_i + y_{i-1}}{(\Delta x)^2} = \frac{M_i}{EI_i}$$

or

$$y_{i+1} - 2y_i + y_{i-1} = \frac{M_i(\Delta x)^2}{EI_i} \tag{7-16}$$

where the subscripts on M and I remind us that each is a function of x. Applying Eq. 7-16 at stations 2 through 14, as indicated by Fig. 7-6(b), we obtain the following set of algebraic equations:

$$y_1 - 2y_2 + y_3 + (0)y_4 + \cdots \qquad \cdots + (0)y_{15} = \frac{M_2}{EI_2}(\Delta x)^2$$

$$(0)y_1 + y_2 - 2y_3 + y_4 + (0)y_5 + \cdots \qquad \cdots + (0)y_{15} = \frac{M_3}{EI_3}(\Delta x)^2$$

$$(0)y_1 + (0)y_2 + y_3 - 2y_4 + y_5 + (0)y_6 + \cdots + (0)y_{15} = \frac{M_4}{EI_4}(\Delta x)^2$$

$$\vdots \qquad\qquad\qquad\qquad\qquad \vdots$$

$$(0)y_1 + (0)y_2 + \cdots \qquad \cdots + (0)y_{12} + y_{13} - 2y_{14} + y_{15} = \frac{M_{14}}{EI_{14}}(\Delta x)^2$$

$$(7\text{-}17)$$

This set of 13 linear algebraic equations contains the 15 deflection terms y_1 through y_{15}. However, since $y_1 = y_{15} = 0$ as known boundary values, Eq. 7-17 constitutes a set of 13 independent equations containing 13 unknowns, the simultaneous solution of which will yield unique solutions for the desired deflections.

The value of M and I at each station must be available as data for solving Eq. 7-17. The computation of these values can either be incorporated in the computer program or be determined manually beforehand and introduced into the computer program as data input, as is done in this example. The following values were determined, using an E value of $30(10)^6$ lb/in.^{2} for the modulus of elasticity of the steel. It should be noted that the I values, at the stations where the cross section changes, are obtained by averaging the I values of the abutting sections.

Station	M_i (lb-in.)	I_i (in.^{4})	$\dfrac{M_i}{EI_i}(\Delta x)^2$ (in.)
1	0	12.57	0.0
2	5,550	12.57	0.0001325
3	11,100	12.57	0.0002649
4	16,650	12.57	0.0003974
5	18,000	12.57	0.0004296
6	19,350	21.63	0.0002684
7	20,700	30.68	0.0002024
8	22,050	30.68	0.0002156
9	23,400	30.68	0.0002288
10	24,750	30.68	0.0002420
11	19,800	30.68	0.0001936
12	14,850	30.68	0.0001452
13	9,900	30.68	0.0000968
14	4,950	17.33	0.0000857
15	0	3.98	0.0

Figure 7-7 Graphical representation of the deflection of the steel shaft of Ex. 7-2

The computer program used to obtain the data shown utilizes the Gauss-Jordan method flow-charted in Fig. 3-4.

The computer printout of the solution is as follows:

```
SOLUTION OF SIMULTANEOUS EQUATIONS BY GAUSS-JORDAN
        METHOD WITH PARTIAL PIVOTING
    X( 1) =       -0.1656066E-02
    X( 2) =       -0.3179636E-02
    X( 3) =       -0.4438303E-02
    X( 4) =       -0.5299572E-02
    X( 5) =       -0.5731229E-02
    X( 6) =       -0.5894497E-02
    X( 7) =       -0.5855359E-02
    X( 8) =       -0.5600613E-02
    X( 9) =       -0.5117066E-02
    X(10) =       -0.4391517E-02
    X(11) =       -0.3472364E-02
    X(12) =       -0.2408010E-02
    X(13) =       -0.1246855E-02
```

A graphical representation of the same results is shown in Fig. 7-7.

The displacement shown at station 10, $y_{10} = 0.005117$ in., compares with a value of 0.005196 in. for the same station obtained by the use of Castigliano's method.[2] It can be seen that the accuracy obtained with the finite-difference method, using just 15 stations, is sufficient for most practical problems. Increasing the number of stations will increase the accuracy of the solution, but the use of an excessive number of stations with the elimination method can lead to a loss in accuracy owing to the large number of calculations introduced in solving the many more simultaneous equations. However, since the set is a tridiagonal one, many more equations can be accurately solved than would be the case if all unknowns were present in each equation. The Gauss-Seidel method can be used for a very large number of stations, but for many practical boundary-value problems the number of stations can be kept small and an elimination method employed, as was done in this example, to obtain solutions quickly with sufficient accuracy.

[2]*Ibid.*

The procedure used to solve Eq. 7-15 in this example is said to be of the *third order*. This means that such a method is capable of yielding exact results if $y(x)$ is a polynomial of the third degree or less. For the shaft used in this example, an analytical solution will show that the displacements can be expressed by five different third-degree polynomials, each applicable to a particular segment of the shaft. However, exact results are not obtained by a third-order numerical method unless $y(x)$ can be expressed over the entire interval of integration with a single polynomial of the third degree or less.

For problems in which $y(x)$ is known to be a polynomial of degree higher than 3, more accurate results can be expected if a numerical procedure of higher order than 3 is used. Methods, known as *fifth-* and *seventh-order* methods, have been developed for use with problems of this type.[3] However, in most engineering problems the degree of accuracy required in the solutions does not warrant the use of higher order procedures, and the third-order method, illustrated in this example, can be used to obtain the desired solutions.

7-4 EIGENVALUE PROBLEMS

Numerous physical systems lead to homogeneous differential equations in which the parameters of the system must have particular values before a solution, which must satisfy certain boundary conditions at the end of the interval of integration, can be obtained. The required parameter values appear in the *characteristic values* or *eigenvalues*.

To illustrate the general nature of eigenvalue problems associated with differential equations, let us consider a slender column of length l subjected to an axial load P, as shown in Fig. 7-8. From beam theory the basic relationship between the curvature d^2y/dx^2 and the internal moment M for the axes shown is

$$\frac{d^2y}{dx^2} = \frac{M}{EI} \tag{7-18}$$

where

$y =$ deflection at any point, in.

$x =$ variable distance along column, in.

$E =$ modulus of elasticity, lb/in.^{2}

$I =$ area moment of inertia of column cross section, in.^{4}

Since y is negative for the configuration shown, and, by convention, the bending moment at any section is positive for this configuration, the bending

[3]F. B. Hildebrand, *Introduction to Numerical Analysis* (New York: McGraw-Hill Book Company, 1974).

Figure 7-8   Slender column subjected to an axial load P

moment M must be equal to $-Py$. With $M = -Py$, Eq. 7-18 becomes

$$\frac{d^2y}{dx^2} + \frac{P}{Ei}\, y = 0 \tag{7-19}$$

or

$$\frac{d^2y}{dx^2} + \lambda y = 0 \tag{7-19a}$$

where $\lambda = P/EI$.

The solution of Eq. 7-19a is

$$y = A \cos \sqrt{\lambda}x + B \sin \sqrt{\lambda}x \tag{7-20}$$

where A and B are constants. Equation 7-20 is easily verified as being a solution by substituting it and its second derivative into Eq. 7-19a.

The *known* boundary conditions for the column are

$$y|_{x=0} = y|_{x=l} = 0 \tag{7-21}$$

Since the slope dy/dx is not known at $x = 0$, only one *initial* condition is known, and therefore one constant, A or B, will be indeterminate. the parameter $\lambda = P/EI$ must have certain values to satisfy the condition that $y = 0$ at $x = l$. The required values of λ necessary to satisfy this condition are eigenvalues. To determine these values of λ, let us now consider the boundary conditions given in Eq. 7-21. Using $y = 0$ at $x = 0$, we find, from Eq. 7-20, that

$$A = 0 \tag{7-22}$$

Similarly, using $y = 0$ at $x = l$, we find that

$$B \sin \sqrt{\lambda}l = 0 \tag{7-23}$$

Since B cannot equal zero for a nontrivial solution, Eq. 7-23 can be satisfied only if

$$l\sqrt{\lambda} = n\pi \qquad n = 1, 2, 3, \ldots$$

Thus, the eigenvalues are

$$\lambda = \frac{n^2\pi^2}{l^2} = \frac{P}{EI} \qquad n = 1, 2, 3, \ldots \tag{7-24}$$

The configurations of the column for the first three eigenvalues, determined by substituting the eigenvalues into Eq. 7-20 with $A = 0$, are shown in Fig. 7-9.

The values of P which satisfy Eq. 7-24, for a given value of EI, are known as the *buckling* or *critical* loads. From a practical point of view, the smallest value of P is of primary importance, since the configurations associated with the larger values of P cannot generally be obtained without failure first occurring under the action of the lowest value of P. The eigenvalue associated with the smallest buckling load is obtained with $n = 1$, so the smallest buckling load is

$$P_{cr} = \frac{\pi^2 EI}{l^2} \tag{7-25}$$

If EI is not a constant but is some function of x, then the solution of Eq. 7-19, given by Eq. 7-20, is not applicable. In most cases in which such a differential equation contains variable coefficients, analytical solutions cannot be obtained, and it becomes necessary to resort to some numerical procedure for finding the eigenvalues.

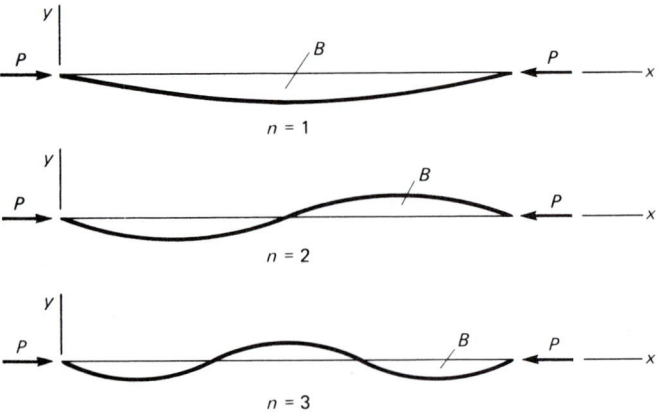

Figure 7-9 Column configurations for first three eigenvalues

The remainder of this chapter will be devoted to the discussion of a finite-difference method for obtaining the solution of homogeneous differential equations such as that given by Eq. 7-19, for example. Such a differential equation can be readily expressed in general finite-difference form as a homogeneous algebraic equation. The application of this general equation for a set of values of the independent variable (at uniformly spaced stations along the column) yields a *set* of homogeneous algebraic equations. The eigenvalues of the set are approximations of the eigenvalues of the differential equation.

The methods discussed in Chap. 3 for determining eigenvalues, the polynomial method, the iteration method, and Jacobi's method (if the coefficient matrix is symmetrical) can be applied in the solution of the algebraic equations resulting from the finite-difference form of the differential equations.

General Numerical Procedure

To develop the general numerical procedure, let us first consider Eq. 7-19a with $\lambda = P/EI$ a constant. Using a *central-difference* expression (see Eq. 5-73) for the second derivative, we may express Eq. 7-19a, in finite difference form, as

$$\frac{y_{i+1} - 2y_i + y_{i-1}}{h^2} + \lambda y_i = 0$$

or as

$$y_{i-1} - (2 - h^2\lambda)y_i + y_{i+1} = 0 \qquad (7\text{-}26)$$

where $h = \Delta x$ is the distance between successive stations along the column (see Fig. 7-10). Applying Eq. 7-26 at stations 2 through n along the column, we can write the system of homogeneous algebraic equations

$$y_1^{\,0} - (2 - h^2\lambda)y_2 \qquad\qquad + y_3 \qquad\quad + (0)y_4 + \cdots\cdots\cdots\cdots + (0)y_n = 0$$

$$y_2 - (2 - h^2\lambda)y_3 \qquad\quad + y_4 + (0)y_5 + \cdots\cdots + (0)y_n = 0$$

$$y_3 - (2 - h^2\lambda)y_4 + y_5 + (0)y_6 + \cdots + (0)y_n = 0$$

$$\cdots\cdots\cdots\cdots\cdots\cdots\cdots\cdots\cdots\cdots\cdots\cdots\cdots\cdots\cdots\cdots\cdots\cdots$$

$$y_{n-1} - (2 - h^2\lambda)y_n + y_{n+1}^{\,0} = 0$$

$$(7\text{-}27)$$

With n increments along the column, Eq. 7-27 yields $n - 1$ equations, the solution of which by the polynomial method involves the expansion of an $n - 1$ by $n - 1$ determinant. From Sec. 3-8 we know that the expansion of

Figure 7-10 Stations along column (n increments)

the determinant yields an $n - 1$ degree polynomial in λ, the roots of which are eigenvalues. Since we used only a finite number of stations along the column, the $n - 1$ eigenvalues obtained will be only approximations of the true eigenvalues of the column. Fortunately, the lowest root or eigenvalue, which, in this problem, is the most important, is the most accurately approximated root value obtained. Improved approximations of all the eigenvalues determined can be obtained by increasing the number of increments. To illustrate, let us first take $h = l/2$ and obtain a first approximation of λ_1. The exact value of λ_1 was found to be $9.87/l^2$ (see Eq. 7-24). With $h = l/2$ (only three stations), and using the boundary conditions $y_1 = y_3 = 0$, we can write, from Eq. 7-27,

$$0 - \left[2 - \left(\frac{l}{2}\right)^2 \lambda\right] y_2 + 0 = 0 \tag{7-28}$$

Thus, Eq. 7-28 shows that the approximation of λ_1 obtained for $h = l/2$ is

$$\lambda_1 = \frac{8}{l^2}$$

To obtain an improved approximation, let us use three increments (four stations) so that $h = l/3$. From Eq. 7-27

$$\left[2 - \left(\frac{l}{3}\right)^2 \lambda\right] y_2 - y_3 = 0$$

$$-y_2 + \left[2 - \left(\frac{l}{3}\right)^2 \lambda\right] y_3 = 0 \tag{7-29}$$

Setting the determinant $|\mathbf{D}|$ of the coefficients of the y's equal to zero gives

$$|\mathbf{D}| = \begin{vmatrix} \left[2 - \left(\frac{l}{3}\right)^2 \lambda\right] & -1 \\ -1 & \left[2 - \left(\frac{l}{3}\right)^2 \lambda\right] \end{vmatrix} = 0$$

Expanding the determinant and simplifying yields the quadratic

$$\lambda^2 - \frac{36}{l^2}\lambda + \frac{243}{l^4} = 0$$

which has the roots

$$\lambda_1 = \frac{9}{l^2} \quad \text{and} \quad \lambda_2 = \frac{27}{l^2}$$

Thus, the approximation $\lambda_1 = 9/l^2$ is considerably closer to the exact value of $9.87/l^2$ than the approximation $8/l^2$ which was obtained by using only two increments. The value $\lambda_2 = 27/l^2$ is an approximation of the second eigenvalue which has the exact value $4(9.87)/l^2$ (see Eq. 7-24). It should now be apparent that the use of four increments $(h = l/4)$ would yield a still better approximation of λ_1 and λ_2 as well as a rough approximation of λ_3.

In general, a very good approximation of the smallest eigenvalue can be obtained by using a reasonable number of increments—say, ten, for example. However, fairly accurate approximations of the higher eigenvalues are obtained only by using a large number of increments. Therefore, unless higher eigenvalues are desired, the required number of increments depends upon the desired accuracy of the approximation of λ_1 (the smallest eigenvalue).

One procedure for qualitatively evaluating the convergence of the approximation of λ_1 to the true value is to compute λ_1 by using successively larger numbers of increments. As the value λ_1 converges to the true value, an increase in the number of increments will cause very little change in successively computed values of λ_1.

Polynomial Method

Let us consider a column having a variable cross section. If the cross section of the column is not uniform, then the coefficient P/EI in the differential equation (see Eq. 7-19) is a variable, since the moment of inertia of the cross section varies along the column.

Denoting the value of I at station i as I_i, Eq. 7-26 becomes

$$y_{i-1} - \left(2 - h^2\frac{P}{EI_i}\right)y_i + y_{i+1} = 0 \tag{7-30}$$

Since the eigenvalues must appear as constants in each of the simultaneous equations resulting from Eq. 7-30, they must be defined in terms of the moment of inertia at some particular station. For example, if we relate the eigenvalues to the moment of inertia at station 1, we write

$$\frac{P}{EI_i} = \left(\frac{I_1}{I_i}\right)\frac{P}{EI_1} = \alpha_i \lambda \tag{7-31}$$

where the variable coefficient $\alpha_i = I_1/I_i$ and $\lambda = P/EI_1$.

Using Eq. 7-30 and the notation of Eq. 7-31, we can write the system of simultaneous equations as

$$\overset{0}{\cancel{y}_1} - (2 - h^2\alpha_2\lambda)y_2 + y_3 + (0)y_4 + \cdots + (0)y_n = 0$$

$$y_2 - (2 - h^2\alpha_3\lambda)y_3 + y_4 + (0)y_5 + \cdots + (0)y_n = 0 \tag{7-32}$$

$$y_3 - (2 - h^2\alpha_4\lambda)y_4 + y_5 + (0)y_6 + \cdots + (0)y_n = 0$$

$$\cdots\cdots\cdots\cdots\cdots\cdots\cdots\cdots\cdots\cdots\cdots\cdots$$

$$y_{n-1} - (2 - h^2\alpha_n\lambda)y_n + \overset{0}{\cancel{y}_{n+1}} = 0$$

Dividing these equations through by the negatives of $h^2\alpha_2$, $h^2\alpha_3$, $\ldots$, $h^2\alpha_n$, respectively, we can express the determinant of the coefficient matrix in the form $|\mathbf{A} - \lambda\mathbf{I}|$ which is suitable for obtaining the characteristic polynomial by the Faddeev-Leverrier method discussed in Chap. 3. The resulting determinant is

$$|\mathbf{D}| = \begin{vmatrix} \left(\dfrac{2}{h^2\alpha_2} - \lambda\right) & -\dfrac{1}{h^2\alpha_2} & 0 & 0 & \cdots & 0 \\[2ex] -\dfrac{1}{h^2\alpha_3} & \left(\dfrac{2}{h^2\alpha_3} - \lambda\right) & -\dfrac{1}{h^2\alpha_3} & 0 & \cdots & 0 \\[2ex] 0 & -\dfrac{1}{h^2\alpha_4} & \left(\dfrac{2}{h^2\alpha_4} - \lambda\right) & -\dfrac{1}{h^2\alpha_4} & \cdots & 0 \\[2ex] \cdots & \cdots & \cdots & \cdots & \cdots & \cdots \\[2ex] 0 & 0 & 0 & \cdots & -\dfrac{1}{h^2\alpha_n} & \left(\dfrac{2}{h^2\alpha_n} - \lambda\right) \end{vmatrix} = 0 \tag{7-33}$$

With n increments along the column, the expansion of this $n - 1$ by $n - 1$ determinant yields an $n - 1$ degree polynomial in λ. The *smallest* root λ_1 of the polynomial will be a close approximation of the smallest value of P/EI_1. The buckling load may then be determined from

$$\lambda_1 = \frac{P}{EI_1} \tag{7-34}$$

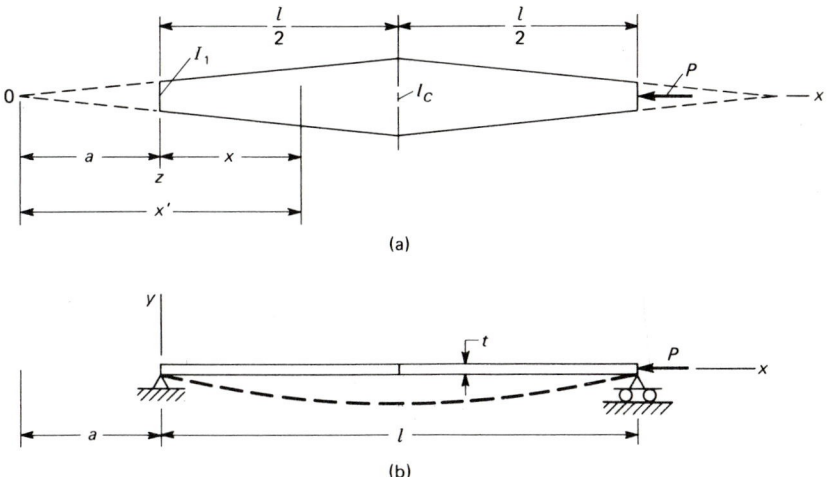

Figure 7-11   Coordinate system for simply supported column of variable cross section

In considering columns of variable cross section with uniform thickness (see Fig. 7-11), the equation

$$I = I_1 \left(\frac{x'}{a} \right)^m \qquad x' \le a + \frac{l}{2} \tag{7-35}$$

might be used to define the moment of inertia of the column about a centroidal axis perpendicular to the xy plane at any cross section of the column, where

x = distance along column (independent variable)
x' = $a + x$ (as shown in Fig. 7-11)
I = moment of inertia about centroidal axis perpendicular to xy plane (plane of bending) anywhere along column
I_1 = moment of inertia about centroidal axis perpendicular to plane of bending at $x' = a$

By using different values for the parameter a and the exponent m, Eq. 7-35 may be used for expressing the moment of inertia at any section of many differently shaped columns of uniform thickness. (For the column shown in Fig. 7-11, $m = 1$.)[4]

[4]S. P. Timoshenko and J. M. Gere, *Theory of Elastic Stability* (New York: McGraw-Hill Book Company, 1961).

EXAMPLE 7-3

Let us consider the column shown in Fig. 7-12. This column has a uniform thickness and a cross section which varies as shown. The shape of this parabolic column is defined by choosing

$a = 206.19$ in.

$m = 2$

$I_c = 1.0$ in.^{4}

Since the column of Fig. 7-12 is symmetrical about $x = l/2$, the values of I, computed from Eq. 7-35 for the stations in the region of $0 < x < l/2$, may also be used for corresponding stations in the region of $x > l/2$.

Referring to Eqs. 7-31 and 7-35, we see that

$$\alpha_i = \frac{I_1}{I_i} = \left(\frac{a}{x_i'}\right)^m$$

or

$$\alpha_i = \left(\frac{a}{a + x_i}\right)^m \tag{7-36}$$

With α_i defined by Eq. 7-36 and dividing the column into ten increments so that h is defined, we can see (from Eq. 7-33) that we are ready to write a program for calculating the elements of the matrix **A** in the determinant of Eq. 7-33, $|\mathbf{A} - \lambda\mathbf{I}| = 0$. We will need to do no further programming, since these elements will then be used as data for the program developed in Chap. 3 for generating the characteristic polynomial coefficients by the Faddeev-Leverrier

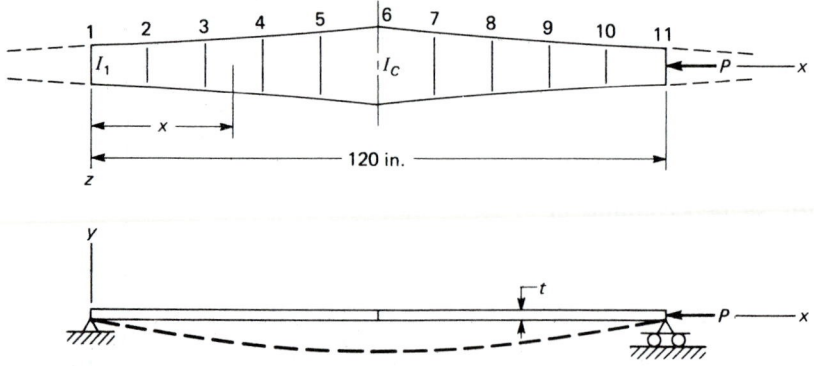

Figure 7-12   Column of Ex. 7-3

method. The roots of the characteristic polynomial will then be determined by Bairstow's method, using the computer program developed in Chap. 2.

The procedure for generating the elements of the matrix for which we wish to determine the eigenvalues is outlined in the flow chart of Fig. 7-13. Note that an even number of column increments should always be used, since there is a whole number of increments in each half of the column. The elements of the matrix are calculated and then printed out by columns for visual inspection, and they are also used as data for the program concerned with generating the characteristic polynomial coefficients.

The FORTRAN names used in the program, the quantities they represent, and the data values used in this example are as follows:

FORTRAN Name	Quantity	Data Values Used in Problem
N	Number of increments into which column is divided for finite-difference representation of the differential equation	
	$$\frac{d^2y}{dx^2} = \frac{M}{EI}$$	10
M	Exponent m of Eq. 7-36 (the exponent describes the column shape)	2
CL	Length of column, in.	120
A1	Distance from point of zero column width (if column were extended to $x' = 0$) to actual end of column, in.	206.19
IC	I_c, the moment of inertia of the cross section of midpoint of column, in.^{4}	1.0
I1	I_1, the moment of inertia of the cross section at end of column, in.^{4}	
RATIO	I_1/I_c	
H	$h (h = \Delta x)$	
X	Variable distance x along the axis of column measured from column end	
NO2P1	$n/2 + 1$	
ALPHA(I)	$\alpha_i = [a/(a + x_i)]^m$	
NO2	$n/2$	
K	Quantity $(n - i + 2)$, where $i = 2, 3, \ldots, n/2$	
L	Order of the **A** matrix, equal to $(n - 1)$	
A(I,J)	Elements of the matrix for which we want the eigenvalues λ	

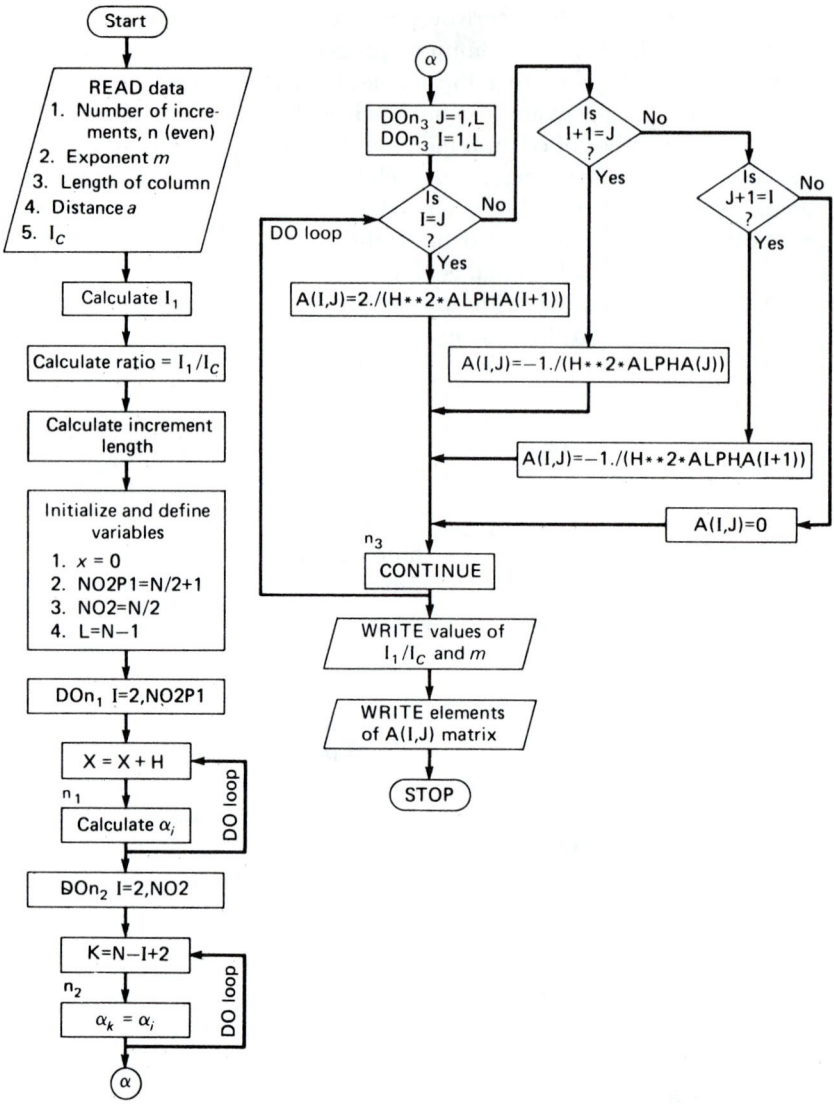

Figure 7-13 Flow chart for the program to generate the matrix **A** of the characteristic polynomial $[\mathbf{A} - \lambda \mathbf{I}] = 0$ for the tapered-column problem

The FORTRAN source program, written to implement the flow chart shown in Fig. 7-13, is as follows:

```
C TAPERED COLUMN PROBLEM—GENERATION OF MATRIX A
      DIMENSION ALPHA(16),A(15,15)
      REAL IC,I1
      READ(5,2)N,M
    2 FORMAT(2I2)
      READ(5,3)CL,A1,IC
    3 FORMAT(3F10.0)
      I1=IC*(A1/(CL/2.+A1))**M
      RATIO=I1/IC
      H=CL/N
      X=0.
      NO2P1=N/2+1
      NO2=N/2
      L=N-1
      DO4I=2,NO2P1
      X=X+H
    4 ALPHA(I)=(A1/(A1+X))**M
      DO5I=2,NO2
      K=N-I+2
    5 ALPHA(K)=ALPHA(I)
      DO12J=1,L
      DO12I=1,L
      IF(I-J)6,9,6
    6 IF(I+1-J)7,10,7
    7 IF(J+1-I)8,11,8
    8 A(I,J)=0.
      GO TO 12
    9 A(I,J)=2./(H**2*ALPHA(I+1))
      GO TO 12
   10 A(I,J)=-1./(H**2*ALPHA(J))
      GO TO 12
   11 A(I,J)=-1./(H**2*ALPHA(I+1))
   12 CONTINUE
      WRITE(6,13)RATIO,M
   13 FORMAT(1H1, 'I1/IC=' ,F6.4,6X, 'M= ' ,I1//)
      WRITE(6,14)
   14 FORMAT(1H , 'FIRST FIVE COLUMNS OF GENERATED MATRIX A' /)
      WRITE(6,15)((A(I,J),J=1,5),I=1,9)
   15 FORMAT(1H ,5E15.7)
      WRITE(6,16)
   16 FORMAT(1H0,/,' LAST FOUR COLUMNS OF GENERATED MATRIX A'/)
      WRITE(6,18)((A(I,J),J=6,9),I=1,9)
   18 FORMAT(1H ,4E15.7)
      WRITE(7,17)((A(I,J),J=1,9),I=1,9)
   17 FORMAT(5E14.7)
      STOP
      END
```

The following computer printout gives the elements of the matrix **A** for which we must determine the eigenvalues:

```
I1/IC=0.6000            M= 2
FIRST FIVE COLUMNS OF GENERATED MATRIX A
 0.1555257E-01 -0.7776283E-02  0.0                    0.0
-0.8655164E-02  0.1731033E-01 -0.8655164E-02  0.0
 0.0           -0.9581085E-02  0.1916217E-01 -0.9581085E-02
 0.0            0.0           -0.1055405E-01  0.2110811E-01
 0.0            0.0            0.0           -0.1157406E-01
 0.0            0.0            0.0            0.0
 0.0            0.0            0.0            0.0
 0.0            0.0            0.0            0.0
 0.0            0.0            0.0            0.0

 0.0
 0.0
 0.0
-0.1055405E-01
 0.2314812E-01
-0.1055405E-01
 0.0
 0.0
 0.0
LAST FOUR COLUMNS OF GENERATED MATRIX A
 0.0            0.0            0.0            0.0
 0.0            0.0            0.0            0.0
 0.0            0.0            0.0            0.0
 0.0            0.0            0.0            0.0
-0.1157406E-01  0.0            0.0            0.0
 0.2110811E-01 -0.1055405E-01  0.0            0.0
-0.9581085E-02  0.1916217E-01 -0.9581085E-02  0.0
 0.0           -0.8655164E-02  0.1731033E-01 -0.8655164E-02
 0.0            0.0           -0.7776283E-02  0.1555257E-01
```

Using the coefficient matrix as data for the program to determine the characteristic polynomial coefficients by the Faddeev-Leverrier method (see Sec. 3-10), we obtain the following computer output:

```
THE CHARACTERISTIC POLYNOMIAL COEFFICIENTS
P(1) THROUGH P(N)
 0.1694143E 00
-0.1198142E-01
 0.4595143E-03
-0.1038747E-04
 0.1407972E-06
-0.1112883E-08
 0.4738090E-11
-0.9169037E-14
 0.5344283E-17
```

These coefficients are substituted into Eq. 3-121, disregarding the term $(-1)^n$, to obtain the characteristic polynomial

$$\lambda^9 - p_1\lambda^8 - p_2\lambda^7 \cdots p_8\lambda - p_9 = 0 \tag{7-37}$$

Using the characteristic polynomial coefficients as input data to the program developed in Chap. 2 for obtaining the roots of polynomials by Bairstow's method, the following is obtained as computer printout:

```
                    REAL PART
CONVERGENCE   IS SLOW              IMAGINARY   PART           ITERATIONS
U=-0.802700E-02   V=0.6873272E -05   DELU= 0.1227109E- 02
                                             DELV=-0.1186479E-05
X( 9)  =        0.003447            0.0                       163
X( 8)  =        0.000980            0.0                       163
X( 7)  =        0.008185            0.000577                  8
X( 6)  =        0.008185           -0.000577                  8
X( 5)  =        0.010393            0.007246                  6
X( 4)  =        0.010393           -0.007246                  6
X( 3)  =        0.009921            0.023195                  4
X( 2)  =        0.009921           -0.023195                  4
X( 1)  =       -0.230838            0.0                       1
```

From this computer printout we can see that the smallest root of the polynomial is 0.000980. Thus, we write for the *smallest* eigenvalue

$$\lambda_1 = \frac{P_{cr}}{EI_1} = 0.000980 \text{ in.}^{-2}$$

For our particular problem $I_c = 1.0$ and $I_1/I_c = 0.6$, as given by the computer printout of the coefficient matrix. Hence $I_1 = 0.6$. For a steel column in which $E = 30 \times 10^6$ psi, the critical or buckling load is

$$P_{cr} = (0.000980)(30 \times 10^6)(0.6)$$

$$= 17,640 \text{ lb}$$

The smallest eigenvalues for tapered columns of the form described by Eq. 7-35 have been determined analytically by Timoshenko.[5] He tabulates values of the dimensionless factor f in the formula

$$P_{cr} = \frac{fEI_c}{l^2}$$

for different values of I_1/I_c and the exponent m (see Eq. 7-35). For $I_1/I_c = 0.6$ and $m = 2$ (the values used in this example), Timoshenko gives $f = 8.51$. The numerical solution by the polynomial method yields

$$f = \frac{Pl^2}{EI_c} = \frac{P}{EI_1}\left(\frac{I_1}{I_c}\right)l^2 = (0.000980)(0.6)(120)^2$$

$$= 8.47$$

[5]*Ibid.*

Thus, the numerical solution is well within the limits of engineering accuracy. Furthermore, it has the advantage of being applicable to any kind of variation of cross section. In addition, approximations to the higher eigenvalues—and thus higher buckling loads—may also be obtained from the polynomial method. For example, the second largest eigenvalue (next to the smallest) shown in the computer printout is $\lambda_2 = 0.003447$. Thus,

$$\lambda_2 = \frac{P_{cr}}{EI_1} = 0.003447 \text{ in.}^{-2}$$

For a steel column ($E = 30 \times 10^6$), the critical load corresponding to λ_2 is

$$P_{cr} = (0.003447)(30 \times 10^6)(0.6)$$

$$= 62{,}046 \text{ lb}$$

The general configuration of the column corresponding to λ_2 is shown in Fig. 7-14.

As previously discussed, the polynomial method results in the best approximation of the smallest eigenvalue. Therefore, we know that the approximation of $\lambda_2 = 0.003447$ is slightly less accurate than the approximation $\lambda_1 = 0.000980$.

Iteration Method

The iteration method discussed in Sec. 3-11 and Sec. 3-12 may also be used for solving eigenvalue problems associated with differential equations of the type discussed in the introductory paragraph of this section. As pointed out in Chap. 3, an advantage of the iteration procedure is that the eigenvectors are obtained simultaneously with the associated eigenvalues, rather than requiring separate operations as in the polynomial method. The following example will illustrate the iteration procedure discussed in Sec. 3-12 in which the sweeping technique is used to obtain the lowest eigenvalues and associated eigenvectors in ascending order.

$$P_{cr} = 62{,}046 \text{ lb}$$

Figure 7-14 General configuration of tapered column corresponding to $\lambda_2 = 0.003447$

EXAMPLE 7-4

Let us again consider the column of Fig. 7-12, which was analyzed in Ex. 7-3 by the polynomial method. In this example we will use the program developed in Sec. 3-12 to obtain the two lowest eigenvalues (lowest buckling loads) and associated eigenvectors. This column has a uniform thickness and a variable cross section for which the moment of inertia varies according to Eq. 7-35. A set of n simultaneous equations describing such a column with a variable cross section is given by Eq. 7-32. Dividing these equations through by $h^2\alpha_2$, $h^2\alpha_3$, $\ldots$, $h^2\alpha_n$, respectively, we obtain the equations in a matrix form, suitable for the iteration method, as

$$
\begin{bmatrix}
\left(\dfrac{2}{h^2\alpha_2} - \lambda\right) & -\dfrac{1}{h^2\alpha_2} & 0 & 0\cdots 0 \\[2mm]
-\dfrac{1}{h^2\alpha_3} & \left(\dfrac{2}{h^2\alpha_3} - \lambda\right) & -\dfrac{1}{h^2\alpha_3} & 0\cdots 0 \\[2mm]
0 & -\dfrac{1}{h^2\alpha_4} & \left(\dfrac{2}{h^2\alpha_4} - \lambda\right) -\dfrac{1}{h^2\alpha_4}\cdots 0 \\[2mm]
\cdots\cdots\cdots\cdots\cdots\cdots\cdots\cdots\cdots\cdots\cdots\cdots \\[2mm]
0 & 0 & 0\cdots-\dfrac{1}{h^2\alpha_n}\left(\dfrac{2}{h^2\alpha_n} - \lambda\right)
\end{bmatrix}
\begin{Bmatrix}
y_2 \\[2mm] y_3 \\[2mm] y_4 \\[2mm] \cdot \\[2mm] y_n
\end{Bmatrix} = \mathbf{0}
$$

The above may be written more compactly as

$$[\mathbf{A} - \lambda \mathbf{I}]\mathbf{Y} = \mathbf{0} \tag{7-38}$$

and we see that the equations are in the form for which the iteration procedure will converge to the largest eigenvalue of the matrix $\mathbf{A}$. However, for convergence to the lowest eigenvalue λ_1, we recall from Sec. 3-12 that the iteration procedure must be applied to equations of the form

$$\mathbf{A}^{-1}\mathbf{X} = \frac{1}{\lambda}\mathbf{X}$$

Using these, convergence is to the lowest eigenvalue λ_1, and then to higher eigenvalues λ_2, λ_3, $\ldots$, in ascending order, as lower eigenvalues are swept out of the equations.

Thus, the matrix $\mathbf{A}$ of Eq. 7-38 must be inverted for input into the program developed in Example 3-10 if the smallest eigenvalues are desired.

The computer output resulting from the application of this program to the column problem of Ex. 7-3, with $\mathbf{A}^{-1}$ as input, is

```
LAMBDA( 1)= 0.9796550E-03
THE ASSOCIATED EIGENVECTOR COMPONENTS ARE
0.1000000E 01
0.1874022E 01
0.2535933E 01
0.2938549E 01
0.3068406E 01
0.2938548E 01
0.2535933E 01
0.1874023E 01
0.1000001E 01

LAMBDA( 2)= 0.3447913E-02
THE ASSOCIATED EIGENVECTOR COMPONENTS ARE
 0.1000000E 01
 0.1556616E 01
 0.1493131E 01
 0.8923209E 00
-0.2788382E-05
-0.8923259E 00
-0.1493137E 01
-0.1556622E 01
-0.1000006E 01
```

Thus, the two smallest eigenvalues found from the iteration procedure are $\lambda_1 = 0.00097965$ and $\lambda_2 = 0.0034479$. These compare with values of $\lambda_1 = 0.000980$ and $\lambda_2 = 0.003447$, respectively, obtained by the polynomial method. Therefore, the smallest buckling load is found to be 17,634 lb as compared with 17,640 lb from the polynomial method. The small difference is obviously insignificant from a design standpoint.

PROBLEMS

7-1. A 120 in. long beam is subjected to a 10,000 lb load as shown in the accompanying illustration. The beam is pinned at the left end and is supported at the right end by an elastic spring of stiffness $k = 5000$

Problem 7-1

lb/in. Write a computer program to obtain the elastic curve by the simultaneous-equation method. Use 6-inch increments (21 stations).

Obtain an analytical solution and compare several of the results from the numerical integration with those from the analytical solution.

7-2. In Ex. 7-2, the differential equation for the elastic curve was taken as

$$\frac{d^2y}{dx^2} = \frac{M}{EI} \qquad \text{(small deflection theory)}$$

This equation for small deflection theory will normally give very accurate results for the deflection y for most practical problems. However, for beams involving large deflections, in which dy/dx is not small compared to 1, the following differential equation for the elastic curve should be used:

$$\frac{d^2y}{dx^2} = \frac{M}{EI}\left[1 + \left(\frac{dy}{dx}\right)^2\right]^{3/2} \qquad \text{(large deflection theory)}$$

Write a computer program using the large deflection theory equation to determine the elastic curve for the beam of Ex. 7-2. Each of the loads on the beam (see Fig. 7-6) is to be increased by a factor of 10. Use the fourth-order Runge-Kutta method for the integration.

Does a comparison of your results with the results obtained in Ex. 7-2 indicate that the use of large deflection theory is necessary for the loads used in this problem?

(partial answer: for $x = 27$ in., $y = -0.05152$ in.)

7-3. The simply supported beam of the accompanying figure is subjected to a uniformly distributed lateral load of $q = 20$ lb/in. and an axial load P. The differential equation of the beam is

$$EI\frac{d^2y}{dx^2} = -Py + \frac{ql}{2}x - \frac{q}{2}x^2$$

where

$E =$ modulus of elasticity of beam

$I =$ moment of inertia of beam cross section

Since the beam is simply supported, the y deflection of the beam is zero at $x = 0$ and $x = l$, and the slope (dy/dx) of the beam is unknown at both $x = 0$ and $x = l$.

Write a FORTRAN program for determining the deflections which define the elastic curve of the beam for various axial loads P. Include in the program the steps necessary to obtain the information required to plot the maximum deflection of the beam for each axial load P as a function of P.

Using the program written, obtain computer solutions for axial loads of 10,000 lb, 20,000 lb, 30,000 lb, and 40,000 lb applied along with the vertical loading specified above. Is the maximum deflection of the beam a linear function of the axial loads P applied?

(partial answer: for $P = 20{,}000$ lb, $y_{max} = -0.8887$ in.)

Problem 7-3

7-4. Work Prob. 7-3 with the following system data:

$$q = 4000 \text{ N/m}$$
$$EI = 26(10)^4 \text{ N·m}^2$$
$$l = 3.0 \text{ m}$$

Computer solutions are to be obtained for axial loads, P, of 45 kN, 90 kN, 135 kN, and 180 kN. Express the results in millimeters.

7-5. The analytical solution of the differential equation of the beam shown in the figure accompanying Prob. 7-3 is

$$y = \frac{qEI}{P^2}\left[(1 - \cos kx) + \left(\frac{\cos kl - 1}{\sin kl}\right)\sin kx\right] + \frac{ql}{2P}x - \frac{q}{2P}x^2$$

where

$$k^2 = \frac{P}{EI}$$

Write a FORTRAN program for evaluating the analytical solution shown. Using the program written and the values of E, I, l, q, and P given in Prob. 7-3, determine the deflections defining the elastic curve of the beam for each value of P.

If Prob. 7-3 has been worked prior to working this problem, select a Δx increment corresponding to that used in Prob. 7-3 and compare the solutions obtained in the two problems at various points along the beam.

7-6. Utilizing the relationship from elementary beam theory

$$EI \frac{d^2y}{dx^2} = M$$

write the necessary moment equations for the beam shown in the accompanying figure, and write a program for determining the elastic curve of the beam using the procedure outlined in Prob. 7-7. Compare the solution obtained with an analytical solution.

$$EI = 18(10)^8 \text{ lb-in.}^2$$

Problem 7-6

7-7. Work the problem of Ex. 7-2 by the trial-and-error method discussed in Sec. 7-2, and compare the results obtained with the deflections found in that example. Use the self-starting modified Euler method for integration. Two initial shaft slopes must be chosen which will be certain to bracket the correct negative slope. Suggested values are 0.0 and -0.002 in./in. Assign the first to the variable name LOW and the second to the variable name HIGH. For an initial dy/dx, use the average of LOW and HIGH. After an integration, the dy/dx value used is assigned to either LOW or HIGH, depending on the results of the integration. For example, if the final y value comes out positive, a larger initial negative slope is required. Therefore, the initial dy/dx value used is assigned to the variable name LOW, and a new initial dy/dx value is determined as the average of LOW and HIGH. Use a Δx value of 0.1 in. and require that the final y value be within 0.0000005 in. of zero. After an essentially correct initial slope has been determined, print out the displacements at 3-in. intervals of beam length. Note that one of three different expressions for the bending moment M as a function of x must be used, depending on the value of x, and that I varies with the section of the shaft in which the x value lies. Use the self-starting modified Euler method. (Note that the predictor equation is not necessary since y'' is a function of x only.)

7-8. The beam shown in part a of the accompanying figure is fixed at A and pinned at B and is thus statically indeterminate. However, looking at the free-body diagram of the beam in part b, we can take moments about an axis through B and obtain the following relationship between the moment at the fixed end and the reaction there:

$$\frac{M_A}{100} + 5000 = R_A$$

Utilizing the relationship from elementary beam theory

$$EI \frac{d^2y}{dx^2} = M$$

write the moment equation of the beam, in terms of M_A, and write a program for determining the elastic curve of the beam, the moment at the fixed end, and the vertical reactions at each end. Use the self-starting modified Euler method, and compare the solution obtained with an analytical solution. (Note that the predictor equation is not necessary since y'' is a function of x only.)

$EI = 10^9\ \text{lb-in}^2$

(a)

(b)

Problem 7-8

7-9. Utilizing the relationship from elementary beam theory

$$EI \frac{d^2y}{dx^2} = M$$

write the necessary moment equations for the beam shown in the accompanying figure, and write a program for determining the elastic curve of the beam by the simultaneous-equation method.

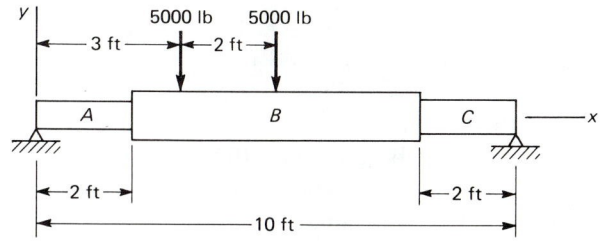

$EI_A = 5(10)^8$ lb-in.^{2} $EI_B = 18(10)^8$ lb-in.^{2} $EI_C = 11(10)^8$ lb-in.^{2}

Problem 7-9

7-10. Utilizing the relationship from elementary beam theory

$$EI \frac{d^2y}{dx^2} = M$$

write the necessary moment equations for the beam shown in the accompanying figure. Then write a program for determining the elastic curve of the beam. Express the deflection y in units of millimeters.

$EI_A = EI_C = 144(10)^4$ N·m^2 $EI_B = 518(10)^4$ N·m^2

Problem 7-10

7-11. Write a computer program to solve the radiating-fin problem of Ex. 7-1 by using the fourth-order Runge-Kutta method for the integration.

7-12. In Ex. 7-1 the temperatures and temperature gradients along a given radiating fin were found. Having found the temperature gradient at $x = 0$, it is possible to determine the amount of heat per hour flowing into the fin by using Fourier's law of heat conduction, $q = -kA \ dT/dx$. Using this we obtain

$$q = -25(0.0025)(-16,639) = 1040 \text{ Btu/hr}$$

In this problem we wish to design a fin of length $L = 0.25$ ft and width $b = 0.5$ ft which will dissipate 1500 Btu/hr. The design variable will be the fin thickness h, with an upper constraint on the thickness of 0.015

ft. The other parameters are the same as in Ex. 7-1. Use a trial-and-error approach employing bisection as explained in Ex. 7-1, modifying the program of that example as required. Choose two values of h which are quite sure to bracket the correct fin thickness you are trying to determine. Suggested values would be 0.0 and 0.015, the latter being the upper constraint. Assign them to the name LOW and HIGH, respectively. For an initial trial run use h equal to the average of LOW and HIGH. With the h determined, calculate an initial temperature gradient from Fourier's law of heat conduction, and then integrate as in Ex. 7-1. After an integration, the value of h used will be assigned to the name LOW or HIGH, depending on the results of the integration, and a new h determined as the average of LOW and HIGH. For example, if the final temperature gradient comes out positive, a larger negative initial temperature gradient is needed. This will require a smaller fin thickness for a given q value, so h will be assigned to the name HIGH and a new h calculated as the average of LOW and HIGH. Trials should continue until the final temperature gradient is within 1°R/ft of zero. Print out the final fin thickness to the nearest 0.0001 ft, and the final temperatures and temperature gradients along the fin.

(answer: $h = 0.0108$ ft.)

7-13. Example 7-1 is concerned with the solution of the radiating-fin problem. The following differential equation, derived in Ex. 7-1, refers to the coordinate system shown in part a of the accompanying figure.

$$\frac{d^2T_1}{dx^2} = \frac{2\sigma\varepsilon_1}{kh} T_1^4$$

where the pertinent initial and final boundary conditions are

$$x = 0 \begin{vmatrix} T_1 = 2000°R \\ \dfrac{dT_1}{dx} = ? \end{vmatrix} \qquad x = L \begin{vmatrix} \\ \dfrac{dT_1}{dx} = 0 \end{vmatrix}$$

The use of a different set of coordinate axes, such as shown in part b of the figure, with the new independent variable y, results in a new differential equation

$$\frac{d^2T_1}{dy^2} = \frac{2\sigma\varepsilon_1}{kh} T_1^4$$

which describes the system.

Considering T_1 as a function of y, determine the pertinent initial and final boundary conditions required to obtain a numerical solution by the trial-and-error approach discussed in Sec. 7-2.

Write a FORTRAN program for solving the differential equation associated with the new set of axes so that the temperature distribution along the fin may be determined. Using this program and the data given in Ex. 7-1, obtain a computer solution of the temperature distribution along the fin.

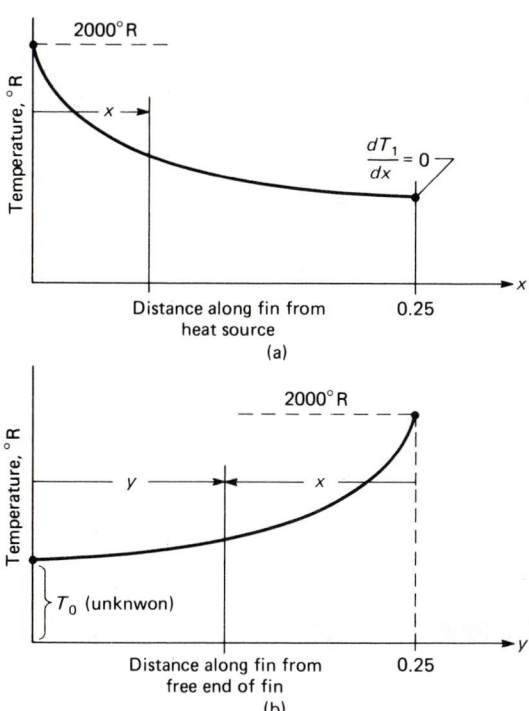

Problem 7-13

7-14. The differential equation for a flexible cable is

$$\frac{d^2y}{dx^2} = -\frac{w(x)}{H} \tag{1}$$

where y is the vertical displacement, $w(x)$ is the load per unit length, and the constant H is the horizontal component of the tension T in the cable. The differential equation is readily derived by setting the summation of forces in the x and y directions equal to zero for a differential segment, as shown in the accompanying illustration. That is,

$$T_1 \sin \theta_1 - T_2 \sin \theta_2 = w(x) \, dx \tag{2}$$

$$H = T_1 \cos \theta_1 = T_2 \cos \theta_2 \quad \text{(a constant)} \tag{3}$$

Eliminating T_1 and T_2 from the first equation gives

$$H(\tan \theta_1 - \tan \theta_2) = W(x)\, dx \qquad (4)$$

where $\tan \theta_1 = dy/dx|_x$ and $\tan \theta_2 = dy/dx|_{x+dx}$. Since

$$\frac{dy/dx|_x - dy/dx|_{x+dx}}{dx} = -\frac{d^2y}{dx^2}$$

Equation 4 yields the differential equation, Eq. 1.

Write a FORTRAN program for obtaining, by the trial-and-error method, the y displacements of the cable shown in the accompanying illustration.

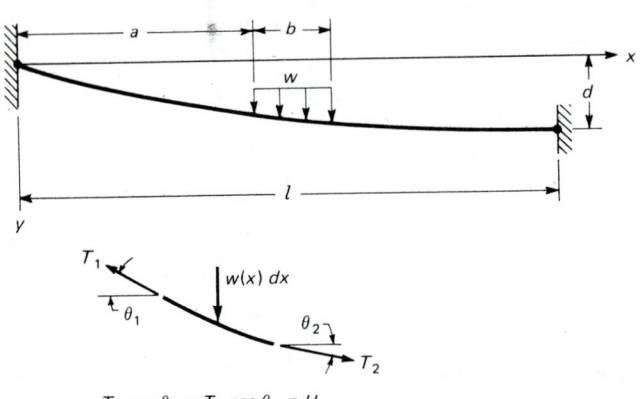

$$T_1 \cos \theta_1 = T_2 \cos \theta_2 = H$$

Problem 7-14

The right end is anchored a distance d below the left end. The pertinent data are as follows:

$$l = 200 \text{ ft} \qquad d = 10 \text{ ft} \qquad a = 100 \text{ ft}$$
$$b = 10 \text{ ft} \qquad h = 10{,}000 \text{ lb} \qquad w = 20 \text{ lb/ft}$$

7-15. Refer to Prob. 7-14 and determine the y displacements of the cable using the following system data as input to the computer program:

$$l = 65 \text{ m} \qquad d = 4 \text{ m} \qquad a = 25 \text{ m}$$
$$b = 7 \text{ m} \qquad H = 45 \text{ kN} \qquad w = 300 \text{ N/m}$$

Express the results in millimeters.

7-16. Referring to Prob. 7-14, write a FORTRAN program for obtaining, by the finite-difference-simultaneous-equation method, the y displacements of the cable.

7-17. Referring to Prob. 7-14, write a FORTRAN program for obtaining the y displacements of the cable and the tension T in the cable at various values of x along the cable. Do not make the assumption that $\sin \theta = \tan \theta = \theta$ for obtaining the values for the tension T.

(partial answer: for $x = 110$ ft, $y = 6.445$ ft, $T = 1.00078(10)^4$ lb)

7-18. The differential equation for the radial displacement u of a point in a thick-walled cylinder is

$$\frac{d^2u}{d\rho^2} + \frac{1}{\rho}\frac{du}{d\rho} - \frac{u}{\rho^2} = 0$$

The radial displacement of point A to A', as shown in the accompanying illustration, is a result of the tangential and radial strains which may be induced by subjecting the inside and outside boundaries of the cylinder to changes in temperature and/or pressures. The relation between the tangential strain ε_t, of a fiber at a distance ρ from the center, and the radial displacement u is $\varepsilon_t = u/\rho$. Assuming that the tangential strains ε_t have been measured on the inside and outside boundaries of a cylinder subjected to an internal pressure and known temperature changes, write a FORTRAN program for obtaining the radial displacements u throughout the cylinder. The tangential strains on the boundaries, as measured with electric-resistance strain gauges, are

$$\varepsilon_t \big|_{\rho=2 \text{ in.}} = 1000 \times 10^{-6} \text{ in./in.}$$

$$\varepsilon_t \big|_{\rho=4 \text{ in.}} = 200 \times 10^{-6} \text{ in./in.}$$

(partial answer: for $\rho = 2.3$ in., $\mu = 0.1702(10)^{-2}$ in.)

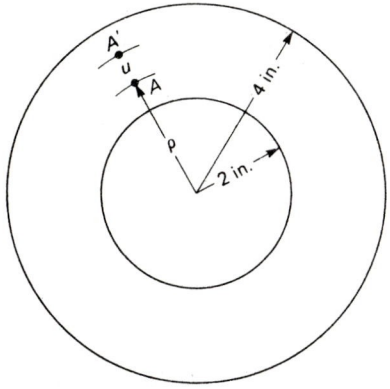

Problem 7-18

7-19. In Prob. 7-18 the differential equation for the radial displacement u in a thick-walled cylinder was given as

$$\frac{d^2u}{d\rho^2} + \frac{1}{\rho}\frac{du}{d\rho} - \frac{u}{\rho^2} = 0$$

Assume a solution to this differential equation of the form

$$u = \sum \alpha_n \rho^n$$

and show that the solution is

$$u = \alpha_1 \rho + \frac{\alpha_2}{\rho}$$

where α_1 and α_2 are constants of integration. If a numerical solution has been obtained for Prob. 7-18, compare these results with the analytical solution.

7-20. The deflection z of a circular membrane which is loaded uniformly with a pressure p is described by the differential equation

$$\frac{d^2z}{dr^2} + \frac{1}{r}\frac{dz}{dr} = -\frac{p}{T}$$

where T is the tension (pounds per linear inch). For a highly stretched membrane, the tension T may be assumed constant for small deflections.

Write a FORTRAN program for obtaining, by the trial-and-error method, the deflections of the annular membrane shown in the accompanying

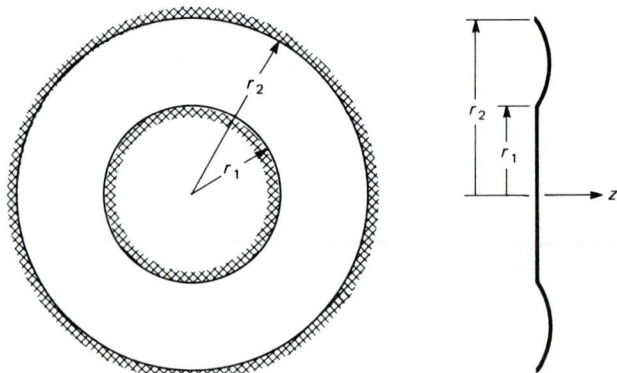

Problem 7-20

illustration. The pertinent data for the membrane, which is fastened at r_1 and r_2, are as follows:

$r_1 = 6$ in. $r_2 = 12$ in.

$T = 100$ lb/in. $p = 5$ psi (uniformly distributed)

7-21. Refer to the annular membrane shown in the figure accompanying Prob. 7-20. The deflection z of the membrane is described by the equation

$$\frac{d^2z}{dr^2} + \frac{1}{r}\frac{dz}{dr} = -\frac{p}{T}$$

in which p is a uniform pressure (pascals), and T is the tension (newtons per linear meter). For a highly stretched membrane the tension may be assumed constant for small deflections. The data for the membrane which is fastened at r_1 and r_2 are as follows:

$r_1 = 160$ mm $r_2 = 300$ mm

$T = 18$ N/mm $p = 35$ kPa

Write a FORTRAN program for obtaining the displacement z of the membrane using the finite-difference–simultaneous-equation method.

7-22. Fluid flowing in a conduit flows by a thin wire of length l and radius r, as shown in the accompanying illustration (part a). The temperature of the fluid flowing by the wire is U, and the temperatures at the ends of the wire in the walls of the conduit are $u(0) = u_0$ and $u(l) = u_e$, as shown in part b of the figure. Thus, heat flows along the wire by conduction, and from the surface of the wire by convection and conduction. Equating the heat flow q_1 into the element to the heat flow $q_2 + q_3$ from the element, as shown in part c of the figure, the differential equation for the temperature u in the wire is found to be

$$\frac{d^2u}{dx^2} = \frac{2K}{kr}u - \frac{2K}{kr}U$$

where

k = thermal conductivity of wire material
r = radius of wire
K = effective conductance of wire surface for heat transfer by convection and conduction

(a)

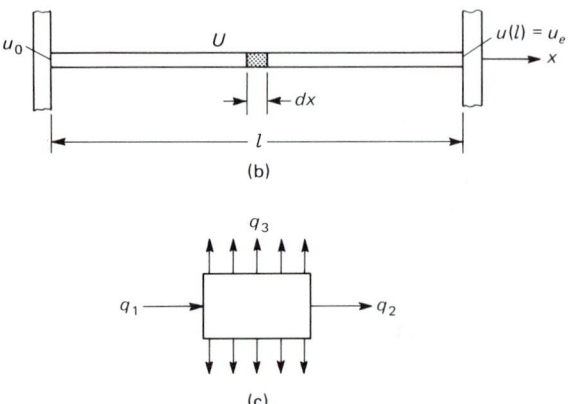

(b)

(c)

The conductance K depends to some extent upon the Reynolds number, which is proportional to the velocity of the fluid. Since the wire cuts across the fluid stream at a bend in the conduit, the velocity of the fluid varies along the length of the wire. Considering that the velocity along the wire increases with x, a reasonable assumption for the variation of K along the wire is

$$K = K_0 + cx$$

where c is a constant, and K_0 is the value of K at $x = 0$.

Write a FORTRAN program for obtaining, by the finite-difference–simultaneous-equation method, the temperature u along the wire.

Problem 7-22

Use the following data:

$$l = 1 \text{ ft}$$

$$r = 0.01 \text{ ft}$$

$$u_0 = 100°F$$

$$u_e = 250°F$$

$$k = 0.035 \text{ Btu}/(\text{sec})(\text{ft})(°F)$$

$$K_0 = 3.8 \text{ Btu}/(\text{sec})(\text{ft}^2)(°F)$$

$$c = 2 \text{ Btu}/(\text{sec})(\text{ft})^3(°F)$$

$$U = 300°F$$

7-23. Solve Prob. 7-22 using the following data:

$$l = 30 \text{ mm}$$

$$r = 300 \text{ mm}$$

$$u_0 = 40°C \text{ (Celsius)}$$

$$u_e = 40°C \text{ (Celsius)}$$

$$k = 190 \text{ J}/(\text{s})(\text{m})(°C)$$

$$K_0 = 60(10)^3 \text{ J}/(\text{s})(\text{m}^2)(°C)$$

$$c = 90(10)^3 \text{ J}/(\text{s})(\text{m}^3)(°C)$$

$$U = 150°C$$

Chapter 8
Introduction to Partial
Differential Equations

8-1 INTRODUCTION

We will now consider the numerical solution of partial differential equations of the general form

$$a \frac{\partial^2 u}{\partial x^2} + b \frac{\partial^2 u}{\partial x\, \partial y} + c \frac{\partial^2 u}{\partial y^2} = f \qquad (8\text{-}1)$$

where, in general, the coefficients a, b, and c are functions of x and y, and f is a function of x, y, u, $\partial u/\partial x$, and $\partial u/\partial y$. Such equations arise in engineering work involving heat transfer, boundary-layer flow, vibrations, elasticity, and so on. It will not be possible, within the scope of this text, to present a comprehensive coverage of the various numerical methods for solving partial differential equations. However, the material presented will provide an introduction to the subject by illustrating some of the most easily understandable and useful methods. The various forms which Eq. 8-1 may take are classified as *elliptic, parabolic,* or *hyperbolic.* The solution of each type will be illustrated by an engineering example.

8-2 ELLIPTIC PARTIAL DIFFERENTIAL EQUATIONS

Elliptic partial differential equations are found in *equilibrium*-type boundary-value problems. In this kind of problem the differential equation will have coefficients such that

$$b^2 - 4ac < 0$$

where a, b, and c are the coefficients associated with Eq. 8-1.[1] Typical examples of this type of differential equation include Laplace's equation

$$\frac{\partial^2 u}{\partial x^2} + \frac{\partial^2 u}{\partial y^2} = 0 \tag{8-2}$$

and Poisson's equation

$$\frac{\partial^2 u}{\partial x^2} + \frac{\partial^2 u}{\partial y^2} = f(x, y) \tag{8-3}$$

where the function $u(x, y)$ must satisfy both the differential equation over a *closed domain* and the boundary conditions on the closed boundary of the domain. A closed solution domain (as opposed to an open-ended domain) is characteristic of elliptic partial differential equations. This is illustrated graphically in Fig. 8-1. The solution domains of parabolic and hyperbolic differential equations are fundamentally different in nature, as they are open-ended domains.

To illustrate a physical situation in which an elliptic partial differential equation arises, let us consider the problem of determining the temperature distribution in a thin homogeneous rectangular plate, insulated perfectly on both faces, with prescribed boundary conditions maintained along the edges of the plate. It will be assumed that the specific heat and thermal conductivity of the plate material do not vary throughout the plate and that the plate is thin enough to consider the heat flow in a direction normal to the insulated faces as negligible.

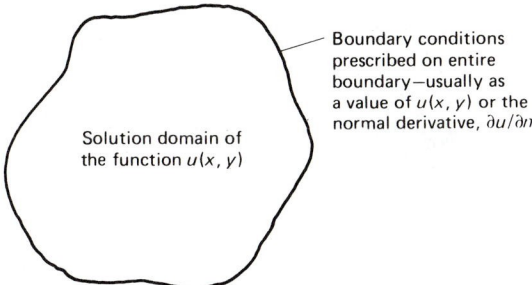

Boundary conditions prescribed on entire boundary—usually as a value of $u(x, y)$ or the normal derivative, $\partial u/\partial n$

Solution domain of the function $u(x, y)$

Figure 8-1   Solution domain of an elliptic partial differential equation

[1]Stephen H. Crandall, *Engineering Analysis* (New York: McGraw-Hill Book Company, 1956), pp. 353ff.

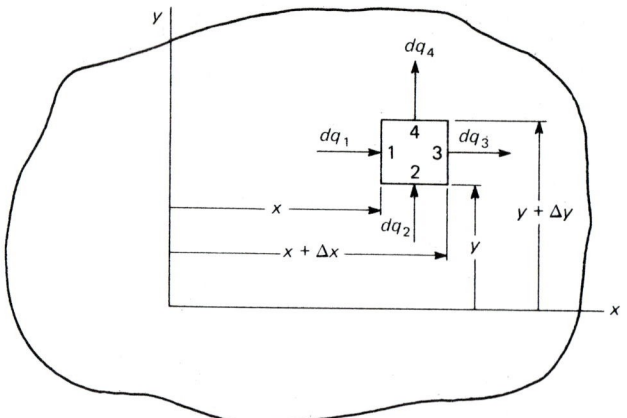

Figure 8-2 Heat entering and leaving an element of a plate in time *dt*

Establishing an *x*-*y* coordinate system on the plate, as shown in Fig. 8-2, we first consider a small element of the plate with dimensions of Δx and Δy. Such an element is shown greatly exaggerated in size in the figure. The quantity of heat entering side 1 of the element in time *dt* is given by Fourier's law of heat conduction as

$$dq_1 = -k(\Delta y)(d)\frac{\partial u}{\partial x}\bigg|_x dt \tag{8-4}$$

where *k* is the coefficient of thermal conductivity, *d* is the thickness of the plate, and $\partial u/\partial x|_x$ is the average temperature gradient over side 1 of the element in the *x* direction. The heat leaving side 3 in time *dt* is

$$dq_3 = -k(\Delta y)(d)\frac{\partial u}{\partial x}\bigg|_{x+\Delta x} dt \tag{8-5}$$

The *net* heat gain of the element in time *dt* due to heat flow in the *x* direction is thus

$$dq_1 - dq_3 = \left[-k(\Delta y)(d)\frac{\partial u}{\partial x}\bigg|_x + k(\Delta y)(d)\frac{\partial u}{\partial x}\bigg|_{x+\Delta x}\right] dt$$

or

$$dq_1 - dq_3 = k(\Delta y)(d)(\Delta x)\left[\frac{\frac{\partial u}{\partial x}\bigg|_{x+\Delta x} - \frac{\partial u}{\partial x}\bigg|_x}{(\Delta x)}\right] dt \tag{8-6}$$

Similarly, the net heat gain in time dt due to heat flow in the y direction is

$$dq_2 - dq_4 = k(\Delta x)(d)(\Delta y)\left[\frac{\left.\frac{\partial u}{\partial y}\right|_{y+\Delta y} - \left.\frac{\partial u}{\partial y}\right|_y}{(\Delta y)}\right] dt \tag{8-7}$$

The *total* net heat gain dQ of the element in time dt is found by adding Eqs. 8-6 and 8-7,

$$dQ = k(\Delta x)(\Delta y)(d)\left[\frac{\left.\frac{\partial u}{\partial x}\right|_{x+\Delta x} - \left.\frac{\partial u}{\partial x}\right|_x}{(\Delta x)} + \frac{\left.\frac{\partial u}{\partial y}\right|_{y+\Delta y} - \left.\frac{\partial u}{\partial y}\right|_y}{(\Delta y)}\right] dt \tag{8-8}$$

The total net heat gain of the element in time dt may also be expressed as

$$dQ = c(\Delta x)(\Delta y)(d)\rho \frac{\partial u}{\partial t} dt \tag{8-9}$$

where c is the specific heat of the plate material, ρ is the weight density, and $\partial u/\partial t$ is the average rate of change of the temperature of the element with respect to time.

Equating Eqs. 8-8 and 8-9 and dividing both sides by $(\Delta x)(\Delta y)(dt)(d)$ gives

$$k\left[\frac{\left.\frac{\partial u}{\partial x}\right|_{x+\Delta x} - \left.\frac{\partial u}{\partial x}\right|_x}{(\Delta x)} + \frac{\left.\frac{\partial u}{\partial y}\right|_{y+\Delta y} - \left.\frac{\partial u}{\partial y}\right|_y}{(\Delta y)}\right] = c\rho \frac{\partial u}{\partial t} \tag{8-10}$$

Letting both (Δx) and (Δy) approach zero and rearranging terms,

$$\frac{\partial u}{\partial t} = \frac{k}{c\rho}\left[\frac{\partial^2 u}{\partial x^2} + \frac{\partial^2 u}{\partial y^2}\right] \tag{8-11}$$

Equation 8-11 is the *two-dimensional heat equation*.

If we are interested in the *equilibrium* or *steady-state* condition, we realize that $\partial u/\partial t = 0$, and Eq. 8-11 reduces to

$$\frac{\partial^2 u}{\partial x^2} + \frac{\partial^2 u}{\partial y^2} = 0 \tag{8-12}$$

The latter is Laplace's partial differential equation which was mentioned earlier in this section as an example of an elliptic partial differential equation. The

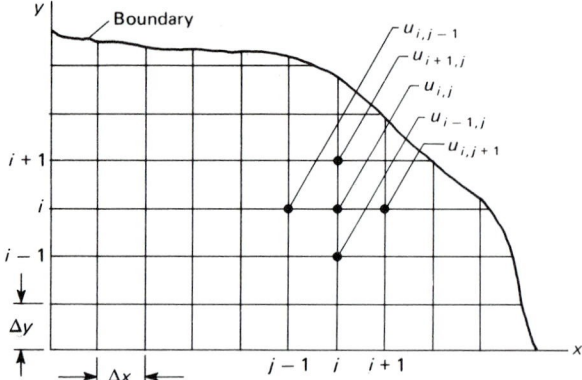

Figure 8-3 Plate temperatures at grid points near intersection of the ith row and jth column of the points

temperature $u(x, y)$ throughout the plate must satisfy this equation, as well as the boundary conditions along the entire boundary of the plate when the plate is in thermal equilibrium. Usually, the boundary is either insulated in part, in which case the *normal derivative* of the temperature at the boundary is equal to zero, and/or the temperature is maintained at a specified value over part or all of the boundary.

We will next develop a numerical method for obtaining the solution of Eq. 8-12. Let us superimpose a lattice or grid with a mesh size of Δx by Δy upon the plate, as shown in Fig. 8-3. The numerical solution will consist of determining the temperatures at the finitely spaced grid points shown. Figure 8-3 shows the temperatures at the grid points in the neighborhood of the intersection of the ith row and jth column. From Eq. 5-79 we can write *central-difference* approximations for the second partial derivatives of the temperature with respect to distance, in the x and y directions, as follows:

$$\frac{\partial^2 u}{\partial x^2} = \frac{u_{i,j+1} - 2u_{i,j} + u_{i,j-1}}{(\Delta x)^2}$$

$$\frac{\partial^2 u}{\partial y^2} = \frac{u_{i+1,j} - 2u_{i,j} + u_{i-1,j}}{(\Delta y)^2}$$

(8-13)

Substituting these finite-difference expressions into Eq. 8-12,

$$\frac{u_{i,j+1} - 2u_{i,j} + u_{i,j-1}}{(\Delta x)^2} + \frac{u_{i+1,j} - 2u_{i,j} + u_{i-1,j}}{(\Delta y)^2} = 0$$

(8-14)

If we use a square mesh so that $\Delta x = \Delta y = h$, Eq. 8-14 reduces to

$$u_{i,j+1} + u_{i,j-1} + u_{i+1,j} + u_{i-1,j} - 4u_{i,j} = 0$$

(8-15)

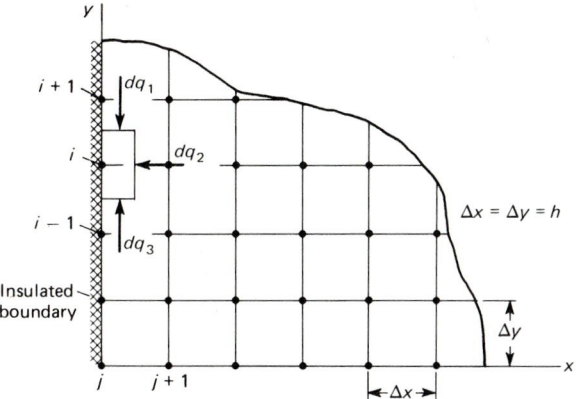

Figure 8-4   Heat flow into half-element on an insulated left boundary

and is referred to as the *Laplacian* difference equation. This equation must hold at every *interior* grid point on the plate.

As mentioned previously, the temperatures at the boundary points are usually known, or the boundary is considered to be perfectly insulated. Insulated boundaries are handled by developing boundary equations. Figure 8-4 shows a *half-element* lying on an *insulated* left boundary of the plate. The *net* heat flowing into this element must equal zero when we are considering a steady-state condition for the plate. The quantity of heat flowing into the three faces of the half-element in time dt are given by the following equations:

$$dq_1 = \left(\frac{khd}{2}\right)\frac{\partial u}{\partial y}\bigg|_{i+1/2} dt = \left(\frac{khd}{2}\right)\left(\frac{u_{i+1,j} - u_{i,j}}{h}\right) dt$$

$$dq_2 = (khd)\frac{\partial u}{\partial x}\bigg|_{j+1/2} dt = (khd)\left(\frac{u_{i,j+1} - u_{i,j}}{h}\right) dt \tag{8-16}$$

$$dq_3 = -\left(\frac{khd}{2}\right)\frac{\partial u}{\partial y}\bigg|_{i-1/2} dt = -\left(\frac{khd}{2}\right)\left(\frac{u_{i,j} - u_{i-1,j}}{h}\right) dt$$

Substituting Eq. 8-16 into the heat-balance equation for the half-element

$$dq_1 + dq_2 + dq_3 = 0$$

yields

(Left) $\qquad u_{i+1,j} + 2u_{i,j+1} + u_{i-1,j} - 4u_{i,j} = 0 \tag{8-17}$

Similarly, the difference equations which apply on the right, upper, and lower *insulated* boundaries of a rectangular plate are

(Right) $\qquad u_{i+1,j} + 2u_{i,j-1} + u_{i-1,j} - 4u_{i,j} = 0$ $\qquad\qquad$ (8-18)

(Upper) $\qquad u_{i,j-1} + 2u_{i-1,j} + u_{i,j+1} - 4u_{i,j} = 0$ $\qquad\qquad$ (8-19)

(Lower) $\qquad u_{i,j-1} + 2u_{i+1,j} + u_{i,j+1} - 4u_{i,j} = 0$ $\qquad\qquad$ (8-20)

Thus, in obtaining a solution for the steady-state heat flow in a rectangular plate, Eq. 8-15 must hold at every *interior* grid point, and Eqs. 8-17 through 8-20 must be satisfied at any appropriate insulated boundaries. (A method for handling irregular or curved boundaries will be discussed on p. 596.) Reviewing the pertinent equations, it can be seen that the problem has been reduced to obtaining the simultaneous solution of a set of linear algebraic equations in the unknown grid-point temperatures u, the total number of equations depending upon the extent of the insulated boundaries and the number of grid points used. If the number of grid points required is not too large, the resulting equations may be solved by the *elimination* methods, discussed in Chap. 3. Usually, however, a rather large number of grid points is desirable, and the number of equations which must be solved simultaneously becomes too large to solve accurately by the elimination methods. In this case the Gauss-Seidel iteration method (see Sec. 3-7) can be employed to obtain a more accurate solution. (In connection with the solution of elliptic partial differential equations, the Gauss-Seidel method is often referred to as Liebmann's method.) The equations which must be solved are of the type which have a dominant coefficient for a different unknown in each equation. In addition, there are many zero coefficients in each equation (only four or five unknowns in each equation have nonzero coefficients). The existence of a dominant coefficient in each equation, as mentioned, is a necessary feature for convergence with the equations which are to be solved by the Gauss-Seidel method, and the presence of zero coefficients is a very convenient feature.

Following the procedure outlined for the Gauss-Seidel method in Sec. 3-7, we first arrange each equation in a form convenient for solving for the unknown with the *largest* coefficient in that equation. In the case we are considering, this unknown will always be $u_{i,j}$. For example, from Eq. 8-15 we obtain

$$u_{i,j} = \frac{u_{i,j+1} + u_{i,j-1} + u_{i+1,j} + u_{i-1,j}}{4} \qquad\qquad (8\text{-}21)$$

All unknown temperatures at the grid points are then assigned initial values on the basis of the best estimate available (the better the estimate, the more rapid the convergence to a solution). In calculating $u_{i,j}$ the values of the temperatures on the right side of Eq. 8-21 consist initially of estimated values or known boundary values. However, as soon as an approximate temperature, at a grid point is calculated, this calculated value supersedes the estimated value and is used as the temperature at that point until it is, in turn, superseded by a new calculated value. Thus, the latest calculated values of the temperatures we are seeking are always used in calculating newer and better values. The applicable equations are used at points on the plate which are selected in some systematic manner, usually either by rows or by columns. The following example illustrates the procedure. (A discussion of a technique for speeding up convergence follows the example.)

EXAMPLE 8-1

Utilizing the digital computer to perform the calculations required by the Gauss-Seidel method, let us determine the temperature distribution in a square plate which has both faces insulated and also has several portions of the edges insulated, as shown in Fig. 8-5. The upper edge and the upper portions of the left and right edges are held at a constant temperature U_T. The bottom edge is maintained at a constant temperature U_B. A grid having ten rows and ten columns of points is superimposed upon the plate, as shown. The left edge is insulated from the bottom up to row $IA = 5$, and the right edge is insulated from the bottom up to row $IB = 8$.

Referring to Eqs. 8-15 through 8-20 and the explanation accompanying Eq. 8-21, we can write the applicable interior and boundary difference equations for this problem as follows:

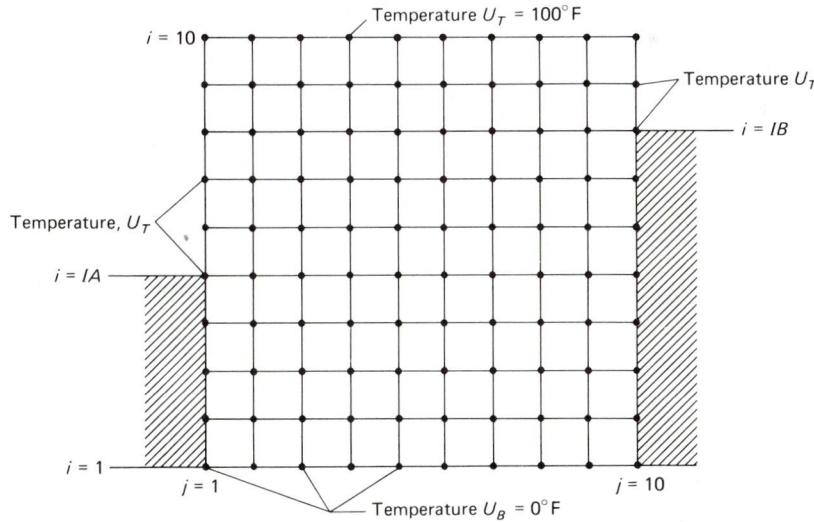

Figure 8-5 Plate of Ex. 8-1

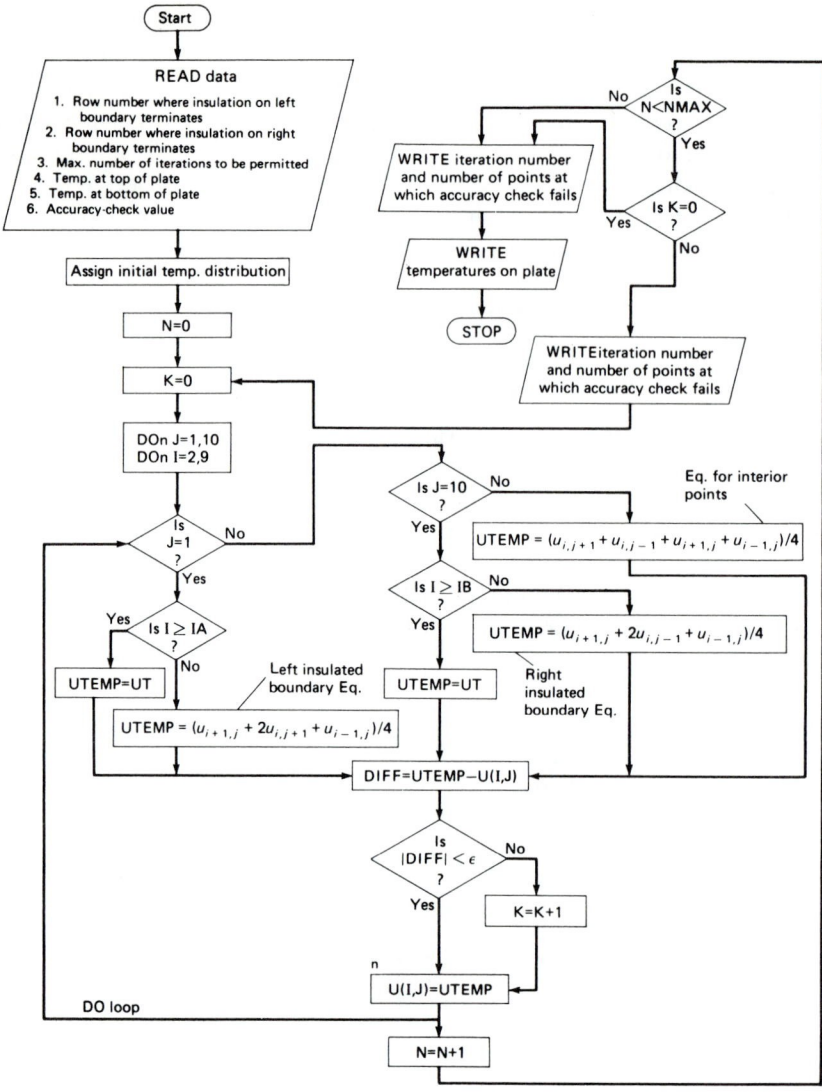

Figure 8-6 Flow chart for Ex. 8-1

(Interior)

$$u_{i,j} = \frac{u_{i,j+1} + u_{i,j-1} + u_{i+1,j} + u_{i-1,j}}{4} \qquad \begin{array}{l} 1 < i < 10 \\ 1 < j < 10 \end{array} \quad \text{(a)}$$

(Insulated portion of left boundary)

$$u_{i,j} = \frac{u_{i+1,j} + 2u_{i,j+1} + u_{i-1,j}}{4} \qquad 1 < i < IA, \quad j = 1 \quad \text{(b)}$$

(Insulated portion of right boundary)

$$u_{i,j} = \frac{u_{i+1,j} + 2u_{i,j-1} + u_{i-1,j}}{4} \qquad 1 < i < IB, \quad j = 10 \text{ (c)} \qquad \text{(8-22)}$$

(Boundaries with temperature U_T)

$$u_{i,j} = U_T \qquad \begin{aligned} &1 \le j \le 10, \qquad i = 10 \\ &IA \le i < 10, \quad j = 1 \\ &IB \le i < 10, \quad j = 10 \end{aligned} \qquad \text{(d)}$$

(Boundary with temperature U_B)

$$u_{i,j} = U_B \qquad 1 \le j \le 10, \, i = 1 \qquad \text{(e)}$$

Equation 8-22, for all i and j values, must be solved simultaneously to obtain the equilibrium temperature over the plate. The initial temperatures at the grid points where the temperatures are unknown are estimated by assuming a linear temperature gradient between U_B at the bottom of the plate and U_T at the top of the plate. The reader should review the steps outlined for employing the Gauss-Seidel method (see p. 198) before studying the flow chart for this problem (Fig. 8-6). The FORTRAN names used for this problem and the quantities they represent are as follows:

FORTRAN Name	**Quantity**	**Value Used in Problem**
U(I,J)	Temperatures at grid points, °F	
IA	Row at which insulation stops on left boundary	5
IB	Row at which insulation stops on right boundary	8
NMAX	Maximum number of iterations desired	100
UT	Temperature at top of plate and portions of left and right boundaries, °F	100
UB	Temperature at bottom of plate, °F	0
EPSI	Accuracy-check value, °F	0.05
I	Grid row number	
J	Grid column number	
N	Number of iterations completed	
K	Number of grid points at which accuracy check fails	
UTEMP	Temporary name for value of U(I,J), °F	
DIFF	Difference in calculated temperatures at a grid point for two successive iterations, °F	

Referring now to the flow chart, it can be seen that one iteration is complete when an approximate value has been computed for each grid point whose temperature is sought. In all iterations the *latest* calculated temperature of each of these grid points is used in each equation in which it appears. After each step in the iteration, the computer is instructed to check the difference between successive calculated values for that grid point. At the end of each iteration, the computer is then instructed to print out the number of grid points at which the value of the temperature has changed from the preceding iteration by more than some predetermined value, epsilon, which defines the accuracy desired. At this time the computer is also instructed to print out the number of iterations completed. When the temperature change at *all* grid points between successive iterations is less than or equal to the prescribed epsilon value, the computer is programmed to print out these temperatures in a tabular array corresponding to the location of the grid points on the plate. The program also has a provision to instruct the computer to print out the temperatures in the form stated if a certain maximum number of iterations is completed before all the grid-point temperatures vary by less than the prescribed epsilon value. This procedure is incorporated to avoid excessive computing time in case the convergence to a solution is slow. Either printout mentioned terminates the program.

The FORTRAN IV computer program used to implement the flow chart shown is as follows:

```
C TEMPERATURE DISTRIBUTION IN A SQUARE PLATE
C SOLUTION BY GAUSS-SEIDEL ITERATION METHOD
      DIMENSION U(10,10)
      READ(5,2) IA,IB,NMAX,UT,UB,EPSI
    2 FORMAT(2I3,I4,2F6.0,F5.2)
      WRITE(6,3)
    3 FORMAT('1','TEMP DIST IN A PLATE BY GAUSS-SEIDEL
                                          ITERATION'/)
      WRITE(6,30)
   30 FORMAT(' ',8X,'ITERATION NUMBER' ,6X,'K VALUE'/)
      DO 4 I=1,10
      DO 4 J=1,10
    4 U(I,J)=UB+(UT-UB)*(I-1.)/9.
      N=0
    5 K=0
      DO 16 J=1,10
      DO 16 I=2,9
      IF(J-1) 9,6,9
    6 IF(IA-I) 7,7,8
    7 UTEMP=UT
      GO TO 14
    8 UTEMP=(U(I+1,J)+2.*U(I,J+1)+U(I-1,J))/4.
      GO TO 14
    9 IF(J-10) 13,10,13
   10 IF(I-IB) 12,11,11
   11 UTEMP=UT
      GO TO 14
```

```
12 UTEMP=(U(I+1,J)+2.*U(I,J-1)+U(I-1,J))/4.
   GO TO 14
13 UTEMP=(U(I,J+1)+U(I,J-1)+U(I+1,J)+U(I-1,J))/4.
14 DIFF=UTEMP-U(I,J)
   IF(ABS(DIFF)-EPSI) 16,15,15
15 K=K+1
16 U(I,J)=UTEMP
   N=N+1
   IF(N-NMAX) 17,20,20
17 IF(K) 18,20,18
18 WRITE(6,19) N,K
19 FORMAT(' ',13X,I4,14X,I4)
   GO TO 5
20 WRITE(6,19) N,K
21 FORMAT('0',10F7.2)
   DO 22 M=1,10
   I=11-M
22 WRITE(6,21) (U(I,J),J=1,10)
   STOP
   END
```

The computer results are shown in the tabular printout below:

```
TEMP DIST IN A PLATE BY GAUSS-SEIDEL ITERATION
```

ITERATION NUMBER	K VALUE	ITERATION NUMBER	K VALUE
1	32	20	68
2	39	21	67
3	52	22	65
4	62	23	62
5	65	24	61
6	68	25	58
7	70	26	56
8	70	27	51
9	73	28	46
10	73	29	43
11	73	30	38
12	73	31	37
13	73	32	34
14	71	33	31
15	71	34	24
16	71	35	17
17	71	36	13
18	71	37	3
19	69	38	0

```
100.00 100.00 100.00 100.00 100.00 100.00 100.00 100.00 100.00 100.00
100.00  97.66  95.64  94.07  93.03  92.51  92.62  93.56  95.84 100.00
100.00  95.03  90.81  87.65  85.53  84.43  84.40  85.80  89.78 100.00
100.00  91.65  84.98  80.20  77.06  75.30  74.78  75.49  77.49  80.08
100.00  86.62  77.29  71.16  67.27  65.00  63.98  63.96  64.63  65.33
100.00  77.59  66.45  59.96  55.95  53.53  52.25  51.79  51.84  51.99
 63.44  57.31  51.05  46.35  43.11  41.02  39.80  39.20  39.01  39.00
 39.19  37.23  34.15  31.35  29.21  27.73  26.81  26.30  26.09  26.04
 18.93  18.29  17.04  15.77  14.72  13.97  13.48  13.20  13.07  13.04
  0.0    0.0    0.0    0.0    0.0    0.0    0.0    0.0    0.0    0.0
```

In recent years much study has been given to ways for speeding the convergence of iterative methods in solving computational problems. The Gauss-Seidel method is iterative, and it has been studied extensively in this regard. A technique called *overrelaxation* has been found to be extremely profitable in speeding the convergence of the Gauss-Seidel method, when applied to the solution of elliptic partial differential equations (the Liebmann process). In place of Eq. 8-21, the equation

$$(u_{i,j})_{\text{new}} = \omega \left(\frac{u_{i,j+1} + u_{i,j-1} + u_{i+1,j} + u_{i-1,j}}{4} \right) + (1 - \omega)(u_{i,j})_{\text{old}}$$

(8-21a)

is used.[2] The parameter ω is known as the *relaxation parameter*. For *overrelaxation* the value of ω lies between 1 and 2; for *underrelaxation*, between 0 and 1. For the Gauss-Seidel method, overrelaxation must be used to speed up convergence. It should be noted that when $\omega = 1$, Eq. 8-21a reduces to Eq. 8-21.

Forsythe and Wasow show that for a square solution domain with a 45-by-45 mesh (1936 interior points), the optimum value of ω is approximately 1.870.[3] They further point out that, in using optimal relaxation in this case, convergence is approximately 30 times faster than for the usual Liebmann process ($\omega = 1$).

Estimating ω_{opt} is an advanced problem beyond the scope of this text, but, for any given situation, it can be determined experimentally (see Prob. 8-3). The value of $\omega = 1.870$ can be used as a guide in choosing a value of ω for a square solution domain where the number of grid points is "large."

Grid Points Near Irregular Boundaries

Since it is obviously not possible to have a rectangular grid fit the boundaries of an irregular domain, we must be concerned, in such instances, with writing equations which are applicable to interior grid points that lie near irregular or curved boundaries.

Consider such a point P in a square mesh, as shown in Fig. 8-7(a). Equation 8-15, which was developed earlier for the interior grid points of a square mesh, does not apply at a grid point such as P, since the grid points C and D are not the defined mesh interval h away from point P. The simplest way to obtain an equation defining the temperature at P, when the boundary temperatures are known, is to make use of linear interpolation. Referring to Fig. 8-7(b), we see that the interpolation may be made either between points A and C or between points B and D. An average of these two interpolations may

[2]George E. Forsythe and Wolfgang R. Wasow, *Finite Difference Methods for Partial Differential Equations* (New York: John Wiley & Sons, 1960), p. 247, eq. 22.4.
[3]*Ibid.*, p. 256.

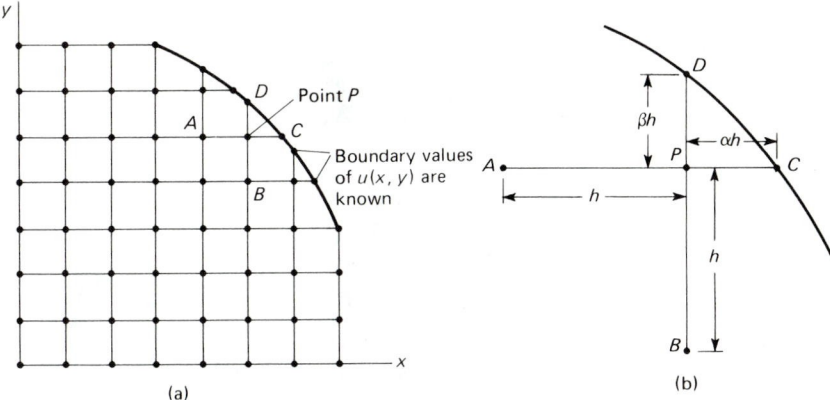

Figure 8-7   Domain with grid points near a curved boundary

also be used. For example, if we linearly interpolate between grid points A and C, we find that

$$u_P = u_A + (u_C - u_A)\left(\frac{h}{h + \alpha h}\right)$$

or

$$u_P = \left(\frac{\alpha}{1 + \alpha}\right)u_A + \left(\frac{1}{1 + \alpha}\right)u_C \qquad (8\text{-}23)$$

Similarly, interpolating between grid points B and D yields

$$u_P = \left(\frac{\beta}{1 + \beta}\right)u_B + \left(\frac{1}{1 + \beta}\right)u_D \qquad (8\text{-}24)$$

An equation such as Eq. 8-23 or 8-24 must be used for each grid point lying close to an irregular boundary.

   If the normal derivative of the function $u(x, y)$ is known at the boundary rather than the temperature $u(x, y)$ itself, the problem of handling irregular boundaries is, in general, more difficult. For example, consider point P near an irregular boundary for which $\partial u/\partial N$ is specified, as shown in Fig. 8-8. To solve the problem it is necessary to write equations defining the temperature at all grid points such as P near the boundary. The value of the normal derivative at G, $\partial u/\partial N|_G$, is known and can be expressed approximately in the following finite-difference form:

$$\left.\frac{\partial u}{\partial N}\right|_G = \frac{u_P - u_F}{\overline{FP}} \qquad (8\text{-}25)$$

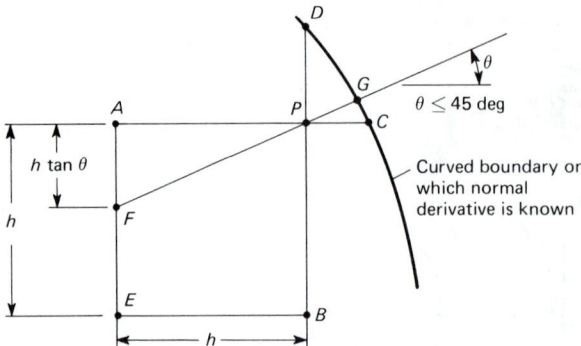

Figure 8-8 Grid points near curved boundary of a plate along which the normal derivative is known

When the angle θ is less than 45 deg, a value of u_F can be obtained by linearly interpolating between the vertically spaced grid points A and E such that

$$u_F = u_A + (u_E - u_A)\frac{h \tan \theta}{h} \tag{8-26}$$

Combining Eqs. 8-25 and 8-26 and expressing the distance $\overline{FP}$ as $h/\cos \theta$, we obtain

$$u_P = \left.\frac{\partial u}{\partial N}\right|_G \left(\frac{h}{\cos \theta}\right) + u_A(1 - \tan \theta) + u_E \tan \theta \tag{8-27}$$

An equation of this type must be used for each grid point close to the irregular boundary. The value of θ for each such grid point will be determined from the geometry of the irregular boundary.

When the angle θ is greater than 45 deg, linear interpolation can be used along a horizonal grid line, such as line EB in Fig. 8-9, to determine an

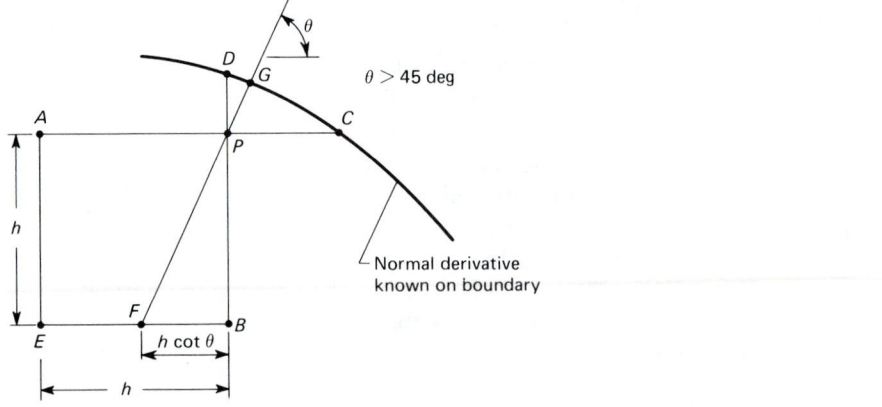

Figure 8-9 Case of a normal derivative making an angle greater than 45 deg with horizontal

expression for the temperature at a grid point such as F. Combining the expression derived from this interpolation with Eq. 8-25 yields the following equation, defining the temperature at grid point P:

$$u_P = \left.\frac{\partial u}{\partial N}\right|_G \left(\frac{h}{\sin \theta}\right) + u_B(1 - \cot \theta) + u_E \cot \theta \tag{8-28}$$

In considering problems with irregular boundaries where the boundary conditions are known normal derivatives, the boundary equations developed previously for rectangular domains (Eqs. 8-17 through 8-20) are obviously not applicable. The equations developed for grid points near irregular boundaries in the preceding paragraphs (Eqs. 8-27 and 8-28), in effect, replace the boundary equations used for rectangular domains. If it is desired to obtain the temperatures at the boundary grid points, they may be calculated by using linear interpolation between the boundary point desired and adjacent grid points whose temperatures were calculated in the solution obtained.

More elaborate (and more accurate) methods have been developed for handling grid points near curved boundaries by the use of two-dimensional Taylor series.[4] Such methods greatly increase the complexity of computer programming, if there are many such grid points to be considered. The resulting increase in accuracy is usually insignificant in most engineering problems.

For some nonrectangular domains it is possible to use non-Cartesian grids to simplify the solution of the problem. For example, polar coordinates may be used with circular domains and triangular and skew coordinates with appropriately shaped domains.[5] However, a discussion of these methods is beyond the scope of this text.

8-3 PARABOLIC PARTIAL DIFFERENTIAL EQUATIONS

Parabolic partial differential equations arise in what are called *propagation* problems. In this type of problem the solution advances outward indefinitely from known initial values, always satisfying the known boundary conditions as the solution progresses. This *open-ended* type of solution domain is illustrated in Fig. 8-10, where the dependent variable is u and the independent variables are x and t. The solution u must satisfy the partial differential equation throughout the open domain, as well as the initial and boundary conditions.

The general partial differential equation, as given by Eq. 8-1, is *parabolic* when the coefficients a, b, and c have values such that

$$b^2 - 4ac = 0$$

An example of a parabolic partial differential equation is found in considering

[4]Crandall, *op. cit.*, pp. 262–264.
[5]M. G. Salvadori and M. L. Baron, *Numerical Methods in Engineering* (Englewood Cliffs, N.J.: Prentice-Hall, Inc., 1961), pp. 237ff.

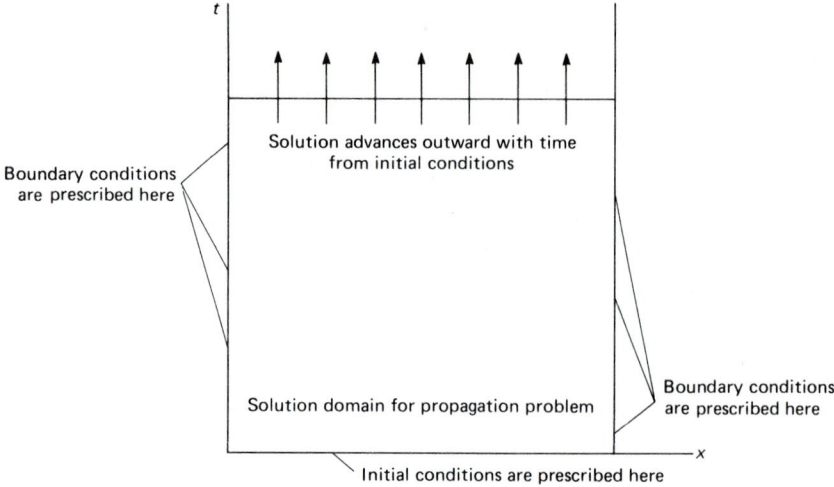

Figure 8-10 Solution domain for a propagation problem

the one-dimensional *transient*-heat-flow problem which is defined by the differential equation

$$\frac{\partial u}{\partial t} = \frac{k}{c\rho}\frac{\partial^2 u}{\partial x^2} \tag{8-29}$$

which may be obtained from the two-dimensional heat equation (Eq. 8-11).

As mentioned previously, the solution $u(x, t)$ propagates with time in a space-time plane, as shown in Fig. 8-10. If we consider a space-time grid, such as the one shown in Fig. 8-11, a solution of Eq. 8-29 will consist of determining the temperature u at each grid point used. To utilize the grid shown, we must put Eq. 8-29 in finite-difference form. Referring to Eqs. 5-79 and 5-81, we find it convenient to substitute a *forward-difference* expression for the first partial such that

$$\frac{\partial u}{\partial t} = \frac{u_{i+1,j} - u_{i,j}}{\Delta t} \tag{8-30}$$

and a *central-difference* expression for the second partial such that

$$\frac{\partial^2 u}{\partial x^2} = \frac{u_{i,j+1} - 2u_{i,j} + u_{i,j-1}}{(\Delta x)^2} \tag{8-31}$$

Substituting these difference equations into Eq. 8-29,

$$u_{i+1,j} = u_{i,j} + \frac{k}{c\rho}\frac{(\Delta t)}{(\Delta x)^2}(u_{i,j+1} - 2u_{i,j} + u_{i,j-1}) \tag{8-32}$$

It can be seen, from Eq. 8-32, that we can obtain the temperature at a particular grid point with coordinates x and $(t + \Delta t)$ in terms of the temper-

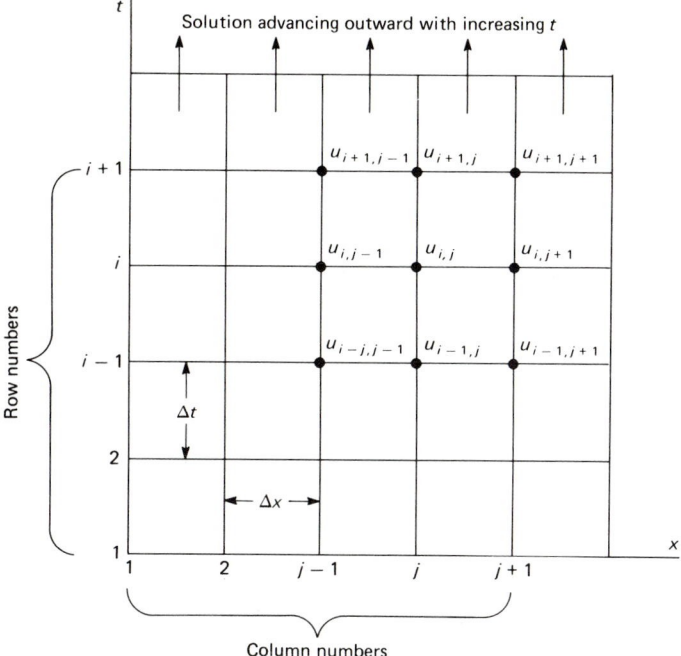

Figure 8-11 Temperature at grid points in the solution domain near ith row and jth column of points

atures at adjacent grid points $(x - \Delta x)$, x, and $(x + \Delta x)$ at a time t. Known initial temperatures and boundary temperatures provide the values necessary to start the calculations which then proceed *row* by *row*, the end points of each row satisfying the given boundary conditions, until some final temperature state (with time) is approximately satisfied as the solution approaches a steady state. This row-by-row progression with time, which continues indefinitely, illustrates the open-ended nature of the solution domain of a parabolic-type partial differential equation.

In solving Eq. 8-32, the stability of the solution obtained is of great importance. It can be shown that the solution will be stable and nonoscillatory for boundary conditions that remain constant with time if[6]

$$\frac{k}{c\rho} \frac{(\Delta t)}{(\Delta x)^2} \leq 0.25$$

The solution obtained will be stable if

$$\frac{k}{c\rho} \frac{(\Delta t)}{(\Delta x)^2} \leq 0.50$$

[6]*Ibid.*, p. 261.

The following example shows in detail the application of Eq. 8-32.

EXAMPLE 8-2

The problem is to determine the transient temperature distribution along a slender rod. The rod, which is shown in Fig. 8-12, is made of aluminum and is 1 ft long. It is assumed to be perfectly insulated at all boundaries except the left end. The pertinent material properties are

$k = 0.0370$ Btu/(sec)(ft)(°F)

$c = 0.212$ Btu/(lb)(°F)

$\rho = 168$ lb/ft^3

and the rod is divided into 12 equal increments by the 13 stations shown.

Figure 8-12 Insulated aluminum bar

Initially, the rod is in a state of thermal equilibrium at a temperature of 100°F. The temperature at the uninsulated end is then suddenly reduced to 0°F, at which time the temperature distribution in the rod assumes a transient state. This state exists until a time at which the temperature everywhere in the rod approaches the final equilibrium state of 0°F. The boundary conditions stated mathematically are

$u(0, t) = 0°F$

$\dfrac{\partial u}{\partial x}(l, t) = 0°F/ft$

and the initial condition is

$u(x, 0) = 100°F$

In the preceding discussion it was shown that the one-dimensional transient-heat-flow equation (Eq. 8-29) can be approximated by the following finite-difference equation:

$$u_{i+1,j} = u_{i,j} + \frac{k}{c\rho} \frac{(\Delta t)}{(\Delta x)^2}[u_{i,j+1} - 2u_{i,j} + u_{i,j-1}] \tag{8-33}$$

The given values of k, c, and ρ establish a thermal diffusivity $(k/c\rho)$ of 0.00104 ft^2/sec. With the number of stations shown in Fig. 8-12, the value of Δx is 1/12 ft. Using these values and referring to the stability criterion discussed earlier, which established that

$$\frac{k}{c\rho} \frac{(\Delta t)}{(\Delta x)^2} \le 0.25$$

for a stable and nonoscillatory solution, we see that the use of a convenient value of $\Delta t = 1.0$ sec will satisfy the requirement for such a solution.

Figure 8-13 shows a space-time grid superimposed upon the solution domain. A careful study of the information contained in this figure will give an excellent insight into the numerical procedures required to obtain a solution of the problem. The temperature is known for each station at $t = 0$, as indicated. An *average* value of 50°F is assumed at station 1 for $t = 0$, as shown, since the temperature at this station is discontinuous at $t = 0$, changing very suddenly from 100°F to 0°F when the transient state is introduced. This average value of 50°F is used only in calculating the temperature at the grid point above station 2 in the row corresponding to $t = \Delta t$. In calculating the temperature at all subsequent grid points above station 2, the *boundary* value of 0°F is used for the temperature at the left-boundary grid points. An additional column of grid points corresponding to an *imaginary* station 14 is included in

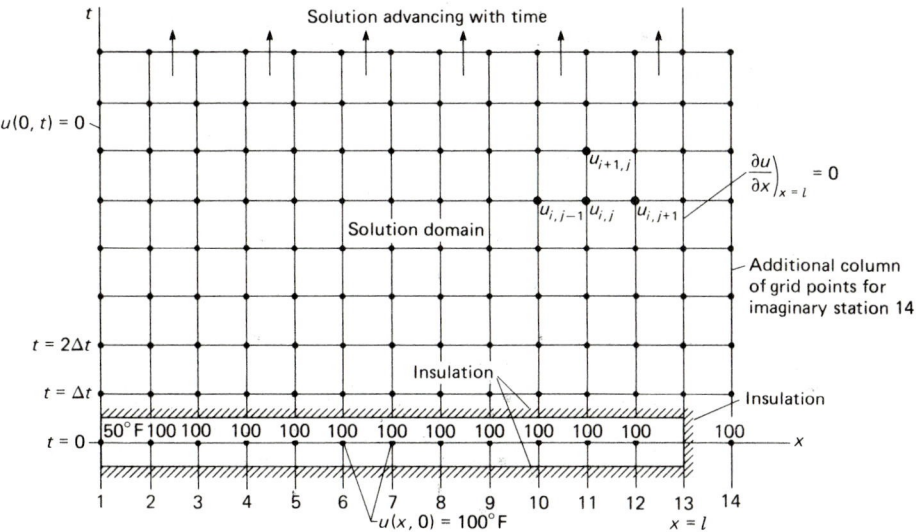

Figure 8-13   Space-time grid for Ex. 8-2

the space-time grid to provide a means of satisfying the boundary condition imposed at the insulated end of the rod. This condition may be expressed, in finite-difference form, as

$$\frac{u_{i,14} - u_{i,12}}{2(\Delta x)} = 0$$

from which

$$u_{i,14} = u_{i,12}$$

Applying Eq. 8-33, the temperature at each grid point from 2 through 13 is determined in the row corresponding to $t = \Delta t$, using the known initial temperatures. The grid point in that row associated with station 14 is then assigned the value calculated for the grid point associated with station 12, thus approximately establishing a zero temperature gradient at station 13. Equation 8-33 is then used again to determine the temperature at grid points 2 through 13 in the next row corresponding to $t = 2\Delta t$, using the grid-temperature values calculated for the *preceding* row. The grid point in this row corresponding to station 14 is then assigned the value calculated for station 12, and the solution advances to the next row, where $t = 3\Delta t$. This procedure is repeated for each subsequent row of grid points until the temperatures at *all* the grid points in a row differ by less than a small predetermined value epsilon from the known final equilibrium temperature of $0°F$. Thus, the solution advances outward with time, the number of rows ultimately calculated in the solution depending upon the time rate at which the temperature of the stations approaches the final equilibrium temperature and the temperature limit desired for the solution, as specified by the value of epsilon chosen. Since the temperature at each station along the rod approaches the final equilibrium temperature of $0°F$ asymptotically in this problem, too small a value of epsilon can result in excessive computing time.

The flow chart for programming this problem for a computer solution is shown in Fig. 8-14 on p. 606. The FORTRAN names and the problem quantities which they represent are as follows:

FORTRAN Name	Quantity	Value Used in Problem
U(J)	Temperature along a row of grid points corresponding to time t, °F	
U1(J)	Temperature along a row of grid points corresponding to time $t + \Delta t$, °F	
UL	Temperature at which left end of rod is held	$0°F$

FORTRAN Name	Quantity	Value Used in Problem
UX	Initial temperature along rod	100°F
DELT	Time increment	1 sec
EL	Length of rod	1 ft
TPR	Time at which printout occurs, sec	
DTPR	Print increment	100 sec
THDIF	Thermal diffusivity, k/cp	0.00104 ft²/sec
B	$k(\Delta t)/cp(\Delta x)^2$	
EPSI	Small value of temperature selected to terminate program. Program terminates when temperature at each station in row is less than UL + EPSI	0.05°F

The FORTRAN IV computer program used to solve the problem is as follows:

```
    DIMENSION U(14),U1(14)
    READ(5,2) UL,UX,DELT,DTPR,EL,THDIF,EPSI
  2 FORMAT(5F4.0,F7.0,F4.0)
    WRITE(6,3)
  3 FORMAT(' ',14X,'TRANSIENT HEAT-FLOW PROBLEM')
    WRITE(6,4)
  4 FORMAT(' ',13X,'(PARABOLIC PARTIAL DIFF EQN.)'//)
    WRITE(6,5)
  5 FORMAT('  TIME',6X,'1',5X,'3',6X,'5',6X,'7',6X,'9',6X,'11',5X,'13'/)
    T=0.
    TPR=DTPR
    B=THDIF*DELT/(EL/12.)**2
    U(1)=(UL+UX)/2.
    DO 6 J=2,14
  6 U(J)=UX
    U1(1)=UL
  7 DO 8 J=2,13
  8 U1(J)=U(J)+B*(U(J+1)-2.*U(J)+U(J-1))
    U1(14)=U1(12)
    T=T+DELT
    IF(T-TPR) 12,9,9
  9 WRITE(6,10) T,(U1(J),J=1,13,2)
 10 FORMAT(' ',F6.0,7F7.2)
    TPR=TPR+DTPR
    DO 11 J=2,13
    DIFF=U1(J)-(UL+EPSI)
    IF(DIFF) 11,12,12
 11 CONTINUE
    STOP
 12 DO 13 J=2,14
 13 U(J)=U1(J)
    U(1)=UL
    GO TO 7
    END
```

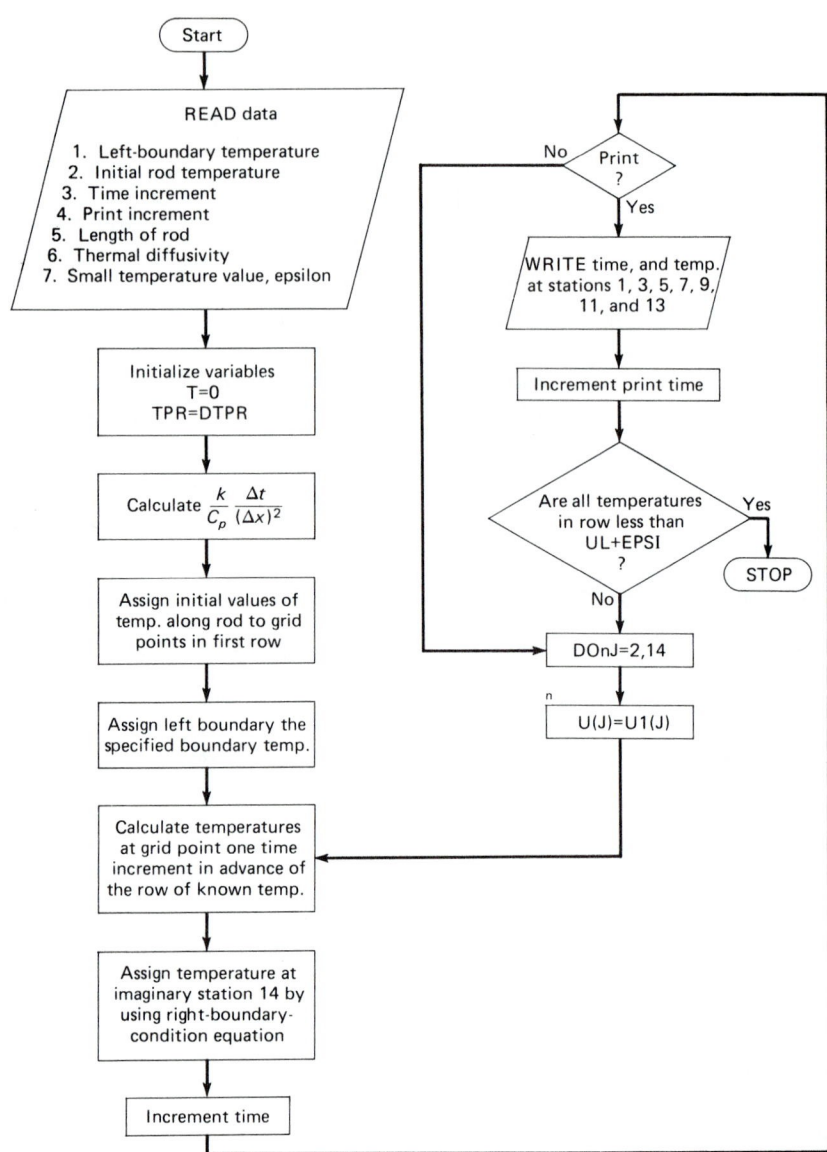

Figure 8-14 Flow chart for Ex. 8-2

The computer results are shown in the following tabular printout:

```
TRANSIENT HEAT-FLOW PROBLEM
(PARABOLIC PARTIAL DIFF EQN.)
  TIME     1       3       5       7       9      11      13
  100.    0.0   28.52   53.49   72.60   85.26   92.16   94.32
  200.    0.0   20.02   38.52   54.18   66.00   73.31   75.78
  300.    0.0   15.29   29.52   41.72   51.06   56.92   58.92
  400.    0.0   11.81   22.81   32.26   39.50   44.06   45.61
  500.    0.0    9.13   17.65   24.96   30.56   34.09   35.29
  600.    0.0    7.07   13.65   19.31   23.65   26.37   27.30
  700.    0.0    5.47   10.56   14.94   18.30   20.41   21.13
  800.    0.0    4.23    8.17   11.56   14.15   15.79   16.34
  900.    0.0    3.27    6.32    8.94   10.95   12.21   12.65
 1000.    0.0    2.53    4.89    6.92    8.47    9.45    9.78
 1100.    0.0    1.96    3.78    5.35    6.56    7.31    7.57
 1200.    0.0    1.52    2.93    4.14    5.07    5.66    5.86
 1300.    0.0    1.17    2.27    3.20    3.92    4.38    4.53
 1400.    0.0    0.91    1.75    2.48    3.04    3.39    3.51
 1500.    0.0    0.70    1.36    1.92    2.35    2.62    2.71
 1600.    0.0    0.54    1.05    1.48    1.82    2.03    2.10
 1700.    0.0    0.42    0.81    1.15    1.41    1.57    1.62
 1800.    0.0    0.33    0.63    0.89    1.09    1.21    1.26
 1900.    0.0    0.25    0.49    0.69    0.84    0.94    0.97
 2000.    0.0    0.19    0.38    0.53    0.65    0.73    0.75
 2100.    0.0    0.15    0.29    0.41    0.50    0.56    0.58
 2200.    0.0    0.12    0.23    0.32    0.39    0.43    0.45
 2300.    0.0    0.09    0.17    0.25    0.30    0.34    0.35
 2400.    0.0    0.07    0.13    0.19    0.23    0.26    0.27
 2500.    0.0    0.05    0.10    0.15    0.18    0.20    0.21
 2600.    0.0    0.04    0.08    0.11    0.14    0.16    0.16
 2700.    0.0    0.03    0.06    0.09    0.11    0.12    0.12
 2800.    0.0    0.02    0.05    0.07    0.08    0.09    0.10
 2900.    0.0    0.02    0.04    0.05    0.06    0.07    0.07
 3000.    0.0    0.01    0.03    0.04    0.05    0.06    0.06
 3100.    0.0    0.01    0.02    0.03    0.04    0.04    0.04
```

The computer printout provides the temperatures at stations 1, 3, 5, 7, 9, 11, and 13 at intervals of 100 sec. The computer printout for stations 3, 5, and 13 is shown in graphical form in Fig. 8-15.

8-4 HYPERBOLIC PARTIAL DIFFERENTIAL EQUATIONS

The general partial differential equation (Eq. 8-1) is hyperbolic when the coefficients a, b, and c have values such that

$$b^2 - 4ac > 0$$

This type of partial differential equation, like the parabolic type, arises in the solution of so-called *propagation* problems. The solution domain of the hy-

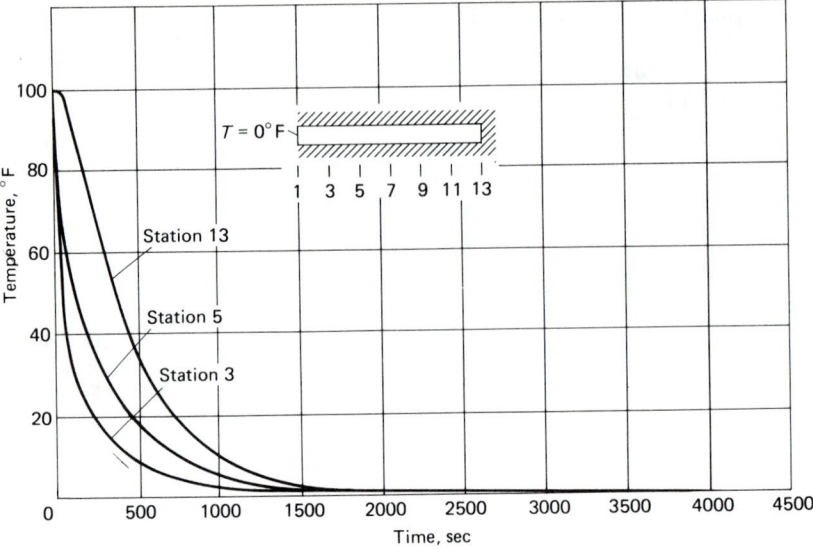

Figure 8-15 Results of numerical solution of Ex. 8-2

perbolic differential equation has the same open-ended characteristic encountered in the solution of parabolic differential equations, consisting of a solution which advances outward indefinitely from known initial conditions while always satisfying specified boundary conditions as the solution progresses.

The *one-dimensional wave equation*

$$\frac{\partial^2 u}{\partial t^2} = a^2 \frac{\partial^2 u}{\partial x^2} \tag{8-34}$$

which is frequently encountered in the areas of physics and engineering, is an example of a hyperbolic partial differential equation. This equation, with appropriate variables and associated physical constants, describes the motion of various types of systems, including the torsional vibrations of cylindrical rods, the longitudinal vibrations of slender rods, the transmission of sound in a column of air, and the transverse vibrations of flexible members in a stressed state.

In the last category mentioned, let us consider the free vibrational characteristics of a length of string tightly stretched between two fixed points such as O and E in Fig. 8-16(a). The general string shape shown (with greatly exaggerated y displacements) represents one vibrational configuration of the string at some instant in time. Figure 8-16(b) shows an enlarged view of the small Δs length element PQ. In deriving the wave equation for the vibrating

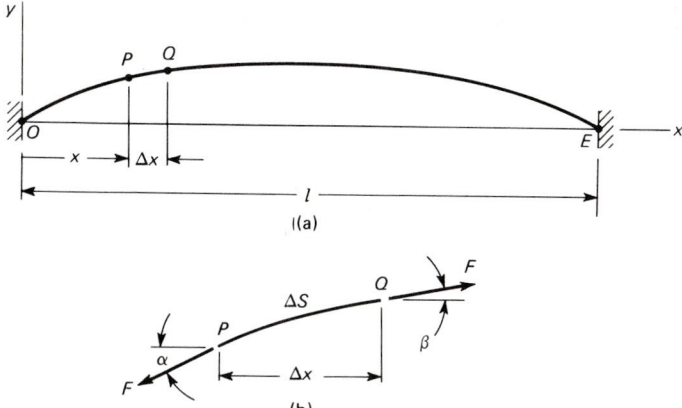

Figure 8-16 Vibrating string and free-body diagram of an element of the string

string, we will make use of the following simplifying assumptions in idealizing the mathematical model which results:

1. For small displacements, $\Delta x = \Delta s$.
2. For small displacements, the additional tension introduced in the string due to its displacement is negligible compared to the initial tension introduced in stretching the string between the supporting points O and E; that is, the tension in the string is considered as constant, with a magnitude equal to the initially applied tension F.
3. The gravity force acting upon the string is negligible compared to the tension in the string.
4. The string is flexible enough to consider the bending and shear stresses developed as negligible compared to the tension in the string.

With these assumptions in mind, the forces acting upon the element are shown in Fig. 8-16(b). Applying Newton's second law of motion in the y direction

$$F \sin \beta - F \sin \alpha = \frac{w}{g}(\Delta x)\frac{\partial^2 y}{\partial t^2} \tag{8-35}$$

where w is the weight per unit length of the string. Since α and β are very small angles, we may use the approximations $\sin \alpha = \tan \alpha$ and $\sin \beta = \tan \beta$ in rewriting Eq. 8-35 as

$$F \tan \beta - F \tan \alpha = \frac{w}{g}(\Delta x)\frac{\partial^2 y}{\partial t^2}$$

Noting that tan α and tan β represent the respective slopes at the ends of the element, we may write

$$F\left[\frac{\left.\dfrac{\partial y}{\partial x}\right|_{x+\Delta x} - \left.\dfrac{\partial y}{\partial x}\right|_{x}}{(\Delta x)}\right] = \frac{w}{g}\frac{\partial^2 y}{\partial t^2}$$

Letting Δx approach zero and rearranging terms,

$$\frac{\partial^2 y}{\partial t^2} = \frac{Fg}{w}\frac{\partial^2 y}{\partial x^2} \tag{8-36}$$

which has the form of Eq. 8-34, where $Fg/w = a^2$.

The solution of Eq. 8-36 exists in a general space-time plane such as the one shown in Fig. 8-17. A numerical solution begins by superimposing a rectangular grid over the solution domain, a portion of which is shown in the figure. The value of the dependent variable y is then determined at all grid points over the desired time interval. The numerical procedure itself begins with the use of the known initial-condition values and proceeds from there in a *row-by-row* progression with time, always satisfying the specified *boundary*

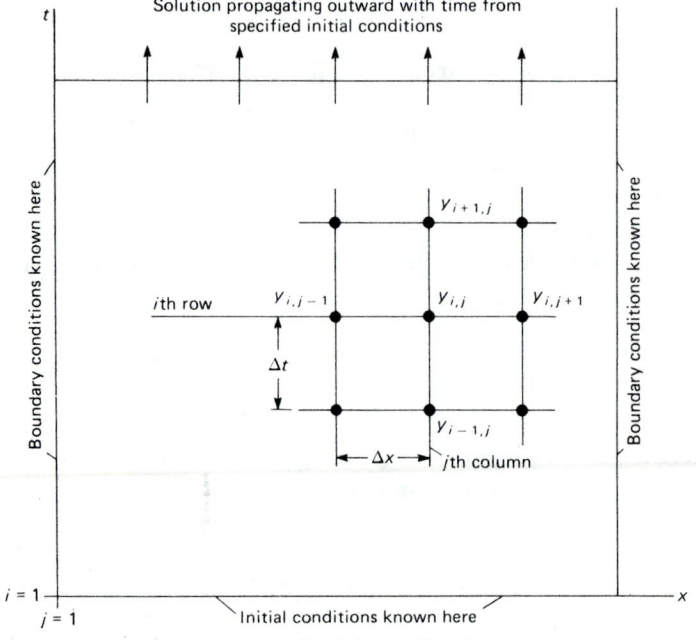

Figure 8-17 Solution domain for the vibrating-string problem

conditions as the solution progresses. (This procedure will be discussed more specifically in the next example.)

Equation 8-36 may be expressed, in finite-difference form, by using the following *central-difference* approximations (see Eq. 5-79) for the two second partial derivatives which appear in the equation:

$$\frac{\partial^2 y}{\partial t^2} = \frac{y_{i+1,j} - 2y_{i,j} + y_{i-1,j}}{(\Delta t)^2}$$

and

$$\frac{\partial^2 y}{\partial x^2} = \frac{y_{i,j+1} - 2y_{i,j} + y_{i,j-1}}{(\Delta x)^2}$$

Substituting these two finite-difference expressions into Eq. 8-36 yields

$$\frac{y_{i+1,j} - 2y_{i,j} + y_{i-1,j}}{(\Delta t)^2} = \frac{Fg}{w}\left(\frac{y_{i,j+1} - 2y_{i,j} + y_{i,j-1}}{(\Delta x)^2}\right)$$

from which

$$y_{i+1,j} = 2y_{i,j} - y_{i-1,j} + C[y_{i,j+1} - 2y_{i,j} + y_{i,j-1}] \tag{8-37}$$

where

$$C = \frac{Fg}{w}\frac{(\Delta t)^2}{(\Delta x)^2}$$

The value of C is important in considering the numerical solution of a partial differential equation, such as Eq. 8-36. It has been shown that an unstable solution is obtained for the wave equation when $C > 1$, that the solution is stable when $C \leq 1$, and that a theoretically correct solution is obtained when $C = 1$.[7] Furthermore, the accuracy of the solution has been shown to decrease as the value of C decreases further and further below the value of 1.

With the preceding discussion in mind it would seem logical to select values for Δx and Δt such that $C = 1$. However, experience reveals that such a selection often results in an inconvenient value of Δt for use in the numerical procedures involved in obtaining a solution. Therefore, it is desirable to select Δx and Δt values which are convenient for use in the numerical procedure and

[7]R. Courant, K. Friedrichs, and H. Lewy, "Über die partiellen Differenzengleichungen der Mathematischen Physik," *Mathematische Annalen*, Vol. 100 (1928), pp. 32–74.

which, at the same time, yield a value of C which is as large as possible consistent with the stability criterion that $C \leq 1$.

The following example illustrates the numerical solution of a hyperbolic partial differential equation as represented by the one-dimensional wave equation.

EXAMPLE 8-3

A string 1.5 ft in length, weighing 0.02 lb/ft, is stretched between supports A and B, as shown in Fig. 8-18, so that the string has an initial tension of 6 lb. The string is then plucked at the two-thirds point, yielding the initial configuration shown in the figure. It is desired to determine various intermediate configurations of the string during the first 0.2 sec after the string is released from rest in the configuration shown. To determine the desired configurations we must calculate the y displacements at various points along the string at various time intervals.

Selecting a value of $\Delta x = 0.1$ ft as a convenient interval for determining stations along the length of the string, we find that for

$$ C = \frac{Fg\,(\Delta t)^2}{w\,(\Delta x)^2} = 1 $$

a value of $\Delta t = 0.00102$ sec must be used. A more convenient value is $\Delta t = 0.001$ sec, the selection of which will yield a value of C only slightly less than 1, which will still assure us of a stable and accurate solution. We next determine that $Fg/w = 9651$ ft²/sec² from the values given for the problem parameters. This latter value, along with the Δx and Δt values selected, is used as input data in the computer program which is shown near the end of this example.

We next sketch a space-time grid such as the one in Fig. 8-19. Since the string is released from rest, the initial conditions are

$$ y(x,0) = \left\{ \begin{array}{ll} 0.005x & (0 \leq x \leq 1.0) \\ -0.01x + 0.015 & (1.0 < x \leq 1.5) \end{array} \right\} $$

$$ \frac{\partial y}{\partial t}(x,0) = 0 $$

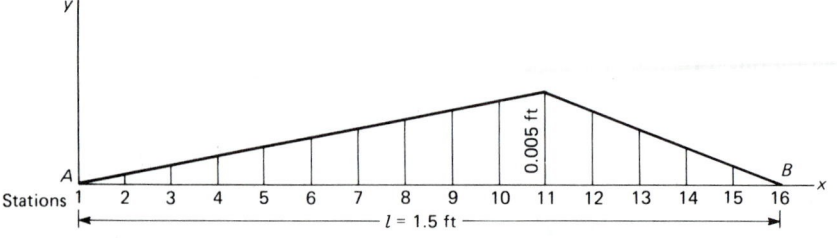

Figure 8-18 Configuration of string at $t = 0$ for Ex. 8-3

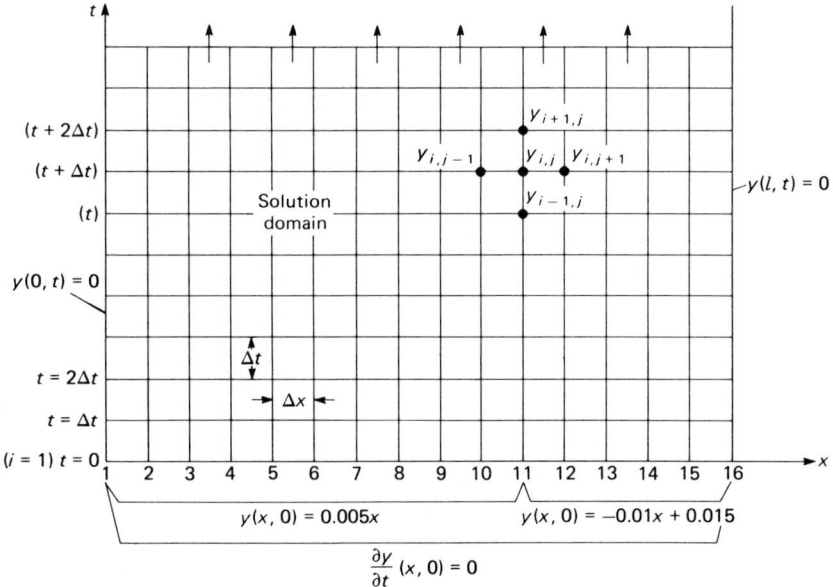

Figure 8-19   Space-time grid for vibrating-string problem

The boundary conditions which must be satisfied are

$$y(0,t) = 0$$

$$y(l,t) = 0$$

The second initial condition shown can be expressed in finite-difference form as

$$\frac{y_{i+1,j} - y_{i-1,j}}{2(\Delta t)} = 0$$

from which

$$y_{i+1,j} = y_{i-1,j} \qquad\qquad\qquad (8\text{-}38)$$

This relationship implies the use of an *imaginary* row of grid points preceding the row identified by $t = 0$ in Fig. 8-19. If we substitute Eq. 8-38 into Eq. 8-37, we obtain the following equation:

$$y_{i+1,j} = y_{i,j} + \frac{C}{2}[y_{i,j+1} - 2y_{i,j} + y_{i,j-1}] \qquad\qquad (8\text{-}39)$$

Equation 8-39 is used to calculate the displacements at the grid points in the row corresponding to $t = \Delta t$, since its use yields values which satisfy the initial condition that the string is released from rest.

The first step in the numerical procedure, then, is to calculate the displacements at grid points 2 through 15 in the row corresponding to $t = \Delta t$ by the use of Eq. 8-39, utilizing the known initial displacements to start the calculating process. Equation 8-37 is then employed to calculate the displacements at grid points 2 through 15 for all subsequent rows in a *row-by-row* progression. The grid points in the vicinity of the ith row and the jth column, shown in Fig. 8-19, illustrate the calculating process, the displacement at each grid point under consideration $(y_{i+1,j})$ being calculated from the previously calculated values at the adjacent grid points shown. The number of rows of grid points calculated obviously depends upon the time interval over which a solution is desired. Thus, the computer solution is usually terminated by adding the Δt increments used and specifying a termination when their sum corresponds to the time interval desired.

In writing the computer program it will not be necessary to use a double-subscripted variable name for identifying the displacements at the various grid points, because all the values calculated need not be stored in memory if we specify a printout of the desired displacements as they are calculated. The numerical procedure discussed shows that it is necessary to retain in memory only the displacements of the last two rows calculated to furnish sufficient data for the ensuing calculation (see Fig. 8-19). Therefore, we will use single-subscripted variable names for identifying the grid points in the pertinent rows, as shown in the following list:

FORTRAN Name	**Quantity**	**Value Used in Problem**
Y(J)	Displacements corresponding to rows of	
Y1(J)	grid points for times t, $t + \Delta t$, and	
Y2(J)	$t + 2\Delta t$, respectively, ft.	
ASQR	$a^2 = Fg/w$	9651 ft^2/sec^2
DELT	Time increment, Δt	0.001 sec
DELX	Increment of string length, Δx	0.1 ft
TPR	Time at which a printout occurs, sec	
DTPR	Print time increment	0.005 sec
T	Time, sec	
C	$C = \dfrac{Fg\,(\Delta t)^2}{w\,(\Delta x)^2}$	
TFIN	Length of time desired for solution interval	0.2 sec

The flow chart for the problem is shown in Fig. 8-20 on page 616. The FORTRAN IV source program, written from the outline provided by the flow chart, is as follows:

```
C THIS PROGRAM DETERMINES DISPLACEMENTS IN A TIGHTLY
                                STRETCHED PLUCKED STRING
      DIMENSION Y(16),Y1(16),Y2(16)
      READ(5,3) (Y1(J),J=1,16)
    3 FORMAT(8F10.0)
      READ(5,3) ASQR,DELT,DELX,DTPR,TFIN,EPSI
C INITIALIZE VARIABLES
      TPR=DTPR
      T=DELT
      C=ASQR*DELT**2/DELX**2
      WRITE(6,4)
    4 FORMAT('1','  TIME',11X,'DISPLACEMENTS AT STATIONS
                                1,3,5,7,9,11,13,
     *15,16'/)
C ASSIGN BOUNDARY VALUES OF ZERO
      Y2(1)=0.
      Y2(16)=0.
C CALCULATE DISPLACEMENTS FOR POINTS IN SECOND ROW OF
                                GRID POINTS
      DO 5 J=2,15
    5 Y2(J)=Y1(J)+.5*C*(Y1(J+1)-2.*Y1(J)+Y1(J-1))
    6 DO 7 J=2,15
      Y(J)=Y1(J)
    7 Y1(J)=Y2(J)
C CALCULATE DISPLACEMENTS FOR POINTS IN SUBSEQUENT ROWS
      DO 8 J=2,15
    8 Y2(J)=2.*Y1(J)-Y(J)+C*(Y1(J+1)-2.*Y1(J)+Y1(J-1))
      T=T+DELT
      IF(ABS(T-TPR)-EPSI) 9,9,6
    9 WRITE(6,10) T,(Y2(J),J=1,15,2),Y2(16)
   10 FORMAT(' ',F6.4,9F8.4)
      TPR=TPR+DTPR
      IF(ABS(T-TFIN)-EPSI) 11,11,6
   11 STOP
      END
```

It should be noted in the program that the displacements at the grid points of the row corresponding to $t = \Delta t$ in Fig. 8-19 are calculated in the DO5J = 2,15 loop using Eq. 8-39, while the displacements at the grid points of subsequent rows are calculated in the DO8J = 2,15 loop using Eq. 8-37, but that all grid points in the process of *being calculated* are identified by the Y2(J) designation.

The computer printout of the displacement-time data for the stations selected is shown on page 617.

Figure 8-21 shows a sketch of the *approximate* string configurations for the various times indicated with the y displacements greatly exaggerated. Although the graphical plot shown was done manually, plotters are available which will display digital readout in graphical form.

The solution shown reveals that the period of vibration of the string is approximately 0.03 sec, since the displacements at each station repeat at approximately this interval. If it were desired to plot the displacement-time curve for a particular station over one cycle, a printout increment of 0.001 sec should be used to obtain enough values to plot a reasonably accurate curve.

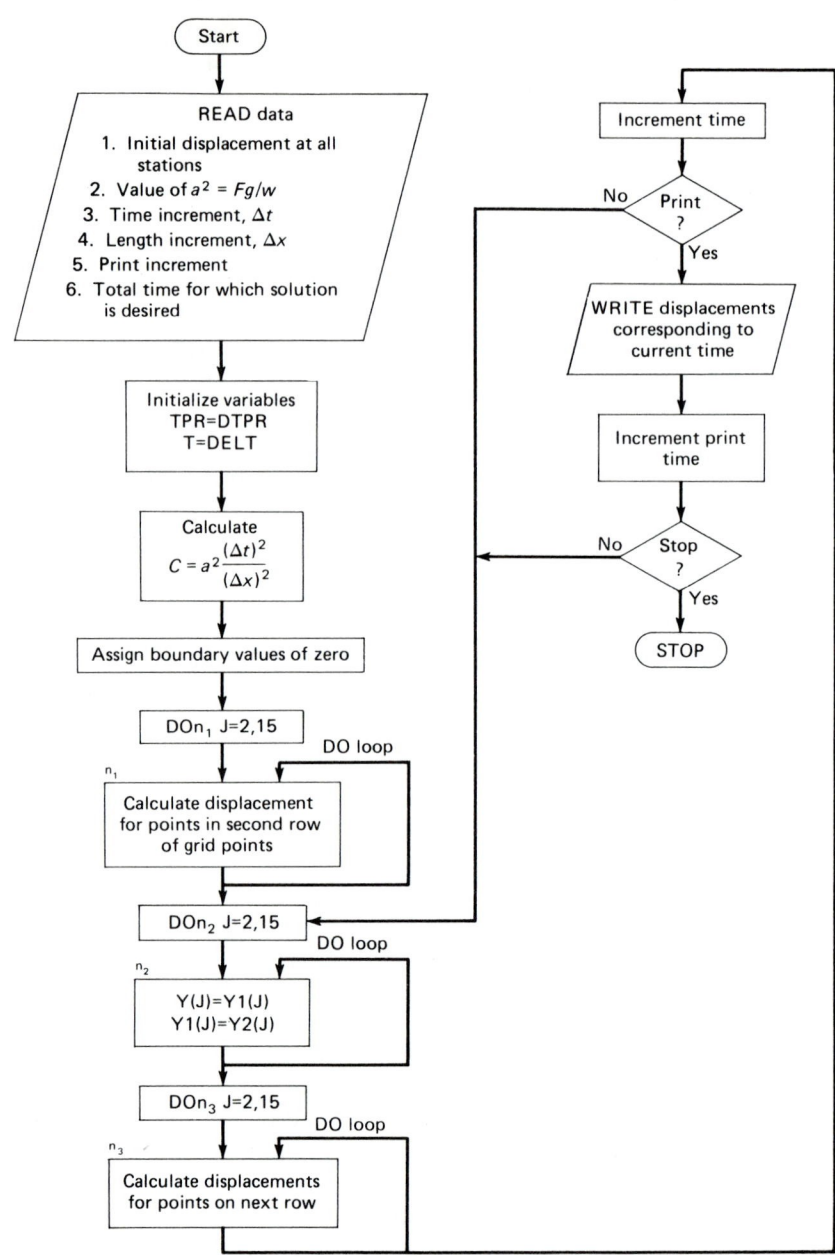

Figure 8-20 Flow chart for Ex. 8-3

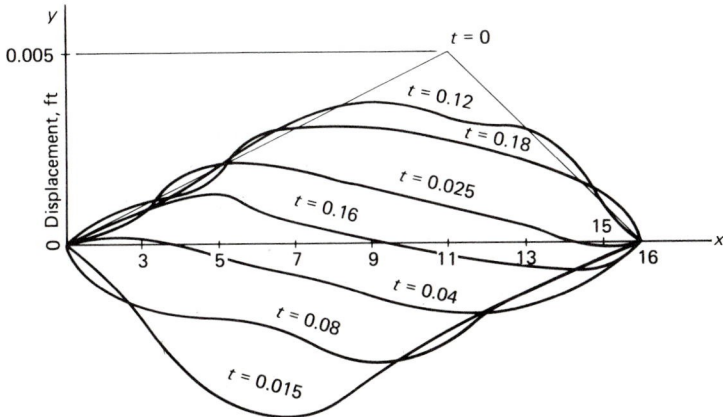

Figure 8-21 String configurations at different times

TIME		DISPLACEMENTS AT STATIONS 1,3,5,7,9,11,13,15,16							
0.0050	0.0	0.0010	0.0020	0.0024	0.0019	0.0014	0.0009	0.0004	0.0
0.0100	0.0	-0.0004	-0.0009	-0.0014	-0.0019	-0.0024	-0.0014	-0.0005	0.0
0.0150	0.0	-0.0020	-0.0041	-0.0046	-0.0035	-0.0025	-0.0015	-0.0005	0.0
0.0200	0.0	-0.0008	-0.0013	-0.0018	-0.0023	-0.0025	-0.0015	-0.0005	0.0
0.0250	0.0	0.0010	0.0021	0.0019	0.0014	0.0010	0.0005	-0.0002	0.0
0.0300	0.0	0.0010	0.0020	0.0031	0.0041	0.0046	0.0030	0.0010	0.0
0.0350	0.0	0.0010	0.0020	0.0028	0.0022	0.0017	0.0012	0.0008	0.0
0.0400	0.0	0.0001	-0.0004	-0.0010	-0.0015	-0.0020	-0.0016	-0.0006	0.0
0.0450	0.0	-0.0019	-0.0040	-0.0045	-0.0035	-0.0026	-0.0016	-0.0005	0.0
0.0500	0.0	-0.0013	-0.0016	-0.0021	-0.0028	-0.0026	-0.0016	-0.0005	0.0
0.0550	0.0	0.0010	0.0020	0.0016	0.0010	0.0004	0.0000	-0.0004	0.0
0.0600	0.0	0.0011	0.0020	0.0030	0.0042	0.0042	0.0031	0.0010	0.0
0.0650	0.0	0.0010	0.0021	0.0030	0.0026	0.0022	0.0016	0.0009	0.0
0.0700	0.0	0.0006	-0.0001	-0.0006	-0.0010	-0.0016	-0.0016	-0.0004	0.0
0.0750	0.0	-0.0021	-0.0037	-0.0042	-0.0036	-0.0026	-0.0015	-0.0005	0.0
0.0800	0.0	-0.0017	-0.0021	-0.0026	-0.0032	-0.0025	-0.0015	-0.0005	0.0
0.0850	0.0	0.0011	0.0015	0.0011	0.0007	0.0002	-0.0005	-0.0005	0.0
0.0900	0.0	0.0010	0.0020	0.0029	0.0041	0.0039	0.0031	0.0009	0.0
0.0950	0.0	0.0010	0.0020	0.0030	0.0032	0.0025	0.0022	0.0010	0.0
0.1000	0.0	0.0008	0.0003	-0.0001	-0.0007	-0.0012	-0.0014	-0.0004	0.0
0.1050	0.0	-0.0022	-0.0034	-0.0039	-0.0037	-0.0024	-0.0015	-0.0005	0.0
0.1100	0.0	-0.0018	-0.0026	-0.0031	-0.0033	-0.0025	-0.0015	-0.0005	0.0
0.1150	0.0	0.0011	0.0012	0.0007	0.0002	-0.0002	-0.0009	-0.0005	0.0
0.1200	0.0	0.0009	0.0020	0.0031	0.0038	0.0034	0.0028	0.0011	0.0
0.1250	0.0	0.0010	0.0020	0.0030	0.0036	0.0027	0.0026	0.0010	0.0
0.1300	0.0	0.0010	0.0009	0.0002	-0.0003	-0.0007	-0.0013	-0.0007	0.0
0.1350	0.0	-0.0020	-0.0030	-0.0035	-0.0036	-0.0025	-0.0016	-0.0005	0.0
0.1400	0.0	-0.0020	-0.0029	-0.0034	-0.0035	-0.0026	-0.0015	-0.0005	0.0
0.1450	0.0	0.0010	0.0009	0.0004	-0.0003	-0.0007	-0.0013	-0.0005	0.0
0.1500	0.0	0.0011	0.0019	0.0032	0.0035	0.0030	0.0024	0.0012	0.0
0.1550	0.0	0.0011	0.0021	0.0030	0.0038	0.0034	0.0028	0.0009	0.0
0.1600	0.0	0.0010	0.0013	0.0006	0.0002	-0.0004	-0.0008	-0.0008	0.0
0.1650	0.0	-0.0019	-0.0026	-0.0030	-0.0034	-0.0026	-0.0015	-0.0004	0.0
0.1700	0.0	-0.0021	-0.0033	-0.0039	-0.0036	-0.0025	-0.0015	-0.0005	0.0
0.1750	0.0	0.0009	0.0003	-0.0002	-0.0005	-0.0012	-0.0014	-0.0005	0.0
0.1800	0.0	0.0010	0.0019	0.0031	0.0031	0.0027	0.0021	0.0012	0.0
0.1850	0.0	0.0009	0.0020	0.0031	0.0038	0.0040	0.0029	0.0011	0.0
0.1900	0.0	0.0010	0.0016	0.0010	0.0006	-0.0000	-0.0003	-0.0005	0.0
0.1950	0.0	-0.0017	-0.0021	-0.0027	-0.0031	-0.0026	-0.0014	-0.0006	0.0
0.2000	0.0	-0.0020	-0.0038	-0.0043	-0.0035	-0.0024	-0.0015	-0.0005	0.0

PROBLEMS

8-1. A rectangular plate is insulated on the left and right boundaries as shown in the accompanying illustration. The temperature at the upper and upper right boundaries and at the lower boundaries are 200°F and 100°F, respectively. Use a pocket calculator to determine the temperature distribution in the plate for the grid shown. Carry out the iterations until the temperature at any station changes less than 2°F between two successive iterations.

(partial answer: $u_{3,2} = 160.1°F$, $u_{4,3} = 188.3°F$)

Problem 8-1

8-2. Write a FORTRAN program for determining the temperature distribution over the triangular plate shown in the accompanying figure. The left boundary is insulated up to and including row $I = IA$, and the right diagonal boundary is completely insulated. A temperature of $U = U_B$ is maintained along the bottom edge of the plate, and a temperature of $U = U_L$ is maintained along the uninsulated portion of the left edge.

Note that the applicable equation on the insulated diagonal boundary is

$$u_{i,j} = \frac{2u_{i,j-1} + 2u_{i-1,j}}{4}$$

This equation can be obtained by considering an imaginary row of grid points having temperatures which are the reflections of temperatures at points situated perpendicularly across the boundary, as shown in the figure. Such a consideration reveals that

$$u_{i-1,j} = u_{i,j+1}$$

and

$$u_{i,j-1} = u_{i+1,j}$$

These relationships are substituted into the general finite-difference form of the differential equation

$$u_{i,j} = \frac{u_{i,j+1} + u_{i,j-1} + u_{i+1,j} + u_{i-1,j}}{4}$$

to obtain the diagonal-boundary equation given.

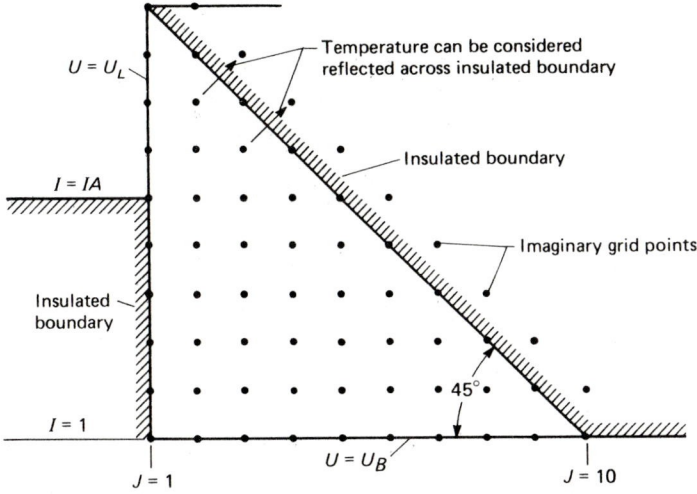

Problem 8-2

8-3. Rewrite the program of Ex. 8-1 to utilize overrelaxation (Eq. 8-21a in place of Eq. 8-21). Run the problem for a range of values of ω between 1 and 2, and determine an approximate value of ω_{opt} for this example.

8-4. Write a FORTRAN program for determining the temperature distribution over the plate shown in the accompanying figure. The left boundary is insulated up to and including row $I = IA$, and the right boundary is completely insulated. A temperature of $U = U_B$ is maintained along the bottom edge of the plate, and a temperature of $U = U_T$ is maintained along the upper edge of the plate and along the upper portion of the left edge, as shown in the figure. Use a grid having a space of $h = l/9$.

Problem 8-4

8-5. Write a FORTRAN program for determining the temperature distribution over the plate shown in the accompanying figure. The left boundary is insulated up to and including row $I = IA$, and the right boundary is completely insulated, as shown in the figure. A temperature of $U = U_B$ is maintained along the bottom edge of the plate, and a temperature of

Problem 8-5

$U = U_T$ is maintained along the portions of the left and upper edges, as shown in the figure. Use a grid spacing of $h = l/9$.

8-6. As shown in the accompanying figure, a 6-in.-square tube, with a 2-in.-square hole in the center portion, carries a fluid having a temperature of 300°F. The outside boundary of the tube is 75°F. Write a FORTRAN program for obtaining the temperature distribution across the tube. Owing to the symmetry of the temperature distribution, it is necessary to calculate the temperatures over only one-fourth of the tube cross section. In using only one-fourth of the tube for obtaining the temperature distribution, it is necessary to satisfy the temperature-gradient conditions of $\partial u/\partial x = 0$ at $x = 3$ in. and $\partial u/\partial y = 0$ at $y = 3$ in.

Problem 8-6

8-7. Refer to Ex. 8-2 and consider that the temperature of the rod at the left end is 0°C and that the initial temperature along the rod is 100°C. Determine whether there are any necessary changes in the program shown if the values for the rod length ($l = 1$ ft) and thermal diffusivity ($k/c\rho = 0.00104$ ft²/sec) are converted to SI units.

8-8. Considering that $X = f(x)$ and that $T = g(t)$, assume a solution of the form

$$u = XT$$

and show that the analytical solution to Ex. 8-2 is

$$u(x,t) = \frac{400}{\pi} \sum_{n=1,3,5,\dots}^{\infty} \frac{e^{-\alpha t}}{n} \sin \frac{n\pi x}{l}$$

where $a^2 = k/c\rho$ and $\alpha = (n\pi a/l)^2$. The analytical solution to the partial differential equation is easily obtained by the separation of variables method. The series solution evolves from expanding $u(x,0) = 100$ in the form of a Fourier series (see Sec. 4-6).

8-9. A 12-in.-square membrane (no bending or shear stresses), with a 4-in.-square hole in the middle, is fastened at the outside and inside boundaries, as shown in the accompanying illustration. If a highly stretched membrane is subjected to a pressure p, the partial differential equation for the deflection w in the z direction is

$$\frac{\partial^2 w}{\partial x^2} + \frac{\partial^2 w}{\partial y^2} = -\frac{p}{T}$$

where T is the tension (pounds per linear inch). For a highly stretched membrane, the tension T may be assumed constant for small deflections.

Utilizing the finite-difference expressions of Eq. 8-13, write a FORTRAN program and obtain the deflections w for a membrane in which

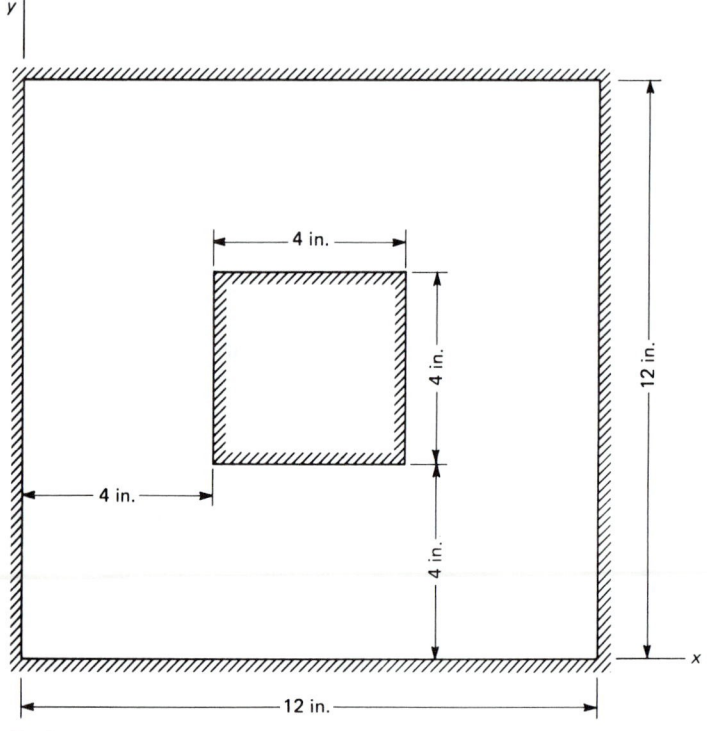

Problem 8-9

$p = 5$ psi (uniformly distributed)

$T = 100$ lb/in.

It should be noted that, owing to symmetry, it is necessary to consider only one-fourth of the membrane. In calculating the deflection over one-fourth of the symmetrical membrane, it is necessary to satisfy the conditions of $\partial w/\partial y = 0$ at $y = 6$ in. and $\partial w/\partial x = 0$ at $x = 6$ in. (This is analogous to an insulated boundary in the temperature-distribution problem discussed in Sec. 8-2.)

(partial answer: for $x = 2$ in. and $y = 2$ in., $w = 0.105$ in.)

8-10. Refer to Prob 8-9 and consider a 0.3-m square membrane with a 0.6-m square hole in the middle in which

$p = 40 \times 10^3$ N/m^2 (uniformly distributed)

$T = 20 \times 10^3$ N/m

8-11. Fluid is flowing through a conduit having a cross section as shown in the accompanying illustration. The partial differential equation for the steady-state velocity ϕ of the fluid is

$$\frac{\partial^2 \phi}{\partial x^2} + \frac{\partial^2 \phi}{\partial y^2} = -\frac{c}{\mu}$$

where c is the absolute value of the pressure gradient in the direction of flow, and μ is the viscosity of the fluid. Noting that the velocity of the fluid is zero on the boundaries, write a FORTRAN program for obtaining

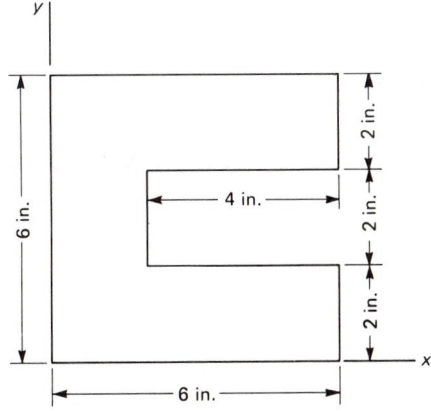

Problem 8-11

the velocity distribution of the fluid. In addition to obtaining the velocities of the fluid flow, the program is to include the calculation of the flow rate Q (volume/sec) where

$$Q = \int_A \phi \, dA$$

The values for c and μ are as follows:

$c = 0.02$ lb/in.^{2}/in. (constant over the cross section)

$\mu = 0.25 \times 10^{-6}$ lb-sec/in.^{2}

8-12. In Prob. 8-11, the 6-in. dimension is to be taken as 0.3 m, the 4-in. dimension as 0.2 m, and the 2-in. dimension as 0.1 m. Determine the steady-state flow velocity ϕ in m/s.

8-13. In Sec. 8-4, the partial differential equation for a tightly stretched string was shown to be

$$\frac{\partial^2 y}{\partial t^2} = \frac{Fg}{w} \frac{\partial^2 y}{\partial x^2}$$

If viscous damping $\left(F_d = -c \frac{\partial y}{\partial t} \Delta x \right)$ is included in the free-body diagram of Fig. 8-16, the differential equation is found to be

$$\frac{\partial^2 y}{\partial t^2} = \frac{Fg}{w} \frac{\partial^2 y}{\partial x^2} - \frac{gc}{w} \frac{\partial y}{\partial t}$$

where c is the viscous damping parameter.

a. Modify the computer program in Ex. 8-3 in order to solve the differential equation with viscous damping.

b. Obtain a solution to Ex. 8-3 if the damping parameter c equals 0.03 lb-sec/ft^2.

(partial answer: for station 7 at $t = 0.1$ sec, $y = 0.00018$ in.)

8-14. Example 8-3 (Sec. 8-4) discusses the numerical solution, on the digital computer, of a vibrating-string problem. The analytical solution of this problem is

$$y(x,t) = \frac{2bl^2}{c(l-c)\pi^2} \sum_{n=1}^{\infty} \frac{1}{n^2} \sin \frac{n\pi c}{l} \cos \frac{n\pi at}{l} \sin \frac{n\pi x}{l}$$

where b is the initial displacement of the string at the point where the string is plucked, and c is the x value at which the string is plucked. The analytical solution is evaluated by summing a number of terms of the series shown, the number of terms summed depending upon the accuracy desired and on the rate of convergence of the series.

Write a FORTRAN program for evaluating the analytical solution for the displacements of the string during one cycle at stations 3, 5, 7, 11, 13, and 15, as indicated by Fig. 8-18 in Ex. 8-3, using the data given in that example. Use all terms in each summation which have a value greater than 0.000001 ft. Use Δt increments of 0.0001 sec.

Compare the results obtained with the results given for corresponding stations in the computer printout included in Ex. 8-3.

8-15. A steel bar has one end fixed, as shown in the accompanying figure. The unrestrained end of the bar is suddenly subjected to a constant force F which is applied as shown in the figure. Sections at various locations along the bar will be displaced longitudinally by the application of such a force, and the displacements $u(x,t)$ at these sections will be functions of both time and location along the bar. Applying Newton's second law to an element of the bar of length dx, determine the partial differential equation describing the displacement of any section along the bar at any time t where

A = cross-sectional area of bar

E = modulus of elasticity of bar

ρ = weight density of bar

l = length of bar

Recall, from strength of materials or theory of elasticity, that the strain in the x direction is given by

$$\varepsilon_x = \frac{\partial u}{\partial x}$$

A = 1 in.^{2}
F = 5000 lb
l = 20 in.
ρ = 0.283 lb/in.^{3}
E = 30 × 10^6 psi
g = 386 in./sec^2

Problem 8-15

It is left to the reader to determine the initial and boundary conditions.

Write a FORTRAN program for determining, by a numerical method, the displacements of the bar at equally spaced stations along the bar at equally spaced time intervals over a total time interval equal to at least one period of the fundamental mode of vibration of the bar. It can be shown that the fundamental period is given by

$$\tau = \frac{4l}{\sqrt{Eg/\rho}}$$

where g is the acceleration of gravity.

Obtain a solution using the values shown in the accompanying figure.

8-16. The analytical solution of Prob. 8-15 is

$$u(x,t) = \frac{8glF}{a^2\pi^2\rho A} \sum_{n=1,3,5,\dots}^{\infty} \frac{(-1)^{(n-1)/2}}{n^2} \sin \frac{n\pi x}{2l}\left(1 - \cos \frac{n\pi at}{2l}\right)$$

where

$$a = \sqrt{\frac{Eg}{\rho}}$$

and the other parameters are as defined in Prob. 8-15 and its accompanying figure.

Write a FORTRAN program for evaluating the series expression for $u(x,t)$. Obtain a solution using the values shown in the figure accompanying Prob. 8-15.

If you have obtained a solution of Prob. 8-15, check the correspondence of the two solutions.

8-17. A circular shaft of length l has a rigid disk attached to each end, as shown in the accompanying figure, and is supported by "frictionless" bearings

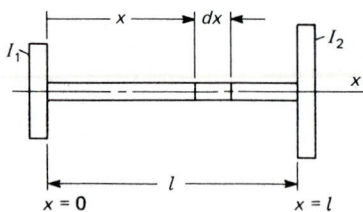

Problem 8-17

(not shown). When free torsional vibrations are initiated in the shaft, the twisting moments on the ends of the elements of length dx (shown in the figure) are

$$GJ \frac{\partial \theta}{\partial x} \quad \text{and} \quad GJ\left(\frac{\partial \theta}{\partial x} + \frac{\partial^2 \theta}{\partial x^2} dx\right)$$

where

G = modulus of rigidity of shaft, lb/in.^{2}

J = polar moment of inertia of shaft cross section, in.^{4}

ρ = weight density of shaft material, lb/in.^{3}

θ = angle of twist at any cross section, radians

By applying the equation $T = I(\partial^2\theta/\partial t^2)$ to the element considered as a free body, show that the partial differential equation describing the angular motion of the shaft for any position x at any time t is

$$\frac{\partial^2 \theta}{\partial t^2} = \frac{Gg}{\rho} \frac{\partial^2 \theta}{\partial x^2}$$

When the shaft is released from rest with a specified initial configuration, the initial conditions are given by the equations

$$\theta(x,0) = f(x)$$

$$\frac{\partial \theta}{\partial t}(x,0) = 0$$

By considering the disks at the ends of the shaft as free bodies and applying the equation $T = I(\partial^2\theta/\partial t^2)$, show that the boundary conditions at the ends of the shaft are given by

$$I_1\left(\frac{\partial^2 \theta}{\partial t^2}\right)_{x=0} = GJ\left(\frac{\partial \theta}{\partial x}\right)_{x=0}$$

and

$$I_2\left(\frac{\partial^2 \theta}{\partial t^2}\right)_{x=l} = -GJ\left(\frac{\partial \theta}{\partial x}\right)_{x=l}$$

where I_1 and I_2 are the mass moments of inertia of the disks about the x axis, as indicated on the accompanying figure.

Write a FORTRAN program for determining θ for equally spaced increments of x and t over a time interval equal to at least one period of the fundamental mode. The period of the fundamental mode is given by

$$\tau = \frac{2\pi l}{\beta a}$$

In the latter equation $a = \sqrt{Gg/\rho}$ and β is the first positive root of the transcendental equation

$$\tan \beta = \frac{(m + n)\beta}{mn\beta^2 - 1}$$

where

$$n = I_2/I_0$$

$$m = I_1/I_0$$

$$I_0 = \rho lJ/g \text{ (mass moment of inertia of shaft about longitudinal axis)}$$

Include in your overall program the steps necessary to determine the fundamental period of the system, and use the value determined as the criterion for stopping the overall program.

As a hint for applying the boundary-condition equations in the solution of the problem, put the boundary equations in difference form by using a *central-difference* expression for each second derivative and *forward-* and *backward-difference* expressions for the respective first derivatives. Use the resulting equations to solve for boundary values of θ as the solution progresses with time.

8-18. Using the program written for Prob. 8-17, determine values of θ for equally spaced x values over a period of time approximately equal to the fundamental period of the system discussed in Prob. 8-17. The shaft is 24 in. long and 2 in. in diameter. The disk on the left end has a mass moment of inertia of 0.25 lb-in.-sec^2, and the disk on the right end has a mass moment of inertia of 0.5 lb-in.-sec^2. The shaft is made of steel such that

$$G = 12(10)^6 \text{ lb/in.}^2$$

$$\rho = 0.286 \text{ lb/in.}^3$$

An initial configuration is given to the shaft by holding the left end fixed and twisting the right end through an angle of 0.04 radian.

8-19. Using the program written for Prob. 8-17, determine values of θ for equally spaced x values over a period of time approximately equal to the fundamental period of the system discussed in Prob. 8-17 in which the system data are as follows:

$l = 0.5$ m (length of shaft)

$d = 0.05$ m (shaft diameter)

$I_1 = 0.03$ kg·m^2 (mass moment of inertia)

$I_2 = 0.06$ kg·m^2 (mass moment of inertia)

$G = 82.7$ GPa (modulus of rigidity)

$\rho = 77.63 \times 10^3$ N/m^3

Chapter 9
Introduction to Digital Computer Simulation Using CSMP (Continuous System Modeling Program)

9-1 INTRODUCTION

Before beginning the study of the CSMP language, let us note the level at which this language fits into the hierarchy of programming languages presently available. The most elementary language, and the language into which programs written in higher level languages must ultimately be translated, is the *machine language* of the computer used. Since a machine-language program written for one particular make and model of computer would not run on another computer, and because of the tedium involved in machine-language coding, engineers seldom write programs in machine language.

The next level of programming language involves the *assembler* or *symbolic* languages. In these, operation codes are symbolic, such as M for "multiply" and A for "add." Addresses may be either numeric or symbolic. Assembler language gives the programmer the advantages of machine language plus some additional advantages such as providing mechanisms for setting up branches to and from assembler-language subroutines. The assembler-language program is translated into machine language by a program called an *assembler*. This language is used primarily by professional programmers and is seldom used by engineers.

At the next level are the so-called *procedural,* or general-purpose, programming languages such as FORTRAN, ALGOL, and PASCAL. A program written in one of the procedural languages is translated into machine language by a *compiler* for that particular language. FORTRAN is the most popular of the procedural languages with engineers at present.

Recently, still higher level languages called special-purpose languages, or problem-oriented languages, have been developed. These languages use words in their vocabulary that are part of the language of the particular discipline for which the program is written. COGO is one example of such a language. It is designed specifically for the solution of surveying problems in civil engineering (COGO is an acronym for coordinate geometry). CSMP is a special-purpose language written specifically for simulating continuous systems on IBM computers. System 360 CSMP[1] will be discussed in this chapter. It is only one of several digital simulation languages currently being used by engineers and is chosen for description here because of the excellent features of the language. The study of one simulation language such as CSMP provides a good background for the study of many of the other simulation languages.

CSMP statements describing the physical system are interpreted and converted by a translator into a FORTRAN IV subroutine called UPDATE, which in turn is compiled and executed with an integration routine (fourth-order Runge-Kutta or some other selected routine) to effect the simulation. No knowledge of integration routines is required to use CSMP. However, an understanding of FORTRAN is very helpful and is assumed in the discussion of CSMP which follows. A knowledge of FORTRAN permits a programmer to supplement CSMP programs extensively by including FORTRAN statements as part of a CSMP program, and/or by the use of FORTRAN subprograms in conjunction with a CSMP program.

9-2 GENERAL NATURE OF A CSMP PROGRAM

Before studying the details of CSMP statements and model structure, let us look at an example problem solved by CSMP to obtain a general idea of the nature of a CSMP program. Figure 9-1 shows a spring-and-mass system, viscously damped by the dashpot shown, and containing the dead spaces represented by the gaps a and b between the mass and the respective springs. When $t = 0$, the mass has zero displacement in the position shown in the figure and a velocity of 8 in./sec, as shown. Considering the mass m as a free body, and applying Newton's second law, the differential equation of motion is obtained as

$$m\ddot{x} + c\dot{x} + f(x) = 0 \tag{9-1}$$

---

[1]*System/360 Continuous System Modeling Program, Users' Manual, CH20-0367-4,* 5th ed. (White Plains, N.Y.: IBM Corporation, Data Processing Division, 1972). This system contains the basic elements of later versions of CSMP. A recent version, CSMP III, is basically S/360 CSMP with extensions. Due to space limitations, these extensions are not included.

where $f(x)$ represents the spring forces acting on the mass. Examining the system, it can be seen that $f(x)$ is given by

$$f(x) = k_2(x - b) \qquad x > b$$

$$f(x) = 0 \qquad a \le x \le b$$

$$f(x) = k_1(x - a) \qquad x < a$$

A complete CSMP program for simulating the system shown in Fig. 9-1 follows:

```
INITIAL
 CONSTANT W=10.0,C=.00259,A=-0.6,B=1.0,K1=.255,K2=1.025
 INCON X0=0.0,XDOT0=8.0
      M=W/386.
      COEF=C/M

DYNAMIC
 NOSORT
      IF(X.GE.0.) GO TO 2
      FOFX=K1*DEADSP(A,0.,X)
      GO TO 3
   2  FOFX=K2*DEADSP(0.,B,X)
   3  CONTINUE
 SORT
      XDDOT=-COEFF*XDOT-FOFX/M
      XDOT=INTGRL(XDOT0,XDDOT)
      X=INTGRL(X0,XDOT)

TERMINAL
      KE=0.5*M*XDOT**2
      WRITE(6,4)KE
   4  FORMAT(' ',E16.7)
 TIMER DELT=.05,OUTDEL=0.2,FINTIM=60.
 METHOD RKSFX
 LABEL SPRING MASS VISCOUSLY DAMPED WITH DEADSPACE
 PRTPLOT XDOT,X,FOFX
 END
 STOP
ENDJOB
```

Let us note first of all that the program is divided into three parts or *segments*. Blank lines have been left between the segments to make them distinct, but the blank lines are not required. The segments are headed by statements consisting of the words INITIAL, DYNAMIC, and TERMINAL. These are the names of the segments. We will learn later that some programs may use only two segments, while some may use only one, the DYNAMIC segment.

In the initial segment we see statements containing the *labels* CONSTANT and INCON, in which the assignments of system variable values and initial conditions are made. As will be shown later, all CSMP data and control state-

$a = -0.6$ in.

$b = 1.0$ in.

$c = 0.00259$ lb-sec/in.

$k_1 = 0.255$ lb/in.

$k_2 = 1.025$ lb/in.

$w = 10$ lb

Figure 9-1   Spring-and-mass system

ments begin with a word called a *label*, which enables the translator to identify what the statement is for. Some control statements consist of a label only. The CONSTANT and INCON statements are followed by two statements having the appearance of FORTRAN arithmetic-assignment statements which calculate the value of the mass M and a variable with the name COEF which is equal to the damping coefficient divided by the mass. These two statements appear in the INITIAL segment rather than the DYNAMIC segment because they are executed only at time equal zero. Statements appearing in the DYNAMIC segment are executed at each interval of time from the start of the simulation to the finish time. Note that M is a *real* variable name and not *integer* as it would be by the predefined type of specification of FORTRAN.

In the DYNAMIC segment we see first an "unsorted" section consisting of statements placed between NOSORT and SORT statements. Statements in an unsorted section will not be reordered by the translator. It should be noted that this section contains a FORTRAN logical IF statement and a FORTRAN unconditional GO TO, as well as arithmetic-assignment statements and a FORTRAN CONTINUE statement. Full use of FORTRAN IV is permissible in an unsorted section.

The DYNAMIC segment in general is sorted, and if any part of it is not to be sorted it must be placed between NOSORT and SORT statements as illustrated. The statements in a sorted section or segment are reordered if necessary by the translator into proper computational sequence, and the user is freed of the responsibility of putting statements in the proper sequence. However, full use of FORTRAN is not permissible in a sorted section of a program.

```
SPRING MASS VISCOUSLY DAMPED WITH DEADSPACE                              PAGE   1

                              MINIMUM              XDOT   VERSUS TIME        MAXIMUM
                             -7.6828E 00                                    8.000CE 00
     TIME          XDOT       I                                              I
0.0             8.0000E 00    +-----------------------------------------------------+
2.0000E-01      7.0260E 00    ---- ------------------------------------------------+
4.0000E-01     -1.2600E C0    -----------------------+
6.0000E-01     -7.6546E 00    +
8.0000E-01     -7.5684E C0    +
1.0000E 00     -6.4429E 00    ---+
1.2000E 00     -2.5556E C0    -----------------------+
1.4000E 00      1.5774E 00    -----------------------------+
1.6000E 00      5.4257E 00    ------------------------------------------+
1.8000E 00      7.1513E C0    ---------------------------------------------------+
2.0000E 00      7.0579E 00    ---------------------------------------------------+
2.2000E 00      4.4652E C0    -----------------------------------------+
2.4000E 00     -3.6666E 00    --------------+
2.6000E 00     -6.8152E C0    --+
2.8000E 00     -6.6794E 00    ---+
3.0000E 00     -5.2724E 00    --------+
3.2000E 00     -1.9046E C0    -----------------------+
3.4000E 00      2.1149E 00    ------------------------------+
3.6000E 00      5.2571E C0    ------------------------------------------+
3.8000E 00      6.3542E 00    --------------------------------------------+
4.0000E 00      6.2284E C0    --------------------------------------------+
4.2000E 00      3.7195E C0    -------------------------------------+
4.4000E 00     -3.4711E 00    --------------+
4.6000E 00     -6.0133E CC    ------+
4.8000E 00     -5.8943E 00    ------+
5.0000E 00     -4.9065E 00    --------+
5.2000E 00     -2.0984E 00    -------------------+
5.4000E 00      1.4455E C0    ---------------------------+
5.6000E 00      4.3741E C0    -------------------------------------+
5.8000E 00      5.5949E C0    -------------------------------------------+
6.0000E 00      5.4951E C0    -------------------------------------------+
6.2000E 00      4.6239E C0    -----------------------------------------+
6.4000E 00     -1.2296E 00    -----------------------+
6.6000E 00     -5.2816E C0    --------+
6.8000E 00     -5.2013E 00    --------+
7.0000E 00     -4.9431E C0    --------+
7.2000E 00     -3.1837E 00    ------------+
7.4000E 00     -2.5824E-C1    -------------------+
7.6000E 00      2.7067E 00    -------------------------------+
7.8000E 00      4.5920E C0    -------------------------------------+
8.0000E 00      4.8491E C0    --------------------------------------+
8.2000E 00      4.7531E C0    --------------------------------------+
8.4000E 00      2.8427E CC    -------------------------------+
8.6000E 00     -2.6444E 00    -------------+
8.8000E 00     -4.5850E 00    ---------+
9.0000E 00     -4.4981E 00    ----------+
9.2000E 00     -4.2242E 00    ----------+
9.4000E 00     -2.6129E C0    --------------+
9.6000E 00     -4.7999E-02    -------------------+
9.8000E 00      2.4842E C0    ------------------------------+
1.0000E 01      4.0293E C0    ------------------------------------+
```

Figure 9-2 A portion of the print-plot output of xDOT versus time

We may also note in the DYNAMIC segment that the function names DEADSP and INTGRL are not standard supplied FORTRAN functions. They are supplied CSMP functions, and there are 34 such functions available. XDDOT, XDOT, and X are the CSMP variable names for $\ddot{x}$, $\dot{x}$, and x, respectively, and are names selected by the programmer.

In the TERMINAL segment we see a calculation made for the kinetic energy of the system (CSMP variable name is KE). This calculation is in the TERMINAL segment because it is made at the end of the simulation using the final value of XDOT. This statement is followed by ordinary FORTRAN WRITE and FORMAT statements. Since the TERMINAL segment is unsorted, full FORTRAN is permissible in this segment. After these FORTRAN statements comes the statement with the label TIMER. This statement is used in this program to assign values to the integration increment of the independent variable, the output increment, and the finish time for the simulation. The next line has the label METHOD and specifies in this program that a fourth-order Runge-Kutta method with fixed step size is to be used in the integration. The next statement with the label LABEL specifies what the output page headings will be. The next statement with the label PRTPLOT specifies that the variables XDOT, X, and FOFX are to be print-plotted. A portion of the output from this program is shown in Fig. 9-2. Unlike a FORTRAN program, the END statement is not the last statement in a CSMP program. In general, there may be more than one END statement, and the last one is followed by STOP and then ENDJOB unless there are FORTRAN subprograms used with the CSMP program, in which case ENDJOB follows the END line of the last subprogram. In the sections which follow, the statements and structure of CSMP programs will be discussed in detail.

9-3 CSMP STATEMENTS

There are three kinds of statements in CSMP. They are

1. structure statements
2. data statements
3. control statements

Structure statements describe the functional relationships between the variables of the program and define the system being simulated. Data statements are used to assign values to variables which are to remain fixed during a particular run, as, for example, an initial condition for the integration of a differential equation. Control statements are used to control certain operations and quantities associated with the translation, execution, and output of the program. An example would be the step size in the integration routine. Control statements are classified as (a) translation control statements, (b) execution control statements, and (c) output control statements.

We will first discuss the rules for writing each of the three kinds of CSMP statements and look at examples of each, and later we will see how complete programs are formed using all three kinds of statements.

9-4 STRUCTURE STATEMENTS

CSMP structure statements are like the arithmetic assignment statements of FORTRAN. They consist of a variable on the left of an equal sign and an expression on the right. The expression may be like an ordinary FORTRAN arithmetic expression. That is, it may consist of a single variable, a single constant, a function, or a combination of these separated by the FORTRAN arithmetic operators. However, in addition to the supplied functions available in FORTRAN such as SIN, COS, SQRT, and so on, there are 34 special CSMP functions available.

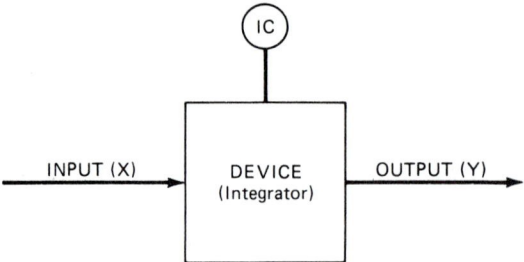

Figure 9-3 Block diagram

One of these, the integrator function, might be used in a structure statement as follows:

$$Y = INTGRL(IC,X)$$ (9-2)

Mathematically this is equivalent to

$$Y = \int_0^t X\, dt + IC$$ (9-3)

The x in Eq. 9-2 is called an *input* to the function. In general, inputs can be expressions (single variables, constants, functions, or combinations of these). IC is the initial condition on Y and is a single variable name or constant. In the functions given in Figs. 9-8 through 9-13, x's are always used for inputs, IC for initial conditions, and P for parameters. Like initial conditions, parameters cannot be general expressions but are single variables or constants. If the system to be simulated is shown in block diagram form, INTGRL is thought of as defining the particular *device*, with Y the output from the function block, X the input, and IC the initial condition as shown in Fig. 9-3.

CSMP programs may be written either from a block diagram representation of the system or from a set of ordinary differential equations. CSMP includes a basic set of functional blocks (functions) similar to the integrator shown in Fig. 9-3 which may be used to represent the components of a system. These functions are given in the section which follows. Examples of programming from a block diagram representation of a system and from ordinary differential equations are given in Sec. 9-9.

Additional examples of structure statements are

```
H = (A+B)/2.
XDOT = INTGRL(XDOTO,-(K*X+C*XDOT)/M)
```

In general, FORTRAN rules apply to the writing of the structure statements and the elements of which they are formed. There are a few differences, however, which are brought out in the following rules governing numerical constants, variables, expressions, and structure statements.

1. In general, numerical constants are considered to be real, regardless of whether or not a decimal point is used, and variables are considered to be real regardless of the initial letter of a variable name. It takes a special control statement (the FIXED statement) to make a variable integer.
2. Real constants are restricted to 12 characters total. For example −126.592E−02 contains the maximum number of characters allowed.
3. If an INTGRL function is included in an expression, it must be the last part of the expression. The expression in the following structure statement illustrates the correct location of the INTGRL function.

```
Y = A*B + INTGRL(IC,X)
```

4. CSMP statements are typed in columns 1 through 72. Columns 73 through 80 are not translated and may be used for identification purposes if desired. Most CSMP statements (all structure statements) may begin in any desired column so long as the statement is within columns 1 through 72. Column 6 is not reserved for continuation as in FORTRAN statements.
5. Most structure statements can be continued (an exception will be noted later under "MACRO functions"), and this is done by concluding the line to be continued with three consecutive decimal points. None of the decimal points can be in columns 73 through 80. Statements should not be continued in the middle of variables or numerical constants. Up to eight continuation lines can be used.
6. Comment statements may be used in a CSMP program for the same purpose for which they are used in a FORTRAN program, to insert explanations in the program to make it more readily understood. In CSMP an asterisk in column 1 denotes a comment line.
7. Statements with a slash in column 1 are not translated but are transferred (with the slash removed) directly to the FORTRAN IV subroutine (called UPDATE) which the translator forms. Up to ten such lines can be used. They are inserted at the beginning of the subroutine and so can be used to insert FORTRAN specification statements (a DIMENSION statement, for example) into the subroutine. These statements must be written according to FORTRAN rules rather than CSMP rules. However, CSMP variables cannot be EQUIVALENCE'd.
8. Blank lines may be used to space statements in the listing.

9-5 CSMP FUNCTIONS

Since CSMP functions are an essential part of structure statements, several of the CSMP functions given in Figs. 9-8 through 9-13 will be explained in more detail than is given by the brief definitions of the functions accompanying the figures.

THE IMPLICIT FUNCTION

This function, which has the general form

```
Y=IMPL(IC,P,FOFY)
```

is used to iteratively solve an equation of the form

$$y = f(y)$$

for y such that

$$|y - f(y)| \le p|y|$$

where IC is the first estimate of the value of Y which must be supplied by the programmer, P is the error bound and also supplied by the programmer, and FOFY is the name appearing to the left of the equal sign in the last statement of the algebraic loop definition of $f(y)$. As an example, suppose we have an equation of the form

$$x = Ce^{-2t}B \sin x$$

which must be solved for x. The following CSMP statements could be used to accomplish this:

```
X=IMPL(XO,ERROR,FUNC)
PART1=C*EXP(-2.*TIME)
PART2=B*SIN(X)
FUNC=PART1*PART2
```

The Arbitrary Function Generator

The arbitrary function generator with linear interpolation can be illustrated by a structure statement having the general form

```
Y=AFGEN(FUNCT,X)
```

FUNCT is the name of a function which has been entered into the computer by means of a data statement called a FUNCTION statement. This data statement will be discussed later. At this time it will suffice to say that the function is entered by giving pairs of values of the independent and dependent variables. Thus, there are values of the dependent variable Y for discrete values of X, but not for a continuous range of X values as would be the case if Y were given as a mathematical function of X. Use of the AFGEN function will give the value of

Figure 9-4 IMPULS function

Y for *any value* of X in the range of X values entered as data, using linear interpolation. The arguments of AFGEN are first the name of the function for which a value of the dependent variable is to be obtained, and second the value of the independent variable in the function when the value of the dependent variable is obtained.

Nonlinear Function Generator

If quadratic interpolation is desired instead of linear interpolation, the nonlinear function generator NLFGEN is used instead of AFGEN. A structure statement using this function would have the form

```
Y=NLFGEN(FUNCT,X)
```

where the arguments are the same as given in the preceding paragraph.

The Impulse Generator

The impulse generator can be used to generate a series of impulses having a value of 1.0, starting at time equal to P_1 and continuing at times equal to $P_1 + kP_2$, where $k = 1, 2, 3, \ldots$. The general form of the function is illustrated by the statement

```
Y=IMPULS(P1,P2)
```

The function is represented graphically in Fig. 9-4. If the spike is to have a value of 2.0 instead of 1.0, the IMPULS function can be multiplied by 2.0. For example,

```
Y=2.*IMPULS(0.,P)
```

gives Y as shown in Fig. 9-5.

Figure 9-5 IMPULS function

The Pulse Generator

The PULSE function can be used to generate a pulse starting at any time a "trigger" is greater than zero and continuing for a minimum width of P. If after the pulse has continued for time P, the trigger value is zero or negative, the pulse will end. The function has the general form

```
Y=PULSE(P,X)
```

The input X, which is usually some selected function of time, triggers the pulse whenever its value is greater than zero, providing a pulse is not already being generated. Graphically the function is as shown in Fig. 9-6.

The IMPULS function can be used to trigger the PULSE function. For example, the statement

```
Y=PULSE(1.,IMPULS(0.,2.))
```

will give a square-wave function as shown in Fig. 9-7.

Other important CSMP functions include the first- and second-order lag functions, the limiter function, the dead-space function, the step function, and the ramp function. These, and others, are shown in Figs. 9-8 through 9-13, which follow.

Figure 9-6 PULSE function

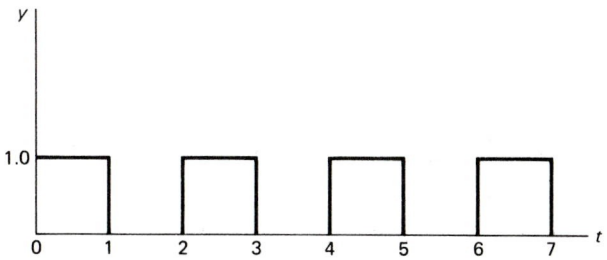

Figure 9-7 PULSE function triggered by IMPULS function

General Form	Function
Y=INTGRL(IC,X) Y(0)=IC Integrator	$Y = \int_0^t X\, dt + IC$ Equivalent Laplace transform: $\dfrac{1}{S}$
Y=DERIV(IC,X) $\dot{X}\,(t=0) = IC$ Derivative	$Y = \dfrac{dX}{dt}$ Equivalent Laplace transform: S
Y=DELAY(N,P,X) P = delay time N = number of points sampled in interval P (integer constant) Dead time (delay)	$Y(t) = X(t - P) \quad t > P$ $Y = 0 \qquad\qquad t < P$ Equivalent Laplace transform: e^{-PS}
Y=ZHOLD (X_1, X_2) Zero-order hold	$Y = X_2 \qquad\qquad X_1 > 0$ $Y = \text{last output} \qquad X_1 \leq 0$ $Y(0)=0$ Equivalent Laplace transform: $\dfrac{1}{S}(1 - e^{St})$

Y=IMPL(IC,P,FOFY)
 	
IC   = first guess
P   = error bound
FOFY = output name of last state-
      ment in algebraic loop
      definition
 	
Implicit function
	$Y = \text{funct}\,(Y)$
	$\|Y - \text{funct}\,(Y)\| \leq P\|Y\|$

Figure 9-8 Mathematical functions. Reprinted by permission from Application Program H20-0240-2 © 1967, 1968 by International Business Machines Corporation

General Form	Function
Y=MODINT(IC,X_1,X_2,X_3) Mode-controlled integrator	$Y = \int_0^t X_3\, dt + IC$ $X_1 > 0$, any X_2 $Y = IC$ $X_1 \le 0$, $X_2 > 0$ $Y =$ last output $X_1 \le 0$, $X_2 \le 0$
Y=REALPL(IC,P,X) Y(0)=IC 1st order lag (real pole)	$P\dot{Y} + Y = X$ Equivalent Laplace transform: $\dfrac{1}{PS + 1}$
Y=LEDLAG(P_1, P_2,X) Lead-lag	$P_2 \dot{Y} + Y = P_1 \dot{X} + X$ Equivalent Laplace transform: $\dfrac{P_1 S + 1}{P_2 S + 1}$
Y=CMPXPL(IC_1,IC_2,P_1,P_2,X) Y(0)=IC_1 $\dot{Y}$(0)=IC_2 2nd order lag (complex pole)	$\ddot{Y} + 2P_1 P_2 \dot{Y} + P_2^2 Y = X$ Equivalent Laplace transform: $\dfrac{1}{S^2 + 2P_1 P_2 S + P_2^2}$

Figure 9-9 System Macros. Reprinted by permission from Application Program H20-0240-2. © 1967, 1968 by International Business Machines Corporation

General Form	Function
Y=FCNSW(X_1,X_2,X_3,X_4) Function switch	$Y = X_2$ $X_1 < 0$ $Y = X_3$ $X_1 = 0$ $Y = X_4$ $X_1 > 0$
Y=INSW(X_1,X_2,X_3) Input switch (relay)	$Y = X_2$ $X_1 < 0$ $Y = X_3$ $X_1 \ge 0$
Y_1,Y_2=OUTSW(X_1,X_2) Output switch	$Y_1 = X_2$, $Y_2 = 0$ $X_1 < 0$ $Y_1 = 0$, $Y_2 = X_2$ $X_1 \ge 0$
Y=COMPAR(X_1,X_2) Comparator	$Y = 0$ $X_1 < X_2$ $Y = 1$ $X_1 \ge X_2$
Y=RST(X_1,X_2,X_3) Resettable flip-flop	$Y = 0$ $X_1 > 0$ $Y = 1$ $X_2 > 0$, $X_1 \le 0$ $Y = 0$ $\left\{\begin{array}{l} X_3 > 0,\ Y_{n-1} = 1 \end{array}\right.$ $Y = 1$ $X_1 \le 0,$ $\left\{\begin{array}{l} X_3 > 0,\ Y_{n-1} = 0 \end{array}\right.$ $Y = 0$ $X_2 \le 0,$ $\left\{\begin{array}{l} X_3 \le 0,\ Y_{n-1} = 0 \end{array}\right.$ $Y = 1$ $\left\{\begin{array}{l} X_3 \le 0,\ Y_{n-1} = 1 \end{array}\right.$

Figure 9-10 Switching functions. Reprinted by permission from Application Program H20-0240-2. © 1967, 1968 by International Business Machines Corporation

General Form	Function		
Y=AFGEN(FUNCT,X) Arbitrary function generator (linear interpolation)	Y = FUNCT (X)		
Y=NLFGEN(FUNCT,X) Arbitrary function generator (quadratic interpolation)	Y = FUNCT (X)	$X_0 \leq X \leq X_n$	
Y=LIMIT(P_1,P_2,X) Limiter	$Y = P_1$ $Y = P_2$ $Y = X$	$X < P_1$ $X > P_2$ $P_1 \leq X \leq P_2$	
Y=QNTZR(P,X) Quantizer	$Y = kP$	$(k - 1/2)P < X \leq (k + 1/2)P$ $k = 0,\ \pm 1,\ \pm 2,\ \pm 3\ldots$	
Y=DEADSP(P_1,P_2,X) Dead space	$Y = 0$ $Y = X - P_2$ $Y = X - P_1$	$P_1 \leq X \leq P_2$ $X > P_2$ $X < P_1$	
Y=HSTRSS(IC,P_1,P_2,X) Y(0)=IC Hysteresis loop	$Y = X - P_2$ $Y = X - P_1$ otherwise	$(X - X_{n-1}) > 0$ and $Y_{n-1} \leq (X - P_2)$ $(X - X_{n-1}) < 0$ and $Y_{n-1} \geq (X - P_1)$ Y = last output	

Figure 9-11 Function generators. Reprinted by permission from Application Program H20-0240-2. © 1967, 1968 by International Business Machines Corporation

General Form	Function	
Y=STEP(P) Step function	$Y = 0 \quad t < P$ $Y = 1 \quad t \geq P$	
Y=RAMP(P) Ramp function	$Y = 0 \quad t < P$ $Y = t - P \quad t \geq P$	
Y=IMPULS(P_1,P_2) Impulse generator	$Y = 0 \quad t < P_1$ $Y = 1 \quad (t - P_1) = kP_2$ $Y = 0 \quad (t - P_1) \neq kP_2$ $k = 0, 1, 2, 3. \ldots$	
Y=PULSE(P,X) P = minimum pulse width Pulse generator with X > 0 as trigger)	$Y = 1 \quad T_k \leq t < (T_k + P)$ or $\qquad X > 0$ $Y = 0 \quad$ otherwise $T_k = $ time of trigger	
Y=SINE(P_1,P_2,P_3) P_1 = delay P_2 = frequency (radians per unit time) P_3 = phase shift in radians Trigonometric sine wave with delay, frequency and phase parameters	$Y = 0 \quad t < P_1$ $Y = \sin(P_2(t - P_1) + P_3) \quad t \geq P_1$	
Y=GAUSS(P_1,P_2,P_3) P_1 = any odd integer P_2 = mean P_3 = standard deviation Noise (random number) generator with normal distribution	Normal distribution of variable Y p(Y) = probability density function	
Y=RNDGEN(P) P = any odd integer Noise (random number) generator with uniform distribution	Uniform idstribution of variable Y p(Y) = probability density function	

Figure 9-12 Signal sources. Reprinted by permission from Application Program H20-0240-2. © 1967, 1968 by International Business Machines Corporation

General Form	Function	
Y=AND(X_1, X_2) And	Y = 1 Y = 0	$X_1 > 0$, $X_2 > 0$ otherwise
Y=NAND (X_1, X_2) Not and	Y = 0 Y = 1	$X_1 > 0$, $X_2 > 0$ otherwise
Y=IOR (X_1,X_2) Inclusive or	Y = 0 Y = 1	$X_1 \leq 0$, $X_2 \leq 0$ otherwise
Y=NOR(X_1,X_2) Not or	Y = 1 Y = 0	$X_1 \leq 0$, $X_2 \leq 0$ otherwise
Y=EOR(X_1,X_2) Exclusive or	Y = 1 Y = 1 Y = 0	$X_1 \leq 0$, $X_2 > 0$ $X_1 > 0$, $X_2 \leq 0$ otherwise
Y=NOT(X) Not	Y = 1 Y = 0	$X \leq 0$ $X > 0$
Y=EQUIV (X_1,X_2) Equivalent	Y = 1 Y = 1 Y = 0	$X_1 \leq 0$, $X_2 \leq 0$ $X_1 > 0$, $X_2 > 0$ otherwise

Figure 9-13 Logic functions. Reprinted by permission from Application Program H20-0240-2. © 1967, 1968 by International Business Machines Corporation

9-6 DATA STATEMENTS

Data statements are typed in columns 1 through 72. They are used to assign values to the variable names constituting the various initial conditions, parameters, and constants of the simulation. In most simulation languages, initial conditions, parameters, and constants[2] are all considered as variables. Initial conditions, which are used with the integrator function and several others, are variables which may or may not change values for different runs of a simulation. Parameters are variables which change values for different runs of a simulation. Constants are variables which do not change values for different runs of a simulation. These three types of variables can be used interchangeably in

[2]Note that the constants discussed here are not the numerical constants of CSMP which are similar to FORTRAN constants, and which were discussed earlier in this chapter. Thus the word "constant" is used in two different ways in CSMP—first, to describe numerical constants consisting of a string of digits, and second, to describe a variable whose value remains constant during a simulation study.

CSMP. INCON, PARAMETER, and CONSTANT statements would usually be used to assign values to variables used as initial conditions, parameters, and constants, respectively. These labels are used merely to make the source program easily understood. However, the programmer may, for example, use a PARAMETER statement to assign values to variables used as initial conditions if he so desires.

As an example of entering initial conditions with an INCON statement, the data statement

```
INCON X0=2.5, XDOT0=0.0
```

assigns the value 2.5 to the name X0 and 0.0 to the name XDOT0. At least one blank must follow any statement label such as INCON. The label can begin in any column. Only the first four characters of data and control statement labels are actually examined (except for COMMON and ENDJOB), so the labels given may be shortened if desired.

As mentioned earlier, parameter and constant statements use the labels PARAMETER and CONSTANT, respectively. Examples are

```
PARAMETER VT=160., VL=440., CD=0.7
CONSTANT PI=3.14159, SIGMA=0.173E-8
```

As many variables as space permits can be assigned values on a data statement. If it is necessary to continue to another line, it is done with three successive decimal points in the same manner that structure statements are continued. That is, any line concluding with three decimal points consecutively is considered to be followed by a continuation line. As many continuation lines as required may be used. Variable names and constants should not be split in continuing from one line to another.

Several runs of a program using different values of a variable can be specified by enclosing in parentheses the several desired values of the variable, separated by commas. For example, if the statement

```
PARAMETER I=.0006, SK=(.669,.671,.680,.692)
```

were used in a program, the program would run four times, with SK having the value .699 in the first run, .671 in the second run, and so forth. If the successive values of the variable have equal incremental changes for each run, such as L = 3.5, 3.6, 3.7, . . . , 4.5, a statement such as

```
PARAMETER I=.0006, L=(3.5,10*0.1)
```

could be used. The value of L in the first run would be 3.5, and there would be ten additional runs with L taking on values of 3.6 through 4.5 with equal increments of 0.1. The repeat constant (10 in the above statement) should be written without a decimal point as shown. A sequence of simulation runs may also be specified using several repeat constants and increments, along with given values of the parameter. For example,

```
PARAMETER TERM=(150.,155.,5*1.0,163.,2*2.0)
```

is equivalent to

```
PARAMETER TERM=(150.,155.,156.,157.,158.,159.,160.,
                                  163.,165.,167.)
```

The maximum number of runs possible in any sequence is 50, and only one multiple-value parameter should be used for each sequence. A sequence of runs due to a multiple-value parameter is terminated by an END statement. After an END statement, more runs can be specified by entering new variable values, as will be explained later in the chapter under "Control Statements" and "CSMP Examples—Run Control," Secs. 9-8 and 9-9, respectively. This is the advantage of using data statements to assign numerical values to variable names instead of using structure statements for that purpose. Assigned in this way, variable values can be changed automatically between successive runs or sequences of runs of a program.

Another important data statement is the FUNCTION statement. It is used for entering into a simulation pairs of values of the independent and dependent variables of a function. Thus, if $y = f(x)$ is available in tabular or graphic form rather than in equation form, the function is specified at discrete intervals by entering pairs of values of the coordinates x and y into the simulation using the FUNCTION statement. These coordinates are for use by the arbitrary function generator (AFGEN) and the nonlinear function generator (NLFGEN) as explained earler under "CSMP Functions." As an example, a function named YOFX might be entered as follows:

```
FUNCTION YOFX=(0.0,4.0),(1.0,4.3),(2.0,5.0),(3.0,6.1),...
(4.0,7.3),(5.0,8.7),(6.0,10.1),(7.0,11.0)
```

In this example, values of x and y are paired off with parentheses. However, the parentheses are optional and may be omitted. The first number of each pair shown is the value of the independent variable, the second that of the corresponding dependent variable. The increments of the independent variable need not be of equal size as they are in the above example, but they must be listed in order of *algebraically* increasing size. FUNCTION is the statement label and must be followed by at least one blank. Any number of continuation lines may be used, and any number of points per function may be specified. There is no restriction on the number of functions defined per simulation.

Let us discuss how the function YOFX, as defined above, could be used in the arbitrary function generator. Suppose that the structure statement

```
Y=AFGEN(YOFX,X)
```

appears in a CSMP program in which the above FUNCTION statement has been used. Y is assigned the value of the function YOFX for whatever value X has in the program. If the value of X is between values given in the FUNCTION statement, the corresponding value of Y is obtained by linear interpolation when AFGEN is used. For example, if X had the value 1.5, then Y would be assigned the value 4.65 with YOFX defined as in the FUNCTION statement above.

Data statements can be in any order and may be mixed with structure statements if desired. However, many CSMP programmers prefer to put data statements near the beginning of the source program, except for those that follow an END statement. Data statements which follow an END statement cause the values of variables to be changed in preparation for another run, or another sequence of runs if a multiple-valued parameter is used. The details of changing parameters for new runs by placing new data statements after an END line will be discussed under "Control Statements" and "CSMP Examples—Run Control."

9-7 MODEL STRUCTURE

Before discussing control statements, let us consider the structure of a CSMP simulation. The "heart" of a continuous system simulator is the built-in process for integration of the differential equations that describe the system. One of the integration methods of numerical analysis must be used. Thus the independent variable (TIME in a CSMP program unless the name is changed by one of the control statements to be discussed later) varies by increments from zero to the finish time. Calculations of the integration routine, and perhaps others as well, must be performed for each increment of time. However, there may be some calculations which need to be made just once for each run, perhaps prior to the run or after the completion of each run. For example, in the differential equation

$$\frac{d^2\theta}{dt^2} = \frac{T_c + k\theta_c}{I_0} - \frac{k}{I_0}\theta$$

the first term on the right of the equal sign is made up of four basic parameters which will not change during a run. There is no need to evaluate this term for each increment of time. It need be done only once prior to the run using a structure statement such as

```
TERM1 = ( TCL + SK*THCL ) /EYE
```

Similarly, there are problems in which calculations must be made at the conclusion of a run using final values of some of the system variables. To satisfy these requirements, CSMP provides the possibility of writing a program in three *segments*, Initial, Dynamic, and Terminal. The Initial segment is intended for those structure statements that are to be executed only once prior to the run.

Many programmers also include data statements in the Initial segment if one is used. The Dynamic segment contains the statements specifying integration of the differential equations, along with any other structure statements which must be executed at each increment of time during the run. The Terminal segment is used for calculations made at the conclusion of a run. In some simulations only a Dynamic segment need be used.

The segments described above consist of one or more *sections*. For many simulations, the Dynamic segment will consist of a single section which has what is called *parallel structure*. In other simulations, one or more *procedural* sections may be required in the Dynamic segment, along with parallel sections.

In an actual physical system, most phenomena occur in parallel. For example, in a spring-mass-damper system the displacement x, velocity $\dot{x}$, and acceleration $\ddot{x}$ are all changing simultaneously. When such a system is simulated on the analog computer, these quantities can all be obtained as output simultaneously. However, with a digital computer these quantities are obtained sequentially, and in a FORTRAN program which is solving such a system, care must be exercised to write the statements in the proper order. Thus the FORTRAN program has what is called procedural structure.

Digital computer simulation, however, is desired to achieve the same effect as the simulation on an analog computer. This is accomplished in a parallel section by means of a sorting algorithm which arranges computations into proper sequence, allowing the programmer to write his statements in any order he desires. This type of section is also called a *sorted* section. The Initial segment of a CSMP simulation is sorted. The Dynamic segment is also sorted, but in some simulations it is necessary to have one or more unsorted sections in this segment. In an unsorted section full use of FORTRAN IV, including the use of branching, input, and output statements is permitted. For such statements FORTRAN rules apply, in general. However, the statements may begin in any column, and column 6 need not be reserved for continuation purposes. If continuation of FORTRAN statements in an unsorted section is required, it is done by CSMP rules; by the use of three successive periods. How an unsorted section may be specified will be explained under "Control Statements." The Terminal segment has procedural structure (is unsorted), and all structure statements are considered to be in the proper order. This allows the full use of FORTRAN IV in the Terminal segment, including the use of FORTRAN branching statements, and input and output statements if desired. This standard structure may be overridden, as will be explained later under "Control Statements."

9-8 CONTROL STATEMENTS

Control statements make specifications having to do with the translation, execution, and output of the simulation, such as specifying the increment of the independent variable of the integration routine, the finish time for the simulation run, and the variables whose values are to be printed out. In general, these statements may appear in any order and may be mixed with structure and data statements. They may begin in any column (except for the ENDJOB, COMMON, and ENDDATA statements) as long as columns 73 through 80 are not used. In this section of the text we will discuss the most commonly used Control statements of the following three types: translation control, execution control, and output control.

Translation Control Statements

• *The* INITIAL *Statement.* As previously discussed under "Model Structure," a CSMP program may be divided into three segments: Initial, Dynamic, and Terminal. A statement with just the label INITIAL on it marks the beginning of the Initial segment.

• *The* DYNAMIC *Statement.* This statement consists of just the label DYNAMIC, and it marks the beginning of the Dynamic segment and the end of the Initial segment. The Dynamic segment is terminated by the TERMINAL statement unless no Terminal segment is used. In this case the END or CONTINUE statement terminates the Dynamic segment.

• *The* TERMINAL *Statement.* This statement consists of just the label TERMINAL, and it marks the beginning of the Terminal segment and the end of the Dynamic segment. The Terminal segment is terminated by the first END or CONTINUE statement.

• *The* END *Statement.* The END statement permits the simulation to accept new data and control statements, and if such statements follow the END statement, a new run is initiated using these new statements. The independent variable (TIME unless the name has been changed) is reset to zero, and initial conditions are reset for the new run. The last END is followed by a STOP, which means that a new run will not be initiated.

• *The* CONTINUE *Statement.* When an END statement is followed by data and/or control statements rather than a STOP statement, the run (or sequence of runs if a multiple-value parameter is used) terminated by the END statement is followed by another simulation using the new variable values. The independent variable TIME is reset to zero, the initial conditions are reset, and a new run is initiated using the new values. However, if the programmer wishes to change a control statement during a simulation, and then wants to continue on from that point in time and not go back to TIME equal zero, he must use a CONTINUE statement instead of an END statement. For example, the programmer might want to change the increment of the independent variable at some point in a simulation. He does not want the solution to start again from TIME equal to zero, so he would use a CONTINUE statement preceding his new control statement rather than an END statement. The use of END and CONTINUE statements for run control will be illustrated in the section "Run Control." The FORTRAN statement CONTINUE, which might also be used in a CSMP program, should always be numbered so that no confusion exists between the CSMP CONTINUE and the FORTRAN CONTINUE. Multivalue parameters should not be used in conjunction with the CONTINUE statement.

• *The* STOP *Statement.* This statement consists of the label STOP only. The STOP follows the last END statement and indicates that no new run is to be initiated.

• *The* ENDJOB *Statement.* The ENDJOB statement follows the STOP unless user-supplied subroutines are used, in which case it follows the last subroutine. The statement consists of the label ENDJOB only, and it must begin in column 1.

• *The* RENAME *Statement.* In CSMP there are certain reserved names such as the name of the independent variable which has the reserved name TIME. The increment of the independent variable has the reserved name DELT. If the integration routine used adjusts the step size based on an error analysis, a minimum step size can be specified by assigning a value to DELMIN. The maximum value of the independent variable is specified by assigning a value to FINTIM. The independent variable increment for printing is called PRDEL, and for print-plot output OUTDEL is used. If any of these quantities are used in structure statements, or in a TIMER statement (an execution control statement in which all but TIME may be assigned values) in the program, these reserved names are used. However, any or all of these six reserved names can be changed by using a RENAME statement. For example, if the independent variable of the problem is a linear distance x rather than time, the programmer might prefer to use the names X, XMAX, and DELTX instead of TIME, FINTIM, and DELT, respectively. A RENAME statement to accomplish these changes would be

```
RENAME TIME=X, FINTIM=XMAX, DELT=DELTX
```

RENAME is the label, and it must be followed by at least one blank. Commas separate the rename specifications. The substitute names X, XMAX, and DELTX replace the reserved names. For example, if the programmer uses the independent variable name in a statement in his program, he would use X instead of TIME. Also, in the printed output the name X will appear as a column heading instead of TIME. A RENAME statement cannot be continued, but more than one RENAME statement can be used if needed. When used, RENAME is usually the first line of a CSMP source program, and it *must* appear before the TIMER statement.

• *The* FIXED *Statement.* All variable names in CSMP are considered real unless they appear in a FIXED statement. This rule also applies to FORTRAN statements appearing in a CSMP program. If it should be necssary to use integer variables in the program with names such as N and JOB, the FIXED statement would be entered as follows:

```
FIXED N,JOB
```

The label FIXED must be followed by at least one blank.

• *The* COMMON *Statement.* When the FORTRAN subroutine UPDATE is formed by the CSMP translator, a COMMON block is established which includes TIME, DELT, DELMIN, FINTIM, PRDEL, and OUTDEL; the variables listed on PARAM-ETER, CONSTANT, and INCON statements; and the variables defined in CSMP structure statements. If the programmer includes user-supplied FORTRAN sub-programs along with his CSMP program (as explained later), he can make these variables available to any of his subprograms by placing CSMP COMMON state-ments at the beginning of the subprograms. The translator replaces these state-ments with the FORTRAN COMMON statements needed. The CSMP COMMON statement consists of just the label COMMON in columns 1 through 6.

• MACRO *Functions.* Statements with the labels MACRO and ENDMAC are used to precede and follow a group of statements, respectively, identifying them as defining a MACRO function. MACRO functions are one of three types of user-defined functions which may be used in a CSMP program. The other two are PROCEDURE functions and FORTRAN subprograms, both of which are discussed later.

Let us first consider a simple MACRO function definition to help clarify the rules concerning these functions which follow. Suppose that in a CSMP program it is necessary to determine the orthogonal components of several vector quan-tities. Instead of writing several groups of similar statements, a MACRO function could be used which might consist of the following statements:

```
MACRO VECTRX,VECTRY=COMPO(VECTOR,THETA)
          VEXTRX=VECTOR*COS(THETA)
          VECTRY=VECTOR*SIN(THETA)
ENDMAC
```

In the above statements

```
VECTRX,VECTRY=COMPO(VECTOR,THETA)
```

is called the *canonical* statement in the MACRO definition. Once having defined the MACRO function, it can be used (referenced) as often as desired.

Before illustrating the referencing of the MACRO function within the sim-ulation structure statements, let us list the rules which must be observed in writing the MACRO definition.

1. VECTRX and VECTRY are dummy names for the outputs of the function, the x and y components of the vector quantity. There may be any number of

outputs. When there are several outputs, as in this example, the dummy names for the outputs are to the left of the equal sign in the MACRO statement and separated by commas. If there is only one output, the single dummy name for the variable is also to the left of the equal sign.

2. The name assigned by the user to the above function is COMPO, and it appears just to the right of the equal sign in the MACRO statement. When the function is referenced in structure statements, the name COMPO must be used.

3. VECTOR and THETA are dummy names for the arguments of the function. They represent, respectively, the magnitude of the vector quantity and the angle in radians which locates the vector with respect to the x axis. In general, they may represent initial conditions, parameters, or other input variables used in the definition of the function outputs.

4. The statements between the MACRO and ENDMAC translation control statements define the output or outputs of the function (define the MACRO). They are self-explanatory in the above example. In general, they may contain any CSMP functions—INTGRL, for example—but FORTRAN logical, branching, or input/output statements are not to be used unless they are within a PROCEDURE function which is embedded within the MACRO function. There should be no data and control statements within the MACRO, and structure statements within a MACRO definition may not be continued. The canonical statement in the MACRO definition may be continued for a total of only four lines. The statements of a MACRO may be written in any order since the translator will automatically sort them to give the correct computational sequence, if this is required. If the MACRO is within a NOSORT section, however, the automatic sorting will not be done. If a PROCEDURE function is embedded within a MACRO function, the statements in the PROCEDURE will be moved as a single entity, but there is no internal sorting of statements within a PROCEDURE.

5. The statement with the label ENDMAC marks the end of the MACRO definition.

6. The group of statements defining the MACRO are placed at the beginning of the CSMP source program ahead of any structure statements in the INITIAL or DYNAMIC segments.

Having seen a simple MACRO definition, and having discussed the rules to be observed for writing such a definition, let us next discuss the referencing or use of the MACRO function within the structure statements of a program.

The following structure statement uses the MACRO function COMPO:

```
VX,VY = COMPO(VELOC,THRAD)
```

Note that this statement has the same format as the canonical statement in the MACRO definition previously discussed. VELOC and THRAD are inputs to, or the real arguments of, the function COMPO, and VX and VY are the outputs of the function. These four names replace the dummy names VECTOR, THETA, VECTRX, and VECTRY, respectively, in the statements of the MACRO definition which calculates the output values.

If the above statement appeared in the Dynamic segment of a CSMP program, values of VX and VY, the x and y components of VELOC, would be calculated at each time interval of the simulation, and they would be available for use in other statements of the simulation. For the MACRO to be a time-saving feature, it would have to be referenced more than once in the simulation.

• PROCEDURE *Functions.* The PROCEDURE function is a type of user-defined function in which FORTRAN IV may be employed along with CSMP structure statements. There is no sorting done within a PROCEDURE, and all executable FORTRAN statements, including branching and input/output statements, may be freely used. We will first look at an example of a PROCEDURE function used in a CSMP program and then point out the rules that must be observed in defining such a function.

The CSMP program containing the PROCEDURE which we will examine is used to determine the dynamic characteristics of a small rocket fired vertically upward. The differential equation of motion of the rocket will include a constant thrust force until burnout, at which time the thrust drops to zero. The vertical acceleration $\ddot{y}$ must be expressed differently during the burn and after the burnout. Therefore, $\ddot{y}$ (CSMP variable name YDDOT) is used as the output of a PROCEDURE function, and FORTRAN logic is employed to transfer control to the correct arithmetic assignment statement defining $\ddot{y}$. The complete CSMP program is as follows:

```
INITIAL
  CONSTANT THRUST=7000.,DK=.008,G=32.17,BURNTM=60.
  INCON YO=0.0,YDOTO=0.0
  A=G*THRUST
  B=DK*G

DYNAMIC
PROCEDURE YDDOT=FUNCT(A,G,BURNTM,TIME,B,YDOT)
      IF(TIME.GE.BURNTM) GO TO 1
      W=3000.-40.*TIME
      YDDOT=A/W-G-B/W*YDOT**2
      GO TO 2
    1 YDDOT=-G-B/(3000.-40.*BURNTM)*SIGN(YDOT**2,YDOT)
    2 CONTINUE
ENDPRO
  YDOT=INTGRL(YDOTO,YDDOT)
  Y=INTGRL(YO,YDOT)

  TIMER DELT=0.1,OUTDEL=2.0,FINTIM=200.
  METHOD RKSFX
  LABEL DYNAMIC CHARACTERISTICS OF A ROCKET
  PRTPLOT YDDOT,YDOT,Y
  END
  STOP
ENDJOB
```

The PROCEDURE consists of the group of statments beginning with the translation control statement having the label PROCEDURE, and it ends with the translation control statement having the label ENDPRO. This group of statements may be inserted anywhere in the Dynamic segment since it will be sorted as a group, but there is no internal sorting of statements within the PROCEDURE.

The following rules govern the writing of PROCEDURE functions:

1. The first line of the PROCEDURE is a translation control statement with the label PROCEDURE. The label is followed by at least one required blank separating the label from the ouputs of the PROCEDURE. In this example there is only one output, YDDOT, but in general there may be any number of outputs. If there are several outputs, they are separated by commas like the outputs in the canonical statement of a MACRO definition. A PROCEDURE statement on which two outputs are given might appear as

```
PROCEDURE SDDOT,THDOT=FOFV(D,M,V,THETA)
```

The output, or outputs, of the PROCEDURE are to the left of the equal sign, while the function name and the input variables of the function are to the right of the equal sign. The input variables are enclosed in parentheses and are separated by commas. The function name in the example being discussed is FUNCT, and the input variables are A, G, BURNTM, TIME, B, and YDOT. A CSMP PROCEDURE function name is just a dummy name because it is not used to reference the function and appears only on the line with the label PROCEDURE. It appears to serve no purpose, but it is required. Any arbitrary name will serve the purpose.
2. In the example program the variable YDDOT is defined within the PROCEDURE. Note that YDDOT appears on the PROCEDURE line as an output. If the function had more than one output, all the variable names for the output variables would be defined in statements following the PROCEDURE statement. Variables other than outputs may also be defined in a PROCEDURE, but they are not available for output by use of the CSMP PRINT or PRTPLOT (print-plot) output control statements. Variables which are defined in a PROCEDURE must be listed as outputs of the PROCEDURE function if they are to appear in output control statements.
3. The PROCEDURE is terminated by a translation control statement with the label ENDPRO.

Note that a PROCEDURE function is used differently from a MACRO function. The statements defining a MACRO are placed ahead of the INITIAL segment, and then the function is referenced as often as desired in the structure statements that follow by using a statement having the same format as the canonical statement of the MACRO definition. The statements defining a PROCEDURE are generally placed right where they are used since a PROCEDURE function is not referenced. It is generally used just once (once at each time interval of the simulation if it appears in the Dynamic segment). The only way it can be used more than once is to embed it in a MACRO definition which may then be referenced a number of times. By embedding a PROCEDURE within a MACRO, it becomes possible to use executable FORTRAN statements, including branching and input/output statements, in the MACRO. However, if a FORTRAN output or input statement is used in a PROCEDURE embedded in a MACRO, the accompanying FORMAT statement should be placed in the Terminal segment, since a FORMAT statement cannot be used in a MACRO. Although a PROCEDURE can be embedded in a MACRO, it should be noted that one PROCEDURE cannot be embedded within another PROCEDURE.

• *The* NOSORT *Statement.* This statement defines the beginning of a section in which statements are not reordered by the translator. Full use of FORTRAN, including the use of branching and input and output, is permissible in an unsorted section. Continuation of the FORTRAN statements, if necessary, is done by CSMP rules, however. An unsorted section would be used in the Initial or Dynamic segments since they are normally sorted. An unsorted section is terminated by a SORT statement or by the statement indicating the beginning of the next segment (Dynamic or Terminal).

If an unsorted section appears in the middle of the Dynamic segment, the Dynamic segment will be separated into three distinct parts, a first part prior to the NOSORT statement, the part following this statement up to a SORT statement, and the part following the SORT statement. The first and third parts will be sorted, but the sorting is confined to within the parts; the translator will not reorder the statements so that they move from the first part to the third part or vice versa.

• *The* SORT *Statement.* This statement defines the beginning of a section in which statements are sorted by the translator. The section is terminated by a NOSORT statement or by the end of the segment.

• DATA *and* ENDDATA *Statements.* If the programmer uses a FORTRAN READ statement (usually placed in a NOSORT section of the Initial segment), he must of course have data statements available for reading. These data statements are placed between CSMP statements having the labels DATA and ENDDATA, and this group of statements follows the END statement. The DATA statement informs the translator that the statements which follow are not CSMP statements and are to be skipped over by the translator. The label ENDDATA must be in columns 1 through 7.

Execution Control Statements

These statements are concerned with the actual execution of the simulation, such as specifying the step size for the integration routine, the finish time for the run, and so forth. They consist of a statement label followed by at least one blank, and then by certain assignments that are made on that particular statement. An execution control statement called a TIMER might appear as follows:

```
TIMER DELT=0.1, PRDEL=0.2, FINTIM=20.0
```

TIMER is the label, while DELT=0.1, PRDEL=0.2, and FINTIM=20.0 are assignments assigning values to the step size for integration, the print increment for output, and the total run time, respectively. As can be seen, successive assignments are separated by commas, Execution control statement labels are TIMER, FINISH, RELERR, ABSERR, and METHOD. Each is explained in the following discussion.

• *The TIMER Statement.* This statement allows the programmer to specify the values of certain system variables as illustrated in the preceding paragraph. These variables all have *reserved* names and will be discussed in turn below.

DELT   This is the name reserved for the increment of the independent variable. The programmer should assign a value to DELT which is a submultiple of the output increment PRDEL and OUTDEL. This would normally be done by choosing a value for DELT first and then making PRDEL and OUTDEL multiples of the chosen value of DELT. If the programmer does not make DELT a submultiple of PRDEL and OUTDEL, the translator adjusts DELT to be a submultiple of the smaller of the two output increments. If neither of the latter has been specified, DELT is made a submultiple of FINTIM/100. If DELT is not specified by the programmer, the translator will assign it a value equal to one-sixteenth of the smaller of PRDEL or OUTDEL, if either or both of the latter have been specified. In general, the programmer should always assign a value of DELT rather than depending upon the translator to assign the value. Roundoff error in the time increment can be avoided by assigning DELT a value equal to $1/2^n$, where n is an integer. Such values (as, for example, .015625 or .0078125) are expressed exactly in binary form.

DELMIN   Two of the integration routines which may be used (the fifth-order predictor-corrector Milne method and the fourth-order Runge-Kutta with variable interval) have an adjustable step size, the adjustment being made based on the results of an error analysis at each step. DELMIN is used to specify a minimum value of DELT. That is, DELT will not be adjustable to less than the value of DELMIN.

FINTIM   This is the maximum value of the independent variable specified for the simulation. In general, FINTIM should be assigned a value which is a multiple of the output increments PRDEL and/or OUTDEL. If this rule is not observed, the translator will adjust its value to the largest multiple of the smallest output increment which is less than the specified value of FINTIM. A value must always be specified for FINTIM, even though the simulation may be terminated before that value is reached. For if a value is not specified, FINTIM is set equal to zero by the translator, and the simulation cannot get started. The independent variable may not always attain the value of FINTIM if the simulation is halted by a FINISH condition (see discussion of the FINISH statement later in this section).

PRDEL   In a simulation study the values of certain variables are normally required as output at specified increments of the independent variable. If these variable values are to be just printed out (not plotted), the output increment has the reserved name PRDEL, and it is assigned a value in the TIMER statement. The smaller of PRDEL and OUTDEL should be a submultiple of the larger, or the smaller will be adjusted so that this is true by the translator. A value of PRDEL should normally always be specified if it is to be used, but if the programmer neglects to do so, its value will be set equal to the value specified for OUTDEL. If a value has not been specified for the latter, the value of PRDEL will be set to FINTIM/100.

OUTDEL   If any of the variables are to have their output values print-plotted, the output increment is called OUTDEL. The programmer should assign a value to OUTDEL if there ia a PRTPLOT statement specifying that certain variables are to have their values print-plotted. If an OUTDEL value is required, but the programmer fails to assign a value, OUTDEL is assigned the value of PRDEL if a value has been specified for the latter. If not, OUTDEL is set equal to FINTIM/100 by the translator. If both PRDEL and OUTDEL are used, the smaller of the two should be a submultiple of the larger, or the smaller will be adjusted by the translator to make it so.

• *The* FINISH *Statement.* Utilizing a FINISH statement, the user can specify conditions for terminating the run other than having the independent value reach a value equal to that of FINTIM. For example, in the rocket problem on page 654 which was used to illustrate a procedure function, a value of 200 sec was used for FINTIM. If the programmer preferred to stop the run when the altitude reached 43,000 ft if this occurred before 200 sec, the FINISH statement could be entered as

```
FINISH Y=43000.
```

Several finish conditions can be specified if desired. Using the rocket problem again as an example, the user might decide to stop the run when the altitude reached 43,000 ft or when the value of $\dot{y}$ became negative. The FINISH statement might then appear as

```
FINISH Y=43000.,YDOT=-.0001
```

Note that YDOT is set equal to a small negative value rather than zero. This is done because the initial value of YDOT is zero, and the FINISH condition would stop the simulation immediately if YDOT were specified as zero in the FINISH statement. As soon as one of the variables Y or YDOT reaches or crosses the specified bound, the run will terminate.

A variable can be used on the right of the equal sign instead of a constant. The specification

```
FINISH X1-X2
```

would cause the run to terminate when X1 and X2 were equal or when their difference changed sign. Up to ten finish conditions can be specified. Finish specifications for one run can be nullified for a subsequent run by means of a RESET statement placed after the END or CONTINUE statement. The RESET statement will be discussed subsequently.

• *The* RELERR *and* ABSERR *Statements.* In the fourth-order Runge-Kutta integration routine with variable step size, the step size is reduced until the following criterion is satisfied:

$$\frac{Y_{t+\Delta t} - Y^s}{A + R|Y_{t+\Delta t}|} \leq 1$$

where Y^s is $Y_{t+\Delta t}$ calculated by Simpson's rule and where A is the *absolute error* and R is the *relative error*. In Milne's fifth-order predictor-corrector method, the step size is reduced until the following criteria are satisfied:

$$\frac{.04|Y^c - Y^p|}{R|Y^c|} \leq 1 \qquad \text{for} \qquad |Y^c| > 1$$

or

$$\frac{.04|Y^c - Y^p|}{R} \leq 1 \qquad \text{for} \qquad |Y^c| \leq 1$$

where Y^p is the predicted value of $Y_{t+\Delta t}$, Y^c is the corrected value, and R is the relative error. The absolute error A and the relative error R may be specified by the programmer. If RELERR is not specified, a value of .0001 will be used. ABSERR is used only with the fourth-order Runge-Kutta method. If it is not specified, .001 is used. The following statements illustrate the specification of relative error and absolute error values.

```
ABSERR XDOT= .0005,X= .0003
RELERR XDOT= .0002,X= .0002
```

• *The* METHOD *Statement.* A method statement consists of the label METHOD followed by a required blank and the name of the integration routine which the programmer wants used for the simulation. One of the following names may be used:

MILNE
This specifies the use of Milne's fifth-order predictor-corrector method with variable step size.

RKSFX
This name specifies that the fourth-order Runge-Kutta method with fixed step size will be used.

RKS
This specifies the fourth-order Runge-Kutta method with variable integration interval. It is the default method which is used if the METHOD statement is omitted.

SIMP
A method based on Simpson's integration rule is specified by this name.

TRAPZ
This name specifies the use of a second-order method variously known as a modified Euler method, an improved Euler method, or the Euler-Gauss method in which a predicted value is obtained by Euler's method (rectangular integration) and a corrected value by trapezoidal integration.

ADAMS
This specifies the use of the second-order Adams integration routine.

RECT
This specifies the use of Euler's method, which employs rectangular integration.

Output Control Statements

Output control statements specify such things as the variable whose values are to be printed and/or print-plotted at specified increments of the independent variable, and page headings for printed or print-plotted output. Their detailed description follows.

• *The* PRINT *Statement.* If the programmer wants values of certain variables printed at each PRDEL interval, he lists those variables, separated by commas, in a PRINT statement as follows:

PRINT X,XD,Y,YD

The label PRINT is followed by at least one required blank. TIME should not be listed in the PRINT statement since it is always printed out automatically when other variables are listed for printing. Listing TIME in the PRINT statement will result in values of TIME being printed *twice* at each interval.

If eight or fewer variables are listed in the PRINT statement, the output will be in column form with the variable names printed as column headings. The independent variable (usually TIME) will be printed in a column at the left side of the page. If 9 to 49 variables are listed in the PRINT statement, the output will be in equation form, such as

X=2.2000E 00

Output values in both column form and equation form have the most significant digit to the left of the decimal point and four digits following the decimal point. Following the number is an E and then a power of 10 by which the number is multiplied.

Only one PRINT statement should be used for each run. If more than one is included, only the last will be used. The PRINT statement can be continued to additional lines by the use of three periods, as previously explained for other kinds of statements. Only real variables should have their values printed out with a PRINT statement. If integer variables are used in a program and their values are to be printed out, their values should be assigned to real variables and the real variable names should appear in the PRINT statement.

• *The* TITLE *Statement.* This statement is used to specify page headings for each page of printed output. It consists of the label TITLE, at least one required blank, and then the heading the user wants to have printed at the top of each page. A typical TITLE statement might be

```
TITLE DYNAMIC CHARACTERISTICS OF A MECHANICAL SYSTEM
                                        WITH BACKLASH
```

No columns beyond number 72 can be used and a TITLE statement cannot be continued. However, several TITLE statements can be used, and this will result in an equal number of lines in the page headings.

• *The* PRTPLOT *Statement.* Using this statement, the programmer specifies the variables whose values are to be plotted versus time, as well as printed. Fig. 9-2 shows a portion of a PRTPLOT output. The PRTPLOT statement used was

```
PRTPLOT XDOT,X,FOFX
```

XDOT versus time is first plotted, with numerical values of TIME and XDOT printed in columns at the left of the page. It is a portion of this first print-plot which is shown in Fig. 9-2. This print-plot is followed by print-plots of X versus time and FOFX versus time.

A statement

```
PRTPLOT XDOT(X,FOFX),XDDOT
```

would cause XDOT to be print-plotted versus time and values of X and FOFX to be printed in columns to the right of the plot. A print-plot of XDDOT versus time would follow. Up to a maximum of three variables can be enclosed in parentheses and printed alongside a print-plot. If constants appear inside parentheses, they specify lower and upper bounds for the print-plot. For example, if the statement

```
PRTPLOT XDOT(-6.0,6.0,X)
```

```
SPRING MASS VISCOUSLY DAMPED WITH DEADSPACE                              PAGE    1

                                MINIMUM          XDOT   VERSUS TIME        MAXIMUM
                                -6.00C0E 00                                6.00C0E 00
   TIME           XDOT          I                                          I        X
0.C             8.CCC0E 00      ---------------------------------------------* 0.0
2.0000E-01      7.0260E 00      ---------------------------------------------* 1.5652E 00
4.0000E-01     -1.2600E 00      --------------------+                          2.2287E 00
6.00C0E-01     -7.6546E 00      *                                             1.1950E 00
8.0000E-01     -7.5684E 00      *                                            -3.3390E-01
1.0000E 00     -6.4425E 00      *                                            -1.7783E 00
1.2000E 00     -2.9556E 00      --------------+                              -2.7490E 00
1.4000E 00      1.5774E 00      ---------------------------+                 -2.8899E 00
1.6000E 00      5.4257E 00      -----------------------------------+         -2.1644E 00
1.8000E 00      7.1513E 00      ----------------------------------------*    -8.6312E-01
2.C000E 00      7.0575E 00      ----------------------------------------*     5.6198E-01
2.2000E 00      4.4652E 00      --------------------------------+             1.8429E 00
2.4000E 00     -3.6666E 00      ----------+                                   1.9319E 00
2.6000E 00     -6.8152E 00      *                                             7.3890E-01
2.8000E 00     -6.6794E 00      *                                            -6.1059E-01
3.C000E 00     -5.2724E 00      ---+                                         -1.8461E 00
3.2000E 00     -1.9046E 00      -----------------+                           -2.5871E 00
3.4000E 00      2.1145E 00      -------------------------+                   -2.5640E 00
3.6000E 00      5.2571E 00      -----------------------------------+         -1.8005E 00
3.8000E 00      6.3542E 00      --------------------------------------*      -5.9935E-01
4.0000E 00      6.2284E 00      --------------------------------------*       6.5887E-01
4.2000E 00      3.7195E 00      ----------------------------+                 1.7724E 00
4.4000E 00     -3.4711E 00      -----------+                                  1.7982E 00
4.6000E 00     -6.0133E 00      *                                             7.2534E-01
4.8000E 00     -5.8943E 00      +                                            -4.6538E-01
5.C000E 00     -4.9065E 00      ----+                                        -1.5809E 00
5.2000E 00     -2.0984E 00      -----------------+                           -2.3043E 00
5.4000E 00      1.4455E 00      ------------------------+                    -2.3706E 00
5.6000E 00      4.3741E 00      -------------------------------+             -1.7677E 00
5.8000E 00      5.5945E 00      ---------------------------------------+     -7.3634E-01
6.C000E 00      5.4951E 00      ---------------------------------------+      3.7373E-01
6.2000E 00      4.6239E 00      --------------------------------+             1.4395E 00
6.4000E 00     -1.2296E 00      --------------------+                         1.8297E 00
6.6000E 00     -5.2816E 00      --+                                           1.0749E 00
6.8000E 00     -5.2013E 00      ---+                                          2.4212E-02
7.C000E 00     -4.9431E 00      ----+                                        -1.0017E 00
7.2000E 00     -3.1837E 00      -----------+                                 -1.8415E 00
7.4000E 00     -2.5824E-01      ------------------------+                    -2.1964E 00
7.6000E 00      2.7067E 00      ---------------------------------+           -1.9422E 00
7.8000E 00      4.5920E 00      ---------------------------------------+     -1.1867E 00
8.C000E 00      4.8491E 00      ----------------------------------------+    -2.2138E-01
8.2000E 00      4.7531E 00      ----------------------------------------+     7.3881E-01
8.4000E 00      2.8427E 00      --------------------------+                   1.5889E 00
8.6000E 00     -2.6444E 00      --------------+                               1.6096E 00
8.8000E 00     -4.5890E 00      -----+                                        7.9124E-01
9.C000E 00     -4.4981E 00      ------+                                      -1.1744E-01
9.2000E 00     -4.2242E 00      -------+                                     -1.0023E 00
9.4000E 00     -2.6129E 00      ---------------+                             -1.7088E 00
9.6000E 00     -4.7599E-02      -------------------------+                   -1.9831E 00
9.8000E 00      2.4842E 00      --------------------------------+            -1.7303E 00
1.0000E 01      4.0293E 00      -----------------------------------+         -1.0561E 00
```

Figure 9-14   Print-plot with upper and lower bounds

appeared in the program on page 632, the XDOT output would appear as shown in Fig. 9-14. Note that the plot of XDOT is "clipped" at 6.0 and −6.0. Comparing this plot with the print-plot of XDOT in Fig. 9-2, it can be seen that the scale for XDOT has been altered so that the clipped plot uses the same page width as the unclipped plot. The printed values of XDOT are the same in the two figures; that is, the printed values are not subject to the bound specified for the plot. If no lower bound is desired, but an upper bound is to be specified, the statement would appear as

```
PRTPLOT XDOT(,6.0,X)
```

If neither bound were specified, the statement would be

```
PRTPLOT XDOT(X)
```

PRTPLOT statements cannot be continued, but several of them may be used, if required, up to a maximum of ten statements for each simulation.

• **The** LABEL **Statement.** The LABEL statement(s) specify page headings for print-plot output. LABEL statements cannot be continued, and multiple LABEL statements cannot be used to obtain multiple lines of page headings. If more than one LABEL statement is used, the first will specify the page headings for the print-plot specified by the first PRTPLOT statement, the second will be associated with the second PRTPLOT statement, and so forth. If there are more PRTPLOT statements than LABEL statements, the print-plots specified by the excess PRTPLOT statements will not have page headings. To nullify a LABEL statement of a previous run prior to a subsequent run, a RESET statement is used, as will be explained later.

• **The** RANGE **Statement.** If the user does not need a complete printout or print-plot of one or more variables, but is interested only in the maximum and/ or minimum values reached by the variables and the times at which these values are reached, these can be obtained with the use of a RANGE statement. For example, in the paratrooper problem of Ex. 6-2, the most pertinent information is the time at which the minimum velocity of the paratrooper is reached. A RANGE statement can be used to obtain this. A PRINT or PRTPLOT statement need not appear in the program. A CSMP program for solving the paratrooper problem is given here, and it is suggested that the reader study the example problem referred to and correlate it with the program, which is

```
INCON XDO=440.,YDO=0.0
CONSTANT TERM=160.,G=32.17
XDD=-G/TERM**2*SQRT(XD**2+YD**2)*XD
YDD=G-G/TERM**2*SQRT(XD**2+YD**2)*YD
XD=INTGRL(XDO,XDD)
YD=INTGRL(YDO,YDD)
V=SQRT(XD**2+YD**2)
TIMER DELT=0.1,FINTIM=20.0
METHOD TRAPZ
RANGE V
END
STOP
ENDJOB
```

This program is an example of one which has only one segment, the Dynamic segment. In such a case, the label DYNAMIC is not required. The printout from this program is

VARIABLE	PROBLEM DURATION 0.0		TO 2.0000E 01	
	MINIMUM	TIME	MAXIMUM	TIME
V	1.4351E 02	6.4000E 00	4.4000E 02	0.0

RANGE statements can be continued by the use of three decimal points, and up to 100 variables can appear in a RANGE statement. In the case of a sequence of runs due to a multiple-value parameter, the values provided by the RANGE statement are for the entire sequence, and the accompanying time value applies just to one run of the sequence. There is nothing in the printout indicating in which run the maximum or minimum occurred. If a CONTINUE statement is used with a RANGE statement following the CONTINUE statement, the values provided are the minimum and maximum values reached during the period following the first finish time. If the RANGE statement precedes the CONTINUE statement, maximum and minimum values will be provided for the periods preceding and following the first finish time. If no range printout is desired for the period following the first finish time, a RESET RANGE statement can be used following the CONTINUE statement to nullify the RANGE specification. In addition, a RANGE specification for one run can be nullified for a subsequent run by use of a RESET statement. Ranges (minimum and maximum values) are automatically printed for all PRTPLOT variables.

• *The* RESET *Statement.* If a program is to run several times because of the use of several END statements, the user can nullify certain specifications used for one or more of the runs by the use of a RESET statement. Then subsequent runs will have that particular specification canceled and the user can enter new specifications if this is desired. RESET can be used to nullify PRINT, PRTPLOT, RANGE, LABEL, RELERR, ABSERR, and FINISH specifications. The statement

```
RESET PRTPLOT
```

would nullify the print-plot specifications of previous runs *and* also all previous LABEL specifications. However, the statement

```
RESET LABEL
```

nullifies only the previous LABEL specifications.

If a statement with just the label RESET on it is used, all previous PRINT, PRTPLOT, RANGE, and LABEL specifications are canceled.

TITLE specifications cannot be nullified by RESET but use of a new TITLE statement after an END or CONTINUE statement will cancel all previous TITLE specifications.

The RESET statement should follow immediately after the END or CONTINUE statement. Use of RESET will be illustrated under "CSMP Examples—Run Control."

9-9 CSMP EXAMPLES—RUN CONTROL

We have previously mentioned several methods for automatically producing a sequence of runs with different data or control statements. We will next consider some examples illustrating these methods, as well as other CSMP features.

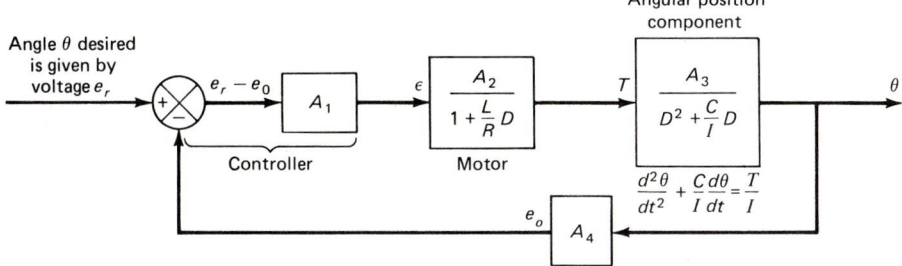

Figure 9-15 Block diagram of an angular-position controller servomechanism

The simplest method for obtaining a sequence of runs where only one parameter, initial condition, or constant is to be changed in value is to specify the multiple values of the quantity on a data statement. The following example illustrates this procedure.

EXAMPLE 9-1

Control systems are often presented in block-diagram form in which the transfer functions of the various system components are shown in blocks. This is illustrated by the diagram of an angular-position controller servomechanism as shown in Fig. 9-15. Following is the data for the system:

L/R = 0.01 sec

c = 0.09 lb-ft/(radians/sec)

I = 0.1 lb-sec^2-ft

A_1 = 5.0

A_2 = 0.01 lb-ft/volt

A_3 = $1/I$ = 10.0 lb^{-1}-sec^{-2}-ft^{-1}

A_4 = 20.0, 10.0, 5.0 volts/radian

It is desired to find the response of the system to a sudden change of the set point voltage, e_r, from 0 to 2 volts and a value of A_4 for suitable system stability. Therefore A_4 is given multiple values on the PARAMETER card. There is a System Macro, the first order lag function (REALPL), which gives the output of a block such as the one representing the motor for a given input and initial condition. There is no System Macro corresponding to the block for the angular position component, so the second-order differential equation for this component is obtained from the transfer function and the INTGRL function used twice to obtain the output θ.

The variable names and the quantities which they represent in the CSMP program are as follows:

Variable Name	Quantity
ESUBR	Set point voltage, e_r, volts
EOUT	Feedback voltage, e_0, which is proportional to the output angle θ, volts
TAU2	$\tau_2 = L/R$, sec
THETA	Output angle, θ, radians
A1,A2,A4	Component gains
RPOLE	Variable name to which the value of the function REALPL is assigned
COEFF	Variable name to which the value of c/I is assigned
C	Damping constant, lb-ft/(radians/sec)
I	Mass moment of inertia of the angular-position component, lb-sec²-ft
TORQUE	Torque output of motor, lb-ft
EPSI	A voltage proportion to $e_r - e_0$
TH2DOT	Angular acceleration of angular-position component, radians/sec²
THDOT	Angular velocity of angular position component, radians/sec
ST	Name to which the value of the step function is assigned
RS	Name to which value of TORQUE/I is assigned

The CSMP program from the block diagram is as follows:

```
INITIAL
 COEFF=C/I
 PARAMETER TAU2=.01,A1=5.,A2=.01,A4=(20.,10.,5.),C=.09,I=.1
DYNAMIC
      RS=TORQUE/I
      TH2DOT=RS-COEFF*THDOT
      THDOT=INTGRL(0.0,TH2DOT)
      TH=INTGRL(0.0,THDOT)
      EOUT=TH*A4
      ERROR=ESUBR-EOUT
      ST=STEP(.5)
      ESUBR=2.*ST
      EPSI=A1*ERROR
      RPOLE=REALPL(0.0,TAU2,EPSI)
      TORQUE=A2*RPOLE
METHOD RKSFX
TIMER DELT=.01,FINTIM=15.,OUTDEL=.05,PRDEL=.05
PRINT TORQUE,ERROR,EPSI,EOUT,ESUBR
LABEL REMOTE POSITION CONTROL SYSTEM
PRTPLT TH
END
STOP
ENDJOB
```

CSMP   RKSFX

TIME	TORQUE	ERROR	EPSI	EOUT	ESUBR
0.0	0.0	0.0	0.0	0.0	0.0
5.0000E-02	0.0	0.0	0.0	0.0	0.0
1.0000E-01	0.0	0.0	0.0	0.0	0.0
1.5000E-01	0.0	0.0	0.0	0.0	0.0
2.0000E-01	0.0	0.0	0.0	0.0	0.0
2.5000E-01	0.0	0.0	0.0	0.0	0.0
3.0000E-01	0.0	0.0	0.0	0.0	0.0
3.5000E-01	0.0	0.0	0.0	0.0	0.0
4.0000E-01	0.0	0.0	0.0	0.0	0.0
4.5000E-01	0.0	0.0	0.0	0.0	0.0
5.0000E-01	0.0	2.0000E 00	1.0000E 01	0.0	2.0000E 00
5.5000E-01	9.8720E-02	1.9832E 00	9.9162E 00	1.6752E-02	2.0000E 00
6.0000E-01	9.6789E-01	1.9206E 00	9.603CE 00	7.94C0E-02	2.0000E 00
6.5000E-01	9.1872E-02	1.8135E 00	9.0675E 00	1.8650E-01	2.0000E 00
7.0000E-01	8.4898E-02	1.6663E 00	8.3314E 00	3.3372E-01	2.0000E 00
7.5000E-01	7.6123E-02	1.4841E 00	7.4206E 00	5.1587E-01	2.0000E 00
8.0000E-01	6.5832E-02	1.2729E 00	6.3643E 00	7.2715E-01	2.0000E 00
8.5000E-01	5.4336E-02	1.0388E 00	5.1938E 00	9.6125E-01	2.0000E 00
9.0000E-01	4.1962E-02	7.8845E-01	3.9422E 00	1.2116E 00	2.0000E 00
9.5000E-01	2.9049E-02	5.2869E-01	2.6434E 00	1.4713E 00	2.0000E 00
1.0000E 00	1.5931E-02	2.6619E-01	1.3310E 00	1.7338E 00	2.0000E 00
1.0500E 00	2.5386E-03	7.4730E-03	3.7365E-02	1.9925E 00	2.0000E 00
1.1000E 00	-9.6169E-03	-2.4129E-01	-1.2065E 00	2.2413E 00	2.0000E 00
1.1500E 00	-2.1446E-02	-4.7441E-01	-2.3721E 00	2.4744E 00	2.0000E 00
1.2000E 00	-3.2287E-02	-6.8682E-01	-3.4341E 00	2.6868E 00	2.0000E 00
1.2500E 00	-4.1915E-02	-8.7411E-01	-4.3706E 00	2.8741E 00	2.0000E 00
1.3000E 00	-5.0141E-02	-1.0327E 00	-5.1636E 00	3.0327E 00	2.0000E 00
1.3500E 00	-5.6820E-02	-1.1599E 00	-5.7994E 00	3.1599E 00	2.0000E 00
1.4000E 00	-6.1850E-02	-1.2537E 00	-6.2686E 00	3.2537E 00	2.0000E 00
1.4500E 00	-6.5171E-02	-1.3133E 00	-6.5663E 00	3.3133E 00	2.0000E 00
1.5000E 00	-6.6770E-02	-1.3384E 00	-6.6919E 00	3.3384E 00	2.0000E 00
1.5500E 00	-6.6675E-02	-1.3298E 00	-6.6490E 00	3.3298E 00	2.0000E 00
1.6000E 00	-6.4954E-02	-1.2891E 00	-6.4454E 00	3.2891E 00	2.0000E 00
1.6500E 00	-6.1715E-02	-1.2185E 00	-6.0923E 00	3.2185E 00	2.0000E 00
1.7000E 00	-5.7094E-02	-1.1208E 00	-5.6042E 00	3.1208E 00	2.0000E 00
1.7500E 00	-5.1259E-02	-9.9967E-01	-4.9983E 00	2.9997E 00	2.0000E 00
1.8000E 00	-4.4401E-02	-8.5881E-01	-4.2941E 00	2.8588E 00	2.0000E 00
1.8500E 00	-3.6727E-02	-7.0249E-01	-3.5125E 00	2.7025E 00	2.0000E 00
1.9000E 00	-2.8456E-02	-5.3514E-01	-2.6757E 00	2.5351E 00	2.0000E 00
1.9500E 00	-1.9813E-02	-3.6126E-01	-1.8063E 00	2.3613E 00	2.0000E 00
2.0000E 00	-1.1026E-02	-1.8537E-01	-9.2685E-01	2.1854E 00	2.0000E 00
2.0500E 00	-2.3129E-03	-1.1843E-02	-5.9214E-02	2.0118E 00	2.0000E 00
2.1000E 00	6.1150E-03	1.5518E-01	7.7589E-01	1.8448E 00	2.0000E 00
2.1500E 00	1.4063E-02	3.1186E-01	1.5593E 00	1.6881E 00	2.0000E 00
2.2000E 00	2.1357E-02	4.5479E-01	2.2740E 00	1.5452E 00	2.0000E 00
2.2500E 00	2.7843E-02	5.81C1E-01	2.9050E 00	1.4190E 00	2.0000E 00
2.3000E 00	3.3394E-02	6.8808E-01	3.4404E 00	1.3119E 00	2.0000E 00
2.3500E 00	3.7913E-02	7.7415E-01	3.8708E 00	1.2258E 00	2.0000E 00
2.4000E 00	4.1327E-02	8.3754E-01	4.1897E 00	1.1621E 00	2.0000E 00
2.4500E 00	4.3599E-02	8.7875E-01	4.3937E 00	1.1213E 00	2.0000E 00
2.5000E 00	4.4716E-02	8.9649E-01	4.4825E 00	1.1035E 00	2.0000E 00
2.5500E 00	4.4697E-02	8.9164E-01	4.4582E 00	1.1084E 00	2.0000E 00
2.6000E 00	4.3586E-02	8.6519E-01	4.3260E 00	1.1348E 00	2.0000E 00
2.6500E 00	4.1455E-02	8.1864E-01	4.0932E 00	1.1814E 00	2.0000E 00
2.7000E 00	3.8394E-02	7.5392E-01	3.7696E 00	1.2461E 00	2.0000E 00

Figure 9-16   Printed output resulting from the PRINT statement

Portions of the printed output and the print-plot output are shown in Figs. 9-16 and 9-17. Although CSMP rules do not prohibit multiplying the System Macro REALPL by a variable, experience reveals that when this is done, the FORTRAN compiler may produce a message indicating that it is an unresolved external reference. Thus, the value of REALPL is first assigned to the variable RPOLE, and the RPOLE is multiplied by A2.

EXAMPLE 9-2

A second method of obtaining sequential runs is by using several END statements followed by new data and/or control specifications. Each run obtained by this method could be a sequence of runs obtained by a multiple-value parameter. To illustrate this, let us consider the following problem. Figure 9-18 represents a simplified model of an automobile suspension system where the automobile is traveling over a bumpy road approximated by a sine curve.

REMOTE POSITION CONTROL SYSTEM   PAGE   1

```
                         MINIMUM         TH      VERSUS TIME       MAXIMUM
                         0.0             A3     = 2.0000E 01       5.6188E-01
   TIME         TH         I                                           I
0.0           0.0          +
5.0000E-02    0.0          +
1.0000E-01    0.0          +
1.5000E-01    0.0          +
2.0000E-01    0.0          +
2.5000E-01    0.0          +
3.0000E-01    0.0          +
3.5000E-01    0.0          +
4.0000E-01    0.0          +
4.5000E-01    0.0          +
5.0000E-01    0.0          +
5.5000E-01    8.3759E-04    +
6.0000E-01    3.9700E-03    +
6.5000E-01    9.3251E-03    +
7.0000E-01    1.6686E-02   -+
7.5000E-01    2.5794E-02   --+
8.0000E-01    3.6357E-02   ---+
8.5000E-01    4.8062E-02   ----+
9.0000E-01    6.0578E-02   -----+
9.5000E-01    7.3566E-02   ------+
1.0000E 00    8.6690E-02   -------+
1.0500E 00    9.9626E-02   --------+
1.1000E 00    1.1206E-01   ---------+
1.1500E 00    1.2372E-01   ----------+
1.2000E 00    1.3434E-01   ----------+
1.2500E 00    1.4371E-01   -----------+
1.3000E 00    1.5164E-01   ------------+
1.3500E 00    1.5799E-01   ------------+
1.4000E 00    1.6269E-01   -------------+
1.4500E 00    1.6566E-01   -------------+
1.5000E 00    1.6692E-01   -------------+
1.5500E 00    1.6649E-01   -------------+
1.6000E 00    1.6445E-01   -------------+
1.6500E 00    1.6092E-01   -------------+
1.7000E 00    1.5604E-01   ------------+
1.7500E 00    1.4998E-01   -----------+
1.8000E 00    1.4294E-01   -----------+
1.8500E 00    1.3512E-01   ----------+
1.9000E 00    1.2676E-01   ---------+
1.9500E 00    1.1806E-01   ---------+
2.0000E 00    1.0927E-01   --------+
2.0500E 00    1.0059E-01   -------+
2.1000E 00    9.2241E-02   -------+
2.1500E 00    8.4407E-02   ------+
2.2000E 00    7.7260E-02   ------+
2.2500E 00    7.0950E-02   -----+
2.3000E 00    6.5596E-02   -----+
2.3500E 00    6.1292E-02   -----+
2.4000E 00    5.8103E-02   -----+
2.4500E 00    5.6063E-02   ----+
2.5000E 00    5.5175E-02   ----+
```

Figure 9-17 Print-plot output resulting from the PRTPLOT statement

Figure 9-18 Simplified model of an automobile suspension system

The motion of the car body, x_1, is desired for various values of damping between the car and the wheel for various automobile speeds.

Application of Newton's second law to masses m_1 and m_2 results in the following simultaneous second-order differential equations describing the system

$$\ddot{x}_1 + \frac{c}{m_1}\dot{x}_1 + \frac{k_1}{m_1}x_1 = \frac{c}{m_1}\dot{x}_2 + \frac{k_1}{m_1}x_2 \tag{9-4}$$

$$\ddot{x}_2 + \frac{c}{m_2}\dot{x}_2 + x_2\left(\frac{k_1 + k_2}{m_2}\right) = \frac{c}{m_2}\dot{x}_1 + \frac{k_1}{m_1}x_1 + \frac{k_2}{6m_2}\sin\frac{2\pi vt}{20} \tag{9-5}$$

Displacements x_1 and x_2 are measured from the static equilibrium positions of masses m_1 and m_2. The initial conditions for the problem are

$$t = 0.0 \begin{vmatrix} x_1 = 0.0 \\ \dot{x}_1 = 0.0 \\ x_2 = 0.0 \\ \dot{x}_2 = 0.0 \end{vmatrix}$$

The problem data are given as

$m_1 = \frac{1}{4}$ the mass of the automobile $= 25$ slugs

$m_2 = $ mass of one wheel $= 2$ slugs

$k_1 = $ spring constant $= 1000$ lb/ft

$k_2 = $ linear spring constant of tire $= 4500$ lb/ft

$c = $ damping constant of dashpot $= 0, 25, 50,$ and 75 lb-sec/ft

$x_1 = $ displacement of automobile body from equilibrium position, ft

$x_2 = $ displacement of wheel from equilibrium position, ft

$x_3 = $ variable describing the profile of the roadway, ft

$v = $ velocity of car $= 30, 60, 90,$ and 120 ft/sec

The automobile velocity will be used as a multiple-value parameter. Each sequence of runs (due to the multiple-value parameter) except the last will be terminated by an END statement followed by a new specification for the damping constant c. A RESET LABEL statement will be used to nullify the LABEL specification of the previous run and a new LABEL will be specified for the subsequent sequence of runs. The last sequence with the damping coefficient equal to 75 lb-sec/ft will be terminated by an END statement followed by a STOP which indicates that no more runs are to follow. The CSMP program to solve this problem is:

```
INITIAL
    CONSTANT PI=3.14159
    PARAMETER C=0.,M1=25.,M2=2.,K1=1000.,K2=4500.,...
V=(30.,60.,90.,120.)
    COEFF1=C/M1
    QUOT1=K1/M1
    COEFF2=C/M2
    QUOT2=(K1+K2)/M2
    A=K2/(6.*M2)
DYNAMIC
    XDDOT1=COEFF1*XDOT2+QUOT1*X2-COEFF1*XDOT1-QUOT1*X1
    XDDOT2=COEFF2*XDOT1+QUOT1*X1+A*SIN(2.*PI*V*TIME/20.)...
    -COEFF2*XDOT2-QUOT2*X2
    XDOT1=INTGRL(0.0,XDDOT1)
    XDOT2=INTGRL(0.0,XDDOT2)
    X1=INTGRL(0.0,XDOT1)
    X2=INTGRL(0.0,XDOT2)

    METHOD RKSFX
    TIMER DELT=.01,FINTIM=15.0,OUTDEL=.05
    LABEL MOTION OF AUTOMOBILE BODY WITH DAMPING
                                     =0.0 LB SEC/FT

    PRTPLOT X1
    END
    RESET LABEL
    PARAMETER C=25.
    LABEL MOTION OF AUTOMOBILE BODY WITH DAMPING
                                     =25.0 LB SEC/FT

    END
    RESET LABEL
    PARAMETER C=50.0
    LABEL MOTION OF AUTOMOBILE BODY WITH DAMPING
                                     =50.0 LB SEC/FT

    END
    RESET LABEL
    PARAMETER C=75.0
    LABEL MOTION OF AUTOMOBILE BODY WITH DAMPING
                                     =75.0 LB SEC/FT

    END
    STOP
ENDJOB
```

Following is the program output for the first 2.5 sec, with zero damping and the car traveling at 30 ft/sec.

```
MOTION OF AUTOMOBILE BODY WITH DAMPING=0.0 LB SEC/FT     PAGE    1
                          MINIMUM        X1    VERSUS TIME         MAXIMUM
                         -2.7211E-01     V = 3.0000E 01          2.6799-01
      TIME           X1        I                                         I
 0.0             0.0           ─────────────────────+
 5.0000E-02      3.1110E-04    ─────────────────────+
 1.0000E-01      6.1430E-03    ─────────────────────+
 1.5000E-01      2.3641E-02    ──────────────────────────+
 2.0000E-01      5.1020E-02    ────────────────────────────+
 2.5000E-01      8.7638E-02    ──────────────────────────────────+
 3.0000E-01      1.2470E-01    ────────────────────────────────────────+
 3.5000E-01      1.5383E-01    ─────────────────────────────────────────+
 4.0000E-01      1.6644E-01    ──────────────────────────────────────────+
 4.5000E-01      1.5357E-01    ─────────────────────────────────────────+
 5.0000E-01      1.1482E-01    ──────────────────────────────────────+
 5.5000E-01      4.9954E-02    ────────────────────────────────+
 6.0000E-01     -3.1307E-02    ─────────────────────────+
 6.5000E-01     -1.1762E-01    ──────────────+
 7.0000E-01     -1.9521E-01    ──────────+
 7.5000E-01     -2.4835E-01    ─+
 8.0000E-01     -2.6887E-01    +
 8.5000E-01     -2.4887E-01    ─+
 9.0000E-01     -1.9174E-01    ──────────+
 9.5000E-01     -1.0471E-01    ───────────────+
 1.0000E 00     -6.1260E-04    ─────────────────────+
 1.0500E 00      1.0242E-01    ───────────────────────────────────+
 1.1000E 00      1.9056E-01    ─────────────────────────────────────────────+
 1.1500E 00      2.4779E-01    ──────────────────────────────────────────────────+
 1.2000E 00      2.6799E-01    ────────────────────────────────────────────────────+
 1.2500E 00      2.4888E-01    ──────────────────────────────────────────────────+
 1.3000E 00      1.9516E-01    ──────────────────────────────────────────────+
 1.3500E 00      1.1923E-01    ──────────────────────────────────────+
 1.4000E 00      3.2475E-02    ──────────────────────────────+
 1.4500E 00     -4.8193E-02    ──────────────────────────+
 1.5000E 00     -1.1269E-01    ──────────────+
 1.5500E 00     -1.5235E-01    ───────────+
 1.6000E 00     -1.6433E-01    ─────────+
 1.6500E 00     -1.5329E-01    ───────────+
 1.7000E 00     -1.2379E-01    ─────────────+
 1.7500E 00     -8.7648E-02    ────────────────+
 1.8000E 00     -5.1863E-02    ──────────────────+
 1.8500E 00     -2.4188E-02    ─────────────────────+
 1.9000E 00     -8.2353E-03    ──────────────────────+
 1.9500E 00     -1.5050E-03    ───────────────────────+
 2.0000E 00     -2.1689E-03    ───────────────────────+
 2.0500E 00     -1.4102E-03    ───────────────────────+
 2.1000E 00      4.9249E-03    ───────────────────────+
 2.1500E 00      2.2030E-02    ──────────────────────────+
 2.2000E 00      5.1045E-02    ────────────────────────────+
 2.2500E 00      8.7065E-02    ──────────────────────────────────+
 2.3000E 00      1.2558E-01    ────────────────────────────────────────+
 2.3500E 00      1.5485E-01    ─────────────────────────────────────────+
 2.4000E 00      1.6765E-01    ──────────────────────────────────────────+
 2.4500E 00      1.5582E-01    ─────────────────────────────────────────+
 2.5000E 00      1.1605E-01    ──────────────────────────────────────+
```

EXAMPLE 9-3

To illustrate the use of the CONTINUE statement in run control, let us use the paratrooper problem of Ex. 6-2. Reviewing the problem briefly, we recall that when a paratrooper jumps from an aircraft which is in straight and level flight, his initial velocity is that of the aircraft. However, after a few seconds it drops below terminal velocity and then slowly increases up to terminal velocity. The optimum time for opening the parachute would generally be at the time of minimum velocity.

In a solution by a numerical method, most accurate results would be obtained by using a rather small integration step size for the first few seconds while the velocity is changing rapidly. After the minimum velocity is reached, and the velocity is changing much more slowly, a larger integration step could be used if it were desired to extend the solution over a period of 20 or 30 sec.

Changing the integration interval, or any other control specifications or data, in the middle of a run is easily accomplished in CSMP. Suppose we wished to use 0.05 sec as an initial value of DELT, and after 10 sec change to a DELT value of 0.5 sec. Also suppose that an initial value of OUTDEL equal to 0.2 sec were desired, with a change to 1.0 sec made after 10 sec. FINTIM is initially given the value 10 sec, DELT a value of 0.05 sec, and OUTDEL a value of 0.2 sec. Then, instead of an END statement, a CONTINUE statement would be used. The simulation would stop after 10 sec to accept new data and/or control specifications, but TIME would not be reset to zero as it would be with an END statement. New DELT, OUTDEL, and FINTIM values would be assigned on a parameter statement following the CONTINUE statement. This would be followed by END and then STOP if no further runs were desired. The print-plots obtained in this manner would be in two parts, one covering the period from 0 to 10 secs, and the other covering the period from 10 to 30 sec. In general, the dependent variable axis would be to a different scale for the two parts.

The simultaneous second-order differential equations which must be solved, and which are derived on pages 438, 439, and 440, are

$$\ddot{x} = -\frac{g}{V_t^2} \sqrt{\dot{x}^2 + \dot{y}^2} \, \dot{x} \qquad (9\text{-}6)$$

$$\ddot{y} = g - \frac{g}{V_t^2} \sqrt{\dot{x}^2 + \dot{y}^2} \, \dot{y} \qquad (9\text{-}7)$$

with initial conditions

$$t = 0 \begin{vmatrix} x = 0.0 \\ \dot{x} = 440 \text{ ft/sec} \\ y = 0.0 \\ \dot{y} = 0.0 \end{vmatrix}$$

The variable names used and the quantities which they represent in the CSMP program are

Variable Name	Quantity
TERM	Terminal velocity, ft/sec
G	Acceleration of gravity, ft/sec^2
XDD	Acceleration in x direction, ft/sec^2
YDD	Acceleration in y direction, ft/sec^2
XD	Velocity in x direction, ft/sec
YD	Velocity in y direction, ft/sec
X	Displacement in x direction, ft
Y	Displacement in y direction, ft
XD0,YD0,X0,Y0	Initial values of XD,YD,X, and Y respectively

The CSMP program is as follows:

```
INCON XD0=440.,X0=0.0,YD0=0.0,Y0=0.0
CONSTANT TERM=160.,G=32.17
XDD=-G/TERM**2*SQRT(XD**2+YD**2)*XD
YDD=G-G/TERM**2*SQRT(XD**2+YD**2)*YD
XD=INTGRL(XD0,XDD)
YD=INTGRL(YD0,YDD)
V=SQRT(XD**2+YD**2)
X=INTGRL(X0,XD)
Y=INTGRL(Y0,YD)
TIMER DELT=0.05,FINTIM=10.0,OUTDEL=0.2
PRTPLOT V,XD,YD,X,Y
METHOD TRAPZ
CONTINUE
TIMER DELT=0.5,FINTIM=30.0,OUTDEL=1.0
END
STOP
ENDJOB
```

The print-plot of velocity versus time for the period from 10 to 30 sec is shown in Fig. 9-19.

```
                                                                      PAGE   1

                             MINIMUM            V      VERSUS  TIME       MAXIMUM
                             1.5054E 02                                   1.5999E 02
     TIME         V              I                                           I
  1.0000E 01   1.5054E 02    +
  1.1000E 01   1.5266E 02    ------------+
  1.2000E 01   1.5442E 02    ----------------------+
  1.3000E 01   1.5583E 02    ------------------------------+
  1.4000E 01   1.5692E 02    ------------------------------------+
  1.5000E 01   1.5775E 02    ------------------------------------------+
  1.6000E 01   1.5837E 02    ----------------------------------------------+
  1.7000E 01   1.5882E 02    -------------------------------------------------+
  1.8000E 01   1.5916E 02    ---------------------------------------------------+
  1.9000E 01   1.5940E 02    ----------------------------------------------------+
  2.0000E 01   1.5957E 02    -----------------------------------------------------+
  2.1000E 01   1.5970E 02    ------------------------------------------------------+
  2.2000E 01   1.5979E 02    ------------------------------------------------------+
  2.3000E 01   1.5985E 02    -------------------------------------------------------+
  2.4000E 01   1.5989E 02    -------------------------------------------------------+
  2.5000E 01   1.5993E 02    -------------------------------------------------------+
  2.6000E 01   1.5995E 02    -------------------------------------------------------+
  2.7000E 01   1.5996E 02    -------------------------------------------------------+
  2.8000E 01   1.5997E 02    -------------------------------------------------------+
  2.9000E 01   1.5998E 02    -------------------------------------------------------+
  3.0000E 01   1.5999E 02    -------------------------------------------------------+
```

Figure 9-19 Velocity-time print-plot for Ex. 9-3

EXAMPLE 9-4

This example will illustrate another method of run control in which the TERMINAL segment is used to change parameter values, and the statement

CALL RERUN

is used to run the simulation again with the new parameter values. A two-point boundary-value problem which is solved in Ex. 7-2 by the finite-difference method will be solved here by the trial-and-error method. The program will illustrate, in addition to the use of the CALL RERUN statement for run control, the use of the FUNCTION data statement and arbitrary function generator, the use of the RENAME statement, and the use of FORTRAN in a NOSORT section of the DYNAMIC segment and the TERMINAL segment.

For the sake of convenience, the problem is restated here. It is desired to determine the elastic curve of the loaded nonuniform circular shaft shown in Fig. 9-20. The differential equation of the elastic curve of the shaft is

$$\frac{d^2y}{dx^2} = \frac{M}{EI}$$

with the following boundary conditions:

$x = 0.0, y = 0.0$

$x = 42.0, y = 0.0$

The initial value of dy/dx is not known. A value of $(dy/dx)|_{x=0}$ must be determined such that the second boundary condition above is satisfied, or very nearly so. The technique used will be to guess at minimum and maximum values of the slope at $x = 0.0$ which we are quite sure will bound the actual slope. We are sure the slope cannot be smaller in magnitude than 0.0, and we are reasonably sure the slope will not be greater (in magnitude) than -0.002. These values will be assigned to the variables MIN and MAX, respectively. The slope used at $x = 0.0$ is calculated in the INITIAL segment as the average of MIN and MAX. Then if y at $x = 42.0$ turns out to be greater than 0.0 as the result of a run, the initial slope must be made larger negatively. This is done by making the initial slope used in the run just completed the MIN value for

Figure 9-20 Loaded nonuniform circular shaft

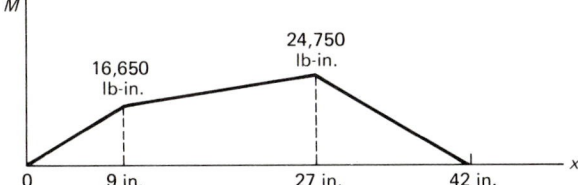

Figure 9-21 Bending-moment diagram for shaft shown in Fig. 9-20

the next run. If y at $x = 42.0$ is less than 0.0, the initial slope must be made smaller negatively. This is done by making the initial slope used in the run just completed the MAX value for the next run. The FORTRAN statements for making these adjustments will be in the TERMINAL segment. Then a CALL RERUN statement will initiate a new run using the new value of MAX or MIN.

When a run is completed where $|y|$ is less than 0.00002 at $x = 42.0$, the adjustment algorithm described above and CALL RERUN will be by-passed and a new run initiated by an END statement. For this final run, a print-plot will be specified.

The bending-moment diagram for the shaft is shown in Fig. 9-21. The moment values at $x = 0$, 9, 27, and 42 in. can be entered using a FUNCTION statement, and the arbitrary function generator will give the correct moment value at any x value using linear interpolation.

```
                                                      PAGE   1

                    MINIMUM              Y     VERSUS  X          MAXIMUM
                   -6.0251E-03                                   5.3859E-06
    X              Y                    I                                  I
 0.0               0.0                  ------------------------------------------------+
 1.0000E 00       -5.6560E-04           ---------------------------------------------+
 2.0000E 00       -1.1263E-03           -------------------------------------------+
 3.0000E 00       -1.6772E-03           ----------------------------------------+
 4.0000E 00       -2.2133E-03           -------------------------------------+
 5.0000E 00       -2.7298E-03           ----------------------------------+
 6.0000E 00       -3.2218E-03           ------------------------------+
 7.0000E 00       -3.6844E-03           --------------------------+
 8.0000E 00       -4.1126E-03           -----------------------+
 9.0000E 00       -4.5016E-03           ------------------+
 1.0000E 01       -4.8470E-03           ------------+
 1.1000E 01       -5.1471E-03           --------+
 1.2000E 01       -5.4006E-03           ------+
 1.3000E 01       -5.6064E-03           ---+
 1.4000E 01       -5.7633E-03           --+
 1.5000E 01       -5.8700E-03           -+
 1.6000E 01       -5.9414E-03           +
 1.7000E 01       -5.9912E-03           +
 1.8000E 01       -6.0190E-03           +
 1.9000E 01       -6.0243E-03           +
 2.0000E 01       -6.0067E-03           +
 2.1000E 01       -5.9656E-03           +
 2.2000E 01       -5.9005E-03           -+
 2.3000E 01       -5.8110E-03           -+
 2.4000E 01       -5.6965E-03           --+
 2.5000E 01       -5.5567E-03           ---+
 2.6000E 01       -5.3909E-03           -----+
 2.7000E 01       -5.1987E-03           ------+
 2.8000E 01       -4.9800E-03           --------+
 2.9000E 01       -4.7362E-03           ----------+
 3.0000E 01       -4.4691E-03           ------------+
 3.1000E 01       -4.1804E-03           ---------------+
 3.2000E 01       -3.8721E-03           ------------------+
 3.3000E 01       -3.5459E-03           ---------------------+
 3.4000E 01       -3.2035E-03           ------------------------+
 3.5000E 01       -2.8468E-03           ---------------------------+
 3.6000E 01       -2.4775E-03           -------------------------------+
 3.7000E 01       -2.0975E-03           ----------------------------------+
 3.8000E 01       -1.7085E-03           -------------------------------------+
 3.9000E 01       -1.3123E-03           ----------------------------------------+
 4.0000E 01       -8.9611E-04           -------------------------------------------+
 4.1000E 01       -4.5227E-04           ----------------------------------------------+
 4.2000E 01        5.3859E-06           ------------------------------------------------+
```

Figure 9-22 Print-plot of Ex. 9-4

The moment of inertia of the cross-sectional area of the shaft will have different values corresponding to the three different diameters. A NOSORT section in the Dynamic segment is used to assign the correct I value for any particular x value. Where there is a sudden change in the cross section of the shaft, the average I value is used.

The CSMP program listing for solving this problem follows, and the print-plot for shaft displacement versus x is shown in Fig. 9-22. Note in the program listing, CALL RERUN in the Terminal segment just precedes the FORTRAN CONTINUE statement to which transfer is made when CALL RERUN is to be by-passed. Experience indicates that for best results, CALL RERUN should be placed in this position. (See the flow chart accompanying Prob. 9-19.)

```
      RENAME TIME=X,DELT=DELX,FINTIM=XMAX
INITIAL
      DYDX0=0.5*(MIN+MAX)
      CONSTANT E=30000000.,MIN=0.0,MAX=-0.002,EPSI=.05
      FUNCTION MOMENT=(0.0,0.0),(9.0,16650.),(27.,24750.),
                                                    (42.0,0.0)
DYNAMIC
      NOSORT
         IF(X.LT.15.)I=12.57
         IF(ABS(X-15.).LT.EPSI)I=21.63
         IF(X.LT.39.0.AND.X.GT.15.+EPSI)I=30.68
         IF(ABS(X-39.0).LT.EPSI)I=17.33
         IF(X.GT.39.0+EPSI)I=3.98
      SORT
      M=AFGEN(MOMENT,X)
      D2YDX2=M/(E*I)
      DYDX=INTGRL(DYDX0,D2YDX2)
      Y=INTGRL(0.0,DYDX)
TERMINAL
         IF(ABS(Y).LT.0.00002)GO TO 3
         IF(Y.GT.0.)GO TO 1
         MAX=DYDX0
         GO TO 2
       1 MIN=DYDX0
       2 CALL RERUN
       3 CONTINUE
      TIMER DELX=0.1,XMAX=42.0
      METHOD TRAPZ
      END
      TIMER OUTDEL=1.0
      PRTPLOT Y,DYDX
      END
      STOP
ENDJOB
```

9-10 FORTRAN SUBPROGRAMS USED WITH CSMP PROGRAMS

Ordinary FORTRAN subprograms can be referenced by a CSMP program. The subprogram statements are placed between the STOP and the ENDJOB statements. If a subprogram has only one output, a function subprogram is generally used. A function subprogram is referenced by using the function name in a CSMP structure statement. To illustrate this, let us again use the shaft-deflection problem considered previously in Ex. 9-4. In the program shown in Sec. 9-9, the bending moment in the shaft at any x value is obtained by using the arbitrary function generator with the CSMP function MOMENT as the first argument, and x as the second. In the program which follows, the magnitude of the bending moment for any x value is obtained from a FORTRAN function supbrogram having the name MOMENT. The statement referencing this subprogram is

```
M=MOMENT(X)
```

The complete listings of the CSMP program and the FORTRAN subprogram used with it follow.

```
    RENAME TIME=X,DELT=DELX,FINTIM=XMAX
INITIAL
    DYDX0=0.5*(MIN+MAX)
    CONSTANT E=30000000.,MIN=0.0,MAX=-0.002,EPSI=.05
DYNAMIC
    NOSORT
        IF(X.LT.15.)I=12.57
        IF(ABS(X-15.).LT.EPSI)I=21.63
        IF(X.LT.39.0.AND.X.GT.15.+EPSI)I=30.68
        IF(ABS(X-39.0).LT.EPSI)I=17.33
        IF(X.GT.39.0+EPSI)I=3.98
    SORT
    M=MOMENT(X)
    D2YDX2=M/(E*I)
    DYDX=INTGRL(DYDX0,D2YDX2)
    Y=INTGRL(0.0,DYDX)
TERMINAL
        IF(ABS(Y).LT.0.00002)GO TO 3
        IF(Y.GT.0.)GO TO 1
        MAX=DYDX0
        GO TO 2
    1 MIN=DYDX0
    2 CALL RERUN
    3 CONTINUE
    TIMER DELX=0.1,XMAX=42.0
    METHOD TRAPZ
    END
    TIMER OUTDEL=1.0
    PRTPLOT Y,DYDX
    END
    STOP
        FUNCTION MOMENT(X)
        REAL MOMENT
        IF(X.GT.9.)GO TO 2
        MOMENT=1850.*X
        RETURN
```

```
  2 IF(X.GT.27.)GO TO 3
    MOMENT=1850.*X-1400.*(X-9.)
    RETURN
  3 MOMENT=1650.*(42.-X)
    RETURN
    END
ENDJOB
```

If a subprogram has more than one output, a subroutine subprogram is used. Instead of using a FORTRAN CALL statement to call the subprogram, a statement similar to the canonical statement of a MACRO definition is used. In the example which follows (again using the shaft problem of Ex. 9-4), the subroutine subprogram BMOMI determines the bending moment and moment of inertia of the shaft cross section for any x value. The subprogram is called with the CSMP statement

```
M,I=BMOMI(X)
```

in which the two outputs are on the left of the equal sign and separated by commas. Any number of outputs is permissible. The translator translates this CSMP statement into the FORTRAN statement

```
CALL BMOMI(X,M,I)
```

which is indicated by the arrow in the subroutine UPDATE (written by the translator) shown below.

```
    SUBROUTINE UPDATE
    COMMON  ZZ9901(5),IZ9901,ZZ9902,IZ9902,ZZ9903,IZ9903,ZZ9991(54)
    COMMON X
  1,DELX   ,DELMIN,XMAX    ,PRDEL  ,OUTDEL,DYDX   ,Y       ,D2YDX2,ZZ0005
  1,DYDXO ,ZZ0003,E        ,MIN    ,MAX    ,EPSI   ,M       ,I       ,ZZ0004
    COMMON ZZ9992(7981),NALARM,IZ9993,ZZ9994(417),KEEP,ZZ9995(489)
  $,IZ0000,ZZ9996(824),IZ9997,IZ9998,ZZ9999(  59)
    REAL        MIN
  1,MAX    ,M        ,I
    GO TO (39995,39996,39997,39998),IZ0000
C    SYSTEM SEGMENT OF MODEL
39995 CONTINUE
    IZ9993= 20
    IZ9997=  2
    IZ9998= 19
    READ(5,39990)(ZZ9999(IZ9999),IZ9999=1,  59)
39990 FORMAT(18A4)
    IZ9901=    160013
    IZ9902=    190017
    IZ9903=        59
    GO TO 39999
C    INITIAL SEGMENT OF MODEL
```

```
39996 CONTINUE
      DYDX0=0.5*(MIN+MAX)
      GO TO 39999
C    DYNAMIC SEGMENT OF MODEL
39997 CONTINUE
 ───→ CALL BMOMI (X,M,I)
      D2YDX2=M/(E*I)
C     DYDX      =INTGRL     (DYDX0      ,D2YDX2      )
C     Y         =INTGRL     (ZZ0003     ,DYDX        )
      ZZ0005=DYDX
      GO TO 39999
C   TERMINAL SEGMENT OF MODEL
39998 CONTINUE
      IF(ABS(Y).LT.0.00002)GO TO 3
      IF(Y.GT.0.)GO TO 1
      MAX=DYDX0
      GO TO 2
1     MIN=DYDX0
2     CALL RERUN
3     CONTINUE
39999 CONTINUE
      RETURN
      END
```

In forming the CALL statement, the translator places the two outputs in the rightmost portion of the argument list with no change in their order. The dummy arguments of the subroutine subprogram must agree in number, order, and mode with the real arguments in the CALL statement generated by the translator. The complete program follows for solving the shaft problem, with a subroutine program to determine the bending moment and moment of inertia.

```
      RENAME TIME=X,DELT=DELX,FINTIM=XMAX
INITIAL
      DYDX0=0.5*(MIN+MAX)
      CONSTANT E=30000000., MIN=0.0,MAX=-0.002,EPSI=.05
DYNAMIC
      M,I=BMOMI(X)
      D2YDX2=M/(E*I)
      DYDX=INTGRL(DYDX0,D2YDX2)
      Y=INTGRL(0.0,DYDX)
TERMINAL
      IF(ABS(Y).LT.0.00002)GO TO 3
      IF(Y.GT.0.)GO TO 1
      MAX=DYDX0
      GO TO 2
    1 MIN=DYDX0
    2 CALL RERUN
    3 CONTINUE
      TIMER DELX=0.1,XMAX=42.0
      METHOD TRAPZ
      END
```

```
      TIMER OUTDEL=1.0
      PRTPLOT Y,DYDX
      END
      STOP
         SUBROUTINE BMOMI(X,M,I)
         REAL M,I
         IF(X.LT.15.)I=12.57
         IF(ABS(X-15.).LT.EPSI)I=21.63
         IF(X.LT.39.0.AND.X.GT.15.+EPSI)I=30.68
         IF(ABS(X-39.0).LT.EPSI)I=17.33
         IF(X.GT.39.0+EPSI)I=3.98
         IF(X.GT.9.)GO TO 2
         M=1850.*X
         RETURN
       2 IF(X.GT.27.)GO TO 3
         M=1850.*X-1400.*(X-9.)
         RETURN
       3 M=1650.*(42.-X)
         RETURN
         END
ENDJOB
```

If a subroutine subprogram has only one output (say, the bending moment in the shaft considered for any x value), the form of the CSMP calling statement would have to be

```
M=BNDMOM(X)
```

with the single output on the left of the equal sign. However, the translator will not recognize this as a statement to be translated into a CALL statement because of the single output. The subprogram BNDMOM could be called with a FORTRAN CALL statement providing it is placed in an unsorted section, as shown below.

```
      RENAME TIME=X,DELT=DELX,FINTIM=XMAX
INITIAL
      DYDX0=0.5*(MIN+MAX)
      CONSTANT E=30000000.,MIN=0.0,MAX=-0.002,EPSI=.05
DYNAMIC
      NOSORT
         IF(X.LT.15.)I=12.57
         IF(ABS(X-15.).LT.EPSI)I=21.63
         IF(X.LT.39.0.AND.X.GT.15.+EPSI)I=30.68
         IF(ABS(X-39.0).LT.EPSI)I=17.33
         IF(X.GT.39.0+EPSI)I=3.98
         CALL BNDMOM(X,M)
      SORT
      D2YDX2=M/(E*I)
      DYDX=INTGRL(DYDX0,D2YDX2)
      Y=INTGRL(0.0,DYDX)
TERMINAL
         IF(ABS(Y).LT.0.00002)GO TO 3
         IF(Y.GT.0.)GO TO 1
```

```
    MAX=DYDXO
    GO TO 2
  1 MIN=DYDXO
  2 CALL RERUN
  3 CONTINUE
TIMER DELX=0.1,XMAX=42.0
METHOD TRAPZ
END
TIMER OUTDEL=1.0
PRTPLOT Y,DYDX
END
STOP
```

An attempt to call the subprogram BNDMOM with a FORTRAN CALL statement placed in a sorted section will result in a diagnostic message as shown below:

```
    RENAME TIME=X,DELT=DELX,FINTIM=XMAX
INITIAL
    DYDXO=0.5*(MIN+MAX)
    CONSTANT E=30000000.,MIN=0.0,MAX=-0.002,EPSI=.05
DYNAMIC
    NOSORT
        IF(X.LT.15.)I=12.57
        IF(ABS(X-15.).LT.EPSI)I=21.63
        IF(X.LT.39.0.AND.X.GT.15.+EPSI)I=30.68
        IF(ABS(X-39.0).LT.EPSI)I=17.33
        IF(X.GT.39.0+EPSI)I=3.98
    SORT
  ————→ CALL BNDMOM(X,M)
****CMSP STATEMENT INCORRECTLY WRITTEN****
```

Generally, when a subprogram is to have a single output, a function subprogram is used.

PROBLEMS

9-1. Write the necessary CSMP statements to generate the function shown in which FINTIM = 30.

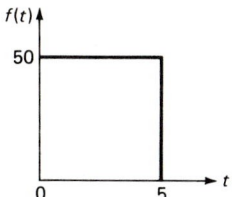

Problem 9-1

9-2. Refer to Ex. 9-1 and use the following data:

$$L/R = 0.01 \text{ sec}$$

$$c = 0.122 \text{ N·m/Rad/sec}$$

$$I = 0.136 \text{ N·m·sec}^2$$

$$A_1 = 5.0$$

$$A_2 = 0.0136 \text{ N·m/volt}$$

$$A_3 = 7.376 \text{ N}^{-1}\text{·m}^{-1}\text{·sec}^{-2}$$

$$A_4 = 20, 10, 5 \text{ volts/radian}$$

Make any necessary changes in the program given in the example, and obtain a print-plot of the angle θ. Compare this print-plot with that shown in Fig. 9-17.

9-3. Refer to Ex. 9-2 and use the following problem data:

$m_1 = \frac{1}{4}$ the mass of the automobile $= 365$ kg

$m_2 = $ mass of one wheel $= 29.2$ kg

$k_1 = $ spring constant $= 14.6$ kN/m

$k_2 = $ linear spring constant of tire $= 65.67$ kN/m

$c = $ damping constant of dashpot $= 0, 364.8, 729.7, 1095$ N·sec/m

$v = $ velocity of car $= 9.14, 18.29, 27.43,$ and 36.58 m/sec

a. Make any modifications necessary in the program given in the example, and obtain a print-plot of the motion of the car body, x_1.

b. Do what is necessary to obtain a print-plot of the displacement of the wheel, x_2.

9-4. The accompanying figure shows the free body of the shaft of Ex. 9-4 in SI units.

Problem 9-4

a. Sketch the moment diagram of the shaft in SI units of kN·mm.
b. Refer to Ex. 9-4 and make any modification necessary in the program given in that example to accommodate SI units, and obtain a print-plot of the beam deflection in millimeters.

9-5. In Ex. 9-4, the differential equation for the elastic curve was taken as

$$\frac{d^2y}{dx^2} = M/EI \quad \text{(small deflection theory)}$$

This equation will normally give very accurate results for the deflection y for most practical problems. However, for beam problems involving large deflections, in which dy/dx is not small compared to 1, the following differential equation for the elastic curve should be used

$$\frac{d^2y}{dx^2} = \frac{M}{EI}\left[1 + \left(\frac{dy}{dx}\right)^2\right]^{3/2} \quad \text{(large deflection theory)}$$

Modify the CSMP program of Ex. 9-4 so that the large deflection theory equation will be used for calculation of the beam deflections.

9-6. Write the necessary CSMP statements to generate the function shown in which $a = 0.5$ sec and FINTIM $= 4.5$ sec.

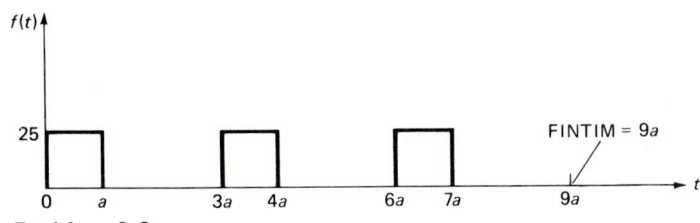

Problem 9-6

9-7. Write the necessary CSMP statements to generate the ramp function shown.

Problem 9-7

9-8. The mass m slides on a surface with a coefficient of friction of μ. Since the friction force, $F = \mu W$, acts in the opposite direction to the velocity $\dot{x}$, the differential equations for motion to the right and left, respectively, are

$$\ddot{x} + \frac{k}{m} x = -\mu g \qquad (\dot{x} > 0) \text{ (right)}$$

$$\ddot{x} + \frac{k}{m} x = \mu g \qquad (\dot{x} < 0) \text{ (left)}$$

where g = acceleration of gravity, 386 in./sec². Use the appropriate switching function to obtain either μg or $-\mu g$ and write a CSMP program for a sequence of nine runs starting with $\mu = 0.1$, and followed by 0.1 increments for subsequent runs. The mass m is to be released from rest so that the initial value of x for each run is the displacement sufficient to overcome the maximum friction force for $k/m = 100$ in./sec². Obtain print-plots of x.

(partial answer: for $x_0 = 20$ and $u = 0.1$ at $t = 1.0$, $x = 1.4893$ in.)

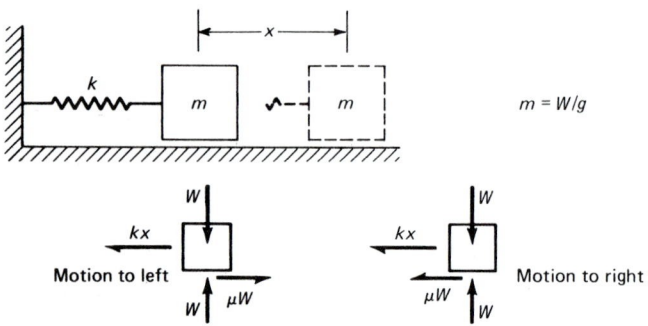

Problem 9-8

9-9. Refer to Prob. 9-8 and work the problem in SI units with $g = 9.81$ m/sec² and $k/m = 2.54$ m/sec².

9-10. The spring and mass system is subjected to a pulse of magnitude F_0 and time duration τ. From the free-body diagram shown and Newton's second law, the differential equation of motion is found to be

$$\ddot{x} + \frac{k_1}{m} x + \frac{[T + k_2(\sqrt{x^2 + l^2} - l)]}{m\sqrt{x^2 + l^2}} x = \frac{F(t)}{m}$$

Problem 9-10

where T is the tension in k_2 when $x = 0$. The system parameter values are as follows:

$k_1 = k_2 = 39.4$ lb/in. $\quad l = 10$ in.

$m = 1.0$ lb-sec^2/in. $\quad T = 394$ lb

$F_0 = 100$ lb $\quad\quad 0.1 \leq \tau \leq 1.0$ sec

Write a CSMP program for a sequence of ten runs starting with $\tau = 0.1$ sec followed by 0.1-sec increments for subsequent runs. Print out minimum and maximum values of x, $\dot{x}$, and $\ddot{x}$.

(partial answer: for $\tau = 0.1$, $x_{min} = -1.68$ in. at 1.983 sec, $x_{max} = 0.67053$ in. at 1.631 sec)

9-11. Utilizing the results obtained in Prob. 9-6, plot x_{max}, $\dot{x}_{max}$, and $\ddot{x}_{max}$ as functions of the pulse duration τ.

9-12. A three-story building is modeled as a lumped mass system as shown. For a ground acceleration of $\ddot{y}$, the differential equations of motion in terms of the mass displacements (q_1, q_2, q_3) relative to the ground are as follows:

$$\ddot{q}_1 + \frac{2c}{m_1}\dot{q}_1 - \frac{c}{m_1}\dot{q}_2 + \frac{(k_1 + k_2)}{m_1}q_1 - \frac{k_2}{m_1}q_2 = -\ddot{y}$$

$$\ddot{q}_2 + \frac{2c}{m_2}\dot{q}_2 - \frac{c}{m_2}(\dot{q}_1 + \dot{q}_3) - \frac{k_2}{m_2}q_1 + \frac{(k_2 + k_3)}{m_2}q_2 - \frac{k_3}{m_2}q_3 = -\ddot{y}$$

$$\ddot{q}_3 + \frac{c}{m_3}\dot{q}_3 - \frac{c}{m_3}\dot{q}_2 - \frac{k_3}{m_3}q_2 + \frac{k_3}{m_3}q_3 = -\ddot{y}$$

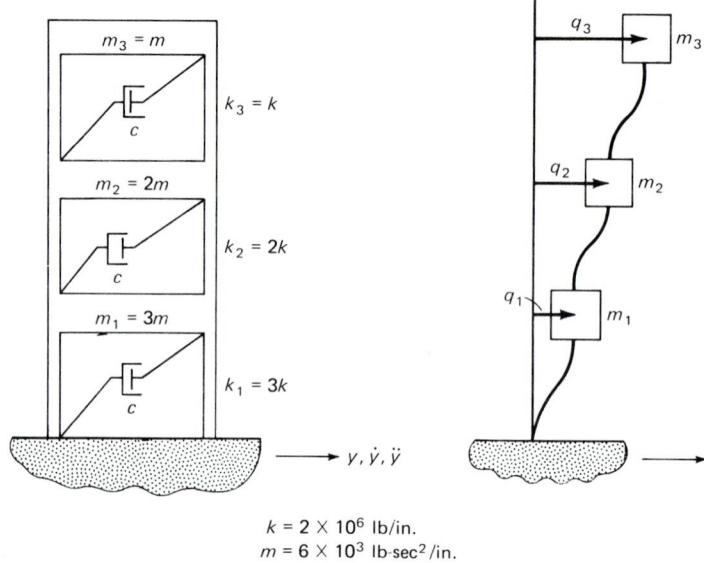

$$k = 2 \times 10^6 \text{ lb/in.}$$
$$m = 6 \times 10^3 \text{ lb-sec}^2/\text{in.}$$
$$c = 2400 \text{ lb-sec/in.}$$

$$1g = 386 \text{ in./sec}^2$$

Problem 9-12

where

$$k = 2 \times 10^6 \text{ lb/in. (all columns)}$$

$$m = 6 \times 10^3 \text{ lb-sec}^2/\text{in.}$$

$$c = 2400 \text{ lb-sec/in. (damping parameter)}$$

It is proposed to study the dynamic response of the structure due to a ground acceleration which is described by the ramp function shown. Write a CSMP program for a sequence of runs in which the buildup time τ of the ramp function has the following values:

```
PARAMETER TAU=(0.4, 9*0.4)
```

Consider that the maximum distortions $(u_1 = q_1,\ u_2 = q_2 - q_1,$

$u_3 = q_3 - q_2)$ are not to exceed 3 in. for no serious damage to occur. Is there any serious damage to the building?

(partial answer: for $\tau = 0.8$ sec, $u_{1min} = -2.6684$ in. at 2.925 sec, $u_{1max} = 1.9642$ in. at 6.235 sec)

9-13. Due to the shape and uniform rotation of the cam, the displacement y of the follower is essentially a sawtooth function with an amplitude of 1 in. and a period of 1 sec. From Newton's second law and the assumption that the follower remains in contact with the cam at all times, the differential equation of motion of the mass m is found to be

$$\ddot{x} + \frac{c}{m}\dot{x} + \frac{2k}{m}x = \frac{k}{m}y$$

Write a CSMP program with a FINTIM of 10 sec and obtain the dynamic response of the mass m for the following system variable values:

$m = 0.1$ lb-sec^2/ft

$k = 20$ lb/ft

$c = 0.2$ lb-sec/ft

Problem 9-13

9-14. Two tanks with cross-sectional areas of A_1 and A_2 are connected together with a pipe of length l and area A_0. The tanks and connecting pipe are filled with a fluid having a mass density of γ lb-sec^2/ft^4. The initial height of the fluid is h in each tank. It is desired to study the dynamic behavior of the two-tank system when a uniform pressure p is suddenly applied to the fluid surface of tank 2. The pressure p is described by the function

$$p = p_0 f(t)$$

where

$$f(t) = 1 \qquad 0 < t < t_0$$
$$f(t) = 0 \qquad t > t_0$$

Due to the blast pressure, the fluid in tank 1 will experience an upward displacement of x_1 and the fluid in tank 2 will experience a downward displacement of x_2. If x_1 and x_2 are not small in comparison to h, the nonlinear differential equation for the system, in terms of x_1 (neglecting friction) is

$$\ddot{x}_1 + \frac{[1 - (A_1/A_2)^2]}{2D}\dot{x}_1^2 + g\frac{[1 + A_1/A_2]}{D}x_1 = \frac{p_0 f(t)}{\gamma D}$$

where

$$D = h[1 + A_1/A_2] + [1 - (A_1/A_2)^2]x_1 + \frac{lA_1}{A_0}$$

$g = 32.2$ ft/sec^2 (acceleration of gravity)

Write a CSMP program for simulation runs for the following parameter values:

$A_1/A_2 = 0.25, 2.0, 5.0$

$\qquad h = 10$ ft, $l = 1$ ft, $A_1/A_0 = 10$

$\quad p_0/\gamma = 100$ ft^2/sec^2, $t_0 = 2$ sec

Print-plots are to be obtained for x_1, $\dot{x}_1$, and $\ddot{x}_1$.

(partial answer: for $A_1/A_2 = 0.25$ and $t = 1.5$ sec, $x_1 = 3.4138$ ft)

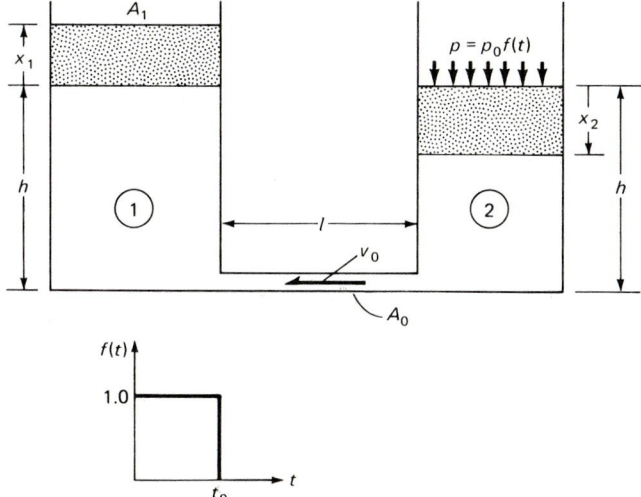

Problem 9-14

9-15. Refer to Prob. 9-14 and determine print-plots for x_1 for the following system data:

$$A_1/A_2 = 0.25, \ 2.0, \ 5.0$$

$$h = 4 \text{ m}$$

$$l = 1 \text{ m}$$

$$A_1/A_0 = 10$$

$$A_1 p_0/\gamma = 300 \text{ m/s}^2$$

$$t_0 = 2 \text{ s}$$

$$g = 9.81 \text{ m/s}^2 \text{ (acceleration of gravity)}$$

9-16. Derive the differential equation given in Prob. 9-14. (*Hint:* Write the kinetic energy T and potential energy V of the system and use Lagrange's equation.) Lagrange's equation is

$$\frac{d}{dt}\!\left(\frac{\partial T}{\partial \dot{q}_i}\right) - \frac{\partial T}{\partial q_i} + \frac{\partial V}{\partial q_i} = Q_i \qquad i = 1, 2, 3, \dots$$

where

q_i = generalized coordinates (x_1 for Prob. 9-10)

T = kinetic energy of the system

V = potential energy of the system

Q_i = generalized nonpotential force associated with the coordinate q_i

The generalized force Q_i includes all forces that add or remove energy from the system. The increment of work dW done by the force Q_i for a differential change dq_i of one of the q_i coordinates is $Q_i \, dq_i$. For the tank system of Prob. 9-14,

$$dW = p_0 f(t) A_2 \, dx_2$$

Since $A_1 x_1 = A_2 x_2$, $dx_2 = (A_1/A_2) \, dx_1$ so that $Q_1 = p_0 f(t) A_1$. The kinetic energy T and potential energy V are

$$T = \frac{\gamma A_1}{2}(h + x_1)\dot{x}_1^2 + \frac{\gamma A_2}{2}(h - x_2)\dot{x}_2^2 + \frac{\gamma A_0}{2} l v_0^2$$

$$V = \gamma g A_2 x_2 \frac{(x_2 + x_1)}{2}$$

To obtain the differential equation in terms of x_1, note that $A_1 x_1 = A_2 x_2 = A_0 v_0$.

9-17. Body A of mass m is subjected to a sinusoidal exciting force $F_0 \sin \omega t$. Body B, also of mass m, is free to move in a vertical slot. A light rod of length l is pinned to both A and B and the force in the spring is zero when $\theta = 0$.

a. Neglect the mass of the rod and coulomb friction and apply Newton's second law to A and B and show that the differential equation of motion in terms of θ is

$$\ddot{\theta} + \frac{c}{m} \cos^2 \theta \dot{\theta} + \frac{g}{l} \sin \theta + \frac{k}{m} \sin \theta \cos \theta = \frac{F_0}{ml} \cos \theta \sin \omega t$$

For small values of θ, the linearized differential equation of motion is

$$\ddot{\theta} + \frac{c}{m} \dot{\theta} + \left(\frac{g}{l} + \frac{k}{m}\right)\theta = \frac{F_0}{ml} \sin \omega t$$

Problem 9-17

b. Write a CSMP program to obtain the maximum steady-state amplitude for the nonlinear equation when $\omega = \omega_n$, where

$$\omega_n = \sqrt{\frac{g}{l} + \frac{k}{m}}$$

The exciting frequency $\omega = \omega_n$ corresponds to resonance for the linear equation of motion. The values for k/m and g/l are 75 and 25, respectively. Thus, $\omega_n = 10$ radians/sec. The response is to be obtained for the following damping values:

$$\frac{c}{m} = 2\xi\omega_n = 4,\ 8,\ 12,\ 16,\ 20$$

where ξ is the damping factor in which $\xi = 1$ corresponds to a critically damped system for small values of θ.

The value for F_0/ml is to be selected so that the steady-state amplitude for the linearized equation does not exceed $\pi/6$ (30 deg) when $\omega = \omega_n$. That is, from vibration theory

$$\theta_{max} = \frac{\pi}{6} = \frac{F_0/ml}{\omega_n^2 2\xi}$$

(partial answer: for $c/m = 8$ and $F_0/ml = 20$, $\theta_{min} = -0.25178$ rad at 1.26 sec, $\theta_{max} = 0.25165$ rad at 1.57 sec)

9-18. The cylinder of radius r, centroidal moment of inertia $\bar{I}$, and mass m rolls without slipping on the moving support. The differential equation of motion of the cylinder, in terms of the displacement u relative to the moving support, is

$$\ddot{u} + \frac{2c}{3m}\dot{u} + \frac{2k}{3m}u = -\frac{2}{3}\ddot{y}$$

or

$$\ddot{u} + 2\xi\left(\frac{2\pi}{\tau}\right)\dot{u} + \left(\frac{2\pi}{\tau}\right)^2 u = -\frac{2}{3}\ddot{y}$$

where

ξ = damping factor as a fraction of critical damping ($\xi_c = 1$)

τ = natural undamped period of the cylinder and spring system, sec

$\ddot{y}$ = acceleration of moving support

Write a CSMP program in order to obtain the maximum response u_{max} in which the acceleration of the support is

$$\ddot{y} = -100 \sin 2\pi t \qquad 0 \le t \le 1$$
$$\ddot{y} = 0 \qquad\qquad\quad 1 < t$$

The maximum response u_{max} is to be obtained for values of the natural period τ ranging from 0.1 to 2 sec for a damping factor of $\xi = 0.1$. A plot of u_{max} as a function of τ is called a *response spectrum*.

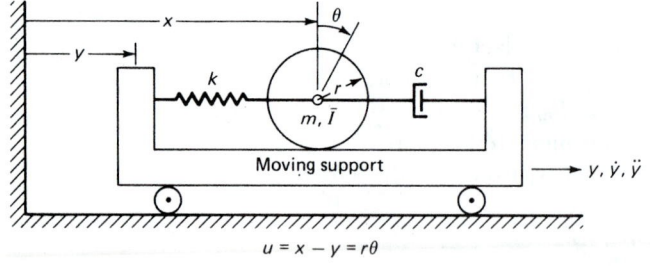

$$u = x - y = r\theta$$

Problem 9-18

9-19. A study is to be made of the trajectory of a pilot ejected from an airplane at various altitudes and various velocities (based on a problem from an

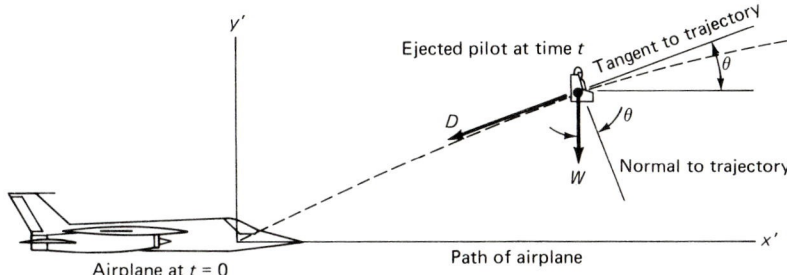

Problem 9-19(a)

IBM CSMP short course). It is important that the ejected pilot and seat mechanism clear the vertical stabilizer by a safe margin.

Let the origin of a fixed x'-y' coordinate system be at the center of mass of the pilot and attached ejection mechanism at the instant ejection begins. In part a of the accompanying figure, the forces which act on the pilot and seat mechanism are shown at some time t after ejection has occurred.

Applying Newton's second law along a tangent to the trajectory, with the direction of the velocity taken as the positive direction, we obtain

$$-D - W \sin \theta = \dot{V}M \tag{1}$$

in which D is the drag force, W is the weight of the pilot and seat, $\dot{V}$ is the tangential acceleration, and M is the mass of the pilot and seat. The drag force D is given by

$$D = \tfrac{1}{2}\gamma C_D S V^2$$

where γ is the mass density of the air, C_D is the drag coefficient, and S is the projected area of the pilot and seat normal to the direction of motion. The air density γ will vary with the altitude.

Applying Newton's second law in the normal direction and taking the direction toward the center of curvature as the positive direction, we obtain

$$W \cos \theta = \frac{MV^2}{\rho} \tag{2}$$

in which V is the velocity of the pilot and seat and ρ is the radius of curvature of the trajectory. The quantity V^2/ρ is the acceleration in the normal direction.

Replacing one of the V's in Eq. 2 by $-\rho\dot\theta$ ($V = -\rho\dot\theta$ since V is positive for a decreasing angle θ), we obtain

$$W \cos \theta = -M\dot\theta V \tag{3}$$

Dividing Eqs. 1 and 3 through by M, and replacing W/M with g, we obtain

$$\frac{dV}{dt} = -\frac{\frac{1}{2}\gamma C_D S V^2}{M} - g \sin \theta \tag{4}$$

and

$$\frac{d\theta}{dt} = \frac{-g \cos \theta}{V} \tag{5}$$

Now let us consider the trajectory of the pilot and seat relative to the airplane as shown in part b of the accompanying figure. Let the x-y coordinate system shown move with the airplane in horizontal flight. The y displacement of the pilot and seat may be obtained at any time t by integrating

$$\frac{dy}{dt} = V \sin \theta \tag{6}$$

The x displacement may be obtained by integrating

$$\frac{dx}{dt} = V \cos \theta - V_a \tag{7}$$

in which V_a is the velocity of the airplane.

Equations 4, 5, 6, and 7 constitute a set of four first-order differential equations to be solved simultaneously. It should be noted, however, that

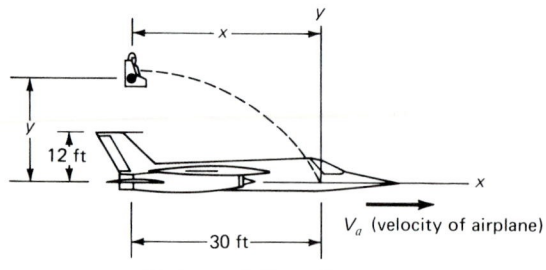

Airplane and pilot at time t

Problem 9-19(b)

Eqs. 4 and 5 are valid only after the seat has cleared the rails ($y > 4$ ft for this problem). Prior to that time

$$\frac{dV}{dt} = 0 \tag{8}$$

and

$$\frac{d\theta}{dt} = 0 \tag{9}$$

are assumed to hold. We are assuming that the pilot and seat reach the ejection velocity relative to the plane, V_e, in a very short time, and that this relative velocity remains constant until the seat clears the rails.

It is suggested that a PROCEDURE be used in the DYNAMIC segment to define dV/dt and $d\theta/dt$ by either Eqs. 4 and 5 or Eqs. 8 and 9, depending upon the value of y. The PROCEDURE is preferred to the use of NOSORT since a PROCEDURE can be moved around as an entity by the translator while a NOSORT section cannot.

The initial conditions are

$$t = 0 \begin{vmatrix} x = 0 \\ y = 0 \\ V = [(V_a - V_e \sin \theta_e)^2 + (V_e \cos \theta_e)^2]^{1/2} \\ \theta = \tan^{-1} \dfrac{V_e \cos \theta_e}{V_a - V_e \sin \theta_e} \end{vmatrix} \tag{10}$$

The angle θ_e is shown in part c of the accompanying figure.

The trajectory study should include velocities, V_a, ranging from 100 to 1000 ft/sec in increments of 100 ft/sec, and altitudes ranging from sea level to 60,000 ft in increments of 1000 ft, and determining the maximum velocity at each altitude for a safe ejection. A safe ejection will be considered one in which y is greater than 20 ft when x equals minus 30 ft.

Problem 9-19(c)

This will result in the center of mass of the pilot and seat passing more than 8 ft above the top of the vertical stabilizer (see part b of the accompanying figure).

The following data values are to be used:

M = mass of pilot and seat, 7.0 slugs

V_e = ejection velocity relative to plane, 40.0 ft/sec

C_D = drag coefficient, 1.0 (dimensionless)

θ_e = angle of ejection, 15.0 deg

S = projected area, pilot and seat, 10.0 ft^2

g = acceleration of gravity, 32.2 ft/sec^2

The mass density of the air at various altitudes is as follows:

Altitude (ft)	γ(lb-sec^2/ft^4)
0	0.002377
1,000	0.002308
2,000	0.002241
4,000	0.002117
6,000	0.001987
10,000	0.001755
15,000	0.001497
20,000	0.001267
30,000	0.000891
40,000	0.000587
50,000	0.000364
60,000	0.000234

Problem 9-19(d)

These values can be entered into the program using a CSMP FUNCTION statement, and the air density at any altitude obtained using the arbitrary function generator.

Begin the study at sea level and a velocity of 100 ft/sec. use a FINTIM of 3.0 sec and a finish condition which will stop the integration when x becomes algebraically less than -30. Thus, when $x \cong -30$ ft, integration will cease, and the TERMINAL segment will be entered. In the TERMINAL segment, the y value should be checked to see if it is greater than 20.0 ft, which indicates a safe ejection. If a safe ejection is indicated, write out the altitude, velocity of the airplane, and the y value. If an ejection is safe at some particular altitude and velocity, it will be safe at all higher altitudes higher than that altitude for all velocities up to that velocity because of the decreasing drag force with higher altitudes. Therefore, after a safe ejection at a given altitude and velocity is indicated, the velocity should be increased by 100 ft/sec and a CALL RERUN used to run again. Eventually an unsafe ejection condition will occur. When it

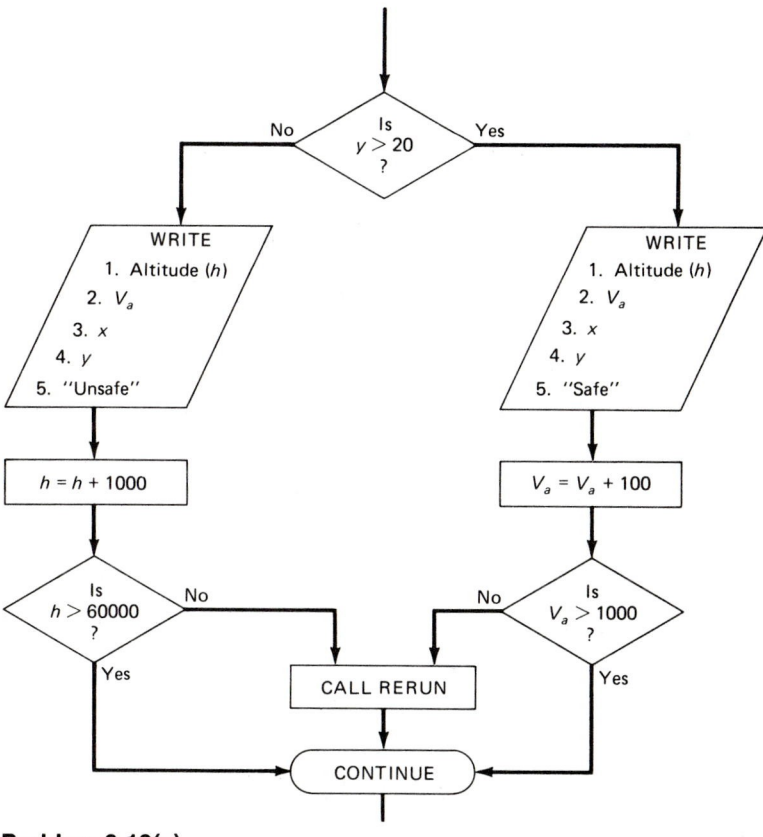

Problem 9-19(e)

does, the altitude should be incremented by 1000 ft with the velocity unchanged. A CALL RERUN statement then causes another run. This continues until a safe ejection again occurs, and the velocity is then incremented as explained earlier. Reruns are made until either the incremented altitude exceeds 60,000 ft or the incremented velocity exceeds 1000 ft/sec. With the data obtained, the altitude-velocity region shown in part d of the accompanying figure can be separated into safe and unsafe parts. With the technique outlined, it will not be necessary to run for all combinations of altitude and velocity.

Use a step size of 0.01 sec and trapezoidal integration. A suggested flow chart for the TERMINAL segment is shown in part e of the accompanying figure.

Appendix A
International System of Units

A-1 NOMENCLATURE OF SI UNITS AND QUANTITIES

In the following table the basic units are length, mass, time, temperature, and current. All other named units and unnamed quantities are derived from fundamental definitions or concepts.

Quantities	Name	SI Notation
length	meter	m
mass	kilogram	kg
time	second	s
temperature	kelvin	K
current	ampere	A
force	newton	N $(kg{\cdot}m/s^2)$
stress, pressure	pascal	Pa (N/m^2)
energy, work	joule	J $(N{\cdot}m)$
power	watt	$W(J/s)$
frequency	hertz	Hz $(1/s)$
potential difference	volt	V (W/A)
resistance	ohm	Ω (V/A)
velocity (linear)	—	m/s
velocity (angular)	—	rad/s
acceleration (linear)	—	m/s^2
acceleration (angular)	—	rad/s^2
moment of force	—	$N{\cdot}m$ $(kg{\cdot}m^2/s^2)$
moment of inertia (area)	—	m^4
moment of inertia (mass)	—	$kg{\cdot}m^2$
impulse (linear)	—	$N{\cdot}s$ $(kg{\cdot}m/s)$
impulse (angular)	—	$N{\cdot}m{\cdot}s$ $(kg{\cdot}m^2/s)$
momentum (linear)	—	$N{\cdot}s$ $(kg{\cdot}m/s)$
momentum (angular)	—	$N{\cdot}m{\cdot}s(kg{\cdot}m^2{\cdot}s)$
weight (specific)	—	N/m^3 $kg/(s^2{\cdot}m^2)$
density (mass)	—	kg/m^3
density (weight)	—	N/m^3
viscosity (absolute)	—	$N{\cdot}s/m^2$ $(Pa{\cdot}s)$

A-2 CONVERSION OF U.S. CUSTOMARY UNITS TO SI UNITS

Multiply (U.S. Customary)	By	To Obtain (SI)
Acceleration (ft/sec^2)	3.048×10^{-1}	m/s^2 (meter/second^2)
Acceleration (in./sec^2)	2.54×10^{-2}	m/s^2 (meter/second^2)
Area (ft^2)	9.2903×10^{-2}	m^2 (meter^2)
Area (in.^{2})	6.4516×10^{-4}	m^2 (meter^2)
Density (lb/ft^3)	1.5708×10^{2}	N/m^3 (newton/meter^3)
Density (lb/in.^{3})	2.7145×10^{5}	N/m^3 (newton/meter^3)
Force (lb)	4.4482	N (newton)
Length (in.)	2.54×10^{-2}	m (meter)
Length (ft)	3.048×10^{-1}	m (meter)
Mass (lb-sec^2/ft)	1.4594×10	kg (kilogram)
Power (horsepower—550 ft-lb/sec)	7.4569×10^{2}	W (watt)
Stress, pressure (psi)	6.8947×10^{3}	N/m^2 or Pa (pascal)
Velocity (ft/sec)	3.048×10^{-1}	m/s (meter/second)
Volume (ft^3)	2.8317×10^{-2}	m^3 (meter^3)
Volume (in.^{3})	1.6387×10^{-5}	m^3 (meter^3)
Work, energy (ft-lb)	1.3558	J (joule)
Work, energy (Btu)	1.0551×10^{3}	J (joule)
Work, energy (kw·h)	3.60×10^{6}	J (joule)

A-3 PREFIXES

The following prefixes are commonly used when very small or very large numbers are involved:

Prefix	Numerical Value	SI Designation
nano	10^{-9}	n
micro	10^{-6}	μ
milli	10^{-3}	m
kilo	10^{3}	k
mega	10^{6}	M
giga	10^{9}	G

For example, the modulus of elasticity E of steel is 2.068×10^{11} Pa (pascals) (30×10^{6} psi), which may also be written as 206.8 GPa (gigapascals).

Appendix B
Matrix Algebra

B-1 MULTIPLICATION

The product of two matrices $\mathbf{A} = [a_{ij}]$ and $\mathbf{B} = [b_{ij}]$ may be written as

$$[a_{ij}][b_{ij}] = [c_{ij}]$$

or, more simply, as

$$\mathbf{AB} = \mathbf{C}$$

The elements c_{ij} of the $\mathbf{C}$ matrix are obtained from

$$c_{ij} = \sum_{k=1} a_{ik}b_{kj} \tag{B-1}$$

where k identifies the kth element in the ith row of $\mathbf{A}$ and the kth element in the jth column of $\mathbf{B}$. To illustrate Eq. B-1, consider the equation

$$\begin{bmatrix} a_{11} & a_{12} & a_{13} \\ a_{21} & a_{22} & a_{23} \\ a_{31} & a_{32} & a_{33} \end{bmatrix} \begin{bmatrix} b_{11} & b_{12} & b_{13} \\ b_{21} & b_{22} & b_{23} \\ b_{31} & b_{32} & b_{33} \end{bmatrix} = \begin{bmatrix} c_{11} & c_{12} & c_{13} \\ c_{21} & c_{22} & c_{23} \\ c_{31} & c_{32} & c_{33} \end{bmatrix}$$

From Eq. B-1, the product of **A** and **B** gives

$$c_{11} = a_{11}b_{11} + a_{12}b_{21} + a_{13}b_{31}$$

$$c_{21} = a_{21}b_{11} + a_{22}b_{21} + a_{23}b_{31}$$

. . . .

. . . .

. . . .

$$c_{33} = a_{31}b_{13} + a_{32}b_{23} + a_{33}b_{33}$$

It should now be apparent that matrix multiplication consists of a *row-on-column* multiplication sequence.

Matrix multiplication is not commutative. That is, $AB \neq BA$. In addition, the product of two matrices AB is defined only if the number of columns in **A** is equal to the number of rows in **B**.

As shown in the following example, the multiplication of a matrix **A** by a *column* matrix **B** results in a column matrix:

$$\begin{bmatrix} 1 & 2 & 3 \\ 3 & 4 & 1 \\ 1 & 2 & 1 \end{bmatrix} \begin{Bmatrix} 1 \\ 2 \\ 3 \end{Bmatrix} = \begin{Bmatrix} (1)(1) + (2)(2) + (3)(3) \\ (3)(1) + (4)(2) + (1)(3) \\ (1)(1) + (2)(2) + (1)(3) \end{Bmatrix} = \begin{Bmatrix} 14 \\ 14 \\ 8 \end{Bmatrix}$$

The *identity* matrix **I**, or *unit* matrix, is an n-by-n matrix with *ones* on the main diagonal and zeros everywhere else. The identity matrix is to matrix algebra what the identity number (one) is to ordinary algebra. That is,

$$IA = AI = A \tag{B-2}$$

Matrix multiplication is associative. That is,

$$ABC = (AB)C = A(BC) \tag{B-3}$$

Premultiplying the product **AB** by **C** means

$$CAB = D$$

If **AB** is to be *postmultiplied* by **C**, then

$$\mathbf{ABC} = \mathbf{E}$$

B-2 MATRIX INVERSION (Also see Section 3-6.)

The inverse of the matrix **A** is denoted as $\mathbf{A}^{-1}$. Also,

$$\mathbf{A}^{-1}\mathbf{A} = \mathbf{I}$$

To invert the matrix

$$\mathbf{A} = \begin{bmatrix} 1 & 1 & 0 \\ 1 & 0 & 1 \\ 1 & 2 & 2 \end{bmatrix}$$

first write the *augmented* matrix

$$\begin{bmatrix} 1 & 1 & 0 & 1 & 0 & 0 \\ 1 & 0 & 1 & 0 & 1 & 0 \\ 1 & 2 & 2 & 0 & 0 & 1 \end{bmatrix}$$

The elements b_{ij} of the inverse matrix $\mathbf{A}^{-1}$ may be obtained by *successive* applications of the following equations on the augmented matrix:

$$b_{i-1,j-1} = a_{ij} - \frac{a_{1j}a_{i1}}{a_{11}} \qquad \begin{cases} 1 < i \le n \\ 1 < j \le m \\ a_{11} \ne 0 \end{cases} \qquad (\text{B-4})$$

$$b_{n,j-1} = \frac{a_{1j}}{a_{11}} \qquad \begin{cases} 1 < j \le m \\ a_{11} \ne 0 \end{cases} \qquad (\text{B-5})$$

where

m = maximum column number

n = maximum row number

i = row number of old matrix **A**

j = column number of old matrix **A**

a = an element of old matrix **A**

b = an element of new matrix **B**

Three successive applications of Eqs. B-4 and B-5 (starting with the augmented matrix) yield

$$\mathbf{A}^{-1} = \begin{bmatrix} \frac{2}{3} & \frac{2}{3} & -\frac{1}{3} \\ \frac{1}{3} & -\frac{2}{3} & \frac{1}{3} \\ -\frac{2}{3} & \frac{1}{3} & \frac{1}{3} \end{bmatrix}$$

B-3 TRANSPOSE OF A MATRIX

The transpose $\mathbf{A}^T$ of $\mathbf{A}$ is obtained by interchanging the rows and columns of $\mathbf{A}$. That is, if

$$\mathbf{A} = \begin{bmatrix} a_{11} & a_{12} & a_{13} \\ a_{21} & a_{22} & a_{23} \\ a_{31} & a_{32} & a_{33} \end{bmatrix}$$

then

$$\mathbf{A}^T = \begin{bmatrix} a_{11} & a_{21} & a_{31} \\ a_{12} & a_{22} & a_{32} \\ a_{13} & a_{23} & a_{33} \end{bmatrix}$$

If $\mathbf{A}$ is a *symmetric* matrix ($a_{ij} = a_{ji}$), then

$$\mathbf{A} = \mathbf{A}^T$$

From the definition of the transpose of a matrix, it follows that

$$[\mathbf{AB}]^T = \mathbf{B}^T\mathbf{A}^T \tag{B-6}$$

B-4 ORTHOGONALITY PRINCIPLE OF SYMMETRIC MATRICES

The matrix equation for a set of n homogeneous algebraic equations may be written as

$$[\mathbf{A} - \lambda\mathbf{I}]\{\mathbf{X}\} = \mathbf{0}$$

or

$$\mathbf{AX} = \lambda\mathbf{X} \tag{B-7}$$

where $\mathbf{A}$ is a square symmetric matrix and the λ's are the eigenvalues corresponding to the eigenvectors $\mathbf{X}$. For the ith and jth eigenvalues and corresponding eigenvectors, we may write from Eq. B-7 the following:

$$\mathbf{AX}_i = \lambda_i\mathbf{X}_i \tag{B-8}$$

and

$$\mathbf{AX}_j = \lambda_j\mathbf{X}_j \tag{B-9}$$

Postmultiplying the transpose of Eq. B-8 by X_j, gives

$$[\mathbf{AX}_i]^{\mathrm{T}}\mathbf{X}_j = \lambda_i\mathbf{X}_i^{\mathrm{T}}\mathbf{X}_j \tag{B-10}$$

From Eq. B-6, we note that $[\mathbf{AX}_i]^{\mathrm{T}} = \mathbf{X}_i^{\mathrm{T}}\mathbf{A}^{\mathrm{T}}$. Thus, Eq. B-10 may be written as

$$\mathbf{X}_i^{\mathrm{T}}\mathbf{A}^{\mathrm{T}}\mathbf{X}_j = \lambda_i\mathbf{X}_i^{\mathrm{T}}\mathbf{X}_j \tag{B-11}$$

Premultiplying Eq. B-9 by $\mathbf{X}_i^{\mathrm{T}}$ gives

$$\mathbf{X}_i^{\mathrm{T}}\mathbf{AX}_j = \lambda_j\mathbf{X}_i^{\mathrm{T}}\mathbf{X}_j \tag{B-12}$$

Noting that $\mathbf{A}^{\mathrm{T}} = \mathbf{A}$, since $\mathbf{A}$ is a symmetric matrix, we obtain upon subtracting Eq. B-12 from Eq. B-11

$$(\lambda_i - \lambda_j)\mathbf{X}_i^{\mathrm{T}}\mathbf{X}_j = 0$$

Since $\lambda_i \neq \lambda_j$, it follows that

$$\mathbf{X}_i^{\mathrm{T}}\mathbf{X}_j = 0 \tag{B-13}$$

which states that the eigenvectors $\mathbf{X}_i$ and $\mathbf{X}_j$ are orthogonal. In summary,

$$\mathbf{X}_i^{\mathrm{T}}\mathbf{X}_j = \begin{cases} 0 & i \neq j \\ M_{ii} & i = j \end{cases} \tag{B-14}$$

With $i = j$, M_{ii} is simply equal to the sum of the squares of the components of $\mathbf{X}_i$.

B-5 ORTHOGONALITY PRINCIPLE OF THE FORM AX = λBX

For many physical problems, the matrix form of a set of homogeneous equations does not occur in the standard form of Eq. B-7, but instead in the form

$$\mathbf{AX} = \lambda\mathbf{BX} \tag{B-15}$$

where $\mathbf{A}$ and $\mathbf{B}$ are square symmetric matrices. By following the procedure of B-4, it is easy to show that the orthogonality of the eigenvectors for matrices of the form of Eq. B-15 is

$$\mathbf{X}_i^T \mathbf{B} \mathbf{X}_j = \begin{Bmatrix} 0 & i \neq j \\ G_{ii} & i = j \end{Bmatrix} \tag{B-16}$$

B-6 PROOF OF CONVERGENCE OF THE POWER METHOD TO THE LARGEST EIGENVALUE AND CORRESPONDING EIGENVECTOR

Assume that the eigenvalues of an $n \times n$ matrix $\mathbf{A}$ are real and distinct so that $|\lambda_1| > |\lambda_2| \geq |\lambda_3| \geq \cdots \geq |\lambda_n|$. The absolute values of some of the distinct eigenvalues may be equal, but $|\lambda_1|$ must be greater than $|\lambda_2|$ for convergence as will become evident in the proof.

Beginning with the matrix $\mathbf{A}$ and an arbitrarily assumed initial vector $\mathbf{X}_0$, and applying the steps on page 224, the following sequence of equations is obtained from r iterations:

$$\mathbf{A}\mathbf{X}_0 = l_1 \left\{ \frac{\mathbf{A}\mathbf{X}_0}{l_1} \right\}$$

$$\mathbf{A}\left\{ \frac{\mathbf{A}\mathbf{X}_0}{l_1} \right\} = l_2 \left\{ \frac{\mathbf{A}^2\mathbf{X}_0}{l_1 l_2} \right\}$$

$$\mathbf{A}\left\{ \frac{\mathbf{A}^2\mathbf{X}_0}{l_1 l_2} \right\} = l_3 \left\{ \frac{\mathbf{A}^3\mathbf{X}_0}{l_1 l_2 l_3} \right\} \tag{B-17}$$

$$\vdots$$

$$\mathbf{A}\left\{ \frac{\mathbf{A}^{r-1}\mathbf{X}_0}{l_1 l_2 \cdots l_{r-1}} \right\} = l_r \left\{ \frac{\mathbf{A}^r\mathbf{X}_0}{l_1 l_2 \cdots l_r} \right\}$$

in which the l's are normalizing factors.

In this proof any number or lowercase letter not in parentheses which appears as a superscript is an exponent. Any superscript of the vector $\mathbf{X}_0$ in parentheses, either alphabetical or numerical, is not an exponent, but rather indicates the number of the iteration in which that particular $\mathbf{X}_0$ was determined in Eq. B-17.

Defining $\mathbf{X}_0^{(0)}$ as $\mathbf{X}_0$, and letting

$$\frac{\mathbf{A}^m\mathbf{X}_0}{l_1 l_2 \cdots l_m} = \mathbf{X}_0^{(m)} \qquad (1 \leq m \leq r) \tag{B-18}$$

Eq. B-17 can be written as

$$\mathbf{A}\mathbf{X}_0^{(m-1)} = l_m\mathbf{X}_0^{(m)} \qquad (m = 1, 2, \ldots, r) \tag{B-19}$$

For distinct eigenvalues of $\mathbf{A}$, the eigenvectors will be linearly independent, and any vector in n-dimensional space can be expressed as a linear combination of the n eigenvectors of matrix $\mathbf{A}$. Thus, the arbitrary vector $\mathbf{X}_0$ can be expressed as

$$\mathbf{X}_0 = a_1\mathbf{X}_1 + a_2\mathbf{X}_2 + \cdots + a_n\mathbf{X}_n$$

or more simply as

$$\mathbf{X}_0 = \sum_{i=1}^{n} a_i\mathbf{X}_i \tag{B-20}$$

Premultiplying Eq. B-20 by $\mathbf{A}^r$ we obtain

$$\mathbf{A}^r\mathbf{X}_0 = \sum_{i=1}^{n} a_i\mathbf{A}^r\mathbf{X}_i \tag{B-21}$$

Noting that $\mathbf{A}\mathbf{X}_i = \lambda_i\mathbf{X}_i$ and that

$$\mathbf{A}[\mathbf{A}\mathbf{X}_i] = \lambda_i[\mathbf{A}\mathbf{X}_i] = \lambda_i[\lambda_i\mathbf{X}_i]$$

it can be seen that

$$\mathbf{A}^2\mathbf{X}_i = \lambda_i^2\mathbf{X}_i$$

Similarly,

$$\mathbf{A}^r\mathbf{X}_i = \lambda_i^r\mathbf{X}_i \tag{B-22}$$

Substituting Eq. B-22 into Eq. B-21 gives

$$\mathbf{A}^r\mathbf{X}_0 = \sum_{i=1}^{n} a_i\lambda_i^r\mathbf{X}_i \tag{B-23}$$

From the definition of Eq. B-18, Eq. B-23 can be written as

$$(l_1, l_2, \ldots, l_r)\mathbf{X}_0^{(r)} = \sum_{i=1}^{n} a_i\lambda_i^r\mathbf{X}_i$$

or as

$$(l_1, l_2, \ldots, l_r)X_0^{(r)} = \lambda_1^r \sum_{i=1}^{n} a_i \left(\frac{\lambda_i}{\lambda_1}\right)^r X_i \tag{B-24}$$

Writing out the summation, we obtain

$$(l_1, l_2, \ldots, l_r)X_0^{(r)} = \lambda_1^r \left[a_1 X_1 + a_2 \left(\frac{\lambda_2}{\lambda_1}\right)^r X_2 + \cdots + a_n \left(\frac{\lambda_n}{\lambda_1}\right)^r X_n \right] \tag{B-25}$$

For sufficiently large r, all the terms of the summation become negligible except for the first one, and

$$(l_1, l_2, \ldots, l_r)X_0^{(r)} = \lambda_1^r a_1 X_1 \tag{B-26}$$

It should be apparent from Eq. B-26 that $X_0^{(r)}$ converges to X_1, which is the eigenvector associated with the eigenvalue having the largest absolute value.

From Eq. B-19 with $m = r$,

$$AX_0^{(r-1)} = l_r X_0^{(r)}$$

After convergence, $X_0^{(r)}$ and $X_0^{(r-1)}$ are essentially equal, and

$$X_0^{(r)} = X_1$$

Thus, $l_r = \lambda_1$, so that

$$AX_1 = \lambda_1 X_1$$

which is in accord with Eq. 3-135.

An examination of Eq. B-25 shows that $X_0^{(r)}$ does not converge to X_1 if $(\lambda_2/\lambda_1)^r$ does not approach zero with increasing r. Therefore, $|\lambda_2|$ cannot equal $|\lambda_1|$ for convergence to X_1 and λ_1. If $\lambda_2/\lambda_1 \cong 1$, convergence may be slow.

If A is symmetric and $X_0^{(0)}$ is orthogonal to X_1, then convergence will not be to X_1 and λ_1. In this case,

$$X_1^T X_0^{(0)} = 0$$

Recalling that $X_0^{(0)} = X_0$, it can be seen from Eq. B-20 that

$$X_1^T X_0^{(0)} = a_1 X_1^T X_1 + a_2 X_1^T X_2 + \cdots + a_n X_1^T X_n \tag{B-27}$$

It then follows from Eq. B-13 that the second and subsequent terms on the right-hand side of Eq. B-27 are equal to zero. But, since $X_1^T X_0^{(0)} = 0$, $a_1 X_1^T X_1$

must also equal zero, which means that $a_1 = 0$, and Eq. B-20 becomes

$$\mathbf{X}_0 = \sum_{i=2}^{n} a_i \mathbf{X}_i$$

Proceeding with equations similar to Eqs. B-21, B-23, B-24, and B-25 will show that convergence will be to $\mathbf{X}_2$ and λ_2 instead of to $\mathbf{X}_1$ and λ_1.

If 1 or more of the eigenvalue ratios in Eq. B-25 is negative, the terms containing those ratios will fluctuate in sign as r changes. These fluctuations may initially give $\mathbf{X}_0^{(r)}$ the appearance of not converging. However, negative eigenvalues are seldom encountered in real physical problems. Convergence in a number of special cases is discussed by Faddeev and Faddeeva.[1]

[1]See D. K. Faddeev and U. N. Faddeeva, *Computational Methods of Linear Algebra*, trans. Robert C. Williams (San Francisco: W. H. Freeman, 1963).

Appendix C
Interpolating Polynomials and Application to Numerical Integration and Differentiation

C-1 INTRODUCTION TO INTERPOLATION

Suppose that we have some tabulated values of a function over a certain range of its independent variable such as shown in Fig. C-1. The problem of *interpolation* is to find the value of the function for some intermediate value of x not included in the table. This x value is assumed to lie within the range of tabulated abscissas. If it does not, the problem of finding the corresponding function value is called *extrapolation*.

Tabular values may be plotted to give us a graphical picture of points through which the function must pass. Connecting the points with a smooth curve gives us a graphical representation of the function. If only a rough approximation of the function value is required for some intermediate x value, it can be obtained by reading the function value directly from the graph. This procedure is called *graphical interpolation*. If the given values of the independent variable are close together, a sufficiently good graphical approximation to the function might be obtained by connecting the points with straight-line segments as shown in Fig. C-2. An intermediate function value could then be obtained by reading it from the graph. An intermediate function value could

x	$f(x)$
0	0
0.2	0.199
0.4	0.389
0.6	0.565
0.8	0.717
1.0	0.841

Figure C-1   Particular x values with $f(x)$

also be obtained analytically by a method based on this piecewise linear approximation of the function. From similar triangles in Fig. C-2,

$$\frac{f(x) - f(x_0)}{x - x_0} = \frac{f(x_1) - f(x_0)}{x_1 - x_0}$$

or

$$f(x) = f(x_0) + \frac{f(x_1) - f(x_0)}{x_1 - x_0} (x - x_0) \tag{C-1}$$

for x values between x_0 and x_1. The use of Eq. C-1 is called linear interpolation, which is familiar to everyone who has used log tables.

A smooth curve passing through the given points can be obtained analytically by assuming the function to be approximated by a polynomial function. This was done in a piecewise manner in the derivation of Simpson's rule in Sec. 5-4 where it was assumed that the actual function could be approximated by second-degree parabolas connecting sets of three successive points. In general, a unique polynomial function of degree n can be determined which passes through $n + 1$ given distinct points. This can be done in a manner similar to that employed in Sec. 5-4 in determining a second-degree parabola which passes through three given points. That is, the nth-degree polynomial passing through the $n + 1$ points may be expressed as

$$f(x) = a_1 x^n + a_2 x^{n-1} + a_3 x^{n-2} + \cdots + a_n x + a_{n+1} \tag{C-2}$$

where the a's are unknown coefficients. The substitution of the $n + 1$ x values and corresponding function values into this equation will give $n + 1$ simultaneous equations in the $n + 1$ unknown a values. This approach was the most simple and direct for deriving Simpson's rule, but for determining higher degree interpolating polynomials, more efficient methods will be derived. However, before proceeding with these derivations, it will be necessary to discuss some basic definitions.

Figure C-2 Graphical approximation of a function with straight-line segments

C-2 DEFINITIONS

Forward Differences

Let $f(x)$ be some function of x. An increment Δx of the independent variable will be denoted by h. The corresponding increment of the function is

$$\Delta f(x) = f(x + h) - f(x)$$

This increment is called the *first forward difference* of $f(x)$ with respect to h. The operator Δ always implies this operation on any function of x on which it operates. Since $\Delta f(x)$ is a function of x, it can be operated on by the operator Δ giving

$$\Delta[\Delta f(x)] = \Delta^2 f(x) = \Delta[f(x + h) - f(x)]$$

Hence

$$\begin{aligned}\Delta^2 f(x) &= [f(x + 2h) - f(x + h)] - [f(x + h) - f(x)] \\ &= f(x + 2h) - 2f(x + h) + f(x)\end{aligned}$$

The function $\Delta^2 f(x)$ is called the *second forward difference* of $f(x)$. Third, fourth, and higher differences are similarly obtained. In summary, the forward difference expressions are

$$\Delta f(x_i) = f(x_i + h) - f(x_i)$$
$$\Delta^2 f(x_i) = f(x_i + 2h) - 2f(x_i + h) + f(x_i)$$

$$\Delta^3 f(x_i) = f(x_i + 3h) - 3f(x_i + 2h) + 3f(x_i + h) - f(x_i)$$

$$\Delta^4 f(x_i) = f(x_i + 4h) - 4f(x_i + 3h) + 6f(x_i + 2h) - 4f(x_i + h) + f(x_i)$$

$$\vdots$$

$$\Delta^n f(x_i) = f(x_i + nh) - nf[x_i + (n - 1)h] + \frac{n(n-1)}{2!} f[x_i + (n - 2)h]$$

$$- \frac{n(n - 1)(n - 2)}{3!} f[x_i + (n - 3)h] + \cdots + (-1)^n f(x_i)$$

in which x_i denotes any specific value for x such as x_0, x_1, and so forth.

The nth difference is often written as

$$\Delta^n f(x_i) = f(x_i + nh) - \binom{n}{1} f[x_i + (n - 1)h] + \binom{n}{2} f[x_i + (n - 2)h]$$

$$- \cdots + (-1)^k \binom{n}{k} f[x_i + (n - k)h] + \cdots + (-1)^n f(x_i)$$

where the symbol

$$\binom{n}{k} = \frac{n(n - 1)(n - 2)(n - 3) \cdots (n - k + 1)}{k!}$$

is the familiar symbol used for binomial coefficients.

If we have a table of function values such as shown in Fig. C-1, a difference table can be formed having entries such as those shown in Fig. C-3. In this table, $f(x_0 + sh)$ is denoted by f_s and $\Delta^k f(x_0 + sh)$ by $\Delta^k f_s$. Each difference is obtained by subtracting the table entry to its upper left from the table entry to its lower left.

Backward Differences

The first backward difference of $f(x)$ with respect to increment h is defined as

$$\nabla f(x) = f(x) - f(x - h)$$

The operator ∇ always implies this operation on the function of x on which it operates, so that

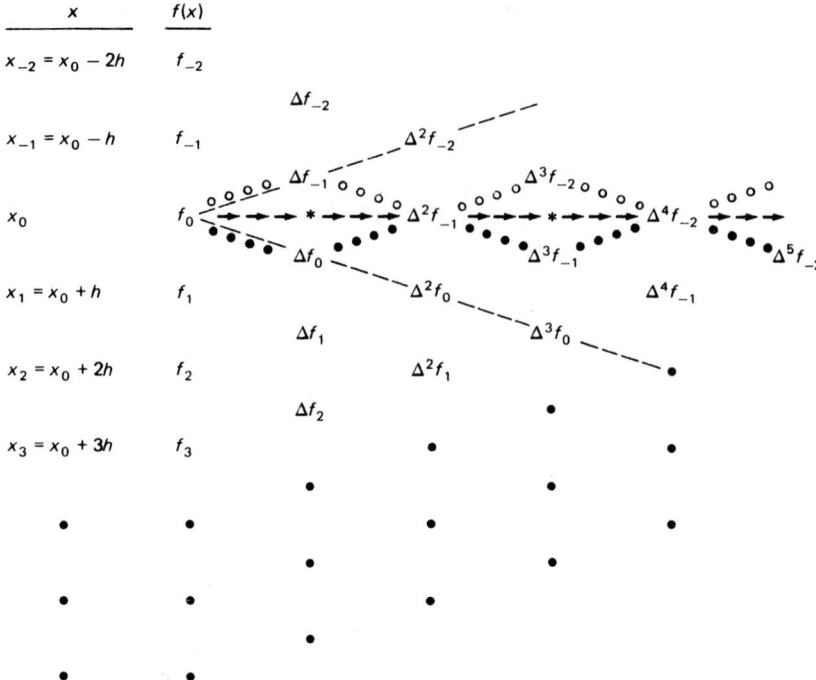

Figure C-3 Difference table

$$\nabla[\nabla f(x_i)] = \nabla^2 f(x_i) = [f(x_i) - f(x_i - h)] - [f(x_i - h) - f(x_i - 2h)]$$
$$= f(x_i) - 2f(x_i - h) + f(x_i - 2h)$$

where x_i denotes any specific values for x such as x_0, x_1, and so forth. In general, $\nabla^n f(x_i) = \nabla[\nabla^{n-1} f(x_i)]$, and the backward differences of $f(x_i)$ are

$$\nabla f(x_i) = f(x_i) - f(x_i - h)$$
$$\nabla^2 f(x_i) = f(x_i) - 2f(x_i - h) + f(x_i - 2h)$$
$$\nabla^3 f(x_i) = f(x_i) - 3f(x_i - h) + 3f(x_i - 2h) - f(x_i - 3h)$$
$$\nabla^4 f(x_i) = f(x_i) - 4f(x_i - h) + 6f(x_i - 2h) - 4f(x_i - 3h) + f(x_i - 4h)$$

$$\vdots \qquad \vdots$$

$$\nabla^n f(x_i) = f(x_i) - \binom{n}{1} f(x_i - h) + \binom{n}{2} f(x_i - 2h) - \cdots$$
$$+ (-1)^n f(x_i - nh)$$

We may also note that

$$\nabla f(x_i) = \Delta f(x_i - h)$$
$$\nabla^2 f(x_i) = \Delta^2 f(x_i - 2h)$$

$$\vdots \qquad \vdots$$

$$\nabla^n f(x_i) = \Delta^n f(x_i - nh)$$

If we let $x_i = x_0$, and use the simplified notation shown in Fig. C-3, the above relationships between the forward- and backward-difference expressions become

$$\nabla f_0 = \Delta f_{-1}$$
$$\nabla^2 f_0 = \Delta^2 f_{-2}$$

$$\vdots \quad \vdots$$

$$\nabla^n f_0 = \Delta^n f_{-n}$$

or, in general,

$$\nabla^k f_s = \Delta^k f_{s-k} \qquad (k = 1, 2, 3, \ldots)$$

Thus, the table in Fig. C-3 can be written with backward-difference notation as shown in Fig. C-4. The numerical values of the table entries would be

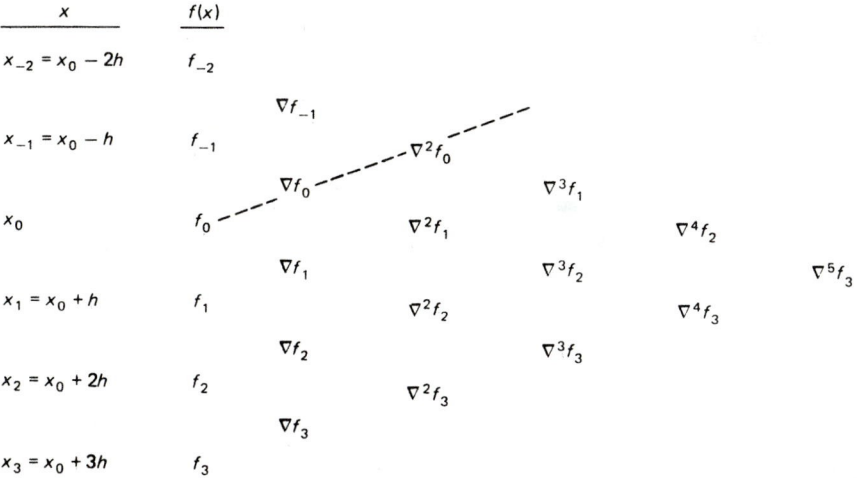

Figure C-4 Table of Fig. C-3 written in backward-difference notation

identical to those in the table of Fig. C-3 for the same function and arguments, and the differences are found as described for that table. The table entries in Fig. C-4 are merely expressed in different notation.

Central Differences

The tables in Figs. C-3 and C-4 can be written in central-difference notation by introduction of the central-difference operator δ defined by

$$\delta^{2n} f(x) = \Delta^{2n} f(x - nh)$$

$$\delta^{2n+1} f(x + h/2) = \Delta^{2n+1} f(x - nh)$$

Using these definitions, the table in Fig. C-3 can be converted to the notation shown in Fig. C-5. Numerical values in this table would be identical to those in the tables of Figs. C-3 and C-4 for the same function and arguments. The tables differ only in the notation used to represent the table entries. For example, the tables of Figs. C-3 through C-5 would all appear as shown in Fig. C-6 for the given function values.

The Averaging Operator

The averaging operator is defined as

$$\mu f(x) = \tfrac{1}{2}[f(x + h/2) + f(x - h/2)]$$

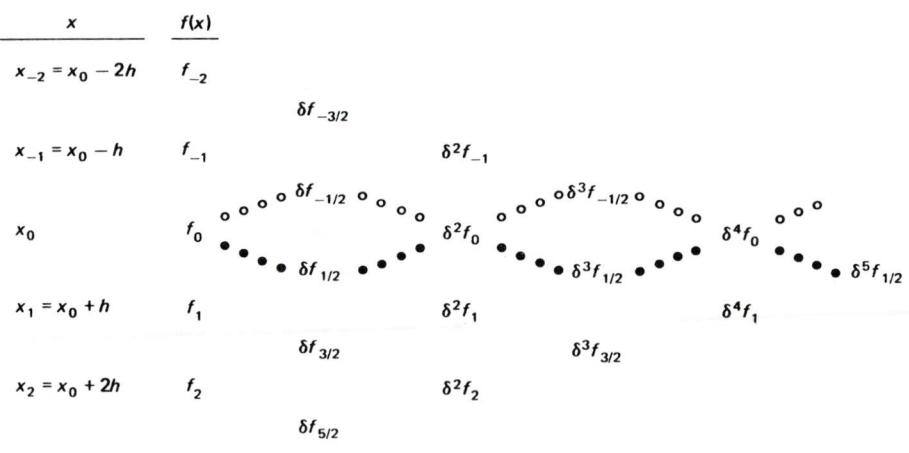

Figure C-5 Table of Fig. C-3 written in central-difference notation

x	$f(x)$				
0	0				
		0.03125			
0.5	0.03125		0.9375		
		0.96875		4.6875	
1.0	1.00000		5.6250		7.50
		6.59375		12.1875		3.75
1.5	7.59375		17.8125		11.25
		24.40625		23.4375	
2.0	32.00000		41.2500		
		65.65625			
2.5	97.65625				

Figure C-6   Numerical values for Figs. C-3, C-4, and C-5

x_0	$f_0 \rightarrow \rightarrow \rightarrow$	$\mu\delta f_0 \rightarrow \rightarrow \rightarrow$	$\delta^2 f_0 \rightarrow \rightarrow \rightarrow$	$\mu\delta^3 f_0 \rightarrow \rightarrow \rightarrow$	$\delta^4 f_0 \rightarrow \rightarrow \rightarrow$
	$\mu f_{1/2}$	$\delta f_{1/2}$	$\mu\delta^2 f_{1/2}$	$\delta^3 f_{1/2}$	$\mu\delta^4 f_{1/2}$	$\delta^5 f_{1/2}$
$x_0 + h$	f_1	$\mu\delta f_1$	$\delta^2 f_1$	$\mu\delta^3 f_1$	$\delta^4 f_1$

Figure C-7   Table of Fig. C-5 with averages from averaging operator inserted

Then,

$$\mu\delta f_0 = \tfrac{1}{2}[\delta f_{1/2} + \delta f_{-1/2}]$$
$$\mu\delta^2 f_{1/2} = \tfrac{1}{2}[\delta^2 f_1 + \delta^2 f_0]$$
$$\mu\delta^3 f_0 = \tfrac{1}{2}[\delta^3 f_{1/2} + \delta^3 f_{-1/2}]$$

and so forth. If these averages are inserted into the table of Fig. C-5 between the values used for averaging, the rows for abscissas x_0 and $x_0 + h$ and the intermediate row become as shown in the table of Fig. C-7. The tables of Figs. C-3 through C-5 and of Fig. C-7 will be referred to later in this appendix when we consider various polynomial interpolation formulas.

Difference Quotients

The operator $\underset{h}{\Delta}$ is defined as follows:

$$\underset{h}{\Delta} f(x) = \frac{f(x + h) - f(x)}{h}$$

The function $\underset{h}{\Delta} f(x)$ is called the *first difference quotient* of $f(x)$. The second difference quotient is

$$\underset{h}{\Delta^2 f(x)} = \underset{h}{\Delta}\left[\underset{h}{\Delta} f(x)\right]$$

$$= \frac{\{[f(x + 2h) - f(x + h)]/h\} - \{[f(x + h) - f(x)]/h\}}{h}$$

$$= \frac{f(x + 2h) - 2f(x + h) + f(x)}{h^2}$$

The nth difference quotient is

$$\underset{h}{\Delta^n f(x)} = \underset{h}{\Delta}\left[\underset{h}{\Delta}^{\,n-1} f(x)\right]$$

It is apparent that

$$\Delta^n f(x) = h^n \underset{h}{\Delta}^{\,n} f(x)$$

Divided Differences

The divided difference of $f(x)$ for the arguments x_k and x_0 will be written $[x_k x_0]$ and is defined as

$$[x_k x_0] = \frac{f(x_k) - f(x_0)}{x_k - x_0}$$

Since

$$[x_0 x_k] = \frac{f(x_0) - f(x_k)}{x_0 - x_k}$$

it is clear that

$$[x_k x_0] = [x_0 x_k]$$

Divided differences of three arguments are defined as follows:

$$[x_k x_0 x_1] = \frac{[x_k x_0] - [x_0 x_1]}{x_k - x_1}$$

or since

$$[x_0x_1] = [x_1x_0]$$

$$[x_kx_0x_1] = \frac{[x_kx_0] - [x_1x_0]}{x_k - x_1}$$

Divided differences of any number of arguments are defined similarly. Thus for $n + 1$ arguments

$$[x_kx_0x_1 \cdots x_{n-1}] = \frac{[x_kx_0x_1 \cdots x_{n-2}] - [x_0x_1x_2 \cdots x_{n-1}]}{x_k - x_{n-1}} \tag{C-3}$$

C-3 POLYNOMIAL APPROXIMATION AND INTERPOLATION

With the definitions previously discussed, we are now in a position to derive many of the well-known interpolating polynomials. We will derive three of these, and give others with a reference to which the interested reader may refer for the derivations. It should be emphasized that there is only one polynomial of degree n passing through $n + 1$ given points. Although the forms of the various polynomials presented will differ, they all yield the same polynomial if the same $n + 1$ points are used.

Newton's General Interpolating Polynomial

If we let $x_k = x$ in Eq. C-3, we have

$$[xx_0x_1 \cdots x_n] = \frac{-[x_0x_1x_2 \cdots x_n]}{x - x_n} + \frac{[xx_0x_1 \cdots x_{n-1}]}{x - x_n}$$

$$[xx_0x_1 \cdots x_{n-1}] = \frac{-[x_0x_1x_2 \cdots x_{n-1}]}{x - x_{n-1}} + \frac{[xx_0x_1 \cdots x_{n-2}]}{x - x_{n-1}}$$

$$[xx_0x_1 \cdots x_{n-2}] = \frac{-[x_0x_1x_2 \cdots x_{n-2}]}{x - x_{n-2}} + \frac{[xx_0x_1 \cdots x_{n-3}]}{x - x_{n-2}}$$

$$\vdots \qquad \vdots$$

$$[xx_0x_1] = \frac{-[x_0x_1]}{x - x_1} + \frac{[xx_0]}{x - x_1}$$

$$[xx_0] = \frac{-f(x_0)}{x - x_0} + \frac{f(x)}{x - x_0}$$

Note that the numerator of the second term of the first equation is given by the second equation, the numerator of the second term of the second equation is given by the third equation, and so forth. Making these substitutions, we obtain

$$[xx_0x_1 \cdots x_n] = \frac{-[x_0x_1x_2 \cdots x_n]}{x - x_n} - \frac{[x_0x_1x_2 \cdots x_{n-1}]}{(x - x_n)(x - x_{n-1})}$$

$$- \frac{[x_0x_1x_2 \cdots x_{n-2}]}{(x - x_n)(x - x_{n-1})(x - x_{n-2})} - \cdots$$

$$- \frac{[x_0x_1]}{(x - x_n)(x - x_{n-1}) \cdots (x - x_1)}$$

$$- \frac{f(x_0)}{(x - x_n)(x - x_{n-1}) \cdots (x - x_0)}$$

$$+ \frac{f(x)}{(x - x_n)(x - x_{n-1}) \cdots (x - x_0)}$$

Solving for $f(x)$ yields

$$f(x) = f(x_0) + (x - x_0)[x_0x_1] + (x - x_0)(x - x_1)[x_0x_1x_2] + \cdots$$

$$+ (x - x_0)(x - x_1)(x - x_2) \cdots (x - x_{n-1})[x_0x_1x_2 \cdots x_n]$$

$$+ R(x)$$

$$(\text{C-4})$$

where the remainder term, $R(x)$, is given by

$$R(x) = (x - x_0)(x - x_1) \cdots (x - x_n)[xx_0x_1 \cdots x_n] \qquad (\text{C-5})$$

If $f(x)$ is a polynomial of degree n, the remainder term is zero for all x. This can be shown as follows. If $f(x)$ is a polynomial of degree n, then

$$[xx_0] = \frac{f(x) - f(x_0)}{x - x_0}$$

is a polynomial of degree $n - 1$. Taking the divided difference of a polynomial lowers the degree by one. Thus, for a polynomial of degree n, $[xx_0x_1]$ is of degree $n - 2$, $[xx_0x_1x_2]$ is of degree $n - 3$, and so forth. Therefore, $[xx_0x_1 \cdots x_{n-1}]$ is of degree zero (is a constant). Hence, $[xx_0x_1 \cdots x_n]$ in Eq. C-5 is equal to zero, and

$$R(x) \equiv 0$$

If $f(x)$ is not a polynomial, we note from Eq. C-5 that the remainder term is zero at $x = x_0$, $x = x_1$, . . . , $x = x_n$, but is not in general elsewhere. If we omit the remainder term from Eq. C-4, we have a polynomial of degree n which coincides with $f(x)$ at $x = x_0, x_1, . . . , x_n$. This polynomial is called an interpolating polynomial, and will be denoted by $p_n(x)$. The basis for using it is the assumption that $p_n(x)$ will be very nearly equal to $f(x)$ for intermediate x values.

Omitting the remainder term in Eq. C-4 gives

$$p_n(x) = f(x_0) + \sum_{S=0}^{n-1} (x - x_0)(x - x_1) \cdots (x - x_S)[x_0 x_1 \cdots x_{S+1}] \qquad \text{(C-6)}$$

which is known as Newton's general interpolating polynomial.

EXAMPLE C-1

Determine the equation of a third-degree polynomial passing through the points (0, 5), (1, 14), (2, 41), and (3, 98) using Newton's general interpolating polynomial. In this example, the abscissas are equally spaced, but they need not be. Also, x_0, x_1, x_2, and x_3 need not be abscissa values necessarily in ascending or descending order. The abscissas, ordinates, and divided differences will first be tabulated in the scheme which follows.

$x_0 \quad f(x_0)$

$\qquad\qquad [x_0 x_1]$

$x_1 \quad f(x_1) \qquad\qquad [x_0 x_1 x_2]$

$\qquad\qquad [x_1 x_2] \qquad\qquad [x_0 x_1 x_2 x_3]$

$x_2 \quad f(x_2) \qquad\qquad [x_1 x_2 x_3]$

$\qquad\qquad [x_2 x_3]$

$x_3 \quad f(x_3)$

Using the scheme above, we obtain

$x \qquad f(x)$

$0 \qquad 5$

$\qquad\qquad\qquad 9$

$1 \qquad 14 \qquad\qquad\qquad 9$

$\qquad\qquad\qquad 27 \qquad\qquad\qquad 2$

$2 \qquad 41 \qquad\qquad\qquad 15$

$\qquad\qquad\qquad 57$

$3 \qquad 98$

Equation C-6, for $n = 3$, is

$$p_3(x) = f(x_0) + (x - x_0)[x_0 x_1] + (x - x_0)(x - x_1)[x_0 x_1 x_2]$$
$$+ (x - x_0)(x - x_1)(x - x_2)[x_0 x_1 x_2 x_3]$$

Substituting values from the table above into Eq. C-6 yields

$$p_3(x) = 5 + (x - 0)9 + (x - 0)(x - 1)9 + (x - 0)(x - 1)(x - 2)2$$
$$= 2x^3 + 3x^2 + 4x + 5$$

The Newton-Gregory Forward-Interpolating Polynomial

Newton's general interpolating polynomial of degree n can be put in a convenient form involving 1st, 2nd, . . . , nth forward differences if the abscissa increment is uniform. By definitions previously given,

$$[x_0 x_1] = \frac{f(x_0) - f(x_1)}{x_0 - x_1} = \Delta_h f(x_0) = \frac{\Delta f(x_0)}{h}$$

If the arguments are equally spaced so that $x_1 = x_0 + h$, $x_2 = x_0 + 2h$, and so forth, then

$$[x_0 x_1 x_2] = \frac{\{[f(x_0) - f(x_1)]/[x_0 - x_1]\} - \{[f(x_1) - f(x_2)]/[x_1 - x_2]\}}{x_0 - x_2}$$

$$= \frac{f(x_0) - 2f(x_1) + f(x_2)}{2h^2}$$

$$= \frac{1}{2!} \Delta^2_h f(x_0)$$

$$= \frac{1}{2!} \frac{\Delta^2 f(x_0)}{h^2}$$

and, in general, if we let $x_S = x_0 + Sh$, we have that

$$[x_0 x_1 x_2 \cdots x_S] = \frac{1}{S!} \frac{\Delta^S f(x_0)}{h^S} \qquad \text{for } S = 1, 2, \ldots, n \tag{C-7}$$

and

$$[x_0 x_1 x_2 \cdots x_n] = \frac{1}{n!} \frac{\Delta^n f(x_0)}{h^n} \tag{C-8}$$

Letting $x_S = x_0 + Sh$ in Eq. C-4 where $S = 1, 2, \ldots, n - 1$, and using the expressions given by Eq. C-7 to substitute for the divided differences in Eq. C-4, we obtain

$$f(x) = f(x_0) + (x - x_0)\frac{\Delta f(x_0)}{h} + \frac{(x - x_0)(x - x_0 - h)}{2!}\frac{\Delta^2 f(x_0)}{h^2} + \cdots$$

$$+ \frac{(x - x_0)(x - x_0 - h)\cdots(x - x_0 - [n - 1]h)}{n!}\frac{\Delta^n f(x_0)}{h^n} + R(x)$$

$$\text{(C-9)}$$

where the remainder, $R(x)$, is given by Eq. C-5 and is

$$R(x) = (x - x_0)(x - x_1)\cdots(x - x_n)[xx_0x_1\cdots x_n]$$

Equation C-9 can be simplified somewhat if we define

$$u = \frac{x - x_0}{h}$$

That is, u is the ratio of the difference between x and x_0 to the increment of the tabulated argument values. This ratio is called the *phase*. Rearranging the equation, we obtain

$$x - x_0 = uh$$

$$x - x_0 - h = uh - h = h(u - 1)$$

$$x - x_0 - 2h = uh - 2h = h(u - 2) \qquad \text{(C-10)}$$

$$\vdots$$

$$x - x_0 - (n - 1)h = uh - (n - 1)h = h(u - n + 1)$$

Making these substitutions into Eq. C-9 and denoting $f(x_0)$ as f_0, $\Delta f(x_0)$ as Δf_0, and so forth, gives

$$f(x) = f_0 + u\Delta f_0 + \frac{u(u - 1)}{2!}\Delta^2 f_0 + \frac{u(u - 1)(u - 2)}{3!}\Delta^3 f_0 + \cdots$$

$$+ \frac{u(u - 1)\cdots(u - n + 1)}{n!}\Delta^n f_0 + R(x)$$

$$\text{(C-11)}$$

Omitting the remainder term of Eq. C-11 gives the Newton-Gregory forward-interpolating polynomial which may be expressed more compactly by using the binomial coefficient notation; it is

$$p_n(x) = f_0 + \binom{u}{1}\Delta f_0 + \binom{u}{2}\Delta^2 f_0 + \binom{u}{3}\Delta^3 f_0 + \cdots + \binom{u}{n}\Delta^n f_0 \qquad \text{(C-12)}$$

Note that the function value f_0 and the differences $\Delta f_0, \Delta^2 f_0, \ldots, \Delta^n f_0$ used in Eq. C-12 appear on a line of long dashes running diagonally downward through the difference table in Fig. C-3.

It may be shown[1] that the remainder term $R(x)$ in Eq. C-11 is equal to

$$\frac{(x - x_0)(x - x_0 - h)(x - x_0 - 2h) \cdots (x - x_0 - nh)}{(n - 1)!} f^{n+1}(\xi)$$

where $f^{n+1}(\xi)$ is the $(n + 1)$st derivative of $f(x)$ evaluated at ξ where $x_0 < \xi < x_n$. Then using Eq. C-10,

$$R(x) = \frac{(uh)(h[u - 1])(h[u - 2]) \cdots (h[u - n])}{(n + 1)!} f^{n+1}(\xi)$$

$$= \binom{u}{n + 1} h^{n+1} f^{n+1}(\xi) \qquad \text{(C-13)}$$

The function $f(x)$ is usually not known, so its $(n + 1)$st derivative would also be unknown. Furthermore, the exact location at which the derivative is to be evaluated is unknown. Thus, the expression for the remainder, which is the difference between the actual function and the interpolating polynomial, is of limited usefulness. One possible use is to compare the coefficient $\binom{u}{n+1}$ of the remainder term with the coefficient of the remainder term of other interpolating polynomials for which one or more different points have been used. The interpolating polynomial with the smallest coefficient in the remainder term usually gives the best approximation of $f(x)$ at the particular x value for which the comparison is made. If the function is known, an upper bound on the error can be established.

EXAMPLE C-2

Using the data given in the table of Fig. C-1, form a difference table. Then using the Newton-Gregory forward-interpolating polynomial (Eq. C-12), approximate $f(.30)$. The difference table for the data from Fig. C-1 is

---

[1] L. M. Milne-Thompson, *The Calculus of Finite Differences* (London: Macmillan & Co. Ltd., 1960), pp. 5, 6.

x	$f(x)$	Δf	$\Delta^2 f$	$\Delta^3 f$	$\Delta^4 f$	$\Delta^5 f$
$x_0 = 0$	0					
		0.199				
$x_0 + h = 0.2$	0.199		.009			
		0.190		.005		
$x_0 + 2h = 0.4$	0.389		$-.014$		.005	
		0.176		$-.010$		.011
$x_0 + 3h = 0.6$	0.565		$-.024$		.006	
		0.152		$-.004$		
$x_0 + 4h = 0.8$	0.717		$-.028$			
		0.124				
$x_0 + 5h = 1.0$	0.841					

Selecting the first tabulated value for x as x_0, the function f_0 and the differences Δf_0, $\Delta^2 f_0$, and so forth, appear on a diagonal running downward to the right as shown by the dashed line in the table.

Substituting values from the table into Eq. C-12, and noting that $x = 0.3$ so that

$$u = \frac{.3 - 0}{.2} = 1.5$$

we obtain

$$p_5(x) = 0 + \binom{1.5}{1}(.199) + \binom{1.5}{2}(-.009) + \binom{1.5}{3}(-.005)$$

$$+ \binom{1.5}{4}(-.005) + \binom{1.5}{5}(.011)$$

$$= 0 + (1.5)(.199) + \frac{(1.5)(.5)}{2!}(-.009) + \frac{(1.5)(.5)(-.5)}{3!}(-.005)$$

$$+ \frac{(1.5)(.5)(-.5)(-1.5)}{4!}(-.005)$$

$$+ \frac{(1.5)(.5)(-.5)(-1.5)(-2.5)}{5!}(.011)$$

$$= 0.2952$$

The function for this example is $f(x) = \sin x$, and $\sin (.30 \text{ radian}) = 0.2955$.

The Lagrangian Interpolating Polynomial

This polynomial is expressed in a form which is more convenient to use than Newton's general interpolating polynomial. Like the latter, it does not require uniform spacing of the abscissa values, nor does x_0, x_1, x_2, . . . necessarily need to be ascending or descending x values.

By definition,

$$[xx_0] = \frac{f(x) - f(x_0)}{x - x_0} = \frac{f(x)}{x - x_0} + \frac{f(x_0)}{x_0 - x}$$

and

$$[xx_0x_1] = \frac{[xx_0] - [x_0x_1]}{x - x_1} = \frac{f(x)}{(x - x_0)(x - x_1)} + \frac{f(x_0)}{(x_0 - x)(x - x_1)}$$

$$- \frac{f(x_0)}{(x_0 - x_1)(x - x_1)} - \frac{f(x_1)}{(x_1 - x_0)(x - x_1)}$$

Combining the second and third terms, and rewriting the fourth term, gives

$$[xx_0x_1] = \frac{f(x)}{(x - x_0)(x - x_1)} + \frac{f(x_0)}{(x_0 - x)(x_0 - x_1)} + \frac{f(x_1)}{(x_1 - x)(x_1 - x_0)}$$

Proceeding in this manner, we finally obtain

$$[xx_0x_1 \cdots x_n] = \frac{f(x)}{(x - x_0)(x - x_1)(x - x_2) \cdots (x - x_n)}$$

$$+ \frac{f(x_0)}{(x_0 - x)(x_0 - x_1)(x_0 - x_2) \cdots (x_0 - x_n)}$$

$$+ \frac{f(x_1)}{(x_1 - x)(x_1 - x_0)(x_1 - x_2) \cdots (x - x_n)} + \cdots$$

$$+ \frac{f(x_n)}{(x_n - x)(x_n - x_0)(x_n - x_1) \cdots (x_n - x_{n-1})}$$

Solving for $f(x)$,

$$f(x) = f(x_0)\frac{(x - x_1)(x - x_2) \cdots (x - x_n)}{(x_0 - x_1)(x_0 - x_2) \cdots (x_0 - x_n)}$$

$$+ f(x_1)\frac{(x - x_0)(x - x_2)(x - x_3) \cdots (x - x_n)}{(x_1 - x_0)(x_1 - x_2)(x_1 - x_3) \cdots (x_1 - x_n)}$$

$$+ f(x_2)\frac{(x - x_0)(x - x_1)(x - x_3) \cdots (x - x_n)}{(x_2 - x_0)(x_2 - x_1)(x_2 - x_3) \cdots (x_2 - x_n)} + \cdots$$

$$+ f(x_n)\frac{(x - x_0)(x - x_1)(x - x_2) \cdots (x - x_{n-1})}{(x_n - x_0)(x_n - x_1)(x_n - x_2) \cdots (x_n - x_{n-1})} + R(x)$$

$$(\text{C-14})$$

where $R(x) = (x - x_0)(x - x_1)(x - x_2) \cdots (x - x_n)[xx_0x_1 \cdots x_n]$.

The remainder of Eq. C-14 is identical with that of Eq. C-4. With the remainder omitted from Eq. C-14, and $p_n(x)$ substituted for $f(x)$, we have the Lagrangian interpolating polynomial

$$p_n(x) = f(x_0)\frac{(x - x_1)(x - x_2) \cdots (x - x_n)}{(x_0 - x_1)(x_0 - x_2) \cdots (x_0 - x_n)}$$

$$+ f(x_1)\frac{(x - x_0)(x - x_2)(x - x_3) \cdots (x - x_n)}{(x_1 - x_0)(x_1 - x_2)(x_1 - x_3) \cdots (x_1 - x_n)}$$

$$+ f(x_2)\frac{(x - x_0)(x - x_1)(x - x_3) \cdots (x - x_n)}{(x_2 - x_0)(x_2 - x_1)(x_2 - x_3) \cdots (x_2 - x_n)} + \cdots$$

$$+ f(x_n)\frac{(x - x_0)(x - x_1)(x - x_2) \cdots (x - x_{n-1})}{(x_n - x_0)(x_n - x_1)(x_n - x_2) \cdots (x_n - x_{n-1})}$$

$$(\text{C-15})$$

EXAMPLE C-3

Given the data

x	$f(x)$
1.20	3.3201
1.70	5.4739
1.80	6.0496
2.00	7.3891

use Eq. C-15 to approximate $f(1.95)$.

Substituting into Eq. C-15 with $n = 3$, gives

$$p_3(1.95) = 3.3201\frac{(1.95 - 1.70)(1.95 - 1.80)(1.95 - 2.00)}{(1.20 - 1.70)(1.20 - 1.80)(1.20 - 2.00)}$$

$$+ 5.4739\frac{(1.95 - 1.20)(1.95 - 1.80)(1.95 - 2.00)}{(1.70 - 1.20)(1.70 - 1.80)(1.70 - 2.00)}$$

$$+ 6.0496\frac{(1.95 - 1.20)(1.95 - 1.70)(1.95 - 2.00)}{(1.80 - 1.20)(1.80 - 1.70)(1.80 - 2.00)}$$

$$+ 7.3891\frac{(1.95 - 1.20)(1.95 - 1.70)(1.95 - 1.80)}{(2.00 - 1.20)(2.00 - 1.70)(2.00 - 1.80)}$$

$$= 7.0290$$

The data given is from the function $f(x) = e^x$, and the value of $e^{1.95}$ to four places is 7.0287, so the error made in using the interpolating polynomial is $-.0003$. It is important to emphasize that the error is the quantity which must be added to the approximation to obtain the exact answer.

C-4 OTHER INTERPOLATING FORMULAS

Interpolating polynomials can be expressed in many different forms. Three forms have been derived. Other classical forms are given here for reference without derivation. For the interested reader, their derivations are given by Milne-Thompson[2] and others.

Newton-Gregory Backward Formula

When interpolating near the end of a table, in order to make sure that the differences required are available in the table, the last abscissa is often designated as x_0, with the previous abscissas designated x_{-1}, x_{-2}, x_{-3}, and so forth. Then the Newton-Gregory backward formula is used. Given in terms of backward-difference notation, it is

$$p_n(x) = f_0 + \binom{u}{1}\nabla f_0 + \binom{u+1}{2}\nabla^2 f_0 + \binom{u+2}{3}\nabla^3 f_0 + \cdots$$
$$+ \binom{u+k-1}{k}\nabla^k f_0 + \cdots + \binom{u+n-1}{n}\nabla^n f_0$$

As before, the phase u is defined as $(x - x_0)/h$, and will be negative for the situation described.

Expressed in forward-difference notation, without the use of the binomial coefficient symbols, the *same* formula is

$$p_n(x) = f_0 + u\Delta f_{-1} + \frac{u(u+1)}{2!}\Delta^2 f_{-2} + \frac{u(u+1)(u+2)}{3!}\Delta^3 f_{-3}$$
$$+ \frac{u(u+1)(u+2)(u+3)}{4!}\Delta^4 f_{-4} + \cdots$$
$$+ \frac{u(u+1)(u+2)\cdots(u+k-1)}{k!}\Delta^k f_{-k} + \cdots$$
$$+ \frac{u(u+1)(u+2)\cdots(u+n-1)}{n!}\Delta^n f_{-n}$$

Note that the differences used in the two different forms of this backward

---

[2]*Ibid.*

formula lie on a diagonal line running upward and to the right from f_0 in the tables of Figs. C-3 and C-4 (shown with a line of dashes) whereas in the forward formulas (see Eq. C-12) the differences were found to lie on a diagonal line running downward and to the right as shown in Fig. C-3 with a line of dashes.

Gauss's Forward Formula

In forward-difference notation, this formula is

$$p_n(x) = f_0 + \binom{u}{1}\Delta f_0 + \binom{u}{2}\Delta^2 f_{-1} + \binom{u+1}{3}\Delta^3 f_{-1} + \binom{u+1}{4}\Delta^4 f_{-2}$$

$$+ \binom{u+2}{5}\Delta^5 f_{-2} + \cdots + \binom{u+k-1}{2k}\Delta^{2k} f_{-k}$$

$$+ \binom{u+k}{2k+1}\Delta^{2k+1} f_{-k} + \cdots$$

In central-difference notation, it becomes

$$p_n(x) = f_0 + \binom{u}{1}\delta f_{1/2} + \binom{u}{2}\delta^2 f_0 + \binom{u+1}{3}\delta^3 f_{1/2} + \binom{u+1}{4}\delta^4 f_0$$

$$+ \binom{u+2}{5}\delta^5 f_{1/2} + \cdots + \binom{u+k-1}{2k}\delta^{2k} f_0$$

$$+ \binom{u+k}{2k+1}\delta^{2k+1} f_{1/2} + \cdots$$

The differences used in this formula lie on zigzag paths in the tables of Figs. C-3 and C-5, which are indicated there by black dots.

Gauss's Backward Formula

In forward-difference notation, this formula is expressed as

$$p_n(x) = f_0 + \binom{u}{1}\Delta f_{-1} + \binom{u+1}{2}\Delta^2 f_{-1} + \binom{u+1}{3}\Delta^3 f_{-2}$$

$$+ \binom{u+2}{4}\Delta^4 f_{-2} + \cdots + \binom{u+k}{2k}\Delta^{2k} f_{-k}$$

$$+ \binom{u+k}{2k+1}\Delta^{2k+1} f_{-k-1} + \cdots$$

In central-difference notation it is

$$p_n(x) = f_0 + \binom{u}{1}\delta f_{-1/2} + \binom{u+1}{2}\delta^2 f_0 + \binom{u+1}{3}\delta^3 f_{-1/2}$$

$$+ \binom{u+2}{4}\delta^4 f_0 + \cdots + \binom{u+k}{2k}\delta^{2k} f_0$$

$$+ \binom{u+k}{2k+1}\delta^{2k+1} f_{-1/2} + \cdots$$

The differences for this formula lie on zigzag paths in the tables in Figs. C-3 and C-5, which are indicated there by small circles.

Stirling's Formula

Stirling's formula is obtained by averaging Gauss's forward and backward formulas. Thus, in forward-difference notation we have

$$p_n(x) = f_0 + \binom{u}{1}\frac{\Delta f_0 + \Delta f_{-1}}{2} + \frac{\binom{u}{2} + \binom{u+1}{2}}{2}\Delta^2 f_{-1}$$

$$+ \binom{u+1}{3}\frac{\Delta^3 f_{-1} + \Delta^3 f_{-2}}{2} + \frac{\binom{u+1}{4} + \binom{u+2}{4}}{2}\Delta^4 f_{-2} + \cdots$$

In central-difference notation with the averaging operator, it becomes

$$p_n(x) = f_0 + \binom{u}{1}\mu\delta f_0 + \frac{u}{2}\binom{u}{1}\delta^2 f_0 + \binom{u+1}{3}\mu\delta^3 f_0 + \cdots$$

$$+ \frac{u}{2k}\binom{u+k-1}{2k-1}\delta^{2k} f_0 + \binom{u+k}{2k+1}\mu\delta^{2k+1} f_0 + \cdots$$

For Stirling's formula the differences used lie on horizontal lines in the tables shown in Figs. C-3 and C-7, which are indicated there by lines of short arrows. At points indicated by an asterisk in Fig. C-3, the averages of the differences above and below are used to obtain the quantities $(\Delta f_0 + \Delta f_{-1})/2$, $(\Delta^3 f_{-1} + \Delta^3 f_{-2})/2$, and so forth.

The Lozenge Diagram

We have seen that the differences for various interpolation formulas can be

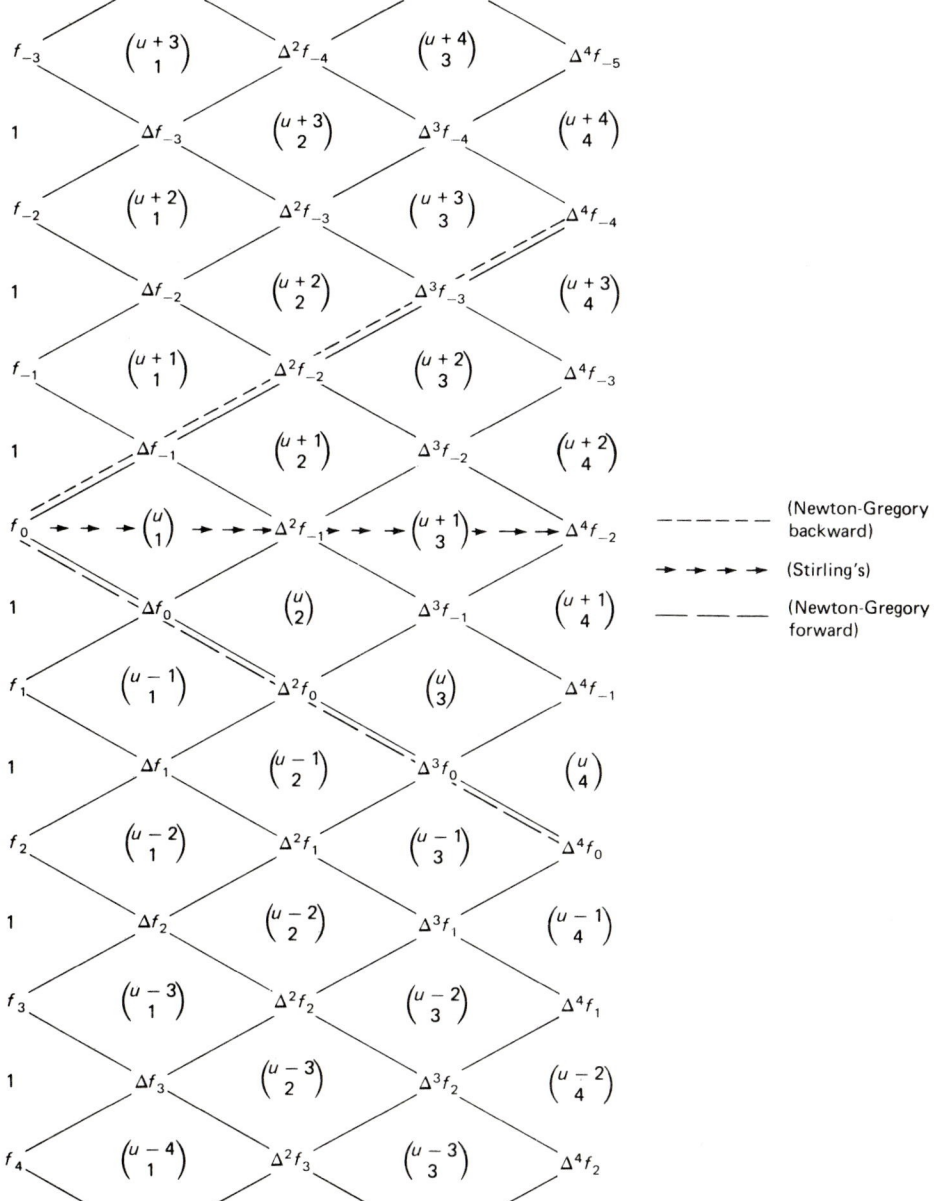

Figure C-8 Lozenge diagram in forward-difference notation

obtained by taking various paths through a difference table. The functions of u used with the differences depends on the path. A lozenge diagram may be used to illustrate the various paths and resulting differences and functions of u for various interpolation formulas. Such a diagram is shown in Fig. C-8 in forward-difference notation.

Interpolation formulas are determined by starting at one of the entries in the first column, usually f_0, and following some path across to the right column. The path may follow a diagonal line, or it may cut horizontally across a lozenge. The rules to be followed for writing the interpolation formula are as follows:

1. The entry in the left column at which the path starts is the first term, and a term is added each time a new column is reached.
2. Steps may be taken from right to left if the terms are subtracted instead of added as in rule 1. However, this is seldom done.
3. The path consists of steps through the diagram. If the slope of a step is positive, the term to be added consists of the product of the difference reached by the step and the function of u immediately below the difference. If the slope of the step is negative, the term to be added consists of the product of the difference reached by the step and the function of u immediately above the difference reached. If the step is horizontal and reaches a function of u, the term added consists of the function of u times the average of the differences above and below. If the step is horizontal and reaches a difference, the term added consists of the product of the difference and the average of the function of u above and below it.

Following the line of long dashes from f_0 in Fig. C-8, for example, gives the Newton-Gregory forward formula, while following the horizontal line of arrows gives Stirling's formula.

Hamming[3] gives a proof that any path chosen will result in a valid interpolation formula, and that if two paths end at the same point, the formulas give identical polynomials even though the entry points into the diagram may not be the same.

C-5 INVERSE INTERPOLATION

Given a table of x values and corresponding $f(x)$ values, interpolation involves finding $f(x)$ for any nontabulated x values which fall within the range of tabulated values. Inverse interpolation, on the other hand, involves finding the value of x corresponding to some given nontabulated $f(x)$ value. For simplicity, let us designate our given function by y. That is,

$$y = f(x)$$

One approach to the problem of inverse interpolation is to consider our x-y relationship to be

$$x = f^{-1}(y)$$

---

[3]Richard W. Hamming, *Numerical Methods for Scientists and Engineers* (New York: McGraw-Hill Book Co., Inc., 1962), pp. 111–115.

	y	$f^{-1}(y)$
$y_0 =$	0.0	0.0
$y_1 =$	0.199	0.2
$y_2 =$	0.389	0.4
$y_3 =$	0.565	0.6
$y_4 =$	0.717	0.8
$y_5 =$	0.841	1.0

Figure C-9 Table of Fig. C-1 rewritten for inverse interpolation

Then the table in Fig. C-1, rewritten for inverse interpolation, is as shown in Fig. C-9. For some nontabulated y value, the corresponding $f^{-1}(y)$ value can be found by one of the interpolation methods previously discussed. Usually the Lagrangian form is used for this purpose since the y values are, in general, not uniformly spaced.

EXAMPLE C-4

Using the data given in Fig. C-9, find the value of x corresponding to a value of 0.25 for y. Since we have six data points given, a fifth-degree interpolating polynomial can be used. Equation C-15, the Lagrangian form, is used with x replaced by y, x_0 by y_0, x_1 by y_1, and so forth. Doing this, we obtain

$$p_5(y) =$$

$$0 + 0.2 \frac{(.25 - 0.)(.25 - .389)(.25 - .565)(.25 - .717)(.25 - .841)}{(.199 - 0.)(.199 - .389)(.199 - .565)(.199 - .717)(.199 - .841)}$$

$$+ 0.4 \frac{(.25 - 0.)(.25 - .199)(.25 - .565)(.25 - .717)(.25 - .841)}{(.389 - 0.)(.389 - .199)(.389 - .565)(.389 - .717)(.389 - .841)}$$

$$+ 0.6 \frac{(.25 - 0.)(.25 - .199)(.25 - .389)(.25 - .717)(.25 - .841)}{(.565 - 0.)(.565 - .199)(.565 - .389)(.565 - .717)(.565 - .841)}$$

$$+ 0.8 \frac{(.25 - 0.)(.25 - .199)(.25 - .389)(.25 - .565)(.25 - .841)}{(.717 - 0.)(.717 - .199)(.717 - .389)(.717 - .565)(.717 - .841)}$$

$$+ 1.0 \frac{(.25 - 0.)(.25 - .199)(.25 - .389)(.25 - .565)(.25 - .717)}{(.841 - 0.)(.841 - .199)(.841 - .389)(.841 - .565)(.841 - .717)}$$

$$= 0.253$$

The table in Fig. C-1 is based on the sine function, so that

$$x = \sin^{-1}(.25) = 0.253$$

to three-digit accuracy, verifying the result obtained by interpolation.

In some cases, the inverse function, $x = f^{-1}(y)$, cannot be well represented by a polynomial even though $y = f(x)$ can be approximated accurately by a polynomial. In such cases, the method just discussed would lead to inaccurate results. A more accurate result could be obtained by determining the polynomial $p_n(x)$ which approximates $f(x)$, replacing $p_n(x)$ with the given value of $f(x)$, and, for the resulting equation, finding the root nearest the approximately known value of x for known $f(x)$ by one of the methods of Chap. 2.

EXAMPLE C-5

Given the data of Ex. C-3, repeated here for convenience, find the value

x	$f(x)$
1.20	3.3201
1.70	5.4739
1.80	6.0496
2.00	7.3891

of x corresponding to a value of 4.0000 for $f(x)$. Since the x values are not equally spaced, we use the Lagrangian form of the interpolating polynomial and determine the third-degree polynomial through the four given points. It is

$$p_3(x) = 3.3201 \frac{(x - 1.70)(x - 1.80)(x - 2.00)}{(1.20 - 1.70)(1.20 - 1.80)(1.20 - 2.00)}$$

$$+ 5.4739 \frac{(x - 1.20)(x - 1.80)(x - 2.00)}{(1.70 - 1.20)(1.70 - 1.80)(1.70 - 2.00)}$$

$$+ 6.0496 \frac{(x - 1.20)(x - 1.70)(x - 2.00)}{(1.80 - 1.20)(1.80 - 1.70)(1.80 - 2.00)}$$

$$+ 7.3891 \frac{(x - 1.20)(x - 1.70)(x - 1.80)}{(2.00 - 1.20)(2.00 - 1.70)(2.00 - 1.80)}$$

$$= 0.899x^3 - 1.810x^2 + 3.830x - 0.223$$

Setting the value of this polynomial equal to 4.000 gives the equation

$$0.899x^3 - 1.810x^2 + 3.830x - 4.223 = 0$$

We know from visual inspection of the tabulated data that x will probably be somewhere in the neighborhood of 1.35. Using an incremental-search technique with a pocket calculator, starting at $x = 1.35$, we find that $x = 1.386$ to four significant digits. Since the data for the table are based on $f(x) = e^x$, this is the correct answer to four significant digits.

C-6 APPLICATION OF POLYNOMIAL APPROXIMATION TO THE DERIVATION OF NUMERICAL INTEGRATION FORMULAS

The Trapezoid Rule

If we let $n = 1$ in Eq. C-11 with the remainder term as given by Eq. C-13, we have

$$f(x) = f_0 + u \, \Delta f_0 + \frac{u(u-1)}{2} h^2 f''(\xi) \qquad x_0 < \xi < x_1$$

Now suppose we integrate this function from x_0 to $x_1 = x_0 + h$. The result is equal to the crosshatched area in the strip under the graph of $f(x)$ shown in Fig. C-10. Since $u = (x - x_0)/h$, we have $dx = h \, du$, and for $x = x_0$, we see that $u = 0$, while for $x = x_1$, $u = 1$. Therefore,

$$\int_{x=x_0}^{x=x_1} f(x) \, dx = \int_{u=0}^{u=1} f(x) h \, du$$

Then, assuming that $f''(\xi)$ is essentially a constant for very small h as u varies from 0 to 1,

$$h \int_{u=0}^{u=1} \left[f_0 + u \, \Delta f_0 + \frac{u(u-1)}{2} h^2 f''(\xi) \right] du$$

$$= h \left[u f_0 + \frac{u^2}{2} \Delta f_0 + \left(\frac{u^3}{6} - \frac{u^2}{4} \right) h^2 f''(\xi) \right]_0^1$$

$$= h \left[f_0 + \frac{1}{2} \Delta f_0 \right] - \frac{1}{12} h^3 f''(\xi)$$

$$= \underbrace{\frac{h}{2} [f_0 + f_1]}_{\text{first term}} - \underbrace{\frac{1}{12} h^3 f''(\xi)}_{\text{second term}} \qquad x_0 < (\xi) < x_1$$

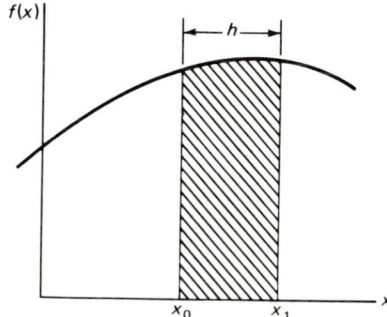

Figure C-10 Graph of function based on Eqs. C-11 and C-13

Using only the first term of this equation, we have the trapezoid rule for the approximate area in one strip under the graph of a function. The second term then becomes the error. This is in agreement with the result obtained from Taylor-series expansions in Chap. 5. The error is said to be "of order h^3", usually written $O(h^3)$.

More Accurate Formulas for the Area in One Strip Under a Curve

Formulas for approximating the area in one strip under a curve with error of any order desired may be derived by letting n take on higher values in Eq. C-11. For example, if we let $n = 2$ in Eq. C-11, and integrate from $x = x_0$ to $x = x_1$, we obtain

$$\int_{x=x_0}^{x=x_1} f(x)\, dx = \int_{u=0}^{u=1} f(x)h\, dx$$

$$= h \int_0^1 \left[f_0 + u\, \Delta f_0 + \frac{u(u-1)}{2!} \Delta^2 f_0 \right.$$

$$\left. + \frac{u(u-1)(u-2)}{3!} h^3 f'''(\xi) \right] du$$

$$= \frac{h}{12}[5f_0 + 8f_1 - f_2] + O(h^4)$$

If we let $n = 3$ in Eq. C-11, and integrate over one strip, we obtain

$$\int_{x=x_0}^{x=x_1} f(x)\, dx = \int_{u=0}^{u=1} f(x)\, h\, du = \frac{h}{24}[9f_0 + 19f_1 - 5f_2 + f_3] + O(h^5)$$

Simpson's Rule

If we take $n = 3$ in Eq. C-11, and integrate the resulting function over two strips, from $x = x_0$ to $x = x_0 + 2h = x_2$, we get the expression for Simpson's rule for two strips, and the error made by using Simpson's rule for the area in those two strips.

$$\int_{x=x_0}^{x=x_2} f(x)\, dx = \int_{u=0}^{u=2} f(x)h\, du$$

$$= h \int_0^2 \left[f_0 + u\, \Delta f_0 + \frac{u^2 - u}{2} \Delta^2 f_0 + \frac{u^3 - 3u^2 + 2u}{6} \Delta^3 f_0 \right.$$

$$\left. + \frac{u^4 - 6u^3 + 11u^2 - 6u}{24} h^4 f''''(\xi) \right] du$$

Assuming that $f''''(\xi)$ is essentially a constant for very small h as u varies from 0 to 2, we obtain

$$\int_{x_0}^{x_2} f(x)\, dx = h\Bigg[uf_0 + \frac{u^2}{2}\Delta f_0 + \left(\frac{u^3}{6} - \frac{u^2}{4}\right)\Delta^2 f_0 + \left(\frac{u^4}{24} - \frac{3u^3}{18} + \frac{2u^2}{12}\right)\Delta^3 f_0$$
$$+ \left(\frac{u^5}{120} - \frac{6u^4}{96} + \frac{11u^3}{72} - \frac{6u^2}{48}\right) h^4 f''''(\xi)\Bigg]_0^2$$

$$\text{(C-16)}$$

Substituting limits gives

$$\int_{x_0}^{x_2} f(x)\, dx = \underbrace{\frac{h}{3}[f_0 + 4f_1 + f_2]}_{\substack{\text{Simpson's rule}\\ \text{expression for}\\ \text{the approximate}\\ \text{area in two strips}\\ \text{under a curve}}} - \underbrace{\frac{1}{90} h^5 f''''(\xi)}_{\text{error term}} \qquad x_0 < (\xi) < x_2$$

$$\text{(C-17)}$$

Equation C-17 is in agreement with the results obtained in Chap. 5. Because the coefficient of $\Delta^3 f_0$ in Eq. C-16 turns out to be zero when the limits are substituted, we need only three ordinate values (we actually use a second-degree parabola) to obtain the accuracy of a third-degree polynomial. This is one of the features of Simpson's rule which makes it appealing.

Newton-Cotes Formulas

If the ordinates of a function $f(x)$ are known for $n + 1$ equally spaced abscissas, we can form an nth-degree polynomial which matches all of the tabulated values. We can then integrate this polynomial over different limits to obtain approximations to the area in different numbers of strips under the curve of $f(x)$. Newton-Cotes formulas result from integration over the limits of abscissa values for which the polynomial matches the tabulated values (x_0 to x_n). Thus, the trapezoid rule and Simpson's rule are special cases of Newton-Cotes formulas for two and three points, respectively. As a further example, let us assume that we have seven points whose abscissas are equally spaced. To obtain a Newton-Cotes formula, we let $n = 7$ in Eq. C-11 and integrate over six strips. After integrating and substituting limits, it turns out that the coefficient of $\Delta^7 f_0$ is zero, so we actually use a sixth-degree polynomial having the accuracy of a seventh-degree polynomial, similar to what occurred in the derivation of Simpson's rule. We obtain the following very accurate seven-point Newton-

Cotes formula with error of order h^9 (this compares with an error of order h^5 for Simpson's rule):

$$\int_{x_0}^{x_6} f(x)\, dx = \int_{u=0}^{u=6} f(x)h\, du$$

$$= \frac{h}{140}[41f_0 + 216f_1 + 27f_2 + 272f_3 + 27f_4$$

$$+ 216f_5 + 41f_6] + O(h^9)$$

$$(C\text{-}18)$$

The error of order h^9 comes from integrating the remainder term in the Newton-Gregory forward formula with $n = 7$.

A table of Newton-Cotes coefficients and orders of error for formulas up to and including the seven-point formula is shown below. This table is a modified version of one given by Milne-Thompson[4] which was taken from Pascal's *Repertorium*. The various coefficients are defined as follows:

$$\int_{x_0}^{x_n} f(x)\, dx = Ch[a_0 f_0 + a_1 f_1 + a_2 f_2 + a_3 f_3 + \cdots + a_n f_n] + O(h^k)$$

No. of Points

$n+1$	C	a_0	a_1	a_2	a_3	a_4	a_5	a_6	k
2	$\frac{1}{2}$	1	1		(trapezoid rule)				3
3	$\frac{1}{3}$	1	4	1	(Simpson's one-third rule)				5
4	$\frac{3}{8}$	1	3	3	1	(Simpson's three-eighths rule)			5
5	$\frac{2}{45}$	7	32	12	32	7			7
6	$\frac{5}{288}$	19	75	50	50	75	19		7
7	$\frac{1}{140}$	41	216	27	272	27	216	41	9

There is little to be gained in accuracy in using a four-point formula over a three-point formula (they have errors of the same order), or a six-point formula over a five-point formula. Odd-point formulas are preferred unless it is necessary to integrate over an odd number of strips. For example, Simpson's three-eighths rule ($n + 1 = 4$) is used to integrate over three strips, but with little more accuracy than Simpson's one-third rule over two strips.

Weddle's Formula

Weddle's formula is a seven-point formula, but it has simpler coefficients than

---

[4]Milne-Thompson, p. 170.

the seven-point Newton-Cotes formula. It may be derived as follows. By definition,

$$\Delta^6 f_0 = f_0 - 6f_1 + 15f_2 - 20f_3 + 15f_4 - 6f_5 + f_6$$

It may also be shown[5] that

$$\Delta^6 f_0 = h^6 f^6(\xi) \qquad x_0 < (\xi) < x_6$$

If we add the first expression given above for $\Delta^6 f_0$ to the bracketed expression in Eq. C-18, and then, to compensate, subtract the second expression given above for $\Delta^6 f_0$, multiplied by $h/140$, from the error term of Eq. C-18, we obtain Weddle's formula, which is

$$\int_{x_0}^{x_6} f(x)\, dx = \frac{3}{10} h[f_0 + 5f_1 + f_2 + 6f_3 + f_4 + 5f_5 + f_6] + O(h^7) \qquad \text{(C-19)}$$

The penalty for the simpler coefficients is an error of order h^7 instead of order h^9 obtained with the Newton-Cotes seven-point formula.

Open Integration Formulas

The Newton-Cotes formulas and others which have been presented thus far are called "closed" formulas. In the case of closed formulas, ordinate values are known at the limits of the integration. To obtain "open" formulas, the range of integration extends beyond the abscissa values for which the ordinates are known. Formulas of the open type are useful in the numerical solution of differential equations.

As an example of the derivation of an open formula, let us derive Eq. 6-114 used in Milne's predictor equation. We let $n = 2$ in Eq. C-11 and integrate from $x = x_0 - h$ to $x = x_0 + 3h$:

$$\int_{x=x_{-1}}^{x=x_3} f(x)\, dx = h \int_{u=-1}^{u=3} f(x)\, du$$

$$= h \int_{-1}^{3} \left[f_0 + u\,\Delta f_0 + \frac{u(u-1)}{2!}\,\Delta^2 f_0 \right.$$

$$\left. + \frac{u(u-1)(u-2)}{3!}\, h^3 f'''(\xi) \right] du$$

$$= h \left[uf_0 + \frac{u^2}{2}(f_1 - f_0) \right.$$

$$\left. + \left(\frac{u^3}{6} - \frac{u^2}{4} \right)(f_2 - 2f_1 + f_0) \right]_{-1}^{3} + O(h^4)$$

$$= \frac{4}{3} h[2f_0 - f_1 + 2f_2] + O(h^4) \qquad \text{(C-20)}$$

[5]*Ibid.*, p. 56.

C-7 APPLICATION OF POLYNOMIAL APPROXIMATION TO THE DERIVATION OF NUMERICAL DIFFERENTIATION FORMULAS

The Newton-Gregory forward-interpolation formula (Eq. C-11) with remainder (Eq. C-13) is

$$f(x) = f_0 + u\,\Delta f_0 + \frac{u(u-1)}{2!}\,\Delta^2 f_0 + \frac{u(u-1)(u-2)}{3!}\,\Delta^3 f_0$$

$$+ \frac{u(u-1)(u-2)(u-3)}{4!}\,\Delta^4 f_0 + \cdots$$

$$+ \frac{u(u-1)(u-2)\cdots(u-n+1)}{n!}\,\Delta^n f_0$$

$$+ \frac{u(u-1)(u-2)\cdots(u-n)}{(n+1)!}\,h^{n+1}f^{n+1}(\xi)$$

(C-21)

Approximations for the derivative of a function will be determined by determining $f'(x)$. Let us note that

$$f'(x) = \frac{df(x)}{du}\frac{du}{dx}$$

and that

$$\frac{du}{dx} = \frac{1}{h}$$

Thus, we can differentiate $f(x)$ with respect to u and multiply by $1/h$ to obtain

$$f'(x) = \frac{1}{h}\left\{ 0 + \Delta f_0 + \frac{1}{2}(2u-1)\Delta^2 f_0 + \frac{1}{6}(3u^2 - 6u + 2)\Delta^3 f_0 \right.$$

$$+ \frac{1}{24}(4u^3 - 18u^2 + 22u - 6)\Delta^4 f_0 + \cdots$$

$$\left. + \frac{d}{du}\left[\binom{u}{n+1} h^{n+1}f^{n+1}(\xi) \right] \right\}$$

(C-22)

Since $f^{n+1}(\xi)$ is an unknown function of u, differentiation of the remainder term as a product cannot be carried out except for $u = 0$, which causes the term containing the derivative of $f^{n+1}(\xi)$ to vanish. Even then the derivative of the remainder term cannot be evaluated exactly because $f^{n+1}(\xi)$ cannot be evaluated. Thus, we will let the derivative of the remainder term constitute our error term which will be $O(h^n)$.

If the derivative is to be evaluated at x_0, then $u = 0$, and

$$f'(x) = \frac{1}{h}\left[\Delta f_0 - \frac{1}{2}\Delta^2 f_0 + \frac{1}{3}\Delta^3 f_0 - \frac{1}{4}\Delta^4 f_0 + \cdots \pm \frac{1}{n}\Delta^n f_0\right] + O(h^n)$$

(C-23)

Differentiating Eq. C-21 with $n = 1$, and letting $u = 0$, only the first term in brackets in Eq. C-23 will remain so that

$$f'(x_0) = \frac{f_1 - f_0}{h} + O(h)$$

This equation agrees with the first of Eq. 5-81 which was derived using the Taylor series. Similarly, if we let $n = 2$ in Eq. C-21, the first two terms of Eq. C-23 will remain, giving

$$f'(x_0) = \frac{1}{h}\left[\Delta f_0 - \frac{1}{2}\Delta^2 f_0\right] + O(h^2)$$

$$= \frac{1}{h}\left[f_1 - f_0 - \frac{1}{2}(f_2 - 2f_1 + f_0)\right] + O(h^2)$$

$$= \frac{-f_2 + 4f_1 - 3f_0}{2h} + O(h^2)$$

This agrees with the first of Eq. 5-82, which was derived using the Taylor series.

If we differentiate Eq. C-21 with $n = 2$, and take $u = 1$ to obtain the derivative at $x = x_1$, we obtain

$$f'(x_1) = \frac{1}{h}\left[\Delta f_0 + \frac{1}{2}(1)\Delta^2 f_0\right] + O(h^2)$$

$$= \frac{1}{h}\left[f_1 - f_0 + \frac{1}{2}(f_2 - 2f_1 + f_0)\right] + O(h^2)$$

$$= \frac{f_2 - f_0}{2h} + O(h^2)$$

Then for the derivative at x_0, we have

$$f'(x_0) = \frac{f_1 - f_{-1}}{2h} + O(h^2)$$

which agrees with the first of Eq. 5-79.

If we differentiate Eq. C-21 with $n = 4$, and take $u = 2$, we obtain the derivative at $x = x_2$ as

$$f'(x_2) = \frac{1}{h}\left[\Delta f_0 + \frac{3}{2}\Delta^2 f_0 + \frac{1}{3}\Delta^3 f_0 - \frac{1}{12}\Delta^4 f_0\right] + O(h^4)$$

$$= \frac{1}{12h}[f_0 - 8f_1 + 8f_3 - f_4] + O(h^4)$$

It now follows that the derivative at x_0 is

$$f'(x_0) = \frac{1}{12h}[f_{-2} - 8f_{-1} + 8f_1 - f_2] + O(h^4)$$

This agrees with the first of Eq. 5-80.

To obtain expressions for the second derivative of $f(x)$, the Newton-Gregory forward equation is differentiated twice. Noting that

$$f''(x) = \frac{d^2 f(x)}{du^2}\left(\frac{du}{dx}\right)^2$$

we obtain

$$f''(x) = \frac{1}{h^2}\left[0 + \frac{1}{2}(2)\Delta^2 f_0 + \frac{1}{6}(6u - 6)\Delta^3 f_0 + \cdots\right] + O(h^{n-1}) \qquad \text{(C-24)}$$

If we take $n = 2$ in Eq. C-21, differentiate twice, and let $u = 0$ to get the second derivative at $x = x_0$, we have only the second term in brackets of Eq. C-24 remaining. Thus,

$$f''(x_0) = \frac{1}{h^2}[f_2 - 2f_1 + f_0] + O(h)$$

This agrees with the second of Eq. 5-81.

If we take $n = 3$ and let $u = 0$, we obtain

$$f''(x_0) = \frac{1}{h^2}[f_2 - 2f_1 + f_0 - (f_3 - 3f_2 + 3f_1 - f_0)] + O(h^2)$$

$$= \frac{1}{h^2}[-f_3 + 4f_2 - 5f_1 + 2f_0] + O(h^2)$$

(C-25)

This agrees with the second of Eq. 5-82.

Proceeding in this manner, the finite-difference approximations for the derivatives given in Chap. 5 in summary form can all be derived.

Index